SPA-BATH ✻ SOLARIUM ✻ EXCELLENT NIGHTLY CABARET ✻

A w
welc
you
Acre
u
rep
being one of the
South West's Top
Family Holiday
Parks.

Set in 44 acres of glorious Cornish countryside, we offer the best in hospitality and have 5 spacious touring areas with electric hitch-up plots.

LUB & SALOON BAR ✻ RESTAURANT & TAKEAWAY ✻ TABLE TENNIS ✻

Although we have the ETB Excellent Award and AA 5 Pennants
e are offering excellent value
r 1995. Cars and awnings will
e free as well as children on certain dates.

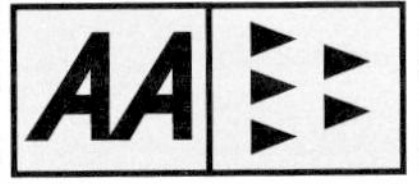

el: 01726 860220
ax: 01726 860877

REAS ✻ FOUR LAKES WITH ON-SITE TACKLE & BAIT SHOP ✻

FOR A VERY SPECIAL HOLIDAY

ACTIVITY
PROGRAMME-ARCHERY,
RIFLE SHOOTING,
ABSEILING, CAVING,
CANOEING, PLUS PRIVATE
THREE ACRE FISHING LAKE

TEL : 01934 742610

FAX : 01934 744950

Staying out...

You love the great outdoors. Sleeping under the stars and waking with the lark. You like the freedom to come and go as you please, to wander in the woods, explore on foot, to breathe fresh air and relax in peaceful surroundings.

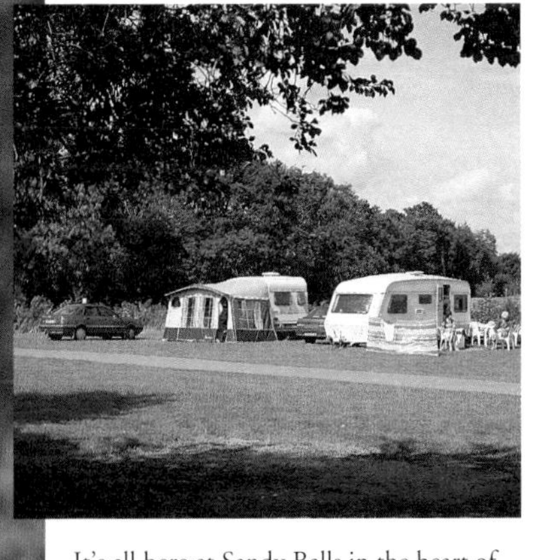

But you also enjoy a good meal, a drink in a cosy country pub, a barbecue on warm summer evenings. Not to mention a dip in an open air pool, a cycle ride along woodland paths... or a pony ride across the moors. You might even fancy a workout in a luxurious new leisure centre complete with multi-gym, solarium, sauna and toning suite. Your children will certainly appreciate an adventure playground, river swimming, art and craft sessions.

eating in

It's all here at Sandy Balls in the heart of the New Forest. The most beautiful holiday location you could imagine, with open field pitches for tents and tourers, mains services, superb toilet and shower blocks, launderette and FREE hot showers. 'Super Pitches' even have Satellite TV hook-up.

Write, phone or fax for FREE colour brochure.
Sandy Balls Estate, Godshill, Fordingbridge, Hampshire SP6 2JY.
Tel: (01425) 653042 Fax: (01425) 653067.

BEACON HILL TOURING PARK

AA RAC

POOLE DORSET

English Tourist Board

Rose award park

Set in 30 acres of lovely English woodland with open grassy spaces and nature rambles, but only minutes from the South's most beautiful beaches; Beacon Hill offers some of the best facilities available at touring parks today plus the delights of Poole, Bournemouth and Dorset's endless tourist attractions.

Attractions
★ Heated Swimming Pool
★ Games Rooms
★ Children's Adventure Playground
★ Tennis Court
★ Riding Nearby
★ Fishing
★ Take-away food
★ Fully licensed Bar
★ Best beaches for windsurfing
★ Fully stocked shop and Off licence

Facilities
★ Free Showers
★ Modern toilets including Disablec
★ Laundry Rooms
★ Hair Driers and Razor Points
★ Dishwashing facilities with free hot water
★ Calor Gas
★ Public Telephone
★ Caravan Rallies welcome
★ Electric Hook-ups

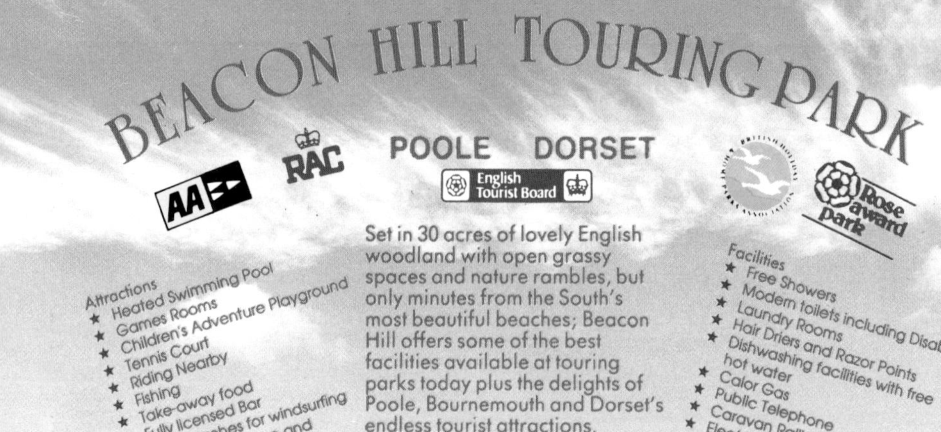

Beacon Hill Touring Park, Blandford Road North,
Poole, Dorset Tel: (01202) 631631

Directions: Situated ¼ mile north from the junction of the A35 and A350 towards Blandford, approximately 3 miles north of Poole

OVERNIGHT STOPS FOR POOLE-CHERBOURG, POOLE-ST, MALO, BRITTANY FERRIES , ONLY 3 MILES FROM FERRY TERMINAL

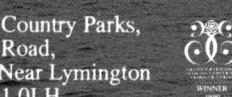

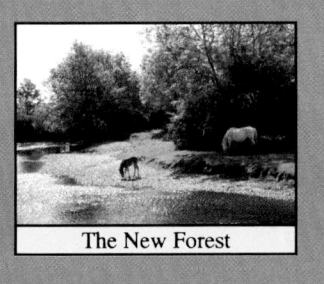

See editorial entry.

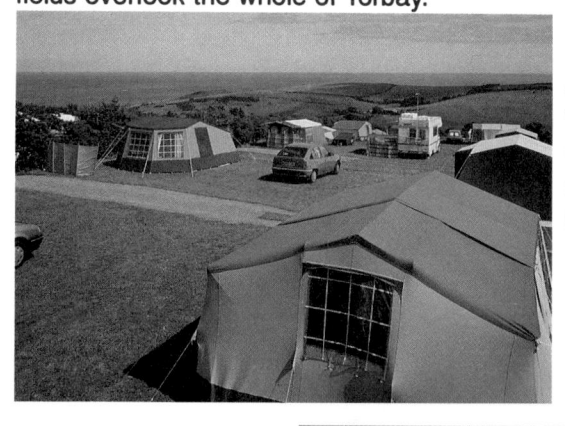

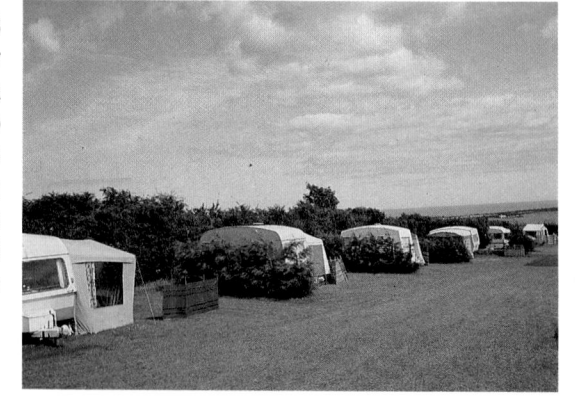

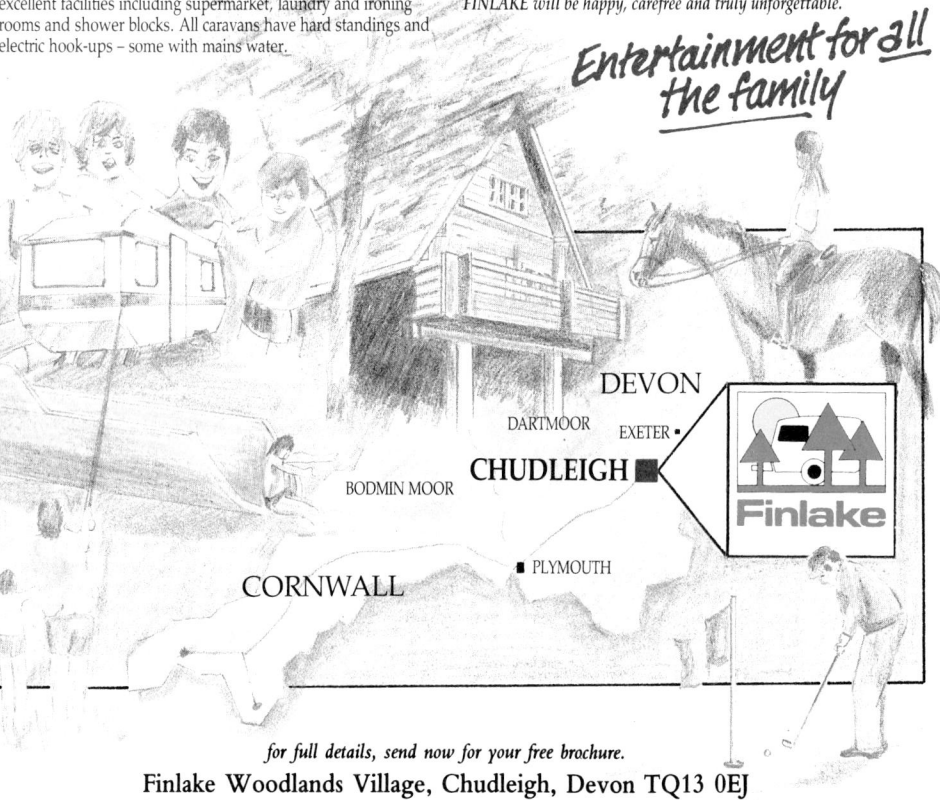

AA

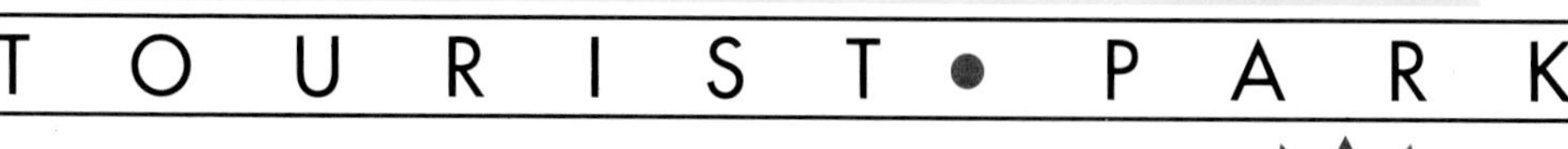

Situated in Wareham Forest with direct access to forest walks. Large, level, well drained pitches together with facilities comparable with the best in Europe. The ideal base for exploring this beautiful part of Dorset.

PROBABLY THE FINEST TOURING PARK IN DORSET

● FREE HOT SHOWERS ● ELECTRIC HOOK-UPS
● SELF SERVICE SHOP ● OFF SALES ● TAKE AWAY FOODS
● LAUNDRETTE ● GAS CYLINDER EXCHANGE ● PAY PHONE
● MOTOR HOME WASTE DISPOSAL ● GAMES ROOM ● CHILDRENS PLAYGROUND
● CHILDRENS POOL ● PUTTING GREEN ● PONY TREKKING
● TENNIS ● BADMINTON ● PRE BOOKABLE PITCHES
● BIKE HIRE ● DOGS ADMITTED ON A LEAD

The Friendly Touring Park

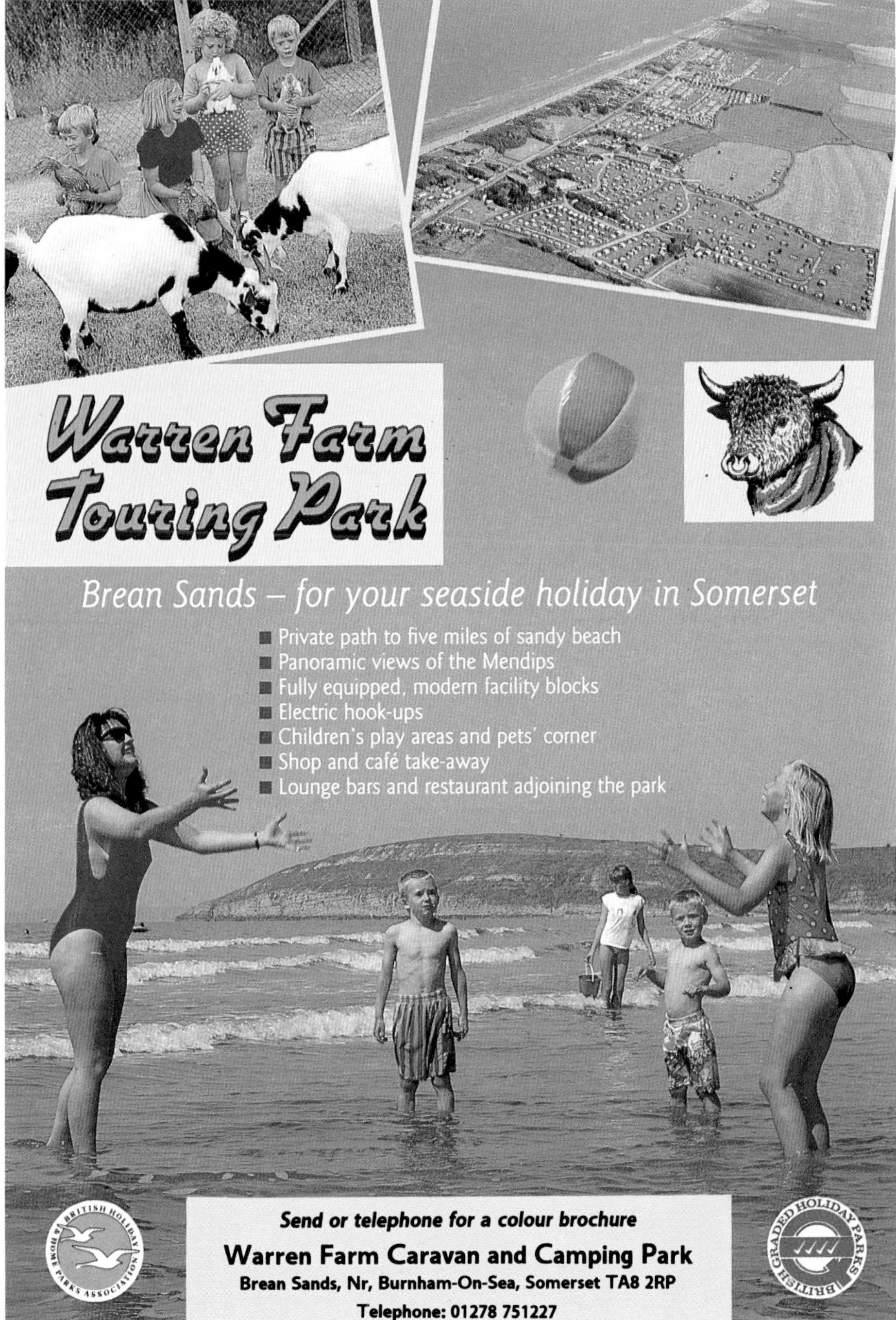
Warren Farm
Touring Park
Brean Sands – for your seaside holiday in Somerset
■ Private path to five miles of sandy beach
■ Panoramic views of the Mendips
■ Fully equipped, modern facility blocks
■ Electric hook-ups
■ Children's play areas and pets' corner
■ Shop and café take-away
■ Lounge bars and restaurant adjoining the park
Send or telephone for a colour brochure
Warren Farm Caravan and Camping Park
Brean Sands, Nr, Burnham-On-Sea, Somerset TA8 2RP
Telephone: 01278 751227
BRITISH HOLIDAY & HOME PARKS ASSOCIATION
BRITISH GRADED HOLIDAY PARKS

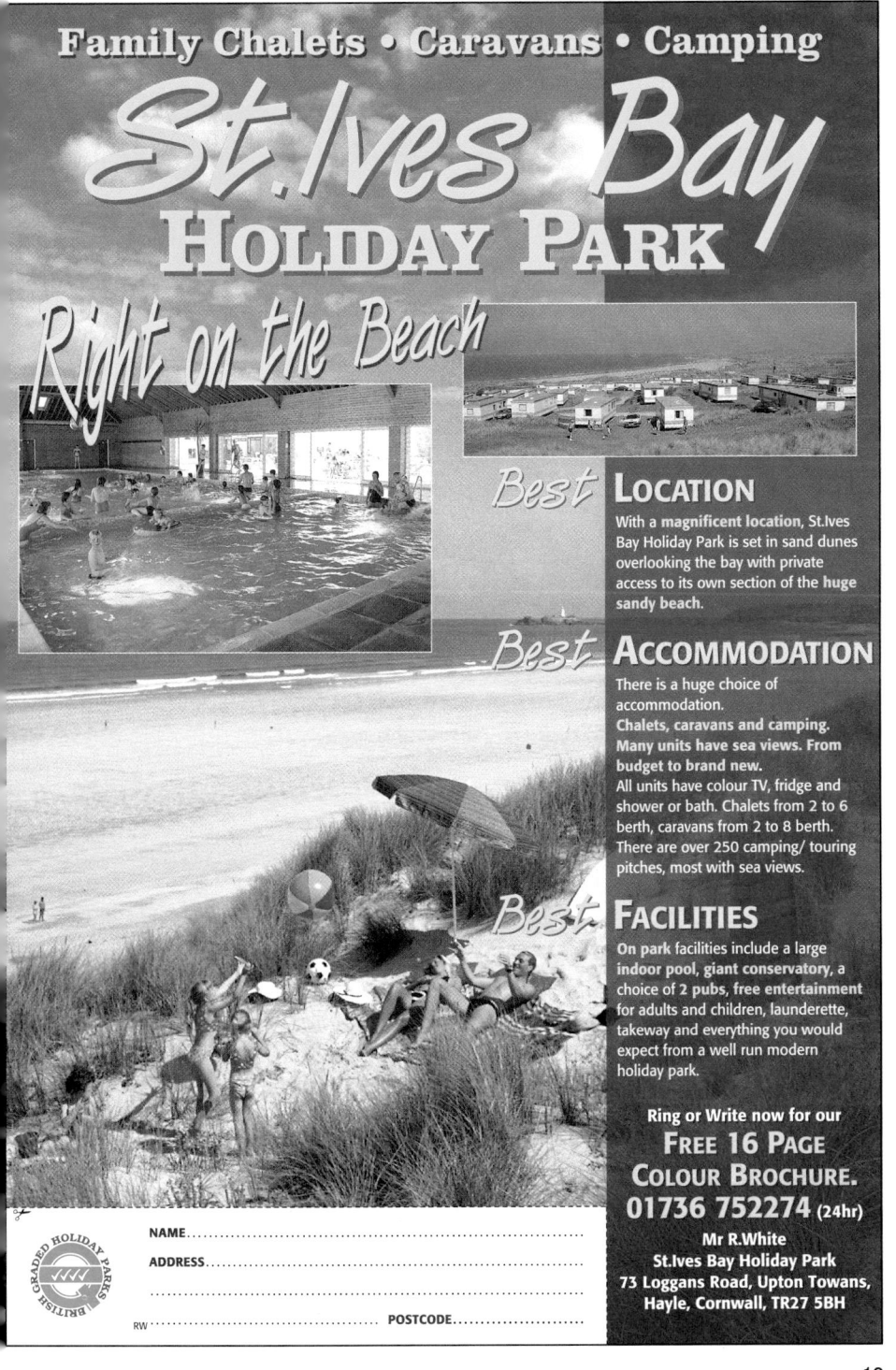

Wareham Forest Tourist Park

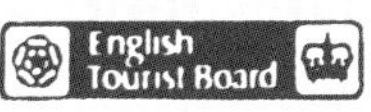

Family run site set in 40 acres of delightful woodlands with open grassy spaces and direct access to Forest walks. Central for lovely Dorset Coastlines and developed to a high standard.

- ☆ Heated Swimming Pool
- ☆ Children's Paddling Pool
- ☆ Indoor Games Room
- ☆ Children's Adventure Playground
- ☆ Long or Short Term Storage
- ☆ Individual Cubicles in toilet block for ladies
- ☆ Fully Serviced Luxury Pitches
- ☆ Launderette
- ☆ Shop/Off Licence
- ☆ Snack Bar Takeaway (Peak Times)
- ☆ Disabled Facilities

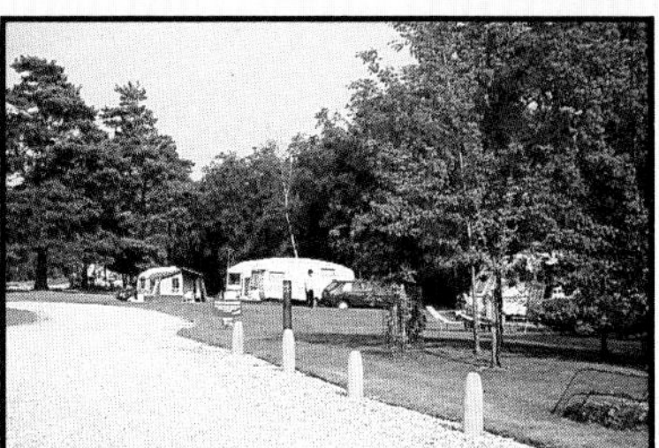

OPEN ALL YEAR

For further details and free coloured brochure

write or phone: Peter & Pam Savage
Wareham Forest Tourist Park
North Trigon Wareham Dorset BH20 7NZ
Tel: Wareham (01929) 551393

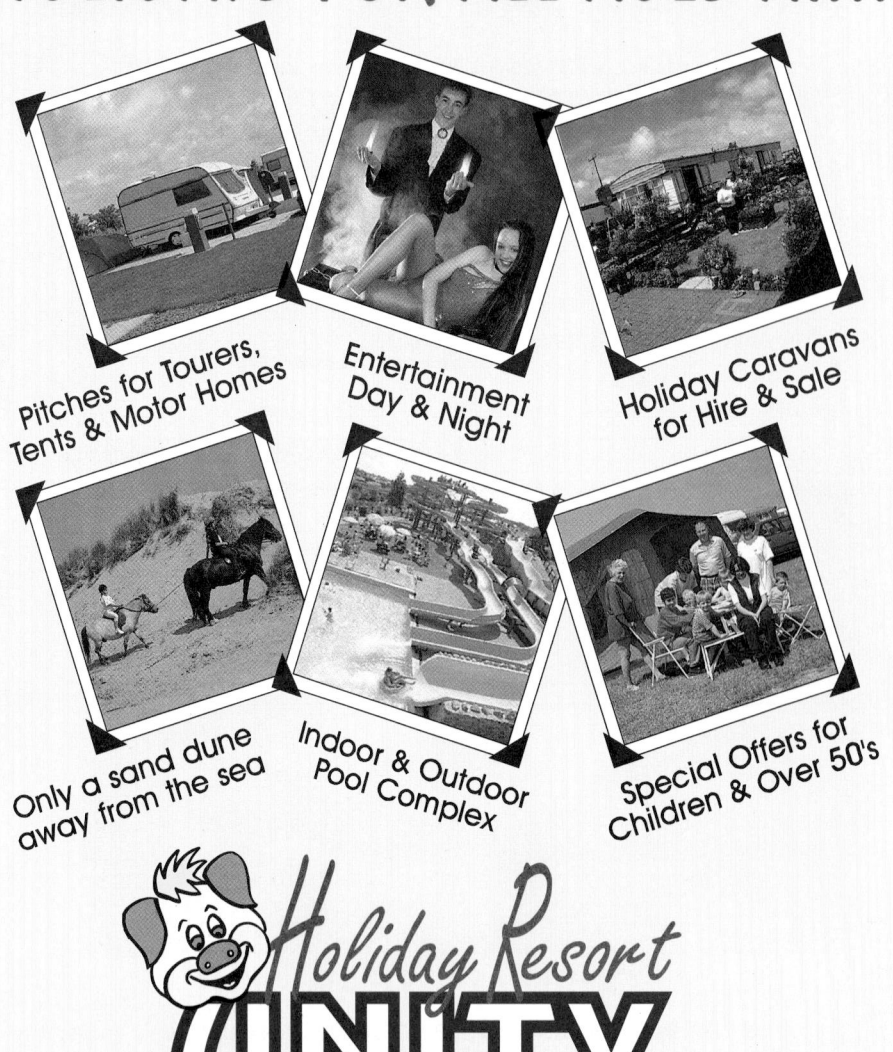

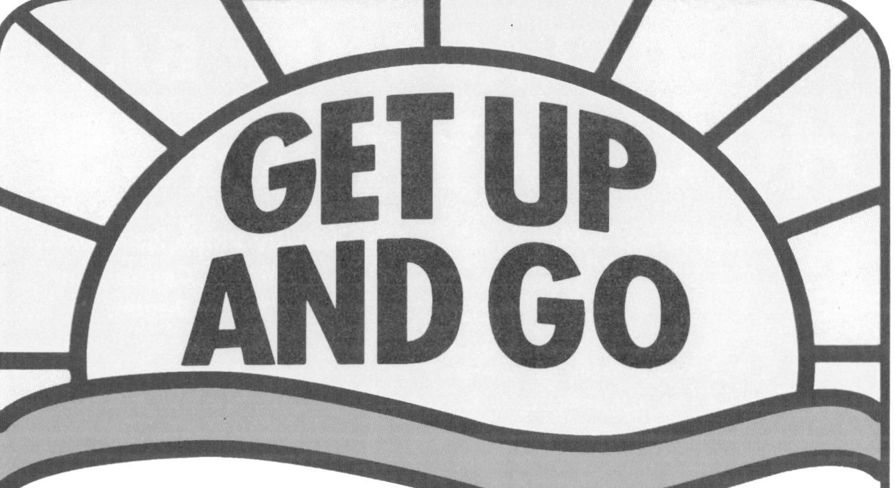

If you're looking for somewhere to pitch your tent or park your tourer – you need look no further than New Beach Touring Park. Because we're right by the beach and provide the very best amenities for the perfect touring holiday.

You can choose a site with or without electrical hook-up to suit your individual requirements. And, naturally, every site has easy access to mains water, disposal points, gas sales and a modern shower and toilet facilities.

What's more, you can take advantage of all the fabulous FREE facilities and entertainment at our Holiday Village next door including:

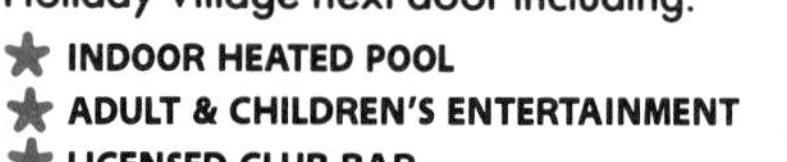

- INDOOR HEATED POOL
- ADULT & CHILDREN'S ENTERTAINMENT
- LICENSED CLUB BAR
- SUPERMARKET PLUS LOTS MORE!

BRITISH GRADED HOLIDAY PARKS

Reserve your site by calling our Holiday Hotline now!

New Beach Holiday Village, Hythe Road, Dymchurch, Kent TN29 0JX

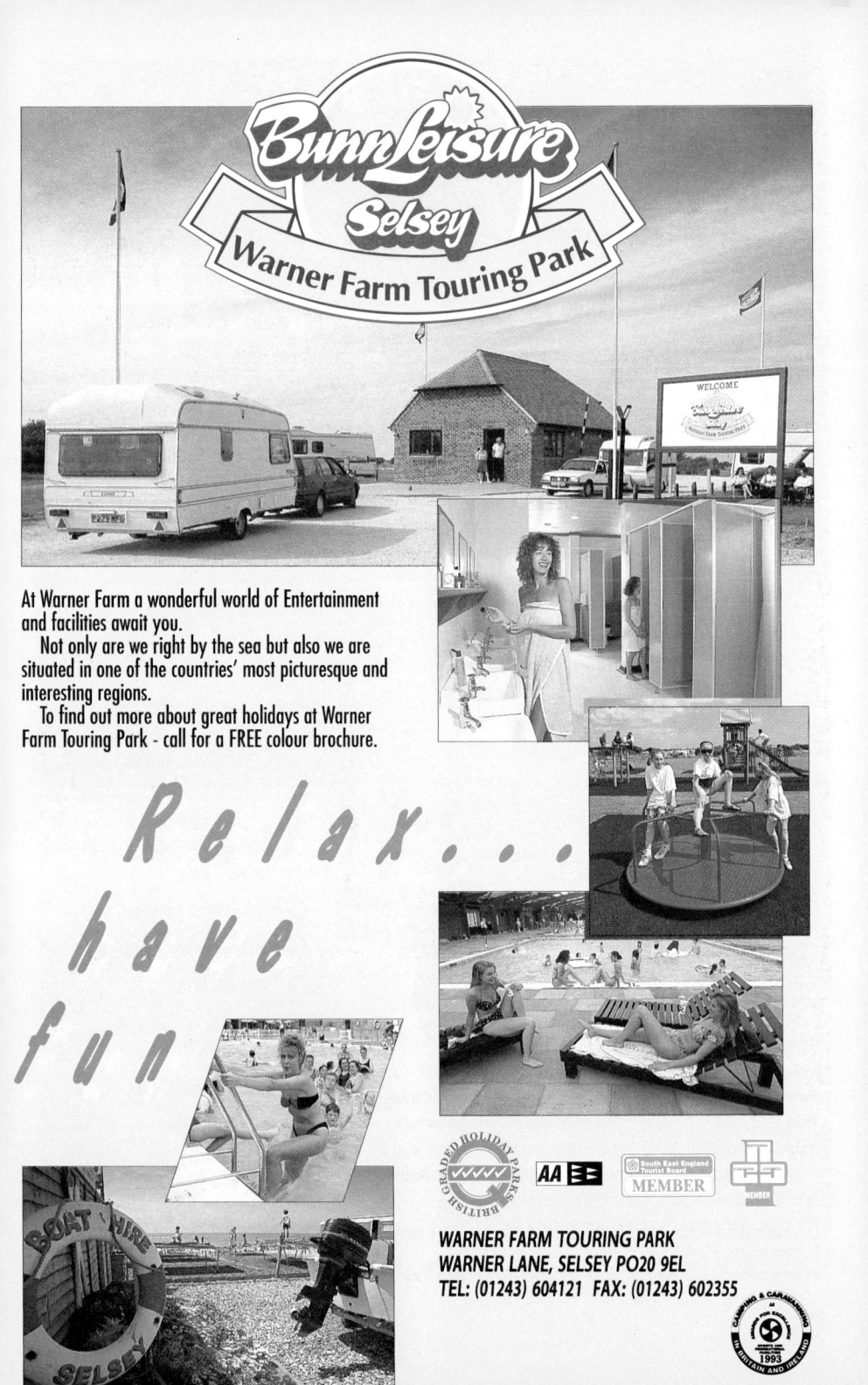

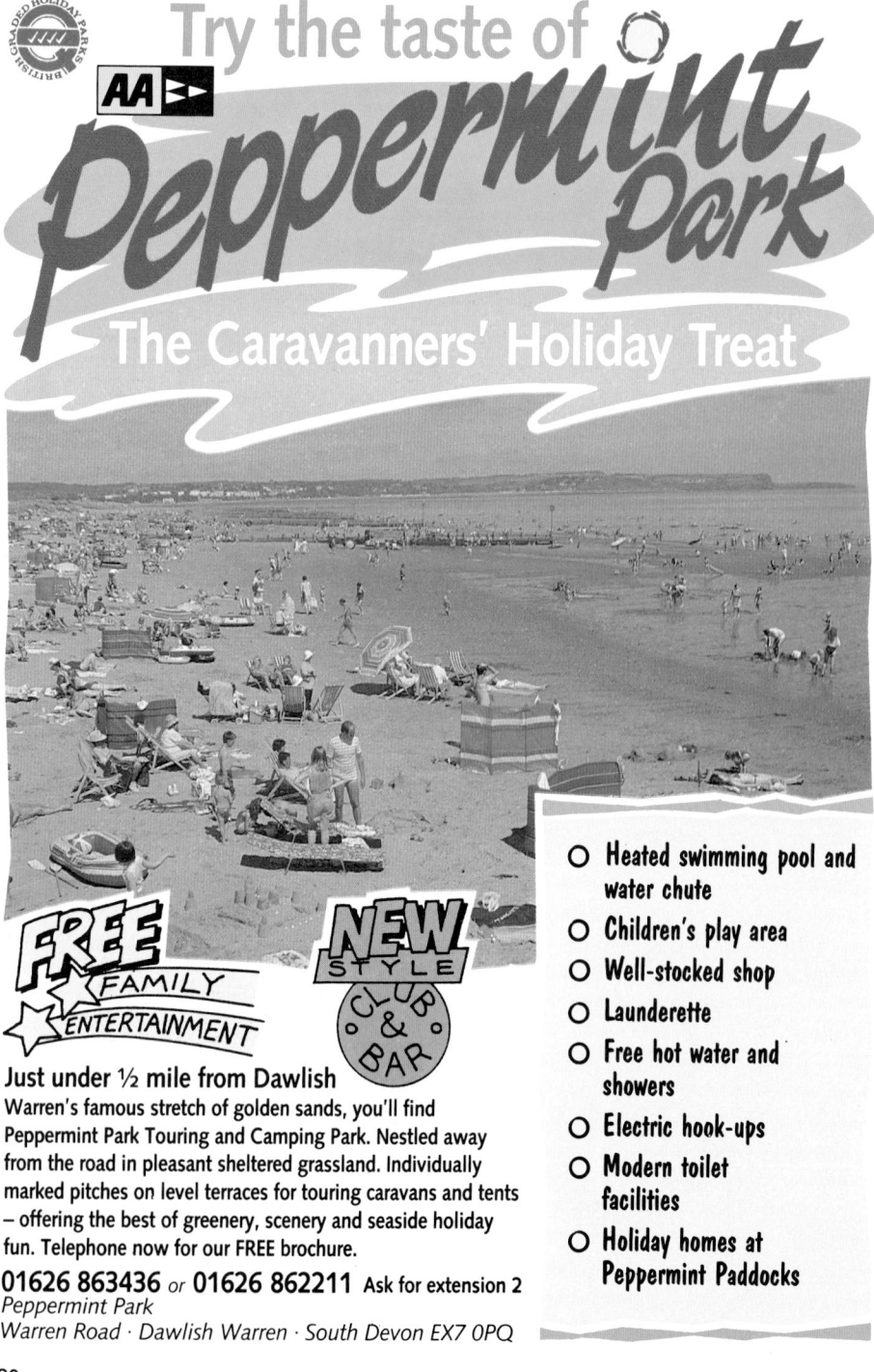

BETWEEN
WATERGATE BAY AND
MAWGAN PORTH NEWQUAY

IN QUIET COUNTRYSIDE CLOSE TO FABULOUS BEACHES

TREVARRIAN
HOLIDAY PARK

"We care about you, we care about your holiday"

Super facilities ★ Heated Pool ★ Individual Pitches ★ Electric Hook-ups ★ No Overcrowding ★ Self Service Shop ★ Laundrette ★ Park Lighting ★ TV/ Video & Games Room ★ Children's Play Area ★ Tennis Court and Pitch & Putt ★ Free Evening ★ Entertainment during Peak Season ★ Modern Toilets & Hot Showers ★ '*Stumbles*' with Club Licence ★ Bar Snacks

RAC

CARAVAN &
CAMPING CLUB

AA

1 **SPECIAL OFFER FOR EASTER...**

for the weekend
Friday, Saturday & Sunday

You must book in advance
Electric Hook-ups extra

2 **...FOR THE OVER 50's**

Special prices on request
Early June and Early Sept.

Activities include -Golf, Dancing, Rambling, Bingo etc.

3 **...FOR YOUNG FAMILIES**

Late June
Especially for parents with children under11. FREE pitch for your caravan or motor home. Special rates, ring for details.

Personally supervised by the proprietors Dave & Tish Phillips.
Write or phone for free colour brochure:
Trevarrian Holiday Park, Mawgan Porth, Newquay, Cornwall

(0637) 860381

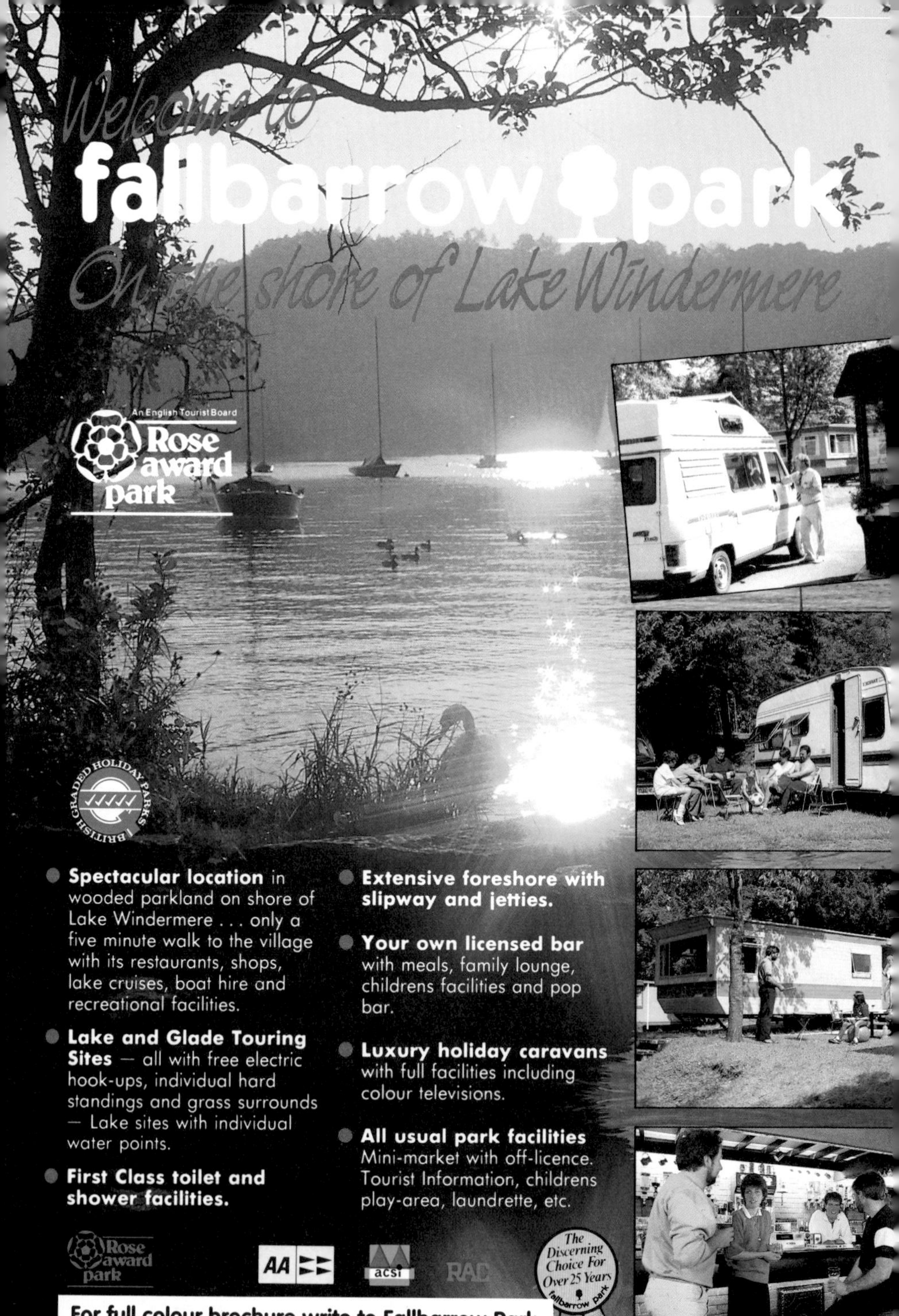

Welcome to
fallbarrow park
On the shore of Lake Windermere
An English Tourist Board
Rose award park
BRITISH GRADED HOLIDAY PARKS
Spectacular location in wooded parkland on shore of Lake Windermere . . . only a five minute walk to the village with its restaurants, shops, lake cruises, boat hire and recreational facilities.
Lake and Glade Touring Sites — all with free electric hook-ups, individual hard standings and grass surrounds — Lake sites with individual water points.
First Class toilet and shower facilities.
Extensive foreshore with slipway and jetties.
Your own licensed bar with meals, family lounge, childrens facilities and pop bar.
Luxury holiday caravans with full facilities including colour televisions.
All usual park facilities Mini-market with off-licence. Tourist Information, childrens play-area, laundrette, etc.
Rose award park
AA
acsi
RAC
The Discerning Choice For Over 25 Years
fallbarrow park
For full colour brochure write to Fallbarrow Park, Windermere, The Lake District LA23 3DL or telephone (015394) 44428.

Woolacombe Sands
HOLIDAY PARK
WOOLACOMBE
NORTH DEVON
Set in beautiful countryside overlooking the sea and Woolacombe's fabulous Golden Sands. First class facilities for Tents & Tourers, which include Showers, Toilets Wash-Basins, Hair dryers, Razor points, Launderette, Ironing room, Shop, Licensed Club, Bar Meals & Take-away, Nightly Entertainment (seasonal).
HEATED INDOOR SWIMMING POOL
Children's Games Room & Play Area. Electric hook ups available.
Booking is advisable especially in Peak Season.
AA
BRITISH GRADED HOLIDAY PARKS
Write for Brochure to: DEPT CG
RICHARDS HOLIDAYS
WOOLACOMBE SANDS HOLIDAY PARK, BEACH ROAD, WOOLACOMBE, NORTH DEVON EX34 7AF.
OR TELEPHONE
01271 870569
Also available self-catering Chalets and Caravans with all amenities

Limefitt Park

The only Campsite to win all 5 AA awards in one year!

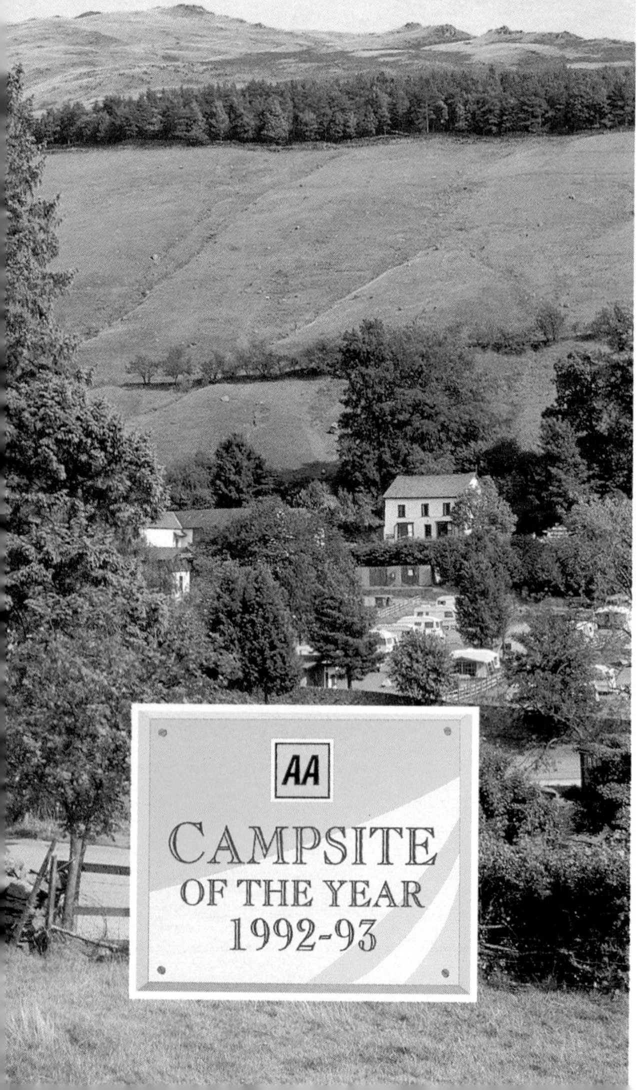

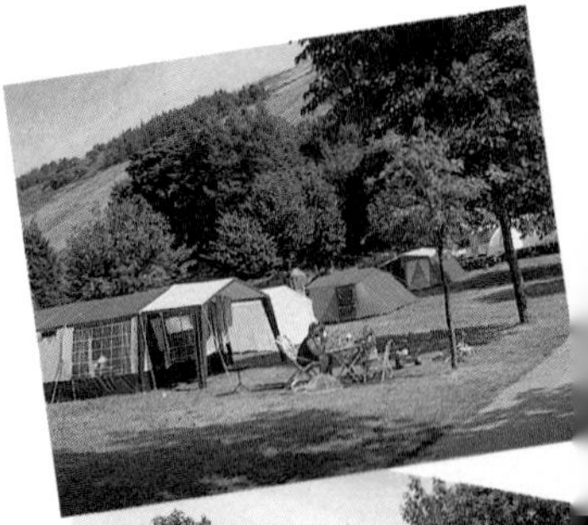

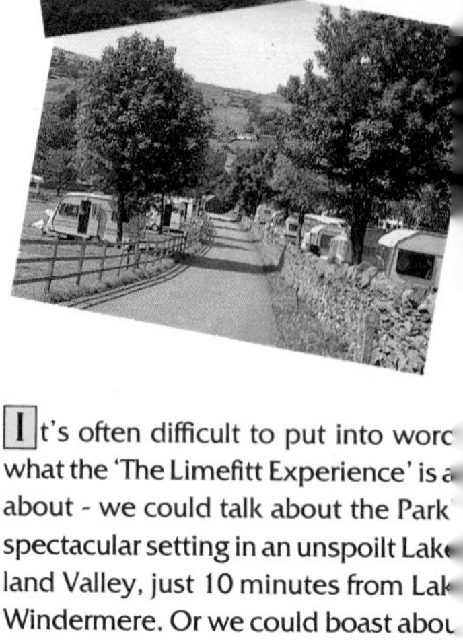

I t's often difficult to put into worc what the 'The Limefitt Experience' is a about - we could talk about the Park' spectacular setting in an unspoilt Lake land Valley, just 10 minutes from Lak Windermere. Or we could boast abou our superb range of facilities includin a Spar shop, parent and toddler room laundrette or our very own traditiona Lakeland Inn.

But possibly the AA summed it a up by calling Limefitt Park 'Campsite c the Year 1992-93'. In fact we were th only campsite to win all 5 AA awards i one year - high praise indeed. We hop you will come and sample Limefitt' delights for yourself.

For a brochure please telephone o write to us, we'd love to hear from you

Limefitt Park

Windermere, The Lake District, LA23 1P.
Telephone: (015394) 32300

Paignton Holiday Park

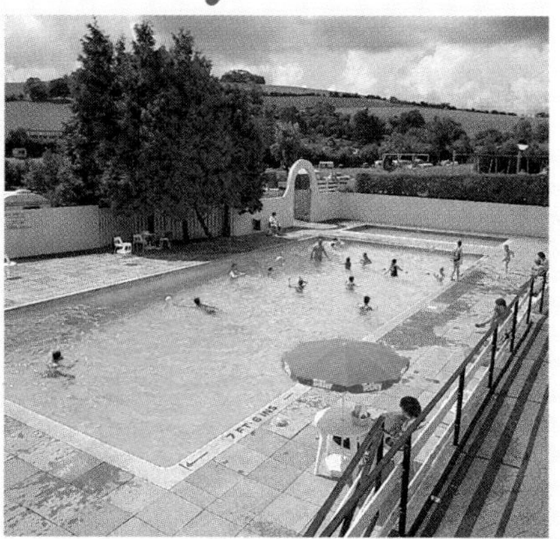

Two parks right in the centre of Torbay have been joined together to offer you the best of both worlds.

A beautifully landscaped Touring and Camping Park and a wide range of luxury Caravan Holiday Homes.

There is a full range of facilities for you to enjoy including a licenced club with entertainment, large heated swimming pool, separate toddlers splash pool, two shops, cafe with terrace, childrens evening play room, two play areas, two fully equipped laundries, and shower facilities for touring caravans and tents.

For free brochure:
Tel: 01803 550504 (24hr answer 01803 521684)
or write to Paignton Holiday Park, Dept. CC, Totnes Rd, Paignton, S. Devon. Tq4 7PY
(Dogs not accepted)

THE HEART OF THE ENGLISH RIVIERA

TOURING IN NORFOLK!

CHOOSE FROM 4 OF THE BEST HOLIDAY PARKS

Set in 250 acres of woodland and heather on the North Norfolk Coast, Kelling Heath is the natural location for those who wish to escape the rigours of everyday life enjoying, if you please, the excellent range of on park facilities.

NATURALLY THE BEST!

KELLING HEATH HOLIDAY PARK

Write for brochure to Mr C. Woods

KELLING HEATH HOLIDAY PARK
Weybourne, Nr Sheringham,
Norfolk, NR25 7HW
Telephone: **01263 588181**

5 Tick, Rose Award: one of Englands highest quality parks. We offer peace, tranquillity with extra large pitches and possibly the highest quality holiday hire caravans to be found.

Write for brochure to Mrs C. Hill

WOODHILL PARK
Cromer Road, East Runton,
Cromer, Norfolk, NR27 9PX
Telephone: 01263 512242

BlueSky HOLIDAY PARK

BRADWELL, GREAT YARMOUTH

It's enjoyment all the way at Blue Sky. $2^{1}/_{2}$ miles from Great Yarmouth with a full range of facilities to help you enjoy your stay, including for children in the Bluey Bear Club.

Write for brochure to Mrs C. Kirk

BLUE SKY LEISURE
Bradwell, Great Yarmouth, Norfolk, NR31 9ED
Telephone: 01493 780571

Relax in peaceful surroundings or join in the family fun, enjoying the excellent on park facilities at Sunfield. $5^{1}/_{2}$ miles from Great Yarmouth yet well placed for exploring the surrounding area and its attractions.

Sunfield HOLIDAY PARK

BELTON, GREAT YARMOUTH

Write for brochure to Mrs C Kirk

BLUE SKY LEISURE
Bradwell, Great Yarmouth,
Norfolk, NR31 9ED.
Telephone: **01493 780571**

For more details on the above Parks refer to advertisements in the Norfolk Section

"Happy Holidays" by the sea at

FRESHWATER HOLIDAY PARK

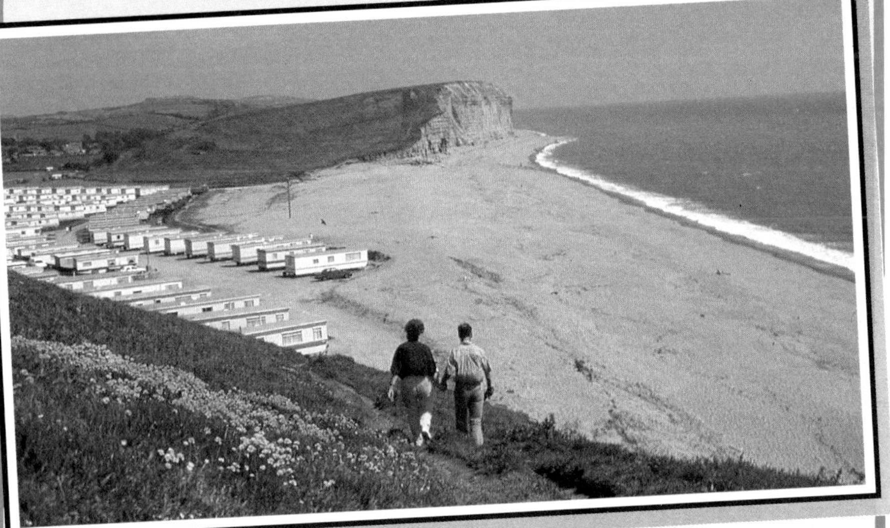

A family site with large Camping and Touring field
•Caravans for hire •Own private beach •Heated swimming pools •Club complex •Entertainment nightly (Whitsun - mid September) •Licensed restaurant •Supermarket •Amusements •Take-away •Free hot showers •Launderette •Horse/Pony rides •Golf course adjoining site •Fine country and Seaside walks •Caravan sales

Colour brochure from Mr C. C. Coads

FRESHWATER HOLIDAY PARK
Burton Bradstock
Near Bridport Dorset DT6 4PT
Telephone: (01308) 897317
Fax: (01308) 897336

SOUTH DEVON'S PREMIER TOURING & CAMPING PARK

"Whatever it takes to make you smile, you'll find it all at Lady's Mile"

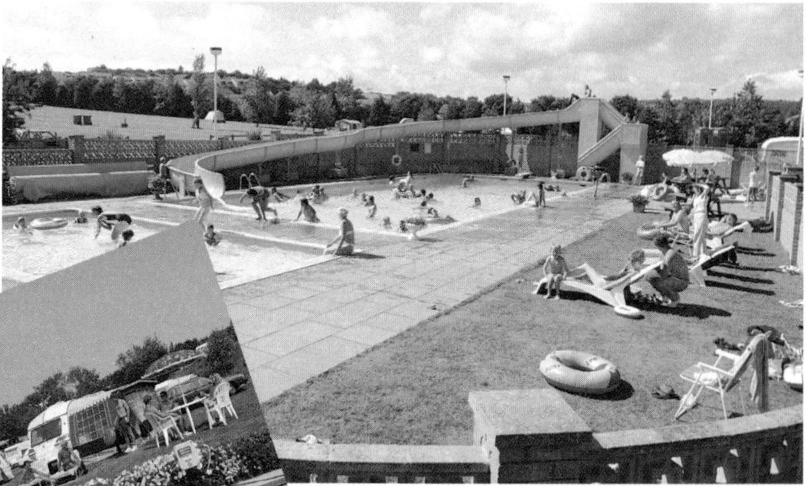

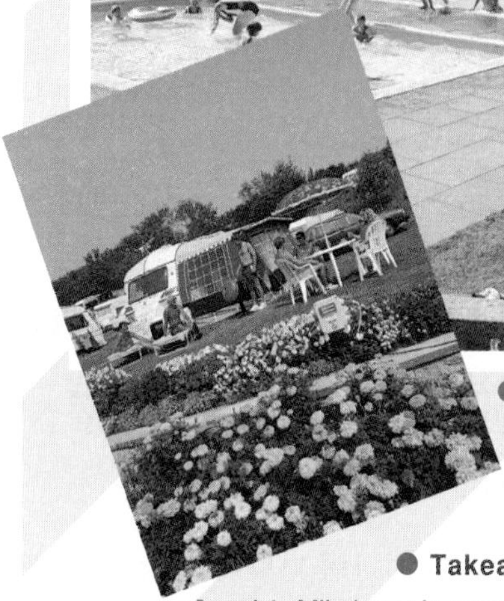

- Heated Swimming Pool with 100' waterslide
- Free Hot Water & Showers ● 2 Launderettes
- Large Mini-market and Off-licence
- Electric Hook-ups ● Rallies Welcome
- Adventure Fort & Play Area
- Takeaway foods ● Self catering apartments

Lady's Mile is set in grassy landscaped grounds and offers the very best in facilities for caravanners and campers. Run by a family with other families in mind, Lady's Mile is the ideal centre from which to spend a go-as-you-please, do-as-you-like holiday. There is plenty to see and do in and around Lady's Mile. We are close to the popular resort of Dawlish and the beautiful golden sands of Dawlish Warren. Our high standards mean we welcome back holiday makers year after year. Send for our free colour brochure.

"Probably the best size pitches in the South West!"

NEW
NINE HOLE GOLF COURSE

Mrs C. Jeffery, Lady's Mile Touring and Camping Park, Freepost, Dawlish, Devon EX7 9YZ

LADY'S MILE

(01626) 863411 (24hr)
FAX (01626) 888689

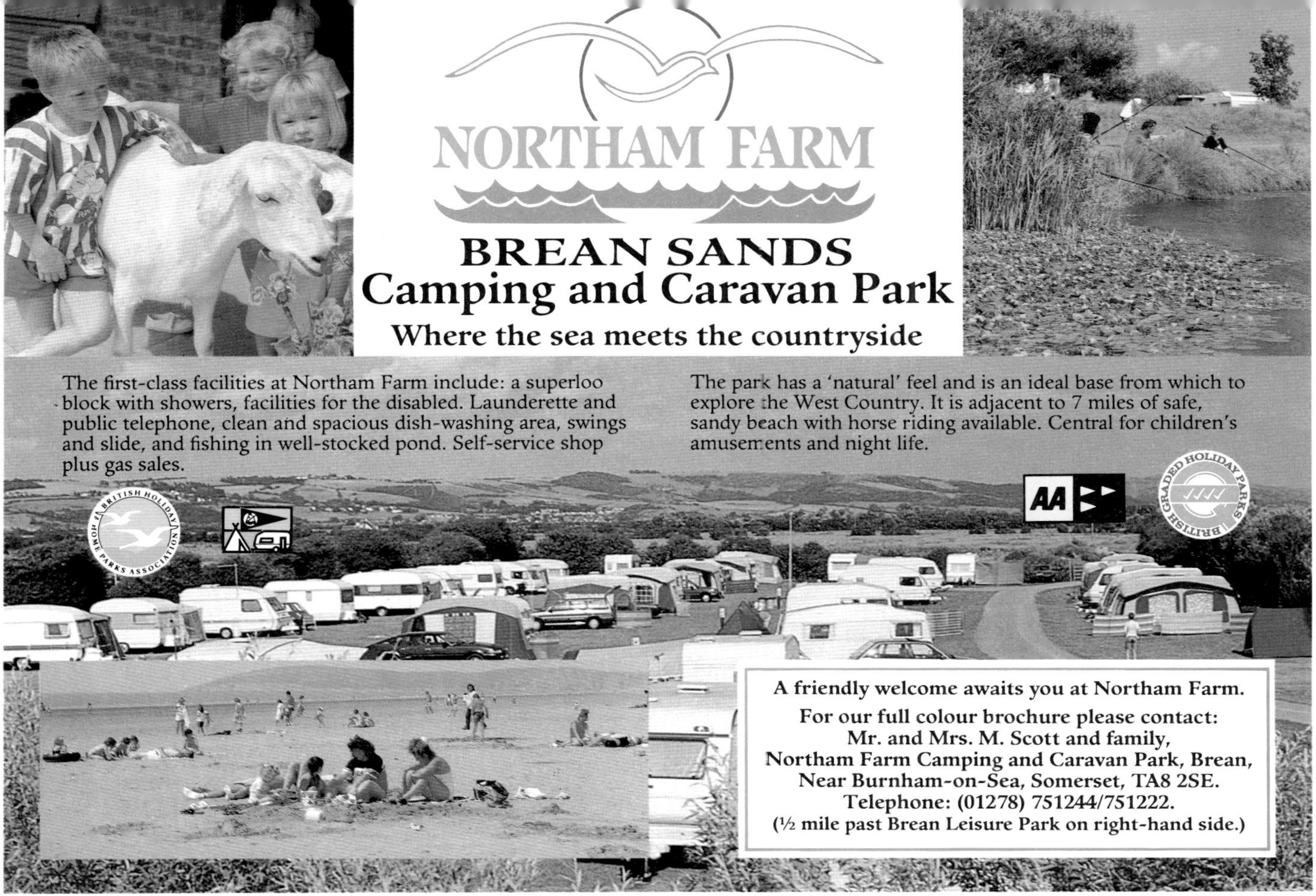

NORTHAM FARM

BREAN SANDS
Camping and Caravan Park

Where the sea meets the countryside

The first-class facilities at Northam Farm include: a superloo block with showers, facilities for the disabled. Launderette and public telephone, clean and spacious dish-washing area, swings and slide, and fishing in well-stocked pond. Self-service shop plus gas sales.

The park has a 'natural' feel and is an ideal base from which to explore the West Country. It is adjacent to 7 miles of safe, sandy beach with horse riding available. Central for children's amusements and night life.

British Holiday Home Parks Association

AA

British Graded Holiday Parks

A friendly welcome awaits you at Northam Farm.

For our full colour brochure please contact:
Mr. and Mrs. M. Scott and family,
Northam Farm Camping and Caravan Park, Brean,
Near Burnham-on-Sea, Somerset, TA8 2SE.
Telephone: (01278) 751244/751222.
(½ mile past Brean Leisure Park on right-hand side.)

Tenting & Touring at its best

FUN FOR ALL THE FAMILY

ON THE BEAUTIFUL PENDINE COAST

- *Serviced pitches available*
- *Lovely secluded holiday park*
- *7 miles of firm golden sands*

- *Family Clubhouse*
- *Indoor swimming pool and complex*
- *Luxury Caravans for hire*

HOLIDAY HOME
OWNERSHIP AVAILABLE!

Pendine Sands Holiday Park,
Nr Camarthen, Dyfed, S Wales

For your free colour brochure phone us today
LO-CALL 0345 443 443

Early Booking Discounts available

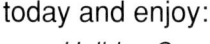

Home Farm
HOLIDAYS
THE ALL YEAR ROUND PARK
Top Class Entertainment nightly Good Friday to end of September

Morfa Lodge Holiday Park
Dinas Dinille, Nr. Caernarfon
Gwynedd LL54 5TP
Tel: 01286 830205

A friendly family run park. Located near a safe sandy beach and with superb mountain views. Central for touring Snowdonia, Anglesey and the Llŷn Peninsula. Luxury 2/3 bedroom caravans for hire. Tourers and tents welcomed.

Phone or write for free colour brochure.

DRAGON AWARD

- ***Outdoor swimming pool***
- ***Licensed Bar with entertainment***
- ***Free Club membership***
- ***Bar meals and take away food***
- ***Snooker / Pool room***
- ***Shop***
- ***Launderette***
- ***Electric hook ups***
- ***Free hot showers***
- ***Disabled toilet***
- ***Children's room***
- ***Children's outdoor playground***

Set midway between Portsmouth, New Forest & Winchester

Just 2 miles off Junc. 8 M27

With so much to see and do on your doorstep, yet within striking distance of the New Forest with its beautiful countryside. The historic city of Portsmouth with HMS Victory and the Mary Rose are only 20 mins away as are Winchester, Romsey, the Motor Museum at Beaulieu, Paultons Park and the wonderful Hampshire coastline.

Riverside Park , on the edge of the picturesque village of Hamble, is a most attractive level grass park with electric hookups, overlooking yachts on the river. Its a fabulous location in 'Howards Way' country encouraging you to explore its many pubs and restaurants tucked away by riverside walks. You won't regret your stay at Riverside!

Ring now for your free colour brochure.

RIVERSIDE PARK
Satchell Lane, Hamble,
Hants SO31 4HR
Telephone 01703 453220

On Hampshire & Dorset Boundary

off the A31 midway between Ringwood and Wimborne
Ideal base for New Forest/Bournemouth Area

Under New Ownership

Phone for our FREE Brochure

Shamba Holiday Park is a family run park, with a commitment to providing a good standard of facilities in a caring, friendly atmosphere. A 7 acre, level, well drained park set in wooded surroundings, situated close to the New Forest, yet within easy reach of Bournemouth and the lovely Dorset coastline.
Fishing, Golf, Sailing, Horse Riding close at hand.

** Licensed Clubhouse *Shop/Off License*
**Take Away Foodbar/Bar Meals*
** Electric Hookups * FREE Showers*
** Childrens Playground *Launderette * Amusements Room*

Ringwood Road, St. Leonards,
Ringwood, Hants. BH24 2SB
Tel: (01202) 873302

MILL FARM CARAVAN AND CAMPING PARK

FIDDINGTON, BRIDGWATER, SOMERSET

Attractive, quiet, sheltered farm site. Between the beautiful Quantock Hills and the sea. Ideal centre for:

SWIMMING, RIDING, BOATING

MEMBER

FREE: Boating, two heated swimming pools, swings, table tennis, colour TV.
Tourist Information, children's play area, canoes for hire, pony rides

Camp shop - Calor/Camping Gas - Off Licence -Restaurant 400 yards - Recommended by Camping Club - Units well spaced
Pay Phone - Clean toilets - Wash Basins - Showers - Shaver Points - Laundry room - Electric hookups - Caravan storage.

Mr & Mrs M.J. Evans TEL: NETHER STOWEY (01278) 732286 For Colour Brochure

NEWPARK HOLIDAY PARK

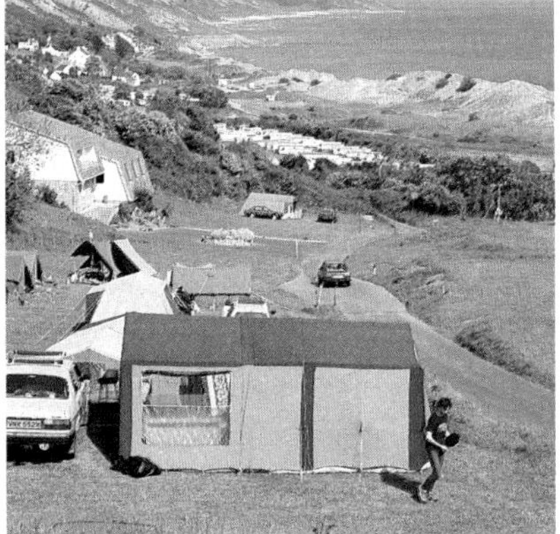

Newpark lies at the edge of the village of Port Eynon which has nestled for centuries on the Gower Peninsula coast. The magnificent beach - within easy walking distance - makes it the ideal place for a family and the broad waters of the Bristol Channel offer a wide range of water sports, safe bathing and the sea fishing for which the bay is renowned.

The countryside surrounding Port Eynon with its quiet lanes and paths, is idea for walking be it a gentle family ramble or an energetic hike.

The village itself has a welcoming pub and a good restaurant, whilst further afield there are a number of good eating places.

Newpark has full facilities for touring caravans, trailer tents and tents. These include a well stocked shop, off licence, play area for children, coin operated launderette, toilet blocks and showers.

The park also has self catering luxury bungalows accommodating up to six people with two bedrooms, bathroom, lounge with dining area, fridge, TV, Patio and everything provided except bed linen and towels.

Newpark Holiday Park, Port Eynon, Gower, South Wales.
Tel: 01792 390292 / 390478 Fax: 01792 391245

Carlyon Bay

Caravan & Camping Park

SUPERB LOCATION WITH FOOTPATH TO BLUE FLAG BEACH

- ★ **AA Britain's Best Sites**
- ★ **Practical Caravan Top 35 Video**
- ★ **England For Excellence Award nomination**
- ★ **AA Outstanding Environment Award 1992, 93 & 94/95**
- ★ **Children's entertainment in peak season**
- ★ **Run by the same Cornish family for 3 generations**

'A Family Affair!"

Carlyon Bay Camping Park, Cypress Avenue, Carlyon Bay, St. Austell, Cornwall PL25 3RE

TEL: 01726 - 812735

FOREST GLADE

International Caravan & Camping Park

ROSE AWARD CARAVAN HOLIDAY PARK

A small country estate surrounded by forest in which deer roam.

LARGE, FLAT, SHELTERED CAMPING/TOURING PITCHES MODERN FACILITIES BUILDING, LUXURY 2/6 BERTH FULL SERVICE HOLIDAY HOMES, ALSO SELF CONTAINED FLAT FOR 2 PERSONS.

FOREST GLADE HOLIDAY PARK, CULLOMPTON, DEVON EX15 2DT

COUNTRY HOLIDAY PARK

Shop, Take Away Food
Adventure Play Area, Games Room,
Electric Hook-up Points. Riding,
Forest & Hill Walks, Gliding, Fishing
& Golf are all nearby.
Freedom for the children, peace
for the adults. Central
for touring S.W. Easy
access coast and moors.
Motor caravans welcome – Facilities for the Disabled. Dogs welcome. Tourers please book in advance.

FREE COLOUR BROCHURE
Tel: (01404) 841381 (Evgs to 9pm)
Fax: (01404) 841593

TRETHEAKE MANOR TOURIST PARK

Veryan, Nr. Truro, Cornwall TR2 5PP

Write or phone Dept CA for colour brochure

Telephone: (01872) 501658

A peaceful park, surrounded by farmland, midway between St Mawes and Mevagissey.

Enjoy the tranquility of the Roseland Peninsula with its mild spring and autumn climate.

Easy access to safe sandy beaches secluded coves and miles of beautiful coastal walks. Close to excellent windsurfing, diving, sailing and riding facilities.

Toilet/Shower block, launderette and dishwashing area all with Free hot water. Children's playground, Games & TV Rooms. Electric and Water hook-ups, some with drainage.

Well stocked campshop, provisions, off licence, gas. Telephone kiosk, Coarse fishing, carp, roach, tench and bream. Indoor/outdoor Bowling and Tennis nearby

Best Placed for Beautiful

NORFOLK

SIXTEEN ACRES OF WOODLAND IN THE HEART OF TRUE NORFOLK COUNTRYSIDE. NEAR TO SANDRINGHAM AND WITHIN EASY REACH OF THE COAST AND BROADS.

- ★ Heated Swimming Pool.
- ★ Miniature Railway
- ★ Well Stocked Shop
- ★ Launderette
- ★ Ironing Room
- ★ Caravans for Hire
- ★ Electric Hook-ups
- ★ Games Room
- ★ Campers Kitchen
- ★ Pets Welcome

Family Run Park for Caravanners, by Caravanners.

OPEN ALL YEAR

Brochure from: Bryan & Hilary Webster
Pentney Park Caravan & Camping Site,
Pentney, Kings Lynn, Norfolk PE32 1HU
Tel: (01760) 337479

"EUROPA PARK"

WOOLACOMBE, N. DEVON. TEL: 01271 870159 / 772

SUPERB CAMPING

PETS WELCOME

ELECTRIC HOOK-UP AVAILABLE

INDOOR HEATED SWIMMING POOL

Wonderful position overlooking Barnstaple Bay, Lundy Island & surrounding countryside.
Full facilities include licensed club and games room. Launderette, Toilets and Showers. Large Children's Play Area. On-site Shop.

"AN INFORMAL AND ENJOYABLE PLACE TO STAY"

Mother Ivey's Bay Caravan Park
Trevose Head, Padstow, Cornwall. PL28 8SL. Tel: 01841 520990

Situated on the coast at Trevose Head with spectacular sea views, our own private sandy beach and one of the cleanest sea-bathing waters in the UK.
Perfect for traditional family holidays, the Park has landscaped grounds, modern facilities, but no clubs! No Bars! No Discos!

Trencreek Farm

HOLIDAY PARK

Hewaswater, St. Austell
Cornwall PL26 7JG

Telephone: St. Austell (0726) 882540

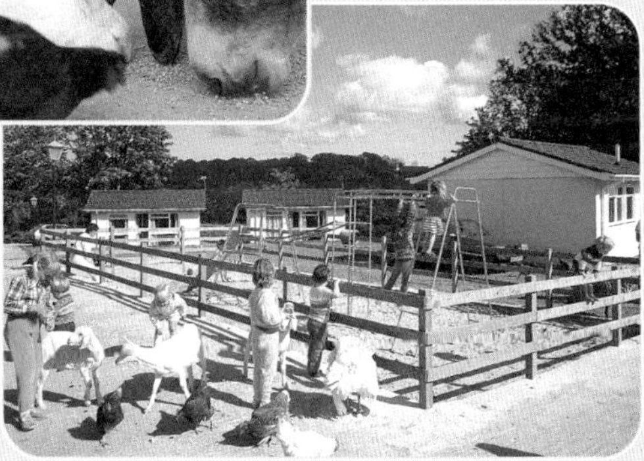

Holiday bungalows, caravans and a fully serviced touring park. All with country views and within easy reach of the sea. No bar or gaming machines, but a swimming pool, tennis court and fishing lake etc. We provide a supervised Kids Club in the main season and the park is safely situated a quarter of a mile off the main road, down our own private lane.

SPECIAL OFFERS: Easter to mid-July.
Self-catering: second week half price.
Touring: £35 per pitch, per week, including electric.

TOURING & TENTING IN NORTH WALES

Brynteg Holiday Park is truly unique. Set in wooded grounds, overlooking superb countryside in idyllic North Wales the park offers a world of fun and enjoyment for the whole family. Whether you want to get away from it with a good book and your fishing rod or dance the night away in the club Brynteg is the ideal venue for holidays and weekend breaks. Situated within easy distance of Caernarfon and Conway Castles and Snowdonia National Park, Brynteg is a firm favourite with the outdoor lover. Enjoy a quiet stroll amidst the most breathtaking scenery North Wales has to offer.

NEW
SWIMMING POOL & LEISURE CENTRE FOR 1995!

For more information or a free colour brochure telephone us now.

B R Y N T E G

Holiday Park

Llanrug, near Caernarfon, Gwynedd. LL55 4RF.

TEL: 0286 871374

UGP 6580

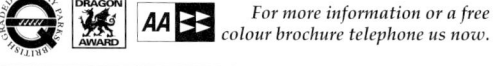

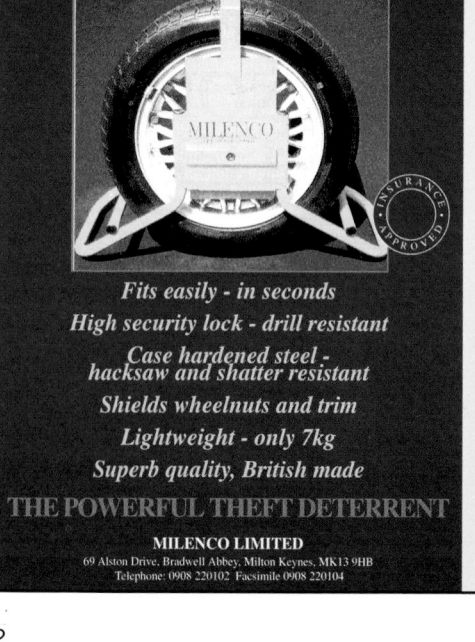

CADE'S

CAMPING TOURING AND MOTOR CARAVAN *SITE GUIDE*

1 9 9 5

Twenty Third Edition

First Published as Camping Site Guide in 1972

Compiled and Edited by Reg Cade

Advertising Sales Manager Andrew Wiltshire Tel: (01908) 643022

Published by
Marwain Publishing Limited,
Marwain House, Clarke Road, Mount Farm, Milton Keynes MK1 1LG.

Designed by
Pepberry Limited,
Marwain House, Clarke Road, Mount Farm, Milton Keynes MK1 1LG.

Computer Typesetting by
Spottiswoode Ballantyne, Colchester, Essex.

Printed by
Warners Midlands plc, Bourne, Lincs.

Distributed by (Newsagents and Bookshops)
Springfield Books Limited,
Springfield House, Norman Road, Denby Dale, Huddersfield HD8 8TH.

(Camping and Caravan Trade)
Marwain Publishing Limited.

ISBN 0 - 905377 - 64 - 8

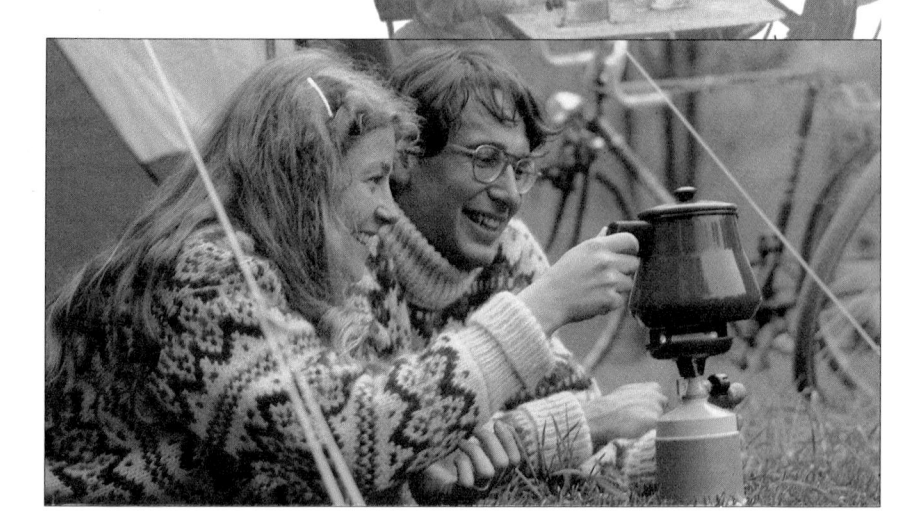

FOREWORD

Bigger and better than ever, it is my pleasure to welcome you to the new revised edition of the most successful publication for touring holidays in Britain.

Reflecting the many changes and improvements taking place now in Britain's tourism industry, **CADE'S CAMPING, TOURING AND MOTORCARAVAN SITE GUIDE** is the only complete, best value guide to give you; discount vouchers, eight page colour road map section, a nationwide Dealer and Retailer section and the most detailed and up to date account of nationwide touring parks. That will enable you to make the most of long touring holidays, short breaks and weekends away in England, Scotland and Wales.

Simply look for the **£** sign and see which parks will give you and your family 50p per night upon redemption of the money off vouchers in the back section of this guide. You can save up to £10 by using one of the vouchers for each night booked and paid for.

Every entry detailed in this guide should provide you with the most essential information on each caravan and camping park enabling you to make the most of your touring holiday. Key symbols make direct comparisons of sites a simple process, the guide will also leave you in no doubt as to whether your interest and requirement is catered for For instance it will inform you as to how many pitches are available, whether the ground is sloping or level, if the park has electric hook-ups and the range of leisure activities available not only on the park, but in the nearby area.

We pride ourselves, as always, on the accuracy of the detailed information in our guide. We must, however, point out that we are not agents of the sites and publish only such information as is supplied to us ny the owner or operator in good faith and cannot therefore be responsible for any conditions or facilities that differ from those published. We would therefore advise you to check directly with the site before booking.

The full addresses and telephone numbers of each site are published to help with your enquiries. Do remember that advance bookings are advised especially in the peak season.

In the meantime, may I wish you successful touring in 1995 and hope you have some enjoyable holidays.

REG CADE
(MANAGING DIRECTOR, MARWAIN PUBLISHING LIMITED)
FOR CADE'S CAMPING, TOURING & MOTORCARAVAN SITE GUIDE.

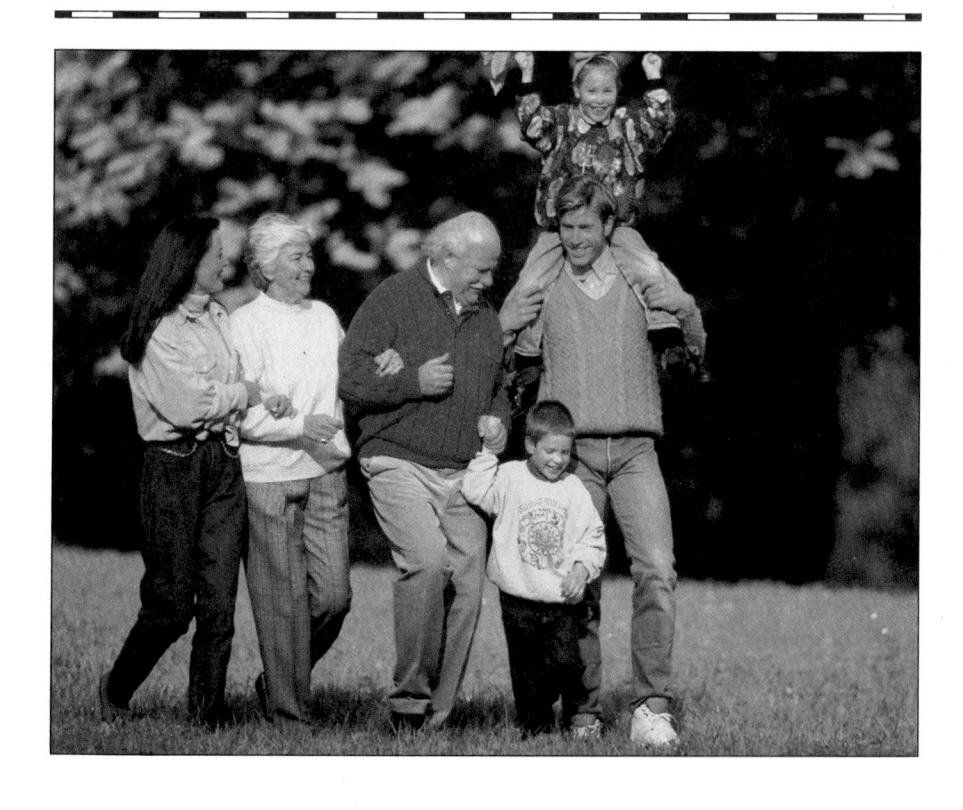

ENGLISH SYMBOLS

Tents
Motor Caravans
Touring Caravans
Nearest Station
Facilities for Disabled
Electricity Hook-ups
No Motorcycles
Flush Toilets
Water
Showers
Shaver Points
Washing Facilities
Ironing Facilities
Launderette
Chem. Toilet Disp.
S Site Shop
M Mobile Shop
l Local Shop
Gas
Public Telephone
Cafe Restaurant
Licensed Club
T.V.
Games Room
Childs Play Area
Swim Pool
Sports Area
No Dogs Allowed
Parking by Unit
Nearby Facilities
Golf
Fishing
Sailing
Boating
Riding
Water-Skiing
Tennis
Climbing
Site accepts Money Off Vouchers

FRANÇAIS SYMBOLES

Tentes
Auto-Caravanes
Caravanes
Gare
Handicapés
Branchments électrique pour caravanes
Motocyclette non admises
Toilettes
Eau
Douches
Prises électrique pour rasoirs
Bains
Repassage
Laverie automatique
Décharge pour W.C. chimiques
S Magasin du terrain
M Magasin mobile
l Magasin du quartier
Gaz
Cabines téléphoniques
Café
Club/Bar patenté
Salle de Télévision
Salle de jeux
Terrain de jeux pour infants
Piscine du terrain
Terrain de sports et de jeux
Chiens interdits
Stationnment à côté de la tente ou de la caravane permis
Le quartier offre:
Golf
Pêche
Voile
Canotage
Equitation
Ski nautique
Tennis
Ascension

INDEX

ENGLAND

AVON

BATH

Bury View, Corston Fields, Bath, Avon, BA2 9HD.
Tel. 873672 Std. 01225.
Nearest Town/Resort Bath.
Directions 5 miles from Bath, situated on A39 Wells road.
Acreage 1¼ **Open** All Year
Access Good **Site** Level
Sites available Total 15.
Facilities
Bath.
Close to Bath, quiet countryside site.

BATH

Newbridge Caravan Park, Brassmill Lane, Bath, Avon, BA1 3JT.
Tel. 428778 Std. 01225
Nearest Town/Resort Bath.
Open All Year
Access Good **Site** Level
Sites available Total 88.
Facilities
Nearby facilities
Bath.
Alongside a river. Ideal touring area and Bath itself. Near a cafe/restaurant.

BATH

Newton Mill Caravan & Camping Park, Newton St. Loe, Bath, Avon, BA2 9JF.
Tel. 333909 Std. 01225.
Nearest Town/Resort Bath.
Directions A4 from Bath towards Bristol, at Globe roundabout B3110 left.
Acreage 43 **Open** All year
Access Good **Site** Level
Sites available Total 195.
Facilities
Nearby facilities
Bath.
Beautiful wooded valley with own Trout stream.

BRISTOL

Salthouse Farm Touring Park, Severn Beach, Bristol, Avon.
Tel. 632274 Std. 01454
Nearest Town/Resort Bristol.
Directions M4 junction 21 take the A403 for 3 miles. At traffic lights turn right onto the B4055 to Severn Beach, site is on the right. M5 junction 17 take the B4055 to traffic lights.
Acreage 2 **Open** April–October
Access Good **Site** Level
Sites available Total 40.
Facilities
Nearby facilities
Alongside an estuary and the New Severn Bridge. Ideal touring.

CLEVEDON

Warrens Holiday Park, Colehouse Lane, Clevedon, Avon, BS21 6TQ.
Tel. 871666 Std. 01275
Nearest Town/Resort Weston-super-Mare.
Directions M5 junction 20, follow road towards Congresbury for 1 mile.
Acreage 8 **Open** March–January
Access Good **Site** Level
Sites available Total 100.
Facilities
Nearby facilities
Yatton.
Fishing.

CONGRESBURY

Oak Farm Touring Park, Weston Road, Congresbury, Avon. BS19 5EB.
Tel. 833246 Std. 01934
Nearest Town/Resort Weston-super-Mare.
Directions 4 miles from junc. 21 on M5, on the A370 midway between Bristol and Weston Super Mare.
Open 31st Mar–October
Access Good **Site** Level
Sites available Total 27.
Facilities
Nearby facilities
Yatton.

WESTON-SUPER-MARE

Ardnave Holiday Park, Kewstoke, Weston-super-Mare, Avon, BS22 9XJ.
Tel. 622319 Std. 01934
Nearest Town/Resort Weston-super-Mare.
Directions Off motorway M5 at junction 21 follow signs to Kewstoke.
Acreage ½ **Open** March–October
Access Good **Site** Level
Sites available Total 12.
Facilities
Nearby facilities
Weston-super-Mare.
Near Beach, Graded 4 Ticks.

WESTON SUPER MARE

Country View Caravan Park, Sand Road, Sand Bay, Weston-super-Mare, Avon, BS22 9UJ.
Tel. 627595 Std. 01943
Nearest Town/Resort Weston-super-Mare.
Directions M5 exit 21, right at Sainsburys onto Queensway, through into Norton Lane, right into Sand Road.
Acreage 4 **Open** March–Oct
Access Good **Site** Level
Sites available Total 120.
Facilities
Nearby facilities
Weston-super-Mare.
200yds from beach, walking distance to National Trust Headland and Woods. Cheddar, Wells, Bath and Wookey Hole a short car ride. Graded 4 Ticks and Rose Award since 1990.

WESTON-SUPER-MARE

Home Farm Kewstoke, Home Farm, Lower Norton Lane, Kewstoke, Weston-super-Mare, Avon, BS22 9YR.
Tel. 636272 Std. 01934
Nearest Town/Resort Weston-super-Mare.
Directions From M5 junction 21 onto the A370 (Weston-super-Mare); within ¾ mile at roundabout turn right into Queensway (signposted Kewstoke and Sand Bay). Continue straight over three roundabouts and follow country lane, at right bend turn left into drive (signposted Home Farm), site on left in 100yds.
Acreage 1 **Open** All Year
Access Good **Site** Level
Sites available Total 5.
Facilities
Nearby facilities
Sandy beach 1 mile, scenic views, ideal for the M5 (3 miles). Caravan entry restricted to Caravan Club Members only.

WESTON-SUPER-MARE

Manor Farm, Grange Road, Uphill, Weston-Super-Mare, Avon.
Tel. 823288 Std. 01934.
Nearest Town/Resort Weston-Super-Mare.
Directions Follow signs to Uphill and Hospital. Just off the A371, opposite Hospital.
Acreage 3 **Open** March–October
Access Good **Site** Lev/Slope
Sites available Total 60.
Facilities
Nearby facilities

≢ Weston-Super-Mare.
Easy access, close to attractions. 2 miles to town centre, close to beach and marina. For enquiries contact : Oak Tree Parks Limited, Oak Tree Park, Locking, Weston-Super-Mare, Avon, BS24 8RG.

WESTON-SUPER-MARE

Norton Farm, Kewstoke, Weston-super-Mare, Avon.
Tel. 623030 Std. 01934
Nearest Town/Resort Weston-super-Mare.
Directions From M5 Junction 21 A370 towards Weston Super Mare in ½ mile right at second roundabout, then follow Queensway to end. Norton Farm is fifth house on right.
Acreage 2 **Open** School Holidays Only
Access Good **Site** Level
Sites available
Facilities
Nearby facilities
≢ Weston-super-Mare.
1 mile beach. 4 miles Weston Super Mare, 3 miles M5.

WESTON-SUPER-MARE

Purn International Holiday Park, A370 Bridgwater Road, Bleadon, Weston-Super-Mare, Avon. BS24 0AN.
Tel. 812342 Std. 01934
Nearest Town/Resort Weston Super Mare.
Directions From North leave M5 at junction 21 A370 into Weston A370 out of Weston – park 2 miles on right next to Anchor Inn, signposted. From South leave M5 junction 22 take signs for Weston on left next to Anchor Inn on A370.
Acreage 3 **Open** March–7th Nov
Access Good **Site** Level
Sites available Total 60.
Facilities
Nearby facilities
≢ Weston Super Mare.
Nearest Park to Weston, Licensed club and our own traditional country pub, The Anchor Inn with restaurant and family room, entertainment, dancing and Karioke. Childrens Bouncing Robin Club with Uncle Chris. 1993 prices held for 1995. RAC appointed 4 Ticks.

WESTON-SUPER-MARE

West End Farm Caravan & Camping Park, Locking, Weston Super Mare, Avon. BS24 8RH.
Tel. 822529 Std. 01934
Nearest Town/Resort Weston Super Mare.

Directions Leave M5 at junc. 21 follow signs for the "International Helicopter Museum" then proceed along the A370 to Heron Public House, turn left onto A371 (to Wells) turn right immediately after Helicopter Museum and follow signs to site.
Acreage 10 **Open** All year
Access Good **Site** Level
Sites available Total 75.
Facilities
Nearby facilities
≢ Weston Super Mare.
2 miles from Weston, ideal touring. Super pitches available.

WINSCOMBE

Netherdale Caravan & Camping Site, Bridgwater Road, Sidcot, Winscombe, Avon BS25 1NH.
Tel. 3481/3007 Std. 0193 484.
Nearest Town/Resort Cheddar.
Directions From Weston-super-Mare follow A371 to join A38 at Sidcot corner, site ¼ mile south. From Wells and Cheddar follow A371 westwards to join A38 a mile south of site.
Acreage 3½ **Open** March–October
Access Good **Site** Lev/Slope
Sites available Total 25.
Facilities
Nearby facilities
≢ Weston-super-Mare.
Excellent walking area, footpath from site to valley and Mendip Hills adjoining. Good views. Ideal touring centre. Many historical places and beaches within easy reach of site. Only individual motorcycles accepted, not groups. Dry ski slope – 3 miles.

BEDFORDSHIRE

RIDGMONT

Rose & Crown, 89 High St. Ridgmont, Beds.
Tel. 280245 Std. 01525
Nearest Town/Resort Woburn/Ampthill.
Directions Midway between Ampthill and Woburn on A507 2 miles south of junc 13 M1.
Acreage 3 **Open** All Year
Access Good **Site** Level
Sites available Total 20.
Facilities
Nearby facilities
≢ Ridgmont.
Adjacent to Woburn Safari Park and 4 miles from Woburn Abbey.

BERKSHIRE

DORNEY REACH

Amerden Caravan Site, Off Old Marsh Lane, Dorney Reach, Nr. Maidenhead, Berkshire.
Tel. Maidenhead 27461 Std. 01628.
Nearest Town/Resort Maidenhead.
Directions Leave M4 junc 7, Slough West, then A4 towards Maidenhead. Third turn left signposted Dorney Reach and caravan site, then first turn right.
Acreage 3 **Open** April–October
Access Good **Site** Level
Sites available
Facilities
Nearby facilities
≢ Taplow.
Near River Thames.

HURLEY

Hurley Caravan & Camping Park, Shepherds Lane, Hurley, Nr. Maidenhead, Berks.
Tel. 823501/824493 Std. 01628
Nearest Town/Resort Maidenhead/Henley-on-Thames.
Directions Maidenhead, A4130 west towards Henley. After 3¼ miles turn right, ¾ mile past East Arms PH into Shepherds Lane. Entrance 200 yards on left.
Acreage 15 **Open** March–October
Access Good **Site** Level
Sites available Total 200.
Facilities
Nearby facilities
≢ Maidenhead.
On picturesque River Thames. Ideal touring centre for Henley, Windsor, Oxford and London. Launching ramp. Walks along riverside and into nearby forest. Site shop in peak season only.

NEWBURY

Oakley Farm Caravan Park, Oakley Farm House, Wash Water, Newbury, Berkshire, RG15 0LP.
Tel. 36581 Std. 01635
Nearest Town/Resort Newbury.
Directions 2¼ miles south of Newbury, off the A343, well signposted off this main road. Take turning adjacent to car sales garage. Site is 380yds on your left.
Acreage 3 **Open** March–October
Access Good **Site** Level
Sites available Total 30.
Facilities
Nearby facilities
≢ Newbury.
Country walks all around the area.

RISELEY
Wellington Country Park, Riseley, Nr Reading, Berks RG7 1SP.
Tel. 326444 Std. 01734
Nearest Town/Resort Reading.
Directions Off junc 11 M4, take A33 to Basingstoke, left turn at roundabout.
Acreage 12 **Open** March–October
Access Good **Site** Level
Sites available Total 58.
Facilities
Nearby facilities
Reading.
Large lake with 350 acres, windsurfing, sailing, canoeing, coarse fishing, nature trails, deer park, Dairy Museum, playground, animal farm, ideal touring base.

WOKINGHAM
California Chalet & Touring Park, Nine Mile Ride, Finchampstead, Wokingham, Berks, RG11 3NY.
Tel. 733928 Std. 01734
Nearest Town/Resort Wokingham.
Directions A321 towards Sandhurst, in 1¼ miles turn right onto B3016. In 1 mile turn right at California crossroads onto the B3430, park is ¼ mile on the right.
Acreage 5¼ **Open** March–October
Access Good **Site** Level
Sites available Total 35.
Facilities
Nearby facilities
Wokingham.
Lakeside, wooded park, ideal for visiting Windsor, Oxford, Thames Valley and London.

BUCKS

BEACONSFIELD
Highclere Farm Country Touring Park, Newbarn Lane, Seer Green, Beaconsfield, Bucks, HP9 2QZ.
Tel. 874505 Std. 01494
Nearest Town/Resort Beaconsfield.
Directions From M40 Junction 2 at Beaconsfield, join A40 to London. Off at Potkiln Lane to Seer Green.
Open March–Janurary
Access Good **Site** Level
Sites available Total 60.
Facilities
Nearby facilities
Seer Green.
A peaceful site within easy reach of London and Windsor.

IVINGHOE
Silver Birch, Silver Birch Cafe, Ivinghoe, Near Leighton Buzzard, Bucks.
Tel. 668348 Std. 01296
Nearest Town/Resort Tring.
Directions Follow B488 out of Tring towards Ivinghoe on the Dunstable road (B488) and we are on the left just before Ivinghoe (3 miles).
Acreage 1½ **Open** March–October
Sites available Total 10.
Facilities
Nearby facilities
Tring.
Near a zoo. Marsworth Reservoirs, Ivinghoe Beacon and many scenic views.

MARLOW
Harleyford Estate Ltd, Henley Road, Marlow, Bucks, SL7 2DX.
Tel. 471361 Std. 01628
Nearest Town/Resort Marlow/Henley on Thames.
Directions Close to M40 junction 4 and M4 junctions 8 and 9 on A4155 between Marlow and Henley.
Acreage 200 **Open** May–September
Access Good **Site** Level
Sites available Total 60.
Facilities
Nearby facilities
High Wycombe.
Estate on beautiful stretch of the River Thames.

CAMBS

BURWELL
Barrons Cove Caravan & Camping Site, Weirs Road, Burwell, Cambridgeshire, CB5 0BP.
Tel. 741547 Std. 01638
Nearest Town/Resort Cambridge/Newmarket.
Directions From Cambridge take B1102 to Burwell from Newmarket take B1103 to Burwell.
Acreage 20 **Open** All year
Access Good **Site** Level
Sites available Total 150.
Facilities
Nearby facilities
Newmarket.
Near to rivers, on the Fens for birdwatching etc, Newmarket Horse Racing. RAC appointed, 3 Pennants and 4 Ticks. You can also call us on 0374 152741.

CAMBRIDGE
Alwyn Camping & Caravan Park, Over Road, Willingham, Cambridgeshire CB4 5EU.
Tel. 260977 Std. 01954.
Nearest Town/Resort Cambridge.
Directions A604 towards Huntingdon for 4 miles turn off at Bar Hill towards Longstanton/Willingham, bare left until you reach Willingham crossroads approx. 4 miles. Turn left and site is about 400 yards on left.
Acreage 5 **Open** March–October
Access Good **Site** Level
Sites available Total 85.
Facilities
Nearby facilities
Cambridge.
Cambridge, Ely, St. Ives. Duxford Air Museum. River Ouse 2½ miles (fishing).

CAMBRIDGE
Highfield Farm Camping Park, Highfield Farm, Long Road, Comberton, Cambridge, CB3 7DG.
Tel. 262308 Std. 01223
Nearest Town/Resort Cambridge.
Directions From Cambridge. Leave A1303/A45 (Bedford) after 3 miles, follow camping signs to Comberton. From M11. Leave junction 12, take A603 (Sandy) for ½ mile then B1046 to Comberton (2 miles).
Acreage 8 **Open** April–October
Access Good **Site** Level
Sites available Total 120.
Facilities
Nearby facilities
Cambridge.
Well maintained, long established family run Touring Park. Close to the historic University City of Cambridge, and the Imperial War Museum, Duxford. Awarded 5 quality symbols (Excellent) in the British Graded Holiday Parks scheme. AA camp site of the year 1991/92 Midlands winner.

CAMBRIDGE
Roseberry Tourist Park, Earith Road, Willingham, Cambs.
Tel. 260346 Std. 01954
Nearest Town/Resort Cambridge.
Directions Leave M11 at junction 16 (Bar Hill) onto the B1050. Site is on the left in 6 miles.
Acreage 9 **Open** Easter–October
Access Good **Site** Level
Sites available Total 80.
Facilities
Nearby facilities
Cambridge.
Ideal for touring Cambridge, Ely, Huntindon area. AA two pennant site. RAC listed. Sheltered orchard site.

HEMINGFORD ABBOTS
Quite Waters Caravan Park, Hemingford Abbots, Huntingdon, Cambs. PE18 9AJ.
Tel. 463405 Std. 01480
Nearest Town/Resort Huntingdon/Cambridge.
Directions North/South off A1 Huntingdon/Cambridge A604/M11 turnoff. 7 miles towards Cambridge turn off at Hemingford Abbots.
Acreage ¼ **Open** April–October
Access Good **Site** Level
Sites available Total 20.
Facilities
Nearby facilities
Huntingdon.
Boating, fishing, country walks, quiet riverside village. AA 3 pennants. E.A.T.B. 4 ticks.

HUNTINGDON
Houghton Mill Camping Park, Mill Street, Houghton, Huntingdon, Cambs, PE17 2BJ.
Tel. 462413 Std. 01480
Nearest Town/Resort St Ives.
Directions Half way between Huntingdon and St Ives off the A1123.
Acreage 9 **Open** April–September
Access Good **Site** Level
Sites available Total 65.
Facilities
Nearby facilities
Huntingdon.
Riverside site in picturesque setting.

HUNTINGDON
Hartford Marina, Wyton, Huntingdon, Cambs, PE17 2AA.
Tel. 454677 Std. 01480
Nearest Town/Resort Huntingdon.
Directions A1123, Huntingdon 3 miles.
Acreage 5 **Open** March–October
Access Good **Site** Level
Sites available Total 31.
Facilities
Nearby facilities
Huntingdon.
River and marina, fishing.

HUNTINGDON
Park Lane (Touring), Park Lane, Godmanchester, Huntingdon, Cambs, PE18 8AF.
Tel. 453740 Std. 01480
Nearest Town/Resort Huntingdon.

Directions From A604 northbound, turn left for Godmanchester/Huntingdon. Follow signs in Godmanchester on lamp posts, turn right at Black Pub Public House to Park Lane.
Acreage 2¼ **Open** March–October
Access Good **Site** Level
Sites available Total 50.
Facilities
Nearby facilities
Huntingdon.
A great deal of History and buildings in the towns of Huntingdon and Godmanchester.

LONGSTOWE
Fox Inn, Old North Road, Bourn, Cambridgeshire, CB3 7UF.
Tel. 719264 Std. 01954
Nearest Town/Resort Cambridge.
Directions Royston A1198 north to Huntingdon, through Bassingbourn and Arrington to Longstowe. Pub is at the crossroads.
Acreage 3 **Open** All year
Access Good **Site** Level
Sites available Total 90.
Facilities
Nearby facilities
Royston.
Cambridge 8 miles, indoor karting 2 miles.

YARWELL
Yarwell Mill Caravan Park, Peterborough, Cambs.
Tel. 782344 Std. 01780
Nearest Town/Resort Stamford.
Directions At Wansford church (A1-A47) intersection follow the Yarwell signs.
Open Easter–October
Access Good **Site** Level
Sites available Total 80.
Facilities
Nearby facilities
Peterborough.
River and Lakeside pitches 1½ miles fishing boating. Nr Nene Valley Railway.

CHESHIRE

ACTON BRIDGE
Woodbine Cottage Caravan Park, Warrington Road, Acton Bridge, Nr. Northwich Cheshire. CW8 3QB.
Tel. 852319/77900 Std. 01606.
Nearest Town/Resort Northwich.
Directions On A49, 4 miles from Northwich, 8 miles south from Warrington.
Acreage 2 **Open** March–October
Access Good **Site** Lev/Slope
Sites available Total 30.
Facilities
Nearby facilities
Acton Bridge.
Gently sloping site on the banks of the River Weaver, overlooking picturesque Cheshire countryside.

CHESTER
Birch Bank Farm, Christleton, Chester, Cheshire.CH3 7QD.
Tel. 335233 Std. 01244
Nearest Town/Resort Chester.
Directions 3 miles turn right off A51 (Chester to Nantwich Road) after Little Chef into Stamford Lane, Second Farm on left.
Acreage 1 **Open** May–October
Access Good **Site** Level
Sites available Total 10.
Facilities
Nearby facilities
Chester.
Quiet, rural, covenient for Chester etc.

CHESTER
Chester Southerly Caravan Park, Balderton Lane, Marlston-cum-Lache, Chester, Cheshire, CH4 9LF.
Tel. 671308 Std. 01244
Nearest Town/Resort Chester.
Directions 3 miles south side of Chester. Turn off the A55 towards Wrexham, at the A483 junction the road sign will immediately direct you to the site.
Acreage 8 **Open** March–November
Access Good **Site** Level
Sites available Total 90.
Facilities
Nearby facilities
Chester.
Chester is noted for its walls, gates, towers and rows (arcaded streets with balconies).

CHESTER
Netherwood Touring Site, Netherwood House, Whitchurch Road, Nr. Chester, Cheshire CH3 6AF.
Tel. Chester 335583 Std. 01244.
Nearest Town/Resort Chester.
Directions On A41, approx. 1 mile from Chester bypass.
Acreage 1½ **Open** March–October
Access Good **Site** Level
Sites available Total 15.
Facilities
Nearby facilities
Chester.
On Shropshire Union Canal. 5 miles from Zoo.

KELSALL
Northwood Hall Country Touring Park, Frodsham Street, Kelsall, Chester, Cheshire, CW6 0RP.
Tel. 752569 Std. 01829.
Nearest Town/Resort Chester.
Directions 7 miles east of Chester off the A54, adjacent to Delamere Forest.
Acreage 5 **Open** All Year
Access Good **Site** Level
Sites available Total 30.
Facilities
Nearby facilities
Chester.
Delamere Forest and the walled city of Chester.

WARRINGTON
Holly Bank Caravan Park, Warburton Bridge Road, Rixton, Warrington, Cheshire WA3 6HU.
Tel. 2842 Std. 0161 775.
Nearest Town/Resort Warrington.
Directions 2 miles from M6 junction 21 on A57 (Irlam) turn right at lights into Warburton Bridge Road entry on left, warrington 5 miles.
Open All year
Access Good **Site** Level
Sites available Total 85.
Facilities
Nearby facilities
Irlam.
Dunham Park, Risley Moss, and ideal touring North Cheshire.

WINSFORD
Lamb Cottage, Camping and Caravan Park, Dalesford Lane, Whitegate, Nr. Northwich, Cheshire CW8 2BN.
Tel. 888491/882302 Std. 01606
Nearest Town/Resort Northwich/Winsford.
Directions Leave M6 at Junction 19 onto A556 to Chester, turn at lights by Sandiway Post Office into Dalesford Lane, site is located 1 mile on right, past garage on the left.
Acreage 4 **Open** March–October
Access Good **Site** Level
Sites available Total 44.
Facilities
Nearby facilities
Cuddington.
Ideal touring, walks in Delamere Forest, 45 mins to Chester, Manchester Airport etc. Discounts for rallies and club outings.

CLEVELAND

GREAT BROUGHTON
Toft Hill Caravan Park, Kirby, Great Broughton, Cleveland, TS9 7HJ.
Tel. 712469 Std. 01642
Nearest Town/Resort Stokesley.
Directions In Stokesley near Junction A172 and A173, take minor road signed Kirby. At Kirby crossroads passed Black Swan on right hand side and take dead end road straight into hills, 1 mile, Farm entrance.
Acreage 2 **Open** April–October
Access Good **Site** Level
Sites available Total 32.
Facilities
Nearby facilities
Scenic views, ideal touring, good walking, rock climbing and hang gliding.

GUISBOROUGH
Tockets Mill, Skelton Road, Guisborough, Cleveland, TS14 6QA.
Tel. 610182 Std. 01287
Nearest Town/Resort Guisborough/Saltburn.
Directions 1 mile out of Guisborough on A173, Whitby Coast Road.
Acreage 38 **Open** March–October
Access Good **Site** Level
Sites available Total 50.
Facilities
Nearby facilities
Saltburn.

CORNWALL

BODMIN
Ruthern Valley Holiday Park, Ruthernbridge, Nr. Bodmin, Cornwall, PL30 5LU.
Tel. 831395 Std. 01208
Nearest Town/Resort Bodmin.
Directions Through Bodmin on A389 towards St. Austell, on outskirts of Bodmin Ruthernbridge signposted right. Follow signs for Ruthern or Ruthernbridge.
Acreage 2 **Open** April–October
Access Good **Site** Level
Sites available Total 30.
Facilities
Nearby facilities
Bodmin Parkway.
Quiet peaceful wooded location centrally based for touring.

BOSCASTLE
Lower Pennycrocker Farm, St. Juliot, Boscastle, Cornwall.
Tel. 250257 Std. 01840
Nearest Town/Resort Boscastle.
Directions 2½ miles north of Boscastle on B3263, turn left signposted Pennycrocker.
Acreage 4 **Open** Easter–September
Access Good **Site** Level
Sites available Total 40.

Facilities
Nearby facilities
Bodmin.
Scenic views, ideal touring.

BOSCASTLE

St. Tinney Farm, St. Tinney, Otterham, North Cornwall, PL32 9TA.
Tel. 261274 Std. 01840
Nearest Town/Resort Boscastle.
Directions Just off the A39 betwqeen Bude and Camelford. 11 miles south of Bude, signposted Otterham.
Acreage 2 **Open** Easter–October
Access Good **Site** Level
Sites available Total 20.
Facilities
Nearby facilities
Bodmin.
Tranquil site with free coarse fishing in the lakes and free riding for children. Friendly farm animals, country walks and close to beaches. Ideal touring centre.

BUDE

Bude Holiday Park, Maer Lane, Bude, Cornwall, EX23 9EE.
Tel. 355955 Std. 01288
Nearest Town/Resort Bude.
Directions Go through Town Centre, pass the golf course towards Crooklets. Park is located at the end of Maer Lane.
Acreage 22 **Open** April–October
Access Good **Site** Level
Sites available Total 250.
Facilities
Nearby facilities
Exeter.
Very close to three beaches, coastal paths, cliff tops and Bude town centre. Entertainment.

BUDE

Budemeadows Touring Holiday Park, Poundstock, Bude, Cornwall, EX23 0NA.
Tel. 361646 Std. 01288
Nearest Town/Resort Bude.
Directions From Bude take A39 south for 3 miles.
Acreage 9 **Open** All year
Access Good **Site** Level
Sites available Total 100.
Facilities
Nearby facilities
Exeter.
1 mile from sandy beaches, cliff walks and rolling surf of Widmouth Bay. Spectactular coastal scenery.

BUDE

Willow Valley Camping Park, Dye House, Bush, Bude, Cornwall. EX23 9LB.
Tel. 353104 Std. 01288
Nearest Town/Resort Bude.
Directions On A39, 1 mile from Stratton on the Stratton to Bideford road. Do not go into Bude.
Acreage 4 **Open** April–October
Access Good **Site** Level
Sites available Total 45.
Facilities
Nearby facilities
Exeter.
Picturesque, friendly family site, sheltered in beautiful Strat valley. 2 miles to sandy, surfing beaches, or small quiet coves. Ideal touring centre.

BUDE

Cornish Coasts Caravan Park, Middle Penlean, Poundstock, Bude, Cornwall, EX23 0EE.
Tel. 361380 Std. 01288
Nearest Town/Resort Bude/ Widemouth Bay.
Directions On seaward side of A39 Bude to Camelford road, 5 miles south of Bude.
Acreage 3 **Open** Easter–October
Access Good **Site** Lev/Slope
Sites available Total 78.
Facilities
Nearby facilities
Exeter.
Superb views over countryside and coast-line, ideal touring location with many beaches nearby. Shop, dogs allowed under strict control peaceful friendly site. Logland play area.

BUDE

Penhalt Farm Holiday Park, Widemouth Bay, Nr. Bude, Cornwall.
Tel. 361210 Std. 01288
Nearest Town/Resort Exeter.
Directions 5 miles south of Bude to Widemouth Bay, then on the Millook road.
Acreage 8 **Open** Easter–October
Access Good **Site** Level
Sites available
Facilities
Nearby facilities
Exeter.
7 berth caravan to let on family camp site, overlooking sea, Widemouth Bay.

BUDE

Red Post Inn and Holiday Park, Launcells, Nr. Bude, Cornwall, EX23 9NW.
Tel. 305 Std. 0128881
Nearest Town/Resort Bude.
Directions Junction A3072 and B3254 roads between Holsworthy and Bude.
Acreage 4 **Open** All year
Access Good **Site** Level
Sites available Total 64.
Facilities
Nearby facilities
Exeter.
Ideal touring area. On bus routes. Basic launderette facility.

BUDE

Sandymouth Bay Holiday Park, Sandymouth Bay, Bude, Cornwall, EX23 9HW.
Tel. 352563 Std. 01288
Nearest Town/Resort Bude.
Directions A39 from Kilkhampton heading south towards Bude. Turn right immediately after Penstowe, through Stibb. In approx ½ mile turn left to Sandymouth Bay.
Acreage 14 **Open** March–October
Access Good **Site** Level
Sites available
Facilities
Nearby facilities
Barnstaple.
Overlooking an award winning beach, scenic views.

BUDE

Upper Lynstone Camping & Caravan Site, Upper Lynstone Farm, Bude, Cornwall.
Tel. 352017 Std. 01288
Nearest Town/Resort Bude.
Directions ½ mile south of Bude on Widemouth Bay road.
Acreage 5 **Open** Easter–October
Access Good **Site** Lev/Slope
Sites available Total 90.
Facilities
Nearby facilities
Exeter.
Within easy reach of good surfing beaches. Access to cliff walks. Only individual motorcycles accepted, not groups.

BUDE

Wooda Caravan Park, Poughill, Bude, Cornwall.
Tel. 352069 Std. 01288
Nearest Town/Resort Bude.
Directions Take road to Poughill 1¼ miles, go through village. At crossroads turn left. Site 200yds along road on right hand side.
Acreage 12 **Open** April–October
Access Good **Site** Lev/Slope
Sites available Total 160.
Facilities

Nearby facilities
Exeter.
Overlooks sea and coastline, woodland walks, coarse fishing, large childrens play area, dog exersise field, short golf course, contact Mrs Q. Colwill ETB grading Excellent 5 Ticks. Sandy beaches 1½ miles. Licensed farm restaurant.

CAMELFORD

Juliots Well Holiday Park, Camelford, Cornwall.
Tel. 213302 Std. 01840
Nearest Town/Resort Tintagel.
Directions Leave Camelford on A39 Wadebridge Road. 1 mile out turn right at Valley Truckle, then first left towards Lanteglos, site 400 yards on right.
Acreage 8¼ **Open** March–October
Access Good
Sites available Total 60.
Facilities
Nearby facilities
Bodmin.
National grading scheme 5 ticks, AA 4 Pennants.

CAMELFORD

Lakefield Caravan Park, Lower Pendavey Farm, Camelford, Cornwall, PL32 9TX.
Tel. 213279 Std. 01840
Nearest Town/Resort Camelford/Tintagel.
Directions 1¼ miles north of Camelford on the B3266 – Boscastle road.
Acreage 5 **Open** Easter–October
Access Good **Site** Level
Sites available Total 30.
Facilities
Nearby facilities
Bodmin.
Scenic views, own lake. Ideal for touring Cornwall.

CARBIS BAY

Chy an Gweal Caravan Park, Carbis Bay Road, St. Ives, Cornwall.
Tel. 796257 Std. 01736
Nearest Town/Resort St. Ives.
Directions Site is on the main St. Ives A3074 road, less than 1 mile from town centre.
Acreage 4 **Open** May–September
Access Good **Site** Level
Sites available Total 50.
Facilities
Nearby facilities
Carbis Bay.
Superb location, less than ½ mile to beach. The only park in St. Ives area that does not accept dogs. Static vans also available.

CARBIS BAY

Carbis Bay Holiday Village, Laity Lane, Carbis Bay, St. Ives, Cornwall.
Tel. 797580 Std. 01736
Nearest Town/Resort St. Ives.
Directions Follow A30 until the Hayle bypass, at large roundabout take the A3074 for St. Ives to Carbis Bay.
Acreage 20 **Open** Witsun–September
Access Good **Site** Lev/Slope
Sites available Total 300.
Facilities
Nearby facilities
St Erth.
Beach, scenic views, walks and historic places.

CARLYON BAY

Carlyon Bay Caravan & Camping Park, "Bethesda", Carlyon Bay, St. Austell, Cornwall.
Tel. 812735 Std. 01726
Nearest Town/Resort St. Austell.
Directions Turn south off the A390 St Austell/St Blazey at the Britannia Inn Roundabout. 500yds turn right into the Avenue of Trees.
Acreage 32 **Open** Easter–3rd Oct
Access Good **Site** Lev/Slope
Sites available Total 180.
Facilities
Nearby facilities
St Austell.
Award winning family park with footpath to golf course and Blue Flag sandy beach.

COVERACK

Penmarth Farm Camp Site, Coverack, Helston, Cornwall.
Tel. 280389 Std. 01326
Nearest Town/Resort Helston.
Directions 10 miles from Helston.
Acreage 2 **Open** March–October
Access Good **Site** Level
Sites available Total 28.
Facilities
Nearby facilities
Cambourne.
¼ mile to beach and walks. Milk, cream and eggs at farm.

CRACKINGTON HAVEN

Hentervene Caravan & Camping Park, Crackington Haven, Nr. Bude, Cornwall.
Tel. 365 Std. 01840 230
Nearest Town/Resort Bude.
Directions 10 miles southwest of Bude, turn off A39 opposite Otterham Garage (Esso), signed Crackington Haven. After 2½ miles turn left onto Cracklington Road at Hentervene sign, park is ½ mile on right – 2 miles from beach.
Acreage 8¼ **Open** All year
Access Good **Site** Level
Sites available Total 35.
Facilities
Nearby facilities
Bodmin.
Ideal touring centre, scenic views, 2 miles to beach. Pets Welcome Off licence, take away meals in season. You can FAX us on 01840 514.

CRANTOCK

Quarryfield Caravan Park, Crantock, Nr. Newquay, Cornwall.
Tel. 872792/876770 Std. 01637
Nearest Town/Resort Newquay.
Directions Off A3075 road to Crantock Village. Bottom of village turn right opposite red telephone kiosk.
Acreage 5 **Open** April–October
Access Good **Site** Level
Sites available Total 125.
Facilities
Nearby facilities
Newquay.
15 minutes walk to beach. Ideal touring site. Bar snacks.

CRANTOCK

Treago Farm, Crantock, Newquay, Cornwall.
Tel. 830277 Std. 01637
Nearest Town/Resort Newquay.
Directions 2¼ miles southwest of Newquay, turn right off the A3075 and follow signposts to West Pentire. Treago is ¼ mile on the left.
Acreage 4 **Open** Easter–October
Access Good **Site** Level
Sites available Total 100.
Facilities
Nearby facilities
Newquay.
Situated between Crantock and Polly Joke beaches. Footpath to both golden, sandy beaches.

FALMOUTH

Pennance Mill Farm Camping Site, Maenporth, Falmouth, Cornwall.
Tel. 312616/317431 Std. 01326
Nearest Town/Resort Falmouth.
Directions From Falmouth take the road to the beaches. Situated between Swanpool beach and Maenporth beach.
Acreage 4 **Open** April–October
Access Good **Site** Level
Sites available Total 60.
Facilities

Nearby facilities
Falmouth.
Situated ½ mile from Maenporth beach, 3 miles from Helford river which is National Trust and 2 miles from Falmouth.

FALMOUTH

Tremorvah Tent Park, Swanpool, Falmouth, Cornwall.
Tel. 312103 Std. 01326
Nearest Town/Resort Falmouth.
Directions Follow international camping signs around Falmouth to Swanpool Beach.
Acreage 3 **Open** Mid May–October
Access Fair **Site** Level
Sites available
Facilities
Nearby facilities
Falmouth.
Family site on hillside to rear of Swanpool beach.

FOWEY

Yeate Farm Camp and Caravan Site, Bodinnick-by-Fowey, Cornwall.
Tel. 870256 Std. 01726
Nearest Town/Resort Fowey.
Directions A38 Liskeard by-pass, fork left A390. Left at East Taphouse B3359 follow signs to Bodinnick. Site on right of Bodinnick ferry road.
Acreage 1 **Open** April–October
Access Good **Site** Level
Sites available Total 30.
Facilities
Nearby facilities
Par/Lostwithiel.
Private quay, slip and storage for small boats. Good walks over mainly National Trust Land. Only individual motorcycles accepted not groups.

FOWEY

Polruan Holiday Centre, Polruan-by-Fowey, Cornwall, PL23 1QH.
Tel. 870263 Std. 01726
Nearest Town/Resort Fowey.
Directions From Plymouth A38 to Dobwalls, left onto A390 to East Taphouse, then left onto B3359. After 4¼ miles turn right signposted Polruan.
Acreage 2 **Open** April–September
Access Good **Site** Lev/Slope
Sites available Total 32.
Facilities
Nearby facilities
Par.
Coastal park surrounded by sea, river and National Trust farmland.

GORRAN HAVEN

Trelispen Caravan and Camping Park, Gorran, St. Austell, Cornwall.
Tel. Mevagissey 843501 Std. 01726.
Nearest Town/Resort Gorran Haven.
Directions From A390 at St. Austell take B3293 for Mevagissey, nearing Mevagissey take road for Gorran Haven, nearing Gorran Haven look for Trelispen Camping Park signs.
Acreage 1½ **Open** April–October
Access Good **Site** Level
Sites available Total 40.
Facilities
Nearby facilities
St. Austell.
Small site in pleasant rural surroundings near impressive cliff scenery and several safe sandy beaches.

HAYLE

Beachside Holiday Park, Hayle, Cornwall.
Tel. 753080 Std. 01736
Nearest Town/Resort Hayle/St Ives.
Directions 1 mile west town off A30. From Camborne into Hayle turn right at putting green. Look for site entrance on right.
Acreage 20 **Open** Easter–September
Access Good **Site** Sloping
Sites available Total 90.
Facilities
Nearby facilities
Hayle.
Adjacent to a sandy beach.

HAYLE

Parbola Holiday Park, Wall, Gwinear, Nr. St. Ives, Cornwall.
Tel. 831503 Std. 01209
Nearest Town/Resort Hayle.
Directions When approaching from the A30 look for the Camborne West interchange and turn left onto the A3047. Turn right at the roundabout on the B3307 (the old A30 road)Connor Downs/Hayle Road carry on for 1½ miles to just before Connor Downs turn left into Gwinear Road and continue for 1½ miles to Carnhell Green then turn right at T junction. Parbola is 1 mile on left.
Acreage 17 **Open** April–September
Access Good **Site** Level
Sites available Total 110.
Facilities
Nearby facilities
No dogs allowed July/August.

HAYLE

Higher Trevaskis Caravan & Camping Park, Station Road, Connor Downs, Hayle, Cornwall, TR22 5DQ.
Tel. 831736 Std. 01209
Nearest Town/Resort Hayle/St Ives.
Directions At Hayle roundabout (Little Chef) on A30 take the first exit (signposted Connor Downs). After 1 mile turn right to Carnhell Green. Park is on the right in ¾ of mile.
Acreage 5¼ **Open** April–October
Access Good **Site** Level
Sites available Total 75.
Facilities
Nearby facilities
Hayle.
Pleasant, secluded, family run, countryside park with good clean facilities. Sheltered fields. Some facilities for the disabled.

HAYLE

Sunny Meadow Holiday Park, Lelant Down, Hayle, Cornwall.
Tel. 752243 Std. 01736
Nearest Town/Resort Hayle/St Ives.
Directions Take the Hayle by-pass, turn off for St Ives to the mini roundabout. Take the first left onto the B3311. We are ¼ mile up on the left.
Acreage ¼ **Open** April–October
Access Good **Site** Level
Sites available Total 10.
Facilities
Nearby facilities
St Erth.

A few miles from both north and south coasts offering ideal opportunity to tour the Peninsula.

HELSTON

Boscrege Caravan Park, Ashton, Helston, Cornwall.
Tel. 762231 Std. 01736
Nearest Town/Resort Praa Sands.
Directions From Helston follow Penzance road (A394) to Ashton, turn right by post office along road signposed to Godolphin and continue about 1½ miles to Boscrege Park.
Acreage 7 **Open** Easter/1 April–October
Access Good **Site** Level
Sites available Total 15.
Facilities
Nearby facilities
Penzance.
Quiet family park in garden setting. No bar. Near sandy beaches. Ideal for exploring West Cornwall. Microwave for campers.

HELSTON

Franchis, Cury Cross Lanes, Helston, Cornwall TR12 7AZ.
Tel. Mullion 240301 Std. 01326.
Nearest Town/Resort Mullion/Helston.
Directions From Helston take the A3083 (Helston to The Lizard road). Franchis 6 miles on from Helston.
Acreage 4 **Open** Easter–October
Access Good **Site** Level
Sites available Total 70.
Facilities
Nearby facilities
Redruth.
Only individual motorcycles accepted, not groups. Sport diving air to 3500 P.S.I. Rose Award Park. Licensed shop on site.

HELSTON

Lower Polladras Camping & Caravan Park, Carleen, Nr. Helston, Cornwall TR13 9NX.
Tel. 762220 Std. 01736
Nearest Town/Resort Helston.
Directions From Helston take the A394 to Penzance and turn right at Riders Garage along the B3302. Aftr ¾ mile turn left to Carleen village. From the A30 turn left in Camborne along the B3303, then take the first right turning after junction of 3303 and 3302.
Acreage 4 **Open** April–October
Access Good **Site** Level
Sites available Total 60.
Facilities
Nearby facilities
Camborne.
Pleasant views of surrounding hills. Ideal touring situation. Childrens adventure playground.

HELSTON

Retanna Country Park, Edgcumbe, Helston, Cornwall TR13 0EJ.
Tel. 40643 Std. 01326.
Nearest Town/Resort Falmouth.
Directions On A394 betwixt Falmouth and Helston (5 miles).
Acreage 8 **Open** April–October
Access Good **Site** Lev/slope
Sites available Total 17.
Facilities
Nearby facilities
Falmouth.
Scenic views. Ideal centre for touring West Cornwall.

ISLES OF SCILLY

Jenford, Bryher, Isles of Scilly, Cornwall.
Tel. 422886 Std. 01720.
Nearest Town/Resort Penzance.
Acreage 1 **Open** April–October
Site Level
Sites available Total 37.
Facilities
Nearby facilities

ISLES OF SCILLY

Troytown Farm, St. Agnes, Isles of Scilly, Cornwall. TR22 OPL.
Tel. Scillonia 22360 Std. 01720
Directions Ship or helicopter from Penzance to St. Mary's inter Island launch to St. Agnes. N.b. Cars are left at Penzance. No caravans. Transport available for luggage and small trailers from Quay to Site (one mile).
Acreage 1¾ **Open** March–October
Site Lev/Slope
Sites available Total 38.
Facilities
Nearby facilities
Penzance.
By beach, sea views to bird sanctuary, Island of Annet, other Islands and Bishops Rock Lighthouse. Very quiet.

LANDS END

Lower Treave Caravan Park, Crows-an-Wra, St. Buryan, Penzance, Cornwall, TR19 6HZ.
Tel. 810559 Std. 01736
Nearest Town/Resort Penzance.
Directions On A30 Penzance/Lands End road, ½ mile west of Crows-an-Wra.
Acreage 4½ **Open** April–15th Oct
Access Good **Site** Level
Sites available Total 80.
Facilities
Nearby facilities
Penzance.
An ideal centre for exploring the Lands End Peninsula.

LANDS END

Cardinney Caravan & Caravan Park, Main A30, Lands End Road, Crows-An-Wra, Lands End, Cornwall, TR19 6HJ.
Tel. 810880 Std. 01736
Nearest Town/Resort Sennen Cove.
Directions From Penzance follow Main A30 to Lands End, approx 5¼ miles. Entrance on right hand side on Main A30, large name board at entrance.
Acreage 5 **Open** Wk before Easter–October
Access Good **Site** Level
Sites available Total 105.
Facilities
Nearby facilities
Penzance.
Sennen Cove Blue Flag, scenic coastal walks, ancient monuments, scenic flights, Minack Ampitheatre, trips to the Isles of Scilly. Ideal for touring Lands End Peninsula. Hard standings.

LAUNCESTON

Chapmanswell Caravan Site, St. Giles on the Heath, Launceston, Cornwall PL15 9SG.
Tel. 211382 Std. 01409.
Nearest Town/Resort Launceston.
Directions Chapmanswell Caravan Park is situated 6 miles from Launceston along the A388 on your left hand side going towards Holsworthy, just past the pub and garage in Chapmanswell.
Acreage 7 **Open** 15th March–October
Access Good **Site** Level
Sites available Total 81.
Facilities
Nearby facilities
Exeter.
Very central for Cornwall and Devon, easy reach of North Devon beaches, Dartmoor and Cornish resorts. Village pub meals 200 yards.

LEEDSTOWN

Calloose Caravan and Camping Park, Leedstown, Hayle, Cornwall.
Tel. Leedstown 850431 Std. 01736.
Nearest Town/Resort Hayle.
Directions Take B3302 from Hayle to

Helston for 4 miles to Leedstown. Site signposted in village.
Acreage 8½ **Open** Easter–October
Access Good **Site** Level
Sites available Total 120.
Facilities
Nearby facilities
Hayle.
Centrally situated for West Cornwall. Sheltered valley site. Skittle alley, crazy golf and takeaway.

LISKEARD

Colliford Tavern Campsite, Colliford Lake, Bodmin Moor, Near St Neot, Liskeard, Cornwall, PL14 6PZ.
Tel. 82335 Std. 01208
Nearest Town/Resort Bodmin.
Directions Just off A30 between Bodmin and Launceston, follow signs to Colliford Lake.
Acreage 3¼ **Open** Easter–October
Access Good **Site** Level
Sites available Total 40.
Facilities
Nearby facilities
Bodmin.
Sheltered site, tranquil haven for wildlife. Good walking. Central touring position. Freehouse with restaurant and accommodation.

LISKEARD

Trenant Chapel House, Trenant Caravan Park, St Neot, Liskeard, Cornwall.
Tel. Liskeard 20896
Nearest Town/Resort Liskeard.
Directions Take St Cleer road off A38 at Dobwalls, 1 mile left SP St. Neot, 1 mile right SP Trennant, ½ mile right SP Trennant.
Acreage 1 **Open** April–October
Site Level
Sites available Total 8.
Facilities
Nearby facilities
Liskeard.
Siblyback and Colliford Reservoirs close, fishing, boardsailing, and bird watching. Site in sheltered corner upper Fowey valley bounded by tributary of Fowey river, close Bodmin moor, ideal walking, touring.

LIZARD

Gwendreath Farm Caravan Park, Kennack Sands, Helston, Cornwall, TR12 7LZ.
Tel. 290666 Std. 01326
Nearest Town/Resort The Lizard.
Directions A3083 from Helston, left on B3293 after R.N.A.S. Culdrose. After Goonhilly Earth Station, take the first right then first left. At end of lane go through Seaview Caravan Site.
Acreage 3 **Open** Easter–October
Access Good **Site** Level
Sites available Total 30.
Facilities
Nearby facilities
Redruth.
Attractive, peaceful family site overlooking the sea in an area of outstanding natural beauty. Short woodland walk to safe sandy beaches.

LIZARD

Sea Acres Holiday Park, Kennack Sands, Nr. Helston, Cornwall, TR12 7LT.
Tel. 290064 Std. 01326.
Nearest Town/Resort Helston.
Directions Take the A3083 out of Helston, 2 miles turn left onto B3293 towards St Keverne. 5 miles on turn right just after Goonhilly Earth Station. Turn left at Kuggar T-Junction, we are half way down the hill on the right.
Acreage 3 **Open** April–October
Access Good **Site** Level
Sites available Total 50.
Facilities
Nearby facilities
Redruth.
Overlooking beach, nine hole pitch & putt and a creche. Childrens swimming pool.

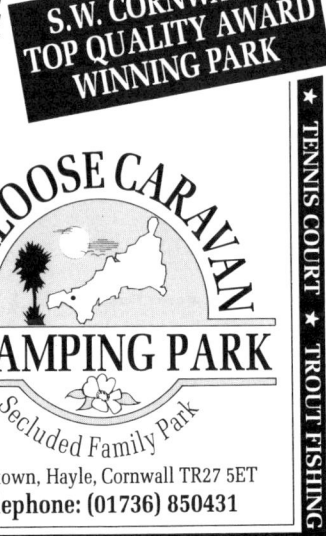

LIZARD

Chy-Carne, Kennack Sands, Ruan Minor, Helston, Cornwall, TR12 7LX.
Tel. 290541 Std. 01326
Nearest Town/Resort Mullion.
Directions From Helston follow A3083, 2 miles turn left B3293 towards St Keverne, 5 miles on, just past Goonhilly Radio Station turn right at Traboe Cross follow road until the T Junction. Turn left then 60 yards on the left.
Acreage 6 **Open** Easter–October
Access Good **Site** Lev/Slope
Sites available Total 14.
Facilities
Nearby facilities
Redruth.
½ mile from clean beach.

LONGDOWNS

Calamankey Campsite, Calamankey Farm Campsite, Longdowns, Penryn, Cornwall TR10 9DL.
Tel. Stithians 860314 Std. 01209
Nearest Town/Resort Falmouth.
Directions A394 from Penryn, 2½ miles.
Acreage 2½ **Open** Easter–October
Access Good **Site** Sloping
Sites available Total 60.
Facilities
Nearby facilities
Penryn.
Beach 4½ miles. Ideal touring. Farming area.

LOOE

Camping Caradon, Trelawne, Looe, Cornwall.
Nearest Town/Resort Polperro/Looe.
Directions From Looe on the A387, take right turn onto B3359. First turning on the right, approx 200yds on the left.
Acreage 2¼ **Open** April–October
Access Good **Site** Level
Sites available Total 85.
Facilities
Nearby facilities
Looe.
Friendly, family run park with rural surroundings.

LOOE

Polborder House Caravan and Camping Park, Bucklawren Road, St. Martin, Looe, Cornwall, PL13 1QR.
Tel. Widegates 265 Std. 0150 34.
Nearest Town/Resort Looe.
Directions East from Looe on B3253, 2 miles turn right signpost Seaton. Site ¾ mile on right.
Acreage 3 **Open** Easter–October
Access Good **Site** Level
Sites available Total 36.
Facilities
Nearby facilities
Looe.
Scenic views, ideal touring, beach 1¼ miles.

LOOE

Talland Barton Caravan Park, Talland Bay, Looe, Cornwall, PL13 2JA.
Tel. 72429 Std. 01503.
Nearest Town/Resort Looe.
Directions Take A387 from Looe towards Polperro. After 1 mile turn left. Follow this road for 1½ miles. The site is on the left hand side by Talland Church.
Acreage 1¼ **Open** Easter–October
Access Poor **Site** Lev/Slope
Sites available Total 30.
Facilities
Nearby facilities

Looe.
Between Looe and Polperro, near a beach. Peaceful countryside, ideal touring.

LOOE

Tencreek Caravan & Camping Park, Looe, Cornwall PL13 2JR.
Tel. 262447 Std. 01503
Nearest Town/Resort Looe.
Directions 1½ miles west of Looe on the A387 Looe to Polperro road.
Acreage 14 **Open** All year
Access Good **Site** Level
Sites available Total 250.
Facilities
Nearby facilities
Looe.
Extensive coastal and countryside views. The nearest park to Looe. Free use of all facilities. Practical Caravan Top 100, E.T.B. 4 Tick Grading and Rose Award.

LOOE

Treble B Holiday Centre, Polperro Road, Looe, Cornwall, PL13 2JS.
Tel. 262425 Std. 01503
Nearest Town/Resort Looe.
Directions 2 miles west Looe on A387 midway between Looe/Polperro.
Acreage 20 **Open** May–September
Access Good **Site** Lev/Slope
Sites available Total 450.
Facilities
Nearby facilities
Looe.
Family site, ideal base for touring all Cornwall. A.A. graded 5 pennant site. R.A.C. appointed. Free coloured brochure. Enquiries to Dept. 06. Free showers.

LOOE

Trelawne Manor Holiday Village, Looe, Cornwall, PL13 2NA.
Tel. 72151 Std. 01503
Nearest Town/Resort Looe.
Directions A38 from Liskeard through Dobwalls, turn left onto the A390 for St. Austell. Go through Taphouse, then turn left onto the B3359. Trelawne is on the left after 8¼ miles.
Open 14 May–10 Sept
Access Good **Site** Level
Sites available
Facilities
Nearby facilities
Liskeard.
Centred around a stately manor house (former home of Lady Jane Grey). Just 1¼ miles from the sea.

LOOE

Trelay Farmpark, Trelay Farm, Pelynt, Looe, Cornwall.
Tel. 220900 Std. 01503.
Nearest Town/Resort Looe/Polperro.
Directions From Looe on A387, take right turn to B3359. Trelay Farm is second turn right before Pelynt.
Acreage 3 **Open** Easter–October
Access Good **Site** Level
Sites available Total 30.
Facilities
Nearby facilities
Looe.
Quiet farm park, ideal for touring. 4 ticks ETB Grading. Motorcycles only accepted at the discretion of the Owner.

LOSTWITHIEL

Downend Camp, Lostwithiel, Cornwall.
Tel. 872363 Std. 01208.
Nearest Town/Resort Lostwithiel.
Directions On the A390.
Acreage 5 **Open** April–October
Access Good **Site** Level
Sites available Total 30.
Facilities
Nearby facilities
Lostwithiel.
Ideal touring, ½ mile to woods.

LOSTWITHIEL

Powderham Castle Tourist Park, Lanlivery, Nr. Fowey, Cornwall.
Tel. 872277 Std. 01208.
Nearest Town/Resort Fowey/St. Austell.
Directions 1½ miles southwest Lostwithiel on A390, turn right at signpost for Lanlivery/Luxulyan, up road 400 yards.
Acreage 10 **Open** April–October
Access Good **Site** Level
Sites available Total 75.
Facilities
Nearby facilities
Lostwithiel.
Quiet uncrowded site, uncommercialised. Central touring position. Canoe and boat hire. Battery charging, freezer pack service. Dish washing and vegetable preparation facilities. Indoor Badmington and soft tennis court, putting green, childrens pool. Winner AA Award for sanitation. ETB 5 Ticks.

MARAZION

Wheal Rodney Carapark, Marazion, Cornwall.
Tel. 710605 Std. 01736.
Nearest Town/Resort Marazion.
Directions ½ mile north Marazion.
Acreage 4¼ **Open** 1 April or Easter–October
Access Good **Site** Level
Sites available Total 45.
Facilities
Nearby facilities
Penzance.
½ mile from safe beach. Sauna, solarium, spa bath on site.

MARAZION

Trevair Touring Site, South Treveneague Farm, St. Hilary, Penzance, Cornwall, TR20 9BY.
Tel. 740647 Std. 01736
Nearest Town/Resort Marazion.
Directions 3 miles from Marazion, B3280 through Goldsithney signposted South Treveneague.
Acreage 3 **Open** End Mar–October
Access Good **Site** Level
Sites available Total 25.
Facilities
Nearby facilities
St Erth.
Set in the peace and quiet of a secluded sunny valley, clean and friendly. Goats, donkey and tame birds.

MAWGAN PORTH

Magic Cove Touring Park, Mawgan Porth, Newquay, Cornwall.
Tel. 860263 Std. 01637
Nearest Town/Resort Newquay.
Directions A30 Bodmin by-pass, turn right 4¼ miles from the end. At the roundabout take the second left (Newquay) then right 400yds past Shell Garage. Pass the airport, T-Junction right to Mawgan Porth. Right after BP Garage and Magic Cover is in 300yds.
Acreage 1 **Open** Easter–October
Access Good **Site** Level

Killigarth Manor Holiday Estate

POLPERRO near LOOE, CORNWALL

A delightful Family run Holiday Estate set in beautiful countryside, close to picturesque Polperro and Talland Bay.

Luxurious new facilities for Tents and Tourers, Toilets, Showers, Wash-Basins, Hairdryers, Razor points. Electric Hookups available.

Heated Indoor Swimming Pool, Adventure Play Areas. Bar, Club/Ballroom with Entertainment. Restaurant, Take-away, Launderette, Ironing room and Shop. (Free Club membership).

EXCELLENT

MEMBER

The family run holiday park – for your family!

Illustrated brochure from Mr. K. MARKS

KILLIGARTH MANOR HOLIDAY ESTATE
POLPERRO, LOOE, CORNWALL PL13 2JQ
TELELEPHONE: 01503 72216

CARAVAN OR TENT INCLUDING 2 PERSONS FROM £7.20 PER NIGHT

S.E.Cornwall's ONLY AA 5 RATED PENNANT SITE

RALLIES WELCOME

Facilities ★ **Heated Swimming Pool ★ Club ★ Dance Hall ★ Disco ★ Games & TV rooms ★ Restaurant ★ Take-Away ★ Shop ★ Laundry ★ Crazy Golf ★ Childrens Play Areas.**

Plus

Treble B Holiday Centre

★ AMPLE MODERN TOILETS ★
★ ELECTRIC POINTS ★
★ FREE HOT SHOWERS ★

and **Seasonal Sites available for Tourers. To Let - Caravans, Flats, Chalets and Superior Farm Cottages.**

LOOE, CORNWALL PL13 2JS **FREE COLOUR BROCHURE TEL: 01503 262425**

TENCREEK Caravan & Camping Park

LOOE, CORNWALL, PL13 2JR

Panoramic views of sea & countryside. Perfectly situated for Looe & Polperro. The nearest park to Looe Beach.

Tents, Touring Caravans and Motor caravans very welcome. Electric hook-ups available. Also fully equipped Rose Award Caravans, sleep 6-8. Families & couples only. Rallies welcome

OPEN ALL YEAR
The nearest park to Looe!

FREE BROCHURE Tel: (01503) 262447/262757

FREE family facilities include: Heated swimming pool · Modern toilets & showers · Adventure park · Shop · Launderette · Dog exercise area · Licensed club with nightly entertainment · two bars · Cafe/take-away · Apartments available in Looe · Golf · Sea · coarse & shark fishing · Boating · Horse riding etc all nearby.

RAC APPOINTED

ROSE AWARD CARAVAN HOLIDAY PARK 1994

Sites available Total 26.
Facilities
Nearby facilities
Newquay.
300yds from beach, ideal for touring Cornwall. Water and drainage on each pitch, hook-ups include T.V. point.

MEVAGISSEY

Tregarton Farm Touring Park, Gorran, St. Austell, Cornwall. PL26 6NF.
Tel. 843666 Std. 01726.
Nearest Town/Resort Mevagissey.
Directions From St Austell south on B3273 signposted Mevagissey. Afetr Pentewan turn right signposted Gorran. Park is on right after 4 miles.
Acreage 8 **Open** April–October
Access Good **Site** Lev/Slope
Sites available Total 150.
Facilities
Nearby facilities
St. Austell.
Quiet family park. Beach $1\frac{1}{4}$ miles. Ideal for touring Cornwall.

MEVAGISSEY

Seaview International, Boswinger, Gorran, St. Austell, Cornwall, PL26 6LL.
Tel. 843425 Std. 01726.
Nearest Town/Resort Mevagissey.
Directions From St. Austell take B3273 to Mevagissey, prior to village turn right. Then follow signs to Gorran.
Acreage 16 **Open** 10th April–September
Access Good **Site** Level
Sites available Total 165.
Facilities
Nearby facilities
St Austell.
Beautiful level park overlooking the sea, surrounded by sandy beaches graded among cleanest in Britain, nearest $\frac{1}{2}$ mile AA Best in Britain Title, and Calor gas Englands best park 1987. Voted among the top ten parks of Europe 1992. Holiday caravans also for hire. You can FAX us on 01726 843358.

MULLION

Teneriffe Farm Caravan Site, A.B. Thomas, Teneriffe Farm, Mullion, Helston, Cornwall TR12 7EZ.
Tel. 240293 Std. 01326.
Nearest Town/Resort Helston.
Directions 10 miles Helston to The Lizard, turn right for Mullion. Take Mullion Cove road, turn left Predannack.
Acreage 3 **Open** Easter–October
Access Good **Site** Lev/Slope
Sites available Total 20.
Facilities
Nearby facilities
Redruth.
Views of sea. S.A.E. required. Tumble drying facility.

MULLION

Mullion Holiday Park, Mullion, Helston, Cornwall, TR12 7LJ.
Tel. 447447 (Bookings) Std. 01392
Nearest Town/Resort Helston.
Directions 3 miles from Helston on A3083 for the Lizard.
Acreage 39 **Open** April–October
Access Good **Site** Level
Sites available Total 150.
Facilities
Nearby facilities
Redruth/Truro.
Close to outstanding coastline and beaches. Ideal park for visiting Cornwall. Indoor swimming pool. When booking please quote CP.

NEWQUAY

Cottage Farm Touring Park, Treworgans, Cubert, Newquay, Cornwall, TR8 5HH.
Tel. 831083 Std. 01637.
Nearest Town/Resort Newquay.
Directions Newqauy to Redruth road A3075, turn right onto High Lanes. Follow signs to Cubert, $1\frac{1}{4}$ miles before Cubert Village turn right signposted Crantock-Wesley Road. Down the lane for $\frac{1}{4}$ mile then turn right signposted Tresean and Treworgans.
Acreage 2 **Open** April–October
Access Good **Site** Level
Sites available Total 45.
Facilities
Nearby facilities
Newquay.
Within easy reach of three National Trust beaches. Small, family site, peaceful and in a rural location.

NEWQUAY

Crantock Plains Touring Park, Nr. Newquay, Cornwall TR8 5PH.
Tel. 830955/831273 Std. 01637.
Nearest Town/Resort Newquay.
Directions From Newquay take Redruth road (A3075), after boating lake on right then garage on left, continue over mini roundabout.Take second signposted road to Crantock site $\frac{1}{2}$ mile down lane on left.
Acreage 3 **Open** Easter–September
Access Good **Site** Level
Sites available
Facilities
Nearby facilities
Newquay.
Quiet family site. Ideal for touring Cornwall.

NEWQUAY

Holywell Bay Holiday Park, (Newquay Holiday Parks Ltd) Holywell Bay, Newquay, Cornwall, TR8 5PR.
Tel. 871111 Std. 0637
Nearest Town/Resort Newquay.
Directions Off A3075 marked Cubert and Holywell Bay (2miles).
Open Mid April–Mid October
Access Good **Site** Lev/Slope
Sites available Total 75.
Facilities
Nearby facilities
Newquay.
Set in peaceful valley, a short level walk from a sandy family beach. Rose Award Caravan Holiday Park, British Graded Holiday Park 5 ticks Excellent. Free swimming pool and 300' waterslide. See our advertisement in the colour section of this guide.

NEWQUAY

Hendra Holiday Park, Newquay, Cornwall. TR8 4NY.
Tel. 875778 Std. 01637
Nearest Town/Resort Newquay.
Directions A30 to Cornwall to Indian Queens, turn right on the A392 Newquay

road at Quintrell Downs. Hendra is 1¼ miles before Newquay Town Centre.
Acreage 36 **Open** April–October
Access Good **Site** Lev/Slope
Sites available Total 600.
Facilities
Nearby facilities
Newquay.
Scenic country views. Waterslide and train rides.

NEWQUAY

Watergate Bay Holiday Park, Watergate Bay, Newquay, Cornwall.
Tel. 860387 Std. 01637
Nearest Town/Resort Newquay.
Directions 4 miles north of Newquay on the B3276 Coast Road to Padstow, Follow directions shown from Watergate Bay.
Acreage 15 **Open** March–November
Access Good **Site** Level
Sites available Total 171.
Facilities
Nearby facilities
Newquay.
¼ mile from Watergate Bay in a rural location in an area of outstanding natural beauty.

NEWQUAY

Monkey Tree Touring Park, Rejerrah, Newquay, Cornwall TR8 5QL.
Tel. 572032 Std. 01872
Nearest Town/Resort Newquay.
Directions From Newquay take A3075 to Redruth, after 4 miles turn left, signposted Zelah. Site 800 metres on the right. From A30 take Perranporth turn B3285, after ¼ mile turn right signed Newquay.
Acreage 12 **Open** April–October
Access Good **Site** Level
Sites available Total 295.
Facilities
Nearby facilities
Newquay.
All flat pitches, surfing beaches few minutes travelling. Quiet family site, ideal touring. Now under New Management. Licensed bar and T.V. and Video room.

NEWQUAY

Newquay Tourist Park, (Newquay Holiday Parks Ltd) Newquay, Cornwall TR8 4HS.
Tel. 871111 Std. 01637
Nearest Town/Resort Newquay.
Directions On A3059 2 miles from Newquay.
Acreage 23 **Open** Mid April–Mid October
Access Good **Site** Lev/Slope
Sites available Total 259.
Facilities
Nearby facilities
Newquay.
Country setting with scenic views. Ideal for touring, free entertainment at licenced club, children welcome. 3 pool complex and giant water slide. AA 5 Pennant, Graded 5 Ticks, Rose Award Park. See advertisment in the colour section of this guide.

NEWQUAY

Perran Quay Tourist Park, Hendra Croft, Rejerrah, Newquay, Cornwall, TR8 5QP.
Tel. 572561 Std. 01872
Nearest Town/Resort Newquay.
Directions On A3075 midway between Newquay and Perranporth.
Open April–October
Access Good **Site** Level
Sites available Total 135.
Facilities
Nearby facilities
Newquay.

NEWQUAY

Newperran Tourist Park, Rejerrah, Newquay, Cornwall.TR8 5QJ.
Tel. 572407 Std. 01872
Nearest Town/Resort Newquay.
Directions Take A30 turn right 2½ miles past the village of Mitchell. On reaching

RAC

A holiday to remember in **NEWQUAY** at

TRELOY TOURIST PARK

A friendly family site for touring vans, tents and dormobiles, convenient for beaches and beauty spots. We cater for families and couples only.

Facilities include:
* Heated swimming pool * Licensed club with family room * Free entertainment * Sports and swimming galas * Cafeteria/takeaway food * Electric hookups * Shop * Laundry * Private washing cubicles * Showers * Games room * TV room * Indoor dishwashing sinks * Adventure playground * COURSE FISHING NEARBY

400 yards from the Park TRELOY GOLF COURSE

Our own superb 9 HOLE PAR 32 GOLF COURSE built to an exceptionally high standard with sculptured American style greens *Golf shop *Clubs for hire *Concessionary green fees for golfers staying at the park *Special golfing competition weeks during April and September *Golfing societies welcome * Coffee Shop * Licensed Clubhouse

Write or telephone please for free colour brochure

TRELOY TOURIST PARK, NEWQUAY.
CORNWALL TR7 47N TEL: 01637 872063

MONKEY TREE TOURING PARK

Rejerrah, Nr. Newquay, Cornwall TR8 5QL

NOW STATIC CARAVANS AVAILABLE

SO YOU'VE COME TO CORNWALL FOR ITS BEAUTY AND CHARM
AND YOU'RE LOOKING FOR SOMEWHERE TO STAY
THEN THE IDEAL SITE IS MONKEY TREE FARM
READ THIS MAP, IT'LL SHOW YOU THE WAY.
IT'S A LOVELY SITE WHERE THE PITCHES ARE FLAT
AND WHEN YOU'RE PARKING YOUR VAN THERE'S NOTHING BETTER
THAN THAT!
THERE'S A HEATED POOL, SAUNA AND SOLARIUM TOO
A GAMES ROOM, CAFE AND SHOP FOR YOU.
THERE'S A TRACTOR CALLED TREVOR WHERE THE
CHILDREN CAN PLAY
AND YOUR DOGS ARE MOST WELCOME
'CAUSE WE FIXED IT THAT WAY.
SO GIVE US A CALL AND BOOK
YOUR PITCH,
OR FOLLOW THE MAP
WE DON'T MIND
WHICH!

RAC · AA · GCC · ANWB · THE CAMPING AND CARAVANNING CLUB · ADAC CAMPING-FUHRER

FREE COLOUR BROCHURE

Tel: (01872)-572032

A3075 at Goonhaven turn right and after ½ mile, sign on righthand side turning on left.
Acreage 25 **Open** Mid May–Mid Sept
Access Good **Site** Level
Sites available Total 270.
Facilities
Nearby facilities
Newquay.
Concessionary green fees, own fishing lake nearby, scenic views and central to nine golden beaches, AA 5 pennants.

NEWQUAY

Resparva House Camping & Caravanning, Summercourt, Newquay, Cornwall TR8 5AH.
Tel. 510332 Std. 01872
Nearest Town/Resort Newquay.
Directions From Newquay A3058 St. Austell Road 8 miles, Site situated old A30 Road.
Acreage 1 **Open** Easter–October
Access Good **Site** Level
Sites available Total 15.
Facilities
Nearby facilities
Truro.
Ideal touring.

NEWQUAY

Summer Lodge Holiday Park, Whitecross, Newquay, Cornwall. TR8 4LW.
Tel. 860415 Std. 01726
Nearest Town/Resort Newquay.
Directions A30 turn right at Indian Queens onto A392. Approx 2 miles along A392 you come to Whitecross, holiday park signposted left.
Acreage 2 **Open** Easter–September
Access Good **Site** Level
Sites available Total 50.
Facilities
Nearby facilities
Newquay.
Set in beautiful countryside and ideally situated for touring. Short distance from beach and main town of Newquay.

NEWQUAY

Trebarber Farm, St. Columb Minor, Newquay, Cornwall, TR8 4JT.
Tel. 873007 Std. 01637
Nearest Town/Resort Newquay.
Directions 3 miles from Newquay on A3059, Newquay to St. Columb Major road.
Acreage 5 **Open** June–September
Access Good **Site** Level
Sites available
Facilities
Nearby facilities
Newquay.
Quiet Ideal family centre for touring, beaches. Walking distance to Porth reservoir (coarse fishing) and to Golf course.

NEWQUAY

Treloy Tourist Park, Newquay, Cornwall, TR8 4JN.
Tel. 872063 Std. 01637
Nearest Town/Resort Newquay.
Directions 5 minutes from Newquay on the A3059 Newquay to St Columb Major Road.
Acreage 11¼ **Open** April–September
Access Good **Site** Lev/Slope
Sites available Total 141.
Facilities
Nearby facilities
Newquay.
Ideal site for touring the whole of Cornwall. Coarse fishing nearby. Own golf course ½ mile, concessionary Green Fees.

NEWQUAY

Trebellan Park, Cubert, Newquay, Cornwall, TR8 5PY.
Tel. 830522 Std. 01637.
Nearest Town/Resort Newquay.
Directions A3075 Newquay to Redruth road, after 2 miles turn right to Holywell Bay/Cubert. Then take the first left.
Acreage 20 **Open** Easter–October
Access Good **Site** Lev/Slope
Sites available Total 158.
Facilities
Nearby facilities
Newquay.
Coastal and country walks, fishing lakes.

NEWQUAY

Trekenning Manor Tourist Park, St Columb, Newquay, Cornwall, TR8 4JF.
Tel. 880462 (Also FAX) Std. 01637
Nearest Town/Resort Newquay.
Directions 7 miles south east of Newquay on junction A30/A39.
Acreage 6¼ **Open** April–October
Access Good **Site** Lev/Slope
Sites available Total 75.
Facilities
Nearby facilities
Newquay.
In grounds of 15th Century manor house. Near to north coast beaches – central Cornwall.

NEWQUAY

Trencreek Holiday Park, Trencreek, Newquay, Cornwall, TR8 4NS.
Tel. Newquay 874210 Std. 01637
Nearest Town/Resort Newquay.
Directions A392 to Quintrell Downs, turn right Newquay East/Porth, at Porth crossroads, ¾ mile outside Newquay, turn left to Trencreek.
Acreage 10 **Open** April–September
Access Good **Site** Level
Sites available Total 150.
Facilities
Nearby facilities
Newquay.
Coarse fishing on site, 15 minutes footpath walk to Newquay, 1 mile by road.

NEWQUAY

Trethiggey Touring Park, Quintrell Downs, Newquay, Cornwall. TR8 4LG.
Tel. 877672 Std. 01637
Nearest Town/Resort Newquay.
Directions Follow main route signposted to Newquay and turn left onto the A3058 at Quintrell Downs, the site is in ¼ mile.
Acreage 15 **Open** 1st March–1st January
Access Good **Site** Level
Sites available Total 157.
Facilities
Nearby facilities
Quintrell Downs.
Peaceful location with scenic views, close to several sandy beaches. English Tourist Board Graded 4 Tick (very good). NO Clubhouse – caravan storage. 12 static caravans to let. Take-away food available.

trevornick
Summer better than others!
Something for everyone and we're only half a mile from the beach! It's all in our brochure!
RING NOW! 01637 830531
AA
AA
EXCELLENT
FOR CAMPERS AND TOURERS
TREVORNICK HOLIDAY PARK, HOLYWELL BAY, NEWQUAY, CORNWALL

Newquay Tourist Park

is great! **For families and couples young and old.**

Fun and entertainment in luscious green parkland with the highest standard facilities and excellent services. **Great, Great Value!**

- Modern Caravans
- Excellent pitches
- Electric hook-ups
- Free showers
- Free 3 pool complex and 200 ft water slide
- Free nightly entertainment
- Children's club
- Self-service shop
- Takeaway

Phone for a colour brochure now!

(01637) 871111 *Please ask for extension 6.*

Newquay Holiday Parks Ltd, 6 Newquay Tourist Park, Newquay, Cornwall TR8 4HS

AA

BETWEEN WATERGATE BAY AND MAWGAN PORTH NEWQUAY

AA RAC

TREVARRIAN holiday Park

IN QUIET COUNTRYSIDE CLOSE TO FABULOUS BEACHES

SPECIAL OUT OF SEASON OFFERS

SEE MAIN ADVERTISEMENT IN COLOUR SECTION FOR FULL DETAILS

ROSECLISTON PARK

TREVEMPER NEWQUAY

☎ 01637 830326

Access VISA AA RAC APPOINTED

HOLIDAY FUN FOR ALL THE FAMILY

- ★ OUTDOOR HEATED POOL
- ★ INDOOR HEATED POOL
- ★ CHILDRENS PADDLING POOL
- ★ LICENSED BAR & CLUB
- ★ FREE ENTERTAINMENT
- ★ AMUSEMENTS
- ★ COLOUR T.V. LOUNGE
- ★ POOL TABLES
- ★ SOLARIUM
- ★ SAUNA
- ★ FIRST CLASS CAMPING & TOURING PITCHES
- ★ DISHWASHING BAYS
- ★ ADVENTURE PLAY AREA
- ★ PUBLIC TELEPHONES
- ★ BUS STOP AT ENTRANCE
- ★ MODERN TOILETS

- ★ HOT SHOWERS
- ★ TAKE—AWAY FOOD BAR
- ★ SELF SERVICE SHOP
- ★ LAUNDERETTE
- ★ ELECTRIC HOOK-UPS
- ★ HARD STANDINGS

THE BEST CHOICE FOR CAMPING & TOURING IN NEWQUAY

HOLIDAY HOTLINE: - Please Ring 01637 830326 For Free Colour Brochure

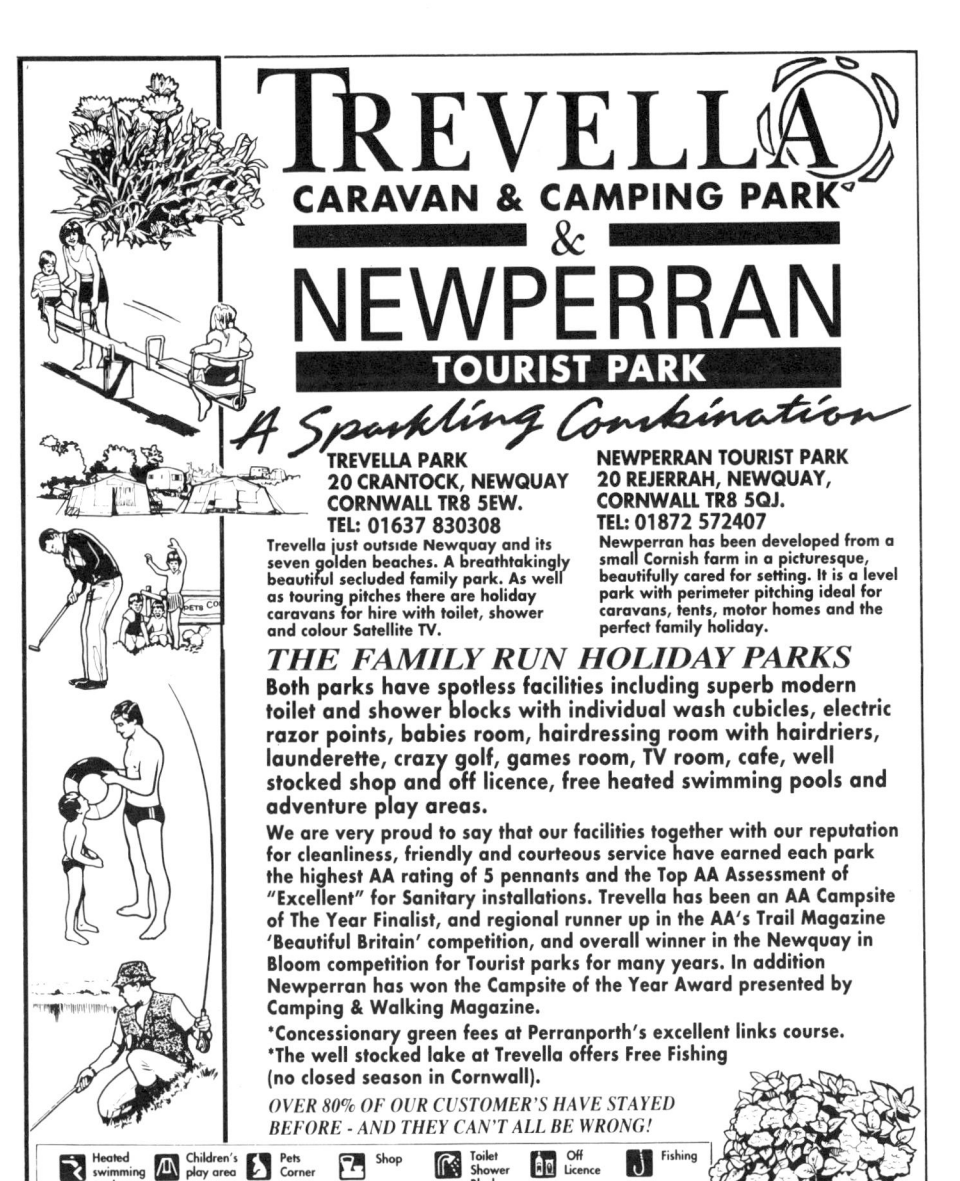

TREVELLA
CARAVAN & CAMPING PARK
&
NEWPERRAN
TOURIST PARK

A Sparkling Combination

TREVELLA PARK
20 CRANTOCK, NEWQUAY
CORNWALL TR8 5EW.
TEL: 01637 830308

Trevella just outside Newquay and its seven golden beaches. A breathtakingly beautiful secluded family park. As well as touring pitches there are holiday caravans for hire with toilet, shower and colour Satellite TV.

NEWPERRAN TOURIST PARK
20 REJERRAH, NEWQUAY,
CORNWALL TR8 5QJ.
TEL: 01872 572407

Newperran has been developed from a small Cornish farm in a picturesque, beautifully cared for setting. It is a level park with perimeter pitching ideal for caravans, tents, motor homes and the perfect family holiday.

THE FAMILY RUN HOLIDAY PARKS

Both parks have spotless facilities including superb modern toilet and shower blocks with individual wash cubicles, electric razor points, babies room, hairdressing room with hairdriers, launderette, crazy golf, games room, TV room, cafe, well stocked shop and off licence, free heated swimming pools and adventure play areas.

We are very proud to say that our facilities together with our reputation for cleanliness, friendly and courteous service have earned each park the highest AA rating of 5 pennants and the Top AA Assessment of "Excellent" for Sanitary installations. Trevella has been an AA Campsite of The Year Finalist, and regional runner up in the AA's Trail Magazine 'Beautiful Britain' competition, and overall winner in the Newquay in Bloom competition for Tourist parks for many years. In addition Newperran has won the Campsite of the Year Award presented by Camping & Walking Magazine.

***Concessionary green fees at Perranporth's excellent links course.**
***The well stocked lake at Trevella offers Free Fishing (no closed season in Cornwall).**

OVER 80% OF OUR CUSTOMER'S HAVE STAYED BEFORE - AND THEY CAN'T ALL BE WRONG!

Heated swimming pool	Children's play area	Pets Corner	Shop	Toilet Shower Block	Off Licence	Fishing
Cafeteria	Launderette	Crazy Golf	Games Room	Television Room	Hair Dressing Room	Babies Room

TELEPHONE FOR COLOUR BROCHURES **01637 830308** ***(24 hours)*** OR CLIP COUPON

Please post to me by return

NAME ____________________

ADDRESS ____________________

☐ **TREVELLA BROCHURE**

☐ **NEWPERRAN BROCHURE**

please tick

NEWQUAY

Trevarrian Holiday Park, Mawgan Porth, Newquay, Cornwall.
Tel. 860381 Std. 01637
Nearest Town/Resort Newquay.
Directions Follow the A30 dual carriageway to end at Bodmin, continuing for 5 miles under railway bridge. Take next turning on right signposted St Mawgan. Follow to roundabout, take Newquay road past Shell Garage and turn right. Follow to T-junction, turn right, ¾ mile.
Acreage 7 **Open** Easter–September
Access Good **Site** Level
Sites available Total 125.
Facilities
Nearby facilities
Newquay.
On the coast road between Mawgan Porth and Watergate Bay. Scenic views with all modern facilities.

NEWQUAY

Trevelgue Holiday Park, Trevelgue Road, Porth, Newquay, Cornwall.
Tel. 851851 Std. 01637
Nearest Town/Resort Newquay.
Directions Located via A30 from Indian Queens, turn right onto A392 towards Newquay. On the outskirts of town turn right along the Porth road B3276. After passing Porth Beach turn right again.
Acreage 10 **Open** March–October
Access Good **Site** Lev/Slope
Sites available Total 90.
Facilities
Nearby facilities
Newquay.
Situated in a beautiful valley only 1¼ miles to Newquay town centre. 5 minutes from Porth Beach.

NEWQUAY

Trevella Park, Crantock, Newquay, Cornwall, TR8 5EW.
Tel. 830308 Std. 01637
Nearest Town/Resort Newquay.
Directions 2 miles south of Newquay on the A3075, turn right signposted Crantock.
Acreage 15 **Open** Easter–October
Access Good **Site** Level
Sites available Total 270.
Facilities
Nearby facilities
Newquay.
½ mile from the beach, concessionary green fees, own fishing lake. AA 5 Pennants.

NEWQUAY

Rosecliston Park, Trevemper, Newquay, Cornwall.
Tel. 830326 Std. 01637
Nearest Town/Resort Newquay.
Directions Take A3075 from Newquay, Rosecliston is 1 mile on left.
Acreage 8 **Open** Whitsun–September
Access Good **Site** Lev/Slope
Sites available Total 130.
Facilities
Nearby facilities
Newquay.
Family site with many facilities on the outskirts of Newquay.

PADSTOW

Dennis Cove Camping, Dennis Cove, Padstow, Cornwall. PL28 8DR.
Tel. 532349 Std. 01841
Nearest Town/Resort Padstow.
Directions Signposted off A389 on outskirts of Padstow Town.
Acreage 5 **Open** Easter–September
Access Good **Site** Lev/Slope
Sites available Total 56.
Facilities
Nearby facilities
Bodmin Parkway.
Site adjoins Camel Estuary and town of Padstow. Scenic views and ideal base for variety of watersports. 5 Touring caravan pitches only. No large groups without prior reservation.

PADSTOW

Mother Iveys Bay Caravan Park, Trevose Head, Padstow, Cornwall. PL28 8SL.
Tel. 520990 Std. 01841
Nearest Town/Resort Padstow.
Directions Padstow to Newquay coast road B3276 4 miles west of Padstow pick up Mother Iveys signs.
Acreage 13 **Open** Easter–October
Access Busy **Site** Lev/Slope
Sites available Total 100.
Facilities
Nearby facilities
Bodmin Parkway.
Own private sandy beach. You can FAX us on 01841 520550.

PADSTOW

Music Water Touring Park, Rumford, Wadebridge, Cornwall. PL27 7SJ.
Tel. 540257 Std. 01841
Nearest Town/Resort Padstow.
Directions Wadebridge A39 to roundabout take B3274 signposted Padstow. Turn left, 2 miles 500yds Park on right.
Acreage 7 **Open** April–October
Access Good **Site** Level
Sites available Total 145.
Facilities

Nearby facilities
Bodmin.
Scenic views, ideal walking, clean friendly family site, splash pool.

PADSTOW

Carnevas Farm Holiday Park, Carnevas Farm, St. Merryn, Padstow, Cornwall, PL28 8PN.
Tel. Padstow 520230 Std. 01841.
Nearest Town/Resort Padstow.
Directions Take Newquay coast road from Padstow, turn right at Tredrea Inn just before getting to Porthcothan Bay. Site ¼ mile up road on right.
Acreage 8 **Open** April–October
Access Good **Site** Lev/Slope
Sites available Total 198.
Facilities
Nearby facilities
Newquay.
Near numerous sandy beaches in lovely rural position, ideal touring, well run family park. AA 3 Pennant site, Rose Award Park 1993 & 1994, English Tourist Board grading system 4 ticks.

PADSTOW

Trerethern Touring Park, Padstow, Cornwall. PL28 8LE.
Tel. 532061 Std. 01841
Nearest Town/Resort Padstow.
Directions On A389 1 mile ssw of Padstow.
Acreage 13¼ **Open** April–October
Access Good **Site** Level
Sites available Total 90.
Facilities
Nearby facilities
Panoramic views, several sandy beaches within 3 miles. Extra large pitches, footpath to padstow. Winter storage, no statics, separate dog exercise area. 4 Ticks, free brochure.

PAR

Par Sands Holiday Park, Par Beach, St. Austell Bay, Cornwall. PL24 2AS.
Tel. 812868 Std. 01726.
Nearest Town/Resort St. Austell/Fowey.
Directions 4 miles east of St Austell on road to Fowey A3082.
Acreage 12 **Open** April–October
Access Good **Site** Level
Sites available Total 200.
Facilities
Nearby facilities
Par.
Alongside safe sandy beach and freshwater wildlife lake. ETB Rose Award 4 Ticks.

PENTEWAN

Pentewan Sands Holiday Park, Pentewan, St. Austel, Cornwall PL26 6BT.
Tel. Mevagissey 843485 Std. 01726
Nearest Town/Resort Pentewan.
Directions From A390 at St. Austell take B3273 south towards Mevagissey. Entrance is 4 miles on left.
Acreage 27 **Open** April–October
Access Good **Site** Level
Sites available Total 470.
Facilities
Nearby facilities
St. Austell.
Large individual marked pitches (many with electric hook-ups) on well equipped site with own safe sandy beach. Tennis on the park.

PENZANCE

Boleigh Farm Site, Boleigh Farm, Lamorna, Penzance, Cornwall.
Tel. 810305 Std. 01736
Nearest Town/Resort Penzance.
Directions Site is 4½ miles southwest of Penzance on the B3315, first on the right after turn to Lamorna Cove.
Acreage 1½ **Open** March–October
Access Good **Site** Level
Sites available Total 30.
Facilities
Nearby facilities

'WAYFARERS' CAMPING SITE

St. Hilary, Penzance, TR20 9EF. Tel: Penzance (01736) 763326

A family campsite in a peaceful rural setting on the B3280, 2 miles east of Marazion. the glorious panorama of Mount's Bay is only one mile distant whilst sandy beaches, coves and the famous 'St. Michaels Mount' are within 2 miles.

NEW **MODERN TOILET FACILITIES. SHOWERS - HOT WATER. LAUNDERETTE. SITE SHOP. CHILDREN'S PLAYPARK**

TOURIST INFORMATION DISPLAYS - HOLIDAY CARAVANS TO LET.

ANWB (Holland) Listed Member of NFSO RAC CARAVAN - CAMPING CLUB

Send for brochure to Malcolm & Rose Judd

ROSEHILL FARM TOURIST PARK

PERRANPORTH CORNWALL

Our friendly 7 acre Touring Park offers level pitches in a rural setting with distant country views, yet only minutes from Perranporth's famous beach. Peace and quiet plus free hot showers, laundry room, games room, shop, play area, electric hook-ups, dog walking field.

No price increase in 1995

AA ▶▶ Brochure from resident proprietors Les & Sue Rolfe, Rosehill Farm Tourist Park, Goonhavern, Truro TR4 9LA Tel: (0872) 572448

CORNWALL REGISTERED ACCOMMODATION 1992

Perranporth Camping & Touring Park

The park, within easy walking distance (approx. 5 minutes) of beach and town, comprises seven acres of well drained sheltered grass land with tarmacadam access roads and all modern facilities.

Mini Supermarket · Swimming Pool · Launderette · Showers and Washrooms · Six berth luxury vans · Adjacent 'Failte Club' with licensed bar, overlooking heated swimming pool and children's paddling pool.

Budnick Road, Perranporth, Cornwall Telephone: Perranporth (0187257) 2174

AA Camping Club Caravan Club British Tourist Authority listed site

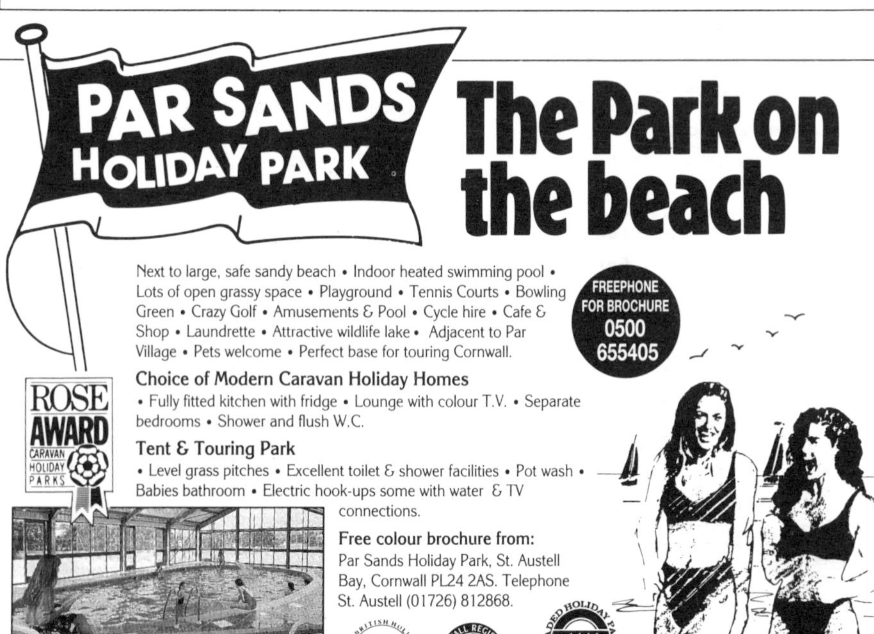

Penzance.
Local Prehistoric Stones, Pipers and Merry Maidens, etc. Sea 1 mile. Coastal walks. Spin dryer. 7 miles to Lands End, 5 miles Minac (open air) theatre.

PENZANCE
Bone Valley Caravan Park, Heamoor Penzance Cornwall TR20 8UJ.
Tel. 60313 Std. 01736
Nearest Town/Resort Penzance.
Directions Follow A30 (Penzance By-pass) to roundabout signposted Heamoor follow road straight through village, turn right at caravan/camping sign, to next caravan/camping sign, turn left.
Acreage 1 **Open** March–7th January
Access Good **Site** Level
Sites available Total 17.
Facilities
Nearby facilities
Penzance.
Clean, friendly, family park, very sheltered with guaranteed personal 24 hour service.

PENZANCE
Garris Farm, Gulval, Penzance, Cornwall TR20 8XD.
Tel. Penzance 65806 Std. 01736
Nearest Town/Resort Penzance.
Directions Leave A30 turning right at Crowlas. Follow road to Chysauster Ancient Village.
Acreage 8 **Open** May–October
Access Good **Site** Sloping
Sites available
Facilities
Nearby facilities
Penzance.

PENZANCE
River Valley Caravan Park, Relubbus, Marazion, Penzance, Cornwall TR20 9ER.
Tel. 763398 Std. 01736
Nearest Town/Resort Marazion.
Directions From Hayle B3302 to Leedstown, turn right onto B3280 to Townsend and straight on to Relubbus.
Acreage 18 **Open** March–5th Jan
Access Good **Site** Level
Sites available Total 90.
Facilities
Nearby facilities
Penzance.
Alongside small stream. Central for touring. Separate area for units with dogs, next to a river walk. No restrictions on length of stay.

PENZANCE
Wayfarers Camping Site, St. Hilary, Penzance, Cornwall TR20 9EF.
Tel. Penzance 763326 Std. 01736
Nearest Town/Resort Marazion.
Directions 2 miles east of Marazion on B3280.
Acreage 4 **Open** March–November
Access Good **Site** Level
Sites available Total 60.
Facilities
Nearby facilities
Penzance.
Quiet, family site. Easy reach Mounts Bay and beaches. Central for West Cornwall touring. Holiday Caravans for hire.

PERRANPORTH
Penrose Farm Touring Park, Goonhavern, Truro, Cornwall TR4 9QF.
Tel. 573185 Std. 01872
Nearest Town/Resort Perranporth.
Directions Leave A30 onto the B3285 signed Perranporth, site 1¼ miles on the left hand side as you enter the village of Goonhavern.
Acreage 6 **Open** April–October
Access Good **Site** Level
Sites available Total 120.
Facilities
Nearby facilities
Newquay/Truro.
Ideal for touring Cornwall. Close to Perranporth beach. 4 Tick Graded.

PERRANPORTH
Perran Sands Holiday Centre, Perranporth, Cornwall, TR6 0AQ.
Tel. 573551 Std. 01872
Nearest Town/Resort Perranporth.
Directions Take the A30 through Cornwall. 3 miles after Mitchell turn right onto the B3285 towards Perranporth. Perran Sands is on the right just before Perranporth.
Acreage 25 **Open** 30 April–8 October
Access Good **Site** Level
Sites available Total 450.
Facilities
Nearby facilities
Truro.
On a cliff top amid dunes and grassland. A short walk from the beach.

PERRANPORTH
Perranporth Camping & Touring Park, Budnick, Perranporth, Cornwall.
Tel. 572174 Std. 01872
Nearest Town/Resort Perranporth.
Directions ¼ mile north east of Perranporth, off B3285 Perranporth/Newquay road.
Acreage 7 **Open** Easter–September
Access Good **Site** Lev/Slope
Sites available Total 180.
Facilities
Nearby facilities
Truro.
¼ mile from town and beach. Easy walking 5 minutes approx.

PERRANPORTH
Rosehill Farm Tourist Park, Goonhavern, Cornwall, TR4 9LA.
Tel. 572448 Std. 01872
Nearest Town/Resort Perranporth.
Directions 200 yds from The New Inn in Goonhavern on the B3285 Perranporth road.
Acreage 6 **Open** Easter–October
Access Good **Site** Lev/Slope
Sites available Total 65.
Facilities
Nearby facilities
Truro & Newquay.
Quiet family site, 1¼ miles from Perranporth beach, ideal touring base. Free hot showers, separate dog walking field. Discount for advance bookings.

PERRANPORTH
Silverbow Park, Goonhavern, Truro, Cornwall, TR4 9NX.
Tel. Perranporth 2347 Std. 0187 257
Nearest Town/Resort Perranporth.
Directions ½ mile south Goonhavern Village, 6 miles south of Newquay on A3075.
Acreage 24 **Open** Easter–October
Access Good **Site** Lev/slope
Sites available Total 100.
Facilities
Nearby facilities
Truro.
Smaller quality park, catering for the more discerning tourist. Spacious layout. A.A. and Calor Award Best Holiday Park in Britain. E.T.B. excellent grading. Two all-weather tennis courts. Short mat bowls.

POLZEATH
South Winds, Old Polzeath Road, Polzeath, Near Wadebridge, Cornwall. PL27 6QU.
Tel. 863267 Std. 01208.
Nearest Town/Resort Wadebridge.
Acreage 7 **Open** Easter–October
Access Good **Site** Level
Sites available Total 100.
Facilities
Nearby facilities
Bodmin Road.
Outstanding views of countryside and sea. You can FAX us on 01208 862080.

POLZEATH

Tristram Caravan & Camping Park, Polzeath, Nr Wadebridge, Cornwall, PL27 6SR.
Tel. 863267/862215 Std. 01208
Nearest Town/Resort Wadebridge.
Acreage 5 **Open** Easter–October
Access Good **Site** Level
Sites available Total 130.
Facilities
Nearby facilities
Bodmin Parkway.
Cliff top site. Direct access onto Polzeath beach. You can FAX us on 01208 862080.

PORTHTOWAN

Porthtowan Tourist Park, Mile Hill, Porthtowan, Truro, Cornwall, TR4 8TY.
Tel. 890256 Std. 01209
Nearest Town/Resort Porthtowan.
Directions Take signpost off A30 Redruth/Porthtowan. Through north country until 'T' junction (1½ miles). Turn right up hill. Site on left just past Woodlands Restaurant.
Acreage 5 **Open** Easter–October
Access Good **Site** Level
Sites available Total 31.
Facilities
Nearby facilities
Redruth.
¾ mile from Porthtowan beach. 2 miles from Portreath beach. Ideal site for touring Cornwall.

PORTREATH

Cambrose Touring Park, Portreath Road, Redruth, Cornwall.
Tel. Porthtowan 890747 Std. 01209
Nearest Town/Resort Redruth/ Portreath.
Directions From Redruth, B3300 (Portreath road) north.
Acreage 3 **Open** Easter–October
Access Good **Site** Level
Sites available Total 50.
Facilities
Nearby facilities
Redruth.
1½ miles sandy beaches, centrally situated as a base from which to tour. Under the personal supervision of the resident proprietors – R.G. & J. Fitton.

PORTREATH

Tehidy Holiday Park, Harris Mill, Redruth, Cornwall TR16 4JQ.
Tel. Redruth 216489 Std. 01209
Nearest Town/Resort Portreath.
Directions Take Redruth Porthtowan exit from A30. Take Porthtowan exit from double roundabout, turn left at first crossroads. Cross next two crossroads Tehidy Holiday Park 200 yards on left pass Cornish Arms Public House.
Acreage 1 **Open** Easter–October
Access Good **Site** Level
Sites available Total 18.
Facilities

Nearby facilities
Redruth.
Near beach, scenic views, ideal touring.

REDRUTH

Venture Caravans Holiday Park, Loscombe Lane, Four Lanes, Redruth, Cornwall, TR16 6LP.
Tel. 216447 Std. 01209.
Nearest Town/Resort Redruth.
Directions A30 to Redruth, A393 to Falmouth, turn right onto B3297 (Helston road), second right after Victoria Pub in Four Lanes.
Acreage 12¼ **Open** April–October
Access Good **Site** Level
Sites available Total 25.
Facilities
Nearby facilities
Redruth.
5 miles to nearest beach, a quiet family park (some statics). Central to tour Cornwalls many tourist attractions. Holiday homes for sale. There is limited access for the disabled. For information please call Keith and Barbara Lewis.

ROSUDGEON

Kenneggy Cove Holiday Park, Higher Kenneggy, Rosudgeon, Penzance, Cornwall. TR20 9AU.
Tel. 763453 Std. 01736
Nearest Town/Resort Penzance.
Directions Off the main A394 7 miles fron Helston 6 miles from Penzance.
Acreage 3¼ **Open** Easter–October
Access Good **Site** Level
Sites available Total 60.
Facilities
Nearby facilities
Penzance.
Quiet family site with spectacular sea views.

RUAN MINOR

The Friendly Camp, Tregullas Farm, Penhale, Ruan Minor, Helston, Cornwall. TR12 7LJ.
Tel. 240387 Std. 01326
Nearest Town/Resort Mullion.
Directions 7 miles south of Helston on left hand side of A3083, just before junction of B3296 to Mullion which is 1 mile.
Acreage 1¼ **Open** April–November
Access Good **Site** Level
Sites available Total 18.
Facilities
Nearby facilities
Redruth.
Nice views, ideal touring, nice moorland walks.

RUAN MINOR

Silver Sands Holiday Park, Kennack Sands, Gwendreath, Ruan Minor, Helston, Cornwall, TR12 7LZ.
Tel. 290631 Std. 01326
Nearest Town/Resort Helston.
Directions On entering Helston take the A3083 Lizard road, pass R.N.A.S. Culdrose then turn left at roundabout onto the B3293 signposted St Keverne. In 4 miles, immediately past Goonhilly Satellite Station, turn right to Kennack. After 1 mile turn left.
Acreage 6 **Open** April–September
Access Good **Site** Lev/Slope
Sites available Total 34.
Facilities
Nearby facilities
Redruth.
800mts to safe sandy beach, ideal touring and walking, quiet family site. In area of outstanding natural beauty.

SALTASH

Dolbeare Caravan & Camping Park, Landrake, Saltash, Cornwall.
Tel. 851332 Std. 01752
Nearest Town/Resort Saltash.
Directions 4 miles west of Saltash, turn off A38 at Landrake into Pound Hill, signposted.
Acreage 9 **Open** All Year
Access Good **Site** Lev/Slope
Sites available Total 60.
Facilities
Nearby facilities
Saltash.
Ideal touring site near Plymouth and coast. Scenic walks. Under the personal supervision of resident proprietors. Caravan storage. Hard standings available. English Tourist Board 4 Ticks.

SALTASH

Stoketon Touring Park, Stoketon Cross, Trematon, Saltash, Cornwall, PL12 4RZ.
Tel. 841447 Std. 01752
Nearest Town/Resort Saltash.
Directions A38, once over Tamar Bridge, 2 miles west (towards Liskeard). Follow signs for Crooked Inn.
Open April–October
Access Good **Site** Lev/Slope
Sites available Total 60.
Facilities
Nearby facilities
Saltash.
First site over the Tamar Bridge, near a river with scenic views. Ideal base for touring. Country inn, home cooked food and real ales adjacent.

SENNEN

Sea View Caravan Park, Sennen, Penzance, Cornwall.
Tel. 871266 Std. 01736
Nearest Town/Resort Sennen.
Directions Left off the A30, ¼ mile from Lands End.
Acreage 4 **Open** Easter–October
Access Good **Site** Level
Sites available Total 60.
Facilities
Nearby facilities
Penzance.
1 mile from Sennen with a Blue Flag beach.

ST. AGNES
Beacon Cottage Farm Camping Park, Beacon Drive, St. Agnes, Cornwall.
Tel. 552347 Std. 01872.
Nearest Town/Resort St. Agnes.
Directions From A30, take B3277 to St. Agnes, take road to the Beacon. Follow signs to site.
Acreage 2 **Open** April–September
Access Good **Site** Level
Sites available Total 50.
Facilities
Nearby facilities
Truro.
On working farm, surrounded by National Trust Land. Sandy beach 1 mile, beautiful sea views.

ST. AGNES
Chiverton Caravan & Touring Park, Blackwater, Near Truro, Cornwall, TR4 8HS.
Tel. 560667 Std. 01872
Nearest Town/Resort St Agnes/Truro.
Directions 5 miles north west of Truro. From the A30 at Chiverton cross roundabout, take the B3277 St Agnes road. In 500yds turn left, park is 200yds on the left.
Acreage 2 **Open** April–October
Access Good **Site** Level
Sites available Total 30.
Facilities
Nearby facilities
Truro.
Ideal touring location, 2 minutes from the A30. Maximum of ¼ hour to most major towns and attractions.

ST. AGNES
Presingoll Farm Caravan & Camping Site, Presingoll Farm, St. Agnes, Cornwall TR5 0PB.
Tel. 552333 Std. 01872.
Nearest Town/Resort St. Agnes.
Directions 1 mile south of St. Agnes on B3277.
Acreage 3¼ **Open** April–October
Access Good **Site** Level
Sites available Total 90.
Facilities
Nearby facilities
Truro.
Ideal centre for touring Cornwall. Site overlooks north coast of Cornwall. Scenic views.

ST. AUSTELL
Penhaven Touring Park, Pentewan Road, St. Austell, Cornwall.
Tel. 843687 Std. 01726.
Nearest Town/Resort Mevagissey.
Directions 3 miles south os St. Austell on the B3273 towards Mevagissey. On the left hand side after the village of London Apprentice.
Open April–October
Access Good **Site** Level
Sites available Total 105.
Facilities
Nearby facilities
St. Austell.
Sheltered valley.

ST. AUSTELL
Trencreek Farm Holiday Park, Hewaswater, St. Austell, Cornwall.
Tel. St. Austell 882540 Std. 01726
Nearest Town/Resort St. Austell.
Directions From St. Austell take A390 towards Truro, after 4 miles fork left onto B3287 (St. Mawes) entrance 1 mile on left.
Acreage 10 **Open** Easter–October
Access Good **Site** Lev/slope
Sites available Total 140.
Facilities
Nearby facilities
St. Austell.
Small working farm with real farm atmosphere. Ideal for families with young children. Coarse fishing lakes. Tennis court, pitch & putt.

ST. AUSTELL
Trewhiddle Holiday Estate, Trewhiddle, St. Austell, Cornwall, PL26 7AD.
Tel. 67011 Std. 01726
Nearest Town/Resort St. Austell.
Directions From St Austell roundabout on the By-Pass, take the B3273 road towards Mevagissey, the site entrance is ¾ mile from the roundabout on the right.
Acreage 9 **Open** January–November
Access Good **Site** Lev/Slope
Sites available Total 105.
Facilities
Nearby facilities
St. Austell.
Set in 16 acres of beautiful grounds, it is renowned for its Rhododendrons and other shrubs and trees.

ST. AUSTELL
Sun Valley Holiday Park, Pentewan Road, St. Austell, Cornwall.
Tel. Mevagissey 843266 Std. 01726.
Nearest Town/Resort Mevagissey.
Directions Take B3273 from St. Austell, site 1 mile past 'London Apprentice', on right.
Acreage 20 **Open** April–October
Access Good **Site** Level
Sites available Total 22.
Facilities
Nearby facilities
St. Austell.
Site situated in woodland and pasture surrounding. 1 mile from sea. Ideal touring centre. Tennis and indoor swimming pool on site.

ST. BURYAN
Tower Park, St. Buryan, Penzance, Cornwall.
Tel. 810286 Std. 01736
Nearest Town/Resort Penzance.
Directions A30 west from Penzance for 3 miles, then B3283 for 2 to St Buryan turn right and bear right. Camp is 300yds.
Acreage 12 **Open** March–October
Access Good **Site** Level
Sites available Total 102.
Facilities
Nearby facilities
Penzance.

ST. BURYAN
Treverven Touring Caravan & Camping Site, Treverven Farm, St. Buryan, Cornwall, TR19 6DL.
Tel. 810221 Std. 01736.
Nearest Town/Resort Penzance.
Directions B3315 midway between Penzance and Lands End.
Acreage 6 **Open** Easter–October
Access Good **Site** Level
Sites available Total 115.
Facilities
Nearby facilities
Penzance.
Near coast, sea views.

ST. DAY
Tresaddern Holiday Park, St. Day, Redruth, Cornwall, TR16 5JR.
Tel. 820459 Std. 01209
Nearest Town/Resort Redruth.
Directions From A30 2 miles east of Redruth take A3047 Scorrier, in 400yds B3298 Falmouth, site 1½ miles on right.
Acreage 3 **Open** Easter–October
Access Good **Site** Lev/Slope
Sites available Total 25.
Facilities
Nearby facilities
Redruth.
Quiet rural site, central for touring south Cornwall.

ST. IVES
Ayr Holiday Park, Ayr, St. Ives, Cornwall.
Tel. 795855 Std. 01736
Nearest Town/Resort St. Ives.
Directions Follow holiday route to St Ives, leave B3306 ½ mile before town centre following signs for Ayr and Porthmeor Beach.
Acreage 2 **Open** April–October
Access Good **Site** Sloping
Sites available Total 40.
Facilities
Nearby facilities
St. Ives.
Near town and beaches, beautiful sea views.

ST. IVES
Penderleath Caravan & Camping Park, Towednack, St. Ives, Cornwall, TR26 3AF.
Tel. 798403 Std. 01736
Nearest Town/Resort St. Ives.
Directions B3311 from St. Ives, after Halsetown first right to Towednack.
Acreage 8 **Open** Easter–October
Access Good **Site** Lev/Slope
Sites available Total 75.
Facilities
Nearby facilities

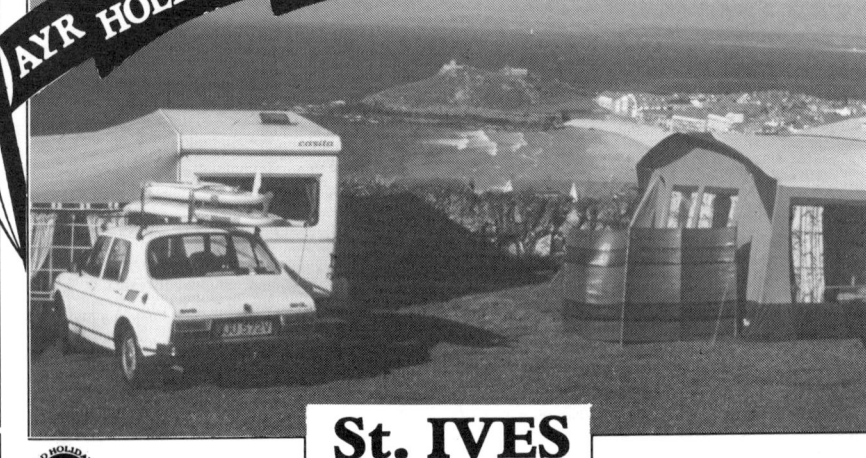

St. Ives.
Set in classified area of outstanding natural beauty with unrivalled views. Peaceful family run site.

ST. IVES

Hellesveor Caravan & Camping Site, Hellesveor Farm, St. Ives, Cornwall, TR26 3AD.
Tel. 795738 Std. 01736
Nearest Town/Resort St. Ives.
Directions 1 mile from the town centre and beaches on the Lands End road (B3306). 5 minutes from bus route.
Acreage ½ **Open** Easter–October
Access Good **Site** Level
Sites available Total 25.
Facilities
Nearby facilities
St. Ives.
Near Lands End coastal path, ideal for touring.

ST. IVES

Polmanter Tourist Park, Polmanter Farm, Halsetown, St. Ives, Cornwall TR26 3LX.
Tel. St. Ives 795640 Std. 01736
Nearest Town/Resort St. Ives.
Directions 2 miles from St. Ives B3311 off B3306.
Acreage 12 **Open** Easter–October
Access Good **Site** Level
Sites available Total 240.
Facilities
Nearby facilities
St. Ives.
2 miles from St. Ives and beaches. Tennis courts on site. Deluxe pitches have water, waste and Cable T.V.

ST. IVES

St. Ives Bay Holiday Park, Upton Towans, Hayle, Cornwall TR27 5BH.
Tel. Hayle 752274 Std. 01736
Nearest Town/Resort Hayle.
Directions A30 from Camborne to Hayle, at roundabout take Hayle turnoff and then turn right onto B3301, 600yds on left enter park at petrol station.
Acreage 12 **Open** May–September
Access Good **Site** Lev/Slope
Sites available Total 200.
Facilities
Nearby facilities
Hayle.
Park adjoining own sandy beach, onto St. Ives Bay. Children very welcome. Pets welcome. Seaviews. Dial-a-Brochure 24 hours, Mr R. White. (see full page colour advertisment).

ST. IVES

Trevalgan Family Camping Park, St. Ives, Cornwall, TR26 3BJ.
Tel. 796433 Std. 01736
Nearest Town/Resort St. Ives.
Directions Follow the holiday route round St. Ives. From the A3306 follow brown camping park signs.
Acreage 5 **Open** May–September
Access Good **Site** Level
Sites available Total 120.
Facilities
Nearby facilities
St. Ives.
Rural park with own stretch of Cornish coast. Superb views and walking. Some facilities for the disabled.

ST. JUST

Kelynack Caravan & Camping Park, Kelynack, St. Just, Nr. Penzance, Cornwall.
Tel. 787633 Std. 01736
Nearest Town/Resort St. Just in Penwith.
Directions From Penzance take A3071 St. Just road, then after 6 miles turn left onto the B3306 Lands End coast road, ½ mile to site sign.
Acreage 2 **Open** April–October
Access Good **Site** Level
Sites available Total 20.
Facilities
Nearby facilities
Penzance.
¾ mile beach, alongside stream in valley setting. Ideal for touring. On coast road. E.T.B. graded very good. Sheltered site.

ST. JUST

Bosavern Garden Caravan Site, Bosavern House, St. Just, Penzance, Cornwall.
Tel. 788301 Std. 01736
Nearest Town/Resort St. Just/Penzance.
Directions Take the A3071 from Penzance towards St. Just. Approximately 550yds before St. Just turn left onto the B3306 signposted Lands End and airport. Bosavern Garden Caravan Park is 500yds from the turn off, behind Bosavern House.
Acreage 2¼ **Open** March–October
Access Good **Site** Level
Sites available Total 12.
Facilities
Nearby facilities
Penzance.
Sea and moorland views, walled garden site surrounded by trees and flowers.

ST. JUST

Levant House, Levant House, Pendeen, Nr. Penzance, Cornwall, TR9 7SX.
Tel. 788795 Std. 01736
Nearest Town/Resort St. Just in Penwith.
Directions 2¼ miles north, left off the B3306 at Trewellard Hotel.
Acreage 2¼ **Open** April–October
Access Good **Site** Lev/Slope
Sites available Total 44.
Facilities
Nearby facilities
Penzance.
Near coastal path, central for touring Lands Peninsula.

ST. JUST

Roselands Caravan and Camping Park, Dowran, St. Just, Penzance, Cornwall TR19 7RS.
Tel. Penzance 788571 Std. 01736.
Nearest Town/Resort Penzance.
Directions Take A3071 from Penzance. Turn left at crossroad ½ mile east of St. Just. Signposted with camping sign and Sancreed 2¾ miles.
Acreage 2 **Open** April–October

Access Good **Site** Level
Sites available Total 20.
Facilities
Nearby facilities
Penzance.
Sea views, close to beaches, scenic walks. Dogs allowed if kept on lead. Static caravans for hire also.

ST. JUST

Trevaylor Caravan and Camping Park, Botallack, St Just, Cornwall.
Tel. 787016 Std. 01736
Nearest Town/Resort Penzance.
Directions Situated on the B3306 Lands End to St Ives road, approx 1 mile to the north of St Just.
Acreage 5 **Open** Mid March–October
Access Good **Site** Level
Sites available Total 85.
Facilities
Nearby facilities
Penzance.
Easy access to the golden sands, white surf from the Atlantic Ocean, rugged cliffs and coastal paths. Off License on site.

ST. MAWES

Trethem Mill Touring Park, St. Just-in-Roseland, Truro, Cornwall.
Tel. 580504 Std. 01872.
Nearest Town/Resort St. Mawes.
Directions St. Austell to St. Mawes A3078.
Acreage 3¾ **Open** April–October
Access Good **Site** Lev/Slope
Sites available Total 84.
Facilities
Nearby facilities
Truro.
St. Mawes.

ST. MERRYN

Trethias Farm Caravan Park, St. Merryn, Padstow, Cornwall.
Tel. Padstow 520323 Std. 01841
Nearest Town/Resort Padstow.
Directions From Wadebridge follow signs to St. Merryn, go past Farmers Arms, third turning right (our signs from here).
Acreage 5 **Open** April–September
Access Good **Site** Level
Sites available Total 40.
Facilities
Nearby facilities
Bodmin Parkway.
Near beach, scenic views.

ST. MERRYN

Trevean Farm Caravan & Camping Park, St. Merryn, Padstow, Cornwall, PL28 8PR.
Tel. 520772 Std. 01841
Nearest Town/Resort Padstow.
Directions From St. Merryn village take the B3276 Newquay road for 1 mile. Turn left for Rumford, site ½ mile on the right.
Acreage 2 **Open** April–October
Access Good **Site** Level
Sites available Total 36.
Facilities
Nearby facilities
Newquay.
Situated near several sandy, surfing beaches.

ST. MERRYN

Tregavone Farm Touring Park, St. Merryn, Padstow, Cornwall, PL28 8JZ.
Tel. 520148 Std. 01841
Nearest Town/Resort Padstow.
Directions Turn right off A39 (Wadebridge- St. Columb) onto A389 (Padstow) come to T junction turn right in 1 mile turn left, entrance on left after 1 mile.
Acreage 4 **Open** March–October
Access Good **Site** Level
Sites available Total 40.
Facilities
Nearby facilities
Newquay.
Quiet family run site situated near sandy surfing beaches, country views, well maintained and grassy.

ST. MERRYN

Treyarnon Bay Caravan Park, Treyarnon Bay, Padstow, Cornwall, PL28 8JR.
Tel. 520681 Std. 01841
Nearest Town/Resort Padstow.
Directions Follow road for Treyarnon from B3276 Newquay to Padstow road. Follow lane and into car park at the bottom of the village. (Holiday park adjoins car park).
Acreage 4 **Open** April–September
Site Sloping
Sites available Total 60.
Facilities
Nearby facilities
Newquay.
Overlooking bay. Ideal for touring, surfing, golf, swimming or just lazing by the sea.

ST. MINVER

Dinham Farm Caravan & Camping Park, St. Minver, Wadebridge, Cornwall, PL27 6RH.
Tel. 812878 Std. 01208
Nearest Town/Resort Wadebridge.
Directions Take B3314, on approaching Polzeath/Rock from Camelford fork right, after 2 miles take left turn at sign for above site 400yds on right.
Acreage 2½ **Open** April–October
Access Good **Site** Lev/Slope
Sites available Total 40.
Facilities
Nearby facilities
Bodmin Parkway.
Overlooking River Camel. New super pitches, hook ups and heated swimming pool.

ST. MINVER

St. Minver Holiday Village, St. Minver, Nr. Wadebridge, Cornwall, PL27 6RR.
Tel. 862305 Std. 01208
Nearest Town/Resort Wadebridge.
Directions Take the A39 from Camelford to Wadebridge, then take the B3314. Turn right at the traffic lights heading for Port Isaac. After 3¼ miles turn left at the road signposted to Rock. The park is 250yds along on the right hand side.
Acreage 6 **Open** 26 March–8 October
Access Good **Site** Sloping
Sites available Total 120.
Facilities
Nearby facilities
Bodmin Parkway.
Set amidst 40 acres of wooded countryside, in the grounds of a lovely old Cornish Manor House.

TINTAGEL

Bossiney Farm Caravan Site, Tintagel, Cornwall. PL34 OAY.
Tel. 770481 Std. 01840
Nearest Town/Resort Tintagel.
Directions ¾ miles from centre of Tintagel on main Boscastle road.
Acreage 2 **Open** April–October
Access Good **Site** Lev/Slope
Sites available Total 20.
Facilities
Nearby facilities
Bodmin Parkway.
Ideal touring centre, near beach, inland views.

TINTAGEL

The Headland Caravan & Camping Park, Atlantic Road, Tintagel, Cornwall. PL34 0DE.
Tel. 770239 Std. 01840.
Nearest Town/Resort Tintagel.
Directions Follow camping/caravan signs from B3263 through village to Headland.
Acreage 4 **Open** Easter–October
Access Good **Site** Lev/Slope
Sites available Total 60.
Facilities
Nearby facilities
Bodmin Parkway.
Three beaches walking distance. Scenic views. Ideal touring centre.

TREVERVA

Menallack Farm, Menallack Farm Treverva, Penryn, Cornwall.
Tel. Falmouth 40333 Std. 01326
Nearest Town/Resort Falmouth/ Helston.
Directions Follow the A39 over the double roundabouts and go straight on towards Helston (A394). Go straight across the first roundabout and take the second exit from the second roundabout (no signpost). In Mabe straight over crossroad. In 2 miles at crossroads turn right to Gweek. In Treverva ¾ mile towards Gweek. Site is on left.
Acreage 1½ **Open** Good Friday–October
Access Good **Site** Lev/slope
Sites available Total 30.
Facilities
Nearby facilities
Falmouth.
Peaceful, isolated, with beautiful views. Easy access to north and south coasts.

TRURO

Carnon Downs Caravan & Camping Park, Carnon Downs, Truro, Cornwall, TR3 6JJ.
Tel. 862283 Std. 01872.
Nearest Town/Resort Truro.
Directions On the A39 Falmouth road, 2¼ miles West of Truro.
Acreage 9 **Open** April–October
Access Good **Site** Level
Sites available Total 150.
Facilities
Nearby facilities
Truro.
Ideally central for touring. Excellent location for sailing and water sports.

TRURO

Chacewater Camping & Caravan Park, Coxhill, Chacewater, Truro, Cornwall.
Tel. St. Day 820762 Std. 01209
Nearest Town/Resort Truro.
Directions From A30 take the A3047 to Scorrier. Turn left at Crossroads Hotel onto the B3298. 1½ miles left to Chacewater ¾ mile sign directs you to the park.
Acreage 6 **Open** Spring Bank Holiday–Sept
Access Good **Site** Level
Sites available Total 80.
Facilities
Nearby facilities
Truro.
Quiet, rural meadow, well off main road. Family run. Ideal for couples and families.

TRURO

Leverton Place, Greenbottom, Nr. Truro, Cornwall, TR4 8QW.
Nearest Town/Resort Truro.
Directions 3 miles west of Truro. Take the A390 to Truro, left at the first roundabout signposted Chacewater. Left at the mini roundabout and Leverton Place is 100yds on the left.
Acreage 10 **Open** All year
Access Good **Site** Level
Sites available Total 110.
Facilities
Nearby facilities
Truro.
Ideal touring and exploring centre for

Liskey

EXCELLENT

The ideal centre for touring and exploring Cornwall. A small, traditional family site with a friendly, relaxed atmosphere.
Just 68 pitches in a garden - like setting with banks of colourful shrubs. Spotlessly clean, modern toilet block with luxury family bathroom and ladies wash cubicles. Shop & Take Away. Adventure Playground and Playbarn.

For brochure, telephone: (01872) 560274 or send a stamp only to: Liskey Touring Park, Greenbottom, TRURO, Cornwall TR4 8QN.

LITTLE BODIEVE HOLIDAY PARK

Wadebridge

Cornwall, PL27 6EG
Telephone: (01208) 812323

AA RAC

- ☆ Excellent touring facilities
- ☆ Luxury caravans for hire
- ☆ Heated swimming pool
- ☆ Licensed clubhouse
- ☆ Shop
- ☆ Games room
- ☆ **Pets Corner**
- ☆ Laundry
- ☆ Superior fully tiled toilet blocks
- ☆ Dishwashing area
- ☆ Electric hook-ups
- ☆ Childrens play equipment
- ☆ Public telephone
- ☆ Crazy golf
- ☆ **Waterslide and Splash pool**

A superior holiday park, probably in one of the best positions for touring all over Cornwall. 20 acres of beautiful touring fields together with our luxury hire units combined together for the ideal family holiday. Family owned and run. Write or telephone for our colour brochure and tariff to resident proprietors Dennis & Barbara Hills, Chris & Karen Berry & Families.

PENROSE FARM TOURING PARK

Goonhavern Nr. Truro, Cornwall TR4 9QF. Telephone: (01872) 573 185

- *QUIET FAMILY PARK- NO CLUB / NO BAR
- * FREE HOT WATER
- * JUST 2.5 MILES FROM PERRANPORTH'S SANDY BEACH
- * ADVENTURE PLAY AREA
- * EXCELLENT CENTRE FOR TOURING CORNWALL
- * ANIMAL CENTRE
- * LEVEL AND SHELTERED PARK
- * SHOP & LAUNDRY
- * DOGS BY ARRANGEMENT

From £4 to £8 per night. Please ring for brochure.

TRETHEAKE MANOR TOURIST PARK

(A tranquil park surrounded by farmland, midway between St. Mawes and Mevagissey

Easy access to uncrowded sandy beaches and secluded coves, sailing, windsurfing, riding and miles of beautiful coastal walks. Most of Cornwall within an hours drive. (Indoor and outdoor Bowls nearby).

Toilet / shower block, dishwashing area and launderette, all with constant free hot water. Games Room. T.V. room. Children's playground. 77 electrical hook ups. 31 with own water supply and 10 all service pitches. Well stocked camp shop. Provisions. Gas. Off licence. Superb coarse fishing. See our colour advertisement in this book.

Colour brochure SAE to:
Dept CA, Tretheake Manor Tourist Park, Veryan, Truro, Cornwall TR2 5PP
(Telephone or Fax) Truro **(01872) 501658**

Cornwall.

TRURO
Liskey Touring Park, Greenbottom, Truro, Cornwall TR4 8QN.
Tel. Truro 560274 Std. 01872
Nearest Town/Resort Truro.
Directions 3½ miles west of Truro, off A390 between Threemilestone and Chacewater.
Acreage 8 **Open** April–September
Access Good **Site** Lev/slope
Sites available Total 68.
Facilities
Nearby facilities
Truro.
Small family site, central for exploring Cornwall. Take away meals hardstandings, adventure play barn, family bathroom, dishwashing sinks. 10 minutes to sea.

TRURO
Summer Valley Touring Park, Shortlanesend, Truro, Cornwall.
Tel. Truro 77878 Std. 01872.
Nearest Town/Resort Truro.
Directions 2 miles out of Truro on Perranporth road (B3284). Sign on left just past Shortlanesend.
Acreage 3 **Open** April–October
Access Good **Site** Level
Sites available Total 60.
Facilities
Nearby facilities
Truro.
Ideal centre for touring Cornwall. British Holiday Parks grading 4 ticks.

TRURO
Tretheake Manor Tourist Park, Veryan, Truro, Cornwall.
Tel. 501658 Std. 01872
Nearest Town/Resort Truro.
Directions 2 miles south of Tregony on the A3078, turn left for Veryan after an Esso station and follow the international signs.
Acreage 9 **Open** April–October
Access Good **Site** Lev/Slpoe
Sites available Total 175.
Facilities
Nearby facilities
St. Austell.
A peaceful park, surrounded by farmland with a range of safe sandy beaches nearby. Centrally placed for visiting all of Cornwall. Coarse fishing (carp and tench) on site.

WADEBRIDGE
Little Bodieve Holiday Park, Wadebridge, Cornwall, PL27 6EG.
Tel. 812323 Std. 01208
Nearest Town/Resort Wadebridge.
Directions 1 mile north of Wadebridge on B3314.
Acreage 20 **Open** March–October
Access Good **Site** Level
Sites available Total 195.
Facilities
Nearby facilities
Bodmin Parkway.
Rose Award family park. 20 acres of level, well mown areas. Ideal touring centre, close to superb beaches. Baby room, crazy golf, pets corner, play area, bar meals, take-away and entertainment in main season.

WADEBRIDGE
The Laurels, Whitecross, Cornwall, PL27 7JQ.
Tel. 813341 Std. 01208
Nearest Town/Resort Wadebridge.
Directions On A39/A389 Wadebridge/Padstow junction.
Acreage 2¼ **Open** Easter–October
Access Good **Site** Level
Sites available Total 30.
Facilities
Nearby facilities
Bodmin Road.
Designated an area of outstanding beauty. Overlooking River Camel, Atlantic Ocean and Bodmin Moor. Set in glorious surroundings.

WADEBRIDGE
Lanarth, St. Kew Highway, Bodmin, Cornwall, PL30 3EE.
Tel. 841215 Std. 01208
Nearest Town/Resort Wadebridge.
Directions On the A39 at St. Kew Highway, 3 miles north east of Wadebridge.
Acreage 10 **Open** April–October
Access Good **Site** Lev/Slope
Sites available Total 86.
Facilities
Nearby facilities
Bodmin.
Set in scenic countryside, surrounded by secluded grounds and gardens. Ideal for touring.

CUMBRIA

ALLONBY
Manor House Caravan Park, Edderside Road, Allonby, Nr Maryport, Cumbria, CA15 6RA.
Tel. 881236 Std. 01900.
Nearest Town/Resort Allonby.
Directions B5300 from Maryport, through Allonby, 1 mile turn right, park 1 mile on right. Signposted on main road.
Acreage 2 **Open** March–15th Nov
Access Good **Site** Level
Sites available Total 30.
Facilities
Nearby facilities
Maryport.
1 mile from beach, quiet park. Ideal for touring North Lakes.

ALSTON
Horse & Waggon Caravan Park, Nentsberry, Alston, Cumbria.
Tel. 382805 Std. 01434
Nearest Town/Resort Alston.
Directions 3 miles east of Alston on the A689.
Acreage ¼ **Open** Mid March–October
Access Good **Site** Level
Sites available Total 10.
Facilities
Nearby facilities
Penrith.
Area of outstanding natural beauty.

AMBLESIDE
Skelwith Fold Caravan Park Ltd, Ambleside, Cumbria LA22 0HX.
Tel. Ambleside 32277 Std. 015394
Nearest Town/Resort Ambleside.
Directions Take A593 Coniston road for 1 mile, turn left onto B5286 Hawkshead road for 1 mile. Site on right.
Acreage 70 **Open** March–15 November
Access Good **Site** Level
Sites available Total 150.
Facilities
Nearby facilities
Windermere.
Ideal central position for exploring lakes.

APPLEBY
Wild Rose Park, Ormside, Appleby, Cumbria, CA16 6EJ.
Tel. 51077 Std. 017683
Nearest Town/Resort Appleby.
Directions Centre Appleby take B6260 Kendal for 1½ miles. Left Ormside and Soulby 1½ miles left, ½ mile turn right.
Acreage 40 **Open** All year
Access Good **Site** Lev/Slope
Sites available Total 184.
Facilities
Nearby facilities
Appleby.
Quiet park in unspoilt Eden Valley, superb views. Midway between Lakes and Yorkshire Dales.

ASKAM IN FURNESS
Marsh Farm, Askam-in-Furness, Cumbria LA16 7AW.
Tel. 62321 Std. 01229
Nearest Town/Resort Barrow-in-Furness.
Directions Leave A590 at Dalton, take A595 from Dalton to Askam, turn left at railway crossing.
Acreage 3 **Open** April–September
Access Good **Site** Level
Sites available Total 40.
Facilities
Nearby facilities
Askam-in-Furness.
Near beach, adjacent golf course. Scenic views.

ASPATRIA
Skiddaw View Caravan Park, Bothel, Carlisle, Cumbria. CA5 2JA.
Tel. 20919 Std. 016973
Nearest Town/Resort Cockermouth/Keswick.
Directions At junction of A591 and A595.
Acreage 3 **Open** April–October
Access Good **Site** Level
Sites available Total 13.
Facilities
Nearby facilities
Carlisle.
Panoramic views of Skiddaw Mountain.

BASSENTHWAITE
Robin Hood Caravan Park, Robin Hood Farmhouse, Bassenthwaite, Keswick, Cumbria CA12 4RJ.
Tel. 76334 Std. 0176 87
Nearest Town/Resort Keswick.
Directions Take A591 North from Keswick for 7 miles, turn right at Castle Inn (signposted Caldbeck) after 1 mile turn right (signposted Robin Hood) site ¼ mile on right.
Acreage 2 **Open** March–November
Access Good **Site** Level
Sites available Total 16.
Facilities
Nearby facilities
Carlisle.
Elevated site, overlooking Bassenthwaite Lake. Easy access to Lakes, Scotland and Coast.

BOUTH

Black Beck Caravan Park, Bouth, Nr. Ulverston, Cumbria.
Tel. 861274 Std. 01229
Nearest Town/Resort Ulverston.
Directions Approx 3 miles from Newby Bridge on the A590 heading towards Ulverston. Right after Steam Railway Station.
Acreage 38 **Open** March–October
Access Good **Site** Level
Sites available Total 75.
Facilities
Nearby facilities
Ulverston.
The site is set in 38 acres of glorious woodland in the heart of the Lake District, with a Beck running its entire length.

BRAMPTON

Irthing Vale Holiday Park, Old Church Lane, Brampton, Nr. Carlisle, Cumbria.
Tel. Brampton 3600 Std. 0169 77.
Nearest Town/Resort Brampton.
Directions ¼ mile from Brampton.
Acreage 4½
Access Good **Site** Level
Sites available Total 40.
Facilities
Nearby facilities
Brampton Junction.
Easy access to Roman Wall, Scottish Borders and Lake District. Swimming nearby.

BROUGHTON IN FURNESS

Birchbank Farm, Birchbank, Blawith, Ulverston, Cumbria.
Tel. 885277 Std. 01229
Nearest Town/Resort Coniston Water.
Directions A5092 ¼ mile west of Gawthwaite turn for Woodland. Site is 2 miles on the right.
Acreage ¼ **Open** May–October
Access Good **Site** Level
Sites available Total 8.
Facilities
Nearby facilities
Kirkby in Furness.
Small farm site, ideal for walking or touring the southern lakes.

CARLISLE

Dalston Hall Caravan Park, Dalston Road, Carlisle, Cumbria.
Tel. 710165/25014 Std. 01228.
Nearest Town/Resort Carlisle.
Directions Leave M6 at junction 42, take road to Dalston. At Dalston turn on to B5299, site on right after ¾ mile.
Acreage 4 **Open** March–October
Access Good **Site** Level
Sites available Total 60.
Facilities
Nearby facilities
Carlisle.
Fishing, ideal for touring Lake District, Hadrian's Wall etc. Nine hole golf course.

CARLISLE

Dandy Dinmont Caravan and Camping Site, Blackford, Carlisle, Cumbria, CA6 4EA.
Tel. 74611 Std. 01228
Nearest Town/Resort Carlisle.
Directions On A7 4½ miles N. of Carlisle. Leave M6 at junc. 44 take Galashiel road to Blackford Church cross roads, then follow site signs.
Acreage 4 **Open** March–October
Access Good **Site** Level
Sites available Total 47.
Facilities
Nearby facilities
Carlisle.
Historic Carlisle-Castle, Cathedral, Roman Wall, Border Country only 45 minutes to Lake District.

CARLISLE

Orton Grange Caravan Park, Wigton Road, Carlisle, Cumbria. CA5 6LA.
Tel. 710252 Std. 01228
Nearest Town/Resort Carlisle.
Directions 4 miles west of Carlisle on A595.
Acreage 6 **Open** All year
Access Good **Site** Level
Sites available Total 50.
Facilities
Nearby facilities
Dalston.
Ideal for touring, north lakes, the Roman Wall plus border country. Camping shop/Tent sales. Tourist Board Grading 4 Ticks.

COCKERMOUTH.

Wyndham Holiday Park, Cockermouth, Cumbria, CA13 9SF.
Tel. 822571/825238 Std. 01900
Nearest Town/Resort Cockermouth.
Directions ½ mile from Cockermouth centre on Old Main Road to Keswick.
Acreage 3 **Open** March–15th Nov
Access Good **Site** Level
Sites available Total 42.
Facilities
Nearby facilities
Carlisle.
Scenic views, Ideal touring. Family entertainment. Lake district.

COCKERMOUTH

Violet Bank Caravan Park, Simonscales Lane, off Lorton Road, Cockermouth, Cumbria, CA13 9TG.
Tel. 822169 Std. 01900

Nearest Town/Resort Cockermouth.
Directions From Cockermouth town centre take the Lorton road (A5292), signed Lorton, Buttermere for about ½ mile then turn right up Vicarage Lane leading to site.
Acreage 6 **Open** March–15th November
Access Good **Site** Level
Sites available Total 30.
Facilities
Nearby facilities
Workington.
Quiet park with superb view. Centre for touring Lakes and fell walking. S.A.E. for brochure and terms.

CONISTON

Coniston Hall Camping Site, Coniston, Cumbria.
Tel. 41223 Std. 015394
Nearest Town/Resort Coniston.
Directions 1 mile south of Coniston.
Acreage 200 **Open** March–October
Site Level
Sites available
Facilities
Nearby facilities
Windermere.
Lake access.

CROOK

Ratherheath Lane Camping and Caravan park, Chain House, Bonningate, Kendal, Cumbria, LA8 8JU.
Tel. 821154 Std. 01539
Nearest Town/Resort Bowness on Windermere.
Directions From Kendal A591 take B5284 to Crook, turn right at sign to Burneside.
Acreage 1 **Open** March–15th November
Access Good **Site** Level
Sites available Total 20.
Facilities
Nearby facilities
Burneside.
Lake District National Park. Pool table on site.

CUMWHITTON

Cairndale Caravan Park, Cumwhitton, Headsnook, Carlisle, Cumbria CA4 9BZ.
Tel. Croglin 896280 Std. 01768
Nearest Town/Resort Carlisle.
Directions Follow A69 to Warwick Bridge and then follow unclassified road through Great Corby to Cumwhitton, approx. 9 miles.
Acreage 2 **Open** March–October
Access Good **Site** Level
Sites available Total 14.
Facilities
Nearby facilities
Carlisle.
Scenic views, ideal touring, quiet site, water and electricity to individual touring sites. Windsurfing nearby.

DENT

Ewegales Farm, Dent, Sedbergh, Cumbria, LA10 5RH.
Tel. 440 Std. 015875
Nearest Town/Resort Sedbergh.
Directions Leave M6 at junction 37 to Sedbergh and Dent. 4 miles east of Dent.
Acreage 11 **Open** All year
Access Good **Site** Level
Sites available
Facilities
Nearby facilities
Dent.
Alongside River.

DENT

High Laning Farm, Dent, Nr. Sedbergh, Cumbria.
Tel. Dent 239 Std. 0158 75.
Nearest Town/Resort Kendal.
Directions Take A684 from Sedbergh southeast 5 miles.
Acreage 4 **Open** All year
Access Good **Site** Level
Sites available Total 80.
Facilities
Dent.
Dent dale has beautiful scenic views, lovely walks, Post Office, church.

DENT

Millbeck Farm, Dent, Sedbergh, Cumbria, LA10 5TB.
Tel. 25272/25424 Std. 015396
Nearest Town/Resort Sedbergh.
Directions From M6 junc. 37 onto A684 to sedbergh on to Dent, site ½ mile west of Dent.
Acreage 1 **Open** Easter–October
Access Good **Site** Lev/Slope
Sites available
Facilities
Nearby facilities
Dent.
Near river, scenic views, ideal for walking. Caravan to let on site.

EGREMONT

Tarnside Caravan Park, Braystones, Beckermet, Cumbria, CA21 2YL.
Tel. 841308 Std. 01946
Nearest Town/Resort Egremont.
Directions Take the A595 south of Whitehaven. When in South Egremont take the B5345.
Acreage 1¼ **Open** All Year
Access Good **Site** Level
Sites available Total 40.
Facilities
Braystones.
Overlooking the sea and West Lake District. Ideal for touring the Lake District and for coastal fishing. Limited facilities for the disabled.

ESKDALE

Fisherground Farm, Eskdale, Cumbria,CA19 1TF.
Tel. 23319 Std. 019467
Nearest Town/Resort Broughton in Furness.
Directions ¾ mile past Broughton on A595 turn RT. up Duddon Valley (signed Ulpha). 4 miles to Ulpha, then turn LT. (signed Eskdale). 6 miles over Birker Moor, descend to Eskdale turn RT. at King George IV Inn. Fisherground is first farm on LT.
Acreage 3 **Open** March–November
Access Good **Site** Level
Sites available Total 30.
Facilities
Nearby facilities
Ravenglass.
Quiet family site, Heart of the Lake District. 7 mile miniature railway 100yds (private station). Adventure playground, pond and laundry.

GOSFORTH

Seven Acres Caravan Park, Holmrook, Cumbria, CA19 1YD.
Tel. 25480 Std. 019467
Nearest Town/Resort Gosforth.

Directions A595 West Cumbria coast road, 1 mile south of Gosforth.
Acreage 7 **Open** March–November
Access Good **Site** Level
Sites available Total 103.
Facilities
Nearby facilities
Seascale.
3 miles from beaches on the west of the Lake District. Good walking and touring. 8 miles to Wasdale Lake/Scafell.

GRANGE-OVER-SANDS

Oak Head Caravan Park, Ayside, Grange-over-Sands, Cumbria.
Tel. Newby Bridge 31475 Std. 015395
Nearest Town/Resort Grange-over-Sands.
Directions M6 junction 36 follow signs for Newby Bridge, site is signposted on left hand side of A590, 2 miles from Newby Bridge, 13 miles from M6.
Acreage 2½ **Open** March–October
Access Good **Site** Lev/slope
Sites available Total 90.
Facilities
Nearby facilities
Grange-over-Sands.
Scenic views, ideal touring. Within easy reach of all lakes.

GREYSTOKE

Whitbarrow Hall Caravan Park, Berrier Greystoke, Penrith, Cumbria CA11 0XB.
Tel. 83456 Std. 017684
Nearest Town/Resort Keswick.
Directions Leave M6 at junction 40, A66 towards Keswick after 8 miles turn right at signpost Hutton Roof site ½ mile from A66.
Acreage 8 **Open** March–October
Access Good **Site** Level
Sites available Total 100.
Facilities
Nearby facilities
Penrith.
Views. 5 miles Ullswater. Lake District.

HAWKSHEAD

The Croft Caravan & Camp Site, North Lonsdale Road, Hawkshead, Nr. Ambleside, Cumbria.
Tel. 36374 Std. 015394.
Nearest Town/Resort Ambleside.
Directions From Ambleside 5 miles on the B5286 at village of Hawkshead.
Acreage 5 **Open** March–November
Access Good **Site** Level
Sites available Total 100.
Facilities
Nearby facilities
Windermere.

HAWKSHEAD

Hawkshead Hall Farm, Hawkshead, Near Ambleside, Cumbria, LA22 0NN.
Tel. 36221 Std. 015394
Nearest Town/Resort Ambleside.
Directions 5 miles from Ambleside on the B5286 on the left hand side of the road.
Acreage 4 **Open** March–15 November
Access Good **Site** Lev/Slope
Sites available Total 50.
Facilities
Nearby facilities
Windermere.
Scenic views.

INGS

Ings Caravan Park, Ings, Staveley, Nr. Kendal, Cumbria LA8 9QF.
Tel. Staveley 821426 Std. 01539
Nearest Town/Resort Windermere.
Directions 300 yards off A591 midway between Staveley and Windermere.
Open March–October
Access Good **Site** Level
Sites available Total 17.
Facilities
Nearby facilities
Windermere.

KESWICK

Ashness Camp Site, Ashness Farm, Keswick, Cumbria. CA12 5UN.
Tel. 77361 Std. 017687
Nearest Town/Resort Keswick.
Directions Take the B5289 from Keswick for 2 miles, turn left signposted Ashness Bridge and Watendath, 1 mile Ashness farm on left.
Acreage 5 **Open** March–November
Access Good **Site** Sloping
Sites available Total 60.
Facilities
Nearby facilities
Penrith.
Centre of lakes, Derwentwater 1 mile, wonderful views from site, fully working farm.

KESWICK

Burns Farm Caravan Site, St. Johns-in-the-Vale, Keswick, Cumbria, CA12 4RR.
Tel. 79225 Std. 017087
Nearest Town/Resort Keswick.
Directions Turn left off the A66 (Penrith to Keswick road) ½ mile past B5322 junction signposted Castlerigg Stone Circle. Site is on the right, farm is on the left. 2¼ miles from Keswick.
Acreage 1¼ **Open** Easter–October
Access Good **Site** Level
Sites available Total 40.
Facilities
Nearby facilities
Penrith.
Ideal touring, walking and climbing. Beautiful views, quiet family site.

KESWICK

Burnside Caravan Park, Underskiddaw, Keswick, Cumbria, CA12 4PF.
Tel. 72950 Std. 017687
Nearest Town/Resort Keswick.
Directions Just off roundabout A66, Carlisle turn off.
Open March–14 November
Access Good **Site** Level
Sites available Total 24.
Facilities
Nearby facilities
Penrith.

KESWICK

Castlerigg Hall Caravan & Camping Park, Castlerigg Hall, Keswick, Cumbria.
Tel. 72437 Std. 017687
Nearest Town/Resort Keswick.
Directions 1¼ miles south east of Keswick off the A591.
Acreage 4 **Open** Easter–Mid November
Access Good **Site** Lev/Slope
Sites available Total 140.
Facilities
Nearby facilities
Penrith.
Scenic views, good walking.

KESWICK

Derwentwater Caravan Park, Crowe Park Road, Keswick, Cumbria, CA12 5EN.
Tel. 72579 Std. 017687
Nearest Town/Resort Keswick.
Directions From A66 take Keswick turn off at roundabout west of town. Turn left at T-Junction, then right at mini roundabout. On brow of hill fork right then right again, keep going until sign on the right for Derwentwater Caravan Park.
Acreage 5 **Open** March–14 November
Access Good **Site** Level
Sites available Total 50.
Facilities
Nearby facilities
Penrith.
On the shores of Derwentwater, lake frontage and a jetty. 5 minute walk to the town centre. Excellent base for outdoor activities in the Northern lakes and Solway Coast.

KESWICK

Dalebottom Holiday Park, Dalebottom, Naddle, Keswick, Cumbria, CA12 4TF.
Tel. Keswick 72176
Nearest Town/Resort Keswick.

Directions Dalebottom situated 2 miles south of Keswick A591 to Ambleside.
Acreage 6 **Open** March–October
Access Good **Site** Lev/slope
Sites available Total 60.
Facilities
Nearby facilities
Keswick.
Scenic views, Ideal for touring.

KESWICK

Scotgate Caravan, and Camping Park, Braithwaite, Keswick, Cumbria CA12 5TF.
Tel. Braithwaite 78343 Std. 017687
Nearest Town/Resort Keswick.
Directions A66 west of Keswick 2 miles. Site at junction with B5292.
Acreage 9 **Open** March–October
Access Good **Site** Level
Sites available Total 165.
Facilities
Nearby facilities
Penrith.
Central for touring Lake District. Situated between Bassenthwaite and Derwentwater Lakes.

KESWICK

Stonethwaite Farm, Borrowdale, Keswick, Cumbria.
Tel. 77234 Std. 0176 87.
Nearest Town/Resort Keswick.
Directions 6¼ miles along Borrowdale Valley from Keswick.
Acreage 9 **Open** April–October
Access Good **Site** Lev/slope
Sites available Total 120.
Facilities
Nearby facilities
Penrith.
Head of valley, alongside river.

KIRKBY LONSDALE

Woodclose Caravan Park, Casterton, Carnforth, Lancs, LA6 2SE.
Tel. 71597 Std. 015242
Nearest Town/Resort Kirkby Lonsdale.
Directions ¼ mile south east of Kirkby Lonsdale on the A65.
Acreage 9¼ **Open** March–October
Access Good **Site** Level
Sites available Total 70.
Facilities
Nearby facilities
Oxenholme.
Near River Lune, within easy walking distance of Lake District, Dales or seaside.

KIRKBY STEPHEN

Bowberhead Caravan Site, Bowberhead Farm, Ravenstonedale, Kirkby Stephen, Cumbria, CA17 4NL.
Tel. 23254 Std. 015396
Nearest Town/Resort Kirkby Stephen.
Directions 4½ miles south of Kirkby Stephen off the A683 road to Sedbergh.
Acreage 1¼ **Open** All year
Access Good **Site** Lev/Slope
Sites available Total 10.
Facilities
Nearby facilities
Kirkby Stephen.
Settle to Carlisle Line, beautiful views, Best fell walking.

KIRKBY THORE

Low Moor, Kirkby Thore, Penrith, Cumbria.
Tel. 61231 Std. 017683
Nearest Town/Resort Appleby.
Directions On A66 Appleby – Penrith.
Acreage 1¼ **Open** April–October
Access Good **Site** Level
Sites available Total 25.
Facilities
Appleby.
Scenic views, ideal touring.

LAMPLUGH

Inglenook Caravan Park, Lamplugh, Workington, Cumbria.
Tel. 861240 Std. 01946
Nearest Town/Resort Cockermouth.
Directions Leave A66 road at Cockermouth and take A5086 road (Egremont). 6 miles on turn left at caravan sign.
Acreage 3½ **Open** March–14 November
Access Good **Site** Level
Sites available Total 36.
Facilities
Nearby facilities
Workington.
Scenic surroundings. Historic interest. Golf 4C. 7 miles beach. Ideal touring and walking area. Luxury holiday homes for hire. A.A. recommended 3 Pennant site and A.A. Award for Excellence. Attractive environment.

LEVENS

Sampool Caravan Park, Levens, Nr. Kendal, Cumbria. LA8 8EQ.
Tel. 52265 Std. 015395
Nearest Town/Resort Kendal.
Directions Kendal – south A6 for 3 miles to slip road onto A591. Follow signs for Milnthorpe to Levens Bridge A6. Turn right onto A590, 250yds on left.
Open 15 March–October
Site Level
Sites available Total 15.
Facilities
Nearby facilities
Oxenholme.
Alongside river, country side, quiet. Handy for lakes.

LONGTOWN

Camelot Caravan Park, Sandysike, Longtown Carlisle. Cumbria.
Tel. 791248 Std. 01228
Nearest Town/Resort Longtown.
Directions On left 1¼ miles south of Longtown on A7, northbound leave M6 at exit 44, take A7 (Longtown) site on right in 4 miles.
Acreage 1¼ **Open** March–October
Access Good **Site** Level
Sites available Total 20.
Facilities
Nearby facilities
Carlisle.
Ideal for Solway coast, Carlisle Settle railway, romantic Gretna Green, base for Hadrians Wall and border towns, Carlisle Castle.

MEALSGATE

The Larches Caravan Park, Mealsgate, Carlisle, Cumbria CA5 1LQ.
Tel. Low Ireby 379 Std. 0196 57.
Nearest Town/Resort Wigton.
Directions 16 miles southwest Carlisle on A595.
Acreage 16 **Open** March–October
Access Good **Site** Lev/slope
Sites available Total 73.
Facilities
Nearby facilities
Wigton.
Ideal site for both beach and Lake District.

MELMERBY

Melmerby Caravan Park, Melmerby, Penrith, Cumbria, CA10 1HE.
Tel. 881311 Std. 01768
Nearest Town/Resort Penrith.
Directions Situated in Melmerby Village on the A686, 10 miles north east of Penrith.
Open Mid-March–October
Access Good **Site** Level
Sites available Total 5.
Facilities
Nearby facilities
Excellent walking country, ideal base for touring North Pennines, Eden Valley and Wales.

MILNTHORPE

Fell End Caravan Park, Slackhead Road, Hale, Milnthorpe, Cumbria LA7 7BS.
Tel. Milnthorpe 62122 Std. 0153 95
Nearest Town/Resort Milnthorpe.
Directions From south leave M6 at junction 35, head north up A6 for 3¼ miles, turn left onto by-road at Brown "Sites" sign, follow lane ¾ mile look for Fell End signs. From north 3¼ miles South Milnthorpe turn right at Brown "Sites" sign, then follow lane as above.
Acreage 28 **Open** March–November
Access Good **Site** Level
Sites available Total 70.
Facilities
Nearby facilities
Arnside.
Leighton Beck R.S.P.B. Bird Reserve. Hot meals to take out. Satellite T.V. to all pitches. Tourist Board Graded Park 5 Ticks. 1994 Calor Award Winner. Best park in England. England for Excellence Silver Award 1992.

MILNTHORPE

Millness Hill Park, Crooklands, Milnthorpe, Cumbria.
Tel. 67306 Std. 015395
Nearest Town/Resort Kendal.
Directions By Junction 36 of the M6 Motorway.
Acreage 1 **Open** March–October
Access Good **Site** Sloping
Sites available Total 31.
Facilities
Nearby facilities
Kendal.
Adjoining Lancaster Canal.

MILNTHORPE

Waters Edge Caravan Park, Crooklands, Milnthorpe, Cumbria LA7 7NN.
Tel. 67708 Std. 015395
Nearest Town/Resort Kendal.
Directions A65 Crooklands, ¾ mile from M6 motorway junction 36.
Acreage 3 **Open** March–November
Access Good **Site** Level
Sites available Total 40.
Facilities
Nearby facilities
Oxenholme.
Set in quiet and pleasant countryside. Lakes, Yorkshire Dales and Morecambe Bay within easy reach.

PENRITH

Beckes Caravan Site, Penruddock, Penrith, Cumbria.
Tel. 83224 Std. 017684
Nearest Town/Resort Penrith.
Directions 7 miles from Penrith, 11 miles from Keswick. 400yds on left from A66 Penrith to Keswick road.
Acreage 3½ **Open** Easter–October
Access Good **Site** Lev/Slope
Sites available Total 23.
Facilities
Nearby facilities
Penrith.
Ideal touring for Lakes.

PENRITH

Lowther Caravan Park, Eamont Bridge, Penrith, Cumbria.
Tel. 63631 Std. 01768
Nearest Town/Resort Penrith.
Directions Juntion 40 M6 take A66 then A6 Shap, entrance to park on right.
Acreage 5 **Open** Mid March–October
Access Good **Site** Lev/Slope
Sites available Total 200.
Facilities
Nearby facilities
Penrith.
River, views, ideal touring, wild life watching, quiet, ideal for families.

PENRITH

Park Foot Caravan & Camping Site, Howtown Road, Pooley Bridge, Penrith, Cumbria. CA10 2NA.
Tel. Pooley Bridge 86309 Std. 0176 84
Nearest Town/Resort Pooley Bridge.
Directions 5 miles southwest of Penrith. Leave M6 at junction 40, then take A66 for Ullswater, next roundabout take A592 then road for Pooley Bridge and 1 mile on Howtown Road to site.
Acreage 15 **Open** March–October
Access Good **Site** Lev/Slope
Sites available Total 323.
Facilities
Nearby facilities
Penrith.
Site off main road and easily accessible. Access to lake for boat launching.

PENRITH

Thacka Lea Caravan Site, Thacka Lea, Penrith, Cumbria. CA11 9HX.
Tel. Penrith 63319 Std. 01768.
Nearest Town/Resort Penrith.
Directions From south, left off A6, past Shell Station north end of town. From north, turn right Grey Bull.
Acreage 1 **Open** March–October
Access Good **Site** Lev/Slope
Sites available Total 25.
Facilities
Nearby facilities
Penrith.
Ten minutes town centre walking. Good touring.

PENRITH

Thanet Well Caravan Park, Greystoke, Penrith, Cumbria. CA11 0XX.
Tel. 84262 Std. 017684
Nearest Town/Resort Penrith.
Directions M6 junction 41 onto D5305 for Wigton, approx 6 miles turn left for Lamonby, follow caravan signs for approx 2 miles to park.
Acreage 3 **Open** March–October
Access Good **Site** Lev/Slope
Sites available Total 20.
Facilities
Nearby facilities
Penrith.
Scenic views, Fell walking, ideal touring.

PORT CARLISLE

Cottage Caravan Park, Port Carlisle, Cumbria CA5 5DJ.
Tel. Kirkbride 51317 Std. 0196 55.
Nearest Town/Resort Carlisle.
Directions 11 miles west of Carlisle on B class coastal road to Bowness-on-Solway.
Acreage 4 **Open** March–October

Sites available Total 20.
Facilities
Nearby facilities
Carlisle.
Good walking near beach on Roman Wall route.

PORT CARLISLE

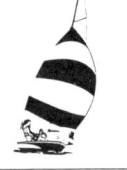

Glendale Caravan Park, Port Carlisle, Nr. Carlisle, Cumbria. CA5 5DJ.
Tel. Kirkbride 51317 Std. 0169 73
Nearest Town/Resort Carlisle.
Directions Take west coast road in Carlisle then fork right at United Biscuits Works, then right fork to Burgh-By-Sands and Bowness On Solway.
Acreage 12 **Open** March–October
Access Good **Site** Level
Sites available Total 20.
Facilities
Nearby facilities
Carlisle.
Near beach, scenic, ideal touring for lakes and north.

PORT HAVERIGG

Butterflowers Holiday Homes, Port Haverigg, Cumbria.
Tel. Millom 2880 Std. 01229 77
Nearest Town/Resort Port Haverigg.
Directions From Millom take A5093 for 400 yards. Turn left for Haverigg, follow beach road.
Acreage 9 **Open** All Year
Access Good **Site** Level
Sites available Total 189.
Facilities
Nearby facilities
Millom.
Adjacent beach, heated swimming pool.

RAVENGLASS

Walls Caravan Camping Park, Ravenglass, West Cumbria.
Tel. Ravenglass 717250 Std. 01229
Nearest Town/Resort Ravenglass/Whitehaven.
Directions A595 into Ravenglass. Site at entrance to village.
Acreage 5 **Open** 28 February–15 November
Access Good **Site** Sloping
Sites available Total 50.
Facilities
Nearby facilities
Ravenglass.
Muncaster castle, Ravenglass and Eskdale miniature railway, Ravenglass Gullery and Nature Reserve, Muncaster watermill, Roman sites in area. All hard standing pitches.

ST. BEES

Beachcomer Caravan Park, St. Bees, Cumbria, CA27 0ES.
Tel. 822777 Std. 01946
Nearest Town/Resort Whitehaven.
Open All Year
Site Level
Sites available Total 18.
Facilities
Nearby facilities
St. Bees.
Near beach, ideal for touring. Start of Coast to Coast walk.

ST. BEES

Seacote Park, St. Bees, Cumbria, CA27 0ES.
Tel. 822777 Std. 01946
Nearest Town/Resort Whitehaven.
Open All Year
Access Good **Site** Lev/Slope
Sites available Total 45.
Facilities
Nearby facilities
St. Bees.
Near the beach, start of Coast to Coast walk. Ideal for touring.

SEDBERGH

Fawcetts Farm, Garsdale, Sedbergh, Cumbria.
Tel. Sedbergh 20502 Std. 015396
Nearest Town/Resort Sedbergh.
Directions 4½ miles east of Sedbergh on the Hawes/Northallerton road.
Acreage 2 **Open** Easter–September
Access Good **Site** Level
Sites available Total 5.
Facilities
Nearby facilities
Garsdale.
Near river and good walks.

SEDBERGH

Lincoln's Inn Camping Site, Firbank, Sedbergh, Cumbria.
Tel. 20567 Std. 015396
Nearest Town/Resort Kendal.
Directions On A684, 8 miles east of Kendal, 3 miles east of M6 junction 37, 2 miles west of Sedbergh.
Acreage ½ **Open** March–October
Site Level
Sites available Total 8.
Facilities
Nearby facilities
Oxenholme.
Alongside river, scenic views, near Howgill Fells for walking. Absolutely no touring caravans.

SEDBERGH

Pinfold Caravan Park, Garsdale Road, Sedbergh, Cumbria, LA10 5JL.
Tel. 20576 Std. 015396
Nearest Town/Resort Sedbergh.
Directions Take A684 through Sedbergh, caravan park 450 yds from village, over Dales Bridge.
Acreage 3 **Open** March–October
Access Good **Site** Level
Sites available Total 38.
Facilities
Nearby facilities
Oxenholme.
Alongside river Rawthey below the Howgill Fells, ideal fell walking and touring. Fishing on the site. Motorcycles are permitted but no groups please.

SILECROFT

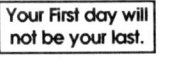

Silecroft Camping & Caravan Site, Silecroft, Near Whicham, Millom, Cumbria. LA18 4NX.
Tel. 772659 Std. 01229
Nearest Town/Resort Silecroft.
Directions From Greenodd, take A5092 for approx 17 miles to coast, turn left at coast road 200 yards on right follow signs.
Acreage 6 **Open** March–October
Access Good **Site** Level

Sites available Total 60.
Facilities
Nearby facilities
Silecroft.
Adjacent to golf course, 100 yards from beach (EEC Approved) in Lake District National Park, 1 mile from Mountain Range. 10 percent discount for advance bookings subject to £10 deposit.

SILLOTH

Moordale Caravan Park, Blitterlees, Silloth, Cumbria.
Tel. 31375 Std. 016973
Nearest Town/Resort Silloth.
Directions From Silloth take the B5300 Silloth to Maryport road. Moordale is about 2 miles on the right hand side.
Acreage 7 **Open** March–October
Access Good **Site** Level
Sites available Total 12.
Facilities S
Nearby facilities
Wigton.
Adjacent to Silloth Golf Course and beach. Ideal for touring Northern lakes and Southern Scotland.

SILLOTH

Rowanbank Caravan Park, Beckfoot, Silloth, Cumbria, CA5 4LA.
Tel. 31653 Std. 016973
Nearest Town/Resort Silloth.
Directions 2 miles South of Silloth on B5300.
Acreage 3¼ **Open** March–November
Access Good **Site** Level
Sites available Total 50.
Facilities
Nearby facilities
Maryport.
Across road from beach on Solway coast, overlooking Scottish Hills.

SILLOTH

Stanwix Park Holiday Centre, Silloth (West), Cumbria.
Tel. Silloth 31671 Std. 016973
Nearest Town/Resort Silloth.
Directions Enter Silloth on B5302, turn left at sea front, 1 mile to West Siloth on B5300. Site on right.
Acreage 4 **Open** Easter–October
Access Good **Site** Level
Sites available Total 121.
Facilities
Nearby facilities
Carlisle.
Large holiday centre with full range of facilities for all the family, indoor and outdoor, including pony trekking. Sunbeds, water shoot, satellite TV. See our display advertisment.

SILLOTH

Tanglewood Caravan Park, Causewayhead, Silloth, Cumbria, CA5 4PE.
Tel. Silloth 31253 Std. 016973
Nearest Town/Resort Silloth.
Directions Take B5302, 1 mile inland from town on Wigton road.
Acreage 2 **Open** Easter–October
Access Good **Site** Level
Sites available Total 31.
Facilities
Nearby facilities
Wigton.
Tree sheltered site, ideal for touring lakes and borders. Pets free of charge.

TEBAY

Tebay Caravan Park, Tebay Service Area, Orton, Penrith, Cumbria, CA10 3SB.
Tel. 24511 Std. 015396
Nearest Town/Resort Kendal.
Directions Leave M6 at Tebay West Services, ¾ mile north of exit 38 and follow signs for Tebay Caravan Park. Access from M6 Southbound via Tebay East Services.
Open Mid-March–October
Access Good **Site** Level
Sites available Total 70.
Facilities
Nearby facilities
Oxenholme.
Ideal touring north/south lakes, Dales, overnight en-route Scotland/South. Quiet, wellkept, sheltered site with a 24-Hour cafe/forecourt.

TROUTBECK

Gill Head Farm, Troutbeck, Penrith, Cumbria, CA11 0ST.
Tel. 79652 Std. 017687
Nearest Town/Resort Keswick.
Directions Just off A66 on A5091 9 miles Keswick, 5 miles Ullswater.
Acreage 10 **Open** April–October
Access Good **Site** Level
Sites available Total 54.
Facilities
Nearby facilities
Penrith.
Ideal touring, scenic views.

TROUTBECK

Moor End Farm Caravan and Camping Site, Moor End Farm, Troutbeck, Penrith, Cumbria, CA11 0SX.
Tel. 779615 Std. 01768

Nearest Town/Resort Keswick.
Directions On A66 9 miles west of junc 40 M6. Turn left for Wallthwaite.
Acreage 2½ **Open** Easter or 1st April–November
Access Good **Site** Sloping
Sites available Total 50.
Facilities
Nearby facilities
Penrith.
Walking.

ULLSWATER

The Quiet Caravan & Camping Site, Ullswater, Nr. Penrith, Cumbria. CA11 0LS.
Tel. Pooley Bridge 86337 Std. 0176 84.
Nearest Town/Resort Pooley Bridge.
Directions Take A592 from Penrith, turn right at lake and right again at Brackenrigg Hotel follow road for 1¼ miles, site on right hand side of road.
Acreage 6 **Open** March–November
Access Good **Site** Lev/Slope
Sites available Total 83.
Facilities
Nearby facilities
Penrith.
Idyllic setting amongst the fells, voted Best Campsite in Britain 1991 by Camping Magazine, AA Northern Campsite of the Year 1989. Excellent grading by English Tourist Board 1995. Large adventure playground and probably the best campsite bar in Britain!.

ULLSWATER

Ullswater Caravan Camping & Marine Park, Watermillock, Penrith, Cumbria CA11 0LR.
Tel. 86666 Std. 0176 84
Nearest Town/Resort Penrith.
Directions A592 from Penrith, turn right at lake and right again at telephone kiosk, signposted Watermillock Church.
Acreage 7 **Open** March–14 November
Access Good **Site** Lev/Slope
Sites available Total 155.
Facilities
Nearby facilities
Penrith.
Lake District National Park. Scenic views. Boat launching and moorings.

ULVERSTON

Bardsea Leisure Park, Priory Road, Ulverston, Cumbria, LA12 9QE.
Tel. 584712 Std. 01229
Nearest Town/Resort Ulverston.
Directions Enter Ulverston, take the second left A5087, 1 mile on the right hand side.
Acreage 10 **Open** All year
Access Good **Site** Level
Sites available Total 83.
Facilities
Nearby facilities
Ulverston.
Steam railway nearby, Stan Laurel Museum, the lakes, Cumbria Crystal. Beautiful scenic walks.

WALNEY ISLAND

South End Caravan Park, Walney, Barrow in Furness, Cumbria.
Tel. 472823 Std. 01229
Nearest Town/Resort Barrow in Furness.
Directions A590 to Barrow, then follow Walney signs. Turn left after crossing bridge to Walney, 4 miles south from there.
Acreage 3 **Open** March–October
Site Sloping
Sites available Total 60.
Facilities
Nearby facilities
Barrow.
Close to beach, good views.

WASDALE

Wasdale National Trust Camp Site,
Wasdale Camp Site, Wasdale, Seascale, Cumbria.
Tel. 26220 Std. 019467
Nearest Town/Resort Gosforth.
Directions Turn east off the A595 on road to Valley Head only. Finger sign at head of lake directs you to the site.
Acreage 8 **Open** Easter–October
Site Sloping
Sites available Total 120.
Facilities
Nearby facilities
Mountains and a lake. Dryer for clothes.

WATERMILLOCK

Cove Camping Park, Lake Ullswater, Watermillock, Penrith, Cumbria CA11 0LS.
Tel. Pooley Bridge 86549 Std. 0176 84.
Nearest Town/Resort Penrith.
Directions Leave M6 at junction 40, turn west follow signs for Ullswater (A592). Turn right at Lake junction, then right at Brackenrigg Hotel. Park is 1½ miles on left. Look for Cove Camping Park sign.
Acreage 2½ **Open** March–November
Access Good **Site** Lev/Slope
Sites available Total 50.
Facilities
Nearby facilities
Penrith.
Peaceful family park, sheltered by nearby Fells. Overlooking Lake Ullswater. Ideal for touring the Lakes. Excellent grading by Tourist Board. 5 Ticks. Freezer for ice packs, hairdryers, hot and cold drinks machine. Battery charging.

WATERMILLOCK

Knotts Hill Caravan Chalet Site, Watermillock, Penrith Cumbria, CA11 0JR.
Tel. 86328 Std. 017684
Nearest Town/Resort Penrith.
Directions A592 from Penrith turn off at Gowbarrow Lodge Grill approx 8 miles from Penrith, entrance ½ mile on right.
Access Good **Site** Lev/Slope
Sites available
Facilities
Nearby facilities
Penrith.

WINDERMERE

Fallbarrow Park, Rayrigg Road, Windermere, Cumbria. LA23 3DL.
Tel. 44428 Std. 015394
Nearest Town/Resort Windermere.
Directions Just north of Bowness village on A592.
Acreage 32 **Open** 15 March–October
Access Good **Site** Level
Sites available Total 81.
Facilities
Nearby facilities
Windermere.
On shore of Lake Windermere. Boating facilities. An A.A. four pennant park. E.T.B. 5 Ticks. Please refer to our colour advertisement.

WINDERMERE

Limefitt Park, Windermere, Cumbria. LA23 1PA.
Tel. Ambleside 32300 Std. 015394
Nearest Town/Resort Windermere.
Directions In Lakeland valley 4 miles north of Windermere on A592 to Ullswater.
Acreage 25 **Open** Easter–October
Access Good **Site** Lev/Slope
Sites available Total 250.
Facilities
Nearby facilities
Windermere.
In valley with river running through, spectacular location/views central lakeland. Pony trekking on site. Undercover cooking and dining facilities. A.A. Campsite of the Year 1992-93. Graded 5 Ticks 'Excellent'.

WINDERMERE

White Cross Bay Leisure Park & Marina, Ambleside Road, Windermere, Cumbria, LA23 1LF.
Tel. 43937 Std. 015394
Nearest Town/Resort Windermere.
Directions Situated 2 miles on the A591 from Windermere centre, going north signposted Ambleside. Leave M6 at junction 36, follow signs to Windermere then Ambleside.
Open March–15 November
Access Good **Site** Level
Sites available Total 125.
Facilities
Nearby facilities
Windermere.
Boat launching Lake Windermere. Central for walking, climbing and touring. Excellent restaurant and facilities. Fishing, sailing, boating, water-skiing and tennis on site.

WINDERMERE

Park Cliffe Camping and Caravan Estate, Birks Road, Tower Wood, Windermere, Cumbria. LA23 3PG.
Tel. 31344 Std. 015395
Nearest Town/Resort Windermere.
Directions M6 junction 36, A590 to Newby Bridge. Turn right onto A592, in 4 miles turn right into Birks Road. Park is roughly ½ mile on the right.
Acreage 25 **Open** March–October
Access Good **Site** Lev/Slope
Sites available Total 250.
Facilities
Nearby facilities
Windermere.
Near to Lake Windermere with outstanding views of lakes and mountains, ideal touring. AA three pennants, RAC, E.T.B. 4 Ticks.

DERBYSHIRE

ASHBOURNE

Bank Top Farm, Fenny Bentley, Ashbourne, Derbyshire.
Tel. 350250 Std. 01335.
Nearest Town/Resort Ashbourne.
Directions Take A515 from town 2 miles. Take B5056, site 200 yards opposite Bentley Brook Inn.
Acreage 2½ **Open** Easter–End September
Access Good
Sites available
Facilities
Nearby facilities
Derby.
Scenic views from site. Area ideal for touring Dovedale and other Dales, also pretty little villages. Viewing gallery to watch the milking of the cows. Washing machine and spin dryer available.

ASHBOURNE

Gateway Park, Osmaston, Near Ashbourne, Derbys.
Tel. 344643 Std. 01335
Nearest Town/Resort Ashbourne.
Directions On A52 12 miles north of Derby – 1 mile south of Ashbourne.
Acreage 15 **Open** April–October
Access Good **Site** Level
Sites available Total 200.
Facilities
Nearby facilities
Derby.
Countryside views, good centre for Dovedale and other Dales, Alton Towers, Chatsworth.

ASHBOURNE

Sandybrook Hall Holiday Park, Sandybrook Hall, Ashbourne, Derbyshire DE6 2AQ.
Tel. 342679 Std. 01335
Nearest Town/Resort Ashbourne.
Directions 1 mile north of Ashbourne on A515. MOT signed.
Acreage 5 **Open** March–November
Access Good
Sites available Total 70.
Facilities
Nearby facilities
Peak District National Park. Near to Alton Towers.

BAKEWELL

Stocking Farm Caravan and Camp Site, Stocking Farm, Calver, Sheffield, S30 1XA.
Tel. Hope Valley 630516
Nearest Town/Resort Bakewell.
Directions Out of Bakewell on the A619 fork lt. onto the B6001 to traffic lights. Turn rt. 1st lt. after Derbyshire Craft Centre, 1st lt. again.
Acreage 1½ **Open** April–October
Access Good **Site** Level
Sites available Total 10.
Facilities
Nearby facilities
Grindleford.
Scenic views, idea touring. Married couples and families only.

BELPER

The Firs Farm Caravan & Camping Park, Crich Lane, Nether Heage, Ambergate, Belper, Derbys, DE56 2JH.
Tel. 852913 Std. 01773
Nearest Town/Resort Ambergate.
Directions 2 miles south of Ambergate turn left off the A6 onto Broad Holme Lane. At top of lane turn left, park is 500yds on the left.
Acreage 3 **Open** All Year
Access Good **Site** Level
Sites available Total 60.
Facilities
Nearby facilities
Ambergate.
Magnificent views, well maintained, landscaped site. Friendly, family run park with a sauna. Host of local attractions.

BUXTON

Cold Springs Farm, Buxton, Derbyshire, SK17 6SS.
Tel. 22762 Std. 01298.
Nearest Town/Resort Buxton.
Directions A5004 from Buxton 1 mile.
Acreage 4 **Open** March–November
Access Poor **Site** Sloping
Sites available Total 25.
Facilities
Nearby facilities
Buxton.
Scenic views. Ideal touring.

BUXTON

Cottage Farm Caravan Park, Blackwell in the Peak, Derbyshire, SK17 9TQ.
Tel. 85330 Std. 01298
Nearest Town/Resort Buxton.
Directions From Buxton, 6 miles east on the A6. Take an unclassified road north signposted.
Acreage 3 **Open** March–October
Access Good **Site** Level
Sites available Total 30.
Facilities
Buxton.
Centre of a National Park, ideal for walking and touring by car.

BUXTON

Limetree Holiday Park, Dukes Drive, Buxton, Derbyshire, SK17 9RP.
Tel. 22988 Std. 01298.
Nearest Town/Resort Buxton.
Directions 1 mile south of Buxton off A515 Ashbourne road, turn left after Buxton Hospital.
Acreage 12¼ **Open** March–October
Access Good **Site** Level
Sites available Total 65.
Facilities
Nearby facilities
Buxton.
Ideal base for touring Peak District. Area of outstanding natural beauty.

BUXTON

Pomeroy Caravan & Camping Park, Street House Farm, Pomeroy, Flagg, Near Buxton, Derbyshire.
Tel. 83259 Std. 01298
Nearest Town/Resort Buxton.
Directions 5 miles south of Buxton on the A515. Site is on the right (signposted) over double cattle grid to tarmac drive.
Acreage 2¼ **Open** April–October
Access Good **Site** Level
Sites available Total 30.
Facilities
Buxton.
Scenic views. Ideal touring, walking and cycling. Central site for the Peak District. National Park site that adjoins Cromford High Peak Trail.

BUXTON

Newhaven Caravan & Camping Park, Newhaven, Nr. Buxton, Derbyshire.
Tel. 84300 Std. 01298
Nearest Town/Resort Buxton.
Directions Midway between Ashbourne and Buxton on A515. At junction with A5012.
Acreage 27 **Open** March–October
Access Good **Site** Level
Sites available Total 110.
Facilities
Nearby facilities
Buxton.
Ideal centre for touring Peak District, National Park and Derbyshire Dales.

CASTLETON

Rowter Farm, Castleton, Sheffield, S30 2WA.
Tel. 620271 Std. 01433
Nearest Town/Resort Buxton.
Directions Off B6061 2¼ miles from village of Castleton near Winnats Pass Blue John Caverns.

COOPER'S CAMP & CARAVAN SITE
Newfold Farm, Edale, Via Sheffield
Derbyshire S30 2ZD

Located in the centre of The Peak District National Park, the small hamlet of Edale, marks the beginning of The Pennine Way. Ideal base for hill walking and touring the peak district: AA Approved site. Facilities include toilet block with hot water, and showers. Post office and shop. Gas supplied. Village pub within 100 yards. Free hot water in hand basins and dishwashing facilities. Caravans for hire. Open all year.

Proprietors - Roger & Penny Cooper.
Tel: (01433) 670372

Acreage 4 **Open** Easter–October
Access Good **Site** Level
Sites available Total 30.
Facilities
Nearby facilities
Hope or Edale.
Near Blue John Cavern, Ideal walking, touring and mountain bike area.

DOVERIDGE
Cavendish Garage, Doveridge, Ashbourne, Derbys, DE6 5JR.
Tel. 562092 Std. 01889
Nearest Town/Resort Uttoxeter.
Directions Main A50 stoke to Derby road, 2 miles Uttoxeter.
Acreage 2 **Open** All Year
Access Good **Site** Level
Sites available Total 15.
Facilities
Uttoxeter.
Alton Towers, Dovedale, Sudbury Hall and many pleasant walks.

EDALE
Cooper's Camp & Caravan Site, New Fold Farm, Edale, Sheffield, Derbyshire, S30 2ZD.
Tel. 670372 Std. 01433
Nearest Town/Resort Hope.
Directions Turn right at Hope Church, 5 miles off the A625. We are in the centre of Edale Village next to the Post Office.
Acreage 7 **Open** All year
Access Good **Site** Sloping
Sites available Total 146.
Facilities
Nearby facilities
Edale.
Ideal base for hill walking.

EDALE
Highfield Farm, Highfield Farm, Edale, Via Sheffield, Derbyshire, S30 2ZJ.
Tel. 670245 Std. 01433
Nearest Town/Resort Buxton.
Directions Leave the A625 at Hope Church, take minor road to Edale. Follow road, pass turning for Edale, at bottom of hill turn right, pass picnic area, access to farm.
Acreage 50 **Open** Easter–October
Access Good **Site** Lev/Slope
Sites available
Facilities
Nearby facilities
Edale.
Good walking country, near Pennine Way. Good views, quiet.

EDALE
Waterside Campsite, Waterside, Barber Booth Road, Edale, Derbys.
Tel. 670215 Std. 01433
Nearest Town/Resort Sheffield.
Directions A625, 18 miles from Sheffield, 10 miles from Buxton.
Open April–September
Access Good **Site** Sloping
Sites available Total 40.
Facilities
Nearby facilities
Edale.
Scenic views, ideal for walking. Pony trekking in the village, 2 miles away.

EDALE
Upper Booth Farm, Mrs. E. Hodgson, Edale, Sheffield, Derbyshire S30 2ZJ.
Tel. 670250 Std. 01433
Nearest Town/Resort Buxton.
Acreage 3 **Open** All year
Site Level
Sites available Total 30.
Facilities
Nearby facilities
Edale.
Ideal centre for walking, climbing, caving etc. 2 miles from start of,and on Pennine Way. Tent numbers limited. Booking advisable. Stream nearby. Camping barn available (for 12).

HARTINGTON
Endon Cottage, Hulme End, Buxton, Derbyshire, SK17 0HG.
Tel. Hartington 84617
Nearest Town/Resort Leek.
Directions From Ashbourne take A515 North for Buxton. After 8 miles take the B5054 via Hartington to Hulme End.
Acreage 3 **Open** Easter–October
Access Good **Site** Sloping
Sites available
Facilities
Nearby facilities
Buxton.
Scenic views. Ideal touring.

HOPE
Laneside Caravan Park, Hope, Derbyshire. S30 2RR.
Tel. 20215 Std. 014 336
Nearest Town/Resort Buxton.
Directions On A625 200yds east of Hope village.
Acreage 5 **Open** Easter–October
Access Good **Site** Level
Sites available Total 135.
Facilities
Nearby facilities
Hope.
Sheltered valley site, ideal walking, touring centre for north Peak District.

HOPE
Hardhurst Farm Caravan & Camping Site, Hardhurst Farm, Hope, Sheffield, S30 2RB.
Tel. 620001 Std. 01433
Nearest Town/Resort Sheffield.
Directions Take the A625 from Sheffield

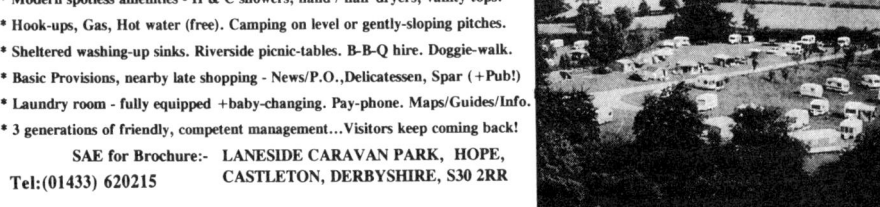

Quiet family riverside site in the most beautiful part of the Peak District National Park.

Laneside Caravan Park

- **Modern spotless amenities - H & C showers, hand / hair dryers, vanity tops.**
- **Hook-ups, Gas, Hot water (free). Camping on level or gently-sloping pitches.**
- **Sheltered washing-up sinks. Riverside picnic-tables. B-B-Q hire. Doggie-walk.**
- **Basic Provisions, nearby late shopping - News/P.O.,Delicatessen, Spar (+Pub!)**
- **Laundry room - fully equipped +baby-changing. Pay-phone. Maps/Guides/Info.**
- **3 generations of friendly, competent management...Visitors keep coming back!**

SAE for Brochure:- LANESIDE CARAVAN PARK, HOPE, CASTLETON, DERBYSHIRE, S30 2RR
Tel:(01433) 620215

travelling for about 12 miles.
Acreage 1¼ **Open** All Year
Access Good **Site** Level
Sites available Total 37.
Facilities
Nearby facilities
Hope.
Scenic views, ideal base for touring the Peak District.

MATLOCK
Haytop Farm Country Park, Whatstandwell, Nr. Matlock, Derbyshire DE4 5HP.
Tel. 852063 Std. 01773
Nearest Town/Resort Matlock.
Directions Leave M1 at junction 28, take A38 to Derby, 6 miles to turn off A610. A610 to Ambergate(A6). Turn right onto A6 at Ambergate then 3 miles to Whatstandwell Bridge. Over bridge then immediatley left at layby. Private drive to site ¼ mile bear right at fork. North from Cromford A6 to Whatstandwell Bridge, 3 miles. Private drive at bridge layby on right. DO NOT CROSS BRIDGE. Bear right up drive. Enquiries at Bungalow (white gates).
Acreage 65
Sites available
Facilities
Nearby facilities
Whatstandwell/Derby.
Fishing, river boating, easy access to A6 and scenic Derbyshire Dales, Historic houses, Crich Tramway Museum, Butterley Railway Museum, Matlock Illuminations. Horse riding nearby. Factory shops in district, natural scenery, wild flowers, birds, village inns, walks abound. Own canoes welcome.

MATLOCK
Pinegroves Caravan Park, High Lane, Tansley, Matlock, Derbys.
Tel. 534815 Std. 01629
Nearest Town/Resort Matlock.
Directions From the M1 take the A38 then the A615 towards Matlock. 2 miles past Wessington, turn left at crossroads into High Lane. Site is 600yds on the left.
Acreage 7 **Open** April–30 October
Access Good **Site** Level
Sites available Total 60.
Facilities
Nearby facilities
Matlock.
Quiet site in woodland and open countryside.

MATLOCK
Sycamore Camping & Caravan Park, Lant Lane, Tansley, Matlock, Derbyshire.
Tel. 55760 Std. 01629
Nearest Town/Resort Matlock.
Directions From Matlock take the A615 to Tansley, turn left into Church Street. 1¼ miles turn left, site is on the right.
Acreage 3¼ **Open** Mid March–Mid November
Access Good **Site** Level
Sites available Total 60.
Facilities
Nearby facilities
Matlock.
Scenic views in an ideal walking country. Lots to do and see.

MATLOCK
Wayside Farm Caravan Park, Matlock Moor, Matlock, Derbyshire.
Tel. 582967 Std. 01629
Nearest Town/Resort Matlock.
Directions 2 miles from Matlock off the A632. Near Matlock Golf Club.
Acreage 1¾ **Open** All Year
Access Good **Site** Sloping
Sites available Total 30.
Facilities
Nearby facilities
Matlock.
Working farm in the lovely Derbyshire Dales. Ideal for touring.

WHALEY BRIDGE
Ringstones Caravan Park, Yeardsley Lane, Furness Vale, Whaley Bridge, Derbyshire.
Tel. 732152 Std. 01663
Nearest Town/Resort Whaley Bridge.
Directions From Whaley Bridge take A6 towards Stockport, in Furness Vale turn left at Pelican crossing (Cantonese resturant on corner).
Acreage 3 **Open** March–October
Access Good **Site** Lev/Slope
Sites available
Facilities
Nearby facilities
Furness Vale.

DEVON

ASHBURTON
Ashburton Caravan Park, Waterleat, Ashburton, Devon, TQ13 7HU.
Tel. 652552 Std. 01364
Nearest Town/Resort Ashburton/Newton Abbot.
Directions Off A38, Ashburton Centre North Street bear right before bridge signposted Waterleat 1½ miles.
Acreage 2 **Open** Easter–October
Access Reasonable **Site** Level
Sites available Total 35.
Facilities
Nearby facilities
Newton Abbot.
In beautiful wooded valley, River Ashburn flowing through. Within Dartmoor National Park.

ASHBURTON
Landscove Camping Site, Landscove, Ashburton, Newton Abbot, Devon.
Tel. 225 Std. 0180426
Nearest Town/Resort Ashburton.
Directions From A38 at Ashburton take Slipway (Peartree). Follow signs to Landscove for 2¼ miles, then left to Woolston Green.
Acreage ¼ **Open** Easter–End of Sept
Site Level
Sites available Total 6.
Facilities
Nearby facilities
Quiet country site by village green. Near Dartmoor and within easy reach of the sea.

ASHBURTON
Parkers Farm Holidays, Higher Mead Farm, Ashburton, Devon TQ13 7LJ.
Tel. 652598 Std. 01364
Nearest Town/Resort Ashburton.

Directions Take the A38 to Plymouth, when you see the sign 26 miles Plymouth take second left at Alston Cross marked Woodland – Denbury. The site is behind the bungalow.
Acreage 5 **Open** April–October
Access Good **Site** Level
Sites available Total 60.
Facilities
Nearby facilities
Newton Abbot.
A real working farm enviroment with goats, sheep, pigs, cows, ducks and rabbits set amidst beautiful countryside.

AXMINSTER

Andrewshayes Caravan Park, Dalwood, Axminster, Devon.
Tel. 831225 Std. 01404.
Nearest Town/Resort Seaton.
Directions A35 Axminster 3 miles. Honiton 6 miles. Take 2nd. turning signpost Dalwood and Stockland. Site entrance 100yds. off A35.
Acreage 10 **Open** Easter/1 April–October
Access Good **Site** Sloping
Sites available Total 90.
Facilities
Nearby facilities
Axminster.
Peaceful, clean park on a working farm, in beautiful countryside. Ideal for family holiday. Easy reach of resorts. New toilet building with family rooms and disabled room.

BARNSTAPLE

Brightlycott Farm Camping & Caravan Site, Brightlycott Farm, Barnstaple, Devon.
Tel. 850330 Std. 01271
Nearest Town/Resort Barnstaple.
Directions On A39 road to Lynton and Lynmouth, 2 miles from Barnstaple, the farm entrance is on the right off main road A39.
Acreage 4 **Open** May–October
Access Good **Site** Lev/Slope
Sites available Total 40.
Facilities
Nearby facilities
Barnstaple.
Panoramic view from the site on modern dairy farm close to beach and moors.

BARNSTAPLE

Lorna Doone Farm, Parracombe, Barnstaple, Devon. EX31 4RJ.
Tel. 262 Std. 015983
Nearest Town/Resort Lynton.
Directions A39 between Barnstable and Lynton.
Acreage 2 **Open** April–October
Access Good **Site** Level
Sites available
Facilities
Nearby facilities
Barnstaple.
Ideal for touring or walking, scenic views.

BIDEFORD

Pusehill Farm Campsite, Pusehill, Westward Ho!, Bideford, Devon.
Tel. 474295 Std. 01237
Nearest Town/Resort Westward Ho!.
Directions Leave Bideford on A39 to Bude, first right to Wootward Ho! D3230. First left to Abbotsham. First right to Pusehill.
Acreage 6 **Open** Easter–September
Site Lev/Slope
Sites available Total 60.
Facilities
Nearby facilities
Barnstaple.
Sandy beach 1 mile away, coastal foot paths. Farm Site.

BRATTON FLEMING

Greenacres Farm Touring Caravan Park, Bratton Fleming, Barnstaple, North Devon, EX31 4SG.
Tel. 763334 Std. 01598
Nearest Town/Resort Barnstaple.
Directions From North Devon link road (A361), turn right at Northaller roundabout (by Little Chef). Take the A399 to Blackmoor Gate, approx 10 miles. Park signed (300yds from the A399).
Acreage 4 **Open** April–October
Access Good **Site** Level
Sites available Total 30.
Facilities
Nearby facilities
Barnstaple.
Moors and coast 5 miles, towns 10 miles. Peaceful, secluded park with scenic views. Ideal for touring, walking and cycling.

BRAUNTON

Lobb Fields Caravan & Camping Park, Saunton Road, Braunton, Devon. EX33 1EB.
Tel. 812090 Std. 01271
Nearest Town/Resort Braunton.
Directions A361 to Braunton, turn left onto B3231. The park is 1 mile on the right.
Acreage 14 **Open** 28th April–September
Access Good **Site** Level
Sites available Total 180.
Facilities
Nearby facilities
Barnstaple.
Facing south with panoramic views. Quiet site with Saunton beach and golf course 1¼ miles away. Dogs on leads.

BRIXHAM
Hillhead Camp, Brixham, Devon TQ5 OHH.
Tel. Off842336 Site853204 Std. 01803
Nearest Town/Resort Brixham.
Directions Follow A380 towards Brixham. Turn on to A379 (Dartmouth) at Prouts Garage (avoiding Brixham town centre.) After B.P. garage Take left fork (Kingswear Lower Ferry) camp 300 yds.
Acreage 12½ **Open** April–October
Site Level
Sites available Total 330.
Facilities
Nearby facilities
Paignton.
Near beaches and river overlooking sea. Panoramic views of sea and country.

BRIXHAM
Centry Touring Caravans & Tents, Mudberry House, Centry Road, Brixham, Devon, TQ5 9EY.
Tel. 853215 Std. 01803
Nearest Town/Resort Brixham.
Directions A3022 to town centre, at traffic lights turn right. Next set of traffic lights turn left and bear right past the Rugby Club, we are ¼ mile ahead.
Acreage 2 **Open** Easter–October
Access Good **Site** Level
Sites available Total 30.
Facilities
Nearby facilities
Paignton.
Within walking distance to the town, harbour and beaches.

BUCKFASTLEIGH
Beara Farm Camping Site, Colston Road, Buckfastleigh, Devon.
Tel. Buckfastleigh 642234 Std. 01364.
Nearest Town/Resort Buckfastleigh.
Directions Coming from Exeter take first left after passing South Devon Steam Railway and Butterfly Centre at Buckfastleigh, signpost marked Beara, fork right at next turning then 1 mile to site, signposted on roadside and junctions.
Acreage 3¼ **Open** All year
Access Good **Site** Level
Sites available Total 45.
Facilities
Nearby facilities
Totnes.
Quiet, select, sheltered site adjoining River Dart. Within easy reach of sea and moors and 1½ miles southeast of Buckfastleigh.

BUCKFASTLEIGH
Churchill Farm, Buckfastleigh, Devon, TQ11 0EZ.
Tel. 642844 Std. 01364
Nearest Town/Resort Buckfastleigh/Buckfast.
Directions Exit A38 at Dartbridge, follow signs for Buckfast Abbey, proceed up hill to crossroads. Turn left into no-through road towards Church Farm entrance opposite church. 1½ miles from A38.
Acreage 2 **Open** All Year
Access Good **Site** Level
Sites available Total 25.
Facilities
Nearby facilities
Totnes.
Stunning views of Dartmoor and Buckfast Abbey, the latter being within easy walking distance as are the Steam Railway, Butterfly Farm, Otter Sanctuary and local inns. Seaside resorts 10 miles.

CHUDLEIGH
Finlake Leisure Park, Chudleigh, Nr Newton Abbot, Devon, TQ13 0EJ.
Tel. 853833 Std. 01626
Nearest Town/Resort Newton Abbot/Teignmouth.
Directions A38 from Exeter, take Chudleigh Knighton/Kingsteignton slip road. A38 from Plymouth, take Chudleigh/Teign Valley exit.
Open Feb ¼ Term–New Year 1996
Access Good **Site** Sloping
Sites available Total 450.
Facilities
Nearby facilities
Newton Abbot.
Ideal touring site for Dartmoor National Park and south Devon coast. Golf, fishing and tennis on site.

CHUDLEIGH
Holmans Wood Tourist Park, Harcombe, Cross, Chudleigh, Devon, TQ13 0DZ.
Tel. 853785 Std. 01626
Nearest Town/Resort Chudleigh.
Directions From Exeter take the A38 Towards Plymouth. Go past the racecourse and after 1 mile take the B3344 for Chudleigh. We are on the left at the end of the sliproad.
Acreage 11 **Open** March–December
Access Good **Site** Level
Sites available Total 144.
Facilities
Nearby facilities
Newton Abbot.
Ideal touring for Dartmoor, Haldon Forest, Exeter and Torbay.

CLOVELLY
Dyke Green Farm, Clovelly, Bideford, Devon EX5 RU.
Tel. Clovelly 431279 Std. 01237.
Nearest Town/Resort Clovelly.
Directions On roundabout at Clovelly Cross.
Acreage 3½ **Open** March–October
Access Good **Site** Level
Sites available
Facilities
Nearby facilities
Barnstaple.
Clovelly village and beach. Sheltered bays, ideal walks etc.

COMBE MARTIN
Stowford Farm Meadows, Combe Martin, Devon. EX34 OPW.
Tel. 882476 Std. 01271
Nearest Town/Resort Combe Martin.
Directions Situated on the A3123 Combe Martin/Woollacombe Road at Berry Down.
Acreage 140 **Open** Easter–October
Access Good **Site** Lev/Slope
Sites available Total 570.
Facilities
Nearby facilities
Barnstaple.

Set in 450 acres of beautiful countryside. Ideal touring site at the heart of North Devon.

COMBE MARTIN

Newberry Farm, Combe Martin, North Devon, EX34 0AT.
Tel. 882333/882334 Std. 01271
Nearest Town/Resort Combe Martin/Ilfracombe.
Directions Leave the M5 at junction 27 and take the A361 to Aller Cross Roundabout. A399 to Combe Martin.
Acreage 6 **Open** Easter–October
Access Good **Site** Level
Sites available Total 100.
Facilities
Nearby facilities
Barnstaple.
On the edge of Exmoor National Park. 5 minute walk to the beach and shops.

CREDITON

Yeatheridge Farm Caravan Park, East Worlington, Crediton, Devon EX17 4TN.
Tel. Tiverton 860330 Std. 01884
Nearest Town/Resort Witheridge.
Directions Leave M5 at junction 27 take A361 to 1st roundabout A396 to mini-roundabout and follow A396 for approx 400yds turn right 200 yds turn left onto B3137 (Old A373) to Witheridge approx 10 miles. Turn left onto B3042 site 3¾ miles on left. Do not enter East Worlington, unsuitable for caravans. From Exeter take A377 to Barnstaple, turn right at Eggesford Station onto B3042, through Chawliegh Village the park is about 4 miles on right.
Acreage 9 **Open** Easter–October
Access Good **Site** Lev/Slope
Sites available Total 85.
Facilities
Nearby facilities
Eggesford.
Indoor heated swimming pools, coarse fishing lakes all free on site. Scenic view from landscape park, working farm with animals. Fishing and riding on site.

CROYDE BAY

Bay View Farm Holidays, Bay View Farm, Croyde, Devon, EX33 1PN.
Tel. 890501 Std. 01271
Nearest Town/Resort Croyde.
Directions At Braunton on A361 turn west on main road B3231 towards Croyde Village.
Acreage 10 **Open** Easter–September
Site Level
Sites available

Facilities
Nearby facilities
Barnstaple.
Near beach, 5 mins walking, Scenic views, ideal touring, booking advisable peak season. S.A.E. for information.

CULLOMPTON

Forest Glade Holiday Park, Cullomptom, Devon EX15 2DT.
Tel. 841381 Std. 01404
Nearest Town/Resort Cullompton.
Directions A373 Cullompton/Honiton, turn for Sheldon at Keeper Cottage Inn, 2½ miles east of Cullompton. Touring caravans via Dunkeswell Road only.
Acreage 10 **Open** Mid March–End October
Access See Directions **Site** Level
Sites available Total 80.
Facilities
Nearby facilities
Honiton/Tiverton Parkway.
Central for southwest twist coast and moors. Large flat sheltered camping pitches. Caravans for hire. Free heated indoor swimming pool and Paddling pool, riding, gliding and Tennis. You can FAX us on 01404 841593.

DARTMOUTH

Leonards Cove, Stoke Fleming, Dartmouth, Devon, TQ6 0NR.
Tel. 770206 (Also FAX) Std. 01803
Nearest Town/Resort Dartmouth.
Directions On A379 2 miles Dartmouth Within village of Stoke Fleming.
Acreage 1 **Open** March–October
Access Good **Site** Lev/Slope
Sites available Total 50.
Facilities
Nearby facilities
Totnes.
On clifftop spectacular views, ½ mile famous Blackpool Sands.

DARTMOUTH

Woodland Leisure Park, Blackawton, Totnes, Devon, TQ9 7DQ.
Tel. 712598/712680 Std. 01803
Nearest Town/Resort Dartmouth.
Directions 4 miles from Dartmouth on main road A3122 (formally B3207).
Acreage 8 **Open** 15th March–15th Nov
Access Good **Site** Level
Sites available Total 80.
Facilities
Nearby facilities
Totnes.
Free entrance to extensive leisure park attached, 75 acres of entertainment. Animal farm and twelve play zones. Paddling pool.

DAWLISH

Peppermint Park, Warren Road, Dawlish Warren, Devon EX7 0PQ.
Tel. 863436/86221 Std. 01626
Nearest Town/Resort Dawlish.
Directions Leave M5 at Exeter and follow A379 signposted to Dawlish then Dawlish Warren.
Acreage 16 **Open** Easter–September
Access Good **Site** Lev/Slope
Sites available Total 300.
Facilities
Nearby facilities
Dawlish Warren.
Closets touring park to Dawlish Warren beach (600 metres). Family run for familes and couples.

DAWLISH

Lady's Mile Touring Caravan & Camping Park, Dawlish, Devon, EX7 0LX.
Tel. Dawlish 863411 Std. 01626.
Nearest Town/Resort Dawlish.
Directions On A379 road 1 mile Exeter side of Dawlish.
Acreage 16 **Open** March–October
Access Good **Site** Level
Sites available Total 486.
Facilities
Nearby facilities
Dawlish.
Family run popular park in green Devon countryside. Ideal touring centre. Short walk to Dawlish Warren beach. 100 foot water slide. Excellent Quality Grading – see our colour advertisement. New 9 hole golf course.

DAWLISH

Golden Sands Holiday Park, Week Lane, Dawlish, South Devon.
Tel. 863099 Std. 01626
Nearest Town/Resort Dawlish.
Directions On the A379 Week Lane, 1 mile Exeter side of Dawlish.
Acreage 2¼ **Open** Easter–October
Access Good **Site** Level
Sites available Total 60.
Facilities
Nearby facilities
Dawlish.
Sandy beach ¼ mile, free entertainment and indoor/outdoor swimming pool.

★ FOR TOURING CARAVANS ★

Close to Dartmouth, a beautiful Town Port and historic centre.

*Shop *Calor Gas *Electric Hook-ups *Beach 3 miles *Laundry Room
*Well kept Toilet and Shower Block ***Torbay and Dartmoor**
within easy reach *Friendly Family Service
*Disabled Facilities *Payphone

Tel: Dartmouth (01803) 832558 *Paul and Dorothy White*

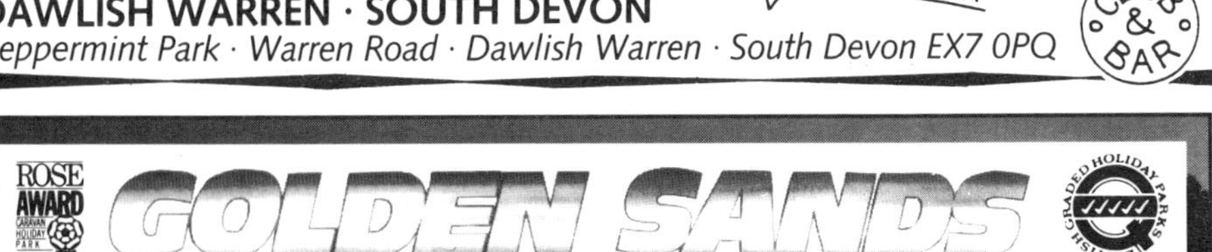

Dawlish Warren, where there is 2 miles of safe sandy beach is just ½ mile away.
Telephone NOW for FREE colour Brochure!
01626 863099

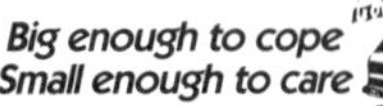

DAWLISH

Leadstone Camping, Warren Road, Dawlish, Devon.
Tel. 864411/872239 Std. 01626
Nearest Town/Resort Dawlish.
Directions Leave the M5 at junction 30 and take signposted road A379 to Dawlish. As you approach Dawlish, turn left on brow of hill, signposted Dawlish Warren. Our site is ¼ mile on right.
Acreage 7 **Open** 16th June–8th September
Access Good **Site** Lev/Slope
Sites available Total 160.
Facilities
Nearby facilities
Dawlish Warren.
Rolling grassland in a natural secluded bowl within ¼ mile of sandy 2 mile Dawlish Warren Beach and nature reserve. Ideally situated for discovering Devon. E.T.B. Graded "Good".

DOLTON

Dolton Caravan Park, The Square, Dolton, Winkleigh, Devon, EX19 8QF.
Tel. 536 Std. 0180 54
Nearest Town/Resort Great Torrington.
Directions From the B3220 turn at the Beacon Garage signposted Dolton. Go into the village and turn right at the Union Inn, the site is at the rear of Royal Oak Inn.
Acreage 2¼ **Open** Easter–September
Access Good **Site** Level
Sites available Total 25.
Facilities
Nearby facilities
Scenic views. Ideal for touring Exmoor and Dartmoor. Walking on the Tarka Trail.

EXETER

Kennford International Caravan Park, Exeter, Devon EX6 7YN.
Tel. 833046 Std. 01392
Nearest Town/Resort Exeter.
Directions ½ mile from end of M5 on A38. 4 miles south of Exeter.
Acreage 8 **Open** All year
Access Good **Site** Level
Sites available Total 120.
Facilities
Nearby facilities
Exeter.
Excellent touring centre in beautiful rural setting with easy access to main roads. Individually hedged sites. Children's adventure playground. Family lounge and bar with takeaway and the very popular log fire cabin.

EXETER

Heazille Barton, Rewe, Exeter, Devon.
Tel. 860253 Std. 01392
Nearest Town/Resort Exeter.
Directions Turn right off the A396 (Exeter to Tiverton road), just past Rewe. Farm is on the right in ½ mile.
Acreage ½ **Open** April–October
Access Good **Site** Level
Sites available Total 5.
Facilities
Nearby facilities
Exeter.
Tranquil site.

EXETER

Haldon Lodge Caravan and Camping Site, Kennford, Nr. Exeter, Devon.
Tel. 832312 Std. 01392
Nearest Town/Resort Exeter.
Directions 4½ miles South of Exeter, ½ mile from end of M5 turn off A38 at Kennford Services. Follow signs for Haldon Lodge turning left through Kennford Village past the Post Office. Proceed to Motorway bridge turning left at Dunchideock, 1 mile to site.
Acreage 4½ **Open** All year
Access Good **Site** Level
Sites available Total 80.
Facilities
Nearby facilities
Exeter.
Peaceful family site with beautiful forest scenery, nature walks, fishing lakes, riding holidays, barbeques, excellent touring centre. Sea and Exeter 15 minutes.

EXMOUTH

Devon Cliffs Holiday Centre, Sandy Bay, Exmouth, Devon, EX8 5BT.
Tel. 223000 Std. 01395
Nearest Town/Resort Exmouth.
Directions Turn off the M5 at exit 30 and take the A376 for Exmouth. At Exmouth follow the signs to Sandy Bay.
Acreage 10 **Open** March–November
Access Good **Site** Lev/Slope
Sites available Total 245.
Facilities
Nearby facilities
Exmouth.
Overlooking the beautiful Sandy Bay, with access to a private beach.

EXMOUTH

Castle Brake Holiday Park, Castle Lane, Woodbury, Near Exeter, Devon, EX5 1HA.
Tel. 232431 Std. 01395
Nearest Town/Resort Exmouth.
Directions A3052 then the B3180 off Woodbury Common. Brown sign for the park and golf course.

KENNFORD INTERNATIONAL CARAVAN PARK

EXETER DEVON EX6 7YN TEL: 01392 833046

M5 A30 EXETER A30 KENNFORD INTERNATIONAL CARAVAN PARK A380 A38

at the centre of the Big 'K'

Jan and Paul Harper welcome you to their 4 Pennant park which provides an exceptionallycomfortable base from which to explore Exeter, Dartmoor and the South Devon resorts of Exmouth,Dawlish and Torquay. The information Room is well stocked and our staff are always happy to help visitors plan their days. For parents with young children, we have provided pitches overlooking the grassy Adventure Playground whilst our other visitors can enjoy the privacy of individually hedged pitches. The pine panelled facilities with free hot showers are kept immaculately clean and are placed centrally in both sections of the Park - no long treks through wet grass for our customers! After a day touring or at the beach, you can return to a quiet drink on the patio, in the Bar or in the Family Lounge, play a game of Pool or enjoy a meal from our Food Bar/Take-a-way. If you prefer to cook, we have a well stocked Shop with an Off Licence. Each evening in the main season we have a log fire in the covered stone fireplace-a focal point on the park and a nice place to sit around at the end of the day! We shall be delighted to send you our full colour brochure.

Advance bookings welcome. AA Four Pennant Rating

Acreage 4 **Open** March–October
Access Good **Site** Level
Sites available Total 42.
Facilities
Nearby facilities
Exmouth.
Peaceful, grassy park with stunning views. Walking in the nearby area. Evening pub style meals, licensed.

EXMOUTH

Webbers Farm Caravan Park, Castle Lane, Woodbury, Exeter, Devon.
Tel. 232276 Std. 01395
Nearest Town/Resort Exmouth.
Directions Leave the M5 junction 30 (Exeter Services) and follow the A376 Exmouth road. At the second roundabout take the B3179 (Budleigh Salterton/Woodbury). From the village centre follow the International signs.
Acreage 8 **Open** Easter–September
Access Good **Site** Lev/Slope
Sites available Total 85.
Facilities
Nearby facilities
Exmouth.
Outstanding view over the River Exe towards Dartmoor. 4 miles from the sea, quiet popular site. Van storage available.

HAWKCHURCH

Hunters Moon Touring Park, Hawkchurch, Axminster, Devon, EX13 5UE.
Tel. 678402 Std. 01297
Nearest Town/Resort Lyme Regis.
Directions From Axminster take A35 towards Dorchester for 3 miles. At main crossroads take left B3165 towards Crewkerne. Follow for 2¼ miles turn left to Hunters Moon.
Acreage 8 **Open** 15th Mar–31st Oct
Access Good **Site** Level
Sites available Total 179.
Facilities
Nearby facilities
Axminster.
All weather bowling greens, super views over Axe Valley.

HOLSWORTHY

Hedley Wood Caravan and Camping Park, Bridgerule, Near Bude, Holsworthy, Devon, EX22 7ED.
Tel. 404 Std. 01288 81
Nearest Town/Resort Bude.
Directions Travel west on A3072 from Holsworthy for 5¼ miles, turn left on B3254 for 2¼ miles turn right, site entrance 500 yards on right (signposted).
Acreage 8 **Open** All Year
Access Good **Site** Lev/Slope
Sites available Total 120.
Facilities
Nearby facilities
16 acre woodland site. Pets welcome. Daily kennelling facility. Static and touring vans for hire and caravan storage available. Clay pigeon shooting.

HOLSWORTHY

Newbuildings, Brandis Corner, Holsworthy, Devon, EX22 7YQ.
Tel. 221305 Std. 01409
Nearest Town/Resort Holsworthy/Bude.
Directions Where the B3218 from Okehampton meets the A3072 Hatherliegh to Holsworthy Road. Newbuildings is at this Cross i.e Dunsland Cross.
Open All Year.
Access Good **Site** Level
Sites available
Facilities
Nearby facilities
Exeter.
Small family farm camping holiday within easy reach of beaches, Dartmoor, Exmoor etc.

Hedley Wood Caravan & Camping Park

RAC Selected Site **Hedley Wood Caravan & Camping Park** **AA**
Bridgerule, Holsworthy, Devon EX22 7ED Tel & Fax 0128881 404
A 16 acre woodland family run site with: Licensed bar & clubroom with children's adventure area. Sheltered and open camping areas. Just 10 minutes drive from the beach. **On-site facilities include:** Licensed bar & clubroom, Shop, laundry, off-licence & all amenities. Static caravans for hire, Nice dogs/pets welcome. Daily kennelling facility, Clay pigeon shoot.
Caravan storage available. **Open All Year.**
Listed Site

Calling All Caravanners and Campers

**** BOWLING ON THE PARK ****
Write or 'phone for brochure
(01297) 678402
Hunters Moon Touring Park
Hawkchurch, Nr. Lyme Regis
Axminster, Devon EX13 5UE

Panoramic Views Over the Beautiful Axe Valley
** All Weather Bowling Greens **
French Boules Pit **
Well Stocked Shop
Electric Hook Ups
Licenced Club ** Barbecues **
Leisure Building With Table Tennis ** Pool ** Darts ** etc.
** Putting Green **
Area of Outstanding Natural Beauty – Sea Side Nearby **

HOLSWORTHY

Noteworthy, Bude Main Road, Holsworthy, Devon.
Tel. Holsworthy 253731 Std. 01409
Nearest Town/Resort Holsworthy/Bude.
Directions 2½ miles west of Holsworthy on A3072.
Acreage 5 **Open** All year
Access Good **Site** Level
Sites available
Facilities
Nearby facilities
Exeter.
Views, 6 miles Cornish coast. Farm site.

HONITON

Otter Valley Park, Northcote Lane, Honiton, Devon, EX14 8ST.
Tel. 44546 Std. 01404
Nearest Town/Resort Honiton.
Directions Off the A30, turn left and left again at first southbound exit. From the town centre, turn left at the A35 Axminster roundabout. Take the first right turn then turn left into Northcote Lane.
Acreage 6 **Open** Late March–Mid September
Access Good **Site** Lev/Slope
Sites available Total 60.
Facilities
Nearby facilities
Honiton.
Ideal touring and holiday base. Spectacular views and 10 miles of coast.

ILFRACOMBE

Big Meadow Camping Park, Watermouth, Ilfracombe, Devon. EX34 9SJ.
Tel. 862282 Std. 01271
Nearest Town/Resort Ilfracombe.
Directions Situated on the A399 coastal road approximately 2 miles from Ilfracombe, opposite Watermouth Castle Tourist Attraction.
Acreage 9 **Open** May–October
Access Good **Site** Level
Sites available Total 125.
Facilities S
Nearby facilities
Barnstaple.
Near Watermouth Harbour, sheltered family site with stream running through.

ILFRACOMBE

Hele Valley Holiday Park, Hele Bay, Ilfracombe, Devon EX34 9RD.
Tel. 862460 Std. 01271
Nearest Town/Resort Ilfracombe.
Directions Take A399 to Ilfracombe turn at signpost Hele village, to bottom of lane, take righthand turning into Holiday Park.
Acreage 4 **Open** April–October
Access Good **Site** Level
Sites available Total 50.
Facilities S
Nearby facilities
Barnstaple.
Near beach and town centre. Ideal for touring. Many tourist attractions nearby and lovely walks.

ILFRACOMBE

Hidden Valley, Coast & Country Park, West Down, Ilfracombe, Devon, EX34 8NU.
Tel. 813837 Std. 01271
Nearest Town/Resort Ilfracombe.
Directions From M5 junction 27 Tiverton/Barnstaple. Follow A361 to Ilfracombe, continue for 8 miles, Hidden valley is on the left.
Acreage 25 **Open** 15th March–15th Nov
Access Good **Site** Level
Sites available Total 135.
Facilities S
Nearby facilities
Barnstaple.
Beautiful wooded valley, ideal touring for Exmoor and North Devons golden coast.

ILFRACOMBE

Little Meadow Camp Site, Watermouth, Ilfracombe, Devon. EX34 9SJ.
Tel. 862222 Std. 01271
Nearest Town/Resort Ilfracombe.
Directions On A399 between Ifracombe and Combe Martin.
Acreage 5 **Open** Whitsun–September
Access Good **Site** Terraced
Sites available Total 100.
Facilities M
Nearby facilities
Barnstaple.
Quiet and peaceful and the best view in Devon.

ILFRACOMBE

Mill Park Touring Site, Berrynarbor, Nr. Ilfracombe. Devon, EX34 9SH.
Tel. 882647 Std. 0271.
Nearest Town/Resort Ilfracombe.
Directions Situated on the A399 coast road between Combe Martin and Ilfracombe near Watermouth Castle. Take the turning opposite the Sawmille Inn signposted to Berrynarbor.
Acreage 15 **Open** 15th March–15th Nov
Access Good **Site** Level
Sites available Total 165.
Facilities S
Nearby facilities
Barnstaple.
Well sheltered site with woodland walks. Own coarse fishing lake. Take away food and an off licence.

ILFRACOMBE

Mullacott Cross Holiday Park, Mullacott Cross, Ilfracombe, Devon, EX34 8NB.
Tel. 862212/862200 Std. 01271
Nearest Town/Resort Ilfracombe.
Directions On A361 1½ miles south of Ilfracombe.
Acreage 5 **Open** Easter–Mid Oct
Access Good **Site** Lev/Slope
Sites available Total 110.
Facilities S
Nearby facilities
Barnstaple.
Excellent centre for touring north Devon.

ILFRACOMBE

Napps Caravan Site, Napps, Old Coast Road, Berrynarbor, Ilfracombe, North Devon.
Tel. 882557 Std. 01271
Nearest Town/Resort Ilfracombe.
Directions On A399, 1¼ miles west of

Combe Martin, turn right onto Old Coast Road (signposted). Site 400yds along Old Coast Road.
Acreage 11 **Open** March–November
Access Good **Site** Level
Sites available Total 250.
Facilities
Nearby facilities
Barnstaple.
Glorious sea and coastal views, beach 200yds. Popular family site with woodland and coastal walks. Summer parking and winter storage available.

ILFRACOMBE

North Morte Farm Caravan & Camping Park, Mortehoe, Woolacombe, Devon, EX34 7EG.
Tel. Woolacombe 870381 Std. 01271
Nearest Town/Resort Ilfracombe.
Directions A361 from Barnstaple, B3343 to Woolacombe, NOT the left turn to Woolacombe. Straight on to Mortehoe.
Acreage 15 **Open** Easter–October
Access Good **Site** Lev/Slope
Sites available Total 175.
Facilities
Nearby facilities
Barnstaple.
Coastal scenic views and walks 500 yards from beach. S.A.E. for details.

IVYBRIDGE

Cheston Caravan & Camping Park, Folly Cross, Wrangaton Road, South Brent, Devon, TQ10 9HF.
Tel. 72586 Std. 01364
Nearest Town/Resort Ivybridge.
Directions From Exeter, after by-passing South Brent, turn left at Wrangaton Cross slip road then right A38. From Plymouth take South Brent (Woodpecker) turn.
Acreage 1¼ **Open** 15th March–15th Jan
Access Good **Site** Level
Sites available Total 23.
Facilities
Nearby facilities
Set in beautiful Dartmoor. Perfect for touring, walking and bird watching. Nearest beach 9 miles. Pets welcome. Easy access from A38.

KINGSBRIDGE

Bolberry House Farm Caravan & Camping Park, Bolberry, Malborough, Kingsbridge, South Devon, TQ7 3DY.
Tel. 561251/560926 Std. 01548
Nearest Town/Resort Salcombe.
Directions Take the A381 Kingsbridge to Salcombe road, turn sharp right at Malborough, through the village and right again round the church. Follow signs to Bolberry ¾ mile on, signposted again, site on right.
Acreage 6 **Open** March–October
Access Good **Site** Level
Sites available Total 75.
Facilities
Nearby facilities
Totnes.
Peaceful rural setting and a friendly family atmosphere. Lovely views down through the valley to the sea. Farm adjoins National Trust land, in an area of outstanding natural beauty for coastal walks. Safe sandy beaches 1 mile. Laundry facilities consist of tumble/spin driers, washing machine, sinks.

KINGSBRIDGE

Island Lodge, Stumpy Post Cross, Kingsbridge, Devon, TQ7 4BL.
Tel. Kingsbridge 852956 Std. 01548
Nearest Town/Resort Kingsbridge.
Directions Travelling from Totnes to Kingsbridge on A381 turn right onto B3194 at Stumpy Post Cross then turn first left into lane leading to site entrance.
Acreage 5 **Open** Easter–October
Access Good **Site** Level
Sites available Total 35.
Facilities
Nearby facilities
Totnes.
Very central for all beaches and villages in the South Hams area. Suitable for families with young children. Small friendly site. Proprietor – Mrs Kay Parker.

KINGSBRIDGE

Karrageen Caravan and Camping Site, Bolberry, Malborough, Kingsbridge, Devon TQ7 3EN.
Tel. 561230 Std. 01548
Nearest Town/Resort Salcombe.
Directions Take A381 Kingsbridge to Salcombe road turn sharp right into Malborough Village, follow signs for Bolberry.
Acreage 7½ **Open** Easter–1st Oct
Access Good **Site** Lev/slope
Sites available Total 60.
Facilities
Nearby facilities
Totnes/Plymouth.
Beaches at Hope Cove only 1 mile away, situated in beautiful scenic countryside, surrounded by National Trust coastline. Parents and Baby room. Superb cliff top walking.

KINGSBRIDGE

Mounts Farm Touring Park, The Mounts, Nr. East Allington, Kingsbridge, South Devon, TQ9 7QJ.
Tel. 521591 Std. 01548

Nearest Town/Resort Kingsbridge.
Directions On the A381 Totnes/Kingsbridge. 3 miles north of Kingsbridge. Entrance from A381 – DO NOT go to East Allington Village.
Acreage 5 **Open** April–October
Access Good **Site** Level
Sites available Total 27.
Facilities
Nearby facilities
Totnes.
In an area of outstanding natural beauty. Ideal for touring all South Devon.

KINGSBRIDGE

Newlands Farm Camping & Caravan Site, Newlands Farm, Slapton, Nr. Kingsbridge, South Devon.
Tel. 580366 Std. 01548
Nearest Town/Resort Kingsbridge.
Directions From Totnes take the A381 towards Kingsbridge, after Halwell take the fourth left signposted Slapton. Go 4 miles to Buckland Cross, proceed ¼ mile, site is on the left hand side.
Acreage 10 **Open** Easter–October
Access Good **Site** Level
Sites available Total 25.
Facilities
Nearby facilities
Totnes.
Fresh water ley, scenic views from site. Near to beaches.

KINGSBRIDGE

Parkland, Sorley Green Cross, Kingsbridge, Devon. TQ7 4AF.
Tel. Kingsbridge 852723 Std. 01548.
Nearest Town/Resort Kingsbridge.
Directions From A381 turn onto B3194 continue to Sorley Green Cross go straight ahead site 100yds on left.
Acreage 3 **Open** All year
Access Good **Site** Level
Sites available
Facilities
Nearby facilities
Central for beaches and touring (river 1 mile). Well sheltered. One pitch with hard standing, hook-up water point and T.V. point (Super Pitch).

LYNTON

Channel View Caravan Park, Manor Farm, Barbrook, Lynton, Devon, EX35 6LD.
Tel. 53349 Std. 01598
Nearest Town/Resort Lynton/Lynmouth.
Directions On main A39, ¾ mile from Barbrook Village.
Acreage 7 **Open** Easter–October
Access Good **Site** Level
Sites available Total 76.
Facilities
Nearby facilities
Barnstaple.
Panoramic views, edge of Exmoor overlooking Lynton/Lynmouth.

LYNTON

Sunny Lyn Caravan & Camping Park, Lynbridge, Lynton, Devon EX35 6NS.
Tel. Lynton 53384 Std. 01598
Nearest Town/Resort Lynton/Lynmouth.
Directions ¾ mile inland from Lynmouth on B3234.
Acreage 3½ **Open** Easter–Early Oct
Access Good **Site** Level
Sites available Total 40.
Facilities
Nearby facilities
Barnstaple.
Trout stream through site. Borders on picturesque 'Lorna Doone' country.

MODBURY

Moor View Touring Park, California Cross, Modbury, Ivybridge, South Devon, PL21 0SG.
Tel. 821485 Std. 01548
Nearest Town/Resort Modbury.
Directions 3 miles east of Modbury on the B3207. From the A38 leave at Wrangaton Cross junction (signed the A3210 Ermington, Ugborough, Yealmpton). Follow camping signs to Moor View.
Acreage 5 **Open** Easter–October
Access Good **Site** Level
Sites available Total 68.
Facilities
Nearby facilities
Plymouth.
Superb views of Dartmoor, peaceful rural setting, sheltered by mature woodland, central for moors, beaches, Plymouth and Torbay. Take-away on site.

MODBURY

Pennymoor Caravan Park, Modbury, Devon.
Tel. 830269/830542 Std. 01548
Nearest Town/Resort Kingsbridge/Salcombe.
Directions Approx 30 miles West of Exeter, leave A38 at Wrangaton Cross. Turn left, then straight across at next crossroads and continue for approx 4 miles. Pass petrol garage on left, then take second left, site is 1 mile on the right.
Acreage 6 **Open** 15 March–15 November
Access Good **Site** Level
Sites available Total 155.
Facilities
Nearby facilities

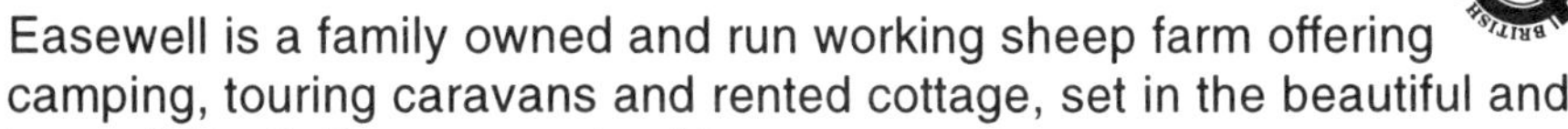

Easewell Farm

HOLIDAY PARK AND GOLF CLUB

MORTEHOE • WOOLACOMBE

Easewell is a family owned and run working sheep farm offering camping, touring caravans and rented cottage, set in the beautiful and tranquil North Devon countryside.

Facilities include • 9 hole golf course • Club house • Indoor heated pool • Takeaway & Restaurant • Adventure playground • Colour Tv • Indoor games room • Dishwashing area • Electric hook-ups • Laundrette
- New modern toilet block
- Free hot showers
- Well stocked shop
- Small beach within walking distance.

MORTEHOE, WOOLACOMBE, N DEVON EX34 7EH • Tel: 01271 870225

DARTMOOR NATIONAL PARK / A38 / PLYMOUTH / MOOR VIEW / TORBAY / BIGBURY / DARTMOUTH / SALCOMBE

PEACEFUL RURAL SETTING, SUPERB VIEWS. IN THE HEART OF SOUTH HAMS COUNTRYSIDE YET QUICK AND EASY ACCESS TO MOORS, BEACHES, PLYMOUTH, TORBAY AND SOUTH DEVON ATTRACTIONS. INDIVIDUAL LARGE LEVEL PITCHES, SOME HARDSTANDING. MODERN SUPERIOR TOILETS & SHOWERS, HIGH PRESSURE, CONSTANT HOT WATER, ALL SCRUPULOUSLY CLEAN. TAKE AWAY, GAMES ROOM, CHILDREN'S PLAYGROUND. PET EXERCISE FIELD. WOODLAND NATURE AREA.

Write or telephone for brochure

MOOR VIEW TOURING PARK, CALIFORNIA CROSS, MODBURY, DEVON PL21 0SG. Tel: 01548 821485

Plymouth.
Peaceful rural site. Ideal touring base. Central to towns, moors, beaches. Bigbury-on-Sea only 5 miles. Holiday caravans to let. New superb toilet/shower block. Free colour brochure.

MODBURY

Southleigh Caravan and Camping Park, Modbury, Devon.
Tel. 830346 Std. 01548
Nearest Town/Resort Kingsbridge.
Directions From A38 turn left past Woodpecker Inn signposted Modbury straight ahead at cross roads now ignoring Modbury signs, 4 miles turn second left past garage 1¼ miles on right.
Acreage 5 **Open** April–September
Access Good **Site** Level
Sites available Total 100.
Facilities
Nearby facilities
Plymouth.
Near Bigbury-on-Sea, easy access Plymouth and the moors and south Devon resorts. Holiday caravans to let.

MORETONHAMPSTEAD

Clifford Bridge Park, Nr. Drewsteignton, Exeter, Devon EX6 6QE.
Tel. 24226 Std. 01647
Nearest Town/Resort Moretonhampstead.
Directions Leave A30 Dual carriage way to Cheriton Bishop, left at Old Thatch 2 miles to crossroads turn right, 1 mile to Clifford.
Acreage 8 **Open** Easter–September.
Access Good **Site** Level
Sites available Total 65.
Facilities
Nearby facilities
Exeter.
The upper Teign valley and Gorge is noted for it's outstanding natural beauty, superb viewpoints and magnificent woodland trails, it's location on Dartmoor National Park makes it a unique touring centre for walking fishing, riding and golf.

MORTEHOE

Easewell Farm Holiday Park, Mortehoe, Nr. Woolacombe, North Devon, EX34 7EH.
Tel. 870225 Std. 01271
Nearest Town/Resort Woolacombe.
Acreage 17 **Open** Easter–September
Access Good **Site** Lev/Slope
Sites available Total 200.
Facilities
Nearby facilities
Barnstaple.
Near beach with scenic views.

MORTEHOE

Warcombe Farm Camping Park, Mortehoe, Near Woolacombe, North Devon, EX34 7EJ.
Tel. 870690 Std. 01271.
Nearest Town/Resort Barnstaple.
Directions Turn left off the A361, Barnstaple to Ilfracombe road at Mullacott Cross roundabout signposted Woolacombe. After 2 miles turn right towards Mortehoe. Site is first on the right in less than a mile.
Acreage 19 **Open** 15th Mar–31st October
Access Good **Site** Level
Sites available Total 145.
Facilities
Nearby facilities
Ilfracombe.
1¼ miles to Woolacombe beach. Panoramic sea views. Well drained level land, family run. Cafe and take-away food available.

NEWTON ABBOT

Dornafield, Dornafield Farm Two Mile Oak, Newton Abbott, Devon TQ12 6DD.
Tel. 812732 Std. 01803
Nearest Town/Resort Newton Abbot.
Directions Take A381 (Newton Abbott to Totnes) in 2¼ miles turn right at Two Mile Oak Inn. In ½ mile turn 1st left site 150 yards on right.
Acreage 14 **Open** 21st March–October
Access Good **Site** Level
Sites available Total 135.
Facilities
Nearby facilities
Newton Abbot.
Beautiful 14th century farmhouse location in tranquil valley with superb facilities. Only motorcyclists belonging to the AA admitted. 'England for Excellence'. Highly Recommended 1991. New golf club 1 mile. 60 'Full Service Pitches' at no extra charge.

NEWTON ABBOT

Lemonford Caravan Park, Bickington, Newton Abbot, Devon, TQ12 6JR.
Tel. 821242 Std. 01626
Nearest Town/Resort Ashburton.
Directions From Exeter along A38 take A382 turnoff, on roundabout take 3rd exit and follow site signs to Bickington. From Plymouth take A383 turnoff, follow road for ¼ mile and turn left onto site.
Acreage 7 **Open** Easter–September
Access Good **Site** Level
Sites available Total 90.
Facilities
Nearby facilities
Newton Abbot.

In a beautiful setting and scrupulously clean. Close to Torbay and the Dartmoor National Park.

NEWTON ABBOT

Stover International Caravan Park, Lower Staple Hill, Newton Abbot, Devon TQ12 6JD.
Tel. 821446 Std. 01626
Nearest Town/Resort Newton Abbot.
Directions A38 to junction of A382, turn towards Newton Abbot and in 600 yards turn right at island signed Trago Mills. Site on left before you reach Trago Mills entrance.
Acreage 18 **Open** 15th March–October
Access Good **Site** Lev/Slope
Sites available Total 200.
Facilities
Nearby facilities
On edge of Dartmoor National Park, 8 miles from many beaches. Ideal touring base. 18 hole golf course immediately adjoining. Some hard standings. Course fishing adjoining. A.A. R.A.C. A.D.A.C. and A.N.W.B. recommended. Indoor heated swimming pool. Luxury 6 berth log cabins for Hire.

NEWTON ABBOT

Ware Barton Caravan Site, Ware Barton, Kingsteignton, Newton Abbot, Devon, TQ12 3QQ.
Tel. Newton Abbot 54025
Nearest Town/Resort Teignmouth.
Directions On A381 Teignmouth to Newton Abbot road.
Acreage 2 **Open** Easter–October
Access Good **Site** Lev/Slope
Sites available Total 50.
Facilities
Nearby facilities
Newton Abbot.
Very central, near sea and moors.

OKEHAMPTON

Bridestowe Caravan Park, Bridestowe, Nr. Okehampton, Devon.
Tel. 261 Std. 0183786
Nearest Town/Resort Bude.
Directions Leave M5 for A30 to Okehampton 3 miles west of Okehampton turn off A30 to Bridestowe village, follow camping signs to site.
Open March–December
Access Good **Site** Level
Sites available Total 53.
Facilities
Nearby facilities
Dartmoor National Park 2 miles, ideal for walking, horse riding and fishing and touring Devon and Cornwall. Within easy reach of coastal resorts.

OKEHAMPTON

Dartmoor View Caravan & Camping Park, Whiddon Down, Nr. Okehampton, Devon.
Tel. 231545 Std. 01647
Nearest Town/Resort Okehampton.
Directions M5 junction 31 take A30 to first island turn left, park ¼ mile on right.
Acreage 5½ **Open** 1st March–30th November
Access Good **Site** Level
Sites available Total 60.
Facilities
Nearby facilities
Exeter.
Ideal touring, scenic views. Tourist Information Centre on site. A.A. 4 pennants. E.T.B. – Excellent. Rose Award. Take-away food.

OKEHAMPTON

Okehampton Motel Caravan Park, Exeter Road, Devon, EX20 1QF.
Tel. 52879/54334 Std. 01837
Nearest Town/Resort Okehampton.
Directions ½ mile off Okehampton By-Pass.
Open All Year
Access Good **Site** Level
Sites available Total 25.
Facilities
Nearby facilities
Exeter.
Any beach north south west with ¼ to 1 hour drive.

OKEHAMPTON

Olditch Caravan & Camping Park, Olditch Farm, Sticklepath, Nr. Okehampton, Devon. EX20 2NT.
Tel. 840734 Std. 01837
Nearest Town/Resort Okehampton.
Directions 4 miles east of Okehampton on old A30, 18 miles west of Exeter.
Acreage 3 **Open** 14 March–14 November
Access Good **Site** Lev/Slope
Sites available Total 32.
Facilities
Nearby facilities
Exeter.
Ideal touring and walking on Dartmoor. Base for all Devon and Cornwall.

THE MOST COMFORTABLE, FUN-PACKED HOLIDAY ON THE RIVIERA

so much to see..... .....do .....and enjoy

Beverley Holidays

Superb accommodation set in 20 acres of beautiful parkland with wonderful views of Torbay. That's a Beverley Holiday. All our luxury caravan homes accommodate 2 to 6 people. An altogether higher level of enjoyment at a sensible price. Beverley Park facilities include: Touring sites, Licensed Club, Indoor and outdoor heated pools, Entertainment, Dancing and cabaret, Sports facilities and Children's activities.

For your FREE full colour brochure phone 01803 843887 (24hrs) or write to Beverley Holidays, Dept 10, Goodrington Road, Paignton, Devon TQ4 7JE.

Designed and built by Caravanners for Caravanners

AA - 4 Pennant and in Top 100 parks in U.K.
RAC - Approved and Recommended
ANWB (Holland) - Highly Recommended
ADAC (Germany) - Highly Recommended
Camping and Caravaning Club - Recommended
Real Automovil Club de Espana - Highly Recommended

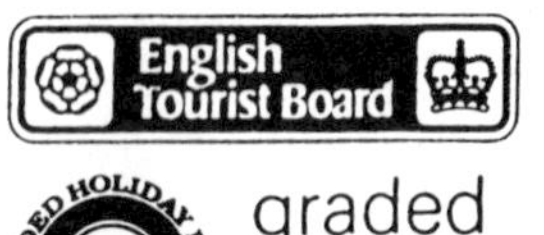

graded Excellent

STOVER *International Caravan Park*

Lower Staple Hill, Newton Abbot, Near Torquay. Tel: (0626) 821446

In the heart of Glorious Devon

Reputed to be one of the most beautiful and luxuriously equipped caravan parks in the U.K.
Three luxury toilet blocks - fully tiled walls and floors, and heated in early and late season and spotlessly clean.
H & C showers - razor points - hair dryers. Two bathrooms complete with bath, shower, washbasin and W.C.
Three chemical disposal points and facilities for emptying **Motorhome Tanks.**
Three enclosed rooms with stainless steel sinks and H & C for pots, pans also separate SS sinks and spin dryers for hand washing clothes, also Launderette and ironing facilities, drying room.
HEATED INDOOR SWIMMING POOL, Children's adventure playground. 200 electric hook-up points.
Facilities for disabled. Bar/Lounge, Games Room, Shop, & Bar meals.
Freezer pack service. Battery charging, Coarse Fishing Lakes & Miniature Steam Railway Golf Course Adjoin our boundary. Caravans - Motorhomes - Tents - Trailer Tents all catered for. Dogs admitted strictly on leash, (NO ROTTWEILERS, PIT BULL TERRIERS OR SIMILAR BREEDS).
BEAUTIFUL 6 BERTH LOG CABIN TYPE HOLIDAY HOMES AND 6 BERTH CARAVANS
FULLY EQUIPPED, FOR SALE SITED OR FOR HIRE. 2 BEDROOM VILLA - SLEEPS 4 ALSO FOR HIRE
SAE please for colour brochure **- This caravan park has been completely redeveloped.**
Open March to 31st October.
STOP PRESS - TWO NEW PUBLIC GOLF COURSES WITHIN 3 MILES.
Directions: A38 to Junction A382, Turn towards Newton Abbot and on 600 yards at island turn right signed Trago Mills.

OKEHAMPTON

'Yertiz' Caravan and Camping Site, Exeter Road, Okehampton, Devon EX20 1QF.
Tel. 52281 Std. 01837
Nearest Town/Resort Okehampton.
Directions From Exeter on A30 take the B3260 signed Okehampton, site on left 50 yards past Motel.
Acreage 3 **Open** All Year
Access Good **Site** Level
Sites available Total 30.
Facilities
Nearby facilities
On the edge of Dartmoor, 30 miles from North and South coasts. Ideal touring centre, good for walking on Dartmoor.

PAIGNTON

Barton Pines, Blagdon Road, Higher Blagdon, Paignton, Devon.
Tel. 553350 Std. 01803
Nearest Town/Resort Paignton.
Directions Take the Torbay Ring Road A380, follow brown tourist signs from the second roundabout.
Acreage 4 **Open** March–October
Access Good **Site** Level
Sites available Total 33.
Facilities
Nearby facilities
Paignton.
Scenic views, near beaches and moors.

PAIGNTON

Beverley Park Holiday Centre, Goodrington Road, Paignton, Devon.
Tel. Churston 843887 Std. 01803
Nearest Town/Resort Paignton.
Directions 2 miles south of Paignton (ring road) A3022. Turn left into Goodrington Road.
Acreage 9½ **Open** Easter–October
Access Good **Site** Level
Sites available Total 194.
Facilities
Nearby facilities
Paignton.
Views across Torbay. Indoor heated swimming pool, tennis court. Sauna.

PAIGNTON

Paignton Holiday Park, Totnes Road, Paignton, Devon.
Tel. 550504 Std. 01803
Nearest Town/Resort Paignton.
Directions 1¼ miles west of Paignton on the A385.
Acreage 20 **Open** March–October
Access Good **Site** Lev/Slope
Sites available Total 250.
Facilities
Nearby facilities
Paignton.
Area of outstanding natural beauty with nearby beaches and attractions of the English Riviera.

PAIGNTON

Byslades Camping and Touring Park, Totnes Road, Paignton, Devon, TQ4 7PY.
Tel. 555072 Std. 01803.
Nearest Town/Resort Paignton.
Directions 2¼ miles west of Paignton on the A385.
Acreage 23 **Open** April–October
Access Good **Site** Level
Sites available Total 150.
Facilities
Nearby facilities
Paignton.

The site is overlooking a beautiful valley and is centrally situated to visit all parts of Devon. Tennis on site.

PAIGNTON

Grange Court Holiday Centre, Grange Road, Goodrington, Paignton, Devon, TQ4 7JP.
Tel. 558010 Std. 01803
Nearest Town/Resort Paignton.
Directions From junc 31 of M5, travel south for approx 20 miles on A380 to junction with A385. Continue south on A380 (Paignton Ring Road) for 1 mile, turn left into Goodrington Road by Esso Filling Station. After ¾ mile turn left into Grange Road and follow signs to park.
Acreage 20 **Open** Mid-Feb–Mid-Jan
Access Good **Site** Sloping
Sites available Total 157.
Facilities
Nearby facilities
Paignton.
Panoramic views over Torbay, close to Goodrington beach.

PAIGNTON

Higher Well Farm Holiday Park, Stoke Gabriel, Totnes, Devon, TQ9 6RN.
Tel. 782289 Std. 01803
Nearest Town/Resort Paignton.
Directions From Paignton take A385 towards Totnes, turn off left at Parkers Arms Hotel. Go 1¾ miles then turn left again, site is 200 yards down road.
Acreage 8 **Open** Easter–October
Access Good **Site** Lev/Slope
Sites available
Facilities
Nearby facilities

Paignton.
Within 4 miles Torbay beaches, 1 mile village Stoke Gabriel and River Dart.

PAIGNTON

Lower Yalberton Holiday Park, Long Road, Paignton, Devon, TQ4 7PH.
Tel. 558127 Std. 01803
Nearest Town/Resort Paignton.
Directions On the south-west side of Paignton, about 2¼ miles from the sea. Turn off the A3022 which bypasses Paignton into Long Road. Site is ¼ mile.
Acreage 25 **Open** May–September
Access Good **Site** Lev/Slope
Sites available Total 543.
Facilities
Nearby facilities
Paignton.
Ideal touring centre yet close to town and beaches. 4 Tick and A.A. 4 Pennants.

PAIGNTON

Marine Park Holiday Centre, Grange Road, Paignton, Devon.
Tel. Churston 843887 Std. 01803
Nearest Town/Resort Paignton.
Directions 2 miles south of Paignton off A379.
Acreage 4 **Open** May–September
Access Good **Site** Lev/Slope
Sites available Total 30.
Facilities
Nearby facilities
Paignton.

PAIGNTON

Ramslade Touring Park, Stoke Road, Stoke Gabriel, Paignton, Devon.
Tel. 782575 Std. 01803
Nearest Town/Resort Paignton.
Directions From Paignton take A385, turn left at Parkers Arms, site 1½ miles on right.
Acreage 9 **Open** 15 March–October
Access Good **Site** Lev/Slope
Sites available Total 135.
Facilities
Nearby facilities
Paignton.
Quiet site. Top Tourist Board Grade – 5 ticks. No dogs high season. Babies bathroom, Logland Play areas and paddling pool with waterfall. You can FAX us on 01803 782828.

PAIGNTON

Whitehill Farm Holiday Park, Stoke Road, Paignton, Devon, TQ4 7PF.
Tel. 782338 Std. 01803
Nearest Town/Resort Paignton.
Directions Turn off A385 at Parkers Arms Public House ½ mile from Paignton Zoo. Park 1 mile from the pub.
Acreage 30 **Open** May–September
Access Good **Site** Lev/Slope
Sites available Total 400.
Facilities
Nearby facilities
Paignton.
Surrounded by rolling countryside. You can FAX us on 01803 782722.

PAIGNTON

Widend Camping Park, Berry Pomeroy Road, Marldon, Paignton, Devon TQ3 1RT.
Tel. Paignton 550116 Std. 01803.
Nearest Town/Resort Paignton/Torquay.
Directions Turn into Five Lanes Road towards Berry Pomeroy off the main Torquay ring road (A380) new duel carriageway at Marldon. Singmore Hotel is on the corner.
Acreage 20 **Open** 15 March–15 November
Access Good **Site** Level
Sites available Total 250.
Facilities
Nearby facilities
Torquay.
A most central site for most of the sea and country amenities in south Devon. S.A.E. for brochure and site fees. 5 ticks, graded excellent.

PLYMOUTH

Riverside Caravan Park, Longbridge Road, Marsh Mills, Plymouth, Devon.
Tel. 344122 Std. 01752
Nearest Town/Resort Plymouth.
Directions On A38 from Exeter, at large roundabout take Plympton Road. First left turn see sign for caravan site and then first right.
Acreage 10¼ **Open** All year
Access Good **Site** Level
Sites available Total 292.
Facilities
Nearby facilities
Plymouth North Road.
Alongside river, shaded valley, quiet and peacful location.

SALCOMBE

Alston Farm Camping & Caravan Site, Nr. Salcombe, Kingsbridge, Devon TQ7 3BJ.
Tel. 561260 Std. 01548
Nearest Town/Resort Salcombe.
Directions Signposted on left of A381 between Kingsbridge and Salcombe towards Salcombe.
Acreage 15 **Open** Easter–October
Access Good **Site** Level
Sites available Total 200.
Facilities
Nearby facilities
Totnes.
Secluded, sheltered site. Dish washing facilities.

SALCOMBE

Higher Rew Farm, Malborough, Kingsbridge, Devon.
Tel. 842681 Std. 01548.
Directions A381 turn right at Malborough follow signs to Soar, then turn left at signpost to Combe and South Sands.
Acreage 5 **Open** Easter–September
Site Lev/Slope
Sites available Total 75.
Facilities
Nearby facilities
Totnes.
Beaches 1 mile. Cliff walks. Tumble and spin dryer. Sinks for clothes wash, washing machine.

SALCOMBE

Sun Park, Soar, Malborough, Nr. Kingsbridge, Devon. TQ7 3DS.
Tel. 561378 Std. 01548
Nearest Town/Resort Salcombe.
Directions A381 fron Kingsbridge to Malborough, turn right through village, follow sign Soar Mill Cove for 1¼ miles, site on right.
Acreage 3¼ **Open** Easter–Mid October
Site Level
Sites available Total 70.
Facilities
Nearby facilities
Totnes.
Overlooking Soar Mill Cove, in an area of outstanding natural beauty. Ideal centre for touring.

SEATON

Leacroft Touring Park, Colyton Hill, Colyton, Devon.
Tel. 552823 Std. 01297
Nearest Town/Resort Seaton/Beer.
Directions A3052 Sidmouth to Lyme Regis road, 2 miles west of Seaton. Turn left at Stafford Cross international caravan sign, site is 1 mile on the right.
Acreage 10 **Open** End March–October
Access Good **Site** Lev/Slope
Sites available Total 138.
Facilities
Nearby facilities
Axminster.
Quiet, peaceful site in open countryside. Picturesque villages nearby and woodland walks. Ideal for touring.

SEATON

Manor Farm Caravan Site, Seaton Down Hill, Seaton, Devon.
Tel. 21524 Std. 01297
Nearest Town/Resort Seaton.
Directions From Lyme Regis A3052, left at Tower Cross, ½ mile entrance on left.
Acreage 22 **Open** April–15th Nov
Access Good **Site** Lev/Slope
Sites available Total 274.
Facilities
Nearby facilities
Axminster.
Glorious scenic views of valley and Lyme Bay. Farm animals, rare breeds. A quiet site only 1 mile from beach.

SIDMOUTH

Oakdown Touring Park, Weston, Sidmouth, Devon, EX10 0PH.
Tel. 680387 Std. 01297
Nearest Town/Resort Sidmouth.
Directions 1½ miles east of Sidford on A3052, take the second Weston turning at the Oakdown sign. Site 50 yards on left.
Also signposted with international Caravan/Camping signs.
Acreage 9 **Open** April–October
Access Good **Site** Level
Sites available Total 120.
Facilities
Nearby facilities
Honiton.
Set in glorious East Devon Heritage coast, near beautiful Weston Valley owned by National Trust, lovely cliff walks. Caravan storage. Fully serviced pitches for touring units. Field trail to nearby world famous Donkey Santurary.

SIDMOUTH

Salcombe Regis Camping and Caravan Park, Salcombe Regis, Sidmouth, Devon, EX10 0JH.
Tel. 514303 Std. 01395
Nearest Town/Resort Sidmouth.
Directions 1½ miles east of Sidmouth signposted off A3052 Coast Road.
Acreage 16 **Open** Easter–October
Access Good **Site** Level
Sites available Total 100.
Facilities
Nearby facilities
Exeter.
Within walking distance from sea in area of outstanding natural beauty. Rose Award

Salcombe Regis

CAMPING & CARAVAN PARK

SIDMOUTH DEVON EX10 0JH

TEL/FAX (01395) 514303

for FREE colour brochure

- Spacious level site with sea views
- Within walking distance of the sea
- Tranquil setting with excellent touring facilities
- Ten luxuriously equipped leisure homes for hire
- Superb walking country

Sidmouth's closest Holiday Park in an area of outstanding natural beauty

---

Oakdown

CARAVAN PARKS

WESTON, SIDMOUTH, DEVON EX10 0PH

Telephone: (01297) 680387

FREE COLOUR BROCHURE WITH PLEASURE

Set amidst the glorious East Devon Heritage Coast, $2\frac{1}{2}$ miles east of Sidmouth, two level, closely mown "EXCELLENT" graded family owned parks. Adjacent to the A3052 for easy access OAKDOWN TOURING PARK (120 units) is landscaped into groves with standard and "Super Pitches" available. The luxurious fully tiled amenities including bathrooms, are centrally heated.

OAKDOWN HOLIDAY HOME PARK (8 luxury Rose Award holiday caravans) nestling in the hamlet of Weston, is adjacent to the beautiful National Trust Valley and beach, marvellous cliff walks and safe bathing.

SIDMOUTH & EAST DEVON'S AWARD WINNING CARAVAN PARKS

HARFORD BRIDGE HOLIDAY PARK. Peter Tavy, Tavistock, Devon PL19 9LS

TELEPHONE: (01822) 810349 FAX: (01822) 810029

This beautiful family run Park is set in Dartmoor National Park with delightful views of Cox Tor. The River Tavy forms a boundary with riverside pitches and other spacious level pitches. Luxury self catering caravan holiday homes and chalets. Tennis, Table Tennis, Fly Fishing, Children's Play Area, Shop, Telephone.

Nearby Golf, Pony Trekking, Swimming, Canoeing and Gliding. Making this an interesting place to stay.

DARTMOOR COUNTRY HOLIDAYS

Peaceful woodland setting next to the River Walkham in the Dartmoor National Park. Ideally placed to explore the beauty of Devon. Small select touring area edged by mature trees and the river for 30 touring caravans, tents and motor caravans. **New Modern toilet block with under-cover washing-up facilities.**

● Purpose-built pine lodges available all year round. High specifications of furnishings and equipment inc. kitchen with oven, hob, microwave and dishwasher. ● 2 golf courses a short drive away. ● Easy walk to village and shops. ● Scenic walks. ● Fishing. ● Dogs accepted. ● Horse-riding nearby. ● Launderette. ● On A386 **Plymouth-Tavistock road.**

MAGPIE LEISURE PARK

Dept CTC, Bedford Bridge, Horrabridge, Yelverton, Devonshire, PL20 7RY.

Telephone: 01822 852651

Brochure & Tariff: 01822 852651

Park. Hook-ups for tents and hard standing for motor caravans.

SOUTH BRENT

Webland Farm Holiday Park, Avonwick, Nr. South Brent, Devon. TQ10 9EX.
Tel. 73273 Std. 01364
Nearest Town/Resort Totnes.
Directions Leave A38 at Marley Head A385 exit, turn right at roundabout and follow Webland signs along lane for about 1¼ miles.
Acreage 5 **Open** 15th March–15th November
Access Good **Site** Lev/Gentle Slope
Sites available Total 35.
Facilities
Nearby facilities
Totnes.
Overlooked by Dartmoor Hills, very quiet country park, well placed for touring the coast and Dartmoor and the many tourist attractions in the area.

SOUTH MOLTON

Romansleigh Holiday Park, Odam Hill, South Molton, North Devon, EX36 4NB.
Tel. 550259 Std. 01769
Nearest Town/Resort Barnstaple.
Directions Take the B3137 South Molton to Witheridge road. Site is signposted right approximately 4 miles from South Molton and 2 miles past Alswear.
Acreage 1 **Open** 31 March–October
Access Good **Site** Level
Sites available Total 20.
Facilities
Nearby facilities
Umberleigh.
Secluded, wooded valley with magnificent all-round views. In the grounds of 14 acres. Ideal touring location.

STARCROSS

Cofton Country Holiday Park, Cofton Farm, Starcross, Dawlish, Devon, EX6 8RP.
Tel. 890111 Std. 01626
Nearest Town/Resort Dawlish Warren.
Directions On A379 Exeter – Dawlish road ¼ mile after fishing village at Cockwood.
Acreage 16 **Open** Easter–October
Access Good **Site** Level
Sites available Total 450.
Facilities
Nearby facilities
Dawlish.
In beautiful rural countryside close to sandy Dawlish Warren beach Clean and tidy family run park. Superb complex and swimming pool, Swan Pub with family lounge and snack bar. Ideal centre to discover Devon. Excellent Quality grading and E.T.B.Rose Award Holiday Park. See our advert on back cover.

STOKENHAM

Old Cotmore Farm Touring Caravan & Camping Park, Old Cotmore Farm, Stokenham, Near Kingsbridge, South Devon, TQ7 2LR.
Tel. 580240 Std. 01548
Nearest Town/Resort Kingsbridge/Dartmouth.
Directions A379 Kingsbridge to Dartmouth road, at mini roundabout in the village of Stokenham take turn signposted Beesands. We have a brown caravan/tent sign at mini roundabout. 1 mile along the lane on the right.
Acreage 5 **Open** March–November
Access Good **Site** Lev/Slope
Sites available Total 50.
Facilities
Nearby facilities
Totnes.
¾ mile to beaches. Sea view from camping field. Picturesque site in the grounds of a 16th Century farmhouse which once belonged to Catherine Parr (last wife of King Henry VIII). Bread delivery every day. Childrens play area planned for 1995. Motorcycles accepted at our discretion.

TAVISTOCK

Harford Bridge Holiday Park, Peter Tavy, Tavistock, Devon.
Tel. 810349 Std. 01822
Nearest Town/Resort Tavistock.
Directions A386 Okehampton road 2 miles north of Tavistock.
Acreage 16½ **Open** March–November
Access Good **Site** Level
Sites available Total 120.
Facilities
Nearby facilities
Plymouth.
Scenic views, riverside pitches, fishing and tennis, ideal touring Dartmoor National Park. W.C.T.B. Rose Award 5 Ticks.

TAVISTOCK

Higher Longford Farm, Moorshop, Tavistock, Devon.
Tel. 613360 Std. 01822
Nearest Town/Resort Tavistock.
Directions Tavistock/Princetown road, 2 miles from Tavistock on the B3357.
Acreage 4 **Open** All year
Access Good **Site** Level
Sites available Total 52.
Facilities
Nearby facilities
Plymouth.
Situated in the Dartmoor National Park, central for touring Devon and Cornwall.

TAVISTOCK

Dartmoor Country Holidays, Magpie Leisure Park, Bedford Bridge, Horrabridge, Yelverton, Devon, PL20, 7RY.
Tel. 852651 Std. 01822
Nearest Town/Resort Tavistock.
Directions 2¼ miles south east of Tavistock off the A386 Plymouth road.
Acreage 8 **Open** 15th March–15th January
Access Good **Site** Level
Sites available Total 30.
Facilities
Nearby facilities
Plymouth.
Wooded level site, situated along banks of River Walkham in Dartmoor National Park. Luxury Pine Lodges sleeping 2-7 also available.

TAVISTOCK

Woodovis Park, Gulworthy, Nr. Tavistock, Devon.PL19 8NY.
Tel. 832968 Std. 01822
Nearest Town/Resort Tavistock.
Directions Take A390 Liskeard road from Tavistock. Site signposted right in 3 miles.
Acreage 14 **Open** March–December
Access Good **Site** Lev/Slope
Sites available Total 55.
Facilities
Nearby facilities
Plymouth.
Scenic views, close to Tamar river. Ideal place for exploring Devon and Cornwall. R.A.C. Three Stars, A.A. Three Stars, A.N.W.B. Approved. E.T.B. Graded Four Ticks. A.A. Award for Environmental Excellance. Heated indoor swimming pool.

TAVISTOCK

Langstone Manor Camping & Caravan Park, Moortown, Tavistock, Devon PL19 9JZ.
Tel. Tavistock 613371 Std. 01822.
Nearest Town/Resort PLymouth.
Directions Take B3357 Princetown/Tavistock road for 1½ miles Langstone Manor signposted off to the right.
Acreage 2½ **Open** 15th March–15th Nov
Site Level
Sites available Total 40.
Facilities
Nearby facilities
Plymouth.
Ideal touring Devon and Cornwall.

TEDBURN ST MARY

Springfield Holiday Park, Tedburn St. Mary, Nr. Exeter, Devon, EX6 6EW.
Tel. 24242 Std. 01647
Nearest Town/Resort Exeter.
Directions From Exeter travel west on A30 from junction 31 of M5 (after 9 miles) take second turning on right signposted Tedburn St Mary, site is 400yds on left.
Acreage 9 **Open** 15th March–30th Oct
Access Good **Site** Terraced
Sites available Total 100.
Facilities
Nearby facilities
Exeter.
On the edge of Dartmoor, ideal for touring central Devon, superb views. 5 Tick and Rose Award Park. A.A. Campsite of the Year 1994, South West Region.

TEIGNMOUTH

Coast View Holiday Park, Torquay Road, Teignmouth, Shaldon, South Devon, TQ14 0BG.
Tel. 872392 Std. 01626
Nearest Town/Resort Teignmouth.
Directions Follow A38 from Exeter, take left fork A380 to Torquay. Proceed aloong A380 for about 6 miles taking the A381 towards Shaldon. Turn right at traffic lights, cross Shaldon bridge and follow main road. Camp is on the right hand side.
Acreage 17
Access Good **Site** Level
Sites available Total 100.
Facilities
Nearby facilities
Teignmouth.

Scenic views across the sea to the South Devon coastline, Devon coast. Ideal for touring.

TEIGNMOUTH

Wear Farm Caravan Site, E. S. Coaker & Co, Newton Road, Bishopsteignton, Nr. Teignmouth, Devon, TQ14 9PT.
Tel. 775249 Std. 01626
Nearest Town/Resort Teignmouth.
Directions Off the A380 take the A381 towards Teignmouth, Wear Farm can be found ¼ a mile on the right from the dual carriageway.
Acreage 5 **Open** Easter–October
Access Good **Site** Lev/Slope
Sites available Total 147.
Facilities
Nearby facilities
Newton Abbot.
Alongside a river, scenic views and ideal touring.

TEIGNMOUTH

Bishopsbrook Camping Park, Newton Road, Bishopsteignton, Teignmouth, Devon.
Tel. 775249 Std. 01626
Nearest Town/Resort Teignmouth.
Directions On A381 Newton Abbot to Teighnmouth Road.
Acreage 2½ **Open** Easter–October
Access Good **Site** Lev/Slope
Sites available Total 77.
Facilities
Nearby facilities
Newton Abbot.
Within walking distance of River Estuary and river beach. Area of outstanding natural beauty, fishing and board sailing nearby.

TIVERTON

West Middlewick Farm, Nomansland, Nr. Tiverton, Devon, EX16 8NP.
Tel. Tiverton 860286 Std. 01884
Nearest Town/Resort Tiverton.
Directions Take the old A373 (now the B3137) W.N.W.from Tiverton, farm is beside road one mile beyond Nomansland, on right (9 miles from Tiverton).
Acreage 3 **Open** All year
Access Good **Site** Level
Sites available Total 15.
Facilities
Nearby facilities
Tiverton Parkway.
Panoramic view towards Exmoor, quiet surroundings, children welcome. Genuine farm.

TIVERTON

Zeacombe House Caravan Park, Zeacombe House, East Anstey, Tiverton, Devon, EX16 9JU.
Tel. 341279 Std. 01398
Nearest Town/Resort Tiverton/South Molton.
Directions Junction 27 of the M5 take the A361 Barnstaple to South Molton road. Travel for 16 miles in a straight direction. Turn right signed Knowstone and travel road for 2¼ miles. Gates are on the left.
Acreage 4¼ **Open** 11 March–October
Access Good **Site** Level
Sites available Total 60.
Facilities
Nearby facilities
Tiverton.
Scenic views across Exmoor, ideal for touring. Flat, landscaped park with flowers, trees and shrubs.

TORQUAY

Widdicombe Farm Holiday Park, The Ring Road, Marldon, Torbay, Devon. TQ3 1ST.
Tel. 558325 Std. 01803.
Nearest Town/Resort Torquay.
Directions At the large roundabout at Newton Abbot, follow signs to Torquay at the next roundabout turn right into Hamlyn Way, straight on at third roundabout, look to right see Widdicombe Farm, continue onto next roundabout, turn back following directions back to Torquay. Widdicombe Farm is ¼ mile on left.
Acreage 10 **Open** Easter–Mid October
Access Good **Site** Level
Sites available Total 200.
Facilities
Nearby facilities
Torquay.
Easy access for caravanners, no narrow country lanes to negotiate. Quiet family run site, known for our hospitality and cleanliness. Lovely setting with scenic views, the nearest site to Torquay. Heated baby bathroom. 50 all weather sites. No discount given on Bargain Breaks or in high season.

TORRINGTON

Greenways Valley, Torrington, Devon. EX38 7EW.
Tel. Torrington 622153 Std. 01805
Nearest Town/Resort Torrington/Westward Ho!.
Directions Site is just one mile from Torrington town centre. Take B3227 (to South Molton) turn right into Borough Road then 3rd left to site entrance.
Acreage 8 **Open** Mid March–October
Access Good **Site** Level
Sites available Total 10.
Facilities
Nearby facilities
Barnstaple.
Peaceful well tended site with a southerly aspect overlooking a beautiful wooded valley, ideal base for touring North Devon. E.T.B. Graded Four Ticks. Tennis on park. You can FAX us on 01805 622320.

TORRINGTON

Smytham Manor Holidays, Smytham Manor, Little Torrington, Devon EX38 8PU.
Tel. 22110 Std. 01805
Nearest Town/Resort Westward Ho!.
Directions 2 miles south Torrington on A386 to Okehampton.
Acreage 15 **Open** Mid March–October
Access Good **Site** Level
Sites available Total 30.
Facilities
Nearby facilities
Barnstaple.
Attractive landscaped grounds, close to moors and beach. Good base for exploring Devon.

TOTNES

Edeswell Farm Country Caravan Park, Edeswell Farm, Rattery, South Brent Devon TQ10 9LN.
Tel. 72177 Std. 01364
Nearest Town/Resort Torbay.
Directions Fron Exeter follow the A38 approx 22 miles ignore Rattery signs leave at Marley Head Junction signposted Paignton, Totnes A358. Site ½ mile on right.
Acreage 6 **Open** March–October
Access Good **Site** Terraced
Sites available Total 46.
Facilities
Nearby facilities
Totnes.
Dartmoor, country site for quiet family holidays but with all facilities. Indoor heated swimming pool.

WATERMOUTH

Watermouth Cove Holiday Park, Berrynarbor, Nr. Ilfracombe, Devon.
Tel. 862504 Std. 01271
Nearest Town/Resort Ilfracombe.
Directions From Ilfracombe, 2 miles on the A399 Coombe Martin road.
Acreage 5 **Open** April–October
Access Good **Site** Level
Sites available Total 90.
Facilities
Nearby facilities
Barnstaple.
Private sandy coves, headland walks, beautiful coastal views.

WINKLEIGH

Wagon Wheels Holiday Village, Winkleigh, Devon. EX19 8DP.
Tel. 83456 Std. 01837
Nearest Town/Resort Okehampton.
Directions On B3220 Crediton to Torrington Road, 1 mile north of the village of Winkleigh.
Acreage 1 **Open** 15th March–October
Access Good **Site** Level
Sites available Total 20.
Facilities
Nearby facilities
Eggesford.
Scenic views of Dartmoor.

WOOLACOMBE

Twitchen Park, Mortehoe, Woolacombe, North Devon, EX34 7ES.
Tel. 870476 Std. 01271
Nearest Town/Resort Woolacombe.
Directions From Barnstaple/Ilfracombe road (A361) to junction with B3343 at Mullacott Cross, first left signposted Woolacombe for 1¾ miles, then right signposted Mortehoe. Park is 1¼ miles on left.
Acreage 20 **Open** April–October
Access Good **Site** Sloping
Sites available Total 131.
Facilities
Nearby facilities
Barnstaple.
Rural, scenic setting, close to Woolacombe's glorious sandy beach and spectacular coastal walks.

WOOLACOMBE

Europa Holiday Village, Station Road, Woolacombe, Devon.
Tel. 870159 Std. 01271
Nearest Town/Resort Woolacombe.
Directions Less than a mile from and above Woolacombe on the right hand side of the main road leading into the resort.
Acreage 11 **Open** Easter–October
Access Good **Site** Lev/slope
Sites available Total 100.
Facilities
Nearby facilities
Barnstaple.
Panoramic views of surrounding countryside and Woolacombe Bay. Quietly situated informal site where well behaved animals (and children!) are welcome.

WOOLACOMBE

Woolacombe Sands Holiday Park, Station Road, Woolacombe, North Devon. EX34 7AF.
Tel. 870569 Std. 01271
Nearest Town/Resort Barnstaple/Ilfracombe.
Directions On the B3343 from Mullacott Cross.
Acreage 10 **Open** Easter–September
Access Good **Site** Lev/Slope
Sites available Total 250.
Facilities
Nearby facilities
Barnstaple.
Near beach, scenic views. Bar snacks and take-away food. Nightly entertainment late May to early September.

WOOLACOMBE

Woolacombe Bay Holiday Village, Sandy Lane, Woolacombe, Devon, EX34 7AH.
Tel. 870221 Std. 01271
Nearest Town/Resort Woolacombe/Ilfracombe.
Directions A361 from Barnstaple, left at roundabout (Mullacott Cross). After 3 miles take right turn to Mortehoe, site is ½ mile on the left.
Acreage 11 **Open** May–September
Site Sloping
Sites available Total 200.
Facilities
Nearby facilities
Barnstaple.
Situated in an unspoilt area of West Country amidst glorious National Trust Hills and breathtaking views of Woolacombe Bay. ¾ mile from beach.

DORSET

BERE REGIS

Rowlands Wait Touring Park, Rye Hill, Bere Regis, Dorset, BH20 7HH.
Tel. 471958 Std. 01929
Nearest Town/Resort Wareham.
Directions Turn left off A35 (Bournemouth/Dorchester) in Bere Regis onto unclassified road signposted Wool/Bovington Camp. After ¾ mile turn right site 300 yards along lane.
Acreage 8 **Open** Easter–October
Access Good **Site** Lev/Slope
Sites available Total 71.
Facilities
Nearby facilities
Wool.
Situated in area of outstanding natural beauty. Within easy reach of coast, direct access from site into heath and woodland. Ideal walking and touring.

BLANDFORD

The Inside Park, Blandford, Dorset. DT11 0HG.
Tel. 453719 Std. 01258
Nearest Town/Resort Blandford Forum.
Directions 1¼ miles south west of Blandford on the road to Winterborne Stickland. Signposted from junction of A350 and A354 on Blandford bypass.
Acreage 13 **Open** Easter–October
Access Good **Site** Lev/Slope
Sites available Total 100.
Facilities
Nearby facilities
Rural environment, ideal for touring, extensive wildlife.

BRIDPORT

Binghams Farm Touring Caravan Park, Binghams Farm, Melplash, Bridport, Dorset, DT6 3TT.
Tel. 488234 Std. 01308
Nearest Town/Resort West Bay/Bridport.
Directions Turn off A35 in Bridport at the roundabout onto A3066, signposted Beaminster. In 1¼ miles turn left into Farm Road.
Acreage 3 **Open** All Year
Access Good **Site** Level
Sites available Total 40.
Facilities
Nearby facilities
Dorchester.
Scenic views, ideal for touring Dorset yet only 3 miles from the coast. In beautiful countryside. This new Award winning park only opened in 1993.

BRIDPORT

Coastal Caravans, Annings Lane, Burton Bradstock, Dorset.
Tel. 897361 Std. 01308
Nearest Town/Resort Bridport.
Directions 3 miles east of Bridport off main Weymouth road, Burton Bradstock Anchor Hotel turn left and the second right.
Acreage 5 **Open** Easter–October
Access Good **Site** Level
Sites available Total 75.
Facilities
Nearby facilities
Dorchester.
1 mile beach, river frontage, scenic views, ideal centre for touring Dorset, Devon and Hampshire.

BRIDPORT

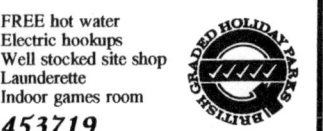

Freshwater Holiday Park, Burton Bradstock, Bridport, Dorset.
Tel. 897317 Std. 01308
Nearest Town/Resort Bridport.
Directions From Bridport take B3157 towards Weymouth site 2 miles on right.
Acreage 40 **Open** Easter–October
Access Good **Site** Level
Sites available Total 500.
Facilities

Nearby facilities
Dorchester.
On beach, cliff walks, golf course adjoining site.

BRIDPORT

Highlands End Farm Holiday Park, Eype, Bridport, Dorset,DT6 6AR.
Tel. Bridport 422139 Std. 01308.
Nearest Town/Resort Bridport.
Directions On approach to Bridport from east (Dorchester) on A35 turn left at roundabout, follow Bridport By-pass. Second roundabout take third exit signposted A35 west 1 mile turn left to Eype and follow signposts.
Acreage 8 **Open** March–October
Access Good **Site** Level
Sites available Total 120.
Facilities
Nearby facilities
Axminsterr.
Exceptional views across Lyme Bay, 500 metres from the beach, indoor heated swimming pool. Hard standing with all weather awning area. British Graded Park – Excellent.

BRIDPORT

West Bay Holiday Park, West Bay, Bridport, Dorset, DT6 4HB.
Tel. 22424 Std. 01308
Nearest Town/Resort Weymouth.
Directions A35 from Dorchester. West Bay is towards the harbour.
Open Easter–End Oct
Access Good **Site** Level
Sites available Total 150.
Facilities
Nearby facilities
Weymouth.
Riverside, next to the harbour. Indoor swimming pool.

BRIDPORT

Uploders Farm, Uploders, Bridport, Dorset, DT6 4NZ.
Tel. 423380 Std. 01308
Nearest Town/Resort Bridport.
Directions A35 3 miles east of Bridport. Just off main road.
Acreage 2 **Open** April–October
Access Good **Site** Level
Sites available Total 25.
Facilities
Nearby facilities
Dorchester.
Beach 4 miles, ideal touring area. Lovely countryside.

CHARMOUTH

Manor Farm Holiday Centre, Manor Farm, Charmouth, Bridport, Dorset DT6 6QL.
Tel. Charmouth 560226 Std. 01297
Nearest Town/Resort Charmouth.
Directions Come off the Charmouth bypass at east end Manor Farm is ¾ mile on right, in Charmouth.
Acreage 30 **Open** All year
Access Good **Site** Lev/Slope
Sites available Total 345.
Facilities
Nearby facilities
Axminster.
Ten minutes level walk to beach, alongside river. in area of outstanding natural beauty. Ideal touring.

CHARMOUTH

Monkton Wylde Farm Caravan Park, Charmouth, Dorset, DT6 6DB.
Tel. 34525 Std. 01297
Nearest Town/Resort Charmouth.
Directions A35 west from Charmouth. At Greenway Head tak B3165 to Marshwood site ½ mile down lane on left.
Acreage 6 **Open** Easter–October
Access Good **Site** Level
Sites available Total 60.
Facilities
Nearby facilities
Axminster.
3 miles from sea. Surrounded by woods and fields, on working farm. Quiet site.

CHARMOUTH

Newlands Caravan Park, Charmouth, Dorset, DT6 6RB.
Tel. 560259 Std. 01297
Nearest Town/Resort Lyme Regis.
Directions From Eastern end of Charmouth by-pass (A35), turn toward Charmouth Village. Site is 100yds on the left hand side.
Acreage 8 **Open** 16 March–October
Access Good **Site** Level
Sites available Total 200.
Facilities
Nearby facilities
Axminster.
150yds from beach.

CHARMOUTH

Wood Farm Caravan & Camping Park, Axminster Road, Charmouth, Bridport, Dorset DT6 6BT.
Tel. Charmouth 560697 Std. 01297.
Nearest Town/Resort Charmouth.
Directions On A35, ½ mile west Charmouth.
Acreage 12
Access Good **Site** Terraced
Sites available Total 216.
Facilities
Nearby facilities
Axminster.
Beach ¾ mile. Country setting. Tennis on site. Indoor heated swimming pool.

NEWLANDS HOLIDAYS
CHARMOUTH
DORSET DT6 6RB

01297
560259

Level sites with super views for tents, tourers, motorhomes, etc.
Some 100 metres from beach. 2 Swimming Pools, Club Shop,
Entertainment, Take-away, Electric Hook-up.
Prices per pitch. No extra charge for people.
FREE COLOUR BROCHURE

Coastal Caravans

Annings Lane, Burton Bradstock,Dorset DT6 4QP

Private, family owned, level Touring Caravan and Camping Park offering peace and seclusion in beautiful Dorset countryside, five minutes from beaches. Modern toilet and shower facilities with free hot water and electricity for shaver and power points. Electric hook-ups. Dogs permitted by arrrangement. Golf, fishing and boating can all be enjoyed within a short distance of the Park. We also have luxury caravans connected to all services for sale or hire.

Write or telephone for brochure:-

(01308) 897361

MANOR FARM HOLIDAY CENTRE

Charmouth, Bridport, Dorset DT6 6QL
Tel: Charmouth (01297) 560226

Modern Facilities including: ★ Electric hook-ups ★ Flush toilets ★ Showers ★ Hair dryers ★ Shaving points ★ Well stocked shop including off licence ★ Coinamatic launderette including ironing facilities ★ Deep sinks for dishes ★ Licensed Bar and family room ★ Telephone Kiosk ★ Children's play area ★ SWIMMING POOL & CHILDREN'S POOL.

Hire one of our Houses, Bungalow or Luxury Caravans or bring your own tent, touring caravan or motor caravan for a restful holiday.

We are close to main A35 and only 10 minutes level walk from beach at Charmouth.

S.A.E. for Brochure to G. Loosmore

CHIDEOCK

Golden Cap Holiday Park, Seatown, Chideock, Nr. Bridport, Dorset.
Tel. 422139 Std. 01308
Nearest Town/Resort Bridport.
Directions On approach to Bridport from east (Dorchester) follow A35 signs around Bridport by-pass. After 2 miles west of Bridport turn left for Seatown, at Chideock park is signposted.
Acreage 10 **Open** March–October
Access Good **Site** Level
Sites available Total 150.
Facilities
Axminster.
100 metres from beach, overlooked by the famous Golden Cap cliff top. Indoor swimming pool available 5 minutes travelling time. Hard standings with all weather awning areas. British Graded Park – very good. Take-away food available.

CHRISTCHURCH

Grove Farm Meadow Holiday Park, Stour Way, Christchurch, Dorset, BH23 2PQ.
Tel. 483597 Std. 01202
Nearest Town/Resort Christchurch.
Directions From Christchurch take the A35 west for 1¼ miles. Turn right at the roundabout near Crooked Bean Restaurant into The Grove. Stour Way is second on the left. Park is at extreme end of Stour Way (signposted).
Acreage 3 **Open** March–October
Access Good **Site** Level
Sites available Total 48.
Facilities
Nearby facilities
Christchurch.
On banks of River Stour. Ideal touring base for Bournemouth, New Forest, Dorset coast and heritage. Tourist Board and Rose Award graded excellent.

CHRISTCHURCH

Longfield Caravan Park, Longfield, Matchams Lane, Hurn, Christchurch, Dorset, BH23 6AW.
Tel. 485214 Std. 01202
Acreage 2¼ **Open** All Year
Access Good **Site** Level
Sites available Total 20.
Facilities
Nearby facilities
Christchurch.
Tents are accepted off peak only.

CHRISTCHURCH

Hoburne Park, Hoburne Lane, Christchurch, Dorset, BH23 4HU.
Tel. 273379 Std. 01425
Nearest Town/Resort Christchurch.
Directions From junction of A35 with A337 at Christchurch, take first exit left onto A337 towards Lymington and then left off next roundabout. Park entrance is 100yds on right.
Acreage 17 **Open** March–October
Access Good **Site** Level
Sites available Total 285.
Facilities
Nearby facilities
Christchurch.
Approx 8 miles from Bournemouth, close to sandy beaches, the New Forest, the Solent and the Isle of Wight.

CHRISTCHURCH

Mount Pleasant Touring Park, Matchams Lane, Hurn, Christchurch, Dorset, BH23 6AW.
Tel. 475474 Std. 01202
Nearest Town/Resort Christchurch.
Directions From Ringwood take A338. At 5 miles take Christchurch exit, at the end of the exit road turn right towards Hurn. At first roundabout take the second exit into Matchams Lane. We are ¾ mile on the right (signposted).
Acreage 7 **Open** March–October
Access Good **Site** Lev/Slope
Sites available Total 170.
Facilities
Nearby facilities
Christchurch.
Nearest camping park to Bournemouth. Lovely forestry setting. English Tourist Board graded Excellent.

CORFE CASTLE

The Woodland Camping Park, Glebe Farm, Bucknowle, Wareham, Dorset, BH20 5NS.
Tel. 480280 Std. 01929
Nearest Town/Resort Swanage/Wareham.
Directions Take Church Knowle and Kimmeridge road off A351 at Corfe Castle ruins site ¾ mile on right.
Acreage 6½ **Open** Easter–October
Site Lev/Slope
Sites available Total 65.
Facilities
Nearby facilities
Direct access onto Purbeck Hills by public footpath, own riding stable. 3 beaches within 5 miles. A quiet family site. SAE for full info.

DORCHESTER

Giants Head Caravan & Camping Park, Old Sherborne Road, Dorchester, Dorset.
Tel. 341242 Std. 01300
Nearest Town/Resort Dorchester.
Directions From Dorchester avoiding bypass, at top of town roundabout take Sherborne Road approx 500 yards fork right at Loaders Garage signposted.
Acreage 3 **Open** March–October
Access Good **Site** Lev/Slope
Sites available Total 50.
Facilities
Nearby facilities
Dorchester.
Ideal touring, wonderful views, good walking. Car is essential. Licensed.

DORCHESTER

Warmwell Country Touring Park, Warmwell, Nr. Dorchester, Dorset, DT2 8JE.
Tel. 852313 Std. 01305
Nearest Town/Resort Weymouth.
Directions From A31 Dorchester to Poole road take the B3390 signposted Warmwell.
Acreage 15 **Open** All Year
Access Good **Site** Level
Sites available Total 190.

Facilities
Nearby facilities
Moreton.
Opposite major leisure attractions.

FERNDOWN

St. Leonards Farm, Ringwood Road, West Moors, Ferndown, Dorset.
Tel. 872637 Std. 01202
Nearest Town/Resort Bournemouth.
Directions 5 miles west of Ringwood on the A31 opposite Gulf Garage.
Acreage 8 **Open** April–September
Access Good **Site** Level
Sites available Total 150.
Facilities
Nearby facilities
Bournemouth.
Pleasant rural style park. Central for Bournemouth, Poole and the New Forest.

LYME REGIS

Cannington Farm Campsite, Cannington Farm, Uplyme, Lyme Regis, Dorset, DT7 3SW.
Tel. 443172 Std. 01297
Nearest Town/Resort Lyme Regis.
Acreage 4¼ **Open** March–October
Access Good/Poor **Site** Level
Sites available Total 30.
Facilities
Nearby facilities
Axminster.
Near the beach with scenic views and ideal touring.

LYME REGIS

Westhayes Caravan Park, Rousdon, Nr. Lyme Regis, Dorset, DT7 3RD.
Tel. Seaton 23456 Std. 01297.
Nearest Town/Resort Lyme Regis/ Seaton.
Directions Leave Axminster on A358 Seaton road, 3 miles turn left at Boshill Cross signposted Lyme Regis, site 1 mile on left.
Acreage 7½ **Open** All year
Access Good **Site** Level
Sites available Total 150.
Facilities
Nearby facilities
Axminster.
Take away/bar meals. Tents during August only. Rallies welcome. Storage facilities. Static caravans for sale.

MORETON

Moreton Glade Touring Park, Station Road, Moreton, Near Dorchester, Dorset.
Tel. 853801 Std. 01305
Nearest Town/Resort Dorchester.
Directions East of the B3390 (Bere Regis to Wemouth road). From Dorchester take the A352 to Warmwell, then the B3390 north of the level crossing at crossways.
Acreage 7 **Open** 16 March–5 January
Access Good **Site** Level
Sites available Total 140.
Facilities
Nearby facilities
10 miles from beach, Warmwell Leisure Centre 1 mile with indoor swimming pool, flume, wave machine, roller rink and soft play area. Multi gym, table tennis, bowls and a dry ski slope. Restaurant/cafe next door.

OWERMOIGNE

Sandyholme Holiday Park, Moreton Road, Owermoigne, Nr. Dorchester, Dorset, DT2 8HZ.
Tel. 852677 Std. 01305
Nearest Town/Resort Dorchester/ Weymouth.
Directions Situated off the A352 Dorchester/Wareham Road – 1 mile through pretty village of Owermoigne.
Acreage 6 **Open** Easter–October
Access Good **Site** Level
Sites available Total 65.
Facilities
Nearby facilities
Moreton.
Quiet family site in Hardy countryside, ideal touring spot with all facilities, situated between Lulworth Cove and Weymouth. Swimming pool nearby.

POOLE

Beacon Hill Touring Park, Blandford Road North, Poole, Dorset, BH16 6AB.
Tel. 631631 Std. 01202
Nearest Town/Resort Poole/ Bournemouth.
Directions Situated ½ mile north from the junction of the A35 and A350 towards Blandford approx 3 miles north of Poole.
Acreage 30 **Open** Easter–September
Access Good **Site** level
Sites available Total 170.
Facilities
Nearby facilities
Poole.
Partly wooded, lovely peaceful setting, scenic views. Proximity main routes. Ideal touring base for Bournemouth, New Forest and Dorset. Coarse fishing and tennis on site. Take away meals.

POOLE

Huntick Farm Caravans, Lytchett Matravers, Poole, Dorset.
Tel. 622222 Std. 01202
Nearest Town/Resort Poole.
Directions Off the A350 Blandford to Poole road. Take the turning to Lytchett Matravers and at the Rose & Crown Public House turn down Huntick Road. The site is ¾ mile on the right.
Acreage 3 **Open** Easter–September
Access Good **Site** Level
Sites available Total 30.
Facilities
Nearby facilities
Poole.
A small, quiet site of grass with wooded surroundings. Convenient for ferries from Poole.

POOLE

Organford Manor Caravans and Holidays, Organford, Poole, Dorset, BH16 6ES.
Tel. 622202 Std. 01202
Nearest Town/Resort Poole.
Directions Approaching from the Poole direction on the A35. At the Lytchett roundabout/junction of the A35/A351 continue on the A35 (signposted Dorchester) for ¼ mile. Take the first left, site first entrance on right.
Acreage 3 **Open** 15 March–October
Access Good **Site** Level
Sites available Total 80.
Facilities

Nearby facilities
Poole/Wareham.
Quiet, secluded site in wooded grounds of 11 acres. House within 10 miles of good beaches from Bournemouth to Swanage. Facilities for the disabled limited, few motorcycles accepted at Proprietors discretion.

POOLE

Pear Tree Farm Caravan & Camping Park, Organford, Poole, Dorset, BH16 6LA.
Tel. 622434 Std. 01202
Nearest Town/Resort Poole.
Directions Take A35 Poole/Dorchester road. Turn onto A351 to Wareham at Lytchett Minster. Turn right within 1 mile signposted Organford. Second site on lefthand side ¼ mile.
Acreage 7½ **Open** April–October
Access Good **Site** Level
Sites available Total 105.
Facilities
Nearby facilities
Wareham.
Quiet, country park, centrally situated for Bournemouth, Poole and Swanage. The New Forest, the Purbeck Hills and the lovely sandy beaches at Sandbanks and Studland Bay are all within easy reach.

POOLE

Merley Court Touring Park, Merley, Wimborne, Nr Poole, Dorset, BH21 3AA.
Tel. 881488 Std. 01202
Nearest Town/Resort Poole.
Directions Direct access from Wimborne bypass south A31 junction A349 Poole road.
Acreage 11 **Open** March–Jan 7th
Access Good **Site** Level
Sites available Total 160.
Facilities
Nearby facilities
Poole.
Bournemouth 8 miles, Poole 4 miles, Purbeck and New Forest 7 miles. A.A. 4 pennant park, R.A.C. appointed, English Tourist Board Caravan Holiday Park of the Year 1991 (Grading "Excellent"). Practical Caravan Magazines "Best Family Park" 1993.

POOLE

Sandford Park, Holton Heath, Poole, Dorset, BH16 6JZ.
Tel. 622513 Std. 01202.
Nearest Town/Resort Poole.
Directions On A351, 8 miles from Poole, 3 miles from Wareham.
Acreage 20 **Open** 31 March–28 October
Access Good **Site** Level
Sites available Total 525.
Facilities
Nearby facilities
Wareham.

POOLE

South Lytchett Manor Caravan Site, Dorchester Road, Lytchett Minster, Poole Dorset. BH16 6JB.
Tel. 622577 Std. 01202
Nearest Town/Resort Poole.
Directions On B3067.
Acreage 10 **Open** April–15 October
Access Good **Site** Level
Sites available Total 150.
Facilities
Nearby facilities
Poole.
Ideal touring.

ST. LEONARDS

Village Holidays, Oakdene Holiday Park, St. Leonards, Ringwood, Dorset.
Tel. 875422 Std. 01202
Nearest Town/Resort Bournemouth.
Directions 3 miles west of Ringwood on A31.
Acreage 55 **Open** 1st Feb–31st Dec
Access Good **Site** Lev/Slope
Sites available Total 435.
Facilities
Nearby facilities
Bournemouth.
Forest walk adjacent to river. Easy access to New Forest and Bournemouth. Late season weekend breaks.

ST. LEONARDS

Oak Hill Camping Site, 234 Ringwood Road, St. Leonards, Ringwood, Dorset.
Tel. 876968 Std. 01202
Nearest Town/Resort Ringwood/Bournemouth.
Directions 3¼ miles west of Ringwood on A31. Opposite Boundary Lane.
Acreage 10 **Open** Easter–October
Access Good **Site** Level
Sites available Total 100.
Facilities
Nearby facilities
Bournemouth.
East access to New Forest and Bournemouth.

ST. LEONARDS

Camping International, 229 Ringwood Road, St. Leonards, Nr. Ringwood, Dorset, BH24 2SD.
Tel. 872817 Std. 01202
Nearest Town/Resort Bournemouth.
Directions 2¼ miles west of Ringwood on A31.
Acreage 8 **Open** March–October
Access Good **Site** Level

Camping International

The New Forest with its quaint villages set in unspoilt open country and full of wild life. Bournemouth with its shops and entertainments. Dorset & Hants coast and country. 60+ places of interest to visit in good or bad weather.

STATISTICALLY THE BEST WEATHER IN THE U.K.

Enjoy all this whilst staying at one of the most popular parks in the area. Designed for the more discerning camper/caravanner who demands superior continental standards along with all of the facilities.

CAMPING INTERNATIONAL HOLIDAY PARK
229 Ringwood Rd., St. Leonard's, Ringwood, Hants BH24 2SD
Telephone: (01202) 872817 Fax: (01202) 861292

BIG, BEAUTIFUL 55 ACRE PARK
2 HEATED INDOOR & OUTDOOR SWIMMING POOLS
CHILDREN'S ADVENTURE PLAYGROUND
ENTERTAINMENTS
BMX TRACK
LICENSED CLUBHOUSE
TEEN'S DISCO
SOLARIUM
MINI GYM & SAUNA
CRAZY GOLF
HORSE RIDING
PONY TREKKING
STABLES
BIKE HIRE
FISHING NEARBY
FOREST WALKS
LAUNDERETTE
GENERAL STORE
BARBECUE
CAFETERIA & TAKEAWAY
PRE-BOOKABLE TOURING & TENT PITCHES
SERVICE PLOTS WITH PLUG-IN MAINS ELECTRIC & WATER
ALSO STATIC HOLIDAY HOMES FOR SALE, ASK FOR DETAILS

A HOLIDAY FOR ALL THE FAMILY

It's not easy finding a holiday all the family will love, whatever their age, whatever their interests... so relax, you've just found it! A Village Holiday offers all-weather fun, excitement and well earned relaxation for mum, dad and the kids–even gran and grandpa! This 55 acre, well equipped caravan /camping park is positioned in beautiful forest surroundings only 8 miles from Bournemouth.

£100 FREE
ENTERTAINMENT VOUCHERS with each 7 day holiday booking

Village Holidays at Oakdene

(SOME FACILITIES ONLY AVAILABLE AT PEAK TIMES)

I enclose S.A.E. for full details ☐ off-peak bargains ☐ Please tick

Name ____________________

Address ____________________

Village Holidays at Oakdene Holiday Park, Dept CTM95, St. Leonards, Ringwood, Hants BH24 2RZ. 24 hr Tele-brochure service: 01202 875422

Sites available Total 205.
Facilities
Nearby facilities
Bournemouth.
New Forest, Bournemouth and coast, ideal touring. You can FAX us on 01202 861292.

ST. LEONARDS

Shamba Holiday Park, 230 Ringwood Road, St. Leonards, Ringwood, Dorset, BH24 2SB.
Tel. 873302 Std. 01202.
Nearest Town/Resort Ringwood.
Directions Just off the A31 midway between Ringwood and Wimborne.
Acreage 5¼ **Open** March–October
Access Good **Site** Level
Sites available Total 150.
Facilities
Nearby facilities
Bournemouth.
Close to the New Forest and Bournemouth.

SHAFTSBURY

Blackmore Vale Filling Station, Sherborne Causway, Shaftsbury, Dorset.
Tel. 852573 Std. 01747
Nearest Town/Resort Shaftsbury.
Open All year
Access Good **Site** Level
Sites available Total 50.
Facilities
Gillingham.
Scenic views, ideal touring.

SWANAGE

"Haycrafts" Caravan & Camping Park, Haycrofts Lane, Harmans Cross, Nr. Swanage, Dorset, BH19 3EB.
Tel. 480572 Std. 01902
Nearest Town/Resort Swanage.
Directions From A351 (Corfe Castle/ Swanage road) turn right opposite Harmans Cross Post Office/general store into Haycrafts Lane. Proceed beyond the village hall on the right and site is a further ½ mile on the left.
Acreage 5 **Open** Easter–September
Access Good **Site** Lev/Slope
Sites available Total 50.
Facilities
Nearby facilities
Small, quality park, immaculately kept, in an area of outstanding natural beauty. Families and couples only. Ideal for walking, cycling and touring. Convenient for Studland beaches. Steam Railway halt 5 minutes walk. ETB Graded 5 Ticks Excellent.

SWANAGE

Sunnydown Farm, Gallows Gore, Langton Matravers, Swanage, Dorset. BH19 8JQ.
Tel. 439385 Std. 01929
Nearest Town/Resort Swanage.
Directions Outside village of Corfe Castle take turning to Langton Matravers Keep to main road until you see sign Sunnydown Farm.
Acreage 5 **Open** End July–End August
Access Good **Site** Lev/Slope
Sites available Total 50.
Facilities
Nearby facilities
Wareham.
Scenic views. Also open Whitsun weekend. Dinosaur Trackway on site. Open days in August. Site belonging to caravan and camping club.

SWANAGE

Tom's Field Camping Site, Tom's Field Road, Langton Matravers, Nr. Swanage, Dorset.
Nearest Town/Resort Swanage.
Acreage 4 **Open** Easter–October
Site Lev/Slope
Sites available Total 100.
Facilities
Nearby facilities
Wareham.
Under new management. The camp has a variety of fields and is well positioned amidst the Purbeck Hills in an area of outstanding natural beauty. Swanage, Corfe Castle and Studland all within easy reach. Access to coastal walk close by.

SWANAGE

Ulwell Cottage Caravan Park, Ulwell, Swanage, Dorset, BH19 3DG.
Tel. 422823 Std. 01929
Nearest Town/Resort Swanage.
Directions 1¼ miles from Swanage on Studland Road. Turn left by telephone box (left hand side) on side of road.
Open April–October
Access Good **Site** Lev/Slope
Sites available Total 70.
Facilities
Nearby facilities
Wareham.
Near sandy beaches, scenic walks and ideal for all water sports.

WAREHAM

Birchwood Tourist Park, North Trigon, Wareham, Dorset, BH20 4DD.
Tel. 554763 Std. 01929
Nearest Town/Resort Wareham.

Directions From Bere Regis follow the A35 towards Poole. After approx 1 mile fork right to Wareham. Birchwood Park is the second park on the right after approx 2 miles.
Acreage 25 **Open** March–October
Access Good **Site** Level
Sites available Total 175.
Facilities
Nearby facilities
Wareham.
Situated in Wareham Forest with direct access to forest walks. Ideal for touring the whole of Dorset.

WAREHAM

Lookout Holiday Park, Stoborough, Wareham, Dorset, BH20 5AZ.
Tel. 552546 Std. 01929
Nearest Town/Resort Wareham.
Directions 1½ miles from Wareham on the A351 to Swanage.
Acreage 15 **Open** April–October
Access Good **Site** Level
Sites available Total 150.
Facilities
Nearby facilities
Wareham.
Ideal location for touring the Purbeck Hills.

WAREHAM

Manor Farm Caravan Park, 1 Manor Farm Cottage, East Stoke, Wareham, Dorset, BH20 6AW.
Tel. Bindon Abbey 462870 Std. 01929.
Nearest Town/Resort Wareham/ Lulworth Cove.
Directions From Wareham take the A352, turn left onto the B3070. At the first crossroads signposted East Stoke turn right. Next crossroads signposted Manor Farm turn right. Park is 300yds on the left.
Acreage 2½ **Open** Easter–September
Access Good **Site** Level
Sites available Total 40.
Facilities
Nearby facilities
Wool/Wareham.
Flat, grass touring park on a working farm in a rural area of outstanding natural beauty, central for most of Dorset. Family run park with clean facilities. Resident Proprietors David & Gillian Topp. A.A. 3 Pennant, RAC Appointed and A.A. Environment Award 1994. No groups or singles.

WAREHAM

Whitemead Caravan Park, Eastburton Road, Wool, Dorset BH20 6HG.
Tel. Bindon Abbey 462241 Std. 01929
Nearest Town/Resort Wareham.
Directions 5 miles west of Wareham A352.
Acreage 5 **Open** April–October
Access Good **Site** Lev/Slope
Sites available Total 90.
Facilities
Nearby facilities
Wool.
In picturesque river valley but flood free. Excellent centre for coast, beaches and touring of beautiful 'Hardy' countryside. Noted for cleanliness and friendliness.

WEYMOUTH

Bagwell Farm Touring Park, Bagwell Farm, Chickerell, Weymouth, Dorset.
Tel. Weymouth 782575 Std. 01305.
Nearest Town/Resort Weymouth.
Directions 4 miles from Weymouth, take the Bridport road, site entrance 500 yards past Victoria Inn on B3157.
Acreage 14 **Open** March–November
Access Good **Site** Lev/Slope
Sites available Total 320.
Facilities
Nearby facilities
Weymouth.

WEYMOUTH

East Fleet Farm Touring Park, Fleet Lane, Chickerell, Weymouth, Dorset, DT3 4DW.
Tel. 785768 Std. 01305
Nearest Town/Resort Weymouth.
Directions 3 miles west of Weymouth on the B3157, left at Chickerell T.A. Camp.
Acreage 20 **Open** 16 March–15 Jan
Access Good **Site** Lev/Slope
Sites available Total 210.
Facilities
Nearby facilities
Weymouth.
On edge of Fleet Water. Area of outstanding natural beauty.

WEYMOUTH

Littlesea Holiday Park, Lynch Lane, Weymouth, Dorset, DT4 9DT.
Tel. 774414 Std. 01305
Nearest Town/Resort Weymouth.
Directions From the outskirts of Weymouth turn right at the first and second roundabouts signposted Portland. At the third roundabout turn left signposted Chickerell, Portland. Go straight across the traffic lights and turn left into Lynch Lane. The Park is at the far end.
Acreage 11 **Open** 26 March–29 October
Site Lev/Slope
Sites available Total 265.
Facilities
Nearby facilities
Weymouth.
Pleasantly set on the sides of a small valley, overlooking The Fleet and Chesil Bank.

WEYMOUTH

Osmington Mills Holidays Ltd, The Ranch House, Osmington Mills, Weymouth, Dorset. DT3 6HB.
Tel. 832311 Std. 01305

Nearest Town/Resort Weymouth.
Directions From the east on the A353 turn left to Osmington Mills 4 miles before Weymouth.
Acreage 12 **Open** Easter–October
Access Good **Site** Sloping
Sites available Total 255.
Facilities
Nearby facilities
Weymouth.
Beautiful situation on Dorset Heritage coast, sea views, rocky beach within walking distance, horse riding and fishing available on the park.

WEYMOUTH
Portesham Dairy Farm Camp Site, Bramdon Lane, Portesham, Weymouth, Dorset, DT3 4HG.
Tel. 871297 Std. 01305
Nearest Town/Resort Weymouth.
Directions 7 miles from Weymouth on B3157 Coast road.
Acreage 3 **Open** 16th Mar–31st October
Access Good **Site** Level
Sites available Total 60.
Facilities
Nearby facilities
Weymouth.
Ideal touring for Chesil area.

WEYMOUTH
Pebble Bank Caravan Park, 90 Camp Road, Wyke Regis, Weymouth, Dorset, DT4 9HF.
Tel. 774844 Std. 01305
Nearest Town/Resort Weymouth.
Directions From harbour roundabout up Boot Hill, turn right at mini roundabout opposite Rodwell Public House onto Wyke Road. Camp Road is 1 mile on the left at the bottom of the hill on apex of sharp right hand bend.
Open April–Early Oct
Access Good **Site** Lev/Slope
Sites available Total 80.
Facilities
Nearby facilities
Good sea views, close to resort centre.

WEYMOUTH
Sea Barn Farm Camping Site, Sea Barn Farm, Fleet, Weymouth, Dorset DT3 4ED.
Tel. 782218 Std. 01305
Nearest Town/Resort Weymouth.
Directions From Weymouth take the B3157, turn left at mini roundabout and sign to Fleet. After 1 mile, turn left to Sea Barn Farm.
Acreage 11 **Open** Easter–October
Site Level
Sites available Total 250.
Facilities
Nearby facilities
Weymouth.
Scenic views over coast and countryside, yet close to Weymouth. Quiet family site. Free membership of West Fleet Holiday Farm Clubhouse. Dog exercise area. Hot water dish washing facilities.

WEYMOUTH
Seaview Holiday Park, Preston, Weymouth, Dorset, DT3 6DZ.
Tel. 833037 Std. 01305
Nearest Town/Resort Weymouth.
Directions Take the A353 from the centre of Weymouth, along the seawall to Preston. Seaview is ½ mile beyond the village, up the hill on the right.
Open Easter–October
Site Sloping
Sites available
Facilities
Nearby facilities
Weymouth.
Nestles on a hillside looking out over the charming Bowleaze Cove.

WEYMOUTH
West Fleet Holiday Farm, Fleet, Weymouth, Dorset. DT3 4EF.
Tel. 782218 Std. 01305
Nearest Town/Resort Weymouth.
Directions From Weymouth take the B3157 4 miles from Weymouth turn left at miniroundabout and sign to Fleet and Moonfleet Manor Hotel, after 1 mile right to West Fleet holiday Farm.
Acreage 11 **Open** Easter–October
Site Level
Sites available Total 250.
Facilities
Nearby facilities
Weymouth.
Beautiful, sheltered location, close mown grass park. Dog exercise area, hot water dishwashing points. Close to Weymouth.

WEYMOUTH
Weymouth Bay Holiday Park, Preston, Weymouth, Dorset, DT3 6BQ.
Tel. 832271 Std. 01305
Nearest Town/Resort Weymouth.
Directions On the A353 Weymouth to Preston road, on the right about 10 minutes drive from Weymouth.
Open Easter–November
Access Good **Site** Level
Sites available Total 110.
Facilities
Nearby facilities
Weymouth.
On a cliff top with excellent indoor and outdoor swimming pools.

WIMBORNE

Charris Camping and Caravan Park, Candy's Lane, Corfe Mullen, Wimborne, Dorset BH21 3EF.
Tel. 885970 Std. 01202
Nearest Town/Resort Wimborne.
Directions A31 Wimborne bypass 1 mile west of Wimborne. Signs for entrance.
Acreage 3 **Open** March–October
Access Good **Site** Lev/Slope
Sites available Total 45.
Facilities
Nearby facilities
Poole.
English tourist board 4 Ticks, A.A. 3 Pennant, R.A.C. approved Caravan Club listed, Caravan and Camping Club listed. Good central site convienient for coast and New Forest. Poole 7½ miles, Bournemouth 8¼ miles. Good overnight stop for Cherbourg ferry. Cafe/restaurant close by.

WIMBORNE

Springfield Touring Park, Candys Lane, Corfe Mullen, Wimborne, Dorset.
Tel. 881719 Std. 01202
Nearest Town/Resort Wimborne.
Directions 1¼ miles west of Wimborne just off main A31.
Acreage 3¼ **Open** Mid March–October
Access Good **Site** Lev/Slope
Sites available Total 45.
Facilities
Nearby facilities
Poole.
Family run park. Free showers and awnings, modern toilet block. Convenient for the Coast and New Forest also ferry. English Tourist Board 4 Ticks. Members of B.H. and H.P.A. All this plus beautiful views over the Stour Valley.

WIMBORNE

Wilksworth Farm Caravan Park, Cranborne Road, Wimborne Minster, Dorset, BH21 4HW.
Tel. 883769/885467 Std. 01202
Nearest Town/Resort Wimborne Minster.
Directions 1 mile north of Wimborne on B3078 to Cranborne.
Acreage 11 **Open** March–October
Access Good **Site** Level
Sites available Total 85.
Facilities
Nearby facilities
Poole.
Quiet, secluded, country park on our family farm. Dogs allowed on leads. Motorcycles accepted sometimes.

DURHAM

BARNARD CASTLE

Thorpe Hall, Wycliffe, Barnard Castle, Durham.
Tel. Teesdale 627230 Std. 01833
Nearest Town/Resort Barnard Castle.
Directions 5 miles east of Barnard Castle and 1½ miles north of A66 near Greta Bridge.
Acreage 2 **Open** April–September
Access Good **Site** Level
Sites available Total 12.
Facilities
Nearby facilities
Darlington.
Near River Tees. Area of historic interest and of great beauty. ETB Graded Four Ticks.

BARNARD CASTLE

West Roods Tourism, West Roods Farm, Boldron, Barnard Castle, County Durham, DL12 9SW.
Tel. 690116 Std. 01833
Nearest Town/Resort Barnard Castle.
Directions Turn right off the A66 (Scotch Corner to Bowes) across the dual carriageway (just past Boldron), at electricity pole and junction box (looks like a watering can with two spouts). Signed Lambhill, West Roods and Roods House into site entrance.
Acreage 1 **Open** April–October
Access Good **Site** Sloping
Sites available Total 16.
Facilities
Nearby facilities
Darlington.
Stone tiled buildings, three Anglo Saxon fields and a Roman Well. Children are welcome. Well used sand pit, swing and rope. Guests are welcome to walk the working farm. Bed & Breakfast available.

BARNARD CASTLE

Winston Caravan Park, Winston, Darlington, Durham.
Tel. Darlington 730228 Std. 01325.
Nearest Town/Resort Barnard Castle.
Directions 5 miles east of Barnard Castle on A67.
Acreage 2 **Open** March–October
Access Good **Site** Level
Sites available Total 20.
Facilities

Nearby facilities
Darlington.
Near to river. Within easy reach of many places of interest.

BISHOP AUCKLAND

Witton Castle Caravan and Camping Site, Witton Le Wear, Bishop Auckland, Co Durham, DL14 0DE.
Tel. 488230 Std. 01388
Nearest Town/Resort Bishop Auckland.
Directions On A68 signposted between Toft Hill and Witton le Wear.
Acreage 30 **Open** March–October
Access Good **Site** Lev/Slope
Sites available Total 280.
Facilities
Nearby facilities
Bishop Auckland.
Set in central Co Durham in an area of outstanding natural beauty.

CONSETT

Manor Park, The Caravan Park, Broadmeadows, Castleside, Consett, Co. Durham, DH8 9HD.
Tel. 501000 Std. 01207
Nearest Town/Resort Consett.
Directions Just off the A68, 3¼ miles south of Castleside (signposted Broadmeadows).
Acreage 7 **Open** April–October
Access Good **Site** Lev/Slope
Sites available Total 45.
Facilities
Nearby facilities
Durham.
Bordering a designated area of outstanding natural beauty.

DURHAM

Finchale Abbey, Finchale Abbey Farm, Durham. DH1 5SH.
Tel. 386 6528 Std. 0191
Nearest Town/Resort Durham.
Directions A167 between Chester-le-Street and Durham.
Acreage 6 **Open** All year
Access Good **Site** Lev/Slope
Sites available Total 80.
Facilities
Nearby facilities
Durham.
Beside river, Finchdale Abbey Priory. Licensed club nearby.

TOW LAW

Viewley Hill Caravan & Camping Site, Viewley Hill Farm, Tow Law, Bishop Auckland, Co. Durham.
Tel. 730308 Std. 01388
Nearest Town/Resort Tow Law.
Directions 2 miles north of Tow Law. Turn off the A68 at Brown Horse Inn crossroad onto B6296 Wolsignham Road. Site is ½ mile on the right.
Acreage ¼ **Open** All Year
Access Good **Site** Level
Sites available Total 5.
Facilities
Nearby facilities
Durham.
Scenic views, 10 miles to Durham City.

WESTGATE-IN-WEARDALE

Westgate Caravan & Camping Site, Britton Hall, Westgate-in-Weardale, Co Durham.
Tel. Weardale 517309 Std. 01388
Nearest Town/Resort Stanhope.
Directions Stanhope 6 miles.
Acreage 1½ **Open** March–October
Access Good **Site** Level
Sites available Total 70.
Facilities
Nearby facilities
Durham.
Riverside site.

ESSEX

BATTLESBRIDGE

Hayes Farm Caravan Park, Hayes Chase, Burnham Road, Battlesbridge, Essex.
Tel. 320309 Std. 01245
Nearest Town/Resort Wickford.
Directions A132 to Burnham.
Acreage 26 **Open** End March–End October
Access Good **Site** Level
Sites available Total 74.
Facilities
Nearby facilities
Wickford.
Alongside river.

BRADWELL-ON-SEA

Saint Lawrence Holiday Park, 10 Main Road, St. Lawrence Bay, Essex, CM0 7LY.
Tel. 779434 Std. 01621
Nearest Town/Resort Saint Lawrence Bay.
Directions Take the B1010 to Latchingdon, first exit off mini roundabout towards Bradwell and follow the brown and white tourism signs to the park.
Acreage 3 **Open** March–8 November
Access Good **Site** Level
Sites available Total 50.
Facilities
Nearby facilities
Southminster.
Alongside river with our own beach, launching ramp and clubhouse. Peaceful and quiet, family run park established in 1950. Ideal for touring. Some facilities for the disabled.

CANVEY ISLAND

Kings Park, Canvey Island, Essex, SS8 8HE.
Tel. 511555 Std. 01268
Nearest Town/Resort Southend-on-Sea.
Directions A13 or A127.
Open December–October
Access Good **Site** Level
Sites available Total 200.
Facilities
Nearby facilities
Benfleet.
Close to shops and beach.

CLACTON ON SEA

Tower Caravan Park, Jaywick, Clacton-on-Sea, Essex CO15 2LF.
Tel. 820372 Std. 01255
Nearest Town/Resort Jaywick/Clacton.
Directions A12 from London or Chelmsford, join A120 at Colchester A133 at Frating. Turn right at Clacton sea front and follow road signs to Jaywick. Tower signposted from Jaywick.
Acreage 10 **Open** April–October
Access Good **Site** Level
Sites available Total 100.
Facilities
Nearby facilities
Clacton-on-Sea.
Adjoining beach. On bus route, quality graded.

CLACTON ON SEA

Silver Dawn Touring Park, Jaywick Lane, Clacton On Sea, Essex, CO16 8BB.
Tel. 421856 Std. 01255
Nearest Town/Resort Clacton on Sea.
Directions From Clacton on Sea turn right on seafront and turn into Jaywick Lane at the T-Junction.
Acreage 6 **Open** April–October
Access Good **Site** Level
Sites available Total 38.
Facilities
Nearby facilities
Clacton.
Usual resort amusements.

COLCHESTER

Colchester Camping & Caravan Park, Cymbeline Way, Lexden, Colchester, Essex.
Tel. 45551 Std. 01206
Nearest Town/Resort Colchester.
Directions From the A12 in any direction, follow tourist signs for caravan park into Colchester on the A134 slip road.
Acreage 12 **Open** All Year
Access Good **Site** Level
Sites available Total 185.
Facilities
Nearby facilities
Colchester.
Close to Britains oldest town, convenient for ferry ports. Ideal for touring East Anglia.

DOVERCOURT

Dovercourt Haven Caravan Park, Low Road, Harwich, Essex, CO12 3TZ.
Tel. 243433 Std. 01255
Nearest Town/Resort Harwich.
Directions A120 to Harwich, at Ramsey roundabout turn right and follow the brown tourist board signs to Dovercourt Haven.
Acreage 6 **Open** March–November
Access Good **Site** Level
Sites available Total 750.
Facilities
Nearby facilities
Parkstone Quay.
Close to sandy beach and continental ferry port. Good base for exploration of coastal country.

MERSEA ISLAND

Waldegraves Farm Holiday Park, Mersea Island, Colchester, Essex, CO5 8SE.
Tel. Colchester 382898 Std. 01206
Nearest Town/Resort Mersea.
Directions From Colchester take B1025, 10 miles to West Mersea. Take left fork to East Mersea, second road to right.
Acreage 10 **Open** March–October
Access Good **Site** Level
Sites available Total 60.
Facilities
Nearby facilities
Colchester.
Grass park, surrounded by trees and lakes. Safe private beach, fishing. Ideal family park. Holiday homes for hire and sale.

ST. OSYTH

Hutleys Touring Park, St. Osyth Beach, St. Osyth, Essex.
Tel. 820712 Std. 01255
Nearest Town/Resort Clacton-on-Sea.
Directions A12 Colchester, B1027 to St. Osyth. Straight through the village to beach (2 miles), park is under the sea wall on the right.
Open March–October
Access Good **Site** Level
Sites available Total 18.
Facilities
Nearby facilities
Clacton-on-Sea.
Near the beach.

SOUTHEND

East Beach Caravan Park, Shoeburyness, Southend-on-Sea, Essex. SS3 9SG.
Tel. 292466 Std. 01702
Nearest Town/Resort Southend-on-Sea.
Directions A127-A1159 to seafront, then follow signs. A13 then follow signs.
Acreage 4¼ **Open** 2nd Sat March–October
Access Good **Site** Level
Sites available Total 45.
Facilities
Nearby facilities
Shoeburyness.
100yds from beach. Safe boating and bathing.

SOUTHMINSTER

Beacon Hill Leisure Park, St. Lawrence Bay, Southminster, Essex, CM0 7LS.
Tel. 779248 Std. 01621
Nearest Town/Resort Maldon.
Directions B1010 to Latchingdon, then mini roundabout towards Bradwell through Mayland Steeple at St. Lawrence left turn sign the stone, St Lawrence Bay ½ mile on right hand side.
Acreage 2 **Open** April–October
Access Good **Site** Level
Sites available Total 50.
Facilities
Nearby facilities
Southminster.
Alongside River Blackwater, ideal touring, walking, all water sports, bird watching, pets welcome, peace and quiet.

SOUTHMINSTER

Steeple Bay Holiday Park, Steeple, Nr. Southminster, Essex, CM0 7RS.
Tel. 773991 Std. 01621
Nearest Town/Resort Southminster.
Directions Turn off the A12 onto the A414, then onto the B1010/B1012 to Latchingdon. At the mini-roundabout follow signs through Mayland, then Steeple Village. After the Blackwater Craft Shop turn left into a small lane. Steeple Bay is just past the farm.
Open March–November

Access Good **Site** Level
Sites available Total 93.
Facilities
Nearby facilities
River setting. The park has its very own Sailing Club and touring guests are able to use our launching ramp for speedboats.

WALLASEA ISLAND

Riverside Village Holiday Park, Wallasea Island, Rochford, Essex. SS4 2EY.
Tel. 258297 Std. 01702
Nearest Town/Resort Southend.
Directions From A127 through Rochford, follow caravan signs for Ashingdon then Wallasea Island. From Chelmsford left at Battlesbridge, past Hullbridge for Ashingdon then Wallasea.
Acreage 5 **Open** March–October
Access Good **Site** Level
Sites available Total 60.
Facilities
Nearby facilities
Rochford.
Alongside River Crouch, Nature reserve, picturesque inns with excellent food. Country walks.

WEELEY

Weeley Bridge Holiday Park, Weeley, Near Clacton-on-Sea, Essex.
Tel. 830403 Std. 01255
Nearest Town/Resort Clacton-on-Sea.
Directions Follow the A12 from London. Take the A133 to Clacton, approximately ½ mile from Weeley roundabout on the right hand side.
Acreage 1¼ **Open** March–October
Access Good **Site** Level
Sites available Total 25.
Facilities
Nearby facilities
Weeley.
Set in a natural woodland area, adjacent to a private, well stocked fishing lake. We have facilities for the disabled but not on touring field.

GLOUCESTER

BOURTON-ON-THE-WATER

Folly Farm, Nr. Bourton-on-the-Water, Cheltenham, Gloucestershire, GL54 3BY.
Tel. 820285 Std. 01451
Nearest Town/Resort Bourton-on-the-Water.
Directions Approximately 2¼ miles west of Bourton-on-the-Water on the A436.
Acreage 2 **Open** All Year
Access Good **Site** Level
Sites available Total 20.
Facilities
Nearby facilities
Moreton-in-Marsh.
Campers and caravanners have free access to poultry and waterfowl exhibition. Garden centre and indoor pet area.

CHELTENHAM

Longwillows, Station Road, Woodmancote, Cheltenham, Gloucestershire.
Tel. 674113 Std. 01242
Nearest Town/Resort Cheltenham.
Directions Take A435 out of Cheltenham towards Evesham, turn off Bishops Cleeve.
Acreage 4 **Open** March–October
Access Good **Site** Level
Sites available Total 80.
Facilities
Nearby facilities
Cheltenham.
Excellent centre for touring the Cotswolds. Licensed pub.

CHELTENHAM

Stansby Caravan Park, The Reddings, Cheltenham, Gloucestershire, GL51 6RS.
Tel. 712168 Std. 01452
Nearest Town/Resort Cheltenham.
Directions M5 junction 11 follow signs to Cheltenham at first roundabout exit at 3 oclock follow signs to site. From Cheltenham follow A40 and signs to site.
Acreage 2½ **Open** February–December
Access Good **Site** Level
Sites available Total 30.
Facilities
Nearby facilities
Cheltenham.
Ideal touring, Cotswolds, Forest of Dean.

CIRENCESTER

Cotswold Hoburne, Broadway Lane, South Cerney, Cirencester, Glos, GL7 5UQ.
Tel. 860216 Std. 01285
Nearest Town/Resort Cirencester.
Directions 4 miles south of Cirencester on A419, follow signposts to Cotswold Hoburne in the Cotswold Water Park.
Acreage 20 **Open** April–October
Access Good **Site** Level
Sites available Total 302.
Facilities
Nearby facilities
Swindon.
In the centre of the Cotswold Water Park – and ideal base for all watersports and nature lovers.

CIRENCESTER

Mayfield Touring Park, Cheltenham Road, Perrotts Brook, Cirencester, Glos.GL7 7BH.
Tel. 831301 Std. 01285
Nearest Town/Resort Cirencester.
Directions On A435 13 miles Cheltenham and 2 miles Cirencester.
Acreage 10 **Open** 20th Mar–31st October
Access Good **Site** Lev/Slope
Sites available Total 64.
Facilities
Nearby facilities
Kemble.
Touring Cotswolds, castles, abbey, wildlife park, local pub five minutes walk – food suitable for children, 16 hardstanding/grass pitches. Board Graded 4 ticks. 6 acres of ground for recreation.

COLEFORD

Forest of Dean Campsites, Campsite Office, Christchurch, Coleford, Glos, GL16 8BA.

Tel. 833057 Std. 0159
Nearest Town/Resort Coleford.
Directions From the A4136, 1 mile north of Coleford, follow international campsite signs. Turn left into Bracelands Drive after ¼ mile.
Open March–October
Access Good **Site** Lev/Slope
Sites available
Facilities
Nearby facilities
Lydney.
35 square miles of mixed woodland, spectacular scenery. Motorcycle acceptance is limited.

DURSLEY
Hogsdown Farm Caravan and Camping Site, Lower Wick, Dursley, Gloucestershire. GL11 6OX.
Tel. 810224 Std. 01453
Nearest Town/Resort Gloucester.
Directions Between Junction 13 and 14 of M5 1 mile off A38, 2 miles from Berkeley.
Acreage 4 **Open** All Year.
Access Good **Site** Level
Sites available Total 40.
Facilities
Nearby facilities
Stroud.
Ideal stop over north, south and touring Cotswold Edge and Way country, Severn Vale. Slimbridge Wild Fowl Trust, Berkeley Castle, Jenner Museum, Weston Burt Arboretum. Cotswold and Severn Way within 2 miles. Oldbury Power Station, butterfly farm and rare animals farm.

GLOUCESTER
Red Lion Caravan & Camping Park, Red Lion, Wainlode Hill, Norton, Gloucestershire.
Tel. Gloucester 730251 Std. 01452.
Nearest Town/Resort Gloucester.
Directions Off A38 at Norton, signposted Wainlode Hill, 5 miles Gloucester.
Acreage 12½ **Open** All year
Access Good **Site** Level
Sites available Total 90.
Facilities
Nearby facilities
Gloucester.
Licensed Inn, hot and cold snacks. On banks of River Severn. Good fishing on site.

LECHLADE
Bridge House Camp Site, Bridge House, Lechlade, Gloucestershire, GL7 3AG.
Tel. Faringdon 252348 Std. 01367
Nearest Town/Resort Lechlade.
Directions Lechlade A361 to Swindon. Opposite Riverside Car Park.
Acreage 3½ **Open** April–October
Site Level
Sites available Total 45.
Facilities
Nearby facilities
Swindon.
Ideal for touring Cotswolds and upper Thames.

MORETON-IN-MARSH
Cross Hands Inn Caravan Park, The Cross Hands, Moreton-in-Marsh, Gloucestershire, GL56 0SP.
Tel. 643106 Std. 01608
Nearest Town/Resort Chipping Norton.
Directions From Chipping Norton take the Worcester road A44. After 3 miles you will see the Inn on your right on the main A44 at the junction of A436.
Acreage 1¼ **Open** All year
Access Good **Site** Level
Sites available Total 18.
Facilities
Nearby facilities
Moreton-in-Marsh.
Ideal touring site for the Cotswolds and only about 20 miles to Stratford-on-Avon.

MORETON VALENCE
Gables Farm Caravan & Camping Site, Gables Farm, Moreton Valence, Glos. GL2 7ND.
Tel. 720331 Std. 01452
Nearest Town/Resort Gloucester.
Directions On A38 6 miles from Gloucester. 2 miles from the M5 junction 13.
Acreage 3 **Open** All year
Access Good **Site** Level
Sites available Total 40.
Facilities
Nearby facilities
Gloucester.
Overnight or local touring. Wetlands trust 6 miles. S.A.E. Gloucester docks and museums.

TEWKESBURY
Brooklands Farm, Alderton, Nr. Tewkesbury, Gloucestershire, GL20 8NX.
Tel. 620259 Std. 01242
Nearest Town/Resort Tewkesbury.
Directions 5 miles from junction 9 M5. Take the A438 Evesham road, continue to Teddington roundabout (approx 3 miles) then follow the B4077 Stow road for a further 3 miles past roundabout site is on the right hand side.
Acreage 10 **Open** 16th Mar–16th January
Access Good **Site** Level
Sites available Total 80.
Facilities
Nearby facilities
Site is situated around a small lake in 20 acres of farmland. Multi service pitches.

TEWKESBURY
Mill Avon Holiday Park, Gloucester Road, Tewkesbury, Gloucestershire.
Tel. 296876 Std. 01684
Nearest Town/Resort Tewkesbury.
Directions In approaching from the M5, follow the A438 into Tewkesbury town centre. Turn left onto the A38 toward Gloucester. Passing the Abbey on the left

and the Bell Hotel on the right, public car park indicated by standard caravan sign on the right.
Open March–October
Access Good **Site** Level
Sites available Total 54.
Facilities
Nearby facilities
Cheltenham.
Abbey in Tewkesbury, Malvern Hill walks, Cotswold villages, Cheltenham and Gloucester. Free fishing on site.

TEWKESBURY

Dawleys Caravan Park, Owls Lane, Shuthonger, Tewkesbury, Gloucestershire, GL20 6EQ.
Tel. 292622 Std. 01684
Nearest Town/Resort Cheltenham/Gloucester.
Directions A38 north from Tewkesbury, approximately 2 miles on the left hand side opposite Eriksons Garage. Or 1¼ miles south on the A38 from the M50 junction 1.
Acreage 3 **Open** 15 March–October
Access Fair **Site** Sloping
Sites available Total 20.
Facilities
Nearby facilities
Cheltenham.
Near a river, secluded rural site, close to the M5 and the M50.

WOTTON UNDER EDGE

Cotswold Gate Caravan & Camping Park, Cononscourt Farm, Bradley, Wotton-under-Edge, Glos, GL12 7PN.
Tel. 843128 Std. 01453
Nearest Town/Resort Wotton-under-Edge.
Directions Site within 4 miles of junction 14 on the M5 and 10 miles of junction 18 on the M4.
Acreage 4 **Open** March–October
Access Good **Site** Level
Sites available Total 60.
Facilities
Nearby facilities
Cotswolds, Severn Bridge and the Bristol Channel. Walking and lovely views.

HAMPSHIRE

ANDOVER

Wyke Down Touring Caravan & Camping Park, Picket Piece, Andover, Hampshire.
Tel. Andover 352048 Std. 01264
Nearest Town/Resort Andover.
Directions International Camping Park Signs from A303 Trunk Road, follow signs to Wyke Down.
Acreage 7 **Open** All year
Access Good **Site** Level
Sites available Total 150.
Facilities
Nearby facilities
Andover.
Ideal touring area. Golf driving range. Country Pub.

BEAULIEU

Decoy Pond Farm, Beaulieu Road, Beaulieu, Brockenhurst, Hants. SO4 7YQ.
Tel. 292652 Std. 01703
Nearest Town/Resort Lyndhurst/Beaulieu.
Directions From Lyndhurst take the B3056 after crossing railway bridge, first drive on left.
Acreage ½ **Open** March–October
Access Good **Site** Level
Sites available Total 4.
Facilities
Nearby facilities
Beaulieu Road.
Ideally situated in the heart of the New Forest riding and fishing available.

BRANSGORE

Harrow Wood Farm Caravan Park, Poplar Lane, Bransgore, Christchurch, Dorset, BH23 8JE.
Tel. 672487 Std. 01425
Nearest Town/Resort Christchurch.
Directions A35 11 miles south west of Lyndhurst, turn right at Cat & Fiddle Public House, 2 miles to Bransgore. Take first right after the school into Poplar Lane.
Acreage 6 **Open** March–6 January
Access Good **Site** Level
Sites available Total 60.
Facilities
Nearby facilities
Hinton Admiral.
New Forest and sea within easy reach.

BRANSGORE

Holmsley Camp Site, Forest Road, Holmsley, Christchurch, Hampshire.
Tel. Lyndhurst 283771 Std. 01703
Nearest Town/Resort New Milton.
Directions Turn west 8 miles southwest of Lyndhurst off A35 and follow Holmsley camp signs
Acreage 89 **Open** Easter–September
Access Good **Site** Level
Sites available Total 700.
Facilities
Nearby facilities
New Milton.
Coast within 5 miles. Booking service available. Owned by the Forestry Commission. Take away food.

BROCKENHURST

Hollands Wood Camp Site, Lyndhurst Road, Brockenhurst, Hampshire, SO42 7QH.
Tel. 283771 Std. 01703
Nearest Town/Resort Brockenhurst.
Directions ¼ mile north of Brockenhurst on A337, signposted.
Acreage 168 **Open** Easter–September
Access Good **Site** Level
Sites available Total 600.
Facilities
Nearby facilities
Brockenhurst.
Scenic views across the New Forest. Booking service available. Owned by the Forestry Commission.

BROCKENHURST

Roundhill Campsite, Beaulieu Road, Brockenhurst, Hampshire, SO42 7QL.
Tel. 283771 Std. 01703
Nearest Town/Resort Brockenhurst.
Directions 1 mile B3055, 2 miles south east of Brockenhurst off A337, signposted.

Acreage 156 **Open** Easter–September
Access Good **Site** Level
Sites available Total 500.
Facilities
Nearby facilities
Brockenhurst.
Motorcyclists' area on campsite available, also rally site and lightweight camping on site. Owned by the Forestry Commission.

CADNAM

Ocknell/Longbeech Campsite, Fritham, Lyndhurst, Hampshire, SO43 7HH.
Tel. 283771 Std. 01703
Nearest Town/Resort Lyndhurst.
Directions B3079 off the A31 at Cadnam, then B3078 via Brook and Fritham.
Acreage 48 **Open** Easter–September
Access Good **Site** Level
Sites available Total 300.
Facilities
Nearby facilities
Two contrasting campsites, one situated on open heath, the other in ancient woodland. Toilets and hot water situated on Ocknell.

FAREHAM

Dibles Park, Dibles Road, Warsash, Southampton, Hants, SO3 6SA.
Tel. Lockseheath 575232 Std. 01489
Nearest Town/Resort Fareham.
Directions Turn left off the A27 (Portsmouth – Southampton) opposite Lloyds Bank into Locks Road (sinposted Warsash). In about 1½ miles at the T-Junction turn right into Warsash Road, in about 300yds turn left into Fleet End Road. Take the first right and we are on the right.
Acreage ¾ **Open** Easter–October
Access Good **Site** Level
Sites available Total 14.
Facilities
Nearby facilities
Swanwick.
Shingle beach 1½ miles.

FORDINGBRIDGE

New Forest Country Holidays, Sandy Balls Estate, Godshill, Fordingbridge, Hampshire, SP6 2JZ.
Tel. 653042 Std. 01425
Nearest Town/Resort Salisbury/Bournemouth.
Directions On B3078, 1½ miles from Fordingbridge. 8 miles from Cadnam. Easy access from M27.
Acreage 120 **Open** All year
Access Good **Site** Level
Sites available Total 340.
Facilities
Nearby facilities
Salisbury.
Open all year round. Edge of New Forest. Supurb woodland setting with high standard of amenities, many walks. Indoor heated pool and leisure complex. Winner of England for Excellence 1993. British Graded Holiday Parks 5 Ticks.

HAMBLE

Riverside Park, Satchell Lane, Hamble, Southampton, Hants. SO3 5HR.
Tel. 453220 Std. 01703
Nearest Town/Resort Southampton.
Directions Exit 8 off M27 (signposted Southampton East) then B3397 to Hamble.
Acreage 2 **Open** March–October
Access Good **Site** Level
Sites available Total 40.
Facilities
Nearby facilities
Hamble/Netley.
Overlooking the Marina and River Hamble with access in village to public hard.
Quaint pubs and restaurants. Easy access to New Forest and many places of interest including HMS Victory, Paultons Fun Park, etc.

HAYLING ISLAND

Fishery Creek Caravan & Camping Park, Fishery Lane, Hayling Island, PO11 9NR.
Tel. 462164 Std. 01705
Nearest Town/Resort Hayling Island.
Directions Turn off A27, cross bridge, follow signs turning left at first roundabout, left after town of Mengham, left into Fishery Lane. Park is at end of lane.
Acreage 8 **Open** March–October
Access Good **Site** Level
Sites available Total 165.
Facilities
Nearby facilities
Havant.
Alongside a beautiful tidal creek, offering peace and tranquility. Own slipway, short path to beach. Fishing on site.

HAYLING ISLAND

Fleet Park, Yew Tree Road, Hayling Island, Hampshire PO11 0QE.
Tel. 463684 Std. 01705
Nearest Town/Resort Havant/Southsea.
Directions Follow A3023 from Havant. Approx. 2 miles on Island turn left into Copse Lane then first right into Yew Tree Road.
Acreage 3 **Open** March–October
Access Good **Site** Level
Sites available Total 75.
Facilities
Nearby facilities
Havant.

Near Ferry Port. Portsmouth/Southsea, Isle of Wight. Easy touring for New Forest and Beaulieu.

HAYLING ISLAND

Lower Tye Camp Site, Copse Lane, Hayling Island, Hants, PO11 0QB.
Tel. 462479 Std. 01705
Nearest Town/Resort Havant.
Directions Exit the M27 or the A317 motorway at Havant. Follow the A3023 from Havant, turn left into Copse Lane. You will see the sign after being on Hayling Island for approx 1¼ miles.
Acreage 5 **Open** March–October
Access Good **Site** Level
Sites available Total 150.
Facilities S
Nearby facilities
Havant.
Near Portsmouth, Isle of Wight, Singlton Open Air Museum, Chichester, excellent beach, all water sports. £6 plus V.A.T. per unit for 2 people. Storage available.

HAYLING ISLAND

Oven Camping Site, Manor Road, Hayling Island, Hampshire PO11 0QX.
Tel. 464695 Std. 01705
Nearest Town/Resort Havant.
Directions Exit M27 or the A37 at Havant. Take the A3023 from Havant, approx 3 miles after crossing bridge onto Hayling Island bear right at the roundabout. Site is on the left in 450yds.
Acreage 10 **Open** March–October
Access Good **Site** Level
Sites available Total 330.
Facilities S
Nearby facilities
Havant.
Excellent touring area for Portsmouth, Chichester, New Forest etc. Safe, clean beaches, excellent for water sports. Caravan storage and rallies.

LYMINGTON

Lytton Lawn, Lymore Lane, Everton, Near Milford-on-Sea, Lymington, Hants, SO41 0TX.
Tel. 642513 Std. 01590
Nearest Town/Resort Lymington.
Directions From Lymington take the A337 towards Everton. Turn left onto the B3058 towards Milford-on-Sea. Second left into Lymore Lane.
Acreage 5 **Open** Easter–October
Access Good **Site** Lev/Slope
Sites available Total 126.
Facilities S
Nearby facilities

Lymington/New Milton.
Views of the Isle of Wight. Beach 1 mile. 2 miles from the beautiful New Forest. Cafe/restaurant, licensed club, swimming pool, games room and sports area available at main park "Shorefield Country Park", approx. 2¼ miles away.

LYNDHURST

Ashurst Camp Site, Lyndhurst Road, Ashurst, Nr. Southampton, Hampshire, SO4 2AA.
Tel. 283771 Std. 01703
Nearest Town/Resort Lyndhurst.
Directions 6 miles southwest of Southampton on A35, signposted.
Acreage 23 **Open** Easter–October
Access Good **Site** Level
Sites available Total 280.
Facilities M I
Nearby facilities
Lyndhurst Road.
Also lightweight camp site for walkers and cyclists. Booking service available. Owned by the Forestry Commission.

NEW MILTON

Bashley Park, Sway Road, New Milton, Hampshire.
Tel. 612340 Std. 01425
Nearest Town/Resort New Milton.
Directions From A35 Lyndhurst/Bournemouth road, take B3055 signposted Sway. Over crossroads at 2¼ miles. Park is ½ mile on left.
Open March–October
Access Good **Site** Level
Sites available Total 400.
Facilities S
Nearby facilities
New Milton.
New Forest – 2 miles from beach, 10 miles Bournemouth. Own golf course, indoor/outdoor pools and tennis. Many facilities. Rose Award for Excellence and England for Excellence Silver Award.

NEW MILTON

Setthorns Camp Site, Wootton, New Milton, Hampshire, BH25 5UA.
Tel. 283771 Std. 01703
Nearest Town/Resort New Milton.
Directions East of the A35 at Holmsley Old Station. Follow signs for site for 2 miles.
Acreage 60 **Open** All Year
Access Good **Site** Level
Sites available Total 320.
Facilities M
Nearby facilities
New Milton.

Booking service available. Owned by the Forestry Commission.

OWER

Green Pastures Farm, Ower, Romsey, Hampshire. SO51 6AJ.
Tel. 814444 Std. 01703
Nearest Town/Resort Romsey.
Directions Site is signposted from A36 and A31 at Ower (exit 2 off M27 – signposted for Salisbury).
Acreage 5 **Open** 15 March–31 October
Access Good **Site** Level
Sites available Total 45.
Facilities S
Nearby facilities
Romsey.
A grassy site on family run farm, within easy reach of the New Forest. Paultons Park 1 mile, convenient for ferries to Isle of Wight and France, from Portsmouth, Southampton and Lymington. Ample space for children to play.

RINGWOOD

The Red Shoot Camping Park, Linwood, Nr. Ringwood, Hampshire BH24 3QT.
Tel. 473789 Std. 01425
Nearest Town/Resort Ringwood.
Directions Fron Ringwood take A338, 2 miles north of Ringwood take right turn signed Moyles Court and Linwood. Follow signs to Linwood.
Acreage 4 **Open** March–October
Access Good **Site** Lev/Slope
Sites available Total 100.
Facilities S
Nearby facilities
Brockenhurst.
Half hour drive to Bournemouth coast, Salisbury and Southampton. Situated in beautiful part of New Forest. Good pub adjacent. Mountain bike hire. Off peak Tariff early and late season.

RINGWOOD

The Copper Kettle, 266 Christchurch Road, Ringwood, Hampshire.
Tel. Ringwood 473904 Std. 01425
Nearest Town/Resort Ringwood.
Directions Off A31 through Ringwood town centre onto B3347, ½ mile from Ringwood town. Opposite petrol station.
Acreage 2½ **Open** March–October
Access Good **Site** Level
Sites available Total 56.
Facilities I
Nearby facilities
Christchurch.
Near River Avon, New Forest, beach. Ideal touring.A.A.3 Pennant.

SOUTHBOURNE

Chichester Camping, 345 Main Road, Southbourne, Emsworth, Hants, PO10 8JH.
Tel. 373202 Std. 01243
Nearest Town/Resort Emsworth.
Acreage 3 **Open** January–October
Access Level **Site** Good
Sites available Total 60.
Facilities
Nearby facilities
Southbourne.
500 yards through footpath to beach. ideal touring.

HERE / WORCS.

ABBEY DORE

The Neville Arms, Abbey Dore, Hereford, HR2 0AA.
Tel. 240319 Std. 01981
Nearest Town/Resort Hereford.
Directions From Hereford take the A465 towards Abergavenny. At Pontrilas take the B4347 on the right, signposted Ewyas Harold. Stay on this road for 3 miles. Pub is on the left, site is on the right.
Acreage 1 **Open** April–November
Access Good **Site** Level
Sites available Total 5.
Facilities
Nearby facilities
Hereford.
Scenic views, ancient Abbey. On the edge of a common, plenty of walks. Licensed Pub.

BROADWAY

Leedons Park Broadway, Childswickham Road, Broadway, Worcs, WR12 7HB.
Tel. 852423 Std. 01386
Nearest Town/Resort Evesham.
Directions Signposted off the A44 Evesham to Broadway road.
Acreage 45 **Open** All year
Access Good **Site** Level
Sites available Total 400.
Facilities
Nearby facilities
Evesham.
Ideal for touring Cotswolds.

CLEVELODE

Riverside Caravan Park, Little Clevelode, Malvern, Worcestershire WR13 6PE.
Tel. Hanley Swan 310475 Std. 01684.
Nearest Town/Resort Malvern.
Directions On B4424 3½ miles east of Malvern on the west bank of the river Severn.
Acreage 4 **Open** March–December
Access Good **Site** Level
Sites available Total 70.
Facilities
Nearby facilities
Good centre for touring. Facilities for fishing and launching boats, tennis. Grade 3 site.

EVESHAM

Ranch Caravan Park, Station Road, Honeybourne, Nr. Evesham, Worcestershire. WR11 5QG.
Tel. Evesham 830744 Std. 01386
Nearest Town/Resort Evesham.
Directions From Evesham take B4035 to Badsey and Bretforton. Turn left to Honeybourne. At village crossroads take Bidford direction, site on left in 400 yards.
Acreage 48 **Open** March–November
Access Good **Site** Level
Sites available Total 120.
Facilities
Nearby facilities
Evesham.
Situated in meadow land in Vale of Evesham on north edge of Cotswolds. Meals available in licensed club.

EVESHAM

Weir Meadow Holiday & Touring Park, Lower Leys, Evesham, Worcestershire.
Tel. 442417 Std. 01386.
Nearest Town/Resort Evesham.
Directions On A44, 500 yards south of town centre.
Acreage 10 **Open** April–October
Access Good **Site** Level
Sites available Total 100.
Facilities
Nearby facilities
Evesham.
Own River Avon frontage, boat moorings. Holiday caravans and chalets for hire. Four minutes walk town centre. One dog only allowed. Free fishing on site for patrons only. Site shop selling ice-cream and caravan accessories. H.E.T.B. Graded 4 Ticks. Hire caravan available for the disabled.

HARTLEBURY

Shorthill Caravan and Camping Centre, Shorthill, Crossway Green, Worcester Road, Hartlebury, Worcs, DY13 9SH.
Tel. 250571 Std. 01299
Nearest Town/Resort Stourport-on-Severn.
Directions Off A449 Kidderminster/Worcester road. Turn left into Little Chef Restaurant after Hartlebury Island. Site at bottom of drive.
Acreage 3 **Open** All year
Access Good **Site** Level
Sites available Total 50.
Facilities
Nearby facilities
Kidderminster.
Ideal touring site. Fishing, golf, boating, fun fair 3 miles. New 3 acre field.

HEREFORD

Upper Gilvach Farm, St. Margarets, Vowchurch, Hereford.
Tel. Michealchurch 618 Std. 0198 123.
Nearest Town/Resort Hereford.
Directions 4 miles off the B4348.
Open Easter–October
Access Good **Site** Level
Sites available Total 20.
Facilities
Nearby facilities
Hereford.

MALVERN

Three Counties Park, Sledge Green, Berrow, Nr. Malvern, Hereford/Worcs, WR13 6JW.
Tel. Birtsmorton 833439 Std. 01684.
Nearest Town/Resort Tewkesbury.
Directions From Tewkesbury take A438 Ledbury road for 6 miles.
Acreage 2 **Open** April–October
Access Good **Site** Level
Sites available Total 50.
Facilities
Nearby facilities
Tewkesbury.
Malvern Hills, Rivers Serven and Avon. Walking, boating, and historic sights.

MALVERN

Oakmere Park, Hanley Swan, Worcester.
Tel. 310375 Std. 01684
Nearest Town/Resort Malvern.
Directions 4 miles south of Malvern, on the B4209. Situated between Malvern and Upton-on-Severn.
Acreage ¼ **Open** Easter–October
Access Good **Site** Level
Sites available Total 8.
Facilities
Nearby facilities
Malvern.
Scenic views and good walking.

MORDIFORD

Lucks-All, Mordiford, Hereford, Herefordshire. HR1 4LP.
Tel. 870213 Std. 01432
Nearest Town/Resort Hereford.
Directions B4224 Hereford to Ross-on-Wye.
Acreage 10 **Open** Easter–October
Access Good **Site** Level
Sites available Total 80.

Facilities
Nearby facilities
Hereford.
Alongside river, scenic views, ideal touring.

OMBERSLEY

Holt Fleet Farm Camping Site, Holt Fleet Farm, Holt Fleet, Worcestershire. WR6 6NW.
Tel. 620512 Std. 01905
Nearest Town/Resort Droitwich.
Directions M5 junc 5 onto A4133 to Ombersley, site 1½ miles from village.
Acreage 9 **Open** April–October
Access Good **Site** Level
Sites available Total 150.
Facilities
Nearby facilities
Droitwich.
Beside the River Severn, ideal touring stopover for Midland beauty spots.

PETERCHURCH

Poston Mill Caravan & Camping Park, Peterchurch, Golden valley, Hereford, HR2 0SF.
Tel. 550225 Std. 01981
Nearest Town/Resort Hereford.
Directions On B4348. 11 miles from Hereford and 11 miles from Hay on Wye.
Acreage 10 **Open** All Year
Access Good **Site** Level
Sites available Total 64.
Facilities
Nearby facilities
Hereford.
Beautiful park, well maintained. On the banks of the River Dore. Highly recommended. You can FAX us on 01981 550885.

ROSS-ON-WYE

Lower Ruxton Farm, Kings Caple, Herefordshire HR1 4TX.
Tel. 840223 Std. 01432
Nearest Town/Resort Ross-on-Wye.
Directions A49 from Ross-on-Wye, 1 mile turn right follow signs for Hoarwithy (Kings Caple 4 miles) across river bridge ½ mile sign to Ruxton second farm on right.
Acreage 8 **Open** Mid July–August
Site Level
Sites available Total 20.
Facilities
Hereford.
Alongside river.

SHRAWLEY

Lenchford Caravan Park, Shrawley, Worcestershire.
Tel. Worcester 620246 Std. 01905
Nearest Town/Resort Worcester.
Directions Take A443 Worcester/Tenbury road. At Holt Heath crossroads, take B4196 to Stourport. Signpost in ¾ mile on right.
Acreage 2 **Open** All year
Access Good **Site** Level
Sites available Total 12.
Facilities
Nearby facilities
Worcester.

STOURPORT-ON-SEVERN

Lickhill Manor Caravan Park, Lickhill Manor, Stourport-on-Severn, Worcestershire DY13 8RL.
Tel. 822024 Std. 01299
Nearest Town/Resort Stourport-on-Severn.
Directions From Stourport town centre proceed 1 mile along Lickhill Road, turn left at sign and follow lane.
Acreage 4 **Open** All year
Access Good **Site** Level
Sites available Total 80.
Facilities
Nearby facilities
Kidderminster.
Alongside river, fishing rights held. Walks through unspoilt Wyre Forest. West Midlands safari park, Severn Valley Railway.

STOURPORT-ON-SEVERN

Lincomb Lock Caravan Park, Worcester Road, Titton, Stourport-on-Severn, Worcestershire.
Tel. 823836 Std. 01299
Nearest Town/Resort Stourport.
Directions A4025 from Stourport, after 1 mile turn right opposite Titton Inn, follow lane.
Acreage 1 **Open** April–October
Access Good **Site** Level
Sites available
Facilities
Nearby facilities
Kidderminster.
Fishing rights on River Severn. Severn Valley Railway. West Midlands safari park. Miles of walks through Wyre Forest.

WORCESTER

Ketch Caravan Park & Moorings, Bath Road, Worcester, WR5 3HW.
Tel. 820430 Std. 01905
Nearest Town/Resort Worcester.
Directions 1¼ miles from Worcester on the A38 heading towards Tewkesbury. 1¾ miles from the M5.
Open April–October
Access Good **Site** Level
Sites available Total 90.
Facilities
Nearby facilities
Worcester.
Alongside the River Severn, views of the Malvern Hills, ideal touring.

WORCESTER

Mill House Caravan & Camping Site, Mill House, Hawford, Worcestershire.
Tel. 451283 Std. 01905
Nearest Town/Resort Worcester.
Directions A449 Worcester to Kidderminster.
Acreage 8½ **Open** Easter–October
Access Good **Site** Level
Sites available Total 150.
Facilities S
Nearby facilities
Shrubhill/Worcester.
Please note motocycles are not allowed into field.

HERTS

BALDOCK

Radwell Mill Lake, Radwell Mill, Baldock, Herts, SG7 5ET.
Tel. 730253 Std. 01462
Nearest Town/Resort Baldock.
Directions Exit 10 A1(M) then A507 towards Baldock, in 500yds turn right (cul de sac) signed Radwell, through village to private drive and site.
Acreage 1 **Open** Easter–November
Access Good **Site** Level
Sites available Total 5.
Facilities
Nearby facilities
Baldock.
Lake, riverside walks, bird watching, quiet garden site.

HODDESDON

Lee Valley Caravan Park, Essex Road, Dobbs Weir, Hoddesdon, Hertfordshire.
Tel. Hoddesdon 462090 Std. 01992
Nearest Town/Resort Hoddesdon.
Directions Hoddesdon exit from A10 turn left at second roundabout.
Acreage 24 **Open** April–October
Access Good **Site** Level
Sites available Total 100.
Facilities
Nearby facilities
Broxbourne.
A quiet riverside setting.

HUMBERSIDE

BARMSTON

Barmston Beach Caravan Park, Sands Lane, Barmston, Nr. Driffield, Humberside, YO25 8PJ.
Tel. 468202 Std. 01262
Directions Take A165 from Bridlington to Hull. The turing to Barmston Beach is signposted about 6 miles south of Bridlington.
Open March–November
Access Good **Site** Level
Sites available Total 16.
Facilities S
Nearby facilities
Bridlington.
Barmston Beach is right next to the beach. Bridlington is a bustling resort with attractive old harbour. Ideal for touring the Yorkshire bealty spots and popular resorts. Part of Haven Holidays.

BARTON-UPON-HUMBER

Silver Birches Tourist Park, Silver Birches, Waterside Road, Barton-Upon-Humber, South Humberside, DN18 5BA.
Tel. 632509 Std. 01652
Nearest Town/Resort Hull/Cleethorpes.
Directions From the A15 or the A1077, follow Humber Bridge signs to Waterside Road. Site is just past the Sloop Public House.
Acreage 1¼ **Open** April–October
Access Good **Site** Level
Sites available Total 24.
Facilities
Nearby facilities
Barton-Upon-Humber.
Next to Barton Clay Pits Nature Reserve. Ideal for touring.

BEVERLEY

Lakeminster Park, Hull Road, Beverley, East Yorkshire, HU17 0PN.
Tel. 882655 Std. 01482
Nearest Town/Resort Beverley.
Directions 1 mile south of Beverley on the main Beverley/Hull road (A1174).
Acreage 5 **Open** All Year
Access Good **Site** Level
Sites available Total 20.
Facilities
Nearby facilities
Beverley.
Family run site, fishing lakes. Ideal touring base for the East Coast, North Yorks, York etc..

BRIDLINGTON

South Cliff Caravan Park, Wilsthorpe, Bridlington, Humberside YO15 3QN.
Tel. 671051 Std. 01262.
Nearest Town/Resort Bridlington.
Directions A165 Bridlington to Hull Road site situated 1¼ miles south of Bridlington.
Acreage 11 **Open** March–November
Access Good **Site** Level
Sites available Total 224.
Facilities
Nearby facilities
Bridlington.
Access through site to award winning sandy beaches "Makis" Leisure Complex, entertainment nightly.

BRIDLINGTON

The Poplars, 45 Jewison Lane, Sewerby, Bridlington, Humberside, YO15 1DY.
Tel. 677251 Std. 01262
Nearest Town/Resort Bridlington.
Directions Take the B1255 to Flamborough, after 2 miles turn left at second leg of the Z bend. Site is 300yds on the left.
Acreage 1½
Access Good **Site** Level
Sites available Total 30.
Facilities
Nearby facilities
¾ mile to the beach, 2 miles to Bridlington centre and 2 miles to Bempton Birds R.S.P.B. Ramp into toilets for the disabled but the cubicles are not very large.

BRIDLINGTON

Shirley Caravan Park, Jewison Lane, Bridlington, Humberside, YO16 5YG.
Tel. 676442 Std. 01262
Nearest Town/Resort Bridlington.
Directions From the roundabout on the A165 take the B1255 to Flamborough for 2 miles. Jewison Lane is on the left and site is on the left after the level crossing.
Acreage 2 **Open** March–November
Access Good **Site** Level
Sites available Total 46.
Facilities
Nearby facilities
Bridlington.

HORNSEA

Springfield Caravan Park, Atwick Road, Hornsea, Humberside.
Tel. 532112 Std. 01964
Nearest Town/Resort Hornsea.
Directions Leave Hornsea on main Bridlington road, site ¼ mile on top of hill.
Acreage 2 **Open** Easter–End October
Access Good **Site** Level
Sites available Total 30.
Facilities
Nearby facilities
Beverley.
Views of the bay.

LEVEN

Dacre Lakeside Park, Brandes Burton, Driffield, Humberside, YO25 8SA.
Tel. 543704 Std. 01964
Nearest Town/Resort Bridlington.
Acreage 4 **Open** March–October
Access Good **Site** Level
Sites available Total 90.
Facilities
Nearby facilities
Beverley.
Alongside a 10 acre lake for wind-surfing and dingy sailing.

SCUNTHORPE

Scunthorpe Caravan Co, Ashfield, Burringham Road, Scunthorpe, Humberside.
Tel. 844781 Std. 01724.
Nearest Town/Resort Scunthorpe.
Directions M180 junction 3 onto the

M181. Turn right at the first roundabout, turn right at the second roundabout, under the viaduct and right at next roundabout onto the B1450. Site is 200yds on the right behind ASDA.

Open All year
Access Good **Site** Level
Sites available Total 10.
Facilities
Nearby facilities
Scunthorpe.
Nature area at the rear of a residential park. 24 miles from Cleethorpes, heritage centre at Grimsby and Normanby Hall and park.

SKIPSEA

Far Grange Park, Windhook, Skipsea, Driffield, Humberside YO25 8SY.
Tel. 468293/468248 Std. 01262.
Nearest Town/Resort Hornsea.
Directions 4¼ miles north of Hornsea on the B1242.
Open March–October
Access Good **Site** Level
Sites available Total 180.
Facilities
Nearby facilities
Bridlington.
Cliff top location with superb views of Bridlington Bay.

SKIPSEA

Mill Farm Country Park, Mill Lane, Skipsea, East Yorkshire, YO25 8SS.
Tel. 468211 Std. 01262
Nearest Town/Resort Hornsea.
Directions A165 Hull to Bridlington road, at Beeford take the B1249 to Skipsea. At crossroads turn right, then first left up Cross Street which leads onto Mill Lane, site is on the right.
Acreage 6 **Open** 1 March–21 October
Access Good **Site** Level
Sites available Total 56.
Facilities
Nearby facilities
Bridlington.
Farm walk, beach nearby. RSPB sites at Bempton and Hornsea. Good centre for many places of local interest.

SKIPSEA

Skipsea Sands, Mill Lane, Skipsea, East Yorkshire, YO25 8TY.
Tel. 468210 Std. 01262
Nearest Town/Resort Bridlington.
Directions 6 miles south of Bridlington on the A165, turn onto the B1242 and follow signs.
Acreage 2 **Open** March–November
Access Good **Site** Level
Sites available Total 48.
Facilities
Nearby facilities
Bridlington.
Only 50yds from the beach, superb sea fishing, childrens mini club, amusements and bingo. Luxurious sportsman and pavillion bars. Static caravans also for rent.

SOUTH CAVE

Waudby Caravan & Camping Park, Brough Road, South Cave, North Humberside, HU15 2DB.
Tel. 422523 Std. 01430
Nearest Town/Resort Hull/Beverley.
Directions Situated 12 miles west of Hull off A63. From Westbound depart A63 at South Cave, park opposite petrol station. From Eastbound depart A63 South Cave, right at top opposite petrol station.
Acreage 1 **Open** April–6th Jan
Access Good **Site** Level
Sites available Total 15.
Facilities
Nearby facilities
Brough.
Scenic walks on Yorkshire Dales. Near to Humber Bridge and Beverley.

STAMFORD BRIDGE

Weir Camping Park, Stamford Bridge, York, YO4 1AN.
Tel. 371377 Std. 01759
Nearest Town/Resort York.
Directions Off the A166 7 miles north-west of Pocklington, 7 miles east of York.
Acreage 2 **Open** March–October
Access Good **Site** Lev/Slope
Sites available Total 60.
Facilities
Nearby facilities

STAMFORD BRIDGE

Fangfoss Old Station Caravan Park, Fangfoss, York, Humberside, YO4 5QB.
Tel. 380491 Std. 01759
Nearest Town/Resort York.
Directions A1079 towards Hull. 7 miles east to Wilberfoss, signposted left to Fangfoss.
Acreage 4 **Open** March–October
Access Good **Site** Level
Sites available Total 45.
Facilities
Nearby facilities
York.
Peaceful country park, easy access to wolds, coast, moors, York etc. Take-away food available on site.

CHANNEL ISLANDS

GUERNSEY

Fauxquets Valley Farm Camping Site, Fauxquets de Bas, Catel, Guernsey, Channel Islands.
Tel. 55460 Std. 01481
Nearest Town/Resort St. Peter Port.
Directions Follow sign for Catel, turn left onto Queens Road. Turn right at the sign for the German Undergroung Hospital.
Acreage 3 **Open** Easter–20 September
Site Level
Sites available Total 90.
Facilities
Nearby facilities
1½ miles from sea, beautiful countryside, quiet site. Fully equipped tents available for hire.

GUERNSEY

La Bailloterie Camp Site, Vale Guernsey, Channel Islands.
Tel. 43636 Std. 01481
Nearest Town/Resort St. Sampsons.
Directions Turn right at roundabout proceed along front until you come to Halfway Plantation. Turn left and proceed to 2nd traffic lights turn right and first left.
Acreage 7½ **Open** May–15th Sept
Access Good **Site** Level
Sites available Total 120.
Facilities
Nearby facilities
Near beach 12 minutes. Fully equiped tents for hire.

JERSEY

Rozel Camping Park, Summerville, St Martin, Jersey, Channel Islands.
Tel. 856797 Std. 01534
Nearest Town/Resort St. Helier.
Directions 5 miles from St. Helier. A6 to Martin's Church then B38 to Rozel.
Acreage 3 **Open** End April–Mid Sept
Site Level
Sites available Total 80.
Facilities
Nearby facilities
1 mile from beach, beautiful countryside. Site surrounded by trees. Modern toilet facilities. You can FAX us on 01534 856127.

ISLE. OF MAN

DOUGLAS

Glen Dhoo Farm Camping Site, Hillberry, Nr. Douglas, Isle of Man.
Tel. Douglas 621254 Std. 01624
Nearest Town/Resort Douglas.
Directions On the A18, 100 yards from Hillberry Corner, travelling from Douglas.
Acreage 12 **Open** April–October
Access Good **Site** Lev/Slope
Sites available Total 70.
Facilities
Nearby facilities
Near Douglas, on TT motorcycle course, in sheltered woodland valley.

PEEL

Peel Camping Park, Derby Road, Peel, Isle of Man.
Tel. 842341 Std. 01624
Nearest Town/Resort Peel.
Directions A20 edge of town signposted.
Acreage 4 **Open** Mid May–Mid Sept
Access Good **Site** Level
Sites available Total 100.
Facilities
Nearby facilities
2 miles T.T. course near sea, central in island, vehicles free.

ST. JOHNS

Ballaspit Farm, Patrick Road, St. Johns, Isle of Man, IM4 3BP.
Tel. 842574 Std. 01624
Nearest Town/Resort Peel.
Acreage 6 **Open** All year
Access Poor **Site** Sloping
Sites available
Facilities
Nearby facilities
Fishing and a mountainous setting.

UNION MILLS

Glenlough Farm Campsite, Glenlough Farm, Union Mills, Isle of Man.
Tel. 851326 Std. 01624
Nearest Town/Resort Douglas.
Acreage 10 **Open** May–September
Site Level
Sites available
Facilities
Nearby facilities
Sheltered site.

ISLE. OF WIGHT

BEMBRIDGE

Whitecliff Bay Holiday Park, Hillway, Whitecliff Bay, Bembridge, Isle of Wight. PO35 5PL.
Tel. 872671 Std. 01983
Nearest Town/Resort Sandown.
Directions B3395 road to Sandown, follow signposts.
Acreage 15 **Open** April–October
Access Good **Site** Lev/Slope
Sites available Total 450.
Facilities
Nearby facilities
Brading.
Situated in pleasant countryside adjoining Whitecliff Bay with sandy beach. Indoor pool and leisure centre, family owned and managed.

BEMBRIDGE

'Carpenters Farm', St. Helens, Ryde, Isle of Wight.
Tel. Bembridge 872450 Std. 01983.
Nearest Town/Resort Sandown.
Directions Sandown 3 miles. Ryde 3 mile.
Acreage 12½ **Open** End of May–September
Access Good **Site** Level
Sites available
Facilities
Nearby facilities
Ryde.
Ideal touring. Swimming pool 3 miles away.

BRIGHSTONE

Grange Farm Camping and Touring Site, Military Road, Brighstone, I.O.W. PO30 4DA.
Tel. 740296 Std. 01983
Nearest Town/Resort Newport.
Directions On coastal road A3055 mid-way from Freshwater to Chale (approx 5mls).
Acreage 2 **Open** March–End October
Access Good **Site** Level
Sites available Total 60.
Facilities
Nearby facilities
Ryde.
Small, working farm on the South West coast, safe swimming, walkers paradise. Fishing, sailing, boating and water-skiing on site aswell as climbing. Cafe/restaurant and licensed club opposite. Motorcycles are accepted but no large groups.

BRIGHSTONE

Chine Farm Camping Site, Military Road, Atherfield Bay, I.O.W. PO38 2JH.
Tel. 740228 Std. 01983
Nearest Town/Resort Freshwater.
Directions East of Freshwater 8 miles on the A3055 Coast Road.
Acreage 5 **Open** May–September
Access Good **Site** Level
Sites available Total 80.
Facilities
Nearby facilities
Own private footpath to beach. Sea view.

3¼ miles Blackgang Chine.

COWES

Comforts Farm Camping Park & Riding School, Comforts Farm, Pallance Road, Northwood, Cowes, Isle of Wight, PO31 8LS.
Tel. 293888 Std. 01983
Nearest Town/Resort Cowes.
Directions From Cowes take the A3020, turn right into The Gates Road at Plessey Radar Site. Turn left into Place Road, after ½ mile bear right into Pallance road. Farm entrance is on the right after passing Travellers Joy Public House
Acreage 8¼ **Open** March–October
Access Good **Site** Lev/Slope
Sites available Total 50.
Facilities
Nearby facilities
Horse riding on site.

COWES

Thorness Bay Holiday Park, Thorness, Isle of Wight, PO31 8NJ.
Tel. 523109 Std. 01983
Nearest Town/Resort Newport.
Directions From Fishbourne, follow signs to Newport and turn off roundabout onto dual carriageway following signs for West Cowes then Yarmouth onto the A3054 (Forest Road) for approx 1 mile. Thorness Bay is signposted.
Open April–October
Access Good **Site** Sloping
Sites available Total 200.
Facilities
Nearby facilities
Pools, riding stables, family club, beaches. On site facilities.

NETTLESTONE

Pondwell Camping and Chalets, Pondwell Hill, Nettlestone, I.O.W.
Tel. 612330 Std. 01983
Directions Signposted from Wightlink Fishbourne. Take A3054 to Ryde then A3055 turning left along B3350 to Seaview. Site is next to Wishing Well Pub.
Acreage 14 **Open** May–September
Access Good **Site** Level
Sites available Total 200.
Facilities
Nearby facilities
Ryde.
Set in countryside with scenic views, walking distance to sea.

NEWCHURCH

Southland Camping Park, Winford Road, Newchurch, Isle of Wight.
Tel. 865385 Std. 01983
Nearest Town/Resort Sandown/Shanklin.
Directions Newport to Sandown road A3056/A3055 through Arreton, after Fighting Cocks Public House take the second left. Continue along road for 1 mile, site is on the left.
Acreage 5¾ **Open** Easter–September
Access Good **Site** Level
Sites available Total 100.
Facilities
Nearby facilities
Lake.
Sheltered, secluded touring park, generous level pitches. Far reaching views over Arreton Valley. 5 Tick (Excellent) Graded Park.

ST. HELENS

Nodes Point Holiday Park, St. Helens, Ryde, Isle of Wight, PO33 1YA.
Tel. 872401 Std. 01983
Directions Approach Ryde on the A3054 to join the A3055 in the town. At Bishop Lovett School (on the left), go straight ahead onto the B330 to St. Helens/Bembridge/Nodes Point.
Acreage 16 **Open** 30 April–1 October
Site Lev/Slope
Sites available Total 240.
Facilities
Nearby facilities
Ryde.
Within 65 acres of parkland running down to the beach.

SANDOWN

Adgestone Camping Park, Lower Adgestone, Nr Sandown, I.O.W. P036 OHL.
Tel. 403432/403989 Std. 01983
Nearest Town/Resort Sandown.
Directions Turn off A3055 at the Fairway by Manor House Pub in Lake, which is between Sandown and Shanklin, pass school and golf course on left, turn right at T junction park 200yds on right.
Acreage 8¼ **Open** Easter–September
Access Good **Site** Level
Sites available Total 200.
Facilities
Nearby facilities
Sandown.
Please refer to main advertisement for full details. You can FAX us on 01983 404955.

Quality Camping at the Islands No 1 Resort!

A family site for tents & caravans within walking distance of the beach. Camping is on level marked pitches with hard road access. The modern tiled toilet block has free hot water to shower & basins. Campers have full use of the facilities at the adjacent Landguard Holidays with its magnificent indoor fun pool, outdoor heated pool and licensed club with entertainment for all.

Landguard Camping
Landguard Manor Road
Shanklin, I.of.W. PO37 7PH
Tel: I of W (01983) 867028

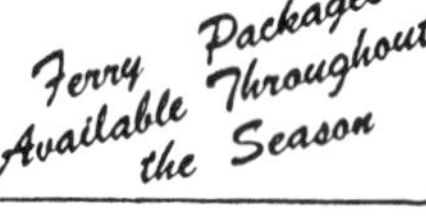

CHEVERTON FARM CAMPING PARK

Newport Road, Apse Heath, Sandown, Isle Of Wight

● **New toilet & shower block for 1994.** ● **Lovely downland views.** ● **Dogs welcome on leads.** **1½ Miles to sandy beaches of Sandown and Shanklin.**

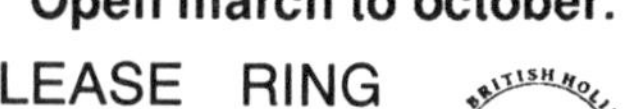

● **Open march to october.**

PLEASE RING
Tel: (01983) 866414
For Brochure

Pick your 1995 Isle of Wight Touring Package Holiday at

Touring Holidays inclusive of site fees, return ferry fares for cars, caravanettes, trailers, touring caravans and up to five passengers.

- Outdoor Heated Swimming Pool
- Adventure Playground • Coarse Fishing

PEAK SEASON PACKAGE
Late Jul - Aug *Prices on application*

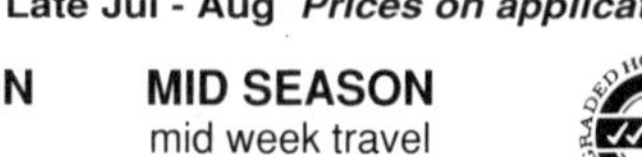

	SPRING/AUTUMN mid week travel	MID SEASON mid week travel
Tents & Caravanettes	**£79.00**	**£112.00**
Trailers, Touring Caravans	**£95.00**	**£139.00**

(These prices are as for 1994)

BOOK ANY DAY TO ANY DAY
WE MAKE THE FERRY RESERVATIONS FOR YOU
Dial-a-Brochure on (01983) 531331 or write to the Resident Proprietor:
MALCOLM N. PEPLOW, The Orchards, Newbridge, Yarmouth, Isle of Wight. PO41 OTS.

SANDOWN
Cheverton Farm Camping Site, Cheverton Farm, Newport Road, Apse Heath, Sandown, Isle of Wight.
Tel. 866414 Std. 01983
Nearest Town/Resort Sandown/Shanklin.
Directions Road number 3056, 500 yards Sandown side of Apse Heath.
Acreage 5 **Open** 1st March–31st October
Access Good **Site** Lev/Slope
Sites available Total 60.
Facilities
Nearby facilities
Sandown.
Near beach, scenic views, country walks.

SANDOWN
Cheverton Copse Caravan & Camping Park, Newport Road, Near Lake, Sandown, Isle of Wight, PO36 0JP.
Tel. 403161 Std. 01983
Nearest Town/Resort Sandown.
Directions On the A3056 Newport/Sandown road, 1¼ miles west of Sandown.
Acreage 1 **Open** May–September
Access Good **Site** Sloping
Sites available Total 26.
Facilities
Nearby facilities
Lake.
Near to all amenities, ideal for touring with superb views.

SANDOWN
Fairway Holiday Park, The Fairway, Sandown, Isle of Wight, PO36 9PS.
Tel. 403462 Std. 01983
Nearest Town/Resort Sandown.
Directions Off Sandown/Shanklin road, into Fairway at Manor House Hotel, Lake. Approx 1 mile from centre of Sandown.
Acreage 5½ **Open** March–September
Access Good **Site** Level
Sites available Total 150.
Facilities
Nearby facilities
Sandown.
Picturesque location, with many facilities, free and easy atmosphere.

SANDOWN
Queen Bower Dairy Caravan Park, Alverstone Road, Queen Bower, Sandown, Isle of Wight.
Tel. 403840 Std. 01983.
Nearest Town/Resort Sandown.
Acreage 2¼ **Open** May–October
Access Good **Site** Level
Sites available Total 20.
Facilities
Nearby facilities
Sandown.
Scenic views, ideal touring. Sell our own produced Dairy products (milk and cream). Public telephone ½ mile.

SHANKLIN
Languard Camping Park, Languard Manor Road, Shanklin, Isle of Wight.
Tel. 867028 Std. 01983
Nearest Town/Resort Shanklin.
Directions A3056 from Newport, ½ mile before Lake Town sign turn right up Whitecross Lane. 400 yards to site.
Acreage 5 **Open** May–September
Access Good **Site** Level
Sites available Total 150.
Facilities
Nearby facilities
Shanklin.
Marked pitches.

SHANKLIN
Lower Hyde Holiday Village, Shanklin, Isle of Wight, PO37 7LL.
Tel. 866131 Std. 01983
Nearest Town/Resort Shanklin.
Directions Approach Shanklin on the A3020, turn left at the traffic lights, go down the High Street and at Boots turn left into Regent Street. Take the third left just before the railway station, then turn right into Landguard Road. The park is on the left.
Acreage 8 **Open** 31 March–8 October
Access Good **Site** Level
Sites available Total 145.
Facilities
Nearby facilities
Shanklin.
Lies within some 55 acres of delightful wooded downland. Just outside Shanklin.

SHANKLIN
Ninham Country Holidays, Shanklin, Isle of Wight.
Tel. 864243 Std. 01983
Nearest Town/Resort Shanklin.
Directions Signposted off Newport/Sandown road (A3056). Sign directions from Safeway Superstore via Whitecross Lane to Ninham.
Acreage 10 **Open** May–September
Access Good **Site** Level
Sites available Total 130.
Facilities
Nearby facilities
Shanklin.
Country park setting close to Islands premier seaside resort.

VENTNOR
Undercliff Riviera Caravan Park, Niton Undercliff, Ventnor, Isle of Wight.
Tel. Niton 730268 Std. 01983
Nearest Town/Resort Ventnor.
Directions 4 miles southwest Ventnor A3055.
Acreage 2 **Open** Easter–September
Access Good **Site** Lev/Slope
Sites available Total 15.
Facilities
Nearby facilities
Shanklin.
Sited in picturesque coastal strip in ground of country house overlooking sea. Site shop in high season only. Stamp for brochure.

YARMOUTH
The Orchards Holiday Caravan & Camping Park, Newbridge, Yarmouth, Isle of Wight. PO41 OTS.
Tel. 531331 Std. 01983
Nearest Town/Resort Yarmouth.
Directions 4 miles east of Yarmouth and 6 miles west of Newport on B3401. Entrance opposite Newbridge Post Office.
Acreage 8 **Open** April–October
Access Good **Site** Lev/Slope
Sites available Total 175.
Facilities
Nearby facilities
Lymington.
Good views of the Downs and Solent. Bookings inclusive of car ferries throughout season. Take-away food and coarse fishing on site. Battery charging, small function/meeting room. Small rallies welcome. You can FAX us on 01983 531666.

SYMBOLS EXPLAINED ON PAGE 47

KENT

ASHFORD

Broadhembury Holiday Park, Steeds Lane, Kingsnorth, Ashford, Kent.
Tel. 620859 Std. 01233
Nearest Town/Resort Ashford.
Directions From junction 10 on M20 take the A2070, then follow signs for Kingsnorth. Turn left at second crossroads in Kingsnorth.
Acreage 5 **Open** All year
Access Good **Site** Level
Sites available Total 55.
Facilities
Nearby facilities
Ashford.
Quiet, country park, every modern amenity, ideal for family holidays, excellent for touring, 10 miles from coast. Quality graded park 5 ticks. Touring not suitable for disabled but caravan hire for disabled persons is available.

ASHFORD

Dean Court Farm, Challock Lane, Westwell, Ashford, Kent, TN25 4NH.
Tel. 712924 Std. 01233.
Nearest Town/Resort Ashford.
Directions Take A252 from Charing on A20 towards Canterbury for 3 miles. On reaching Challock, turn right signposted Westwell. Farm is 1 mile on the right.
Acreage 3 **Open** All year
Access Good **Site** Sloping
Sites available Total 30.
Facilities
Nearby facilities
Charing.
Quiet, very good walking on North Downs Way and good for touring. Good stop-over site for channel ports, Folkestone and Dover.

BIDDENDEN

Spilland Farm Holiday & Tourist Park, Benenden Road, Biddenden, Kent.
Tel. 291379 Std. 01580
Nearest Town/Resort Biddenden/Tenterden.
Directions A262 from Biddenden, 1 mile fork right, park ¼ mile on right.
Acreage 6 **Open** April–September
Access Good **Site** Sloping
Sites available Total 65.
Facilities
Nearby facilities
Headcorn.
Centre for tourists, castles etc, yet 15 miles to coast at Rye. 4 miles grass airfield, flying lessons, parachuting.

BIDDENDEN

Woodlands Park, Tenterden Road, Biddenden, Ashford, Kent.
Tel. 291216 Std. 01580
Nearest Town/Resort Tenterden/Hastings.
Directions On A262, 3 miles north of Tenterden. 15 miles south of Maidstone.
Acreage 10 **Open** March–October
Access Good **Site** Level
Sites available Total 100.
Facilities
Nearby facilities
Headcorn.
Quiet, country site. Ideal for tourist centre.

BIRCHINGTON

Two Chimneys Caravan Park, Shottendane Road, Birchington, Thanet, Kent.
Tel. 841068/843157 Std. 01843
Nearest Town/Resort Margate.
Directions 1½ miles Birchington, turn right into park lane at Birchington Church, left fork "RAF Manston". First left onto B2049 site ½ mile on right.
Acreage 10 **Open** March–October
Access Good **Site** Level
Sites available Total 90.
Facilities
Nearby facilities
Birchington.
Country site, ideal touring centre, 3 miles Margate, 13 miles Canterbury. Sauna, solarium and spa bath. British graded Holiday Parks 4 ticks. Tennis court on site.

BIRCHINGTON

Thanet Way Caravan Co, Frost Farm, Frost Lane, St. Nicholas-at-Wade, Birchington, Kent.
Tel. 847219 Std. 01843.
Nearest Town/Resort Minis Bay.
Directions On A299 from London to Margate.
Open March–October
Access Good **Site** Lev/Slope
Sites available Total 10.
Facilities
Nearby facilities
Birchington.
Quiet country site, 1½ miles from beach. Walking.

BIRCHINGTON

Quex Caravan Park, Park Road, Birchington, Kent.
Tel. 841273 Std. 01843.
Nearest Town/Resort Margate/Ramsgate.
Directions Follow road signs to Margate, when in Birchington turn right at mini roundabout (signposted Margate). Approximately 100yds after roundabout take the first turning on the right and then right again as directed by Tourist Board signs.
Open March–October
Access Good **Site** Level
Sites available Total 50.
Facilities
Nearby facilities
Birchington.
Ideal base for touring Thanet and Canterbury areas.

CANTERBURY

Red Lion Caravan Park, Old London Road, Dunkirk, Near Canterbury, Kent, ME13 9LL.
Tel. 750661 Std. 01227
Nearest Town/Resort Canterbury.
Directions 5 miles – Take the A2 London bound, turn off at park sign ¼ mile for Dunkirk. 3 miles – At the end of the M2 (junction 7) take the A2 Canterbury bound. Immediately take park sign 3 miles for Dunkirk.
Acreage 1 **Open** All Year
Access Good **Site** Level
Sites available Total 25.
Facilities
Nearby facilities
Canterbury.
Orchard and country routes, gardens to visit, Canterbury city, Dover 15 miles, beaches 5 miles, Channel Tunnel 17 miles. Cafe/restaurant in the adjoining pub.

CANTERBURY

The Rose and Crown, Stelling Minnis, Canterbury Kent CT4 6AS.
Tel. 709265 Std. 01227
Nearest Town/Resort Canterbury.
Directions 6 miles south of Canterbury on B2068.
Acreage 1 **Open** March–October
Access Good **Site** Level
Sites available Total 30.
Facilities
Nearby facilities
Canterbury East.
Rural.

CANTERBURY

Yew Tree Caravan Park, Stone Street, Petham, Canterbury, Kent, CT4 5PL.
Tel. 700306 Std. 01227
Nearest Town/Resort Canterbury.
Directions 4 miles south of Canterbury on the B2068, turn right by the Chequers Public House, park entrance is on the left

hand side.
Acreage 2 **Open** March–October
Access Good **Site** Lev/Slope
Sites available Total 30.
Facilities
Nearby facilities
Canterbury East.
Small picturesque park overlooking the Chartham Downs. Scenic views, large swimming pool, ideal touring base.

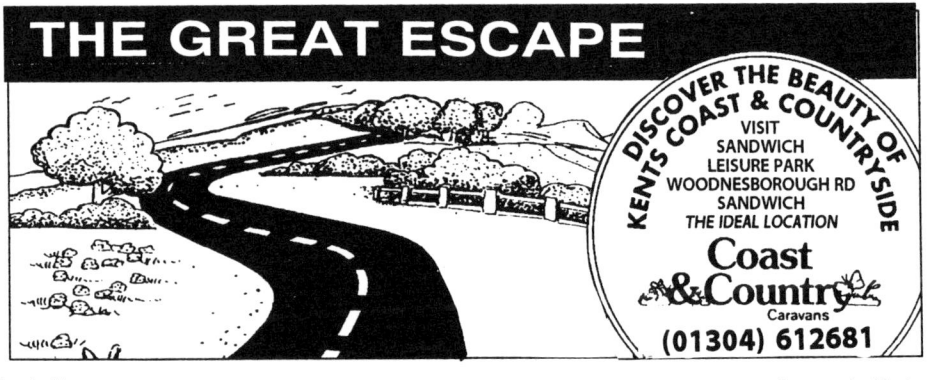

DEAL

Clifford Park Caravans, Clifford Park, Thompson Close, Walmer, Deal, Kent, CT14 7PB.
Tel. 373373 Std. 01304
Nearest Town/Resort Deal.
Directions A258, Deal 1 mile and Dover 5 miles.
Acreage ¼ **Open** March–30 October
Access Good **Site** Level
Sites available Total 15.
Facilities
Nearby facilities
Walmer.
Ideal touring area for day trips to France or the beaches.

DEAL

Leisurescope Holiday Caravan Park, Golf Road, Deal, Kent, CT14 6RG.
Tel. 363332 Std. 01304
Nearest Town/Resort Deal.
Directions If approaching from the A2 take the A258 to Deal. Follow road onto the seafront heading north, follow seafront road. At T-Junction turn right into Golf Road, go past the golf clubhouse to Leisurescope.
Acreage 1½ **Open** March–October
Access Good **Site** Level
Sites available Total 55.
Facilities
Nearby facilities
Deal.
300yds from the sea, scenic views, walking and cycling. Fishing and golf. Quiet and peaceful park.

DEAL

Sutton Vale Country Club, Sutton-By-Dover, Kent, CT15 5DH.
Tel. 374155 Std. 01304
Nearest Town/Resort Deal.
Directions A2 Dover road, take Whitfield roundabout, down Archers Court Road, 4 miles, opposite McDonalds.
Open March–January
Access Good **Site** Level
Sites available Total 14.
Facilities
Nearby facilities
Deal.
Scenic countryside.

DOVER

Hawthorn Farm, Martin Mill, Dover, Kent, CT15 5LA.
Tel. 852658 Std. 01304
Nearest Town/Resort Dover/Deal.
Directions 2¼ miles from St Margaret's Bay. Near Dover on the A258 from Dover towards Deal.
Acreage 15 **Open** March–October
Access Good **Site** Level
Sites available Total 250.
Facilities
Nearby facilities
Martin Mill.
Beautifully landscaped. Extremely convenient for crossing to France. Country setting with seaside facilities nearby.

DYMCHURCH

New Beach Holiday Village Touring Park, Hythe Road, Dymchurch, Kent, TN29 0JX.
Tel. 872234 Std. 01303
Nearest Town/Resort Hythe.
Directions Situated on the main coast road between Hythe and Dymchurch (A259).
Acreage 15 **Open** March–9th Janurary
Access Good **Site** Level
Sites available Total 250.
Facilities
Nearby facilities
Folkestone.
Near beach.

EASTCHURCH

Warden Springs Caravan Park, Warden Point, Eastchurch, Sheppey, Kent, ME12 4HF.
Tel. 880216 Std. 01795
Nearest Town/Resort Sheerness.
Directions M20 junction 7 or M2 junction 5 to the A249. A249 to Sheppey, B2231 to Eastchurch.
Acreage 2 **Open** March–October
Access Good **Site** Sloping
Sites available Total 48.
Facilities
Nearby facilities
Sheerness.
Near beach, scenic views, fishing.

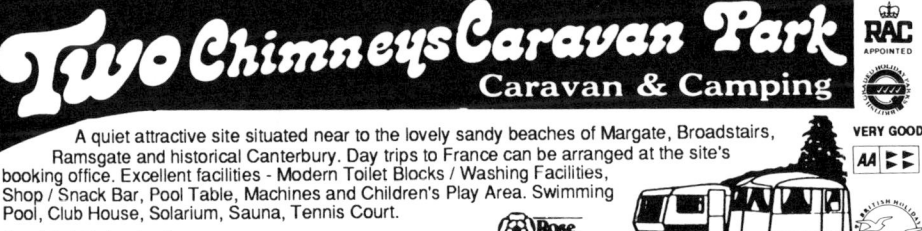

FOLKESTONE

'Black Horse Farm', 385 Canterbury Road, Densole-Swingfield, Folkestone, Kent, CT18 7BG.
Tel. 892665 Std. 01303.
Nearest Town/Resort Folkestone.
Directions 4 miles from Folkestone on A260 to Canterbury. Site on left, 100 yards past Black Horse Inn on right.
Acreage 4 **Open** January–December
Access Good **Site** Level
Sites available Total 45.
Facilities
Nearby facilities
Folkestone.
Ideal centre for touring east Kent. Telephone 9a.m.-8p.m. Convenient for Channel ferries. Quality Graded 4 Ticks.

FOLKESTONE

Varne Ridge Caravan Park, 145 Old Dover Road, Capel, Nr. Folkestone, Kent.
Tel. 251765 Std. 01303
Nearest Town/Resort Dover/Folkestone.
Directions Main A20 midway between Folkestone and Dover.
Acreage 1¼ **Open** March–January
Access Good **Site** Level
Sites available Total 18.
Facilities
Nearby facilities
Folkestone.
Close to ferry terminals and the Channel Tunnel.

LEYSDOWN-ON-SEA

Priory Hill Holiday Park Ltd, Wing Road, Leysdown, Isle of Sheppey, Kent, ME12 4QT.
Tel. 510267 Std. 01795
Nearest Town/Resort Leysdown.
Directions A2, M2 or M20 from London to the A249 signposted to Sheerness. B2231 to Leysdown.
Acreage 1¼ **Open** Mid March–October
Access Good **Site** Level
Sites available Total 55.
Facilities
Nearby facilities
Sheerness.
Very near the beach, alongside a coastal park with Pitch & Putt. Indoor heated swimming pool, sauna and sun-bed.

MINSTER

Wayside Caravan Park, Way Hill, Minster, Ramsgate, Kent, CT12 4HW.
Tel. 821272 Std. 01843
Nearest Town/Resort Ramsgate.
Directions ¼ mile East of Minster Village on the B2048.
Acreage ¼ **Open** 1st March–30th October
Access Good **Site** Level
Sites available Total 7.
Facilities
Nearby facilities
Minster.

MINSTER ON SEA

Irwin Park Ltd, The Broadway, Minster-on-Sea, Sheerness, Kent, ME12 2DF.
Tel. 875211 Std. 01795
Nearest Town/Resort Sheerness.
Directions 2 miles from Sheerness. M2 junction 5, A249 to Isle of Sheppey, onto B2231 then first left to Minster.
Open March–October
Access Good **Site** Level
Sites available Total 100.
Facilities
Nearby facilities
Sheerness.
Near to beach and open country. Ideal boating, sailing, wind-surfing and fishing. 2 miles to Holland Ferry for stop-over.

OTFORD

East Hill Farm Caravan Park, East Hill Road, Nr. Kemsing, Sevenoaks, Kent. TN15 6YD.
Tel. 522347 Std. 01959.
Nearest Town/Resort Sevenoaks.
Directions Off the A225 – telephone for directions.
Open April–October
Access Good/Poor **Site** Level
Sites available Total 20.
Facilities
Nearby facilities
Otford.

RAMSGATE

Pine Meadow Touring Park, Spratling Court Farm, Manston, Ramsgate, Kent, CT12 5AN.
Tel. 587770 Std. 01843
Nearest Town/Resort Ramsgate.
Directions From A256 junction take B2050 west towards Manston village, in 500 yards turn right, signposted Pine Meadow.
Acreage 3 **Open** April–September
Access Good **Site** Level
Sites available Total 40.
Facilities
Nearby facilities
Ramsgate.
Sheltered rural site, 10 minutes from Margate, Broadstairs and Ramsgate (Sally Line Terminal). 4 Tick park.

RAMSGATE

Manston Caravan & Camping Park, Manston Court Road, Manston, Ramsgate, Kent.
Tel. 823442 Std. 01843
Nearest Town/Resort Ramsgate.
Directions From the M2 follow the A299 and join the A253 to Ramsgate. Turn left onto the B2048 then first right (Kent International Airport) to join the B2050. As you pass the airport entrance take the next turn left for 500yds.
Acreage 7 **Open** April–October
Access Good **Site** Level
Sites available Total 100.
Facilities
Nearby facilities
Ramsgate.
Quiet, family park. Motorcycles are sometimes accepted.

RAMSGATE

Viking Caravan Club, Foads Lane, Cliffsend, Nr. Ramsgate, Kent, CT12 5JH.
Tel. 588081 Std. 0843
Nearest Town/Resort Ramsgate.
Directions Follow Canterbury/London sign A253. At the third roundabout turn left, follow Sandwich direction A256, take the first turning on the right at Cliffsend Road. Site is signposted from the third roundabout.
Acreage 6 **Open** March–October
Access Good **Site** Level
Sites available Total 40.
Facilities
Nearby facilities
Ramsgate.
Near beaches, Historical attractions, RAF Manston Aircraft Museum and good leisure facilities.

SANDWICH

Sandwich Leisure Park, Woodnesborough Road, Sandwich, Kent, CT13 0AA.
Tel. 612681 Std. 01304
Nearest Town/Resort Sandwich.
Directions Take A257 to Sandwich and follow brown campsite signs to park.
Acreage 14 **Open** March–October
Access Good **Site** Level
Sites available Total 100.
Facilities
Nearby facilities
Sandwich.

SHEERNESS

Sheerness Holiday Park, Halfway Road, Sheerness, Kent, ME12 3AA.
Tel. 662638 Std. 01795
Nearest Town/Resort Sheerness.
Directions From M20 or M2 take the A249 towards Sheerness, then the A250 into the town. We are ½ mile from the town centre.
Acreage 4 **Open** Easter–October
Access Good **Site** Level
Sites available Total 86.
Facilities
Nearby facilities
Sheerness.

WEST KINGSDOWN

'To The Woods', Botsom Lane, West Kingsdown, Nr. Sevenoaks, Kent TN15 6BN.
Tel. Farningham 863751 Std. 01322.
Nearest Town/Resort West Kingsdown.
Directions A20 West Kingsdown facing London Clearways Cafe on left next turning Botsom Lane.
Acreage 3 **Open** All year
Access Poor **Site** Level
Sites available Total 40.
Facilities
Nearby facilities
Swanley.
Easy access via Swanley to centre of London. Margate, Dover etc, only 1 hour by car. Winter and all year caravan storage available.

WHITSTABLE

Primrose Cottage Caravan Park, Golden Hill, Whitstable, Kent CT5 3AR.
Tel. Whitstable 273694 Std. 01277.
Nearest Town/Resort Whitstable.
Directions On A299, 1 mile east of Whitstable roundabout.
Acreage ½ **Open** March–October
Access Good **Site** Level
Sites available Total 10.
Facilities
Nearby facilities
Whitstable.

WROTHAM

Thriftwood Caravan Park, Plaxdale Green Road, Stansted, Nr. Wrotham, Kent.
Tel. 822261 Std. 01732
Nearest Town/Resort Sevenoaks.
Directions On A20 on top of Wrotham Hill, 3½ miles south of Brands Hatch, exit 2A,M20 signposted with international camping signs.
Acreage 10 **Open** March–January
Access Good **Site** Level
Sites available Total 150.
Facilities
Nearby facilities
Borough Green.
35 minutes by train to London, convenient for southern ports.

LANCASHIRE

BENTHAM

Riverside Caravan Park, Wenning Avenue, Bentham, Lancaster, Lancashire.
Tel. 61272 Std. 015242
Nearest Town/Resort Bentham.
Directions Follow caravan signs off the B6480 at the Black Bull Hotel in Bentham
Acreage 10 **Open** March–October
Access Good **Site** Level
Sites available Total 60.
Facilities
Nearby facilities
Bentham.
Free fishing for trout and sea trout adjacent to the site. Electric points for tourers.

BLACKPOOL

Gillett Farm Caravan Park, Peel Road, Nr. Blackpool, Lancs, FY4 5JU.
Tel. 761676 Std. 01253
Nearest Town/Resort Blackpool.
Directions Blackpool junction 4 on M55 turn left to Lytham 400yds to traffic lights. Turn right and immediate left into Peel Road. 350yds second site on the right.
Acreage 12 **Open** March–October
Access Good **Site** Slightly Sloping
Sites available Total 76.
Facilities
Nearby facilities
Blackpool.
Within easy reach of Blackpool, Lytham St Annes and Fleetwood. Graded 4 Ticks.

BLACKPOOL

Newton Hall Holiday Centre, Staining Road, Staining, Blackpool, Lancashire.
Tel. 882512 Std. 01253
Nearest Town/Resort Blackpool.
Directions 2¼ miles east from Blackpool Tower off the B5266, right at Newton Arms Hotel, park is 700 mts on the right.
Acreage 1 **Open** 1st March–31st October
Access Good **Site** Level
Sites available Total 32.
Facilities
Nearby facilities
Blackpool North.
Ideal touring centre for all of Blackpools attractions. Flat, green bowling complex on site.

BLACKPOOL

Mariclough - Hampsfield, Preston New Road, Peel, Blackpool, Lancs.
Tel. 761034 Std. 01253
Nearest Town/Resort Blackpool.
Directions M55 junction 4, first left onto the A583. At Kirkham go through traffic lights, site 200yds on the left.
Acreage 2 **Open** Easter–November
Access Good **Site** Level
Sites available Total 50.
Facilities
Nearby facilities
Blackpool/Kirkham.
Flat, mowed grass, sheltered park. Off license.

BLACKPOOL

Pipers Height Caravan & Camping Park, Peel Road, Peel, Blackpool, Lancashire.
Tel. 763767 Std. 01253
Nearest Town/Resort Blackpool.
Directions Exit M55 junction 4 take the first turning left (signed airport) on the A583. At the first set of lights turn right then sharp left. Site is first on the right. Site 2 miles from the M55.
Acreage 11 **Open** March–October
Access Good **Site** Level
Sites available Total 150.
Facilities
Nearby facilities
Blackpool.

BLACKPOOL

Richmond Hill Caravan Park, 352 St. Anne's Road, Blackpool, Lancashire.
Tel. 344266 Std. 01253
Nearest Town/Resort Blackpool.
Directions We are situated in Blackpool south shore. Near Airport.
Acreage 1 **Open** March–October
Access Good **Site** Level
Sites available Total 15.
Facilities
Nearby facilities
Blackpool South.
Near beach, theatres, piers, pleasure beach.

BLACKPOOL

Under Hill Farm, Peel, Nr. Blackpool, Lancashire FY4 5JS.
Tel. 763107 Std. 01253.
Nearest Town/Resort Blackpool.
Directions Site is situated on the A583 road, ½ mile from M55 motorway and 3½ miles east of Blackpool.
Acreage 6 **Open** Easter–October
Access Good **Site** Sloping
Sites available Total 60.
Facilities
Nearby facilities
Blackpool.
There are many attractions only 3 miles from the site, zoo, parks, beach. Electric hook-ups when available.

CARNFORTH

Bolton Holmes Farm, Bolton-le-Sands, Carnforth, Lancashire LA5 8ES.
Tel. 732854 Std. 01524
Nearest Town/Resort Lancaster/Morecambe.
Directions Travel north on A6. Take first left after Royal Hotel, Mill Lane, Bolton-le-Sands.
Open April–September
Access Good **Site** Sloping
Sites available Total 30.

Facilities
Nearby facilities
Carnforth.
Scenic views. On shore side.

CARNFORTH

Capernwray House, Capernwray, Carnforth, Lancs, LA6 1AE.
Tel. 732363 Std. 01524
Nearest Town/Resort Carnforth/Kirby Lonsdale.
Directions Leave the M6 junction 35 and follow signs for Over Kellet. At the village green turn left signposted Capernwray. Site is 2 miles on the right.
Acreage 5¼ **Open** March–October
Access Good **Site** Lev/Slope
Sites available Total 60.
Facilities
Nearby facilities
Carnforth.
Near a canal, beautiful scenery and good walking. 10 minutes to the beach. Swimming pool around the corner.

CARNFORTH

Detron Gate Farm, Bolton-le-Sands, Nr. Carnforth, Lancashire LA5 9TN.
Tel. 732842/733617 Std. 01524
Nearest Town/Resort Morecambe.
Directions 2¼ miles A6 south, exit 35 from M6.
Acreage 16 **Open** March–October
Access Good **Site** Lev/Slope
Sites available Total 195.
Facilities
Nearby facilities
Carnforth.
Near Morecambe, ideal touring Dales and Lakes.

CARNFORTH

Holgate's Caravan Parks Ltd, Cove Road, Silverdale, Nr. Carnforth, Lancashire LA5 0SH.
Tel. 701508 Std. 01524
Nearest Town/Resort Morecambe.
Directions 5 miles northwest of Carnforth, between Silverdale and Arnside.
Acreage 10 **Open** 21 Dec–7 Nov
Access Good **Site** Lev/Slope
Sites available Total 70.
Facilities
Nearby facilities
Silverdale.
On Morecambe Bay. In area of outstanding natural beauty. Indoor swimming pool, spa bath, sauna, solarium, licensed lounge bar. Restricted facilities during Winter months.

CARNFORTH

Morecambe Lodge Caravan Park, Shore Lane, Bolton-le-Sands, Carnforth, Lancs, LA5 8JP.
Tel. 823260/824361 Std. 01524
Nearest Town/Resort Morecambe/Lancaster.
Directions A6 north from Lancaster, 4 miles to Bolton-le-Sands, turn left onto coastal road A5105 at traffic lights. 200yds turn right by the first house and follow this road to the beach. Site is on the left before the beach.
Acreage 1¼ **Open** March–October
Access Good **Site** Level
Sites available Total 25.
Facilities
Nearby facilities
Carnforth.
Direct access to the beach, peaceful with beautiful views of lakes, hills. Noted for spectacular sunsets.

CARNFORTH

Sandside Farm Caravan & Camping Park, The Shore, Bolton-le-Sands, Carnforth, Lancashire LA5 8JS.
Tel. 822311 Std. 01524
Nearest Town/Resort Carnforth.
Directions A6 from junc 35 (M6) through Carnforth, turn right at Little Chef in Bolton Le Sands.
Acreage 6 **Open** March–October
Access Good **Site** Lev/Slope
Sites available Total 140.
Facilities
Nearby facilities
Carnforth.
Scenic views on shoreside overlooking Morecambe Bay, ideal touring lakes and dales. Childrens sand pit.

CLITHEROE

Three Rivers Park, Eaves Hall Lane, West Bradford, Near Clitheroe, Lancs, BB7 3JG.
Tel. 23523 Std. 01200
Nearest Town/Resort Clitheroe.
Directions Junction 31 off M6, take the A59 towards Clitheroe. Turn off at West Bradford/Pimlico sign straight into West Bradford. Turn left at the T-Junction and then first right into Eaves Hall Lane. We are at the top.
Acreage 7 **Open** All Year.
Access Good **Site** Lev/Slope
Sites available Total 146.
Facilities
Nearby facilities
Clitheroe.
Scenic views of Pendle Hill and walks alongside the River Ribble.

COCKERHAM

Cockerham Sands Country Park, Cockerham, Near Lancaster, Lancs. LA2 0BB.
Tel. 751387 Std. 01524
Nearest Town/Resort Lancaster.
Directions Leave M6 at Junction 33 take A6 (Garstang/Glasson Dock) for 1¼ miles, turn right onto Cockerham Road for 2 miles, turn right in 2¼ miles turn left opposite Thurnham Hall at sign saying park 3 miles.
Open March–October
Access Good **Site** Level
Sites available Total 9.
Facilities
Nearby facilities
Lancaster.
Adjacent to the park safe shore and River Lune. Club complex with cabaret and disco. Snooker, pool and darts. T.V. and pool lounge.

CROSTON

The Royal Umpire Caravan Park, Southport Road, Croston, Near Preston, Lancs, PR5 7HP.
Tel. 600257 Std. 01772
Nearest Town/Resort Southport.
Directions 10 miles East of Southport, 5 miles West of Chorley, on A581 midway between A59 and the A49.
Acreage 60 **Open** Mid Dec–Early Nov
Access Good **Site** Level
Sites available Total 200.
Facilities
Nearby facilities
Croston.
Landscaped touring park, ideally situated year-round holiday venue. Immaculate toilet blocks, 2 laundrettes, well-stocked licensed shop, satellite TV rental, fabulous full size fort/adventure playground. Caring dog owners welcomed. Midweek discounts. Phone for a colour brochure. Cafe 200yds.

GARSTANG

Claylands Caravan Park, Robinson's Caravans, Cabus, Garstang, Nr. Preston, Lancs.
Tel. Forton 791242 Std. 01524
Nearest Town/Resort Garstang/Blackpool.
Directions 2 miles north of Garstang, signposted directly off the A6.
Acreage 14 **Open** March–October
Access Good **Site** Level
Sites available Total 64.
Facilities

Nearby facilities
Preston.
Ideally situated on the banks of the River Wyre with beautiful views of the Trough of Bowland.

GARSTANG

Six Arches Caravan Park, Scorton, Garstang, Nr. Preston, Lancashire.
Tel. 791683 Std. 01524
Nearest Town/Resort Blackpool.
Directions On A6, 3 miles north of Garstang, turn east at Little Chef down Station Lane, then turn first left.
Acreage 13 **Open** March–October
Access Good **Site** Level
Sites available Total 16.
Facilities
Nearby facilities
Lancaster.
The caravan park is situated on the banks of the River Wyre and is just ½ mile from the beautiful village of Scorton. Blackpool and Morecambe are just half an hour by car, and only 45 minutes from the Lake District.

GISBURN

Todber Caravan Park, Burnley Road, Gisburn, Clitheroe, Lancashire BB7 4JJ.
Tel. 445322 Std. 01200
Nearest Town/Resort Nelson/Clitheroe.
Directions On A682, Nelson, 1½ miles from A59 at Gisburn (A59 Preston to Skipton Road.
Acreage 4 **Open** March October
Access Good **Site** Lev/Slope
Sites available Total 100.
Facilities
Ideal touring Yorkshire Dales, Bronte country, good views Ribble Valley.

GISBURN

Rimington Caravan Park, Hardacre Lane, Gisburn, Nr. Clitheroe, Lancs, BB7 4EE.
Tel. 445355 Std. 01200
Nearest Town/Resort Clitheroe.
Directions Travelling east on the A59, enter Gisburn and turn right onto the A682 signposted Nelson. After 1 mile fork right and site is on the right in 400yds.
Acreage 2 **Open** March–October
Access Good **Site** Level
Sites available Total 25.
Facilities
Nearby facilities
Clitheroe.
Quiet, family owned park set in lovely countryside with quality facilities and amenities.

LONGRIDGE

Beacon Fell View Caravan Park, Higher Road, Longridge, Nr. Preston, Lancashire, PR3 2TY.
Tel. 785434 Std. 01772
Directions Leave M6 at junction 32, take Garstang signs onto the A6. At traffic lights turn right, follow to Longridge. DO NOT take the sign for Beacon Fell. At Longridge go across the roundabout, keep left at the White Bull. Park is 1 mile on the right.
Open March–October
Site Level
Sites available Total 100.
Facilities
Nearby facilities
Preston.
Scenic views of Ribble Valley. Ideal centre for touring.

LYTHAM ST.ANNES

Eastham Hall Caravan Park, Saltcoates Road, Lytham St. Annes, Lancashire.
Tel. 737907 Std. 01253
Nearest Town/Resort Lytham St. Annes.
Directions Take A584 to Lytham St. Annes, right onto B5259. Site 1 mile on right.
Acreage 15 **Open** March–October
Access Good **Site** Level
Sites available Total 160.
Facilities
Nearby facilities
Lytham St. Annes.

LYTHAM ST ANNES

Sea View Caravan Park, Bank Lane, Warton, Lancs, PR4 1TD.
Tel. 679336 Std. 01772
Nearest Town/Resort Lytham/St Annes.
Directions Just off the A584 (Preston to Lytham road), 2 miles east of Lytham. 8 miles west of Preston.
Acreage 3 **Open** March–October
Access Good **Site** Level
Sites available Total 9.
Facilities
Nearby facilities
Lytham.
Estuary views and walks (Lancashire coastal way) quiet location Within easy reach of Blackpool.

MORECAMBE

Broadfields Caravan & Camping Park, 276 Oxcliffe Road, Morecambe, Lancs, LA3 3EH.
Tel. 410278 Std. 01524

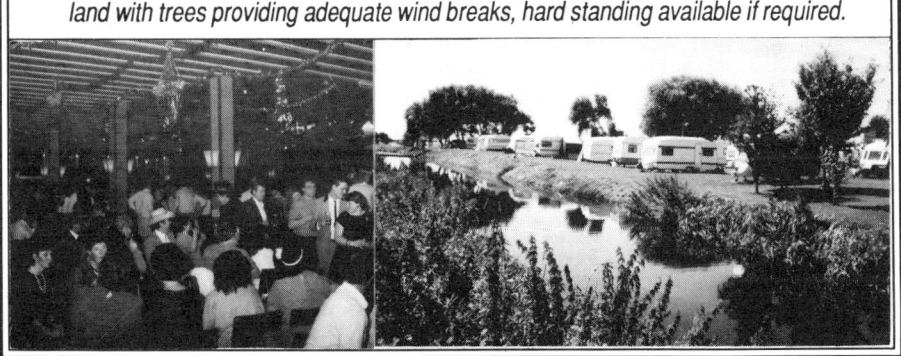

Nearest Town/Resort Morecambe/ Lancaster.
Directions Junction 34 off the M6, follow the A589 Morecambe and Heysham road. At the first big roundabout keep left. Follow signs for Middleton and Overton. Site is on the right in about 1 mile.
Acreage 2¼ **Open** March–October
Access Good **Site** Level
Sites available Total 45.
Facilities
Nearby facilities
Morecambe.
10 minutes from Morecambe Prom, ¾ hour drive to the Lake District.

MORECAMBE

Melbreak Camp Site, Carr Lane, Middleton, Nr. Morecambe, Lancashire.
Tel. 852430 Std. 01524
Nearest Town/Resort Morecambe.
Directions Take A589 out of Morecambe. Follow signs to Middleton. Turn right by church. Site ½ mile on left.
Acreage 1½ **Open** March–October
Access Good **Site** Level
Sites available Total 50.
Facilities
Nearby facilities
Morecambe.
Site is ½ mile from Middleton Sands and 3 miles from seaside attractions of Morecambe.

MORECAMBE

Venture Caravan Park, Langridge Way, Westgate, Morecambe, Lancashire, LA4 4TQ.
Tel. 412986 Std. 01524
Directions Exit 34 on the M6, A683 to Lancaster then the A589 to Morecambe and Heysham. Through two roundabouts, the third roundabout at Shrimp turn left signposted Heysham. In ¾ mile turn right at the school, Langridge Way and go straight ahead to the park.
Acreage 17¼ **Open** All Year
Access Good **Site** Level
Sites available Total 327.
Facilities
Nearby facilities
Morecambe.

MORECAMBE

The Regent Leisure Park, Westgate, Morecambe, Lancashire.
Tel. 413940 Std. 01524
Nearest Town/Resort Morecambe.
Directions Leave M6 at junction 34 heading for Lancaster then Morecambe, turn 1st left at third large roundabout, we are then 1¼ miles on the left.
Open March–January
Access Good **Site** Level
Sites available Total 25.
Facilities
Nearby facilities
Morecambe.
Ideal centre for exploring lakes and dales, club complex with cabaret/disco and childrens indoor adventureland. E.T.B. Rose Award and Graded Excellent Quality Grading.

ORMSKIRK

Abbey Farm Caravan Site, Dark Lane, Ormskirk, Lancashire.
Tel. 572686 Std. 01695
Nearest Town/Resort Ormskirk.
Directions From the M6 junction 27 onto the A5209 to Parbold and Newburgh. Turn left onto the B5240 and an immediate right into Hobcross Lane. Park is 1¼ miles on the right. From the M58 junction 3 onto the B5240. At the T-Junction turn left and right onto the B5240, turn left into Hobcross Lane. Park is 1¼ miles on the right.
Acreage 6 **Open** All year.
Access Good **Site** Level
Sites available
Facilities
Nearby facilities
Good golf centre. Ideal for visiting Liverpool, Southport, Wigan, Chorley and Manchester. Bathroom available. Undercover washing up area. British Graded Holiday Park 5 Ticks. Dog exercise field. Late night arrivals area. Lending Library. Bar.B.Q area and recreational field.

POULTON-LE-FYLDE

River Wyre Caravan Park, 30 Mains Lane, Singleton, Poulton-le-Fylde, Blackpool, Lancs, FY6 7LG.
Tel. 883368 Std. 01253
Nearest Town/Resort Blackpool.
Directions M55 junction 3, follow Fleetwood signs to first set of traffic lights, turn left. Go straight through next set of traffic lights and park is 200yds on the right hand side.
Open March–October
Access Good **Site** Level
Sites available
Facilities
Nearby facilities
Poulton-le-Fylde.
Riverside site, ideal touring, good fishing pond and a club on site.

POULTON-LE-FYLDE

Meadowcroft Caravan Park, Garstang Road, Great Eccleston, Nr. Blackpool, Lancs, PR3 0ZQ.
Tel. 670266 Std. 01995
Nearest Town/Resort Blackpool.
Directions Leave the M55 at junction 3 onto the A585 in the direction of Fleetwood to the traffic lights. Turn right onto the A586 for 1¼ miles, park is signed on the right.
Open March–October
Access Good **Site** Level
Sites available Total 45.
Facilities
Nearby facilities
Poulton-le-Fylde.
Scenic views, 10 minute walk to the market village.

PREESALL

Willowgrove Caravan Park, Sandy Lane, Preesall, Poulton-Le-Fylde, Lancashire, FY6 0EJ.
Tel. 811306 Std. 01253
Nearest Town/Resort Blackpool.
Directions M6, M56 turn off Fleetwood, turn off on A588. After Stalmine take the B5377 to Preesall. At T-Junction turn right to caravan park, 400yds on the left.
Acreage 5 **Open** Easter–October
Access Good **Site** Level
Sites available Total 60.
Facilities
Nearby facilities
Poulton.
Own private lake, fishing and birdwatching.

THORNTON

Kneps Farm Holiday Park, River Road, Thornton-Cleveleys, Lancashire.
Tel. 823632 Std. 01253
Nearest Town/Resort Blackpool.
Directions Approach is on the A585. At the roundabout turn right for Little Thornton, then turn right again at the church into Stanah Road. This leads to River Road and the entrance is facing traffic approaching a bend.
Acreage 10 **Open** March–October
Access Good **Site** Level
Sites available Total 65.
Facilities
Nearby facilities
Poulton-le-Fylde.
Situated in the Wyre Estuary Country Park with easy access to coastal resorts of Blackpool, Wyre and Fylde.

LEICESTERSHIRE

OAKHAM

Ranksborough Hall Caravan & Camping, Ranksborough Hall, Langham, Nr. Oakham, Leics.
Tel. 722984 Std. 01572
Nearest Town/Resort Oakham.
Directions Main A606 to Langham Village.
Acreage 13 **Open** All Year
Access Good **Site** Level
Sites available Total 110.
Facilities
Nearby facilities
Oakham.

WOLVEY

Villa Farm Caravan & Camping Park, Villa Farm, Wolvey, Nr. Hinckley, Leics, LE10 3HF.
Tel. 220493/220630 Std. 01455.
Nearest Town/Resort Hinckley.
Directions M6 junction 2 then take B4065 and follow caravan and camping signs. M69 junction 1 follow signs for Wolvey then caravan and camping signs.
Acreage 7 **Open** All year
Access Good **Site** Level
Sites available Total 110.
Facilities
Nearby facilities
Hinckley.
A quiet site ideally located to explore the many places of interest in the Midlands.

LINCOLNSHIRE

ALFORD

Woodthorpe Hall Leisure Park, Woodthorpe, Alford, Lincs, LN13 0DD. Tel. 450294 Std. 01507
Nearest Town/Resort Alford/ Mablethorpe.
Directions From Alford, A1104 for 3 miles then the B1373, site 1 mile. From Louth, A157 for 10 miles then the B1373, site 1¼ miles.
Acreage 40 **Open** March–January
Access Good **Site** Level
Sites available Total 120.
Facilities
Nearby facilities
Delightfully wooded area, pleasant for walks around our farm and 6 miles to Mablethorpe.

BOSTON

White Cat Caravan & Camping Park, Shaw Lane, Old Leake, Boston, Lincolnshire.
Tel. Boston 870121 Std. 01205
Nearest Town/Resort Boston/ Skegness.
Directions 8 miles from Boston on the A52 Skegness road, then take the first right (opposite B1184).
Acreage 2½ **Open** Mid March–Mid November
Sites available Total 40.
Facilities
Nearby facilities
Boston.
Ideal touring for Fens, wild life marshes, Skegness resort. Permanent tourer sites available.

BOSTON

The Plough, Swineshead Bridge, Boston, Lincs, PE20 3PT.
Tel. 820300 Std. 01205
Nearest Town/Resort Boston/ Skegness.
Directions Site is on the main A17 Sleaford (12 miles) to Kings Lynn road. 7 miles from Boston.
Acreage 3 **Open** March–October
Access Good **Site** Level
Sites available Total 60.
Facilities
Nearby facilities
Public House in own 5 acre area alongside South Witham River for fishing.

HOLBEACH

Matopos, Main Street, Fleet Hargate, Holbeach, Nr. Spalding, Lincs.
Tel. 422910 Std. 01406
Nearest Town/Resort Holbeach.
Directions From Spalding take the A151 to Holbeach. Continue for a further 3 miles to Fleet Hargate, turn right into the village just before the A151 joins the A17.
Acreage 3 **Open** March–October
Access Good **Site** Level
Sites available Total 45.
Facilities
Nearby facilities
Kings Lynn.
Spalding Flower Festival.

HOLBEACH

Whaplode Manor Caravan Park, Whaplode Manor, Saracens Head, Holbeach, Lincs.
Tel. 422837 Std. 01406
Nearest Town/Resort Holbeach.
Directions Just off the A17, 3 miles north of Holbeach.
Acreage 2 **Open** Easter–November
Access Good **Site** Level
Sites available Total 20.
Facilities
Spalding.
Quiet country.

INGOLDMELLS

Country Meadow Holiday Park, Anchor Lane, Ingoldmells, Skegness, Lincs, PE25 1LZ.
Tel. 874455 Std. 01754
Nearest Town/Resort Skegness.
Directions 4 miles north of Skegness on the A52 to Ingoldmells. When leaving the village turn right into Anchor Lane and park is ¼ mile on the left.
Acreage 15 **Open** Easter–October

Access Good **Site** Level
Sites available Total 200.
Facilities
Nearby facilities
Skegness.
Easy walk to the beach and village. Looking out onto farm land but close to amusements.

INGOLDMELLS

Hardy's Touring Site, Sea Lane, Ingoldmells, Skegness, Lincs, PE25 1PG.
Tel. 874071 Std. 01754
Nearest Town/Resort Skegness.
Directions 4 miles north of Skegness on the A52 to Ingoldmells. Turn right at Ship Public House, we are ¼ mile down Sea Lane.
Acreage 4 **Open** Easter–October
Access Good **Site** Level
Sites available Total 126.
Facilities
Nearby facilities
Skegness.
5 minutes walk from the beach and village centre.

INGOLDMELLS

Valetta Farm Caravan Site, Mill Lane, Addlethorpe, Skegness, Lincs.
Tel. 763758 Std. 01754
Nearest Town/Resort Skegness.
Directions Turn left off the A158 (Horncastle to Skegness road) in Burgh-le-Marsh at the signpost Ingoldmells and Addlethorpe. Follow signposts for Ingoldmells for 3 miles, turn right by disused mill into Mill Lane. Site is on the left in 150yds.
Acreage 2 **Open** 25 March–20 October
Access Good **Site** Level
Sites available Total 35.
Facilities
Nearby facilities
Skegness.
1 mile from the beach, quite a pretty site in the country.

LINCOLN

Hartsholme Country Park, Skellingthorpe Road, Lincoln, Lincolnshire.
Tel. 686264 Std. 01522
Nearest Town/Resort Lincoln.
Directions 3 miles south of City centre, situated on main Lincoln to Skellingthorpe road. Signposted from A46 bypass.
Open March–October
Access Good **Site** Level
Sites available Total 50.
Facilities
Nearby facilities
Lincoln.
Scenic views, ideal touring. Adjacent to Swanholme Lakes local Nature Reserve.

LONG SUTTON

Foremans Bridge Caravan Park, Sutton St James, Nr. Spalding, Lincolnshire.
Tel. 85346 Std. 01945
Nearest Town/Resort Spalding/Kings Lynn/Wisbech.
Directions From the A17 take the B1390 to Sutton St James, site is on the left after 2 miles.
Acreage 2¼ **Open** March–November
Access Good **Site** Level
Sites available Total 40.
Facilities
Nearby facilities
Spalding/Kings Lynn.
40 minutes away from the beach, fishing alongside park. Ideal for touring the Fens. 5 holiday statics for hire also. 2 miles to a restaurant.

MABLETHORPE

Golden Sands Holiday Centre, Quebec Road, Mablethorpe, Lincs, LN12 1QJ.
Tel. 472671/477871 Std. 01507
Nearest Town/Resort Mablethorpe.
Directions From Mablethorpe town centre, follow the sea front road to the North end for Golden Sands.
Acreage 23 **Open** 26 March–29 October
Access Good **Site** Level
Sites available Total 400.
Facilities
Nearby facilities
Skegness.
Next to rolling dunes and the finest sandy beach for miles.

MABLETHORPE

Denehurst Guest House & Camp Site, Alford Road, Mablethorpe, Lincs, LA12 1PX.
Tel. 472951 Std. 01507
Nearest Town/Resort Mablethorpe.
Directions From Mablethorpe town centre, head towards Alford on the A1104. Just past the Rix Garage on the left, approx 50 yds further is Denehurst Guest House and Camp Site.
Acreage 1
Access Good **Site** Level
Sites available Total 20.
Facilities
Nearby facilities
1 mile from sandy beaches, ideal touring in the Lincolnshire Wolds.

MARKET DEEPING

The Deepings Caravan & Camping Park, Outgang Road, Market Deeping, Lincolnshire, PE6 8LQ.
Tel. 344335 Std. 01778
Nearest Town/Resort Market Deeping.
Directions Park is 2 miles from Market

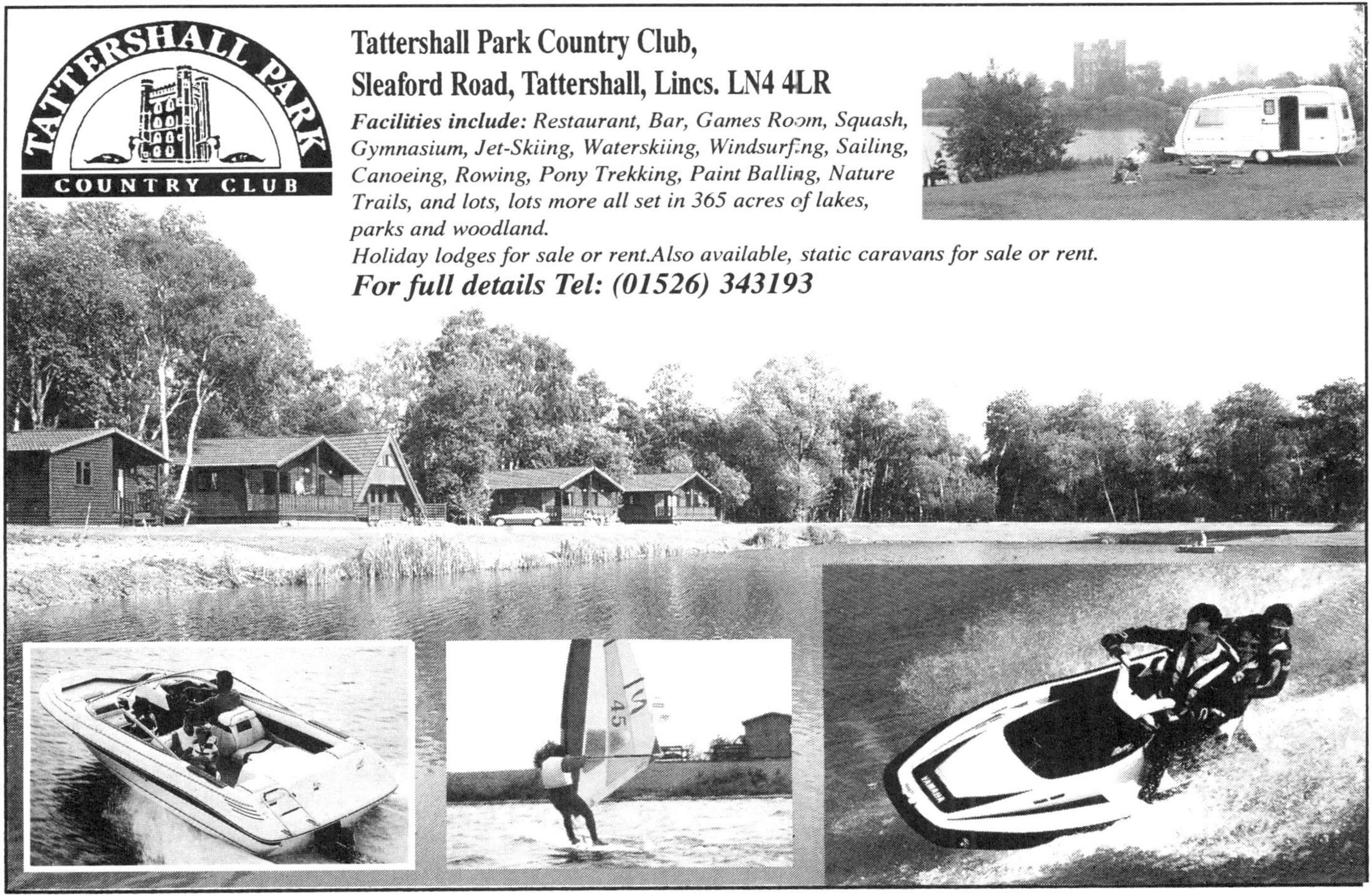
TATTERSHALL PARK
COUNTRY CLUB
Tattershall Park Country Club,
Sleaford Road, Tattershall, Lincs. LN4 4LR
Facilities include: Restaurant, Bar, Games Room, Squash, Gymnasium, Jet-Skiing, Waterskiing, Windsurfing, Sailing, Canoeing, Rowing, Pony Trekking, Paint Balling, Nature Trails, and lots, lots more all set in 365 acres of lakes, parks and woodland.
Holiday lodges for sale or rent.Also available, static caravans for sale or rent.
For full details Tel: (01526) 343193
45

Deeping, on the A16 Spalding road. Take the first left after The Goat Inn.
Open February–December
Access Good **Site** Level
Sites available Total 90.
Facilities
Nearby facilities
Peterborough.

MARKET DEEPING

Tallington Lakes, Barholm Road, Tallington, Stamford, Lincolnshire.
Tel. 347000 Std. 01778
Nearest Town/Resort Stamford.
Directions Off the A1 at Stamford, through the centre following signs. A16 Spalding/Market Deeping for 6 miles. Go through the village of Tallington, over the level crossing and take the first left (farm shop on the corner). Entrance is 200yds on the right.
Acreage 25 **Open** All Year
Access Good **Site** Level
Sites available Total 95.
Facilities
Nearby facilities
Stamford.
Tallington Lakes is a watersports centre offering some of the best water-skiing, jetskiing, sailing and wind-surfing in the country.

MARKET RASEN

The Rother Cafe Camp Site, Gainsborough Road, Middle Rasen, Nr. Market Rasen, Lincolnshire LN8 3JU.
Tel. 842433 Std. 01673
Nearest Town/Resort Market Rasen.
Directions 1½ miles west of Market Rasen, on east side of A631/A46 junction. Site at rear of Rother Cafe.
Acreage 2 **Open** March–October
Access Good **Site** Level
Sites available Total 45.
Facilities
Nearby facilities
Market Rasen.
Tree and hedge screened. Natural, relaxed country site. Good overnight stop and touring centre.

MARKET RASEN

Walesby Woodland Caravan Park, Walesby Road, Market Rasen, Lincolnshire.
Tel. 843285 Std. 01673
Nearest Town/Resort Market Rasen.
Directions In Market Rasen, take the B1203 to Tealby. After ¾ mile, turn left onto unclassified road to Walesby. ¼ mile on the left, enter lane. Site entrance 150 yards on right, signposted.
Acreage 2½ **Open** March–1st November
Access Good **Site** Level
Sites available Total 60.
Facilities
Nearby facilities
Market Rasen.
Ideal sight seeing. Lincoln 16 miles. Set in forestry land, many walks. Total peace yet close to town. 20 miles from beach. A.A. 3 Pennant R.A.C. Appointed. Tourist Board five ticks. Calor Gas Runner-up Green Award 1993.

METHERINGHAM

The White Horse Inn Holiday Park, Dunston Fen, Metheringham, Lincoln, LN4 3AP.
Tel. 398341 Std. 01526
Nearest Town/Resort Metheringham.
Directions From Dunston follow signs for Dunston Fen, River Witham 5 miles down Fen Road.
Acreage 1 **Open** February–December
Access Good **Site** Level
Sites available Total 10.
Facilities
Nearby facilities
Metheringham.
Alongside river.

NORTH SOMERCOTES

Lakeside Holiday Park, North Somercotes, Nr. Louth, Lincolnshire LN11 7RB.
Tel. 358428 Std. 01507
Nearest Town/Resort Mablethorpe.
Directions Located on A1031 Grimsby/Mablethorpe coast road.
Acreage 15 **Open** April–October
Access Good **Site** Level
Sites available Total 400.
Facilities
Nearby facilities
Grimsby.
Ideal touring area, near to Mablethorpe beaches, golf courses etc.

SKEGNESS

Hill View Fishing Lakes & Touring Caravan Park, Skegness Road (A52), Hogsthorpe, Nr. Skegness, Lincs, PE24 5NR.
Tel. 872979 Std. 01754
Directions On the A52, 7 miles from Skegness towards Mablethorpe.
Acreage 2¼ **Open** 15 March–30 October
Access Good **Site** Level
Sites available Total 45.
Facilities
Nearby facilities
Skegness.
Ideal touring, two well stocked fishing lakes.

SKEGNESS

North Shore Holiday Centre, Elmhirst Ave, Roman Bank, Skegness, Lincolnshire.
Tel. 763815/762051 Std. 01754
Nearest Town/Resort Skegness.
Directions A52 (Mablethorpe), 500yds from the A158 junction.
Open March–October
Access Good **Site** Level
Sites available Total 250.
Facilities
Nearby facilities
Skegness.
Near the beach, Pitch & Putt, Crazy Golf, tennis, bowls and boule all on site.

SKEGNESS

Riverside Caravan Park, Wainfleet Bank, Wainfleet, Skegness, Lincolnshire.
Tel. Skegness 880205 Std. 01754
Nearest Town/Resort Skegness.
Directions A52 Boston to Skegness. 5 miles southwest of town. Turn off to Wainfleet from Bypass.
Acreage 1 **Open** Mid March–Mid October
Access Good **Site** Level
Sites available Total 24.
Facilities
Nearby facilities
Wainfleet.
Alongside river, very quiet and secluded. Electric points for all tourers and tents.

SKEGNESS

Southview Leisure Park, Burgh Road, Skegness, Lincs.
Tel. 764893 Std. 01754
Nearest Town/Resort Skegness.
Directions On the main A158.
Open March–September
Access Good **Site** Level
Sites available Total 100.
Facilities
Nearby facilities
Skegness.
New leisure centre on the park aswell as a nine hole golf course.

SLEAFORD

Low Farm Touring Park, Spring Lane, Folkingham, Sleaford, Lincolnshire, NG34 0SJ.
Tel. 497322 Std. 01529
Nearest Town/Resort Sleaford.
Directions 9 miles south of Sleaford on the A15. Go through village, turn right opposite the petrol station.
Acreage 2¼ **Open** Easter–October
Access Good **Site** Lev/Slope
Sites available Total 36.
Facilities
Nearby facilities
Sleaford.

SPALDING

Lake Ross Caravan Park, Dozens Bank, West Pinchbeck, Spalding, Lincolnshire.
Tel. Spalding 761690 Std. 01775
Nearest Town/Resort Spalding.
Directions Take A151 Spalding/Bourne.
Open April–October
Access Good **Site** Level
Sites available
Facilities
Nearby facilities
Spalding.
By lakeside. Also rivers within walking distance. Fishing on site. Ramp into club for wheelchairs.

STAMFORD

Casterton Caravan & Camping, Casterton Hill, Stamford, Lincolnshire.
Tel. 481481 Std. 01780
Nearest Town/Resort Stamford.
Directions On the B1081 between Stamford and Great Casterton.
Acreage 1¾ **Open** All year
Access Good **Site** Level
Sites available Total 30.
Facilities
Nearby facilities
Stamford.
Near Rutland Water and Burley House. 1¼ miles to a swimming pool.

SUTTON-ON-SEA

Cherry Tree Site, Huttoft Road, Sutton-on-Sea, Lincs, LN12 2RU.
Tel. 441626 Std. 01507
Nearest Town/Resort Sutton-on-Sea.
Directions Take the A52 from Sutton-on-Sea, 1¼ miles on the left hand side. Entrance via a lay-by. Tourist Board signs on road.
Acreage 3 **Open** March–October
Access Good **Site** Level
Sites available Total 60.
Facilities
Nearby facilities
Skegness.
Beach, golf course and Lincolnshire Wolds.

WAINFLEET ALL SAINTS

Riverside Caravan Park, Wainfleet Bank, Wainfleet, Skegness, Lincs, PE24 4ND.
Tel. 880205 Std. 01754

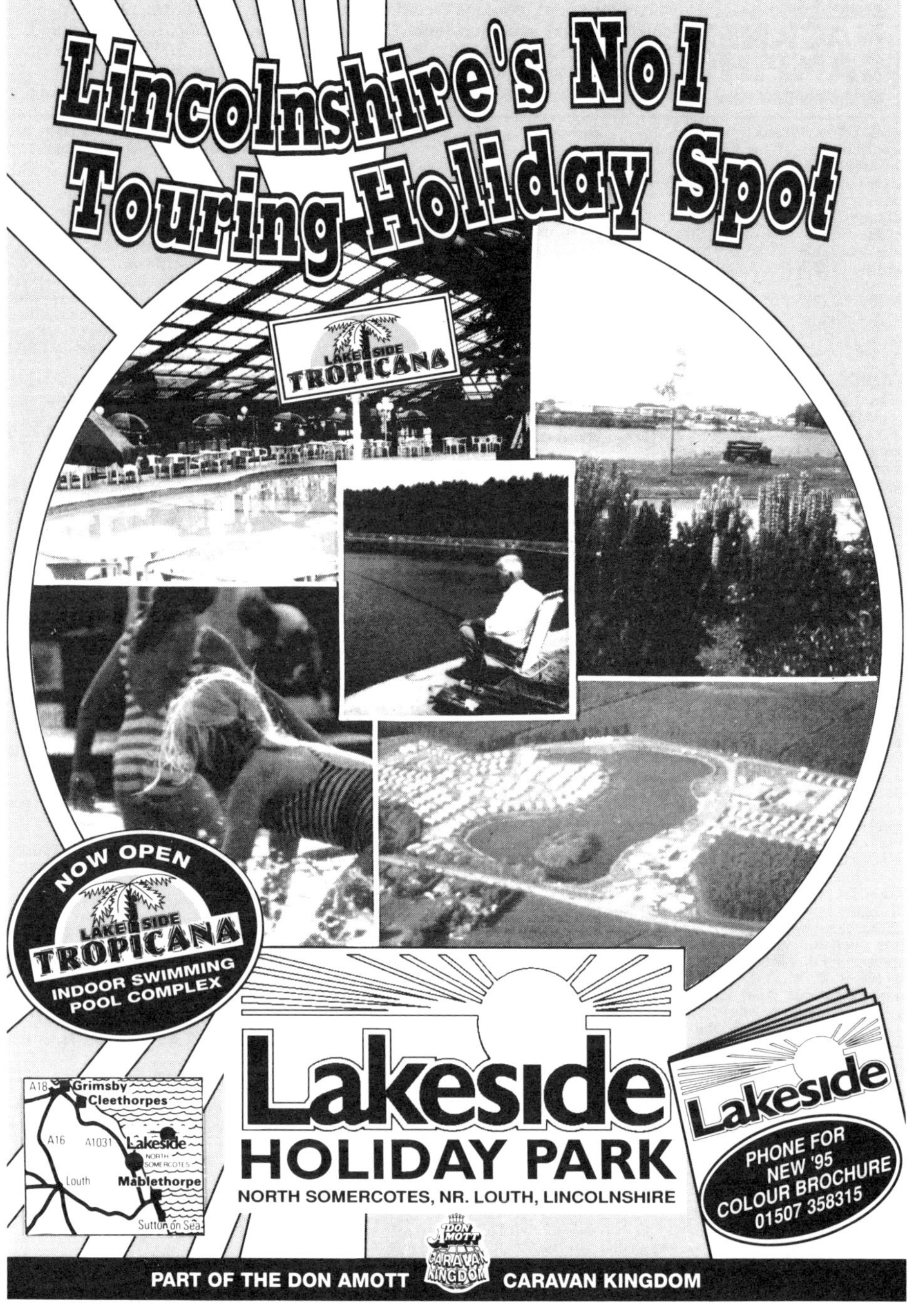
Lincolnshire's No 1
Touring Holiday Spot
LAKESIDE TROPICANA
NOW OPEN
LAKESIDE TROPICANA
INDOOR SWIMMING POOL COMPLEX
Lakeside
HOLIDAY PARK
NORTH SOMERCOTES, NR. LOUTH, LINCOLNSHIRE
A18
Grimsby
Cleethorpes
A16
A1031
Lakeside
NORTH SOMERCOTES
Louth
Mablethorpe
Sutton on Sea
Lakeside
PHONE FOR NEW '95 COLOUR BROCHURE 01507 358315
DON AMOTT CARAVAN KINGDOM
PART OF THE DON AMOTT CARAVAN KINGDOM

Nearest Town/Resort Skegness.
Directions Turn off the A52 at signpost Wainfleet All Saints B1195. Follow signs, turn left at sign Wainfleet Bank. Site in 1 mile.
Acreage 1 **Open** 15 March–15 October
Access Good **Site** Level
Sites available Total 12.
Facilities M
Nearby facilities
Wainfleet.
Beach 6 miles, fishing and boating adjacent. Ideal for cycling.

WAINFLEET ALL SAINTS

Swan Lake, Culvert Road, Wainfleet, Skegness, Lincolnshire.
Tel. 880469 Std. 01754
Nearest Town/Resort Skegness.
Directions Between Skegness A52 heading towards Boston, into Wainfleet. Follow tourist signs for Swan Lake. 6 miles from Skegness.
Open March–October
Access Good **Site** Level
Sites available
Facilities S
Nearby facilities
Thorpe Culvert.
Ideal touring, 2 acre fishing lake no closed season. Very attractive site. Minicom available for the deaf.

WOODHALL SPA

Bainland Country Park, Horncastle Road, Woodhall Spa, Lincs, LN10 6UX.
Tel. 352903 Std. 01526
Nearest Town/Resort Horncastle/Skegness.
Directions From Horncastle on the B1191, 6 miles on the left just past the petrol station (Mager). Or from Woodhall Spa on the B1191, 1¼ miles on the right before the petrol station.
Acreage 12 **Open** All Year
Access Good **Site** Level
Sites available Total 150.
Facilities S I
Nearby facilities
Lincoln/Metheringham.
On the edge of the Wolds in the centre of Lincolnshire. Own 18 hole Par 3 golf course and a bowling green.

WOODHALL SPA

Jubilee Caravan & Camping Site, Stixwould Road, Woodhall Spa, Lincolnshire, LN10 6QH.
Tel. 352448 Std. 01526
Nearest Town/Resort Lincoln/Skegness.
Directions A158 Lincoln/Horncastle road.
Acreage 4 **Open** April–October
Access Good **Site** Level
Sites available Total 100.
Facilities S I
Nearby facilities
Lincoln.
Scenic views, ideal touring.

LONDON

ACTON

Tent City, Old Oak Common Lane, East Acton, London, W3 7DP.
Tel. 743 5708 Std. 0181
Nearest Town/Resort London.
Directions Turn off the A40 (Westway) onto Old Oak Common Lane, under the railway bridge. Tent City is on the right.
Acreage 3 **Open** June–7 September
Site Level
Sites available Total 450.
Facilities S M I
Nearby facilities
East Acton.

CHINGFORD

Lee Valley Campsite, Sewardstone Road, Chingford, London E4 7RA.
Tel. 529 5689 Std. 0181
Nearest Town/Resort Chingford.
Directions Leave M25 at junction 26, follow signs for Waltham Abbey, turn left at traffic lights, site is 2 miles on right.
Acreage 12 **Open** Easter–October
Access Good **Site** Lev/Slope
Sites available Total 200.
Facilities S
Nearby facilities
Chingford.
Ideal for touring London. Nearest London Underground Station Walthamstow Central.

EDMONTON

Lee Valley Leisure Complex (Picketts Lock), Meridian Way, Edmonton, London, N9.
Tel. 6666 Std. 0181 345
Directions Signposted from the A406 and the A110, situated on the A1055.
Acreage 6 **Open** All year
Access Good **Site** Level
Sites available Total 200.
Facilities I
Nearby facilities
Lower Edmonton.
Good base for London. Golf course on site and other facilities include squash, badminton, table tennis, roller skating, creche, sauna and a cinema.

HACKNEY

Hackney Camping, Millfields Road, Hackney, London, E5 0AR.
Tel. 985 7656 Std. 0181
Nearest Town/Resort London.
Directions From Dover A2 Blackwall Tunnel A102 (Clapton/Hackney direction). Kenworthy Road, Davbenay Road, Mandeville Street, go over Cow Bridge where Mandeville Street meets Millfields Road.
Acreage 3 **Open** 18 June–30 August
Access Good **Site** Level
Sites available Total 200.
Facilities S I
Nearby facilities
Pleasant, peaceful site, very close to central London. Alongside a canal. Free cooking facilities etc. Swimming pool ¼ mile.

LEYTON

Eastway, Lee Valley Cycle Circuit, Temple Mills Lane, Newham, London E15.
Tel. 6084 Std. 0181 534
Directions A102(M) north from Blackwall Tunnel, follow sign for 'Leyton' onto A106 and then signs to Eastway Centre.
Acreage 4 **Open** April–September
Access Good **Site** Level
Sites available Total 120.
Facilities
Underground-Leyton.
Camp site is part of 40 acre landscaped parkland, only 4 miles from City of London.

WEST DRAYTON

'Riverside Mobile Park & Touring Park', Thorney Mill Road, West Drayton, London.
Tel. West Drayton 446520 Std. 01895
Nearest Town/Resort West Drayton.
Directions M4 near London Airport to West Drayton post office, Swan Road, Thorney Mill Road.
Acreage 2 **Open** All year
Access Good **Site** Level
Sites available Total 33+.
Facilities S I
Nearby facilities
West Drayton.
Near riverside. Night halts only. Showers 40p per person. Cash on arrival. Arrivals not later than 7.00 pm. No tents. No cheques. Not less than two nights bookings by phone only. Night halts only not a holiday site. Calor Gaz. Dogs allowed on lead.

MERSEYSIDE

SOUTHPORT

Brooklyn Park & Country Club, Gravel Lane, Banks, Southport, Merseyside, PR9 8BU.
Tel. 28534 Std. 01704
Nearest Town/Resort Southport.
Directions Off the A565 at Banks roundabout, 1 mile Southport.
Open March–7 January
Access Good **Site** Level
Sites available Total 100.
Facilities
Nearby facilities
Southport.
1 mile outside Southport with its many attractions. Beach, botanical gardens, Lord St. Shopping and theatres. Cafe/restaurant at weekends only.

SOUTHPORT

Leisure Lakes, Mere Brow, Tarleton, Preston, Merseyside, PR4 6JX.
Tel. 813446 Std. 01772
Nearest Town/Resort Southport.
Directions 6 miles outside Southport on the Southport to Preston road, A565.
Acreage 10 **Open** All Year
Access Good **Site** Level
Sites available Total 100.
Facilities
Nearby facilities
Southport.
35 acres of lakes, surrounded by woodland.

NORFOLK

BARFORD

Swans Harbour Caravan & Camping Park, Barford Road, Marlingford, Norwich, Norfolk.
Tel. 759658 Std. 01603
Nearest Town/Resort Norwich.
Directions Turn off Norwich Southern Bypass onto the B1108 (Norwich to Watton). 2¼ miles turn right at crossroads signposted Marlingford. Follow brown tourist signs to the site.
Acreage 4 **Open** All Year
Access Good **Site** Level
Sites available Total 50.
Facilities
Nearby facilities
Wymondham.
Alongside the upper reaches of River Yare. Ideal centre for touring Norfolk.

BARNEY

The Old Brick Kilns, Little Barney, Fakenham, Norfolk, NR21 0NL.
Tel. 878305 Std. 01328
Nearest Town/Resort Fakenham.
Directions 6 miles from Fakenham on the A148 to Cromer. Turn right onto the B1354 Aylsham road. After 100yds turn right and follow site signs to Little Barney.
Open March–October
Access Good **Site** Level
Sites available Total 60.
Facilities
Nearby facilities
Kings Lynn.
Central location for all North Norfolk attractions.

BLAKENEY

Long Furlong Cottage Caravan Park, Blakeney-Saxlingham Road, Wiveton, Nr. Holt, Norfolk, NR25 7DD.
Tel. 740833 Std. 01263
Nearest Town/Resort Blakeney/Holt.
Directions From Holt turn off right at Sharrington (A148). Follow signs to 1 mile outside Langham, then turn right at the crossroads (signposted Blakeney). Site is approx. 5 miles from Holt.
Acreage 2 **Open** All Year
Access Good **Site** Lev/Slope
Sites available Total 34.
Facilities
Nearby facilities
Sheringham.
Sheltered and well drained site set in an apple orchard. Central position for local attractions.

CAISTER-ON-SEA

The Old Hall Holiday Park, High Street, Caister-on-Sea, Great Yarmouth Norfolk
Tel. 720400 Std. 01493
Nearest Town/Resort Great Yarmouth.
Directions Take A149 northwards from Great Yarmouth turn right at roundabout near Yarmouth Stadium. Park next to Caister Police Station/opposite Caister Church.
Acreage 4 **Open** Easter–September
Access Good **Site** Level
Sites available Total 34.
Facilities
Nearby facilities
Great Yarmouth.
Family run, close to beach (ten minutes walk), ideal centre for touring.

FOREST PARK, CROMER

Value for money - Families Only touring park.
Enjoy an unforgettable touring holiday in this 85 acre oasis of mature trees and parkland.
Forest Park, Northrepps Road, Cromer, Norfolk NR27 0JR

Telephone: (01263) 513290

Please refer to our main advertisement in the front colour

Beeston Regis Caravan & Camping Park

CROMER ROAD, WEST RUNTON, CROMER, NORFOLK NR27 9NG

Tel: (01263) 823614 for further details and brochure

44 acres beautifully situated caravan and camping park with panoramic views overlooking the sea and direct access to sandy beach, next to the town of Sheringham on A149 to Cromer. Hot showers, pay phone, dogs allowed, shop open every day. Group camping by arrangement.

SEACROFT
CAMPING & CARAVAN PARK

SEACROFT CAMPING PARK is situated 1mile west of Cromer on the A149 coastal road.
The well screened camping area is approximately five acres, it is divided by rows of shrubs and offer fine sea views.
There is a heated swimming pool and an additional field for recreation.

Licensed Restaurant
open to Non Residents

RUNTON ROAD, CROMER, NORFOLK NR27 9NJ

TEL: (01263) 511722

CAISTER-ON-SEA

Grasmere Caravan Park, Bultitudes Loke, Yarmouth Road, Caister-on-Sea, Great Yarmouth, Norfolk, NR30 5DH.
Tel. 720382 Std. 01493
Nearest Town/Resort Great Yarmouth.
Directions Enter Caister from roundabout near Yarmouth Stadium at Yarmouth end of bypass. After ½ mile turn sharp left just past Esso garage.
Acreage 2 **Open** April–Mid October
Access Good **Site** Level
Sites available Total 46.
Facilities
Nearby facilities
Great Yarmouth.
½ mile from beach, 3 miles to centre of Great Yarmouth. Advance bookings taken for touring site pitches. Each pitch with it's own electric, water tap and foul water drain.

CLIPPESBY

Clippesby Holidays, Clippesby, Nr. Gt. Yarmouth, Norfolk NR29 3BJ.
Tel. 369367 Std. 01493
Nearest Town/Resort Acle.
Directions A1064 from Acle, 2 miles turn left onto the B1152. ¼ mile turn left opposite village sign. A149 from Potter Heigham, ½ mile turn right on B1152, 2 miles turn right.
Acreage 34 **Open** Easter–October
Access Good **Site** Level
Sites available Total 80.
Facilities
Nearby facilities
Acle.
A quiet family run park, in the heart of Broadlands National Park near nature reserves and coastal resorts. With a choice of woodland glades or sheltered parkland, table tennis, swimming, lawn tennis and cottages in the grounds. ETB Excellent grading, AA 3 Pennants, RAC Appointed. Booking advisable.

CROMER

Manor Farm Camp Site, Manor Farm, East Runton, Cromer, Norfolk. NR27 9PR.
Tel. Cromer 512858 Std. 01263
Nearest Town/Resort Cromer.
Directions 1½ miles west of Cromer. Turn off A148 at signpost 'East Runton'.
Acreage 16 **Open** Easter–September
Access Good **Site** Lev/Slope
Sites available
Facilities
Nearby facilities
Cromer.
Spacious, quiet, family run farm site. Panoramic sea and woodland views. Ideal for families. Separate field for dog owners.

CROMER

Roman Camp & Caravan Park, West Runton, Nr. Cromer, Norfolk NR27 9ND.
Tel. 837256 Std. 01263
Nearest Town/Resort Cromer/ Sheringham.
Directions Cromer to King's Lynn. A148 right to West Runton. Cromer to Sheringham. A149 left at West Runton.
Acreage 1 **Open** Easter–1 October
Access Good **Site** Level
Sites available Total 12.
Facilities
Nearby facilities
West Runton.
Near beach, scenic views.

CROMER

Seacroft Camping & Caravan Park, Runton Road, Cromer, Norfolk, NR27 9NJ.
Tel. 511722 Std. 01263
Nearest Town/Resort Cromer.
Directions 1 mile west of Cromer on A149 coast road.
Acreage 5 **Open** 20th March–October
Access Good **Site** Gently Sloping
Sites available Total 118.
Facilities
Nearby facilities
Cromer.
Well screened camping area divided by rows of shrubs. Fine sea views.

CROMER

Woodhill Camping & Caravan Park, Cromer Road, East Runton, Cromer, Norfolk, NR27 9PX.
Tel. 512242 Std. 01263
Nearest Town/Resort Cromer.
Directions Set between East and West Runton on the seaside of the A149 Cromer to Sheringham road.
Acreage 32 **Open** April–October
Access Good **Site** Lev/Slope
Sites available Total 390.
Facilities
Nearby facilities
West Runton.
Peaceful and tranquil, cliff top site, fantastic views, walks and beaches. All facilities new or recently re-built. 2 acres of field for dog excercising. Free barbecue area. E.T.B. 5 Ticks of Excellent Grading.

DISS

Willows Camping & Caravan Park, Diss Road, Scole, Norfolk.
Tel. Diss 740271 Std. 01379
Nearest Town/Resort Diss.
Directions 200yds off the A140 roundabout at Scole in the direction of Diss.
Acreage 4 **Open** May–September
Access Good **Site** Level
Sites available Total 32.
Facilities
Nearby facilities
Diss.

GREAT YARMOUTH

Blue Sky Caravan Park, Burgh Road, Bradwell, Gt. Yarmouth, Norfolk NR31 9ED.
Tel. 780571 Std. 01493
Nearest Town/Resort Great Yarmouth.
Directions Take Burgh Road at junction of A12/A143. Blue Sky Park is 1½ miles down road on left.
Acreage 7 **Open** April–October
Access Good **Site** Level
Sites available Total 240.
Facilities

Nearby facilities
Great Yarmouth.
Centrally situated for sandy beaches at Great Yarmouth and for touring the Norfolk Broads and Coastline.

GREAT YARMOUTH

Bureside Holiday Park, Boundary Farm, Oby, Nr. Great Yarmouth, Norfolk, NR29 3BW.
Tel. 369233 Std. 01493
Nearest Town/Resort Great Yarmouth.
Directions At Acle take A1064 over Acle Bridge, take first left onto B1152 then second left then first left, then first right.
Acreage 12 **Open** End M.B.H.–Mid Sept
Access Good **Site** Level
Sites available Total 170.
Facilities
Nearby facilities
Acle.
Miles of riverside walks with views over open Broadland, ideal for fishing and boating. No all male parties.

GREAT YARMOUTH

Burgh Castle Marina & Caravan Park, Nr. Great Yarmouth, Norfolk. NR31 9PZ.
Tel. 780331 Std. 01493
Nearest Town/Resort Gorleston-on-Sea.
Directions A143. At 2 miles southwest from Gorleston roundabout fork right for Belton and Burgh Castle then ¾ mile turn right and entrance ¾ mile on left.
Acreage 15 **Open** All year.
Access Good **Site** Level
Sites available Total 60.
Facilities
Nearby facilities
Great Yarmouth.
Own salt water harbour, slipway, pontoons, boat park, public bar. Licensed pub.

GREAT YARMOUTH

Liffens Holiday Park, Burgh Castle, Great Yarmouth, Norfolk NR31 9QB.
Tel. 780357 Std. 01493
Nearest Town/Resort Great Yarmouth.
Directions From Great Yarmouth, signs for Lowestoft/Beccles to roundabout where A12 and A143 meet take the sign for Burgh Castle, 2 miles to T junction right, follow tourist signs to Liffens.
Acreage 12 **Open** Easter–October
Access Good **Site** Level
Sites available Total 150.
Facilities
Nearby facilities
Great Yarmouth.
Family holiday park close to old Roman fortress yet 10 minutes from Gt. Yarmouth. 2 bars/entertainment/cabaret. 2 heated pools. Free colour brochure.

GREAT YARMOUTH

Seashore Holiday Centre, North Denes, Great Yarmouth, Norfolk, NR30 4HG.
Tel. 851131 Std. 01493
Nearest Town/Resort Great Yarmouth.
Directions From Great Yarmouth take the A149 north towards Caister. Turn right at the second set of traffic lights, signposted to the Sea Front and Racecourse. Continue to the sea and turn left, Seashore is on the left.
Acreage 4 **Open** 31 March–9 April
Access Good **Site** Level
Sites available
Facilities
Nearby facilities
Great Yarmouth.
Situated at the end of the prom, overlooking the sea.

GREAT YARMOUTH

Willowcroft Camping & Caravan Park, Staithe Road, Repps with Bastwick, Great Yarmouth, Norfolk, NR29 5JU.
Tel. 670380 Std. 01692
Nearest Town/Resort Potter Heigham.
Directions 10 miles from Great Yarmouth on the Potter Heigham road, into Church Road, then Staithe Road.
Acreage 2 **Open** All Year
Access Good **Site** Level
Sites available Total 44.
Facilities
Nearby facilities
Acle.
Two minute walk from site to river. Fishing, excellent for walks and bikes etc. Quiet park. Disabled facility plans passed for 1995.

GREAT YARMOUTH

Sunfield Holiday Park, Station Road, Belton, Great Yarmouth, Norfolk, NR31 9NB.
Tel. 781234 Std. 01493
Nearest Town/Resort Great Yarmouth.
Directions From Great Yarmouth follow A143, turn right off duel carriageway to Belton. Once in Belton follow brown tourist site signs.
Acreage 16 **Open** April–October
Access Good **Site** Level
Sites available Total 150.
Facilities
Nearby facilities
Great Yarmouth.
The ideal base for touring the Norfolk Coast and countryside. Also close to Great Yarmouth.

FOR THE BEST IN GREAT YARMOUTH HOLIDAYS FOR 1995
IT'S ENJOYMENT ALL THE WAY!
The Blue Sky Club offers; ● Sparkling entertainment, live music, discos, dancing, cabaret and competitions. For children, the Bluey Bear Club ● Heated leisure pool ● Children's play area ● Family fun centre ● Crazy golf ● Supermarket ● Hot food take-away ● Launderette ● 2 1/2 miles from Great Yarmouth's famous Golden Mile ● Centrally situated for exploring the area and its attractions ● Touring Caravan and Tent pitches. Full facilities including electric hook-ups. Luxury holiday caravans for hire.
BlueSky
HOLIDAY PARK
BRADWELL, GREAT YARMOUTH
● Lively entertainments programme centred at the Sunfield Club. Live music, discos, dancing and competitions ensure fun for all ● Bar meals ● Heated leisure pool ● Children's play area ● Bowls and putting green ● Hot food take-away ● Supermarket ● Launderette ● 5 1/2 miles from Great Yarmouth ● Well located for enjoying the Norfolk/Suffolk coastline and delightful Norfolk Broads ● Touring Caravan and Tent pitches. Excellent facilities including disabled. Electric hook- ups. Luxury holiday caravans for hire.
Sunfield
HOLIDAY PARK
BELTON, GREAT YARMOUTH
ROSE AWARD
CARAVAN HOLIDAY PARKS
Write for colour brochure to Mrs. C. Kirk
BLUE SKY LEISURE
BRADWELL,
GREAT YARMOUTH,
NORFOLK NR31 9ED.
BLUE SKY LEISURE
A SYMBOL OF QUALITY
TELEPHONE
01493 780571
BRITISH GRADED HOLIDAY PARKS

GREAT YARMOUTH
Vauxhall
HOLIDAY PARK
NEW FOR '95
• Over 300 sites for touring caravans & tents
• Luxury NEW Indoor Pool for '95
• FREE 5 Star Entertainment
• All-electric sites
• Grass & Hard Standings
• Awnings Free
ALL WEATHER FUN
PRACTICAL CARAVAN
TOP 100 PARK
AA
QUOTE REF 8
PHONE 01493 857231 FOR YOUR FREE BROCHURE
8 ACLE NEW ROAD, GREAT YARMOUTH NR30 ITB
UNHITCH, PITCH AND RELAX

GREAT YARMOUTH

Vauxhall Holiday Park, 8 Acle New Road, Great Yarmouth, Norfolk.
Tel. 857231 Std. 01493
Nearest Town/Resort Great Yarmouth.
Directions Situated on approach to Great Yarmouth on A47 from Norwich.
Acreage 20 **Open** Easter then–Mid May-Sept
Access Good **Site** Level
Sites available Total 300.
Facilities
Nearby facilities
Great Yarmouth.
Ideal centre for attractions of Great Yarmouth and for exploring the famous Norfolk Broads.

GREAT YARMOUTH

Welcome Farm Tourist Centre, Butt Lane, Burgh Castle, Great Yarmouth, Norfolk, NR31 9PY.
Tel. 780481 Std. 01493
Nearest Town/Resort Great Yarmouth.
Directions 1 mile from the main A143 Great Yarmouth to Beccles road. 3 miles from Great Yarmouth.
Acreage 12 **Open** Easter–October
Access Good **Site** Level
Sites available Total 300.
Facilities
Nearby facilities
Great Yarmouth.
Rural location, scenic walks and views. Bar, lounge, take-away shop and an outdoor swimming pool.

GREAT YARMOUTH

Wild Duck Chalet Caravan & Camping Park, Great Yarmouth, Norfolk.
Tel. 780268 Std. 01493
Nearest Town/Resort Great Yarmouth.
Directions From Yarmouth take Gorleston road (A143) straight to first roundabout Beccles Road to dual carriageway, first left signposted Belton.
Acreage 60 **Open** Easter–October
Access Good **Site** Lev/Slope
Sites available Total 150.
Facilities
Nearby facilities
Great Yarmouth.
Pine Tree park. Triangle for Yarmouth, Gorleston, Lowestoft and Broads. Motorcycles not in large groups, 2/3 by arrangement.

HADDISCOE

Pampas Lodge, Beccles Road, Haddiscoe, Norfolk.
Tel. Aldeby 677265 Std. 01502
Nearest Town/Resort Beccles.
Directions A143 Beccles/Great Yarmouth, centre of village.
Acreage 3 **Open** March–October
Access Good **Site** Level
Sites available Total 40.
Facilities
Nearby facilities
Haddiscoe.
1 mile river.

HARLESTON

Lone Pine, Low Road, Wortwell, Harleston, Norfolk.
Tel. Homersfield 788596 Std. 01986
Nearest Town/Resort Harleston.
Directions 2¼ miles from Harleston, 5 miles from Bungay, east off A143 to Wortwell, turn south at Bell Inn into low road.
Acreage 2 **Open** 1 May–September
Access Good **Site** Lev/Slope
Sites available Total 24.
Facilities
Nearby facilities
Diss.
Overlooking beautiful Waveney Valley, near river, ideal touring East Anglia. Alternative telephone: Harleston 01379 852423.

HARLESTON

Little Lakeland Caravan Park, Wortwell, Harleston, Norfolk, IP20 0HG.
Tel. Homersfield 788646 Std. 01986
Nearest Town/Resort Harleston.
Directions Turn off A143 (Diss to Lowestoft) at roundabout signposted Wortwell in village turn right about 300 yards after Bell P.H. at bottom of lane turn right into site.
Acreage 4 **Open** March–7th Jan
Access Good **Site** Level
Sites available Total 40.
Facilities
Nearby facilities
Diss.
Half acre fishing lake, site library.

HEMSBY

Long Beach Caravan Park, Hemsby, Great Yarmouth, Norfolk.
Tel. 730023 Std. 01493
Nearest Town/Resort Great Yarmouth.
Directions Take A149 north from Great Yarmouth, then B1159 on roundabout on Caister bypass. At Hemsby turn right on Beach Road, then second left at King's Loke signposted Longbeach.
Acreage 2 **Open** Easter–October
Access Good **Site** Level
Sites available Total 40.
Facilities

Nearby facilities
Great Yarmouth.
30 acres private sandy beach. Ten minutes drive to Great Yarmouth.

HUNSTANTON

The Chequers Inn, Thornham, Kings Lynn, Norfolk, PE36 6LY.
Tel. 512229 Std. 01485
Nearest Town/Resort Hunstanton.
Directions On main coast road A149 from Kings Lynn, approx 25 miles. Pub is adjacent to a garage.
Open April–October
Access Good **Site** Level
Sites available Total 7.
Facilities
Nearby facilities
Kings Lynn.
RSPB sanctuaries and close to protected beaches.

HUNSTANTON

Heacham Beach Holiday Park, South Beach Road, Heacham, Hunstanton, Norfolk, PE31 7DD.
Tel. 570270 Std. 01485
Nearest Town/Resort Hunstanton.
Directions A149 from King's Lynn to Hunstanton and Heacham is the first village after Snettisham. Turn left at the sign for Heacham Beach and fork left about a mile along this road.
Acreage 1 **Open** 31 March–8 October
Site Level
Sites available Total 25.
Facilities
Nearby facilities
Kings Lynn.

HUNSTANTON

The Orchards Caravan Park, Heacham, King's Lynn, Norfolk, PE31 7HG.
Tel. 570327 Std. 01485
Nearest Town/Resort Hunstanton.
Directions Turn off A149 Hunstanton/King's Lynn road at traffic island into Heacham Village (not Heacham Beaches), park is straight through next to public hall and bowling green.
Open All year.
Access Good **Site** Level
Sites available Total 18.
Facilities
Nearby facilities
King's Lynn.
Seaside village in beautiful West Norfolk. Motor Caravans only. Able to join membership of Licensed Club. Please make cheques payable to J PIGNEY.

HUNSTANTON

Searles Holiday Centre, South Beach, Hunstanton, Norfolk.
Tel. 534211 Std. 01485
Nearest Town/Resort Hunstanton.
Directions South of Hunstanton on B1161 off A149.
Acreage 50 **Open** Easter–October
Access Good **Site** Level
Sites available Total 250.
Facilities
Nearby facilities
King's Lynn.
Beach 100yds, Caravans over 17 feet in length by arrangement. Indoor swimming pool.

KING'S LYNN

Woodlakes Holiday Park, Holme Road, Stow Bridge, King's Lynn, Norfolk.
Tel. 810414 Std. 01553
Nearest Town/Resort King's Lynn.
Directions Take A10 from King's Lynn (approx 8 miles) turn right at South Runcton, through the village of Runcton Holme to the crossroads. Turn left and Woodlakes 1 mile (B road).
Acreage 12 **Open** March–October
Access Good **Site** Level
Sites available Total 100.
Facilities
Nearby facilities
Downham Market.
20 miles to nearest beach, ideal scenic views from river banks. Many Historical houses close by, famous Norfolk Broads.

KING'S LYNN

Pentney Park Caravan & Camping Site, Pentney, King's Lynn, Norfolk. PE32 1HU.
Tel. 337479 Std. 01760
Nearest Town/Resort King's Lynn.

Woodlakes HolidayPark

. . . the ideal centre for exploring East Anglia

FOR TOURING CARAVANS, MOTOR CARAVANS AND TENTS

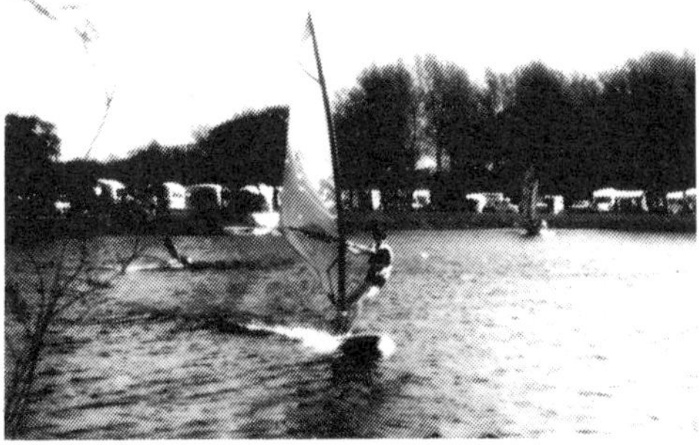

This site gives you the chance to do a spot of quiet fishing, boating, exploring or just relaxing in this beautifully tranquil part of Norfolk. WOODLAKES set in 66 acres of woods and lakes, is the ideal centre for touring East Anglia's attractive sandy beaches, charming countryside, inland waterways, including the famous Norfolk Broads.

- CHILDREN'S PLAY AREAS. ROW BOAT HIRE.
- **EXCELLENT COURSE AND TROUT FISHING ON 24 ACRES OF ADJOINING LAKES.**
- WOODLAND FOR PLEASANT WALKS.
- SHOP AND RECEPTION.
- RECREATION ROOM.
- MODERN TOILET BLOCKS. WITH H. & C. FOR SHOWERS. WASH BASINS, ETC.
- LEVEL PITCHES IN SUNNY OR
- SHADED POSITIONS.
- RAC, AA, NFSO, CC.

Send SAE for brochure and information to:

Woodlakes, Holme Road,
Stowbridge, Kings Lynn
PE34 3PX
Tel: (01553) 810414

SHERINGHAM, NORFOLK

For a Breath of Fresh Air!

Stay in 250 acres of woodland and heather

Situated in an area of outstanding beauty, Kelling Heath is the completely natural choice for visitors with touring caravans and tents. There are miles of woodland walks through this natural wildlife reserve, including a specially prepared 2½ mile nature trail.

The park's elevated location commands magnificent views of the coast and sea. The historic North Norfolk Railway runs to Sheringham from the Park boundary.

- Heated leisure pool
- Tennis courts
- Nature and trim trails
- Children's adventure playgrounds
- Licensed bars, entertainment, bar meal selection and take-away
- Family fun centre
- Supermarket
- Launderette and ironing room
- Hot showers and flush toilets
- Luxury holiday homes for hire
- Holiday homes for sale

Turn North at Site sign at Bodham on A148, or turn South off A149 at Weybourne Church.

Booking is advisable at all times

BRITISH GRADED HOLIDAY PARKS ✓✓✓✓✓ EXCELLENT

ROSE AWARD CARAVAN HOLIDAY PARKS

Write for brochure to Mr. C. Woods

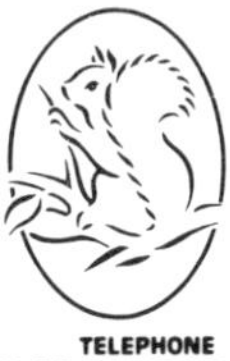

KELLING HEATH HOLIDAY PARK

BLUE SKY LEISURE
A Blue Sky Leisure Park

TELEPHONE
01263 588181

WEYBOURNE NR. SHERINGHAM
NORFOLK NR25 7HW

NATURALLY THE BEST!

LUXURY HOLIDAY HOMES, TOURING CARAVANS AND TENTS

Directions Situated on A47 midway between Kings Lynn and Swaffham, entrance 150 yards from junction of B1153 with A47.
Acreage 16 **Open** All year
Access Good **Site** Level
Sites available Total 200.
Facilities
Nearby facilities
King's Lynn.
Ideal touring base set in woodland and clearings, easy reach of coast and Broadlands.

METHWOLD
Warren House Caravan Site, Brandon Road, Methwold, Thetford, Norfolk, IP27 4RH.
Tel. 728238 Std. 01366
Nearest Town/Resort Brandon.
Directions B1106, 5 miles.
Acreage 4 **Open** March–October
Access Good **Site** Level
Sites available Total 40.
Facilities
Nearby facilities
Brandon.
Forestry. Motorcycles are accpeted in certain cases.

MUNDESLEY
Sandy Gulls New Cliff Top Touring Park, Cromer Road, Mundesley, Norfolk.
Tel. 720513 Std. 01263
Nearest Town/Resort Cromer.
Directions South along the coast road for 4 miles.
Open Easter–October
Access Good **Site** Level
Sites available Total 40.
Facilities
Nearby facilities
Cromer.
Cliff top location.

NORTH WALSHAM
Two Mills Touring Park, Old Yarmouth Road, Scarborough Hill, North Walsham, Norfolk, NR28 9NA.
Tel. 405829 Std. 01692
Nearest Town/Resort North Walsham.
Directions Take old Yarmouth road out of North Walsham, (parellel to bypass) Two Mills is 1 mile south on left hand side.
Acreage 5 **Open** 1st March–3rd Jan
Access Good **Site** Level
Sites available Total 59.
Facilities
Nearby facilities
North Walsham.
Quiet secluded park for ADULTS ONLY. Ideal base for discovering North Norfolk. Clean, heated toilet block, cubicles for the ladies. Day kennels for dogs. You can relax here.

POTTER HEIGHAM
Causeway Cottage Caravan Park, Bridge Road, Potter Heigham, Nr. Great Yarmouth, Norfolk.
Tel. 670238 Std. 01692
Nearest Town/Resort Great Yarmouth.
Directions Potter Heigham is between Great Yarmouth and Norwich. Turn off the A149 at Potter Heigham, we are 250yds from the river and old bridge.
Acreage ¼ **Open** March–October
Access Good **Site** Level
Sites available Total 5.
Facilities
Nearby facilities
Great Yarmouth.
250yds from shops and hotels, fishing, boating and walking. 6 miles from Golden Sands beach.

PULHAM ST MARY
Waveney Valley Horse Holidays, Airstation Farm, Pulham St Mary, Diss, Norfolk.
Tel. 741228 Std. 01379
Nearest Town/Resort Diss.
Directions Take A140 at Scole, travel north for 3 miles. Turn right into Dickleborough, at church turn right, 2 miles, first left then first left again.
Acreage 5 **Open** Easter–October
Access Good **Site** Level
Sites available Total 25.
Facilities
Nearby facilities
Diss.
Pleasant rural countryside, river, Waveney 3 miles. Good local fishing.

REEDHAM
Reedham Ferry Camping & Caravan Park, Reedham Ferry Inn, Reedham, Norwich, Norfolk.
Tel. 700429 Std. 01493
Nearest Town/Resort Acle/Great Yarmouth.
Directions Acle 7 miles on B1140 to Reedham Ferry.
Acreage 4 **Open** Easter–September
Access Good **Site** Level
Sites available Total 20.
Facilities
Nearby facilities
Reedham.
Next to river adjoining Reedham Ferry Inn, selling traditional country ales.

SCRATBY
Scratby Hall Caravan Park, Scratby, Great Yarmouth, Norfolk, NR29 3PH.
Tel. 730283 Std. 01493
Nearest Town/Resort Great Yarmouth.
Directions 5 miles north of Great Yarmouth, off the B1159, signed.
Acreage 4 **Open** Easter–Mid October
Access Good **Site** Level
Sites available Total 108.
Facilities
Nearby facilities
Great Yarmouth.
Close to the beach and conveniently situated for visiting the Norfolk Broads.

SEA PALLING
Golden Beach Holiday Centre, Beach Road, Sea Palling, Norwich, Norfolk, NR12 0AL.
Tel. Stalham 598269 Std. 01692
Nearest Town/Resort Stalham.
Directions Site entrance just 200yds from the beach. From Norwich take the A1151 through Wroxham to Stalham, then turn left at the B1151 to Sea Palling. Turn left down beach road.
Acreage 7 **Open** March–1 November
Access Good **Site** Level
Sites available Total 50.
Facilities
Nearby facilities
Wroxham.
200yds from the beach, 3 miles from the Norfolk Broads.

SHERINGHAM
Beeston Regis Caravan & Camping Park, Cromer Road, West Runton, Nr. Sheringham, Norfolk, NR27 9NG.
Tel. 823614 Std. 01263
Nearest Town/Resort Sheringham.
Directions A149 through Sheringham towards Cromer, 1 mile outside Sheringham.
Acreage 44 **Open** Easter–September
Access Good **Site** Level
Sites available Total 420
Facilities
Nearby facilities
Sheringham.
Overlooking sea, easy access to beach.

SHERINGHAM
Kelling Heath Caravan Park, Weybourne, Nr. Sheringham, Norfolk, NR25 7HW.
Tel. 588181 Std. 01263
Nearest Town/Resort Sheringham.
Directions Turn north at site sign at Bodham on the A148 or turn south off the A149 at Weybourne Church.
Acreage 75 **Open** 19th March–October
Access Good **Site** Level
Sites available Total 300.
Facilities
Nearby facilities
Sheringham.
A 250 acre estate of woodland and heather, with magnificent views of the Weybourne coastline.

SHERINGHAM
Woodlands Caravan Park, Holt Road, Upper Sheringham, Sheringham, Norfolk, NR26 8TU.
Tel. 823802 Std. 0263
Nearest Town/Resort Sheringham.
Directions 4 miles east of Holt, off the A148.
Acreage 20 **Open** March–October
Access Good **Site** Lev/Slope
Sites available Total 286.
Facilities
Nearby facilities

WoodHill
Peaceful & Friendly
Park
SET BETWEEN
SHERINGHAM & CROMER
IN PRETTY NORTH NORFOLK
Award winning Woodhill Park is one of Norfolk's finest parks. From it there are magnificent views of the surrounding North Norfolk Coast and Countryside. This coastal park is operated to a very high standard and offers peace, tranquillity and a superb range of luxury caravan holiday homes.
WE WELCOME ALL TOURING CARAVANS, TENTS AND MOTOR HOMES.
• All Toilet/Shower buildings recently built or refurbished
• Launderette • Mini Market • Over 100 Super Size Electric Hook-Up Pitches • Children's Playground • Courtesy Barbecue Area
Send for brochure to Mrs. C. Hill
WOODHILL PARK
CROMER ROAD, EAST RUNTON, CROMER, NORFOLK NR27 9PX.
Telephone: 01263 512242
BLUE SKY LEISURE
A Blue Sky Leisure Park
ROSE AWARD
CARAVAN HOLIDAY PARK
BRITISH GRADED HOLIDAY PARKS
EXCELLENT

Surrounded by woodlands on two sides, fields and trees on the remaining two sides. In an area of outstanding natural beauty.

SNETTISHAM

Diglea Caravan and Camping Park, Beach Road, Snettisham, Norfolk, PE31 7RA.
Tel. Dersingham 541367 Std. 01485
Nearest Town/Resort Hunstanton.
Directions King's Lynn/Hunstanton A149, turn left off Snettisham bypass, park and beach $1\frac{1}{4}$ miles.
Acreage 6 **Open** April–October
Access Good **Site** Level
Sites available Total 200.
Facilities
Nearby facilities
King's Lynn.
Peaceful, family run park in a rural setting. Beach and RSPB sanctuary close by. Rally field available.

STANHOE

The Rickels Caravan & Camping Site, Bircham Road, Stanhoe, Kings Lynn, Norfolk, PE31 8PU.
Tel. 518671 Std. 01485
Nearest Town/Resort Hunstanton.
Directions From Kings Lynn take the A148 to Hillington, turn left onto the B1153 to Great Bircham. Fork right onto the B1155 to the crossroads, straight over. Site is 100yds on the left.
Acreage $2\frac{1}{4}$ **Open** March–October
Access Good **Site** Lev/Slope
Sites available Total 30.
Facilities
Nearby facilities
Kings Lynn.

Local beaches, stately homes, Sandringham and market towns. Childrens Television.

SWAFFHAM

Breckland Meadows Touring Park, Lynn Road, Swaffham, Norfolk, PE37 7AY.
Tel. 721246 Std. 01760
Nearest Town/Resort Kings Lynn/Hunstanton.
Directions Take the A47 from Kings Lynn to Swaffham, approx 15 miles. Take the first exit off the dual carriageway, site is $\frac{1}{4}$ mile before Swaffham town centre.
Acreage 2 **Open** 20 March–October
Access Good **Site** Level
Sites available Total 25.
Facilities
Nearby facilities
Kings Lynn.
Central for touring, ideal for walking Swaefas Way and Peddars Way.

THETFORD

The Dower House Touring Park, East Harling, Norwich, Norfolk, NR16 2SE.
Tel. East Harling 717314 Std. 01953
Nearest Town/Resort Norwich.
Directions From Thetford take A1066 East for 5 miles, fork left at camping sign onto unclassified road, site on left after 2 miles signposted.
Acreage 20 **Open** 20th March–October
Access Good **Site** Level
Sites available Total 160.
Facilities
Nearby facilities
Harling Road.
Set in Thetford Forest, the site is spacious and peaceful. Although we have a bar, we have no amusement arcade or gaming machines.

NORTHANTS

NORTHAMPTON

Billing Aquadrome, Crow Lane, Great Billing, Northampton, Northamptonshire.
Tel. 408181 Std. 01604
Nearest Town/Resort Northampton.
Directions On the A45 east of Northampton, 7 miles from M1 junction 15.
Acreage 235 **Open** 20 March–5 November
Access Good **Site** Level
Sites available Total 755.
Facilities
Nearby facilities
Northampton.
Flat, level grassland bordering the River Nene. Motorcycles accepted if camping.

THRAPSTON

Mill Marina, Midland Road, Thrapston, Northants, NN14 4JR.
Tel. 732850 Std. 01832
Nearest Town/Resort Thrapston.
Directions A14 (old A604)/A605 into Thrapston. 500 yards from mini roundabout signposted.
Acreage 5 **Open** April–December
Access Good **Site** Level
Sites available Total 42.
Facilities
Nearby facilities
Kettering.
Riverside site with fishing and boat trips. Swimming pool nearby.

OVERSTONE SOLARIUM

CARAVAN HOLIDAY HOME PARK

SET IN NORTHAMPTONSHIRES BEAUTIFUL ROLLING COUNTRYSIDE

- ✱ **ENJOY** Three all weather tennis courts and nine squash courts
- ✱ **ENJOY** Miles of walks through wooded and lakeside settings
- ✱ **ENJOY** Free fishing in well stocked lakes with carp up to 30 pounds in weight
- ✱ **ENJOY** The heated outdoor swimming pool
- ✱ **ENJOY** A drink or meal in the pleasant surroundings of the Lakeside Club

Peaceful and beautiful are the words to describe the setting at Overstone. 115 acres of wooded parkland in the rolling countryside of Northamptonshire.

Tourers welcome-all the facilities of the Holiday Home Park are available.

Tourers welcome all the facilities of the Holiday Home Park are available including electric hook ups.

DONT DELAY - BOOK TODAY!

OVERSTONE SOLARIUM

PHONE **(01604) 645255**

ECTON LANE, SYWELL
NORTHAMPTONSHIRE NN6 0BO

Billing Aquadrome

Northampton's Leisure Park

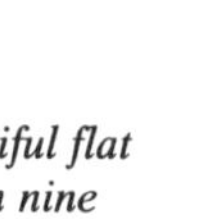

Billing Aquadrome Limited, Crow Lane, Great Billing, Northampton NN3 9DA

HAS something for everyone. 235 acres of beautiful flat countryside and woodland. Boating, fishing from nine lakes, fairground, crazy golf, pedloes, amusement centres, bars, restaurants ... the list is endless!

NEW FOR 1995 is a multi purpose sports and leisure centre, and the new Billing Mill Development of bars and restaurants.

Tourers, tents and motorhomes are welcomed. New and used Holiday Homes for sale. Call now for a brochure on ***(01604) 408181.***

S

NORTHUMBRIA

ALNWICK
Cherry Tree Farm, Edlingham, Alnwick, Northumberland.
Tel. 574635 Std. 01665
Nearest Town/Resort Alnwick.
Directions 5 miles west of Alnwick on Alnwick Rothbury road.
Acreage 1 **Open** Easter–October
Access Good **Site** Lev/Slope
Sites available Total 20.
Facilities
Nearby facilities
Alnmouth.
Attractive streamside site, scenic views, ideal touring.

ASHINGTON
Sandy Bay Caravan Park, North Seaton, Ashington, Northumberland, NE63 9YD.
Tel. 815055 Std. 01670
Nearest Town/Resort Ashington.
Acreage 7 **Open** March–November
Access Good **Site** Level
Sites available Total 40.
Facilities
Nearby facilities
Morpeth.
Sandy Bay nestles on the edge of the River Wansbeck estuary with miles of golden Northumbrian sand.

ASHINGTON
Wansbeck Riverside Park, Ashington, Northumberland, NE63 8TX.
Tel. 812323 Std. 01670
Nearest Town/Resort Ashington.
Directions 1 mile south west of Ashington, just off A1068.
Acreage ¼ **Open** All year
Access Good **Site** Sloping
Sites available Total 74.
Facilities
Nearby facilities
Morpeth.
Picturesque riverside site, ideal for Northumberland. Special rates October-March.

BAMBURGH
Glororum Caravan Park, Glororum, Bamburgh, Northumberland.
Tel. 214457 Std. 01668.
Directions Caravan Park 1 mile from Bamburgh on Adderstone (B1341) or from A1 take B1341 Adderstone towards Bamburgh, 4 miles.
Open April–October
Access Good **Site** Level
Sites available Total 100.
Facilities
Nearby facilities
Berwick-upon-Tweed.
Caravan Park is set in peaceful surroundings. Nearby lovely beach. Within easy reach of Holy Island, Farne Islands, Cheviots. No single sex parties.

BAMBURGH
Seafield Caravan Park, Seafield Road, Seahouses, Northumberland, NE68 7SP.
Tel. 720628 Std. 01665
Nearest Town/Resort Seahouses.
Directions B1340 east off the main A1 to the coast.
Acreage 1 **Open** March–January
Access Good **Site** Level
Sites available Total 20.
Facilities
Nearby facilities
Chathill.
In the centre of the village, near to a beach, scenic views and the harbour.

BEADNELL
Beadnell Links Ltd, The Chimes, Beadnell, Chathill, Northumberland. NE67 5BU.
Tel. 720993 Std. 01665
Nearest Town/Resort Beadnell.
Directions B1340 to Beadnell, thereafter signed.
Open April–October
Access Good **Site** Level
Sites available Total 20.
Facilities
Nearby facilities
Chathill.
Site near beach.

BELFORD
Blue Bell Farm Caravan & Camp Site, West Street, Belford, Northumberland.
Tel. 213368 Std. 01668
Nearest Town/Resort Berwick-on-Tweed.
Directions 15 miles north of Alnwick. Stay on the A1, turn left at Belford sign (right if going south). In Belford Village centre take Wooler Road, site is 150yds on the right.
Acreage 2 **Open** February–October
Access Good **Site** Level
Sites available Total 30.
Facilities
Nearby facilities
Berwick-on-Tweed.
Ideal touring, beaches, golf, walks, hills and climbing.

BELFORD
Budle Bay Camp & Caravan Site, Waren Mill, Bamburgh, Northumberland, NE70 7EE.
Tel. 213362 Std. 01668
Nearest Town/Resort Berwick-on-Tweed.
Directions 15 miles north of Alnwick. Stay on the A1, turn right at Belford sign towards Bamburgh, Waren Mill and Budle Bay. Site is 2 miles down this road.
Acreage 7 **Open** April–October
Access Good **Site** Level
Sites available Total 200.
Facilities
Nearby facilities
Berwick.
Alongside a river, near the beach. Bird watching area. Ideal for divers.

BERWICK-UPON-TWEED
Marshall Meadows Farm, Berwick-upon-Tweed, Northumberland, TD15 1UT.
Tel. 307375 Std. 01289
Nearest Town/Resort Berwick.
Directions 2¼ miles north of Berwick off the A1.
Open Easter–October
Access Good **Site** Level
Sites available Total 40.
Facilities
Nearby facilities
Berwick.
Quiet site on cliff edge.

BERWICK-UPON-TWEED
Ord House Caravan Park, East Ord, Berwick-upon-Tweed, Northumberland, TD15 2NS.
Tel. 305288 Std. 01289
Nearest Town/Resort Berwick-upon-Tweed.
Directions Take East Ord road from bypass, follow caravan signpost.
Acreage 42 **Open** March–October
Access Good **Site** Lev/Slope
Sites available Total 60.
Facilities
Nearby facilities
Berwick-upon-Tweed.
Sheltered tree lined estate with 18th century mansion house containing licenced club.

CORBRIDGE-ON-TYNE
Barrasford Park Caravan and Camping Site, 1, Front Drive, Barrasford Park, near Hexham, Northumberland, NE48 4BE.
Tel. 681210 Std. 01434
Nearest Town/Resort Corbridge.
Directions Signposted 8 miles north of Corbridge on the A68.
Acreage 60 **Open** April–October
Access Good **Site** Sloping
Sites available Total 30.
Facilities
Nearby facilities
Corbridge.
6 miles from Hadrian's Wall, ideal break for travellers to and from Scotland.

HALTWHISTLE
Yont the Cleugh, Coanwood, Haltwhistle, Northumberland.
Tel. 320274 Std. 01434
Nearest Town/Resort Haltwhistle.
Directions Signposted 4½ miles from A69 at Haltwhistle.
Acreage 5 **Open** March–January
Access Good **Site** Level
Sites available Total 30.
Facilities
Nearby facilities
Haltwhistle.
Rural site. Scenic views. Near main Roman Wall site.

HAYDON BRIDGE

Poplars Riverside Park, Eastland Ends, Haydon Bridge, Hexham, Northumberland, NE47 6BY.
Tel. 684427 Std. 01434
Nearest Town/Resort Hexham.
Directions Onto A69, then 6 miles.
Acreage 1 **Open** March–October
Access Good **Site** Level
Sites available Total 11.
Facilities
Nearby facilities
Haydon Bridge.
Hadrian's Wall country, free fishing on site, 2 minutes to the village.

HEXHAM

Causey Hill Caravan Park, Causey Hill, Hexham, Northumberland.
Tel. 604647/602834 Std. 01434
Nearest Town/Resort Hexham.
Directions From town centre Blanchland Road, to Hexham Racecourse.
Open April–October
Access Good **Site** Sloping
Sites available Total 30.
Facilities
Nearby facilities
Hexham.
Scenic views, near Roman Wall. Tourist Board Graded 4 Ticks. A.A. Classified 3 Pennants.

HEXHAM

Springhouse Farm Caravan Park, Slaley, Hexham, Northumberland.
Tel. 673241 Std. 01434
Nearest Town/Resort Hexham.
Open March–October
Access Good **Site** Sloping
Sites available Total 20.
Facilities
Nearby facilities
Hexham Station.
Quiet, surrounded by forest. Panoramic views, excellent country walks.

MORPETH

Percy Wood Caravan Park, Swarland, Nr. Morpeth, Northumberland, NE65 9JW.
Tel. 787649 Std. 0670.
Nearest Town/Resort Alnwick.
Directions From the A1 turn off to Swarland and follow caravan signs.
Acreage 60 **Open** March–Janurary
Access Good **Site** Lav/Slope
Sites available Total 80.
Facilities
Nearby facilities
Morpeth.
Ideal base for touring coast and country. Adjacent to a golf course and forest walks.

OTTERBURN

Byrness Caravan Park, Cottonshope, Burnfoot, Nr. Otterburn, Northumberland, NE19 1TF.
Tel. 520259 Std. 01830
Nearest Town/Resort Jedburgh/Hexham.
Directions Adjacent to A68 – 17 miles to Jedburgh, 28 miles to Hexham, 38 miles to Newcastle.
Acreage 3 **Open** 1st March–31st October
Access Good **Site** Level
Sites available Total 36.
Facilities
Nearby facilities
Hexham.
Surrounded by Cottonshope, Burn and River Rede. Ideal walking and touring base. 6 miles south of the Scottish Border at Carter Bar. Situated in Border Forest Park.

ROTHBURY

Coquetdale Caravan Park, Whitton, Rothbury, Morpeth, Northumberland.
Tel. Rothbury 20549 Std. 01669
Nearest Town/Resort Rothbury.
Directions ½ mile southwest of Rothbury on road to Newtown.
Acreage 1½ **Open** Easter–October
Access Good **Site** Level
Sites available Total 50.
Facilities
Nearby facilities
Morpeth.
Beautiful views. Ideal situation for touring Borders and coast. All units are strictly for families and couples only.

ROTHBURY

Clennel Hall, Clennel, Alwinton, Morpeth, Northumberland.
Tel. 50341 Std. 01669
Nearest Town/Resort Rothbury.
Acreage 13¼ **Open** February–December
Access Good **Site** Level
Sites available Total 50.
Facilities
Nearby facilities
Morpeth.
Rural countryside, alongside a small river.

WOOLER

Highburn House Caravan & Camping Park, Wooler, Northumberland.
Tel. 281344/281839 Std. 01668
Nearest Town/Resort Wooler.
Directions Off A1 take A697 to Wooler town centre, at the top of Main Street take left turn, 400 metres on left is our site.
Acreage 12 **Open** April–December
Access Good **Site** Level
Sites available Total 100.
Facilities
Nearby facilities
Berwick.
River runs through middle of site, beautiful view over hills and valley.

WOOLER

Riverside Caravan Park, Wooler, Northumbria, NE71 6EE.
Tel. 281447 Std. 01668
Nearest Town/Resort Wooler.
Directions From Newcastle follow signs for Morpeth, then Colstream, thus joining the A697 to Wooler. From Scotland take the A697 from Coldstream to Wooler. Riverside lies on the south-east outskirts of the town.
Open 31 March–29 October
Sites available Total 98.
Facilities
Nearby facilities
Situated on the edge of Northumbria National Park.

NOTTS

CARLTON-ON-TRENT

Carlton Manor Caravan Park, Ossington Road, (off A1), Carlton-on-Trent, Nr. Newark, Nottinghamshire.
Tel. 821573 Std. 01636
Nearest Town/Resort Newark.
Directions A1 north towards Doncaster. Site is 7 miles north of Newark. Signposted on the A1.
Acreage 2 **Open** April–October
Access Good **Site** Level
Sites available Total 22.
Facilities
Nearby facilities
Newark.
We do allow individual motor cyclists, but not groups. Clean site Warden on site at all times. Emergency phone on site at Wardens. Doctor in village. Train spotting on site. Shops and fishing in village. Pubs, library, hairdressers etc. all nearby. Shop open between 8am and 8pm.

HOLME PIERREPONT

Holme Pierrepont Caravan & Camping Park, National Watersports Centre, Adbolton Lane, Holme Pierrepont, Notts, NG12 2LU.
Tel. 821212 Std. 01159
Nearest Town/Resort Nottingham.
Directions 3 miles south east of Nottingham. Off the A52 Nottingham/Grantham road.
Acreage 18 **Open** Easter–October
Access Good **Site** Level
Sites available Total 300+.
Facilities
Nearby facilities
Nottingham.

NOTTINGHAM

Manor Farm, Thrumpton, Nottinghamshire, NG11 0AX.
Tel. 830341 Std. 01159
Nearest Town/Resort Nottingham.
Directions From M1 junction 24, take the A453 Nottingham south, in 3 miles turn left. In 100 yds turn right. At next junction turn left, site immediately on right.
Acreage 3 **Open** All year
Access Good **Site** Level
Sites available Total 20.
Facilities
Nearby facilities

Nottingham.
Good walks, fishing in the village on River Trent. We charge a small extra fee for electric and awnings.

NOTTINGHAM

Moor Farm Trailer Park, Moor Road, Calverton, Nottingham, NG14 6FZ.
Tel. 652426 Std. 01159
Nearest Town/Resort Nottingham.
Directions From Nottingham A60/A614, second right onto the B6386. Take the first right into Calverton Village.
Open All year
Access Good **Site** Level
Facilities
Nearby facilities
Lowdham.
River, ideal touring.

NOTTINGHAM

Thornton's Holt Camping Park, Stragglethorpe, Radcliffe-on-Trent, Notts. NG12 2JZ.
Tel. 332125 Std. 01159
Nearest Town/Resort Nottingham.
Directions 3 miles east of Nottingham turn south of A52 towards Cropwell Bishop. Park is ¼ mile on left.
Acreage 8 **Open** All Year
Access Good **Site** Level
Sites available Total 90.
Facilities
Nearby facilities
Radcliffe-on-Trent.
Indoor heated swimming pool. Only 3 miles from Nottingham. Ideal base for touring Sherwood Forest and Vale of Belvoir.

TUXFORD

Orchard Park, Marnham Road, Tuxford, Newark, Notts, NG22 0PY.
Tel. 870228 Std. 01777
Nearest Town/Resort Retford.
Directions 1¼ miles south east of A1, off A6075 Lincoln Road, turn right in ¾ mile onto the Marnham Road – site on right in ¾ mile.
Acreage 5¼ **Open** March–October
Access Good **Site** Level
Sites available Total 50.
Facilities
Nearby facilities
Retford.
Peaceful location, ideal for Sherwood Forest and many attractions river fishing 3 miles.

WORKSOP

Riverside Caravan Park, Worksop Cricket Club, Central Avenue, Worksop, Notts, S80 1ER.
Nearest Town/Resort Worksop.
Directions At the roundabout on the junction with the A57/A60 Mansfield, follow international site signs towards the town centre.
Acreage 4¼ **Open** March–January
Access Good **Site** Level
Sites available Total 45.
Facilities
Nearby facilities
Worksop.
Ideal for touring Notts, Derbys and South Yorks areas. Few miles to the M1 and A1 roads.

OXFORDSHIRE

BLETCHINGDON

Diamond Farm Caravan & Camping Park, Islip Road, Bletchington, Oxford, Oxon OX5 3DR.
Tel. 350909 Std. 01869.
Nearest Town/Resort Oxford.
Directions A34 from Oxford towards the M40. After 4 miles turn left onto B4027, site is 1 mile on the left.
Acreage 3½ **Open** All Year
Access Good **Site** Level
Sites available Total 37.
Facilities
Nearby facilities
Islip.
Ideal centre for Oxford, Blenheim Palace and the Cotswolds.

CHARLBURY

Cotswold View Caravan & Camping Site, Enstone Road, Charlbury, Oxford.
Tel. 810314 Std. 01608
Directions From A44 Oxford to Stratford-on-Avon road, take the B4022 to Charlbury just south of Enstone. Site is 2 miles on the left.
Acreage 7 **Open** April–October
Access Good **Site** Lev/Slope
Sites available Total 90.
Facilities
Tennis on site.

CHIPPING NORTON

Chipping Norton Camping Site, Chadlington, Oxon, OX7 3PN.
Tel. 641993 Std. 01608
Nearest Town/Resort Chipping Norton.
Directions On the A361, 1¼ miles south of Chipping Norton.
Acreage 4¼ **Open** 20 March–1 November
Access Good **Site** Level
Sites available Total 80.
Facilities
Nearby facilities
Kingham.
Ideal touring base for the Cotswolds.

CHIPPING NORTON

Churchill Heath Caravan Park, Kingham, Chipping Norton, Oxon, OX7 6UJ.
Tel. 658317 Std. 01608
Nearest Town/Resort Chipping Norton.
Directions 6 miles from Stow-on-the-Wold, 4 miles from Chipping Norton on the B4450.
Acreage 6 **Open** All Year
Access Good **Site** Level
Sites available Total 50.
Facilities
Nearby facilities
Kingham.
Bourton-on-the-Water, ideal touring. In the centre of the Cotswolds.

HENLEY-ON-THAMES

Swiss Farm International Camping, Marlow Road, Henley-on-Thames, Oxfordshire. RG9 2HY.
Tel. 573419 Std. 01491
Nearest Town/Resort Henley-on-Thames.
Directions ½ mile north of Henley on Marlow road A4155.
Acreage 14 **Open** March–October
Access Good **Site** Sloping
Sites available Total 180.
Facilities
Nearby facilities
Henley.
Beautiful old bridge town famous for its Regatta. British Graded Holiday Parks 3 Tick.

OXFORD

Cassington Mill Caravan Park, Eynsham Road, Cassington, Witney, Oxford. OX8 1DB.
Tel. 881081 Std. 01865
Nearest Town/Resort Oxford.
Directions A40 west of Oxford, 3 miles on left. A40 east, 1 mile from Eynsham on the right.
Acreage 4 **Open** April–October
Access Good **Site** Level
Sites available Total 83.
Facilities
Nearby facilities
Oxford.
River, close to Oxford and Blenheim Palace. Boating on site.

OXFORD

Oxford Camping International, 426 Abingdon Road, Oxford, Oxfordshire OX1 4XN.
Tel. Oxford 246551 Std. 01865
Nearest Town/Resort Oxford.
Directions South side of Oxford take A4144 to City centre, 100yds (90 metres) on left to the rear of Touchwoods Outdoor Life Centre, signposted.
Acreage 5 **Open** All Year
Access Good **Site** Level
Sites available Total 129.
Facilities
Nearby facilities
Oxford.
Historic city $1\frac{1}{4}$ miles, River Thames $\frac{1}{2}$ mile, ideal touring centre.

WALLINGFORD

Bridge Villa International Camping & Caravan Park, Crowmarsh Gifford, Wallingford, Oxfordshire OX10 8HB.
Tel. 836860 Std. 01491
Nearest Town/Resort Wallingford.
Directions A4130/500 metres.
Acreage 4 **Open** March–October
Access Good **Site** Level
Sites available Total 111.
Facilities
Nearby facilities
Cholsey.
Within 400 metres of River Thames.

WITNEY

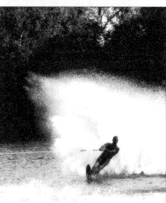

Hardwick Parks, Downs Road, Standlake, Nr. Witney, Oxon, OX8 7PZ.
Tel. 300501 Std. 01865
Nearest Town/Resort Witney.
Directions A415 Witney to Abingdon road, signposted 4 miles out of Witney on the main road.
Acreage 40 **Open** April–October
Access Good **Site** Level
Sites available Total 250.
Facilities
Nearby facilities
Oxford.
On the edge of the Cotswolds. Ideal for all watersports, two lakes on park for fishing, sailing and water-skiing.

WITNEY

Lincoln Farm Park, High Street, Standlake, Nr Witney, Oxon. OX8 7RH.
Tel. 300239 Std. 01865
Nearest Town/Resort Witney.
Directions $5\frac{1}{2}$ miles southeast Witney on the A415 to Abingdon.
Acreage 4 **Open** April–October
Access Good **Site** Level
Sites available Total 61.
Facilities
Nearby facilities
Oxford.
Situated in the heart of classic Oxfordshire Village. Private leisure club with swimming pool, spa pool and sauna. Graded 5 Ticks. Member of Best of British Caravan and Camping Parks. Advance booking recommended.

SYMBOLS EXPLAINED ON PAGE 47

SHROPSHIRE

BISHOPS CASTLE

Cwnd House Farm, Wentnor, Bishops Castle, Shropshire.
Tel. Linley 650237 Std. 01588
Nearest Town/Resort Church Stretton.
Directions Cwnd House Farm is on Longden Pulverbatch road from Shrewsbury (13 miles) Bishops Castle is southwest off A489 from Craven Arms.
Acreage 2 **Open** May–October
Access Good **Site** Level
Sites available Total 10.
Facilities
Nearby facilities
Church Stretton.
Farm site, Scenic views, Ideal touring centre.

BISHOPS CASTLE

Green Caravan Park, Wentnor, Nr. Bishops Castle, Shropshire. SY9 5EF.
Tel. 650605/650231 Std. 01588
Nearest Town/Resort Bishops Castle.
Directions From A5 Shrewsbury, take A488 19 miles South to A489 (Lydham Heath) East $\frac{3}{4}$ mile. Turn at caravan signpost. Park is 3 miles on the left.
Acreage 15 **Open** April–October
Access Good **Site** Level
Sites available Total 140.
Facilities
Nearby facilities
Craven Arms.
Alongside river, scenic, ideal touring and walking centre.

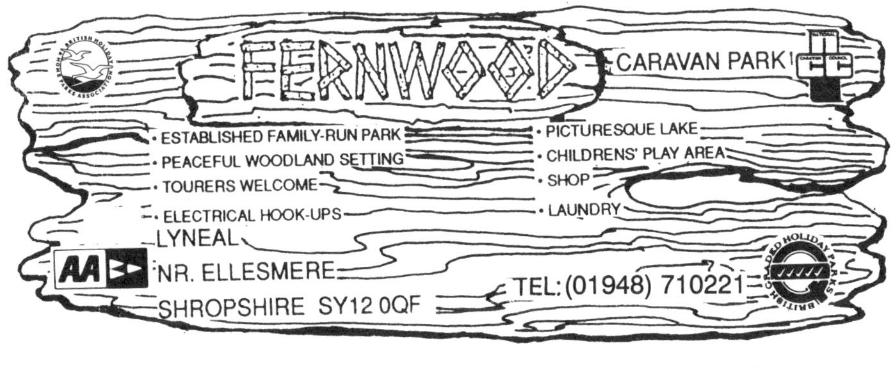

BRIDGNORTH
Camp Easy, Rays Farm, Billingsley, Bridgnorth, Salop, WV16 6PF.
Tel. 841255 Std. 01299
Nearest Town/Resort Bridgnorth.
Directions Off the B4363 midway between Bridgnorth and Cleobury Mortimer, signposted Rays Farm.
Acreage 11 **Open** May–September
Site Lev/Slope
Sites available Total 15.
Facilities
Nearby facilities
Kidderminster.
Select quiet site in beautiful wooded valley. Many rare farm animals eg. deer, highland cattle, goats, pigs, owls, turkeys etc. Tents and all equipment provided. Customers tents, caravans etc. not permitted.

BRIDGNORTH
Stanmore Hall Touring Park, Stourbridge Road, Bridgnorth, Shropshire.
Tel. Bridgnorth 761761 Std. 01746
Nearest Town/Resort Bridgnorth.
Directions 1¼ miles from Bridgnorth on A458 to Stourbridge.
Acreage 6 **Open** March–6 Jan
Access Good **Site** Level
Sites available Total 120.
Facilities
Nearby facilities
Wolverhampton.
Sited around lake and amongst trees, ideal site for Severn Valley Railway and Iron Bridge museums. Motorcycles accepted but families only. Graded 5 Ticks.

CHURCH STRETTON
Wayside Inn, Marshbrook, Church Stretton, Shropshire, SY6 6QE.
Tel. 781208 Std. 01694
Nearest Town/Resort Church Stretton.
Directions 12 miles south of Shrewsbury, 2 miles south of Church Stretton on the A49. Turn right over level crossing at Marshbrook, inn is on the right.
Acreage 2 **Open** All Year
Access Good **Site** Level
Sites available Total 80.
Facilities
Nearby facilities
Church Stretton.
Alongside a stream, quiet and secluded site in the countryside. Ideal for walking and touring. Motorcycles are accepted but limited.

CLEOBURY MORTIMER
The Blount Arms Caravan Park, Forest Park, Cleobury Mortimer, Kidderminster, Shropshire, DY14 9BD.
Tel. 270423 Std. 01299
Nearest Town/Resort Cleobury Mortimer.
Directions A4117, 2¼ miles east.
Acreage 1 **Open** March–October
Access Good **Site** Level
Sites available Total 30.
Facilities
Nearby facilities
Kidderminster.
Edge of the Wyre Forest. West Midlands Safari Park, Severn Valley Railway and Ludlow Castle nearby.

CRAVEN ARMS
Glenburrell Farm, Horderley, Craven Arms, Shropshire.
Tel. 672318 Std. 01588
Nearest Town/Resort Ludlow.
Directions 3 miles northwest of Craven Arms. 9 miles Ludlow from A49. 1½ miles on A489. Farm site near the Long Mynd.
Open April–October
Access Good **Site** Level
Sites available
Facilities
Craven Arms.
Alongside river, scenic views, ideal touring, near Ironbridge.

CRAVEN ARMS
Kevindale, Broome, Craven Arms, Salop, SY7 0NT.
Tel. 326 Std. 015887
Nearest Town/Resort Craven Arms.
Directions From Craven Arms which is situated on the A49 Hereford to Shewsbury road, take the B4368 Clun/Bishops Castle road in 2 miles take B4367 Knighton road 1¼ miles turn right into Broome Village.
Acreage 2 **Open** All Year
Access Good **Site** Level
Sites available Total 12.
Facilities
Nearby facilities
Broome.
Scenic views, near village inn with good food, close to Mid Wales Border, ideal walking.

ELLESMERE
Fernwood Caravan Park, Lyneal, Nr. Ellesmere, Shropshire.
Tel. Bettisfield 710221 Std. 01948
Nearest Town/Resort Ellesmere.
Directions A495 from Ellesmere signposted Whitchurch. In Welshampton, right turn on B5063 signed Wem. Over canal bridge right sign Lyneal.
Acreage 7 **Open** March–November
Access Good **Site** Lev/Slope
Sites available Total 60.
Facilities
Nearby facilities
Wem.
25 acres woodland open to caravanners. Lake with wildfowl and fishing.

ELLESMERE
Talbot Caravan Park, Sparbridge, Talbot Street, Ellesmere, Shropshire, SY12 0HH.
Tel. 622408/622285 Std. 01691
Nearest Town/Resort Ellesmere.
Directions On A495 (A528) Ellesmere to Shrewsbury road.
Acreage 1 **Open** March–November
Access Good **Site** Level
Sites available Total 25.
Facilities
Nearby facilities
Gobowen.
Near Mere, lakes, Cremorne Gardens.

KINNERLEY
Cranberry Moss Camping & Caravan Park, Kinnerley, Oswestry, Shropshire SY10 9DY.
Tel. 741444 Std. 01743
Nearest Town/Resort Oswestry.
Directions 8 miles south east of Oswestry and 11 miles north west of Shrewsbury. Leave A5 for B4396, site 300yds on the left. Signposted on the A5.
Acreage 4 **Open** April–October
Access Good **Site** Level
Sites available Total 60.
Facilities
Shrewsbury.
Ideal touring. Country park, walks.

LUDLOW
Westbrook Park, Little Hereford, Ludlow, Salop, SY8 4AU.
Tel. 711280 Std. 01584
Nearest Town/Resort Ludlow.
Directions 3 miles west of Tenbury Wells on A456, enter village of Little Hereford. Turn left after passing over River Teme bridge and travel on by road for 300yds. Turn into park on left by the road junction.
Acreage 8 **Open** March–10th Jan
Access Good **Site** Level
Sites available Total 38.
Facilities
Nearby facilities
Ludlow.
In pretty orchard close to River Teme, ¼ mile to fishing. On well maintained quality park, short walk to local inn for refreshments and food. Bowling nearby.

NESSCLIFFE
Royal Hill Camping Site, Royal Hill, Edgerley, Kinnerley, Oswestry, Salop, SY10 8ES.
Tel. 741242 Std. 01743
Nearest Town/Resort Oswestry.
Directions 3 miles from the A5 at Nesscliffe. Follow Pentre Melverley signs.
Acreage 2 **Open** April–October

Access Good **Site** Level
Sites available
Facilities
Nearby facilities

SHREWSBURY
Cartref Caravan & Camping Site, Cartref, Fords Heath, Nr. Shrewsbury, Shropshire.
Tel. 821688 Std. 01743
Directions From Shrewsbury bypass A5 trunk road take the A458 Welshpool West. 2 miles to Ford Village, turn south at Ford, follow camp signs.
Acreage 1½ **Open** Easter–October
Access Good **Site** Level
Sites available Total 25+.
Facilities
Shrewsbury.
Ideal touring, overnight stop. One holiday caravan for hire. Peaceful countryside.

WEM
Lower Lacon Caravan Park, Wem, Shropshire. SY4 5RP.
Tel. 232376 Std. 01939
Nearest Town/Resort Wem.
Directions From Wem over crossings, left 1 mile on left. From the A49 take B5065 for Wem 3 miles on right.
Acreage 48 **Open** All Year
Access Good **Site** Level
Sites available Total 270.
Facilities
Nearby facilities
Wem.
Take away food.

WHITCHURCH
Green Lake Farm Caravan & Camping Site, Green Lane Farm, Prees, Whitchurch, Shropshire, SY13 2AH.
Tel. 840460 Std. 01948
Nearest Town/Resort Whitchurch.
Directions 4¼ miles south south east of Whitchurch. Turn right off the A41 (Whitchurch to Newport) onto the A442 signposted Telford. In 150yds turn right at the crossroads (signposted Prees). Site entrance on the right 200yds white farm house.
Acreage 3 **Open** March–October
Access Good **Site** Level
Sites available Total 20.
Facilities
Nearby facilities
Prees.
Unspoilt North Shropshire, close to Hawkstone Park Follies and Golf Course.

WHITCHURCH
Brook House Farm, Grindley Brook, Whitchurch, Salop.
Tel. 664557 Std. 01948
Nearest Town/Resort Whitchurch.
Directions Site on main A41 road 1 mile north of Whitchurch. First farm coming North from Whitchurch.
Acreage 1 **Open** March–November
Access Good **Site** Level
Sites available
Facilities
Nearby facilities
Whitchurch.
Ideal for touring Wales and Chester.

SOMERSET

BRIDGWATER
The Fairways International Touring Caravan and Camping Park, Woolavington Corner, Bath Road, Bawdrip, Bridgwater, Somerset, TA7 8PP.
Tel. 685569 Std. 01278
Nearest Town/Resort Bridgwater.
Directions 3¼ miles on Glastonbury side of Bridgwater. 1½ miles off M5 junction 23 at junction A39 and B3141.
Acreage 5¾ **Open** 1st March–15th Nov
Access Good **Site** Level
Sites available Total 200.
Facilities
Nearby facilities
Bridgwater.
Ideal for touring Somerset. Off Licence.

BRIDGWATER
Mill Farm Caravan & Camping Park, Fiddington, Bridgwater, Somerset, TA5 1JQ.
Tel. 732286 Std. 01278
Nearest Town/Resort Bridgwater.
Directions Leave M5 at junction 23 or 24, take A39 west for 6 miles. Turn right to Fiddington, then follow camping signs.
Acreage 12 **Open** All year
Access Good **Site** Level
Sites available Total 250.
Facilities
Nearby facilities
Bridgwater.
Free boating, canoe and trampoline hire on site. Walking, riding, fishing. Quantock Hills 2 miles. Beach 4 miles. Exmoor, Cheddar Gorge, Wookey Caves within easy reach. Tourist Information Room. Free swimming and paddling pools. Children's pony rides on site. Off licence, large sandpit, Splash Pool.

BURNHAM-ON-SEA
Home Farm Holidays Touring Caravan & Camping Park, Edithmead, Nr. Burnham-on-Sea, Somerset, TA9 4HD.
Tel. 788888 Std. 01278.
Nearest Town/Resort Burnham-on-Sea.
Acreage 40 **Open** All Year
Access Good **Site** Level
Sites available Total 850.
Facilities
Nearby facilities
Ideal for touring.

BURNHAM-ON-SEA
Northam Farm Caravan and Touring Park, Brean, Nr. Burnham-on-Sea, Somerset.
Tel. 751244/751222 Std. 01278
Nearest Town/Resort Burnham-on-Sea.
Directions M5 Junction 22. Follow signs to Brean, ¼ mile past Leisure Park on righthand side.
Acreage 20 **Open** Easter–October
Access Good **Site** Level
Sites available Total 350.
Facilities
Nearby facilities
Weston-super-Mare.
Ideal base for seeing Somerset. 200 metres to safe sandy beach. Family entertainment within east walking distance. Excellent facilities, fishing lake on park. Take-away food. You can FAX us on 01278 751150.

HOLIDAY CENTRE LTD
Coast Road, Somerset TA8 2RB
Tel: Brean Down (01278) 751235
Tel: Caravan Sales (01278) 751602
Fax: Brean Down (01278) 751539

Try Unity Farm for a super, fun packed, water splashing, roller coaster, caravan and camping holiday. Situated in 200 acres of level meadowland, only a sand dune away from Brean Sands, With views over open countryside towards Cheddar. The park accepts tents, touring caravans, motor homes and has holiday homes for hire and sale. Facilities include an indoor and outdoor pool complex with giant waterslides, an 18 hole golf course, funfair with over 30 attractions, fishing lake, bars with entertainment and a childrens 'Piglet Club'.

YOU WILL NOT FIND BETTER VALUE ANYWHERE ELSE IN THE SOUTH - WEST

THE FAIRWAYS

INTERNATIONAL TOURING CARAVAN AND CAMPING PARK

BATH ROAD,
BAWDRIP, BRIDGWATER,
SOMERSET TA7 8PP
Telephone: (01278) 685569 or 423840

Set in beautiful surroundings. 1 miles off Junction 23 of the M5 motorway.

• Excellent toilet facilities with showers • Private wash cubicles • Hair dryer • Electric shaver points • Babies room • Facilities for disabled inc. shower • Launderette • Ironing and dishwashing facilities • Hook ups • Gas • Shop with Off Licence • Games room • Play area • Chemical disposal • Telephone •

Easy reach seaside. All sports facilities and places of historical interest.

IN THE HEART OF SOMERSET CIDER COUNTRY

MILL FARM

CARAVAN AND CAMPING PARK

FIDDINGTON BRIDGEWATER SOMERSET TA5 1JQ

SWIMMING, RIDING, BOATING

A unique, quiet, friendly & sheltered country park. Situated at the foot of the beautiful Quantock Hills beside a picturesque stream. The ideal family site.

FREE: Three Heated Swimming Pools. Boating on shallow lake. Sand pit.

Games /TV Room, Ropes, Swings and slides, Trampolines for hire.

Tourist Information Room. Farm Pets.

Clean, modern toilet & shower blocks. Laundry room, Pay phone. Well stocked shop. Off licence. Hot take-away during high season. Excellent Pub & Restaurant nearby.

Ponies & Canoes For Hire **Caravan Storage**

OPEN ALL YEAR

Separate meadows for rallys
Mr & Mrs M.J. Evans
Tel: Nether Stowey (01278) 732286

REFER ALSO TO OUR ADVERT IN THE FRONT COLOUR SECTION
Phone or write for colour brochure

BURNHAM ON SEA

Burnham On Sea Sports Club, Stoddens Road, Burnham On Sea Somerset.
Tel. 751235 Std. 01278
Nearest Town/Resort Burnham On Sea.
Directions M5 junction 22 follow brown signs over roundabout at next roundabout exit right signposted Middle Burnham. After 600yds fork left, entrance on right over cattle grid approx 300 yds.
Acreage 23 **Open** All Year.
Access Good **Site** Level
Sites available Total 20.
Facilities
Nearby facilities
Highbridge.
Ideal base for touring West Country. A small, wuiet park. 1 mile from the town centre and beach.

BURNHAM-ON-SEA

Southfield Farm Caravan Park, Brean, Nr. Burnham-on-Sea, Somerset TA8 2RL.
Tel. 233 Std. 01278751
Nearest Town/Resort Burnham-on-Sea.
Directions 4 miles north along coast road from Burnham-on-Sea (well signposted). Site is in Brean village.
Acreage 10 **Open** Spring Bank Holiday–September
Access Good **Site** Level
Sites available
Facilities
Nearby facilities
Weston-super-Mare.
Adjacent beach, good centre for touring Somerset. Local entertainments nearby.

BURNHAM-ON-SEA

Warren Farm Touring Park, Brean Sands, Burnham-on-Sea, Somerset, TA8 2RP.
Tel. 751227 Std. 01278
Nearest Town/Resort Burnham-on-Sea.
Directions Leave M5 at junction 22, follow signs to Burnham-on-Sea, Berrow and Brean on the B3140. Site is 1¼ miles past the leisure centre.
Acreage 50 **Open** April–Mid October
Access Good **Site** Level
Sites available Total 500.
Facilities
Nearby facilities
Weston-super-Mare.
Flat, grassy, family park with excellent facilities. 100 metres from 5 miles of sandy beach.

BURNHAM-ON-SEA

Unity Farm Holiday Centre, Coast Road, Brean Sands, Somerset.
Tel. 751235 Std. 01278
Nearest Town/Resort Burnham-on-Sea.
Directions Leave M5 at junction 22. Follow signs for Berrow and Brean, site on right 4½ miles from M5.
Acreage 150 **Open** Easter–October
Access Good **Site** Level
Sites available Total 600.
Facilities
Nearby facilities
Weston-super-Mare.
200 yards from 7 mile beach, own leisure centre, with 30 fun fair attractions and pool complex with 3 giant water slides and 18 hole golf course, fishing lake and horse riding. Family entertainment from end of May till end of September. Special offers for young families and OAPs in June and September.

CHARD

Alpine Grove Touring Park, Alpine Grove, Forton, Chard, Somerset, TA20 4HD.
Tel. 63479 Std. 01460
Nearest Town/Resort Chard.
Directions Take the A30 from Crewkerne to Chard. At Cricket St Thomas Wild Life Park follow official camping & caravan signs, on the B3167 turning right at crossroads. Site is on the right.
Acreage 7½ **Open** Easter–September
Access Good **Site** Level
Sites available Total 40.
Facilities
Nearby facilities
Crewkerne.
Shaded by mature oak trees and screened by Rhododendrons. Ideal touring centre.

CHARD

Snowdon Hill Farm, "The Beeches", Catelgate Lane, Wambrook, Chard, Somerset.
Tel. 63213/66828 Std. 01460
Nearest Town/Resort Chard.
Directions Just off main A30 Chard to Exeter road.
Acreage 3 **Open** April–November
Access Good **Site** Level
Sites available Total 5.
Facilities
Nearby facilities
Axminster.
25 minutes to coast, 4 miles to wildlife park at Cricket St. Thomas, ideal touring, scenic views. Lovely country walks, good food at local pubs. Swimming pool in Chard 1 mile away.

BUCKLEGROVE CARAVAN & CAMPING PARK

FREE HEATED INDOOR POOL

Enjoy the peace and beauty of the Somerset Countryside at this family run Holiday Park situated at the foot of the Mendip Hills midway between the Cathederal City of Wells and the famous Cheddar Gorge.

☆ Modern toilet facilities with bathroom, dishwashing, free showers, Disabled facilties ☆ Children's play area ☆ Licensed Bar and Conservatory ☆ Well stocked shop ☆ Launderette ☆ Electric hook-up ☆ Gas sales ☆ Holiday homes for hire/sale ☆ Summer & Winter storage ☆ Bus stop at entrance ☆ Separate camping field for Dog Owners

RODNEY STOKE, CHEDDAR, SOMERSET BS27 3UZ Tel: (01749) 870261

CHARD

South Somerset Holiday Park, The Turnpike, Howley, Chard, Somerset, TA20 3EA.
Tel. 62221/66036 Std. 01460
Nearest Town/Resort Chard.
Directions 3 miles west of Chard on the A30.
Acreage 7 **Open** All Year
Access Good **Site** Level
Sites available Total 110.
Facilities
Nearby facilities
Crewkerne.
Scenic views and ideal touring.

CHEDDAR

Broadway House Holiday, Touring Caravan & Camping Park, Cheddar, Somerset.
Tel. 742610 Std. 01934
Nearest Town/Resort Cheddar Gorge.
Directions Exit 22 (M5) 8 miles. Follow brown tourist signs for Cheddar Gorge. We are midway between Cheddar and Axbridge on the A371.
Acreage 25 **Open** March–November
Access Good **Site** Level
Sites available Total 400.
Facilities
Nearby facilities
Weston-super-Mare.
Centrally situated in wonderful touring area, i.e. Wells, Bristol and Weston-super-Mare.

CHEDDAR

Bucklegrove Caravan and Camping Park, Rodney Stoke, Cheddar, Somerset, BS27 3UZ.
Tel. 870261 Std. 01749
Nearest Town/Resort Wells/Cheddar.
Directions Midway Between Wells and Cheddar on A371.
Open March–November
Access Good **Site** Lev/Slope
Sites available Total 125.
Facilities
Nearby facilities
Weston Super Mare.
Ideal touring centre at foot of Mendip Hills, scenic views, walking.

CHEDDAR

Froglands Farm Caravan and Camping Park, Froglands Farm, Cheddar, Somerset.
Tel. 742058 Std. 01934
Nearest Town/Resort Cheddar/Weston-super-Mare.
Directions On main A371, 150yds past village church.
Acreage 4 **Open** Easter–October
Access Good **Site** Level
Sites available Total 68.
Facilities
Nearby facilities
Weston-super-Mare.
Walking distance, village shops, pubs, Gorge and Caves.

CHEDDAR

Longbottom Farm, Shipham, Near Winscombe, Somerset, BS19 2RW.
Tel. 743166 Std. 01934
Nearest Town/Resort Cheddar/Bristol.
Directions Bristol A38, left to Shipham after Churchill traffic lights (1¼ miles).
Acreage ¼ **Open** All Year
Access Good **Site** Level
Sites available Total 20.
Facilities
Nearby facilities
Backwell.
Walking, mountain bikes and trekking nearby.

CHEDDAR

Ragwood Farm Camping & Caravanning Site, Ragwood Farm, Clewer, Cheddar, Somerset.

WARREN FARM CARAVAN AND CAMPING PARK
BREAN SANDS, BURNHAM-ON-SEA,
SOMERSET
TEL: 01278 751227

Flat, grassy park. 100 metres from five miles of sandy beach. Family park with excellent facilities.

Please refer to main advertisement for full details in the colour section of this guide.

COUNTRY VIEW

CARAVAN & TOURING PARK

SAND RD, SAND BAY, WESTON-SUPER-MARE, AVON BS22 9UJ

Small family "Rose Award" park only 200 yards to beach.

Luxury caravans for hire. Separate field for Tourers & Tents.

An ideal park for touring Somerset's many attractions

Comprehensive Facilities Include:

- *Heated swimming pool*
- *Sun Patio*
- *Childrens play area*
- *Large games room*
- *Shop*
- *Showers*
- *Laundry etc.*

For a colour brochure tel: (01934) 627595

Tel. 742254 Std. 01934
Nearest Town/Resort Cheddar.
Directions Half way between Cheddar and Wedmore on the B3151. In Clewer turn right at the toll house.
Acreage 4 **Open** May–October
Access Good **Site** Level
Sites available Total 65.
Facilities
Nearby facilities
Weston-super-Mare.
Good views, secluded site near a river. Good for touring.

CHEDDAR
Splott Farm, Blackford, Near Wedmore, Somerset, BS28 4PD.
Tel. 641522 Std. 01278
Nearest Town/Resort Burnham-on-Sea/Cheddar.
Directions Leave M5 at junction 22, 2 miles to Highbridge, take B3139 Highbridge/Wells road, about 5 miles.
Acreage $4\frac{1}{4}$ **Open** May–September
Access Good **Site** Gentle Slope
Sites available Total 40.
Facilities
Nearby facilities
Highbridge.
Views of Mendip Hills (and Quantocks), very peaceful site, ideal touring. Weston-super-Mare, Wells, Cheddar, Burnham-on-Sea, Wookey. Very rural area.

CHEDDAR
Rodney Stoke Inn, Rodney Stoke, Nr. Cheddar, Somerset.
Tel. 870209 Std. 01749
Nearest Town/Resort Cheddar.
Directions On the main A371, 3 miles from Cheddar towards Wells, on the right.
Acreage 3 **Open** All Year
Access Good **Site** Level
Sites available Total 32.
Facilities
Nearby facilities
Weston-super-Mare.
Quiet site behind 'All-Day' pub. Walks and scenic views. Easy access to Cheddar, Wells and Weston-super-Mare.

CROWCOMBE
Quantock Orchard Caravan Park, Crowcombe, Nr. Taunton, Somerset, TA4 4AW.
Tel. 618618 Std. 01984
Nearest Town/Resort Minehead.
Directions A358 from Taunton to Minehead for 10 miles. Turn left just before the village of Crowcombe towards steam railway. Site is on the left.
Acreage $3\frac{1}{4}$ **Open** All Year
Access Good **Site** Level
Sites available Total 74.
Facilities
Nearby facilities
Taunton.
Scenic views, ideal touring area. Mountain bike hire.

DULVERTON
Lakeside Caravan Park, Higher Grants Farm, Exbridge, Dulverton, Somerset, TA22 9BE.
Tel. 24068 Std. 01398
Nearest Town/Resort Dulverton.
Directions Leave the M5 junction 27. Take the A361 towards Barnstaple, turn right onto A396 at first roundabout. Turn left at the next roundabout, straight on at the Black Cat and stay on the A396. Park is 3 miles on the left hand side.
Acreage 4 **Open** 3 March–29 October
Access Good **Site** Lev/Slope
Sites available Total 50.
Facilities
Nearby facilities
Lovely views, ideal for touring Exmoor. Fly fishing on site. Dog walking field.

EXFORD
Westermill Farm, Exford, Minehead, Somerset, TA24 7NJ.
Tel. 238 Std. 0164383
Nearest Town/Resort Exford.
Directions Leave Exford on Porlock Road. After $\frac{1}{2}$ mile fork left. Continue 2 miles past another campsite until "Westermill" seen on tree. Fork left.
Acreage 6 **Open** End March–End Oct
Access Poor **Site** Level
Sites available Total 60.
Facilities
Nearby facilities
Taunton.
Beautiful, secluded site beside a river. Fascinating 500 acre farm with Waymarked walks. Centre Exmoor National Park. Log cottages and farmhouse cottage for hire. You can FAX us on 0164383 660.

GLASTONBURY
The Old Oaks Touring Park, Wick Farm, Wick, Glastonbury, Somerset, BA6 8JS.
Tel. 831437 Std. 01458
Nearest Town/Resort Glastonbury.
Directions A361 2 miles from town centre left at signpost Wick 1 Mile.
Acreage $2\frac{1}{2}$ **Open** March–October
Access Good **Site** Lev/Slope
Sites available Total 40.
Facilities
Nearby facilities
Castle Cary.
Lovely tranquil setting, scenic views, private course fishing. Small working farm.

ILMINSTER
Stewley Cross Caravan Park, Stewley Cross, Ashill, Ilminster, Somerset.
Tel. 480314 Std. 01823

Nearest Town/Resort Ilminster/Taunton.
Directions M5 junction 25 head east towards Yeovil along the A358, 6 miles at Porteus Petrol Station. Along A303 turn onto A358 towards Taunton/M5.
Acreage ¼ **Open** April–October
Access Good **Site** Level
Sites available Total 5.
Facilities
Nearby facilities
Taunton.
Ideal touring centre.

ILMINSTER

Thornleigh Caravan Park, Hanning Road, Horton, Ilminster, Somerset, TA19 9QH.
Tel. 53450 Std. 01460
Nearest Town/Resort Ilminster.
Directions A303 West Ilminster, take the A358 signposted Chard. ½ mile turn right signposted Horton and Broadway. Site on the left opposite the filling station, ¾ mile.
Acreage 1¼ **Open** March–October
Access Good **Site** Level
Sites available Total 20.
Facilities
Nearby facilities
Crewkerne.
Flat site, ideal for touring Somerset and Devon. Gymnasium, sauna and solarium on site. 6 miles to Cricket St Thomas Wildlife Park twinned with Crinkley Bottom.

MARTOCK

Southfork Caravan Park, Parrett Works, Martock, Somerset, TA12 6AE.
Tel. 825661 Std. 01935
Nearest Town/Resort Martock.
Directions Situated 2 miles north west of A303 (between Ilchester and Ilminster). From A303 east of Ilminster, at roundabout take second exit signposted South Petherton and follow camping signs. From A303 west of Ilchester, after Cartgate roundabout (junction with A3088 to Yeovil) take exit signposted Martock and follow camping signs.
Acreage 2 **Open** All Year
Access Good **Site** Level
Sites available Total 30.
Facilities
Nearby facilities
Yeovil.
Set in beautiful countryside by River Parrett. Numerous places of interest nearby for all age groups. Ideal base for touring.

MINEHEAD

Blue Anchor Park, Blue Anchor, Nr. Minehead, Somerset, TA24 6JT.
Tel. 821360 Std. 01643
Nearest Town/Resort Minehead.
Directions From A39 at Williton, travel west for 4 miles to Carhampton and turn right onto B3191 signposted Blue Anchor. Park is 1½ miles on right.
Acreage 5 **Open** March–October
Access Good **Site** Level
Sites available Total 103.
Facilities
Nearby facilities
Minehead.
On waters edge, an ideal base from which to explore Exmoor and this beautiful coastline.

MINEHEAD

Minehead & Exmoor Caravan Park, Porlock Road, Minehead, Somerset TA24 8SN.
Tel. 703074 Std. 01643
Nearest Town/Resort Minehead.
Directions Main A39 offically signposted 1 mile from centre of Minehead.
Acreage 2 **Open** March–1 November
Access Good **Site** Level
Sites available Total 50.
Facilities
Nearby facilities
Minehead.
Ideal touring site 1 mile from Minehed centre and beach.

MINEHEAD

Totterdown Farm Camp Site, Mr & Mrs B.T. Halse, Totterdown Farm, Timberscombe, Nr. Minehead, Somerset TA24 7TA.
Tel. 841317 Std. 01643
Nearest Town/Resort Minehead.
Directions Take Tiverton Road A396 from Dunster 2 miles. Farm in layby on left before Timberscombe village.
Acreage 8 **Open** Mid July–Mid September
Access Good **Site** Lev/Slope
Sites available Total 22.
Facilities
Nearby facilities
Taunton.
Very near Dunster village, near river Avill, beautiful view of Exmoor.

PORLOCK

Burrowhayes Farm Caravan & Camping Site and Riding Stables, West Luccombe, Porlock, Nr. Minehead, Somerset, TA24 8HU.
Tel. 862463 Std. 01643
Nearest Town/Resort Minehead.
Directions 5 miles west of Minehead on A39, left hand turning to West Luccombe, site ½ mile on the right.
Acreage 8 **Open** 15 March–October
Access Good **Site** Lev/Slope
Sites available Total 140.
Facilities
Nearby facilities
Taunton.
Riding stables on site. Picturesque setting with oak woods and open moorland as a backdrop. Walks start from the site.

PORLOCK

Porlock Caravan Park, Highbank, Porlock, Nr. Minehead, Somerset. TA24 8NS.
Tel. 862269 Std. 01643
Nearest Town/Resort Minehead.
Directions A39 from Minehead to Lynton, take the B3225 in Porlock to Porlock Weir. Site signposted.
Acreage 3½ **Open** Mid March–October
Access Good **Site** Level
Sites available Total 40.
Facilities
Nearby facilities
Taunton.
Scenic views, Ideal touring and walking.

SHEPTON MALLET

Greenacres Camping, Barrow Lane, North Wootton, Nr. Shepton Mallet, Somerset, BA4 4HL.
Tel. 890497 Std. 01749
Nearest Town/Resort Wells.
Directions From Wells take the A39, turn left at Brownes Garden Centre. Site signposted in the village.
Acreage 4½ **Open** May–September
Site Level
Sites available Total 30.
Facilities
Nearby facilities
Castle Cary.
An award winning family site. Peacefully set within sight of Glastonbury Tor.

SHEPTON MALLET

Manleaze Caravan Park, Cannards Grave, Shepton Mallet, Somerset.
Tel. 342404 Std. 01749
Nearest Town/Resort Shepton Mallet.
Directions 1 mile south of Shepton Mallet on A371.
Acreage ¾ **Open** All year
Access Good **Site** Level
Sites available Total 25.
Facilities
Nearby facilities
Castle Cary.

SHEPTON MALLET

Old Down Caravan & Camping Park, Emborough, Bath, Somerset, BA3 4SA.
Tel. 232355 Std. 01761
Nearest Town/Resort Midsomer Norton.
Directions From Shepton Mallet take the A37 towards Bristol, after 6 miles turn right onto the B3139. Site is on the right opposite Old Down Inn.
Acreage 4 **Open** April–October
Access Good **Site** Level
Sites available Total 25.
Facilities
Nearby facilities
Bath.
A level field with an ancient oak tree as the centre. Piece of a large recreation area. Ideal touring centre.

SHEPTON MALLET

Phippens Farm, Stoke St. Michael, Oakhill, Nr. Bath, Somerset.
Tel. 840395 Std. 01749
Nearest Town/Resort Shepton Mallet.
Directions A367 Bath/Shepton Mallet road. Turn into Stoke St. Michael road in village of Oakhill sit on right hand side (1½ miles).
Acreage 7 **Open** Easter–September
Access Good **Site** Level
Sites available
Facilities
Frome.
Good touring area. Longleat, Bath, Cheddar, Wookey Hole, Bristol, Wells, etc.

STREET

Bramble Hill Camping Site, Bramble Hill, Walton, Nr. Street, Somerset, BA16 9RQ.
Tel. 42548 Std. 01458
Nearest Town/Resort Street.
Directions A39 1 mile from Street, 2 miles from Glastonbury.
Acreage 3½ **Open** April–September
Access Good **Site** Level
Sites available Total 60.
Facilities
Nearby facilities
Castle Cary/Taunton.
Quiet site. Caravan storage also available.

TAUNTON

Ashe Farm Caravan & Camp Site, Ashe Farm, Thornfalcon, Taunton, Somerset TA3 5NW.
Tel. Taunton 442567 Std. 01823
Nearest Town/Resort Taunton.
Directions 4 miles southeast Taunton on A358, turn right at 'Nags Head' towards West Hatch, ¼ mile on right.
Acreage 7 **Open** April–October
Access Good **Site** Level
Sites available Total 30.
Facilities
Nearby facilities
Taunton.
Ideal touring centre, easy reach of Quantock and Blackdown Hills.

TAUNTON

Holly Bush Park, Culmhead, Taunton, Somerset, TA3 7EA.
Tel. 421515 Std. 01823
Nearest Town/Resort Taunton.
Directions From Taunton follow signs for the Racecourse and Corfe on the B3170, 3¼ miles from Corfe turn right at crossroads towards Wellington. Turn right at the next T-Junction, site is 200yds on the left.
Acreage 2¼ **Open** March–January
Access Good **Site** Level
Sites available Total 40.
Facilities
Nearby facilities
Taunton.
Area of outstanding natural beauty.

WATCHET

Doniford Bay Holiday Park, Watchet, Somerset, TA23 0TJ.
Tel. 632423 Std. 01984
Nearest Town/Resort Watchet.
Directions Leave the M5 at exit 24. Follow Minehead signs on the A39 until you reach West Quantoxhead. Fork right after St. Audries Garage to Doniford Bay, the park is signposted.
Acreage 5 **Open** 26 March–8 October
Site Level
Sites available Total 120.
Facilities
Nearby facilities
Taunton.
Overlooking the sea.

WATCHET

Warren Farm, Watchet, Somerset.
Tel. 31220 Std. 01984
Nearest Town/Resort Watchet.

Directions B3191, 1 mile from Watchet on the Blue Anchor Road.
Acreage 13 **Open** Easter–End September
Access Good **Site** Lev/Slope
Sites available Total 100.
Facilities
Nearby facilities
Taunton.
275 acre working farm, adjacent to a beach. Good centre for Quantock hills and Exmoor. Established in 1928 by the same family. Open for rallies by appointment only. Facilities for the disabled available by 1995.

WELLS

Chewton Cheese Dairy, Priory Farm, Chewton Mendip, Bath, BA3 4NT.
Tel. 241666 Std. 01761
Nearest Town/Resort Wells.
Directions On A39 6 miles north east of Wells.
Open All year
Access Good **Site** Level
Sites available Total 25.
Facilities
Nearby facilities
Bath.
Cheese dairy on site, wooded picnic area and gardens, ideal for visiting Wells, Bath, Cheddar, and Mendip Hills.

WELLS

Homestead Park, Wookey Hole, Wells, Somerset.BA5 1BW.
Tel. 673022 Std. 01749
Nearest Town/Resort Wells.
Directions Leave Wells by A371 towards Cheddar, turn right for Wookey Hole. Site 1¼ miles on left in village.
Acreage 2 **Open** Easter–October
Access Good **Site** Level
Sites available Total 55.
Facilities
Nearby facilities
Bristol/Bath.
Sheltered on bank of River Axe, Wookey Hole Caves, National Trust Area, Mendip Hills, walking, climbing. Leisure Centre nearby.

WELLS

Mendip Heights Camping & Caravan Park, Priddy, Wells, Somerset BA5 3BP.
Tel. 870241 Std. 01749
Nearest Town/Resort Wells.
Directions On A39 north from Wells, turn left at Green Ore crossroads onto B3135 towards Cheddar and follow campsite signs.
Acreage 4½ **Open** April–October
Access Good **Site** Level
Sites available Total 90.
Facilities

Nearby facilities
Bristol/Bath/Weston-super-Mare.
Quiet family site in area of outstanding natural beauty. Ideal for touring and walking. Gliding nearby.

WELLS

Ye Olde Punch Bowl Inn & Restaurant, Henton, Wells, Somerset, BA5 1PD.
Tel. 672212 Std. 01749
Nearest Town/Resort Wells.
Directions 3 miles from Wells on B3139 to Wedmore/Burnham on Sea. Park is on the right hand side just as you enter the village. Midway between Wells and Wedmore exit M5 junction 22.
Acreage 1 **Open** Easter–End September
Access Good **Site** Level
Sites available Total 5.
Facilities
Nearby facilities
Taunton.
Central for Cheddar 8 miles. 12 miles to Wookey Hole Caves and coast. Open views from site of the Mendip Hills and Cheddar Valley with a small stream. Toilets open during pub opening hours only, advised own on board toilet. Small fee for awnings.

WILLITON

Home Farm Holiday Centre, St. Audries Bay, Williton, Somerset.
Tel. Williton 632487 Std. 01984
Nearest Town/Resort Williton / Watchet.
Directions Leave M5 at Junction 23, follow A39 towards Minehead for 17 miles. At West Quantoxhead take first right turn after St. Audries Garages (signposted Blue Anchor, Doniford and Watchet) B3191 take first right turning in ½ mile to our drive.
Open All year
Access Good **Site** Terraced
Sites available Total 30.
Facilities
Nearby facilities
Taunton.
Private beach, good base for touring Exmoor. West Somerset Railway – two miles.

WIVELISCOMBE

Bouchers Farm Camping Site, Bouchers Farm, Waterrow, Wiveliscombe, Taunton, Somerset.
Tel. Wiveliscombe 623464 Std. 01984
Nearest Town/Resort Wiveliscombe.
Directions 10 miles west Taunton on B3227 First left after Waterrow.
Acreage 4 **Open** 1 April–1 October
Access Good **Site** Level
Sites available Total 100.
Facilities
Nearby facilities
Taunton.
Alongside river with scenic views. £3 per night, tent or caravan.

STAFFS

CHEADLE

Star Caravan & Camping Park, Nr. Alton Towers, Cheadle, Stoke-on-Trent, Staffs, ST10 3DW.
Tel. 702256/308530 Std. 01538
Nearest Town/Resort Cheadle.
Directions Situated off the B5417, ¾ mile from Alton Towers.
Acreage 50 **Open** 1st February–31st December
Access Good **Site** Lev/Slope
Sites available Total 188.
Facilities
Nearby facilities
Stoke.
Situated in the centre of beautiful countryside within 9 miles of Leek, Uttoxeter and Ashbourne Town. Within easy reach of the Peak District and Dovedale. Cafe/Restaurant nearby. English Tourist Board Graded Parks 3 Tick.

CHEADLE

Hales Hall Caravan Park, Oakamoor Road, Cheadle, Staffs.
Tel. 753305 Std. 01538
Nearest Town/Resort Cheadle.
Directions Take the B5417 from Cheadle, signposted Oakamoor. Site is ¾ mile on the left.
Acreage 8 **Open** Easter–November
Access Good **Site** Sloping
Sites available Total 50.
Facilities
Nearby facilities
Stoke-on-Trent.
4 miles to Alton Towers, Peak District, Wedgwood and other potteries and Gladstone Pottery Museum.

LEEK

Glencote Caravan Park, Churnet Valley, Station Road, Cheddleton, Nr. Leek, Staffs, ST13 7EE.
Tel. 360745 Std. 01538
Nearest Town/Resort Leek.
Directions 3½ miles south of Leek off the A520 (Stone to Leek road).
Acreage 6 **Open** April–October
Site Level
Sites available Total 50.
Facilities

Nearby facilities
Stoke-on-Trent.
Situated in the heart of Churnet Valley. Railway Museum and canalside pub close by, near to Alton Towers. H.E.T.B. Graded 4 Tick.

LONGNOR

Longnor Wood Over 50's Caravan & Camping Park, Longnor, Nr. Buxton, Derbyshire, SK17 0LD.
Tel. 83648 Std. 01298
Nearest Town/Resort Buxton.
Directions A515 from Buxton, 7 miles to Longnor. From Longnor follow caravan site signs for 1½ miles.
Acreage 7 **Open** Easter–October
Access Good **Site** Lev/Slope
Sites available Total 47.
Facilities
Nearby facilities
Buxton.
Ideal location for walking and tourist attractions, Chatsworth and Blue John Mines.

RUGELEY

Silvertrees Caravan Park, Stafford Brook Road, Rugeley, Staffordshire WS15 2TX.
Tel. 582185 Std. 01889
Nearest Town/Resort Rugeley.
Directions From A51 take unclassified road towards Penkridge at traffic lights After two miles turn right by a white fence, entrance 100 yards on left.
Acreage 10 **Open** April–October
Access Good **Site** Lev/Slope
Sites available Total 100.
Facilities
Rugeley.
Set on Cannock Chase, a designated area of outstanding natural beauty, 18 miles Alton Towers.

TAMWORTH

Drayton Manor Park, Nr. Tamworth, Staffordshire.
Tel. 287979 Std. 01827
Nearest Town/Resort Fazeley.
Directions M42 junction 9, A4091 main road passes entrance. 3 miles from junction 9. A5 at Fazeley ¼ mile.
Acreage 4 **Open** Easter–October
Access Good **Site** Level
Sites available Total 100.
Facilities
Nearby facilities
Tamworth.
Within a 250 acre theme park and zoo. Take-aways and bars, garden centre. 41 rides, games and attractions. Only one dog per unit is permitted. Childrens play area and swimming pool locally. Licensed bar with T.V.

SUFFOLK

BECCLES

Waveney Lodge Caravan Site, Waveney Lodge, Elms Road, Aldeby, Beccles, Suffolk.
Tel. Aldeby 677445 Std. 01502
Nearest Town/Resort Beccles.
Directions Turn off the A146 Beccles to Norwich road at Gillingham roundabout onto the A143 Great Yarmouth road. Turn right in 1 mile to Aldeby, first left at top of hill into Elms Road. Site is on the right in ½ mile.
Acreage 1 **Open** All Year
Access Good **Site** Level
Sites available Total 15.
Facilities
Nearby facilities
Access to the Broads, near sandy beaches. Ideal for touring Norfolk and East Suffolk. ETB British Graded Holiday Parks 2 Ticks.

BECCLES

Waveney River Centre, Burgh-St-Peter, Nr. Beccles, Suffolk.
Tel. 677343 Std. 01502
Nearest Town/Resort Lowestoft/Great Yarmouth.
Directions Signpost at Haddiscoe on the A143.
Acreage 5 **Open** Easter–October
Access Good **Site** Lev/Slope
Sites available Total 30.
Facilities
Nearby facilities
Beccles.
Overlooking River Waveney.

BUNGAY

Outney Meadow Caravan Park, Outney Meadow, Bungay, Suffolk, NR35 1HG.
Tel. 892338 Std. 01986
Nearest Town/Resort Bungay.
Directions Entrance is signposted from the junction of the A143 and A144 at Bungay.
Acreage 6 **Open** Easter–October
Access Good **Site** Level
Sites available Total 45.
Facilities
Nearby facilities
Beccles.
Beside the River Waveney and common.

BURY ST EDMUNDS

The Dell Touring Park, Beyton Road, Thurston, Bury St Edmunds, Suffolk. IP31 3RB.
Tel. 270121 Std. 01359
Nearest Town/Resort Bury St Edmunds.
Directions Take A45 eastbound 6 miles from Bury follow Thurston signs.
Open All Year.
Access Good **Site** Level
Sites available Total 100.
Facilities
Nearby facilities
Thurston.
Ideal for touring East Anglia. 1 hour from Cambridge, Norwich and coast. E.A.T.B. 3 Ticks.

DARSHAM

Haw Wood Caravan Site, Darsham, Suffolk, IP17 3QT.
Tel. 248 Std. 0198 684
Nearest Town/Resort Lowestoft.
Directions Approx. 30 miles north of Ipswich on the A12. Turn right 1 mile after Darsham level crossing at the Happy Eater. Caravan park is ¼ mile on the right.
Acreage 7 **Open** April–October
Access Good **Site** Level
Sites available Total 40.
Facilities
Nearby facilities
Darsham.
Near the beach, ideal touring and bird watching. Peaceful and quiet.

DUNWICH

Cliff House, Minsmere Road, Dunwich, Saxmundham, Suffolk, IP17 3DQ.
Tel. 73282 Std. 01728
Nearest Town/Resort Southwold.
Directions From A12, at Blythburgh take the B1125 to Dunwich. Follow signs to Dunwich Heath.
Acreage 30 **Open** April–October
Access Good **Site** Level
Sites available Total 121.
Facilities
Nearby facilities
Yoxford.
Beach frontage, adjoining National Trust and Minsmere Bird Reserve. Suffolk Heritage Coast.

EYE

Honeypot Camp and Caravan Park, Wortham, Eye, Suffolk, IP22 1PW.
Tel. 783312 Std. 01379
Nearest Town/Resort DISS.
Directions Four miles south west of Diss, on south side A143, towards Bury St. Edmunds.
Acreage 5¼ **Open** April–November
Access Good **Site** Level
Sites available Total 32.
Facilities
Nearby facilities
Diss.
Recommended family run inland touring site, Norfolk/Suffolk centre, Steam Museum 2 miles. Quiet and peaceful surroundings. Fishing on site. Lakeside pitches. Free colour illustrated brochure. Established over 30 years.

FELIXSTOWE

Suffolk Sands Holiday Park, Carr Road, Felixstowe, Suffolk, IP11 8TS.
Tel. 273434 Std. 01394
Nearest Town/Resort Felixstowe.
Directions Take the A45 into Felixstowe and turn right at the first roundabout. Go straight across the next roundabout, continue along Walton Avenue to the

Discover
Coastal Suffolk
TOURING & CAMPING SITES.
HOLIDAY HOMES FOR SALE.
Enjoy weekends and holidays. Sail, swim, fish, ski. Quiet beaches, estuaries, castles, wildlife parks, sports centres. Pine forests, heathland. Potteries, art studios. Bird sanctuaries. Unhurried. Real England. New motor roads London and Midlands.
THE MOON & SIXPENCE
LAKESIDE SETTING. SANDY BEACH.
Convenient Woodbridge, Felixstowe. Secluded location, continental atmosphere. Club, family room. Log cabin, barbeque. Play area.
CAKES & ALE
Convenient Leiston, Aldeburgh, Southwold, Dunwich, Minsmere. Superb touring, bird watching, cycling. Spacious friendly park. Quiet uncommercialised. Shop, club tennis courts, table tennis, play area.
PRIORY PARK
BEACH AND ESTUARY FRONTAGE. GOLF.
Superb south facing location, panoramic views over estuary. Sail, swim, fish, ski. Close Ipswich. Heated swimming pool, club dating to 13th century, bars, meals. Own 9 hole golf course. Hard tennis courts. Nature trails. play area. Open all year.
COASTAL SUFFOLK LEISURE
Priory Park
Ipswich Suffolk IP10 0JT
Tel Ipswich 727393
Name
Address
For details please return this coupon to: Coastal Suffolk Leisure, Priory Park, Ipswich, Suffolk IP10 0JT Tel: Ipswich 727393
Cades.

traffic lights. Turn right and after 200yds bear right into Carr Road. The park is on the left.
Acreage 3 **Open** Easter–November
Access Good **Site** Level
Sites available Total 96.
Facilities
Nearby facilities
Situated right by the seafront.

HALESWORTH

The Garage, St. Lawrence, Beccles, Suffolk.
Tel. Ilketshall 781241 Std. 01986
Nearest Town/Resort Halesworth.
Directions Situated on A144, 3½ miles north Halesworth, 5½ miles south Bungay.
Acreage 1 **Open** All year
Access Good **Site** Level
Sites available Total 12.
Facilities
Nearby facilities
Halesworth.
Ideal touring centre. Situated in rural area, 12 miles coast.

IPSWICH

Low House Touring Caravan Centre, Low House, Bucklesham Road, Foxhall, Ipswich, Suffolk, IP10 0AU.
Tel. 659437 – Evenings Std. 01473
Nearest Town/Resort Ipswich/Felixstowe.
Directions Turn off A45 Ipswich Ring Road (South) via slip road onto the A1156 (signposted East Ipswich). In 1 mile turn right, in ¼ mile turn right signposted Bucklesham. Site is on the left in ½ mile.
Acreage 3¼ **Open** All Year
Access Good **Site** Level
Sites available Total 30.
Facilities
Nearby facilities
Ipswich.
Ornamental Tree Walk and Pets Corner. Temporary membership of sports centre (opposite) available. Large stores nearby (Sainsburys etc.), licensed club opposite. Dogs are allowed if kept on leads.

IPSWICH

Priory Park, Ipswich, Suffolk IP10 0JT.
Tel. 727393 Std. 01473
Nearest Town/Resort Ipswich.
Directions Travelling east along A45 Ipswich southern by-pass take first exit after River Orwell Road bridge. turn left towards Ipswich following caravan/camping signs. 300yards from by-pass on left, follow signs to Priory Park.
Acreage 85 **Open** All year
Access Good **Site** Lev/Slope
Sites available Total 100.
Facilities
Nearby facilities
Ipswich.
Superb historic setting. Frontage onto River Orwell. Magnificent south facing panoramic views. 9 hole golf course and hard tennis court within the park grounds. Club adventure play area, nature trails, access to foreshore. Holiday lodges for hire. Holiday Homes for sale.

LEISTON

Cakes & Ale, Abbey Lane, Leiston, Suffolk.
Tel. Leiston 831655 Std. 01728
Nearest Town/Resort Leiston/Aldeburgh.
Directions Leave A12 taking B1121 Saxmundham, Benhall, Sternfield in Saxmundham take B1119 signposted Leiston proceed for 3 miles then take byroad left following signs to park.
Acreage 45 **Open** April–October
Access Good **Site** Level
Sites available Total 100.
Facilities
Nearby facilities
Saxmundham.
2 miles best beach in area. Excellent base for coastal Suffolk, Southwold, Dunwich, Minsmere, Aldeburgh. Launderette, tennis courts and table tennis on park.

LOWESTOFT

Chestnut Farm, Gisleham, Lowestoft, Suffolk.
Tel. Lowestoft 740227 Std. 01502
Nearest Town/Resort Lowestoft.
Directions 3 miles south of Lowestoft on A12 turn west at southern roundabout at Kessingland bypass (opposite Suffolk wildlife park) singposted Rushmere/Mutford/Gislehan, then second turing on left, then first drive on left.
Acreage 3 **Open** 1 April–31 October
Access Good **Site** Level
Sites available Total 20.
Facilities
Nearby facilities
Oulton Broad.
Scenic views, close to Wildlife Park. Fishing on farm, 2½ miles to beach, golf course 3 miles.

LOWESTOFT

Heathland Beach Caravan Park, London Road, Kessingland, Suffolk.
Tel. 740337 Std. 01502
Nearest Town/Resort Lowestoft.
Directions 3 miles south of the A12 on the B1437. 1 mile north of Kessingland Village.
Acreage 11 **Open** April–30 October
Access Good **Site** Level
Sites available Total 106.
Facilities
Nearby facilities
Lowestoft.
Surrounded by farmland, beach.

LOWESTOFT

North Denes Caravan & Camping Site, North Denes, Lowestoft, Suffolk.
Tel. 573197 Std. 01502
Nearest Town/Resort Lowestoft.
Directions From A12, through Lowestoft follow signs "North Denes".
Acreage 15 **Open** April–October
Access Good **Site** Level
Sites available Total 400.
Facilities
Nearby facilities
Lowestoft Central.
Very close to beach, sea views, grassy site.

LOWESTOFT

Broad View Caravans, Marsh Road, Oulton Broad, Suffolk, NR32 3PW.
Tel. 565587 Std. 01502
Nearest Town/Resort Lowestoft.
Directions From Beccles A146 into Oulton Broad. At traffic lights bear left over railway bridge, Marsh Road is on the left. Very sharp so continue to roundabout and come back round then into Marsh Road.
Acreage 1 **Open** April–October
Access Good **Site** Level
Sites available Total 15.
Facilities
Nearby facilities
Oulton Broad South.
Alongside the Broads, fishing and boating.

SAXMUNDHAM

Lakeside Leisure Park, Saxmundham, Suffolk, IP17 2QP.
Tel. 603344 Std. 01728
Nearest Town/Resort Saxmundham.
Directions From Ipswich travelling north on the A12, turn left onto the B1119 following signs. Approximately 1 mile off the A12.
Acreage 35 **Open** Easter–October
Access Good **Site** Level
Sites available Total 200.
Facilities
Nearby facilities
Saxmundham.
Ideal touring base, coarse and Carp fishing on site.

SOUTHWOLD

Southwold Harbour Caravan Park, Ferry Road, Southwold, Suffolk, IP18 6ND.
Tel. 722486 Std. 01502
Nearest Town/Resort Southwold.
Directions A12 to Blythburgh take the A1095 to Southwold. Turn right at the Kings head Public House and follow road to the harbour.
Open April–October
Access Good **Site** Level
Sites available Total 200.
Facilities M
Nearby facilities
Close to the beach, harbour and the old town of Southwold. Ideal for fishing, walking and cycling.

WOODBRIDGE

Sandlings Centre, Lodge Road, Hollesley, Woodbridge, Suffolk.
Tel. 411202 Std. 01394
Nearest Town/Resort Woodbridge.
Directions Take A1152 off A12 passed Woodbridge across Milton Traffic Lights and onto B1083 Bawdsey Road, turn left at T junction, Shottisham. Drive out of Village 1¼ miles on left.
Acreage 4 **Open** March–January
Site Level
Sites available Total 39.
Facilities
Nearby facilities
Woodbridge.
Natural History Information Centre on site. Ideal area for walking, bird watching etc.

WOODBRIDGE

The Moon and Sixpence, Newbourne Road, Waldringfield, Woodbridge, Suffolk, IP12 4PP.
Tel. 736650 Std. 01473
Nearest Town/Resort Woodbridge.
Directions Turn off A12, Ipswich Eastern By-Pass, onto unclassified road signposted Waldringfield, Newbourn. Follow caravan direction signs.
Acreage 5 **Open** April–October
Access Good **Site** Level
Sites available Total 75.
Facilities
Nearby facilities
Woodbridge.
Picturesque location. Sheltered, terraced site. Own private lake and sandy beach. You can FAX us on 01473 736270.

SURREY

HAMBLEDON

The Merry Harriers, Hambledon, Surrey.
Tel. Wormley 682883 Std. 01428
Nearest Town/Resort Godalming.
Directions Leave Godalming on B2130 and follow Hambledon signs approx. 4 miles.
Acreage 1 **Open** All year
Access Good **Site** Level
Sites available Total 25.
Facilities
Nearby facilities
Witley.
Unspoilt countryside, opposite country pub.

SUSSEX

ARUNDEL

Maynards Caravan & Camping Park, Crossbush, Arundel, West Sussex, BN18 9PQ.
Tel. 882075 Std. 01903
Nearest Town/Resort Arundel/ Littlehampton.
Directions ¾ mile from Arundel on A27, turn left into car park of Howards Hotel going east on Worthing/Brighton road.
Acreage 3 **Open** All Year
Access Good **Site** Level
Sites available Total 70.
Facilities
Nearby facilities
Arundel.
Very central for touring. 3 miles to sea, ¾ mile to river. Arundel Castle and Bird Sanctuary.

BATTLE

Brakes Coppice Farm Park, Forewood Lane, Crowhurst, East Sussex, TN33 0SJ.
Tel. 830322 Std. 01424
Nearest Town/Resort Battle.
Directions Turn right off the A2100 (Battle to Hastings road) 2 miles from Battle. Follow signs to Crowhurst, 1¼ miles turn left into site.
Acreage 3¼ **Open** March–October
Access Good **Site** Sloping
Sites available Total 30.
Facilities
Nearby facilities
Crowhurst.
Secluded, 11 acre, woodland park with level pitches. Fishing on site.

BEXHILL-ON-SEA

Cobbs Hill Farm Caravan & Camping Park, Watermill Lane, Bexhill-on-Sea, East Sussex, TN39 5JA.
Tel. 213460 Std. 01424
Nearest Town/Resort Bexhill-on-Sea.
Directions From Bexhill take the A269, turn right into Watermill Lane. Site is 1 mile on the left.
Acreage 7 **Open** April–October
Access Good **Site** Level
Sites available Total 45.
Facilities
Nearby facilities
Bexhill-on-Sea.
Quiet countryside, on a small farm.

BILLINGHURST

Limeburners (Camping) Ltd, Limeburners, Newbridge, Billinghurst,Sussex,RH14 9JA.
Tel. 782311 Std. 01403
Nearest Town/Resort Billinghurst.
Directions 1½ miles west of billinghurst on A272, turn left on B2133 150yds on left.
Open April–October
Access Good **Site** Level
Sites available Total 40.
Facilities
Nearby facilities
Public house attached, lunch time and evening food.

BOGNOR REGIS

Copthorne Caravan Park, Rose Green Road, Bognor Regis, Sussex, PO21 3ER.
Tel. 262408 Std. 01243
Nearest Town/Resort Bognor Regis.
Directions 2 miles from Bognor, take B2166 and turn left at third roundabout. Copthorne is approx 200 metres on the right nearly opposite Esso garage.
Acreage 6 **Open** April–September
Access Good **Site** Level
Sites available Total 4-6.
Facilities
Nearby facilities
Bognor Regis.
Established 1945 – 1995. Mainly static park with a small touring field. Ideal access to Chichester, Goodwood and South Downs.

CHICHESTER

Bell Caravan Park, Bell Lane, Birdham, Nr. Chichester, Sussex.
Tel. 512264 Std. 01243
Nearest Town/Resort Chichester.
Directions From Chichester take the A286 towards Wittering for approx. 4 miles. At Birdham turn left into Bell Lane, site is 500yds on the left.
Acreage ¼ **Open** March–October
Access Good **Site** Level
Sites available Total 15.
Facilities
Nearby facilities
Chichester.

CHICHESTER

Red House Farm, Bookers Lane, Earnley, Chichester, Sussex, PO20 7JG.
Tel. 512959 (Also Fax) Std. 01243
Nearest Town/Resort Bracklesham Bay.
Directions From Chichester turn south on A286 signposted "Witterings". 5 miles south turn left at Birdham Garage towards Bracklesham Bay, ½ mile turn left again into Bookers Lane, site is on the left.
Acreage 4 **Open** Easter–October
Access Good **Site** Level
Sites available Total 100.
Facilities
Nearby facilities
Chichester.
In countryside, quiet and spacious. 1 mile from beach and shops. Childrens adventure playground. Camping Gaz only.

DIAL POST

Wincaves Camping & Caravan Park, Ashurst Lane, Dial Post, Nr. Horsham, West Sussex, RH13 8NX.
Tel. 710923 Std. 01403
Nearest Town/Resort Worthing.
Directions ½ mile south of Dial Post on the A24 (London- Worthing Road).
Acreage 15 **Open** All year.
Access Good **Site** Level
Sites available Total 100.
Facilities
Nearby facilities
Horsham.
Wood/downland walks adjoining seasonal pitches, storage facilities Central for touring South East.

EAST GRINSTEAD

Longacres Caravan & Camping Park, Newchapel Road, Lingfield, Surrey, RH7 6LE.
Tel. 833205 Std. 01842
Nearest Town/Resort East Grinstead.
Directions From the M25 junction 6 take the A22 aouth towards East Grinstead. At Newchapel roundabout turn left onto the B2028 towards Lingfield. Site is on the right in 700yds.
Acreage 18 **Open** All Year
Access Good **Site** Lev/Slope
Sites available Total 60.
Facilities
Nearby facilities

Lingfield.
Quad bikes, Go Karts, fishing and tourist information on site. Ideal to visit London, Surrey, Kent and Sussex.

EAST WITTERING

Gees, 127 Stocks Lane, Bracklesham Bay, East Wittering, Nr. Chichester, Sussex.
Tel. 690223 Std. 01243
Nearest Town/Resort Chichester.
Directions Chichester A24, A288 East Wittering/Bracklesham Bay.
Open March–August
Access Good **Site** Level
Sites available Total 25.
Facilities
Nearby facilities
Chichester.
Near beach.

FERRING

Onslow Caravan Park, Onslow Drive, Ferring-by-Sea, Nr. Worthing, Sussex.
Tel. Worthing 243170 Std. 01903
Nearest Town/Resort Worthing.
Directions 4 miles from Worthing to Ferring on A259.
Open March–October
Access Good **Site** Level
Sites available Total 4.
Facilities
Nearby facilities
Goring.
Near beach. English Tourist Board Graded 5 Ticks.

HAILSHAM

The Old Mill Caravan Park, Chalvington Road, Golden Cross, Hailsham, East Sussex, BN27 3SS.
Tel. Chiddingly 872532 Std. 01825
Nearest Town/Resort Hailsham/Eastbourne.
Directions 4 miles north west of Hailsham. Turn left off the A22 just before Golden Cross Inn car park. Site is 150yds on the left of Chalvington Road.
Acreage 2 **Open** April–October
Access Good **Site** Level
Sites available Total 26.
Facilities
Nearby facilities
Polegate.
Ideal touring for beach, downland and countryside. Pitches are available for own static holiday caravans.

HALLAND

Bluebell Caravan Park, Shortgate, Nr. Halland, East Sussex.
Tel. 264303 Std. 01903
Nearest Town/Resort Brighton/Eastbourne.
Directions From the A27 Lewes towards East Grinstead, A26 then B2192 Ringmer/Halland, 3¼ miles from Ringmer on the Halland road.
Acreage 1 **Open** March–October
Access Good **Site** Level
Sites available Total 30.
Facilities
Nearby facilities
Lewes.
Scenic views, central for touring. Attractions and many sports. Contact Address : 76 Mendip Road, Durrington, West Sussex, BN13 2LS.

HASTINGS

Carters Farm, Elm Lane, Pett, Nr. Hastings, East Sussex TN35 4JD.
Tel. Pett 813206/812244 Std. 01424
Nearest Town/Resort Hastings.
Directions On A259 towards Rye, right turn for Pett at Gustling, signposted after that.
Acreage 12 **Open** Easter–October
Access Good **Site** Lev/Slope
Sites available Total 100.
Facilities S I
Nearby facilities
Hastings.
Farm site, family run, few restrictions, family run.

HASTINGS

Old Coghurst Farm Caravan & Camping Park, Rock Lane, Three Oaks, Hastings, East Sussex, TN35 4NX.
Tel. 753622 Std. 01424
Nearest Town/Resort Hastings.
Directions 3 miles north east of Hastings. 1¾ miles south east of Westfield from the A28 and 1¾ miles from the A259, Three Oaks turning.
Acreage 4 **Open** March–October
Access Good **Site** Lev/Slope
Sites available Total 60.
Facilities S I
Nearby facilities
Three Oaks.
Picturesque site surrounded by rolling countryside. 3¼ miles to a sandy/shingle beach. Tennis on site.

HASTINGS

Shearbarn Holiday Park, Barley Lane, Hastings, East Sussex. TN35 5DX.
Tel. 423583 Std. 01424
Nearest Town/Resort Hastings.
Directions A259 towards Folkestone 400yds from seafront turn right into Harold Road (opposite Stables Theatre) approx ¼ mile turn right into Gurth Road. Turn left at end of Gurth Road into Barley Lane. Booking office approx ¼ mile on right.
Acreage 16 **Open** March–January
Access Good **Site** Level
Sites available Total 450.
Facilities S
Nearby facilities
Hastings.
Close to beach, beautiful views of sea and country park.

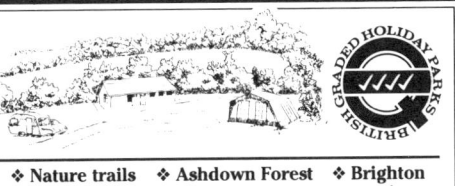

HEATHFIELD

Greenviews Caravan Park, Broad Oak, Heathfield, East Sussex, TN21 8RT.
Tel. 863531 Std. 01435
Nearest Town/Resort Heathfield.
Directions Approximately 1¼ miles on the A267.
Acreage 3 **Open** April–October
Access Good **Site** Level
Sites available Total 10.
Facilities
Ideal touring, approx. 15 miles from Eastbourne.

HENFIELD

Harwoods Farm, West End Lane, Henfield, West Sussex.
Tel. Henfield 492820 Std. 01273
Nearest Town/Resort Horsham/Brighton.
Directions From Henfield village on A281 turn opposite White Hart pub. 2 miles into West End lane, signposted in Henfield Highstreet.
Acreage 1¾ **Open** Easter–October
Access Good **Site** Level
Sites available Total 35.
Facilities
Nearby facilities
Horsham/Brighton.
Small, sheltered site near River Adur. Miles of walking along river and local footpaths. Limited fishing available. Booking advised Bank Holidays. (2) Deep earth closets. No youth clubs. Only individual motorcycles accepted, not groups. No trailer caravans.

HENFIELD

Downsview Caravan Park, Bramlands Lane, Woodmancote, Near Henfield, West Sussex, BN5 9TG.
Tel. 492801 Std. 01273
Nearest Town/Resort Brighton.
Directions Signed off the A281 in the village of Woodmancote. 2¼ miles from East Henfield and 6¼ miles north of Brighton.
Acreage 4 **Open** Mid March–Mid Nov
Access Good **Site** Level
Sites available
Facilities
Nearby facilities
Brighton/Hassocks.
Specialists in peace and quiet. Near to Brighton and South Downs. NO play-grounds or discos etc. Waste water hook-ups available.

HENFIELD

North Tottington Sands Farm, Tottington Drive, Small Dole, Henfield, Sussex BN5 9XZ.
Tel. Henfield 493157 Std. 01273
Nearest Town/Resort Brighton.
Directions Turn first left off A2037 (Henfield/Upperbeeding). After Small Dole sign into Tottington Drive, farm at end.
Acreage 4 **Open** March–November
Access Good **Site** Level
Sites available Total 25.
Facilities
Nearby facilities
Shoreham.
Small farm site near South Downs. Beach 5 miles, Brighton and Worthing 10 miles.

HORAM

Horam Woodland View Touring Park, Horebeech Lane, Horam, Heathfield, East Sussex TN21 0HR.
Tel. 3597 Std. 014353
Nearest Town/Resort Hailsham.
Directions Off A267 Heathfield to Hailsham Road, at Horam take road opposite Merrydown Wine Company ¼ mile down is site entrance.
Open Easter–October
Access Good **Site** Level
Sites available Total 25.
Facilities
Nearby facilities
Small quiet site, pretty countryside, good walks, many places to visit.

HORAM

Horam Manor Touring Park, Horam, Nr. Heathfield, East Sussex. TN21 0YD.
Tel. 813662 Std. 01435
Nearest Town/Resort Heathfield/Eastbourne.
Directions On A267, 3 miles south of Heathfield, 10 miles north of Eastbourne.
Acreage 7 **Open** March–October
Access Good **Site** Sloping
Sites available Total 90.
Facilities
Nearby facilities
Eastbourne.
A tranquil rural setting, but with plenty to do on the estate, and many places to visit. See our seperate advertisment.

LITTLEHAMPTON

White Rose Touring Park, Mill Lane, Wick, Nr. Littlehampton, West Sussex, BN17 7PH.
Tel. 716176 Std. 01903
Nearest Town/Resort Littlehampton.
Directions From Arundel (A27) take A284 south. Mill Lane on left 1½ miles from A27/A284 Junction, just past Six Bells public house.
Acreage 6 **Open** 15th March–15th January
Access Good **Site** Level
Sites available Total 127.
Facilities
Nearby facilities
Arundel.
Ideal location for countryside and beach. 2 miles from Arundel Castle. Credit card telephone bookings accepted (essential for Bank Holidays and peak periods).

PEVENSEY BAY

Bay View Tourist Park, Old Martello Road, Pevensey Bay, Nr. Eastbourne, East Sussex.
Tel. 768688 Std. 01323
Nearest Town/Resort Eastbourne.
Directions 2 miles from Eastbourne centre off the A259.
Acreage 3¼ **Open** Easter–October
Access Good **Site** Level
Sites available Total 55.
Facilities
Nearby facilities
Pevensey Bay.
Scenic views, near a beach, ideal for touring.

SEAFORD

Buckle Caravan Park, Marine Parade, Seaford, East Sussex, BN25 2QR.
Tel. 897801 Std. 01323
Nearest Town/Resort Seaford.
Directions Between Newhaven and Seaford, just off the A259.
Acreage 8 **Open** March–2 January
Access Good **Site** Level
Sites available Total 150.
Facilities
Nearby facilities
Bishopstone.
Adjoining beach. Newhaven Ferry 2 miles, Brighton 12 miles and Eastbourne 8 miles.

SEDLESCOMBE

Whydown Farm Tourist Caravan Park, Whydown Farm, Crazy Lane, Sedlescombe, East Sussex, TN33 0QT.
Tel. 870147 Std. 01424
Nearest Town/Resort Battle/Hastings.
Directions Travelling south on A21, turn left into Crazy Lane, 100 yds past junction A21/B2244, opposite Black Brooks Garden Centre.
Acreage 2 **Open** 1st March–31st October
Access Good **Site** Level
Sites available Total 26.
Facilities
Nearby facilities
Battle.
Ideal touring, 15 minutes to the beach. Countryside and Hastings.

SELSEY

Warner Farm Touring Park, Warner Lane, Selsey, West Sussex.
Tel. 604121 Std. 01243
Nearest Town/Resort Chichester.
Directions From the A27 Chichester take the B2145 to Selsey. On entering Selsey turn right into School Lane. Follow signs for Warner Farm Touring Park.
Acreage 10 **Open** March–October
Access Good **Site** Level
Sites available Total 200.
Facilities
Nearby facilities
Chichester.
Near beach.

UCKFIELD

Honeys Green Farm Caravan Park, Easons Green, Framfield, Uckfield, East Sussex, TN22 5RE.
Tel. 840334 Std. 01825
Nearest Town/Resort Uckfield/Lewes.
Directions Turn off A22 (Uckfield – Eastbourne) at Halland roundabout onto B2192 signposted Blackboys/Heathfield, site ½ mile on left.
Acreage 2 **Open** Easter–October
Access Good **Site** Level
Sites available Total 22.
Facilities
Nearby facilities
Uckfield/Lewes.
Small peaceful rural park, coarse fishing lake, walks.

WEST WITTERING

Wicks Farm Camping Park, Redlands Lane, West Wittering, Chichester, Sussex, PO20 8QD.
Tel. 513116 Std. 01243
Nearest Town/Resort West Wittering/ Chichester.
Directions From Chichester A286 for Birdham. Then B2179 for West Wittering.
Acreage 2¼ **Open** April–October
Access Good **Site** Level
Sites available Total 40.
Facilities
Nearby facilities
Chichester.

WINCHELSEA

Rye Bay Caravan Park, Pett Level Road, Winchelsea Beach, Sussex, TN36 4NE.
Tel. 226340 Std. 01797
Nearest Town/Resort Rye.
Directions 3 miles west of Rye and 7 miles east of Hastings.
Open March–October
Access Good
Sites available Total 70.
Facilities
Nearby facilities
Rye.
Direct frontage to the beach.

WISBOROUGH GREEN

Bat & Ball, Newpound Lane, Wisborough Green, West Sussex, RH14 0EH.
Tel. 700313 Std. 01403
Nearest Town/Resort Billinghurst.
Directions From Billinghurst (A29) take the A272 west for Petworth. After 2 miles turn right onto the B2133 for Guildford. Site is 1 mile on the left hand side.
Acreage 3 **Open** All Year
Access Good **Site** Level
Sites available Total 40.
Facilities
Nearby facilities
Billingshurst.
Good views, walking and touring. Very close to a river.

TYNE & WEAR

ROWLANDS GILL

Derwent Park Caravan and Camping Park, Derwent Park, Rowlands Gill, Tyne and Wear, NE39 1LG.
Tel. 543383 Std. 01207
Nearest Town/Resort Rowlands Gill.
Directions 7 miles S.W. of Newcastle on Tyne. In Rowlands Gill at junction of A694/ B6314.
Acreage 3 **Open** April–September
Access Good **Site** Level
Sites available Total 50.
Facilities
Nearby facilities
Metro Centre.
Beside the River Derwent, in Derwent walk country park, ideal location for touring Northumbria. Near Gateshead Metro Centre and Beamish.

WARWICKSHIRE

LONG COMPTON

Mill Farm, Long Compton, Shipston-on-Stour, Warwickshire.
Tel. Long Compton 663 Std. 0160 884
Nearest Town/Resort Moreton-on-Marsh.
Directions Turn off A3400 west for Barton-on-the-Heath. Site on right in ½ mile.
Acreage 3 **Open** March–October
Access Good **Site** Level
Sites available Total 10.
Facilities
Moreton-in-Marsh.
Fringe of the Cotswolds.

SHIPSTON ON STOUR

Parkhill Farm, Idlicote Road, Halford, Shipston on Stour, Warks.
Tel. 661452 Std. 01608
Nearest Town/Resort Shipston on Stour.
Directions A429 Fosse Way to Halford, turn for Idlicote road ¾ mile on fork.
Acreage 5 **Open** Easter–October
Access Good **Site** Lev/Slope
Sites available
Facilities
Nearby facilities
Moreton in Marsh.
By River Stour.

SOUTHAM

Holt Farm, (N.G. & A.C. Adkins), Southam, Leamington Spa CV33 0NJ.
Tel. 812225 Std. 01926
Directions From Southam By-Pass, follow camping and caravan signs. Site is 3 miles from Southam off Priors Marston, Priors Hardwick Road.
Acreage 1½ **Open** April–October
Access Good **Site** Level
Sites available Total 45.
Facilities
Nearby facilities
Leamington Spa.
Ideal touring centre for Mid Warwickshire. Near canal.

STRATFORD-UPON-AVON

Dodwell Park, Evesham Road, Stratford-upon-Avon, Warwickshire CV37 9SR.
Tel. Stratford 204957 Std. 01789
Nearest Town/Resort Stratford-upon-Avon.
Directions 2 miles southwest of Stratford on B439 (formerly the A439) - Not the racecourse site.
Acreage 2 **Open** All year
Access Good **Site** Lev/Slope
Sites available Total 50.
Facilities
Nearby facilities
Stratford-upon-Avon.
Shakespeare Theatre and Cotswolds. B.T.A. Graded 4 Ticks.

STRATFORD-UPON-AVON

Elms Caravan Park, Elms Camp, Tiddington, Stratford-upon-Avon, Warwicks.
Tel. 292312 Std. 01789
Nearest Town/Resort Stratford-upon-Avon.
Directions On the B4086, 1½ miles from Stratford-upon-Avon.
Acreage 10 **Open** April–October
Access Good **Site** Level
Sites available Total 80.
Facilities
Nearby facilities
Stratford-upon-Avon.
Riverside site.

STRATFORD-UPON-AVON

Island Meadow Caravan Park, Aston Cantlow, Warwickshire, B95 6JP.
Tel. 488273 Std. 01789
Nearest Town/Resort Stratford-upon-Avon.
Directions From the A46 or the A3400 follow signs for Aston Cantlow Village. Park is ½ mile west of the village in Mill Lane.
Acreage 3 **Open** March–October
Access Good **Site** Level
Sites available Total 80.
Facilities
Nearby facilities
Wilmcote.
Small, quiet island with fishing, adjacent to a picturesque village. Ideal centre for Shakespear country.

STUDLEY

Outhill Caravan Park, Outhill, Studley, Warwicks, B80 7DY.
Tel. 852160 Std. 01527
Nearest Town/Resort Henley-in-Arden.
Directions From A435 (Birmingham to Evesham road) turn towards Henley-in-Arden on A4189. Take third turning to the right (approx 1¼ miles), check in at Outhill Farm (first on left).
Acreage 11 **Open** April–October
Access Good **Site** Level
Sites available Total 15.
Facilities
Peace and quite.

WILTSHIRE

CALNE

Blackland Lakes Holiday and Leisure Centre, Stockley Lane, Calne, Wilts, SN11 0NQ.
Tel. 813672 Std. 01249
Nearest Town/Resort Calne.
Directions Site is signposted from A4 east of Calne.
Acreage 17 **Open** All Year
Access Good **Site** Level
Sites available Total 180.
Facilities
Nearby facilities
Chippenham.
Rural, quiet, scenic views, ideal touring centre, coarse fishery, nature trail, good childrens play equipment, family fitness course (trim trail) Special facilities for motor caravans, car/van wash, covered barbecue for parties, groups welcome. 35 hardstandings for winter use, please book.

CHIPPENHAM

Piccadilly Caravan Site, Folly Lane (Gastard Road), Lacock, Chippenham, Wiltshire.
Tel. Lacock 730260 Std. 01249
Nearest Town/Resort Chippenham/ Melksham.
Directions Turn right off A350 Chippenham/Melksham Road,5 miles south of Chippenham, close to Lacock. Signposted to Gastard (with caravan symbol), site is after the Nurseries.
Acreage 2½ **Open** April–October
Access Good **Site** Level
Sites available Total 40.
Facilities
Nearby facilities
Chippenham.
Close National Trust village of Lacock. Ideal touring centre.

CRICKLADE

Second Chance Caravan Park, Marston Meysey, Wltshire, SN6 6SN.
Tel. 810675 Std. 01285
Nearest Town/Resort Cricklade.
Directions Between Swindon and Cirencester on the A419. Turn off at the Fairford signpost and caravan park signs. Proceed approx. 3 miles then turn left at the Castle Eaton signpost. We are on the left.
Acreage 2 **Open** March–November
Access Good **Site** Level
Sites available Total 26.
Facilities
Nearby facilities
Swindon.
Riverside location, private fishing and access for your own canoe, to explore upper reaches of Thames. Ideal base for touring the Cotswolds.

DEVIZES

Bell Caravan and Camping Site, Andover Road, Lydeway, Devizes, Wilts. SN10 3PS.
Tel. 840230 Std. 01380
Nearest Town/Resort Devizes.
Directions 3 miles south east of Devizes on Andover A342 road.
Acreage 3 **Open** Easter–October
Access Good **Site** Level
Sites available Total 30.
Facilities
Pewsey.
Ideal touring, Stonehenge, Avebury and Bath. Off License.

DEVIZES

Lakeside, Rowde, Devizes, Wiltshire.
Tel. 722767 Std. 01380
Nearest Town/Resort Devizes.
Directions 1 mile from Devizes on A342 towards Chippenham.
Acreage 6¼ **Open** April–October
Access Good **Site** Level
Sites available Total 55.
Facilities
Nearby facilities
Chippenham.
Pub within 500yds, restaurant and bar food. Well stocked, 2 acre fishing lake on site.

MALMESBURY

Burton Hill Caravan and Camping Park, Arches Lane, Burton Hill, Malmesbury, Wiltshire.
Tel. 822585/822367 Std. 01666
Nearest Town/Resort Malmesbury.
Directions Turn off the A429 into Arches Lane, opposite Malmesbury Hospital. ½ mile south of Malmesbury off the Chippenham road.
Acreage 1½ **Open** April–November
Access Good **Site** Level
Sites available Total 30.
Facilities
Nearby facilities
Chippenham.
A quiet site on the edge of Cotswolds. Dogs welcome.

MARLBOROUGH

Hill-View Caravan Park, Oare, Marlborough, Wiltshire.
Tel. 63151/62271 Std. 01672
Nearest Town/Resort Marlborough.
Directions On A345, 6 miles south of Marlborough on Pewsey/Amesbury road.
Open Easter–September
Access Good **Site** Level
Sites available Total 10.
Facilities
Nearby facilities
Pewsey.
Place of historic interest and scenic views. SAE for enquiries. Graded 4 Ticks. Booking is advisable.

NETHERHAMPTON

Coombe Nurseries Caravan Park, Race Plain, Netherhampton, Salisbury, Wilts. SP2 8PN.
Tel. 328451 Std. 01722
Nearest Town/Resort Salisbury.
Directions Take A36-A30 Salisbury – Wilton road, turn off at traffic lights onto A3094 Netherhampton – Stratford Tony road, cross on bend following Stratford Tony road, 2nd left behind racecourse, site on right, signposted.
Acreage 3 **Open** All year
Access Good **Site** Level
Sites available Total 48.
Facilities
Nearby facilities
Salisbury.
Adjacent to racecourse (flat racing), ideal touring, lovely views.

ORCHESTON

Stonehenge Touring Park, Orcheston, Near Shrewton, Wiltshire.
Tel. 620304 Std. 01980
Nearest Town/Resort Salisbury.
Directions On A360 11 miles Salisbury, 11 miles Devizes.
Acreage 2 **Open** All year.
Access Good **Site** Level
Sites available Total 30.
Facilities
Nearby facilities
Salisbury.
Stonehenge 5 miles, Salisbury plain, easy reach Bath and the New Forest. AA 3 Pennants. BGHP 4 ticks. Take Away Food.

SHREWTON

Brades Acre, Tilshead, Salisbury, Wiltshire. SP3 4RX.
Tel. Shrewton 620402 Std. 01980
Nearest Town/Resort Salisbury/ Devizes.
Directions A360, 10 miles to Devizes, 13 miles to Salisbury.
Acreage 1½ **Open** All year
Access Good **Site** Level
Sites available Total 35.
Facilities

Nearby facilities
Salisbury.
Touring for Stonehenge, Salisbury Cathedral, Wilton and Longleat Houses. Avebury for riding.

WESTBURY
Woodland Park, Brokerswood, Nr. Westbury, Wiltshire. BA13 4EH.
Tel. Westbury 822238 Std. 01373
Nearest Town/Resort Westbury/Trowbridge.
Directions 4 miles Westbury, 5 miles Trowbridge, 5 miles Frome, left off A361 Southwick onto unclassified 1¼ miles on left, turn at Standerwick on A36.
Acreage 1 **Open** All year
Access Good **Site** Level
Sites available Total 30.
Facilities
Nearby facilities
Westbury.
Site adjoins an 80 acre area of forest open to the public together with a museum, lake, Narrow Gauge Railway, etc.

WHITEPARISH
Hillcrest Campsite, Southampton Road, Whiteparish, Nr.Salisbury, Wilts. SP5 2QW.
Tel. 884471 Std. 01794
Nearest Town/Resort Salisbury.
Directions 8 miles from Salisbury on A36. Travelling towards Southampton, one mile from A27 junction at Brickworth Garage on left.
Acreage 3 **Open** All year
Access Good **Site** Lev/slop
Sites available Total 35.
Facilities
Nearby facilities
Salisbury.
Central to Salisbury, Winchester,New Forest. Ideal for overnight stop before channel crossing.

NORTH YORKS

AYSGARTH
Westholme Caravan Park, Aysgarth, Leyburn, North Yorks, DL8 3SP.
Tel. 663268 Std. 01969
Nearest Town/Resort Leyburn.
Directions Follow the A684 from Leyburn to Hawes 7½ miles.
Acreage 4 **Open** March–October
Access Good **Site** Level
Sites available Total 75.
Facilities
Nearby facilities
Darlington.
Alongside stream, scenic views, ideal touring centre. Fishing.

BARDEN
Howgill Lodge, Barden, Nr. Skipton, North Yorkshire, BD23 6DJ.
Tel. 720655 Std. 01756
Nearest Town/Resort Bolton Abbey.
Directions Turn off B6160 at Barden Tower, site 1 mile on right.
Acreage 4 **Open** April–October
Access Narrow **Site** Terraced
Sites available Total 30.
Facilities
Nearby facilities
Skipton.
Beautiful views, ideal for walking or touring.

BENTHAM
Riverside Caravan Park, Wenning Avenue, Bentham, Nr. Lancaster, North Yorkshire.
Tel. 61272 Std. 015242
Nearest Town/Resort Bentham.
Directions Off B6480 at Black Bull Hotel in Bentham and right before crossing river.
Acreage 9 **Open** March–October
Access Good **Site** Level
Sites available Total 30.
Facilities
Nearby facilities
Bentham.
Riverside site, ideal for touring, with free fishing. E.T.B. 4 Ticks.

BEDALE
Pembroke Caravan Park, 19 Low Street, Leeming Bar, Northallerton, North Yorkshire, DL7 9BW.
Tel. 422652 Std. 01677
Nearest Town/Resort Bedale.
Directions A1 Leeming Services, right onto A684 to Leeming Bar. Keep left, crossroads into Leases Road. ½ mile on the right.
Acreage 1¼ **Open** March–October
Access Good **Site** Slight Slope
Sites available Total 14.
Facilities
Nearby facilities
Northallerton.
Between teh Yorkshire Dales and North Yorks Moors.

EASINGWOLD
Easingwold Caravan & Camping Site, White House Farm, Thirsk Road, Easingwold, York, North Yorks, YO6 3NF.
Tel. 821479 Std. 01347
Nearest Town/Resort York.
Directions On A19 15 miles north of York, 1 mile north of Easingwold.
Acreage 5 **Open** Easter–October
Access Good **Site** Level
Sites available Total 30.
Facilities
Nearby facilities
York/Thirsk.
Ideal touring. Near North Yorkshire Moors National Park, Dales and York.

EASINGWOLD
Hollybrook Touring Caravan Park, Penny Carr Lane, Off Stillington Road, Easingwold, York. YO6 3EU.
Tel. 821906 Std. 01347
Nearest Town/Resort York.
Directions From A19 (York/Thirsk) turn right on entering Easingwold. Signpost- ed Stillington ¼ mile turn right, into narrow lane, site on right.
Acreage 2 **Open** March–December
Access Good **Site** Level
Sites available Total 30.
Facilities
Nearby facilities
York.
Ideal touring centre, North Yorks Moors, Dales, East Coast Resorts Owned by Caravanners.

FILEY
Crows Nest Caravan Park, Gristhorpe, Filey, North Yorkshire.
Tel. 582206 Std. 01723
Nearest Town/Resort Filey/Scarborough.
Directions Off A165 north of Filey, south of Scarborough.
Acreage 12 **Open** March–October
Access Good **Site** Lev/Slope
Sites available
Facilities
Nearby facilities
Scarborough.

FILEY
Primrose Valley Holiday Centre, Primrose Valley, Near Filey, North Yorkshire, YO14 9RF.
Tel. 513771 Std. 01723
Nearest Town/Resort Filey.
Directions Take the A165 Scarborough to Bridlington road. You will see our signpost about a mile from the Filey turn-off.
Acreage 10 **Open** March–October
Site Lev/Slope
Sites available Total 140.
Facilities
Nearby facilities
Filey.
Situated on a cliff top with access to a large sandy beach. Excellent facilities include swimming pools and evening entertainment.

FILEY
Reighton Sands Holiday Park, Reighton Gap, Nr. Filey, North Yorks, YO14 9SJ.
Tel. 890476 Std. 01723
Nearest Town/Resort Filey.
Directions We are signposted opposite the garage at Reighton, on the A165 Filey to Bridlington road, and are located just 1 mile off this road.
Acreage 20 **Open** 19 March–16 October
Access Good **Site** Lev/Slope
Sites available Total 327.
Facilities
Nearby facilities
Filey.
On a cliff top with access to a beach.

GRASSINGTON
Hawkswick Cote Farm Caravan Park, Arncliffe, Nr. Skipton, North Yorks, BD23 5PX.
Tel. 770226 Std. 01756
Nearest Town/Resort Skipton.
Directions B6160 Dales road from Skipton. North from Grassington, through Kilnsey, left to Arncliffe. 1½ miles on left hand side.
Acreage 2 **Open** April–October
Access Good **Site** Level
Sites available Total 40.
Facilities
Nearby facilities
Skipton.
Beautiful quiet countryside.

GRASSINGTON
Threaplands House Camping & Caravan Park, Threaplands House Farm, Cracoe, Nr. Skipton, North Yorks, BD23 6LD.
Tel. 730248 Std. 01756
Nearest Town/Resort Skipton.
Directions Follow B6265 from Skipton to Cracoe. At end of straight road keep giong straight on down the lane. Site is ½ mile. 6 miles from Skipton.
Acreage 8 **Open** March–October
Access Good **Site** Level
Sites available Total 30.
Facilities
Nearby facilities
Skipton.
Ideal for walking and touring the Yorkshire Dales. Public telephone and cafe/restaurant ¼ mile away.

GRASSINGTON

Wood Nook Caravan Park, Skirethorns, Threshfield, Skipton, North Yorks. BD23 5NU.
Tel. 752412 Std. 01756
Nearest Town/Resort Grassington.
Directions From Skipton take the B6265 to Threshfield then the B6160 for 100yds. Turn left after garage into Skirethorns Lane, signposts at 600yds and 300yds entrance clearly marked Wood Nook on the left.
Acreage 3 **Open** March–October
Access Good **Site** Level
Sites available Total 48.
Facilities
Nearby facilities
Skipton.
Quiet, secluded, ideal for touring and walking.

HARROGATE

Ripley Caravan Park, Ripley, Harrogate, N.Yorks. HG3 3AU.
Tel. 770050 Std. 01423
Nearest Town/Resort Harrogate.
Directions From Harrogate take A61 to Ripon after 3 miles at Ripley roundabout take B6165 Knaresborough Road site 300 yards on left.
Acreage 18 **Open** Easter–October
Access Good **Site** Level
Sites available Total 100.
Facilities
Nearby facilities
Harrogate.
Ideal site for touring Dales, Harrogate and York. A level and quiet family site. British Tourist Board Graded 5 Ticks.

HARROGATE

Rudding Holiday Park, Follifoot, Harrogate, North Yorkshire.
Tel. 870439 Std. 01423
Nearest Town/Resort Harrogate.
Directions 3 miles south of Harrogate between A61 Leeds/Harrogate road and A661 Wetherby/Harrogate road.
Acreage 30 **Open** March–October
Access Good **Site** Level
Sites available Total 141.
Facilities
Nearby facilities
Harrogate.
Set in 50 acres of parkland, peaceful Yorkshire countryside. Heated swimming pool, 18 hole golf course and driving range.

HARROGATE

Bilton Park, Village Farm, Bilton Lane, Harrogate, North Yorkshire HG1 4DH.
Tel. 863121 Std. 01423
Nearest Town/Resort Harrogate.
Directions A59 Harrogate ring road, turn at Dragon Hotel into Bilton Lane. Site 1 mile.
Acreage 8 **Open** April–October
Access Good **Site** Level
Sites available Total 25.
Facilities
Nearby facilities
Harrogate.
River. Conference and Exhibition town. Ideal touring.

HARROGATE

Warren House Caravan Site, Warsill, Ripley, Harrogate, North Yorkshire.
Tel. 620683 Std. 01765
Nearest Town/Resort Harrogate/Pateley Bridge.
Directions Harrogate (A61), Ripley roundabout (B6165), ½ mile right Fountains Abbey, over crossroads left at next two junctions, take sign Warsill.
Acreage 7 **Open** Easter–October
Access Good **Site** Lev/Slope
Sites available
Facilities
Harrogate.
Gateway to Yorkshire Dales, Brimham Rocks, Fountains Abbey. Dogs Strictly on lead.

HAWES

Bainbridge Ings Caravan & Camping Site, Hawes, North Yorkshire DL8 3NU.
Tel. 667354 Std. 01969
Nearest Town/Resort Hawes.
Directions Approaching Hawes from Bainbridge on the A684 turn left at the signpost marked Gayle and we are 300yds on at the top of the hill.
Acreage 3¼ **Open** April–October
Access Good **Site** Level
Sites available Total 55.
Facilities
Garsdale.
A quiet, clean, family run site with beautiful views and only ¼ mile from Hawes. Motorcycles are accepted but not in large groups.

HAWES

Shaw Ghyll Farm, Simonstone, Hawes, North Yorkshire.
Tel. 667359 Std. 01969
Nearest Town/Resort Hawes.
Directions 2 miles north of Hawes following the Muker road.
Acreage 2½ **Open** March–October
Access Good **Site** Level
Sites available Total 30.

Facilities
Nearby facilities
Quiet sheltered site, ideal for walks and families, pleasant aspect, river and lovely scenic walks

HELMSLEY

Foxholme Touring Caravan Park, Harome, Helmsley, York, North Yorkshire YO6 5JG.
Tel. 770416 Std. 01439
Nearest Town/Resort Helmsley.
Directions A170 towards Scarborough ½ mile turn right to Harome, turn left at church, through village, follow caravan signs.
Acreage 6 **Open** Easter–October
Access Good **Site** Level
Sites available Total 60.
Facilities
Nearby facilities
Malton.
Ideal touring area. Near National Park, Abbeys, Herriot country.

HELMSLEY

Wren's of Ryedale, Gale Lane, Nawton, North Yorkshire.
Tel. Helmsley 71260 Std. 01439
Nearest Town/Resort Scarborough/York.
Directions Leave Helmsley by A170. 2½ miles to Beadlam, pass White Horse Inn and church on left, in 50 yards turn right. Site 700 yards down lane.
Acreage 3½ **Open** April–October
Access Good **Site** Level
Sites available Total 45.
Facilities
Nearby facilities
Malton.
Situated on edge of Yorkshire Moors National Park. Very good centre for touring. Attractive, quiet, family run site.

HELMSLEY

Golden Square Caravan Park, Oswaldkirk, York, North Yorkshire.
Tel. 788269 Std. 01439
Nearest Town/Resort Helmsley.
Directions 2 miles south of Helmsley. First right off the B1257 to Ampleforth.
Acreage 10 **Open** March–October
Access Good **Site** Level
Sites available Total 110.
Facilities
Nearby facilities
Thirsk/Malton.
Surrounded by open countryside and woodland with magnificent views of North Yorkshire Moors. Swimming pool nearby.

HELMSLEY

Wombleton Caravan Park, Moorfield Lane, Wombleton, Kirbymoorside, North Yorks.
Tel. 431684 Std. 01751
Nearest Town/Resort Kirbymooorside/Helmsley.
Directions Leave Helmsley by A170 for 4 miles, turn right for Wombleton go through Wombleton ½ mile on left.
Acreage 6 **Open** March–October
Access Good **Site** Level
Sites available Total 78.
Facilities
Nearby facilities
Malton.
Ideal touring, scenic view, near Yorkshire Dales National Parks and Herriot country. Caravans to let and seasonal pitches available. Tourist Board Graded 5 Tick.

HINDERWELL

Fern Farm, 30 High Street, Hinderwell, Saltburn, North Yorkshire, TS13 5JH.
Tel. 840350 Std. 01947
Nearest Town/Resort Whitby.
Directions Midway between Runswick Bay and Staithes. Near Port Mulgrave.
Acreage 3
Access Good **Site** Level
Sites available
Facilities
Nearby facilities
Whitby/Saltburn.
1 mile to the beach, Cleveland Way Walk, North Yorkshire Moors and a National Park. Views of the Moors from the site.

INGLETON

The Trees Caravan Park, Westhouse, Ingleton, North Yorkshire.
Tel. 41511 Std. 015242
Nearest Town/Resort Ingleton.
Directions From Ingleton, travel 1¼ miles along the A65 towards Kirkby Lonsdale (about ¼ mile past the A687 junction – Country Harvest). Turn left at signpost for Lower Westhouse, site is on the left in 50yds.
Acreage 3 **Open** April–October
Access Good **Site** Level
Sites available Total 29.
Facilities
Nearby facilities
Bentham.
Set in beautiful country scenery. Ideal for walking and touring. Mountains, caves and waterfalls nearby.

KNARESBOROUGH

Kingfisher Caravan Park, Low Moor Lane, Farnham, Knaresborough, North Yorks.
Tel. 869411 Std. 01423
Nearest Town/Resort Knaresborough.
Directions From Knaresborough take A6055 1¼ miles. Turn left to Farnham Village in Farnham, turn left, park approx 1 mile on the left.
Acreage 10 **Open** March–October
Access Good **Site** Level
Sites available Total 50.
Facilities
Nearby facilities
Knaresborough.
Ideal touring base for Dales, convenient for Harrogate and York. Adjacent private fishing and golf range.

KNARESBOROUGH

Lido Caravan Park, Wetherby Road, Knaresborough, North Yorks, HG5 8LR.
Tel. 865169 Std. 01423
Nearest Town/Resort Knaresborough.
Directions On B6164 Knaresborough to Wetherby road, off A59 (A1 4 miles).
Acreage 20 **Open** 1st April–31st October
Access Good **Site** Lev/Slope
Sites available Total 300.
Facilities
Nearby facilities
Knaresborough.
Alongside River Nidd. Motorcycles accepted in couples only. Fishing on site.

KNARESBOROUGH

Scotton Park Caravans, New Road, Scotton, Knaresborough, North Yorkshire.
Tel. Harrogate 864413 Std. 01423
Nearest Town/Resort Knaresborough.
Directions Leave Knaresborough (A59) on the B6165, site 1½ miles out of town, at right turn to Scotton village.
Acreage 8 **Open** March–January
Access Good **Site** Lev/Slope
Sites available Total 93.
Facilities
Nearby facilities
Knaresborough.
Ideal touring for Dales. Quiet family run site. Bus stop at entrance. Holiday vans available for letting. S.A.E. for brochure. Motorcyclists accepted by advanced booking only.

LEEDS

Moor Lodge Caravan Park, Blackmoor Lane, Bardsey, Leeds, Yorkshire, LS17 9DZ.
Tel. 572424 Std. 01937
Nearest Town/Resort Leeds/Wetherby.
Directions Turn right after Toby Steak House New Inn on the A58 coming from Wetherby towards Leeds.
Open All Year
Access Good **Site** Level
Sites available Total 10.
Facilities
Nearby facilities
Leeds.
Scenic views, ideal touring.

LEYBURN

Constable Burton Hall Caravan Park, Constable Burton, Near Leyburn, North Yorkshire, DL8 5LJ.
Tel. 450428 Std. 01677
Nearest Town/Resort Leyburn.
Directions From the A1 take the A684 in a westerly direction for 9 miles. Park is on the right after the village.
Acreage 10 **Open** April–October
Access Good **Site** Lev/Slope
Sites available Total 120.
Facilities
Nearby facilities
Northallerton.

MASHAM

Fearby Caravan & Camping Site, Rear of Black Swan Hotel, Fearby, Masham, Ripon, North Yorkshire.
Tel. 689477 Std. 01765
Nearest Town/Resort Masham.
Directions Turn left off A6108 800yds past filling station. Site is 2 miles on the left hand side at the rear of the Black Swan in Fearby.
Acreage 2 **Open** March–October
Access Good **Site** Level
Sites available Total 50.
Facilities
Nearby facilities
Northallerton.
Small site overlooking Burn Valley in beautiful countryside. Ideal for walking.

MUKER IN SWALEDALE

Usha Gap Camp & Caravan Site, Usha Gap, Muker, Richmond, North Yorkshire.
Tel. Richmond 886214 Std. 01748
Nearest Town/Resort Hawes.
Directions From Richmond on the B6270 for 20 miles.
Acreage 1 **Open** All year
Access Good **Site** Level
Sites available Total 35.
Facilities
Nearby facilities
Darlington.
Alongside small river, beautiful scenery. Good walking country and good centre for touring by car. Near moors.

NORTHALLERTON

Hutton Bonville Caravan Park, Church Lane, Hutton Bonville, Northallerton, N. Yorks, DL7 0NR.
Tel. 881416 Std. 01609
Nearest Town/Resort Northallerton.
Directions 4 miles north of Northallerton on the main A167.
Acreage 5 **Open** March–October
Access Good **Site** Lev/Slope
Sites available Total 75.
Facilities
Nearby facilities
Northallerton.
Scenic views and central for touring the Yorkshire coast, Moors and Dales.

OSMOTHERLEY

Cote Ghyll Caravan Park, Osmotherley, Northallerton, North Yorks. DL6 3AH.
Tel. 883425 Std. 01609
Nearest Town/Resort Northallerton.
Directions Leave A19 at junction of A684 Northallerton turnoff. Follow Osmotherley signs to village, then caravan signs uphill from village cross. Entrance ½ mile on right.
Open April–October
Access Good **Site** Sloping
Sites available Total 57.
Facilities
North Yorkshire Moors, ideal touring.

PATELEY BRIDGE

Heathfield Caravan Park, Wath Road, Pateley Bridge, Harrogate, North Yorkshire HG3 5PY.
Tel. Harrogate 711652 Std. 01423
Nearest Town/Resort Pateley Bridge.
Directions Take Ramsgill road, turn left in 1 mile.
Acreage 2 **Open** April–October
Access Good **Site** Level
Sites available
Facilities
Nearby facilities
Harrogate.
Scenic views, ideal touring, walking, etc.

PATELEY BRIDGE

Studford Farm Caravan & Camping Site, Studford Farm, Lofthouse, Harrogate, North Yorks, HG3 5SG.
Tel. 755210 Std. 01423
Directions To Lofthouse off the B6265 at Pateley Bridge 7 miles. ½ mile beyond Lofthouse bear left signposted Stean. Site is within 200yds.
Acreage 2 **Open** April–October
Access Good **Site** Level
Sites available Total 20.
Facilities
Nearby facilities
Harrogate.
Excellent walking, scenic Dale views and alongside a river. Ideal for touring the Yorkshire Dales.

PATELEY BRIDGE

Westfield, Westfield Farm, Heathfield, Pateley Bridge, Harrogate, North Yorks.
Tel. 711410 Std. 01423
Nearest Town/Resort Pateley Bridge.
Directions From Pateley Bridge 1 mile turn left to Heathfield after 100yds turn left to continue on this road through Heathfield caravan site. We are third site.
Acreage 3 **Open** April–October
Access Single Track. **Site** Lev/Slope
Sites available
Facilities
Nearby facilities
Harrogate.
Small farm site along stream in quiet Yorkshire Dales location. Holiday chalet for hire.

PATELEY BRIDGE

Riverside Caravan Site, Pateley Bridge, Harrogate, N.Yorks, HG3 5HL.
Tel. 711383/711320 Std. 01423
Nearest Town/Resort Harrogate/Ripon.
Directions From Harrogate take B6165, in Pateley Bridge go over river and turn right, site is ¼ mile up Ramsgill road.
Acreage 4½ **Open** April–October
Access Good **Site** Level
Sites available
Facilities
Nearby facilities
Harrogate.
Alongside river, scenic views, ideal touring and walking.

PICKERING

Flamingo Land Holiday Village, Kirby Misperton, Malton, North Yorkshire, YO17 0UX.
Tel. 668300 Std. 01653
Nearest Town/Resort Malton/Pickering.
Directions Off A169 Malton to Pickering road.
Open Easter–October
Access Good **Site** Sloping
Sites available Total 250.
Facilities
Nearby facilities
Malton.
Gently sloping site close to country and coast.

PICKERING

Spiers House Campsite, Cropton, Pickering, North Yorks, YO18 8ES.
Tel. 591 Std. 017515
Nearest Town/Resort Pickering.
Directions Take A170 westwards from Pickering and at Wrelton turn north to Cropton, continue from there on the Rosedale Road for 1 mile wher site is signposted at the edge of Cropton Forest.
Acreage 10 **Open** 31st March–1st Oct
Access Good **Site** Lev/Slop
Sites available Total 150.
Facilities
Nearby facilities
Malton.
Site located in an extensive open grassland area and there are several way marked walks in the adjoining forest. An ideal base to explore the surrounding moors and coast. No advance bookings accepted for less than 7 nights.

PICKERING

Sun Inn, Normanby, Sinnington, North Yorks, YO6 6RH.
Tel. 431051 Std. 01751
Nearest Town/Resort Pickering.
Directions 6 miles south west of Pickering off the A170. Turning off is between Helmsley and Pickering.
Acreage ¼ **Open** April–October
Access Good **Site** Level
Sites available Total 30.
Facilities
Nearby facilities
Malton.
Own river, scenic views and pub on site. 10 minutes from the North Yorkshire Moors.

PICKERING

Upper Carr Touring Park, Upper Carr Lane, Opposite Black Bull, Pickering, North Yorks YO18 7JP.
Tel. Pickering 73115 Std. 01751
Nearest Town/Resort Pickering.
Directions From Pickering take A169 Malton Road due south, at 2 miles turn left opposite Black Bull Pub. Site 50 yards on left.
Acreage 4 **Open** March–October
Access Good **Site** Level
Sites available Total 80.
Facilities
Nearby facilities
Malton.
Ideal touring, on edge of North Yorks Moors, 30 mins drive to Scarborough, nearby forest walks and drives. 5 minutes drive to North York Moors Steam Railway.

PICKERING

Wayside Caravan Park, Wrelton, Pickering, North Yorkshire. YO18 8PG.
Tel. 72608 Std. 01751
Nearest Town/Resort Pickering.
Directions 2½ miles west of Pickering off A170 just past the village of Wrelton. Signposted off the main road on right.
Acreage 4½ **Open** Easter–Early October
Access Good **Site** Level
Sites available Total 72.
Facilities
Nearby facilities
Malton.
Ideal touring for North Yorks Moors, Historic Railway, scenic views.

RICHMOND

Brompton-on-Swale Caravan Park, Brompton-on-Swale, Richmond, North Yorkshire.
Tel. 824629 Std. 01748
Nearest Town/Resort Richmond.
Directions Exit A1 at Catterick A6136. Follow B6271 to Richmond and drive through Brompton-on-Swale. Park on left 1 mile out of Brompton. 1¼ miles south east of Richmond.
Acreage 7¼ **Open** April–October
Access Good **Site** Level
Sites available Total 150.
Facilities
Nearby facilities
Darlington/Northallerton.
Situated in a peaceful natural setting on the banks of the River Swale which provides fishing and walks.

RICHMOND

Fox Hall Caravan Park, Ravensworth, Nr. Richmond, North Yorkshire.
Tel. 718344 Std. 01325
Nearest Town/Resort Richmond.
Directions From Scotch Corner take the A66 west bound. 5 miles along turn left to Ravensworth. Site is 300yds on the right.
Acreage 3¼ **Open** April–October
Access Good **Site** Level
Sites available Total 10.
Facilities
Nearby facilities
Darlington.
Scenic views and ideal touring.

RICHMOND

Swaleview Caravan Park, Reeth Road, Richmond, North Yorkshire.
Tel. 823106 Std. 01748
Nearest Town/Resort Richmond.
Directions On A6108, 3 miles west town.
Acreage 4 **Open** March–October
Access Good **Site** Level
Sites available Total 50.
Facilities
Nearby facilities
Darlington.
Beautiful area in National Park by side of River Swale. Central for coasts and lakes.

RIPON

Gold Coin Farm, Galphay, Ripon, North Yorks, HG4 3NJ.
Tel. 658508 Std. 01765
Nearest Town/Resort Ripon.
Directions Take Pateley Bridge road from Ripon (B6265) turning right after 1 mile.
Acreage 6 **Open** All year
Access Good **Site** Lev/Slope
Sites available
Harrogate.
Scenic views, ideal touring, Lightwater Valley.

RIPON

Sleningford Watermill, North Stainley, Ripon, North Yorks, HG4 3HQ.
Tel. 635201 Std. 01765
Nearest Town/Resort Ripon.
Directions 5½ miles N.W. of Ripon (turning at clock tower) onto A6108, between North Stainley and West Tanfield.
Acreage 14 **Open** Easter–October
Access Good **Site** Level
Sites available Total 80.
Facilities
Nearby facilities
Picturesque riverside, fishing and canoeing access, quiet rural site, birds, wildflowers etc. Ideal for touring Herriot country and Dales.

RIPON

Winksley Banks Holiday Park, Galphay, Ripon, North Yorkshire.
Tel. 658439 Std. 01765
Nearest Town/Resort Ripon.
Directions 4 miles from Ripon, 1 mile north of Winksley Village on the unlisted road to Kirkby Malzeard.
Acreage 1 **Open** March–October
Access Good **Site** Sloping
Sites available Total 10.
Facilities
Nearby facilities
Harrogate.
In an area of designated outstanding natural beauty. Free fishing in a river running through the park.

RIPON

Woodhouse Farm Caravan & Camping Park, Winksley, Nr. Ripon, North Yorkshire HG4 3PG.
Tel. 658309 Std. 01765
Nearest Town/Resort Ripon.
Directions Take B6265 from Ripon 3½ miles. Right at the Winksley/Grantley signpost. Follow site signs for 2¼ miles.
Acreage 15 **Open** April–October
Access Good **Site** Level
Sites available Total 120.
Facilities
Nearby facilities
Harrogate.
An attractive, quiet, country site with excellent facilities. Ideal for touring Yorkshire Dales. Luxury holiday vans available for letting. On site coarse fishing lake. SAE for Brochure.

RIPON

The Yorkshire Hussar Inn Holiday Caravan Park, Markington, Harrogate, Yorkshire, HG3 3NR.
Tel. 677327 Std. 01765
Nearest Town/Resort Harrogate/Ripon.
Directions 1 mile west of A61 (Harrogate/Ripon road). Ripon 5 miles. Harrogate 7 miles.
Acreage 5 **Open** April–October
Access Good **Site** Level
Sites available Total 40.
Facilities
Nearby facilities
Harrogate.
Ideal touring centre. Site at rear of Inn. Garden setting in village. Ideal touring centre for the Dales. Fountains Abbey 1¼ miles.

ROBIN HOOD'S BAY

Middlewood Farm Holiday Park, Robin Hood's Bay, Whitby, North Yorkshire.
Tel. 880414 Std. 01947
Nearest Town/Resort Whitby.
Directions Scarborough – Whitby A171 Road, turn to Robin Hood's Bay / Fylingthorpe, turn right at Village Crossroads.
Acreage 2
Access Good **Site** Level
Sites available Total 50.
Facilities
Nearby facilities
Whitby.
Super luxury toilet facilities with free hot showers, laundry, campers kitchen, private bathrooms for hire. Adventure playground. A walkers, artists and wildlife paradise. Close to beach, Rose Award 5 Tick Park.

SCARBOROUGH

Arosa Caravan & Camping Park, Ratten Row, Seamer, Scarborough, North Yorkshire YO12 4QB.
Tel. 862166 Std. 01723
Nearest Town/Resort Scarborough.
Directions 4 miles south of Scarborough on A64 York/Scarborough road.
Acreage 5 **Open** March–January
Access Good **Site** Level
Sites available Total 92.
Facilities
Nearby facilities
Seamer.
Ideal touring site for North Yorkshire Moors, Wolds and east coast beaches.

SCARBOROUGH

Cayton Village Caravan Park, Dept 1, Mill Lane, Cayton Bay, Scarborough, YO11 3NN.
Tel. 583171 Std. 01723
Nearest Town/Resort Scarborough.
Directions 3 miles south of Scarborough off A165 at Cayton Bay traffic lights. Turn right onto Mill Lane. The park is on the right hand side in ½ mile. From A64 take the B1261 signposted Filey. At Cayton Village take the second left after Blacksmiths Arms onto Mill Lane. The park is 150yds on the left hand side.
Acreage 10 **Open** Easter–October
Access Good **Site** Level
Sites available Total 200.
Facilities
Nearby facilities
Seamer.
Next to Conservation Village Church, Pub, ¼ mile from beach. Winter telephone number 01904 624630.

SCARBOROUGH

Jasmine Caravan Park, Cross Lane, Snainton, Scarborough, North Yorkshire YO13 9BE.
Tel. 859240 Std. 01723
Nearest Town/Resort Scarborough/Pickering.
Directions Turn off the A170 in Snainton Village opposite junior school, ¾ mile signposted.
Acreage 4 **Open** March–Janurary
Access Good **Site** Level
Sites available Total 70.
Facilities
Nearby facilities
Scarborough.
Scenic, quiet park within easy reach of forest, moors, coast and wolds. Ideal cycling and walking in the immediate vicinty. Personal supervision. S.A.E.

SCARBOROUGH

Flower of May Holiday Park, Lebberston Cliff, Scarborough, North Yorks. YO11 3NU.
Tel. 584311/582324 Std. 01723
Nearest Town/Resort Scarborough.
Directions 3 miles south of Scarborough off A165 signposted at roundabout.
Acreage 13 **Open** Easter–September
Access Good **Site** Level
Sites available Total 300.
Facilities
Nearby facilities
Scarborough.
Acclaimed as one of the best privately owned holiday parks in the country, the Flower of May provides the most comprehensive facilities, right on the coast between Scarborough and Filey.

SCARBOROUGH

Lebberston Touring Caravan Park, Home Farm, Beckfield, Lebberston, Scarborough, North Yorks. YO11 3PF.
Tel. Scarborough 582254 Std. 01723
Nearest Town/Resort Scarborough.
Directions From A64 or A165 take B1261 to Lebberston and follow signs.
Acreage 7½ **Open** May–September
Access Good **Site** Lev/Slope
Sites available Total 125.
Facilities
Nearby facilities
Scarborough.
Quiet, country site, situated on farm. Most pitches on outside overlooking Yorkshire Wolds, Vale of Pickering. Dogs on lead, dog area. Individual pitches.

SCARBOROUGH

Blue Dolphin Holiday Centre, Gristhorpe Bay, Filey, North Yorks, YO14 9PU.
Tel. 515155 Std. 01723
Nearest Town/Resort Filey.
Directions Off the A165 between Scarborough and Filey.
Acreage 30 **Open** Easter–1st wk Oct
Access Good **Site** Sloping
Sites available Total 410.
Facilities
Nearby facilities
Filey.
Overlooking the Yorkshire Wolds.

SCARBOROUGH

Jacobs Mount Caravan and Camping Site, Stepney Road, Scarborough, North Yorks, YO12 5NL.
Tel. 361178 Std. 01723
Nearest Town/Resort Scarborough.

LEBBERSTON TOURING CARAVAN PARK

Home Farm, Beckfield, Main Street
Lebberston, Scarborough
North Yorkshire YO11 3PF
Telephone Scarborough 582254
(S.T.D. 01723-582254)

Lebberston Touring Caravan Park

This quiet country site is situated a mile off the coastline south of Scarborough (5 miles), the largest of Yorkshire's resorts with extensive sandy beaches, wide promonades and many indoor and outdoor activities. A rugged deep sided headland with a ruined castle on its summit seperates two lovely bays. Other beaches south of the site are Filey (3 miles), Flamborough Head incorporating Bempton Cliff bird sanctuary and Bridlington.

From £5.50 per night and £10 Booking Deposit.

Proprietors: C.J. and A.C. Jackson

SCARBOROUGH - *Yorkshire's Warmest Welcome*

SCALBY MANOR CARAVAN & CAMPING PARK

This scenic park is set in 20 acres of countryside. A footpath takes you down to the beach and Scarborough's North Bay and with the town centre just three miles away, the setting is just perfect for a relaxing holiday.

Enjoy over 45 miles of superb seaside, set against the backcloth of the North York Moors National Park. Heritage, tradition, festivals . . . family fun or big time stars . . . quiet times or 24 hour action. You'll see why there's so much more to the seaside than the sea.

(For full details of facilities see listing under Scarborough)

FOR DETAILS AND BOOKING FORMS PLEASE CONTACT:

Caravan Booking Office, Tourist Information Centre,
St. Nicholas Cliff, Scarborough, North Yorkshire YO11 2EP
Telephone: (01723) 366212

the happy family Flower of May holiday park

RAC AA

Widely acclaimed as one of the best privately owned holiday parks in the country, the Flower of May is constantly updated to provide the most comprehensive facilities, right on the coast between Scarborough and Filey.

*** Lounge Bar and Family Lounge**
*** Children's safety play area**
*** Self Service Shop**
*** Fish and Chip Shop**
*** Cafe * Special terms early and late season - ask for details***

NEW! LEISURE COMPLEX

to make the most of your holiday. Including indoor heated swimming pool and paddling pool, superb squash courts, fully equipped gym, games room with pool and snooker.

Please send for colour brochure from the resident proprietors:
Mr & Mrs J. G. Atkinson,
Dept. I, Flower of May,
Lebbeston Cliff,
Scarborough YO11 3NU
Telephone (01723) 584311

Directions 2 miles west of Scarborough on the A170 Thirsk Road.
Acreage 5 **Open** March–October
Access Good **Site** Lev/Slope
Sites available Total 56.
Facilities
Nearby facilities
Scarborough.
Set in Mature woodland in beautiful countryside, yet only 2 miles from Scarborough beaches and attractions. Touring caravan rallies catered for off-peak. ETB 5 Tick Graded (Excellent), Rose Award RAC Appointed AA 3 pennants Caravan Club Listed. Bar with family room.

SCARBOROUGH

Scalby Manor Caravan & Camping Park, Burniston Road, Scarborough, North Yorkshire.
Tel. 366212 Std. 01723
Nearest Town/Resort Scarborough.
Directions Located 2 miles north of Scarborough Town Centre on the coast road to Whitby, A165. Follow signposts to Burniston/Whitby.
Acreage 20 **Open** Easter–October
Access Good
Sites available Total 375.
Facilities
Nearby facilities
Scarborough.
The site offers an ideal touring base for the North Yorkshire National Park and Moors and yet only 2 miles from the resort of Scarborough.

SCARBOROUGH

Spring Willows Touring Park, Main Road, Staxton, Scarborough, North Yorks, YO12 4SB.
Tel. 891505 Std. 01723
Nearest Town/Resort Scarborough.
Directions Exit the A64 at Staxton onto the A1039 to Filey. Entrance is on the right in 100yds.
Acreage 10 **Open** March–December
Access Good **Site** Level
Sites available Total 184.
Facilities

Nearby facilities
Childrens Club during high season. Ideal for touring.

SCARBOROUGH

St.Helens Caravan & Camping Park, Wykeham, Scarborough, N.Yorks YO13 9QD.
Tel. 862771 Std. 01723
Nearest Town/Resort Scarborough.
Directions A170 Pickering – Scarborough road 6 miles west of Scarborough.
Acreage 32 **Open** All year
Access Good **Site** Level
Sites available Total 250.
Facilities
Nearby facilities
Scarborough.
Set in North York Moors National Park. An ideal base to explore moors and coastal resorts. Family park, play equipment, baby baths. Take-away food. A.A. Campsite of the Year 1994.

SELBY

Bay Horse Inn, York Road, Barlby, Selby, North Yorks.
Tel. 703878 Std. 01757
Nearest Town/Resort Selby.
Directions In village centre 1¾ miles north on A19 from Selby.
Acreage 1 **Open** All year
Access Good **Site** Level
Sites available Total 12.
Facilities
Nearby facilities
Selby.
15 minutes from York, 5 minutes from Selby (driving) buses pass site, old english pub.

SETTLE

Knight Stainforth Hall, Stainforth, Settle, North Yorkshire.
Tel. 822200 Std. 01729
Nearest Town/Resort Settle.
Directions A65 Settle/Kendal. Turn opposite Settle High School. 2½ miles along Stackhouse Lane.
Acreage 6 **Open** March–October
Access Good **Site** Sloping
Sites available Total 100.

Facilities
Nearby facilities
Settle.
Riverside. Near to potholes. Ideal walking and touring. You can FAX us on 01729 823387.

SKIPTON

Eshton Road Caravan Site, Eshton Road, Gargrave, Nr. Skipton, North Yorkshire, BD23 3PN.
Tel. 749229 Std. 01756
Nearest Town/Resort Skipton.
Directions 4¼ miles from Skipton, A65 follow lakes signs.
Acreage 1¼ **Open** All year
Access Good **Site** Level
Sites available Total 30.
Facilities
Nearby facilities
Gargrave.
Alongside Leeds Liverpool Canal. Central for Dales.

SKIPTON

Lower Heights Farm, Silsden, Keighley, North Yorkshire, BD20 9HW.
Tel. 653035 Std. 01535
Nearest Town/Resort Skipton.
Directions 1 mile from Silsden off A6034.
Acreage 2 **Open** Easter–November
Access Good **Site** Level
Sites available Total 5.
Facilities
Nearby facilities
Keighley.
Scenic views. Yorks Dales and Bronte Country.

SLINGSBY

Robin Hood Caravan and Camping Park, Green Dyke Lane, Slingsby, North Yorkshire.
Tel. 628391 Std. 01653
Nearest Town/Resort Malton.
Directions From Malton take B1257 westwards 6 miles to Slingsby. Turn right and right again.
Acreage 4 **Open** March–October
Access Good **Site** Level
Sites available Total 48.
Facilities

Nearby facilities
Malton.
Sheltered site, Ideal touring site for North Yorkshire Moors, coast, Ryedale, Castle Howard and York. A.A. 3 Pennant and E.T.B. 4 Ticks. A family run site with modern, fully tiled and cubicled wash room.

TADCASTER

Whitecote Caravan Park, Ryther Road, Ulleskelf, Nr. Tadcaster, North Yorks, LS24 9DY.
Nearest Town/Resort York
Open March–January
Access Good **Site** Level
Sites available Total 18.
Facilities
Nearby facilities
Church Fenton.
River fishing on site. Near parklands and York.

THIRSK

Beechwood Caravan Park, Beechwood House, South Kilvington, Thirsk, North Yorkshire, YO7 2LZ.
Tel. 522348 Std. 01845
Nearest Town/Resort Thirsk.
Directions ¼ mile north of Thirsk on the A61. Thirsk to A19 Teeside.
Open March–October
Access Good **Site** Level
Sites available Total 30.
Facilities
Thirsk.
Ideal touring centre for moors, dales and market towns.

THIRSK

Nursery Caravan Park, Rainton, Thirsk, North Yorkshire.
Tel. 577277 Std. 01845
Nearest Town/Resort Thirsk.
Directions South from Thirsk on the A168 4 miles, take filter lane to Topcliffe. Right over river bridge and continue to T-Junction, turn right, park is ½ mile on the right.
Open March–October
Access Good **Site** Level
Sites available Total 30.
Facilities
Nearby facilities
Thirsk.
Very peaceful site situated halfway between Ripon and Thirsk. Ideal for touring local Abbeys, coastal resorts and York.

THIRSK

Quernhow Caravan & Camp Site, Great North Road (A1), Sinderby, Nr. Thirsk, North Yorkshire.
Tel. Thirsk 567221 Std. 01845
Nearest Town/Resort Ripon.
Directions Beside the A1 (west side) 9 miles north of Boroughbridge and 17 miles south of Scotch Corner near junction A61 and B6267.
Acreage 4 **Open** All year
Access Good **Site** Level
Sites available Total 50.
Facilities
Thirsk.
Ideal centre touring Yorkshire Dales. Holiday chalet to rent.

WETHERBY

Maustin Caravan Park, Kearby with Netherby, near Wetherby, North Yorkshire.LS22 4DP.
Tel. 288 6234 Std. 0113
Nearest Town/Resort Harrogate/Wetherby.
Directions A61 three right turns, after crossing River Wharfe at bottom of Harewood Bank. A1 from Wetherby through Sicklinghall to Kearby.
Acreage 2 **Open** March–October
Access Good **Site** Level
Sites available Total 13.
Facilities
Nearby facilities
Suits couples, flat green bowling, quiet, easy reach of many small towns and dales.

WHITBY

Burnt House Holiday Park, Ugthorpe, Nr. Whitby, North Yorks, YO21 2BG.
Tel. 840448 Std. 01947
Nearest Town/Resort Whitby.
Directions 8½ miles north of Whitby on A171, towards Guisborough, signposted Ugthorpe, 275 yards on right.
Acreage 7 **Open** March–October
Access Good **Site** Level
Sites available Total 99.
Facilities
Nearby facilities
Whitby.
Ideal base for touring coast or countryside, 4 miles to beach. Fully serviced static caravans for sale and hire.

WHITBY

Northcliffe Holiday Park, High Hawsker, Whitby, North Yorkshire.
Tel. Whitby 880477 Std. 01947
Nearest Town/Resort Whitby.
Directions South from Whitby 3 miles, turn left B1447 to Robin Hood's Bay.
Open Easter–October
Access Good
Sites available Total 30.
Facilities
Nearby facilities
Whitby.
Scenic views. Lovely walks. Overlooking sea. All mains service – hard standing touring pitches. New Woodland Shop and Tea-Room with pizza take-away. You can FAX us on 01947 880972.

WHITBY

Rigg Farm Caravan Park, Stainsacre, Whitby, North Yorkshire YO22 4LP.
Tel. Whitby 880430 Std. 01947
Nearest Town/Resort Whitby.
Directions Approaching Whitby from Teeside or Scarborough on A171, take B1416. 1¼ miles south of Ruswarp turn into unclassified road signposted Sneatonthorpe/Hawsker/Stainsacre. Site within 2 miles on left.
Acreage 3 **Open** March–October
Access Good **Site** Level
Sites available Total 20.
Facilities
Nearby facilities
Whitby.

WHITBY
Sandfield House Farm Caravan Park, Sandsend Road, Whitby, North Yorkshire, YO21 3SR.
Tel. 602660 Std. 01947
Nearest Town/Resort Whitby.
Directions 1 mile north of Whitby on the A147 coast road. Opposite Whity Golf Course.
Acreage 12 **Open** March–October
Access Good **Site** Level
Sites available Total 50.
Facilities
Nearby facilities
Whitby.
Sea views, ½ mile from sandy beach (2 miles long). Set in undulating countryside.

WHITBY
York House Caravan Park, Hawsker, Whitby, North Yorkshire.
Tel. 880354 Std. 01947
Nearest Town/Resort Whitby.
Directions 3 miles south of Whitby on the A171, signposted.
Acreage 4¼ **Open** March–October
Access Good **Site** Lev/Slope
Sites available Total 59.
Facilities
Nearby facilities
Whitby.
Scenic views of the sea, Whitby and North Yorkshire Moors.

WHITBY
"Serenity" Touring Caravan & Camping Park, High Street, Hinderwell, Whitby, North Yorks, TS13 5JH.
Tel. 841122/840523 Std. 01947
Nearest Town/Resort Whitby.
Directions Take B1266 off A171 Whitby to Guisborough Moor road. To T-Junction turn left onto A174. 1 mile Hinderwell. Site entrance in village on left signed "Serenity".
Acreage 3 **Open** March–October
Access Good **Site** Level
Sites available Total 20.
Facilities
Nearby facilities
Whitby.
A very quiet, sheltered and secure family site with lovely country views. ½ mile from the sea. Marvellous coastal, country and moorland walks. Village shops, public telephone and pubs all nearby.

WHITBY
Whitby Holiday Park, Saltwick Bay, Whitby, North Yorks, YO22 4JX.
Tel. 602664 Std. 01947
Nearest Town/Resort Whitby.
Directions As you approach Whitby, look for signs directing you to Whitby Abbey. Follow Green Lane to the T-Junction, turn right then look for caravan signs.
Acreage 14 **Open** 31 March–October
Site Sloping
Sites available Total 250.
Facilities
Nearby facilities
Whitby.
Overlooks Saltwick Bay.

YORK
Cawood Holiday Park, Caravan and Camping Centre, Ryther Road, Cawood, Selby, North Yorks. YO8 0TT.
Tel. 268450 Std. 01757
Nearest Town/Resort Selby.
Directions From A1 or York take B1222 to Cawood lights, turn on B1223 for 1 mile towards Tadcaster, site on the left.
Acreage 8 **Open** March–January
Access Good **Site** Level
Sites available Total 70.
Facilities
Nearby facilities
Selby/York.
Ideal country site, twixt York and Selby, 1 hour from coast, 9 miles from A1. Caravans and tents set amongst oak trees, some with views over fishing lake. Caravans and luxury bungalows to rent, some specifically adapted with disabled facilities. ETB Grading 5 Ticks, RAC Listed, AA 4 Pennant.

YORK
Chestnut Farm Caravan Park, Acaster Malbis, York, North Yorkshire, YO2 1UQ.
Tel. 704676 Std. 01904
Nearest Town/Resort York.
Directions Travelling east on the A64 towards York, turn left up sliproad to roundabout (signposted Copmanthorpe and Acaster Malbis). Straight over roundabout and over flyover then left into Copmanthorpe. Follow signs to Acaster Malbis (2 miles).
Acreage 2 **Open** April–October
Access Good **Site** Level
Sites available Total 25.
Facilities
Nearby facilities
York.
Family run park in a pretty village by the River Ouse. 3¼ miles from the centre of York.

YORK
Moor End Farm, Acaster, Malbis, York, Yorkshire YO2 1UQ.
Tel. York 706727 Std. 01904
Nearest Town/Resort York.
Directions Off A64 going west turn off at Copmanthorpe and follow symbols and Acaster signs to village.
Acreage 1 **Open** April 1st–October
Access Good **Site** Level
Sites available Total 15.
Facilities
Nearby facilities
York.
Working dairy farm and small friendly site. ETB 4 Ticks. Dish washing facilities.

YORK
Naburn Lock Caravan Site, Naburn, York, YO1 4RU.
Tel. 728697 Std. 01904
Nearest Town/Resort York.
Directions A19 Selby to York B1222 from outside York through Naburn village ½ mile on right.
Acreage 5 **Open** April–October
Access Good **Site** Level
Sites available Total 50.
Facilities
Nearby facilities
York.
Ideal centre for York, Yorkshire Dales, Moors etc. Bike hire, hourly bus to York, daily River Bus to York.

YORK
The Old Post Office Camp Site, Mill Cottage, Mill Lane, Acaster Malbis, York, YO2 1UL.
Tel. 706288 Std. 01904
Nearest Town/Resort York.
Directions 4 miles south west of York, via Bishopethorpe in the village of Acaster Malbis.
Acreage ½ **Open** April–October
Access Good **Site** Level
Sites available Total 20.
Facilities
Nearby facilities
York.
Riverside camping, ideal for visiting York.

YORK
Mount Pleasant Caravan Village, Acaster, Malbis, York, North Yorkshire.
Tel. 707078 Std. 01904
Nearest Town/Resort York.
Directions From York via Bishopthorpe or Copmanthorpe. Follow signs for 'Acaster Airfield'.
Acreage 11 **Open** March–November
Access Good **Site** Level
Sites available Total 120.
Facilities
Nearby facilities
York.
Near river. Good centre for visiting York, Yorkshire Dales, North Yorkshire Moors, Wolds, etc.

YORK
Swallow Hall Caravan Park, Swallow Hall, Crockey Hill, York YO1 4SG.
Tel. 448219 Std. 01904
Nearest Town/Resort York.
Directions A64 then turn south on A19 between York and Selby then turn east at Crockey Hill, to Wheldrake – Site 2 miles.
Acreage 5 **Open** March–October
Access Good **Site** Level
Sites available Total 30.
Facilities
Nearby facilities
York.
10 mins from York city centre, woodland walks and Yorkshire Moors. 18 hole golf course on site.

SOUTH YORKS

BARNSLEY
Cinderhill Farm, Cawthorne, Barnsley, South Yorkshire, S75 4JA.
Nearest Town/Resort Barnsley/Penistone.
Directions Take A635 to Cawtrorne, at Post Office take Dorton Road. At the end of 30 mph limit turn left down a concrete lane to site.
Acreage 2 **Open** All year
Access Good **Site** Level
Sites available
Facilities
Barnsley.
Streamside, grassy site in lovely countryside. Ideal for touring.

BARNSLEY
Earth's Wood Caravan Park, Bank End Lane, Barnsley Road, Clayton West, Huddersfield, South Yorks, HD8 9LJ.
Tel. 863211/864266 Std. 01484
Nearest Town/Resort Huddersfield.
Directions From Huddersfield, follow the A635 onto the A636. Turn off the A636 at Junction Inn, pass through Clayton West. Site is 1 mile from the A636 junction.
Acreage 2 **Open** March–October
Access Good **Site** Level
Sites available Total 45.

Facilities
Nearby facilities
Huddersfield/Barnsley.
Flat, grassy site, sheltered by a band of trees. Close to swimming baths and a water sports centre.

BARNSLEY

Greensprings Touring Park, Rockley Lane, Worsbrough, Barnsley, South Yorks, S75 3DS.
Tel. 288298 Std. 01226
Nearest Town/Resort Barnsley.
Directions Junction 36 on M1. A61 to Barnsley, take left turn after $\frac{1}{2}$ mile signed to Pilley. Site is $\frac{1}{4}$ mile along this road.
Acreage 4 **Open** April–October
Access Good **Site** Lev/Slope
Sites available Total 60.
Facilities
Nearby facilities
Barnsley.
Country site, well wooded, pleasant walks. Convenient from M1. Ideal location for Sheffield venues.

HATFIELD

Hatfield Marina, Old Thorne Road, Hatfield, Doncaster, South Yorkshire.
Tel. 841572 Std. 01302
Nearest Town/Resort Doncaster.
Directions Leave the M18 at junction 5, follow the A18 into Hatfield. Signposted at entrance to the village.
Open All Year
Access Good **Site** Level
Sites available Total 45.
Facilities
Nearby facilities
Doncaster.
Part of a watersports centre – visitors centre, craft available for public hire. Sailing, canoeing and wind-surfing.

ROTHERHAM

Thrybergh Country Park, Doncaster Road, Thrybergh, Rotherham, South Yorks, S65 4NU.
Tel. 850353 Std. 01709
Nearest Town/Resort Rotherham.
Directions Situated 5 miles from the A1(M) and M1 and 3 miles from the M18 on the main Rotherham to Doncaster road (A630). Between the villages of Thrybergh and Hooton Roberts.
Acreage 1$\frac{3}{4}$ **Open** April–September
Access Good **Site** Level
Sites available Total 18.
Facilities
Nearby facilities
Rotherham.
Within a country park. 35 acre lake with fly fishing, sailing, canoeing and wind-surfing.

SHEFFIELD

Fox Hagg Farm, Lodge Lane, Rivelin, South Yorkshire.
Tel. 230 5589 Std. 0114
Nearest Town/Resort Sheffield.
Directions Off A57.
Acreage 2 **Open** April–October
Access Good **Site** Level
Sites available Total 60.
Facilities
Nearby facilities
Sheffield.
Outskirts of Peak District. Ideal touring, scenic views.

WEST YORKS

BINGLEY

Harden & Bingley Caravan Park, Goit Stock Lane, Harden, Bingley, West Yorks.
Tel. 273810 Std. 01535
Nearest Town/Resort Bingley.
Directions From Bingley take the B6429 to Harden Village. Turn left onto Wilsden Road, just before bridge turn right into Goit Stock Lane and follow signs.
Acreage 1$\frac{1}{2}$ **Open** April–October
Access Poor **Site** Level
Sites available Total 20.
Facilities
Bingley.
Beautiful, secluded valley with woodland and a stream. Lovely walks.

HEBDEN BRIDGE

Pennine Camp Site, High Greenwood House, Heptonstall, Hebden Bridge, W. Yorks.
Tel. 842287 Std. 01422
Nearest Town/Resort Hebden Bridge.
Directions From Hebden Bridge take Heptonstall road then follow tent and caravan signs.
Acreage 5 **Open** All year
Access Good **Site** Sloping
Sites available Total 50.
Facilities
Nearby facilities
Hebden Bridge.

KEIGHLEY

Springs Farm Caravan Park, Lothersdale, Keighley, West Yorkshire.
Tel. 632533 Std. 01535
Nearest Town/Resort Skipton.
Directions Main Keighley/Skipton road, turn onto Colne road. Proceed for $\frac{1}{4}$ mile to Crosshills, turn right to Lothersdale and follow caravan signs on roadside, for 3$\frac{1}{4}$ miles.
Acreage 3$\frac{1}{2}$ **Open** April–October
Access Good **Site** Sloping
Sites available Total 37.
Facilities
Nearby facilities
Skipton/Keighley.
Picturesque site overlooking hills & trout lake. Ideal for touring Dales and Moors, etc. Booking essential at all times. Regret no hikers or organised parties.

KEIGHLEY

Upwood Holiday Park, Upwood House, Blackmoor Road, Oxenhope, Near Haworth, Keighley, West, Yorks, BD22 9SS.
Tel. 643254 Std. 01535
Nearest Town/Resort Haworth.
Directions A629 Keighley/Halifax to Denholme. Just before village, left onto B6141 Oxenhope. Turn right in 1$\frac{1}{2}$ miles into Blackmoor Road, site is on the right in $\frac{3}{4}$ mile.
Acreage 12 **Open** April–October
Access Good **Site** Level
Sites available Total 70.
Facilities
Nearby facilities
Keighley.
Ideal for touring and walking. Country, panoramic views, Bronte country. Close to Yorkshire Dales, Worth Valley and steam railway.

LEEDS

Roundhay Caravan & Camping Site, Elmete Lane, Roundhay, Leeds, West Yorkshire, LS8 2LG.
Tel. 265 2354 Std. 0113
Nearest Town/Resort Leeds.
Directions A58 from the city centre (4$\frac{1}{4}$ miles). A6120 from west to A58 junction. A1 to A58 from north. A1 and M62 from south and east.
Acreage 7 **Open** April–December
Access Good **Site** Level
Sites available Total 60.
Facilities
Nearby facilities
Leeds City.
Roundhay Park with Tropical World. Temple Newsam House, Kirkstall Abbey and many other places of interest.

SHIPLEY

Crook Farm Caravan Park, Glen Road, Baildon, Bradford, West Yorkshire.
Tel. Bradford 584339 Std. 01274
Nearest Town/Resort Shipley.
Directions 2 miles from Shipley, 1 mile Baildon, follow Glen signs from Baildon.
Open 7th March–7th Janurary
Access Good **Site** Sloping
Sites available Total 30.
Facilities
Nearby facilities
Shipley.
Scenic views. Good touring country.

WALES

CLWYD

ABERGELE

Ty Mawr Holiday Park, Towyn Road, Towyn, Abergele, Clwyd, LL22 9HG.
Tel. 832079 Std. 01745
Nearest Town/Resort Abergele.
Directions On the A548 between Rhyl and Abergele, ½ mile west of Towyn.
Acreage 27
Access Good **SitM●Level**
Sites available Total 485.
Facilities
Nearby facilities
Abergele.
A short distance from the sandy beach of Colwyn Bay, close to Snowdonia.

COLWYN BAY

Dinarth Hall, Rhos-on-Sea, Colwyn Bay, Clwyd.
Tel. 548203 Std. 01492
Nearest Town/Resort Rhos on Sea.
Directions A55 to Rhos-on-Sea then B5115.
Acreage 4 **Open** Whitsun–September
Access Good **Site** Level
Sites available Total 50.
Facilities
Nearby facilities
Colwyn Bay.
Close to sea and within reach of Snowdonia.

COLWYN BAY

Bron-y-Wendon Touring Caravan Park, Wern Road, Llanddulas, Colwyn Bay, Clwyd, LL22 8HG.
Tel. 512903 Std. 01492
Nearest Town/Resort Colwyn Bay.
Directions Follow the A55 into North Wales and take the Llanddulas junction (A547). Follow the tourist information signs to the park.
Acreage 8 **Open** 21 March–October
Access Good **Site** Lev/Slope
Sites available Total 130.
Facilities
Nearby facilities
Colwyn Bay.
All pitches have coastal views. 300yds to beach. Site is ideal for seaside and touring.

COLWYN BAY

Ty-Ucha Farm, Tan-y-Graig Road, Llysfaen, Colwyn Bay, Clwyd, LL29 8UD.
Tel. Colwyn Bay 517051 Std. 01492
Nearest Town/Resort Colwyn Bay.
Directions A55 then the A547 to Llysfaen, turn to Highlands Road, then Tan-y-Graig Road. 3 miles south east of Colwyn Bay.
Acreage 1 **Open** May–October
Site Level
Sites available Total 20.
Facilities
Colwyn Bay.
Ideal for touring.

COLWYN BAY

Westwood Caravan Park, Ffordd Y Llan, Llysfaen, Colwyn Bay, North Wales.
Tel. 517410 Std. 01492
Nearest Town/Resort Colwyn Bay.
Directions A547 from A55 and follow sign for Old Colwyn, turn into Highlands road.
Open Easter–October
Access Good **Site** Sloping
Sites available Total 88.
Facilities
Nearby facilities
Colwyn Bay.
Central for several attractions, sea and country views.

CORWEN

Y Felin Caravan Park, Llandrillo, Corwen, Clwyd, LL21 0TD.
Tel. 84333 Std. 01490
Nearest Town/Resort Bala.
Directions A5 to Corwen, take the B4401 into Llandrillo Village, keep left after the church, park in 500yds.
Acreage 2 **Open** Easter–October
Access Good **Site** Level
Sites available
Facilities
Nearby facilities
Wrexham.
Very quiet and private, alongside a river.

CORWEN

Glan Ceirn Caravan Park, Ty Nant, Corwen, Clwyd, LL21 0RT.
Tel. 420346 Std. 01490
Nearest Town/Resort Corwen/Betws-y-Coed.
Directions Between Corwen and Betws-y-Coed just off the A5. Coming from Betws-y-Coed take the second right after Cerrigydrudion over a samll bridge and 300yds along the lane. From Corwen turn left after Glan Ceirn signs over a small bridge, 300yds on the left.
Acreage 1 **Open** March–October
Access Good **Site** Level
Sites available Total 10.
Facilities
Nearby facilities
Ruabon.
Picturesque site bordering Snowdonia National Park. Trout fishing on site. Ideal for touring North and West Wales.

CORWEN

Hendwr Caravan Park, Llandrillo, Corwen, Clwyd, LL21 0SN.
Tel. 440210 Std. 01490
Nearest Town/Resort Corwen/Bala.
Directions From Corwen (A5) take the B4401 for 4 miles, turn right at sign Hendwr. Site is on the right in ¼ mile. From Bala take the A494 for 1½ miles, turn right onto the B4401 via Llandrillo. Site is 1 mile north on the left.
Acreage 2¼ **Open** April–October
Access Good **Site** Level
Sites available Total 60.
Facilities
Nearby facilities
Ruabon.
Alongside a river, good walking, pony trekking and fishing. Wonderful views and an excellent touring centre for North Wales.

CORWEN

Llawr-Betws Caravan Park, Corwen, Clwyd, LL21 0HD.
Tel. 460224 Std. 01490
Nearest Town/Resort Corwen/Bala.
Directions From A5 past Corwen, turn left at second traffic lights onto the A494 Bala road. Site is signposted in 2 miles.
Acreage 3 **Open** March–October
Access Good **Site** Level
Sites available Total 65.
Facilities
Nearby facilities
Ruabon.
Fishing on site. Outdoor and indoor games room.

DENBIGH

Caer-Mynydd Caravan Park, Saron, Denbigh, Clwyd LL16 4TL.
Tel. 550302 Std. 01745
Nearest Town/Resort Denbigh.
Directions Ruthin to Denbigh A525 turn by swimming pool Denbigh for Prion and Saron approx 4¼ miles, near Saron Chapel.
Acreage 2 **Open** March–October
Access Good **Site** Level

Sites available Total 29.
Facilities
Nearby facilities
Rhyl.
Fishing, boating, 10 minute drive to beach. Sports area and swimming pool 4¼ miles.

DENBIGH
Station House Caravan Park, Bodfari, Denbigh, Clwyd, LL16 4DA.
Tel. 710372 Std. 01745
Nearest Town/Resort Denbigh.
Directions From the A541 Mold to Denbigh road, turn onto the B5429 in the direction of Tremeirchion. Site is immediately on the left by cream house.
Acreage 2 **Open** April–October
Access Good **Site** Level
Sites available Total 26.
Facilities
Nearby facilities
Rhyl.
Attractive site with scenic views. Ideal touring centre. Offa's Dyke path 400yds. Close to two inns (400yds).

DENBIGH
Tyn-yr-Eithin, Mold Road, Denbigh, Clwyd, LL16 4BH.
Tel. 813211
Nearest Town/Resort Denbigh.
Acreage 6 **Open** April–October
Access Good **Site** Level
Sites available Total 80.
Facilities
Nearby facilities
Rhyl.
Scenic views.

LLANGOLLEN
Pont Bell, Glan Llyn, Glyn Ceiriog, Llangollen, Clwyd.
Tel. 718320 Std. 01691
Nearest Town/Resort Llangollen.
Acreage 1 **Open** Easter–September
Access Good **Site** Level
Sites available Total 7.
Facilities
Nearby facilities
Chirk.
Alongside a river. Ideal for touring.

LLANGOLLEN
Wern Isaf Farm, Llangollen, Clwyd.
Tel. 860632 Std. 01978
Nearest Town/Resort Llangollen.
Directions Up behind Bridgend Hotel over canal bridg turn right into Wern road first farm on right.
Acreage 4 **Open** Easter–October
Access Good **Site** Lev/Slope
Sites available Total 40.
Facilities
Nearby facilities
Ruabon.
Scenic views, ideal walking, touring.

MOLD
Fron Farm, Hendre, Mold, Clwyd.
Tel. 741217 Std. 01352
Nearest Town/Resort Mold.
Directions From Mold take Denbigh road A541. 1 mile past Hendre turn right for Rhes-y-cae. Fron Farm is 3rd turning on right (including farm lanes).
Acreage 3 **Open** April–October
Access Good **Site** Level
Sites available Total 45.
Facilities
Nearby facilities
Flint.
Scenic views of the Clwydian Mountains. Ideal for touring. Free hot showers.

PRESTATYN
Nant Mill Farm Caravan & Tenting Park, Nant Mill, Prestatyn, Clwyd, LL19 9LY.
Tel. 852360 Std. 01745
Nearest Town/Resort Prestatyn.
Directions ½ mile east of Prestatyn on A548 coast road.
Acreage 5 **Open** Easter–October
Access Good **Site** Lev/Slope
Sites available Total 150.
Facilities
Nearby facilities
Prestatyn.
Near town shops. ½ mile beach, ideal to tour north Wales. Hotel bar meals 200yds.

PRESTATYN
Presthaven Sands Holiday Park, Gronant, Prestatyn, Clwyd, LL19 9TT.
Tel. 856471 Std. 01745
Nearest Town/Resort Prestatyn.
Directions Take the A548 out of Prestatyn towards Gronant. The park is signposted left, then entrance is ½ mile further on the right.
Acreage 12 **Open** Easter–November
Access Good **Site** Level
Sites available Total 100.
Facilities
Nearby facilities
Prestatyn.
Alongside 2 miles of beaches and sand dunes. Very flat park.

PRESTATYN
Tan-Y-Don Caravan Park, 263 Victoria Road, Prestatyn, Clwyd, LL19 7UT.
Tel. 853749 Std. 01745
Nearest Town/Resort Prestatyn/Rhyl.
Directions Main A548 coast road between Prestatyn and Rhyl – close to Ffrith beach.
Open 7th March–October
Access Good **Site** Level
Sites available Total 8.
Facilities
Nearby facilities
Prestatyn.
Near beach, ideal touring for coastal and inland roads. Licensed club only 100yds.

RHYL
Henllys Farm Camping & Touring Site, Towyn Road, Towyn, Abergele, Clwyd.
Tel. 351208 Std. 01745
Nearest Town/Resort Rhyl.
Directions On A548 south side, near Towyn.
Acreage 11 **Open** Whitsun–September
Access Good **Site** Level
Sites available Total 280.
Facilities
Rhyl.
½ mile from beach.

RUABON
James' Caravan Park, Ruabon, Nr. Wrexham, Clwyd, LL14 6DW.
Tel. 820148 Std. 01978
Nearest Town/Resort Llangollen.
Directions 5 miles south of Wrexham, 5 miles east of Llangollen on the junction of A483 and the A539 Llangollen road.
Acreage 8 **Open** All Year
Access Good **Site** Lev/Slope
Sites available Total 40.
Facilities
Nearby facilities
Ideal accessable touring park.

RUTHIN
Llanbenwch Farm, Llanfair D.C. Ruthin Clwyd, LL15 2SH.
Tel. 702340 Std. 018242
Nearest Town/Resort Ruthin.
Directions On A525 3 miles south of Ruthin.
Open All year
Site Sloping
Sites available
Facilities
Nearby facilities
Wrexham.
Beautiful scenery facing Clwydian range.

ST. ASAPH
Penisar Mynydd Caravan Park, Caerwys Road, Rhuallt, St. Asaph, Clwyd, LL17 0TY.
Tel. 582227 Std. 01745
Nearest Town/Resort Rhyl/Prestatyn.
Directions From Chester take the A55 expressway. 1 mile past Sundawn Nurseries and Teapot Cafe take a right turn. From Conway take the first left at the top of Rhuallt Hill. Well signed off the A55 expressway.
Acreage 2 **Open** Easter–October
Access Good **Site** Level
Sites available Total 30.
Facilities
Nearby facilities
Rhyl/Prestatyn.
Scenic views and walks, ideal for touring.

WREXHAM
Plassey Touring Caravan & Leisure Park, Eyton, Wrexham, Clwyd.
Tel. 780277 Std. 01978
Nearest Town/Resort Wrexham.
Directions 4 miles from Wrexham (south) take the A483 Chester/Oswestry by-pass. Turn left onto the B5426 for 'Plassey', follow brown and cream signs.
Acreage 9 **Open** March–8 November
Access Good **Site** Level
Sites available Total 120.
Facilities
Nearby facilities
Wrexham.
Ideal for family holidays and touring North Wales. Many on-site amenities. Beautiful countryside. Toilets only for the disabled and motorcycles accepted but not on the field. Golf and fishing on site.

WREXHAM
Bangor-on-Dee Racecourse, Overton Road, Bangor-on-Dee, Wrexham, Clwyd, LL13 0DA.
Tel. 780740 Std. 01978
Nearest Town/Resort Wrexham.
Directions Turn off the A525 Wrexham to Whitchurch road through Bangor Village onto the Overton road (B5426).
Acreage 3 **Open** End March–October
Access Good **Site** Level
Sites available Total 100.
Facilities
Nearby facilities
Wrexham.
Quiet site looking across the River Dee to the Welsh mountains.

DYFED

ABERAERON

Brynarian Caravan Park, Cross Inn, Llanon, Dyfed, SY23 5NA.
Tel. 272231 Std. 01974
Nearest Town/Resort Aberaeron.
Directions Llanryhstud turn on the B4337 to Cross Inn. Take the first right then left at crossroads into the park.
Acreage 2 **Open** March–October
Access Good **Site** Level
Sites available Total 12.
Facilities
Nearby facilities
Aberystwyth.

ABERAERON

Wide Horizons Caravan Park, Aberaeron, Dyfed, SA46 0ET.
Tel. 570043 Std. 01545
Nearest Town/Resort Aberaeron.
Directions ¼ mile south of Aberaeron on the A487 Aberystwyth to Cardigan coast road.
Acreage 2 **Open** April–October
Access Good **Site** Sloping
Sites available Total 30.
Facilities
Nearby facilities
Aberystwyth.

ABERPORTH

Caerfelin Caravan Park, Aberporth, Dyfed.
Tel. 810540 Std. 01239
Nearest Town/Resort Aberporth.
Directions Turn off A487 at Blaenannerch onto B433, enter village of Aberporth. Turn right at St. Cynwyls church, park 200 yards on left.
Acreage 2 **Open** April–September
Access Good **Site** Lev/Slope
Sites available Total 16.
Facilities
Nearby facilities
Carmarthen.
Well sheltered site overlooking sea. Some five minutes walk to sandy beaches.

ABERPORTH

Pilbach Caravan Park, Bettws Evan, Aberporth, Dyfed.
Tel. 851434 Std. 01239
Nearest Town/Resort Aberporth.
Directions From A487 take B4333 (Newcaste Emlyn road), first left, first right, first left.
Acreage 15 **Open** March–October
Access Good **Site** Level
Sites available Total 65.
Facilities
Nearby facilities
Aberystwyth.
B.H.P.A. 5 ticks grading and Dragon award park.

ABERYSTWYTH

Aberystwyth Holiday Village, Penparcau Road, Aberystwyth, Dyfed.
Tel. 624211/2 Std. 01970
Nearest Town/Resort Aberystwyth.
Directions Take A487 out of Aberystwyth, south ½ mile.
Acreage 6 **Open** March–October
Access Good **Site** Level
Sites available Total 152.
Facilities
Nearby facilities
Aberystwyth.
Panoramic views of Aberystwyth, Cardigan Bay and the Rheidol Valley.

ABERYSTWYTH

Ocean View, North Beach, Clarach Bay, Aberystwyth, Dyfed.
Tel. 623361 Std. 01970
Nearest Town/Resort Aberystwyth.
Directions Take the A487 Aberystwyth to Machynlleth toad. Just north of Aberystwyth turn onto the B4572 for Clarach Bay. Ocean View is on the right as you head for the beach.
Open March–October
Access Good **Site** Level
Sites available Total 24.
Facilities
Nearby facilities
Aberystwyth.
Small select park, short walk to popular beach. Glorious views, ideal touring area of magic Mid-Wales.

ABERYSTWYTH

Riverside Park, Lon Glanfred, Llandre, Nr. Aberystwyth, Dyfed.
Tel. 820070 Std. 01970
Nearest Town/Resort Aberystwyth/Borth.
Directions North of Aberystwyth on the A487, take the B4353 to Llandre/Borth. After Llandre Post Office Stores take the second right into Lon Glanfred. Entrance in 500yds.
Open March–October
Access Good **Site** Level
Sites available Total 30.
Facilities
Nearby facilities
Borth.
Peaceful, secluded family park beside a trout stream. Only 2 miles from beach.

ABERYSTWYTH

Rhoslawdden, Moriah, Capel Seion, Aberwystwyth, Dyfed, SY23 4EA.
Tel. 612585 Std. 01970
Nearest Town/Resort Aberystwyth.
Directions Aberystywyth to Devils Bridge 3 miles from Aberystwyth.
Acreage 2
Access Good **Site** Level
Sites available
Facilities
Nearby facilities
Aberystwyth.

AMROTH

Little Kings Park, Ludchurch, Nr. Amroth, Dyfed.
Tel. 330 Std. 0183 483
Nearest Town/Resort Amroth/Saundersfoot.
Directions A477 south west from St Clears on Tenby road. After Llanteg Village and petrol station turn left signposted Amroth/Ludchurch. After 1 mile turn right to Ludchurch and site is at top of hill on left.
Acreage 10 **Open** Easter–September
Access Good **Site** Level
Sites available Total 85.
Facilities
Nearby facilities
Kilgetty.
1¼ miles to beach, views of sea. Covered, heated swimming pool.

AMROTH

Pantglas Farm, Tavernspite, Whitland, Dyfed, SA34 0NS.
Tel. 618 Std. 01834 83
Nearest Town/Resort Amroth.
Directions A477 towards Tenby take the B4314 at Red Roses crossroads to Tavernspite 1¼ miles, take the middle road at the village pump. Pantglas is ½ mile down on the left.
Acreage 3¼ **Open** Easter–October
Access Good **Site** Level
Sites available Total 45.
Facilities
Nearby facilities
Whitland.
Pretty, family run, Wales in Bloom Award Winning Park. Clean toilets and showers, pets and a super play area. Caravan storage facility. Short walk to village shop. Easy reach of Tenby, Saundersfoot and Amroth.

BORTH

Brynowen Holiday Park, Borth, Dyfed, SY24 5LS.
Tel. 871366 Std. 01970
Nearest Town/Resort Aberystwyth.
Directions Take B4353 off the A487, Aberystwyth to Machynlleth road. Brynowen is on the left just before Borth.
Acreage ¾ **Open** Easter–October
Access Good **Site** Level
Sites available Total 18.
Facilities S
Nearby facilities
Borth.
Beach, scenic views, golf, fishing, boating and other water sports. Limited facilities for the disabled. Bar snacks available.

BORTH

Glanlerry Caravan Park, Borth, Dyfed, SY24 5LU.
Tel. 871413 Std. 01970
Nearest Town/Resort Borth.
Open April–October
Access Good **Site** Level
Sites available Total Good.
Facilities M
Nearby facilities
Borth.
Sheltered touring area, alongside a river bank with spectacular scenery. Beach ½ mile.

BORTH

Ty Craig Holiday Park, Llancynfelin, Nr. Borth, Dyfed, SY20 8PU.
Tel. 832339 Std. 01970
Nearest Town/Resort Borth.
Directions 2 miles off the A487 at Trer'ddol onto the B4353. On the left hand side of road by the church.
Acreage 2 **Open** March–October
Access Good **Site** Level
Sites available Total 20.
Facilities S
Nearby facilities
Near to beach for swimming and surfing. Near to mountains for walking and hiking.

BORTH

Cambrian Coast Holiday Park, Borth, Dyfed, SY24 5JU.
Tel. 871233 Std. 01970
Nearest Town/Resort Borth.
Directions Adjoining sea front, B4353 Borth road (off A487 Machynlleth to Aberystwyth road). Entrance to site is 1¼ miles north of Borth Village.
Open March–October
Access Good **Site** Level
Sites available
Facilities S
Nearby facilities
Borth.
Near the beach, adjacent to a golf course and a nature reserve. Ideal touring base.

BORTH

The Mill House Caravan & Camping Park, Dolybont, Borth Ceredigion, Dyfed SY24 5LX.
Tel. 871481 Std. 01970
Nearest Town/Resort Borth.
Directions On Aberystwyth/Machynlleth road A487, turn west at Rhydypennau Garage corner (between Talybont and Bow Street) onto B4353 through Llandre. Proceed 1 mile, on Borth B4353 stop under railway bridge, fork right into Dolybont Village singposted. First right before hump-back bridge in Village.
Acreage 7 **Open** Easter–October
Access Good **Site** Level
Sites available Total 40.
Facilities
Nearby facilities
Borth.
Delightful site beside stream, own fishing and river swimming. 1 mile Borth seaside, safe bathing, rock pools and sand hills.

BURRY PORT

Shoreline Leisure Home Park, Burry Port, Dyfed, SA16 0HD.
Nearest Town/Resort Burry Port.
Directions Leave the M4 at junction 48 onto the A4138 to Llanelli. Then take A484 to Burry Port and follow harbour signs.
Acreage ¼ **Open** April–October
Access Good **Site** Level
Sites available Total 10.
Facilities S
Nearby facilities
Burry Port.
Adjoining beach. Near to a country park and harbour. Central for South Wales.

CARDIGAN

Allt-y-Coed, St. Dogmaels, Cardigan, Dyfed.
Tel. 612673 Std. 01239
Nearest Town/Resort Cardigan.
Directions Cardigan/St. Dogmaels/ Poppit Sands coast road from Poppit Sands, past Youth Hostel for 1 mile. Over the cattle grid and follow coastal footpath signs.
Acreage 2 **Open** All Year
Access Good **Site** Level
Sites available
Facilities
Nearby facilities
Fishguard.
Pembrokeshire coast path goes past the site. Dolphins, seals, falcons, rare birds, wild flowers and panoramic views.

CARDIGAN

Llety Caravan Park, Tresaith, Aberporth, Cardigan, Dyfed.
Tel. 810354 Std. 01239
Nearest Town/Resort Aberporth.
Directions Take the B4333 Newcastle Emlyn to Aberporth road. Turn right to Tresaith in 1½ miles, second park on the left.
Acreage 2 **Open** March–October
Access Good **Site** Level
Sites available Total 20.
Facilities
Nearby facilities
Aberystwyth.
Scenic views over Cardigan Bay. 200yds from the beach.

CARDIGAN

Penralltllyn, Cilgerran, Cardigan, Dyfed, SA43 2PR.
Tel. 682350 Std. 01239
Nearest Town/Resort Cardigan.
Directions Cardigan (4¼ miles) to Llechryd Bridge (on Cardigan/Newcastle Emlyn road). Follow signs from bridge to caravan park (1¼ miles).
Acreage 1¼ **Open** Easter–November
Access Good **Site** Lev/Slope
Sites available Total 20.
Facilities
Nearby facilities
Carmarthen.
Beaches, fishing in River Teifi, canoeing also in the river or on the farm pond. Walks and an old railway etc. nearby.

CARDIGAN

Tygwyn Caravan Park, Tygwyn, Mwnt, Cardigan, Dyfed, SA43 1QH.
Tel. 612164 Std. 01239
Nearest Town/Resort Cardigan.
Directions Follow the Mwnt signs from Cardigan 5 miles.
Acreage 1 **Open** April–October
Access Good **Site** Level
Sites available
Facilities
Nearby facilities
Carmarthen.
Near beach, quiet, ideal touring, scenic views, farm animals. Sea the seals and dolphins in the Bay.

CARMARTHEN

Coedhirion Farm Parc, Llanddarog, Carmarthen, Dyfed, SA32 8BH.
Tel. 275666 Std. 01267
Nearest Town/Resort Carmarthen.
Directions Just off the A48 dual carriageway, 9 miles west of M4 junction 49 and 6 miles east of Carmarthen. Near the village of Llanddarog.
Acreage 3 **Open** Easter–Christmas
Access Good **Site** Level
Sites available Total 20.
Facilities
Nearby facilities
Carmarthen.
Very conveniently situated for overnight stays, or as a base for touring Pembrokeshire and Gower.

DEVILS BRIDGE

Erwbarfe Farm, Devils Bridge, Aberystwyth, Dyfed.
Tel. Ponterwyd 665 Std. 0197 085
Nearest Town/Resort Aberystwyth.
Directions On A4120 midway between Devils Bridge and Ponterwyd.
Acreage 5 **Open** March–October
Access Good **Site** Level
Sites available Total 50.
Facilities
Nearby facilities
Aberystwyth.
Narrow Gauge railway at Devils Bridge, well known tourist area.

DEVILS BRIDGE

The Woodlands Caravan Park, Devils Bridge, Aberystwyth, Dyfed, SY23 3JW.
Tel. 890233 Std. 01970
Nearest Town/Resort Devils Bridge.
Directions 12 miles East of Aberystwyth on A4120 in Devils Bridge village and 300yds from bridge. Or 3 miles S.W. of Ponterwyd, turn off A44 at Ponterwyd.
Acreage 8 **Open** Easter–October
Access Good **Site** Level
Sites available Total 60.
Facilities
Nearby facilities
Devils Bridge.
Quiet country site adjoining farm. Ideal for walking,bird watching touring, fishing.

FISHGUARD

Fishguard Bay Caravan Park, Dinas Cross, Newport, Dyfed, SA42 0YD.
Tel. 415 Std. 013486
Nearest Town/Resort Fishguard.
Directions Take A478 Cardigan road from Fishguard for 1½ miles. Turn left at sign.
Acreage 5 **Open** March–December
Access Good **Site** Lev/Slope
Sites available Total 50.
Facilities
Nearby facilities
Fishguard.
Superb cliff top location offering excellent views and walks along this 'Heritage' coast of Pembrokeshire.

FISHGUARD

Gwaun Vale Holiday Touring Park, LLanychaer, Fishguard, Dyfed SA65 9TA.
Tel. 874698 Std. 01348
Nearest Town/Resort Fishguard.
Directions From Fishguard take the B4313 Gwaun Valley/Llanychaer Road for

$1\frac{1}{4}$ miles, touring park on the right hand side.
Acreage 2 **Open** March–9th January
Access Good **Site** Level
Sites available Total 31.
Facilities
Nearby facilities
Fishguard.
Ideal touring park, peaceful and quiet, with beautiful views, walks and within easy reach of beaches. British Graded 4 Ticks. AA 3 pennants.

HAVERFORDWEST
Brandy Brook Caravan & Camping Site, Rhyndaston, Hayscastle, Haverfordwest, Dyfed.
Tel. 840272 Std. 01348
Nearest Town/Resort Haverfordwest.
Directions A487 from Haverfordwest, signposted Brandy Brook at Roch Motel. About $3\frac{1}{4}$ miles from that sign.
Acreage 20 **Open** Easter–September
Access Adequate **Site** Slight Slope
Sites available Total 41.
Facilities
Haverfordwest.
In a pretty valley near a trout stream. Natural countryside with no built up areas near.

HAVERFORDWEST
Creampots Touring Caravan & Camping Park, Havenway, Broad Haven, Haverfordwest, Dyfed, SA62 3TU.
Tel. 781776 Std. 01437
Nearest Town/Resort Haverfordwest.
Directions Take B4131 Broad Haven road from Haverfordwest to Broadway (5 miles). Turn left and Creampots is the second site on the right (500yds).
Acreage 7 **Open** Easter–October
Access Good **Site** Level
Sites available Total 65.
Facilities
Nearby facilities
Haverfordwest.
Ideal touring base, $1\frac{1}{4}$ miles from safe, sandy beach and coastal path at Broad Haven.

HAVERFORDWEST
Redlands Touring Caravan Park, Little Haven, Haverfordwest, Dyfed. SA62 3UU.
Tel. 781301 Std. 01437
Nearest Town/Resort Little Haven.
Directions $6\frac{1}{4}$ miles southwest of Haverfordwest, on B4327 Dale Road.
Acreage 5 **Open** Easter–Mid September
Access Good **Site** Level
Sites available Total 60.
Facilities
Nearby facilities
Haverfordwest.
Small well run site in Pembrokeshire Natural Park, within easy reach of coastal park and superb sandy beaches.

HAVERFORDWEST
Pelcomb Cross Farm Caravan Site, Pelcomb Cross Farm, Pelcomb Cross, Haverfordwest, Dyfed.
Tel. Camrose 710431 Std. 01437
Nearest Town/Resort Haverfordwest.
Directions On the A487 from Haverfordwest to St. Davids. 3 miles from Haverfordwest.
Acreage 2 **Open** March–December
Access Good **Site** Level
Sites available Total 30.
Facilities

Haverfordwest.
Central for beaches, National Park and numerous tourist attractions.

HAVERFORDWEST
Scamford Caravan Park, Keeston, Haverfordwest, Pembrokeshire, Dyfed, SA62 6HN.
Tel. 710304
Nearest Town/Resort Newgale.
Directions From Haverfordwest take the A487 towards St. Davids. In approx. $4\frac{1}{4}$ miles turn right at Keeston, then follow signs for Scamford Caravan Park.
Open April–October
Access Good **Site** Level
Sites available Total 5.
Facilities
Nearby facilities
Haverfordwest.
Ideal location for many beaches, coast path, Preseli Hills, Milford Haven Waterway, etc..

HAVERFORDWEST
The Rising Sun, St. David's Road, Pelcomb Bridge, Haverfordwest, Dyfed.
Tel. 765171 Std. 01437
Nearest Town/Resort Haverfordwest.
Directions Take St. David's Rd from Haverfordwest. Site is about $1\frac{1}{2}$ miles on left hand side at the bottom of a hill just past Pelcomb Bridge sign.
Acreage $2\frac{1}{4}$ **Open** April–October
Access Good **Site** Lev/Slope
Sites available Total 30.
Facilities
Nearby facilities
Haverfordwest.
Close to many quiet beautiful beaches, ideal centre for touring.

KILGETTY
Heritage Court Caravan Park, Heritage Court, Pleasant Valley, Stepaside, Near Narberth, Dyfed.
Tel. 812464 Std. 01834
Nearest Town/Resort Tenby.
Directions Carmarthen/Red Roses/ Stepaside road. At the start of dual carriageway turn left off A477 for Stepaside. Left over bridge, follow signs for Wisemans Bridge, signposts for Heritage Court.
Acreage 4 **Open** March–November
Access Good **Site** Level
Sites available Total 150.
Facilities
Nearby facilities
Kilgetty.
Near beach, alongside stream in a scenic, wooded valley. Historic walks and ancient monuments on site.

KILGETTY
Masterland Farm Touring Caravan & Tent Park, Broadmoor, Kilgetty, Pembrokeshire.
Tel. 813298 Std. 01834
Nearest Town/Resort Tenby.
Directions After Carmarthen take main A40 to St. Clears, then take the A477 to Broadmoor. Turn right at Cross Inn Public House, Masterland Farm is 300yds on your right.
Acreage 8 **Open** March–October
Access Good **Site** Level
Sites available Total 25.
Facilities
Nearby facilities

Kilgetty.
Ideal touring, close to leisure parks etc..

KILGETTY
Ryelands Caravan Park, Ryelands Lane, Kilgetty, Dyfed.
Tel. 812369 Std. 01834
Nearest Town/Resort Saundersfoot/ Tenby.
Directions Turn left after railway bridge in Kilgetty into Ryelands Lane. Site in $\frac{3}{4}$ mile on the right.
Acreage 5 **Open** March–30 October
Access Good **Site** Lev/Slope
Sites available Total 45.
Facilities
Kilgetty.
Set in open countryside with views to the west, north and east.

LAMPETER
Hafod Brynog Caravan Park, Ystrad Aeron, Felinfach, Lampeter, Dyfed. SA48 7PG.
Tel. 470084 Std. 01570
Nearest Town/Resort Aberearon.
Directions On main A482 Lampeter to Aberaeron road, 5 miles.
Acreage 8 **Open** March–October
Access Good **Site** Lev/Slope
Sites available Total 30.
Facilities
Nearby facilities
Aberystwyth.
Scenic views.

LAMPETER
Moorlands Caravan Park, Llangyby, Nr Lampeter, Dyfed.
Tel. 543 Std. 0157045
Nearest Town/Resort Lampeter.
Directions $4\frac{1}{2}$ miles approx. on the A485 Lampeter to Tregaron road.
Acreage 2 **Open** Easter–October
Access Good **Site** Level
Sites available Total 10.
Facilities
Nearby facilities
Aberystwyth.
Ideal touring centre, 12 miles from Cardigan Bay.

LAUGHARNE
Broadway Caravan Park, Laugharne, Dyfed.
Tel. 427272 Std. 01994
Nearest Town/Resort Laugharne.
Open March–October
Access Good **Site** Level
Sites available
Facilities
Nearby facilities
Whitland.

LITTLE HAVEN
Hasguard Cross Caravan Park, Hasguard Cross, Haverfordwest, Dyfed SA62 3SL.
Tel. 781443 Std. 01437
Nearest Town/Resort Little Haven.
Directions B4327 out of Haverfordwest 7 miles on the Dale road. Turn right Hasguard crossroads. Site entrance 100 yards on right.
Acreage 3 **Open** All Year
Access Good **Site** Level
Sites available Total 60.
Facilities
Nearby facilities
Haverfordwest.
Near many beaches nearest $1\frac{1}{4}$ miles.

LITTLE HAVEN

Howelston Caravan and Camping Site, Littlehaven, Haverfordwest, Dyfed.
Tel. 781253 Std. 01437
Nearest Town/Resort Haverfordwest.
Directions Off B4327 6 miles S.W. of Haverfordwest, turn right at Hasgaurd Cossroads and right again in ¼ mile. Site on left in ½ mile.
Acreage 5 **Open** April–September
Access Good **Site** Lev/Slope
Sites available Total 60.
Facilities
Nearby facilities
Haverfordwest.
1 mile from nearest beach. Site overlooking St. Brides Bay. Freezing and dish washing facilities.

LITTLE HAVEN

South Cockett Caravan and Camping Park, Broadway, Little Haven, Haverfordwest, Dyfed, SA62 3TU.
Tel. 781296/781760 Std. 01437
Nearest Town/Resort Broad Haven.
Directions From Haverfordwest take B4341 road for Broad Haven for about 6 miles, turn left at official camping signs, site 300yds.
Acreage 6 **Open** Easter–October
Access Good **Site** Level
Sites available Total 75.
Facilities
Nearby facilities
Haverfordwest.
Scenic views, ideal touring, near beach, coastal path nearby.

LLANDDEUSANT

Cross Inn and Black Mountain Caravan Park, Cross Inn, Llanddeusant, Llangadog, Dyfed.
Tel. 4621 Std. 01550
Nearest Town/Resort Llandovery.
Directions From Llandovery A40 to Trecastle turn right to Llanddeusant, site on right 9 miles. From B4069 Bryamman to Llangadog road, turn over bridge opposite Three Horseshoes carry on 3 miles.
Acreage 5 **Open** All year
Access Good **Site** Lev/Slope
Sites available Total 40.
Facilities
Nearby facilities
Llangadog.
Area of outstanding natural beauty in Brecon Beacons National Park.

LLANDOVERY

Erwlon Caravan & Camping Site, Llandovery, Dyfed.
Tel. 20332 Std. 01550
Nearest Town/Resort Llandovery.
Directions Adjoining A40 from Brecon to Llandovery.
Acreage 4 **Open** All year
Access Good **Site** Level
Sites available Total 40.
Facilities
Nearby facilities
Llandovery.
In a beautiful part of Wales.

LLANFARIAN

Morfa Bychan Holiday Park, Llanfarian, Aberystwyth, Dyfed.
Tel. 617254 Std. 01970
Nearest Town/Resort Aberystwyth.
Directions 1 mile south of Aberystwyth.
Acreage 5 **Open** April–October
Access Good **Site** Lev/Slope
Sites available Total 60.
Facilities
Nearby facilities
Aberystwyth.
Beach, walking, beautiful countryside.

LLANGRANOG

Greenfields Holiday Park, Plwmp, Llandysul, Dyfed, SA44 6HF.
Tel. 654333 Std. 01239
Nearest Town/Resort Llangranog.
Directions Just off the A487 between Aberaeron and Cardigan at Pentregat on the B4321 to Llangranog.
Acreage 3 **Open** March–10 January
Access Good **Site** Sloping
Sites available Total 50.
Facilities
Nearby facilities
Aberaeron.
Set in 33 acres of beautiful rural surroundings. Just 5 minutes from a golden beach at Llangranog.

LLANON

Woodlands Caravan Park, Llanon, Nr Aberystwyth, Dyfed, SY23 5LX.
Tel. 202342 Std. 01974
Nearest Town/Resort Aberaeron.
Directions 5 miles north of Aberaeron A487. Left at sign.
Acreage 4 **Open** April–October
Access Good **Site** Level
Sites available Total 80.
Facilities
Nearby facilities
Aberystwyth.
250 yards from beach, 300 yards from main road. Tree screened site, small river.

MAENCHLOCHOG

Rosebush Caravan Park, Belle Vue House, Rosebush, Narberth, Dyfed, SA66 7QT.
Tel. 532206 Std. 01437
Nearest Town/Resort Fishguard.
Directions B4313 to A40 passes through Rosebush. 1 mile from B4329, Cardigan to Haverfordwest.
Acreage 1¼ **Open** March–October
Access Good **Site** Level
Sites available Total 50.
Facilities
Nearby facilities
Clynderwen.
Coarse fishing on park.

MANORBIER

Park Farm Caravans, Manorbier, Tenby, Dyfed.
Tel. 871273 (Site Office) Std. 01834
Nearest Town/Resort Tenby.
Directions 5 miles west of Tenby on A4139 take second turning left for Manorbier.
Acreage 7 **Open** Easter–October
Access Good **Site** Level
Sites available Total 70.
Facilities
Nearby facilities
Manorbier.
Footpath to beach. For ENQUIRIES please telephone 01646 672583.

MARLOES

East Hook Farm, Marloes, Haverfordwest, Dyfed.
Tel. 636291 Std. 01646
Nearest Town/Resort Haverfordwest.
Directions From Haverfordwest take B4327 to Dale. Turn off to Marloes and East Hook Farm is 1 mile from Marloes towards Martins Haven on coast path.
Acreage 5 **Open** All Year
Access Good **Site** Level
Sites available Total 5.
Facilities
Nearby facilities
Haverfordwest.
Sea views, near beaches both sides of the Peninsula and on Pembs coastal path.

MILFORD HAVEN

Sandy Haven Caravan Site Limited, Sandy Haven, Herbrandston, Haverfordwest, Dyfed.
Tel. 698844/693180 Std. 01646
Nearest Town/Resort Milford Haven.
Directions A40 to Haverfordwest. A4076 to Milford Haven, follow Dale Rd. to Herbrandston Village ¼ mile.
Acreage 1 **Open** Whitsun–September
Access Good **Site** Lev/Slope
Sites available Total 30.
Facilities
Nearby facilities
Milford Haven.
Sandy beach, river, coastal path, scenic views. In National Park.

NARBERTH

Allensbank, Providence Hill, Narberth, Dyfed, SA67 8RF.
Tel. 860243 Std. 01834
Nearest Town/Resort Narberth.
Directions Take A487 Tenby road, caravan park 1 mile from town on left hand side of road.
Open Easter–September
Access Good **Site** Level
Sites available Total 11.
Facilities
Nearby facilities
Narberth.
Tourist Board Graded 4 Ticks. Bar and pool.

NARBERTH

Dingle Caravan Park, Jesse Road, Narberth, Dyfed, SA67 7DP.
Tel. 860482 Std. 01834
Nearest Town/Resort Amroth.
Open Easter–October
Access Good **Site** Level
Sites available Total 30.
Facilities
Nearby facilities
Narberth.
In the town yet surrounded by fields. Ideal touring, other beautiful beaches and hills within easy distance. Cafe/restaurant and swimming pool nearby.

NARBERTH

Wood Office Caravan & Tent Park, Cold Blow, Narberth, Dyfed, SA67 8RR.
Tel. 860565 Std. 01834
Nearest Town/Resort Narberth.
Directions 3 miles from A40. Ponblewin roundabout, A478, B4314.
Acreage 2 **Open** Good Friday–September
Access Good **Site** Level
Sites available Total 40.
Facilities
Nearby facilities
Narberth.
Scenic views, ideal touring (central Pembrokeshire). Oakwood Park 3 miles.

NARBERTH

New Park, Landshipping, Narberth, Dyfed, SA67 8BG.
Tel. 891284 Std. 01834
Nearest Town/Resort Narberth.
Directions Travelling west, turn left off A40 at Canaston Bridge onto A4075. Turn right at Canaston Bowls towards Martletwy/Landshipping, 2 miles turn right and 200yds turn left. Entrance on left within 1 mile.
Acreage 1 **Open** Easter–October
Access Good **Site** Level
Sites available Total 15.
Facilities
Nearby facilities
Narberth.
Ideal touring, walking, river within 1 mile.

NARBERTH

Noble Court Caravan Park, Redstone Road, Narberth, Dyfed, SA67 7ES.
Tel. 861191 Std. 01834
Nearest Town/Resort Narberth.
Directions ½ mile north of Narberth on B413 road and ½ mile south of A40 on B4313.
Acreage 3 **Open** March–October
Access Good **Site** Lev/Slope
Sites available Total 92.
Facilities
Nearby facilities
Narberth.
Conveniently situated for travel to all Pembrokeshire beaches and countryside also Pembrokeshire National Park. Quiet family caravan park with amenities for all ages.

NEWCASTLE EMLYN

Afon Teifi Caravan and Camping Park, Pentrecagal, Newcastle Emlyn, Dyfed. SA38 9HT.
Tel. 370532 Std. 01559
Nearest Town/Resort Newcastle Emlyn.
Directions 2 miles east on the A484, 100 yards past garage.
Acreage 6 **Open** All Year
Access Good **Site** Level
Sites available Total 110.
Facilities
Nearby facilities
Carmarthen.
Alongside river, ideal touring centre, good family site, ideal for children. W.T.B. Graded 5 Ticks.

NEWGALE

Newgale Beach Holiday Park, Newgale, Haverfordwest, Dyfed, SA62 6BD.
Tel. 710675/710812 Std. 01437
Nearest Town/Resort Haverfordwest.
Directions Follow the A487 to St. Davids from Haverfordwest. At Newgale turn left signposted to Nolton Haven for ½ mile. The second turning on the left takes you to the park.
Acreage 2 **Open** March–October
Access Good **Site** Level
Sites available Total 15.
Facilities
Nearby facilities
Haverfordwest.
Alongside beach with scenic views.

NEWPORT

'Morawelon', Parrog, Newport, Dyfed, SA42 0RW.
Tel. 820565 Std. 01239
Nearest Town/Resort Fishguard/Cardigan.
Directions A487 from Fishguard, 7 miles to Newport. A487 from Cardigan, 12 miles to Newport. Turn down road signposted Parrog Beach or Parrog at the western end of town. Morawelon is the last house at the end of the road by the quay wall.
Acreage 5 **Open** Easter–Mid Oct
Access Good **Site** Lev/Slope
Sites available Total 85.
Facilities
Nearby facilities
Fishguard.
Direct access to the beach and sea, scenic views over the bay, ideal centre for Windsurfers, sailing etc. Canoe hire available, Salmon river fishing and coastal path walking. All accessable from the site. Boat park by the quay wall. Tourist Board Verified.

NEW QUAY

Frondeg Caravan Park, Gilfachreda, Nr. New Quay, Dyfed, SA45 9SP.
Tel. Llanarth 580491 Std. 01545
Nearest Town/Resort New Quay.
Directions Take A487 from Aberystwyth to Llanarth, then take the B4342 to New Quay for approx. 1 mile to Gilfachreda Village.
Acreage 1 **Open** Easter–October
Access Good **Site** Level
Sites available Total 10.
Facilities
Nearby facilities
Aberystwyth.
Quiet, secluded site near a small river leading to safe, sandy bathing beaches, 10 minutes walk. New Quay harbour town, 2 miles by road.

NEW QUAY

Wern Mill Camping Site, Gilfachrheda, New Quay, Dyfed SA45 9SP.
Tel. 580699 Std. 01545
Nearest Town/Resort New Quay.
Directions From Aberystwyth take the A487 via Aberaeron to Llanarth. Gilfachrheda is located 1½ miles from Llanarth on the B4342 to New Quay road.
Acreage 2½ **Open** Easter–October
Access Good **Site** Level
Sites available Total 50.
Facilities
Nearby facilities
Aberystwyth.
Very sheltered site, ½ mile from two sandy beaches. Ideal centre for touring mid Wales. Idyllic walks. Family site. No motorcycles.

PEMBROKE

Upper Portclew Farm, Freshwater East, Pembroke, Dyfed.
Tel. Lamphey 672112 Std. 01646
Nearest Town/Resort Freshwater East.
Directions 3 miles southeast of Pembroke.
Acreage 3 **Open** Whitsun–10 September
Site Level
Sites available
Facilities
Nearby facilities
Lamphey.
Near beach, National Park.

PUMPSAINT

Maesbach Caravan Park, Ffarmers, Llanwrda, Dyfed, SA19 8EX.
Tel. 650413 Std. 01558
Nearest Town/Resort Aberavon.
Directions From A40 at Llanwrda take the A482 (Lampeter road), after passing through Pumpsaint take the second turning on the right at the side of Royal Oak Public House. Follow signs for 2 miles.
Acreage 4½ **Open** March–October
Access Good **Site** Level
Sites available Total 30.
Facilities
Nearby facilities
Roman Gold Mines, working Water Mill, bird reserve and a reservoir. Scenic views from the site. Some disabled facilities.

PUMPSAINT

Penlanwen, Pumpsaint, Llanwrda, Dyfed. SA19 8RR.
Tel. 650667 Std. 01558
Nearest Town/Resort Lampeter.
Directions 7 miles northwest of Llandovery, take A40, turn right onto A482 at Llanwrda, past Bridgend Inn on left and look for site signs. From Lampeter take A482 for 8Miles to Pumpsaint.
Acreage 3 **Open** All year
Access Good **Site** Level
Sites available Total 20.
Facilities
Nearby facilities
Llandovery.
Scenic views, guided tour of gold mines with cafe and shop. Pony trekking, ideal for families.

RED ROSES

South Carvan Caravan Park, Tavernspite, Whitland, Dyfed. SA34 0NL.
Tel. 451 Std. 0183 483
Nearest Town/Resort Whitland.
Directions From St. Clears take A477 to Tenby at Red Roses turn right 1¾ miles down road into village of Tavernspite.
Acreage 7 **Open** April–September
Access Good **Site** Level
Sites available Total 45.
Facilities
Nearby facilities
Whitland.

ST.CLEARS

Parciau Bach Caravan Park, St. Clears, Dyfed, SA33 4LG.
Tel. 230647 Std. 01994
Nearest Town/Resort St. Clears.
Directions From St. Clears traffic lights take Llanboidy Road. In a 100 yards fork right, then first right, first right.
Acreage 5 **Open** March–December
Access Good **Site** Lev/Slope
Sites available Total 25.
Facilities
Nearby facilities
Beautiful tranquil site, ideal touring. T.V. Hook-up.

ST. DAVIDS

Caerfai Bay Caravan & Tent Park, St. Davids, Pembrokeshire, SA62 6QT.
Tel. 720274 Std. 01437
Nearest Town/Resort St. Davids.
Directions Turn off the A487 (Haverfordwest to St. Davids road) in St. Davids opposite the Grove Hotel at the Caerfai signpost. Entrance to the park is at the end of the road, ¼ mile on the right.

Open April–October
Access Good **Site** Lev/Slope
Sites available Total 80.
Facilities
Nearby facilities
Haverfordwest.
Magnificent sea views and coastal scenery. 200yds from award winning Caerfai bathing beach. Immediately adjacent to Pembrokeshire coastal path.

ST. DAVIDS

Nine Wells Caravan & Camping Park, Nine Wells, Solva, Nr. Haverfordwest, Dyfed, SA62 6UH.
Tel. 721809 Std. 01437
Nearest Town/Resort Haverfordwest.
Directions From Haverfordwest take A487 to Solva. ¼ mile past Solva turn left at Nine Wells. Site clearly signposted.
Acreage 4½ **Open** Easter–October
Access Good **Site** Lev/Slope
Sites available Total 70.
Facilities
Nearby facilities
Haverfordwest.
Sandy beach ¾ mile. Walk the coastal footpath to Solva. About 5 minute walk to cove and coastal footpath and Iron Age Fort, down National Trust Valley.

ST. DAVIDS

Park Hall Camping Park, Maerdy Farm, Penycwm, Haverfordwest, Dyfed.
Tel. 721606/721282 Std. 01437
Nearest Town/Resort Haverfordwest.
Directions 12 miles from Haverfordwest on the A487 and 6 miles from St. Davids. Turn at R.A.F. Brawdy.
Acreage 7 **Open** March–October
Access Good **Site** Level
Sites available Total 100.
Facilities
Nearby facilities
Haverfordwest.
Near beach, scenic views. Ideal touring, fishing on private lake.

ST.DAVIDS

Prendergast Caravan and Camping Park, Cartlett Lodge, Trefin, Haverfordwest, Dyfed. SA62 5AL.
Tel. 831368 Std. 01348
Nearest Town/Resort St. Davids/Fishguard.
Directions From Haverfordwest take A40 towards Fishguard, until Letterston. Turn left on B4331 until you reach A487. Turn left for St. Davids in about 2½ miles. Turn right by sign for Trefin.
Acreage ½ **Open** April–September
Access Good **Site** Lev/Slope
Sites available Total 12.
Facilities
Nearby facilities
Haverfordwest.
Lovely walks along coastal path.

SARNAU

Talywerydd Caravan & Camping Park, Penbryn, Near Sarnau, Llanysul, Dyfed, SA44 6QY.
Tel. 810322 Std. 01239
Nearest Town/Resort Cardigan.
Directions From Cardigan take second Penbryn turn off A487. From Aberystwyth take second Penbryn turn off A487. Talywerydd 500 yds on the left.
Acreage 4 **Open** Easter–September
Access Good **Site** Level
Sites available Total 20.
Facilities
Nearby facilities
Aberystwyth.
Scenic views over Cardigan Bay, ideal for touring west Wales. Penbryn beach 1 mile away. Bed & Breakfast.

SARNAU

Brynawelon Touring Caravan Park, Sarnau, Llandysul, Dyfed, SA44 6RE.
Tel. 654584 Std. 01239
Nearest Town/Resort Cardigan.
Directions Travelling north on A487 take a right turn at Sarnau crossroads, site is 550yds on the left.
Acreage 2 **Open** April–October
Access Good **Site** Level
Sites available Total 30.
Facilities
Nearby facilities
Carmarthen.
2 miles to Penbryn Beach. Rural surroundings, quiet family site.

SARNAU

Treddafydd Caravan Site, Treddafydd, Sarnau, Llandysul, Dyfed.
Tel. 654551 Std. 01239
Nearest Town/Resort Cardigan.
Directions 10 miles north of Cardigan on A487 and 30 miles south of Aberystwyth, turn by Sarnau church then first left.
Acreage 3 **Open** Easter–October
Access Good **Site** Sloping
Sites available Total 10.
Facilities
Nearby facilities
Carmarthen/Aberystwyth.
1 mile from the fine sandy beach of Penbryn.

SAUNDERSFOOT

Moreton Farm Leisure Park, Moreton, Saundersfoot, Dyfed, SA69 9EA.
Tel. 812016 Std. 01834
Nearest Town/Resort Tenby/Saundersfoot.
Directions From St. Clears o the A477, turn left onto A478 for Tenby. Site is on left 1¼ miles, opposite chapel.
Acreage 12 **Open** March–December
Access Good **Site** Level
Sites available Total 60.
Facilities
Nearby facilities
Saundersfoot.
1 mile of safe golden beach. Own fishing lake. Dragon Award.

SAUNDERSFOOT

Moysland Farm Camping Site, Tenby Road, Saundersfoot, Dyfed, SA69 9DS.
Tel. Saundersfoot 812455
Nearest Town/Resort Saundersfoot/Tenby.
Directions M4 to Kilgetty, turn left to tenby. Site is on right hand side of road before New Hedges roundabout.
Acreage 4 **Open** Whitsun–September
Access Good **Site** Level
Sites available Total 40.
Facilities
Nearby facilities
Saundersfoot.
Beach ¼ mile, ideal centre for touring. Tents for hire.

SAUNDERSFOOT

Trevayne Farm, Saundersfoot, Dyfed, SA69 9DL.
Tel. 813402 Std. 01834
Nearest Town/Resort Saundersfoot/Tenby.
Directions A40 to St. Clears A477 to Kilgetty. A478 towards Tenby, approx 2½ miles from Tenby turn left for Saundersfoot, right for New Hedges and left again for Trevayne ¾ mile.
Acreage 7 **Open** Easter–October
Access Good **Site** Level
Sites available Total 100.
Facilities
Nearby facilities
Tenby.
Situated on coast with lovely sandy beach and scenery. 25 electricity hook-ups available for touring caravans.

Rowston Holiday Park is a landscaped, family run site, ideally situated just one mile from Tenby and Saundersfoot. Its acres of colourful grounds slope gently towards the sea at Waterwynch, a few hundered yards away. This delightful sandy cove is a secluded sun trap with safe bathing, and rock pools for the children. Rowston is one of the highest graded parks of the area and offers its guests a relaxing holiday in a variety of luxury caravans and sumptuous pine lodges, at very competative prices. A number of fully serviced super touring pitches are available and family tents are always most welcome. Rowston prides it self on its friendly atmosphere and its range of facilities. Here is the perfect base from which to explore the beaches, cliffs and coves of the renowned Pembrokeshire Coastal National Park.

ROWSTON HOLIDAY PARK,
NEW HEDGES,NR. TENBY,
PEMBROKESHIRE SA70 8TL

BRITISH GRADED HOLIDAY PARKS

Where families make friends....

For our FREE colour brochure TEL: (01834) 842178

TENBY

Buttyland Farm Touring Caravan and Tent Park, Manorbier, Nr Tenby, Dyfed.
Tel. 871278 Std. 01834
Nearest Town/Resort Tenby.
Directions Take A4139 from Tenby by pass Penally through Lydstep village, straight over next crossroads our park on right.
Acreage 10 **Open** March–October
Access Good **Site** Level
Sites available Total 110.
Facilities
Nearby facilities
Manorbier.
Beach 1 mile, ideal touring.

TENBY

Kiln Park Holiday Centre, Marsh Road, Tenby, Dyfed, SA70 7RB.
Tel. 844121 Std. 01834
Nearest Town/Resort Tenby.
Directions From Tenby A4139 towards Pembroke, approx 1 mile on left hand side is Kiln Park.
Acreage 30 **Open** March–October
Access Good **Site** Level
Sites available Total 310.
Facilities
Nearby facilities
Tenby.
5 minutes walk from sandy beach. Tenby has usual resort amusements.

TENBY

Lodge Farm Caravan and Camping Park, Lodge Farm, New Hedges, Tenby, Dyfed.
Tel. 842468 Std. 01834
Nearest Town/Resort Tenby/Saundersfoot.
Directions Approaching Tenby on A478, turn left at New Hedges roundabout, first right , through village, Lodge farm entrance opposite minimarket.
Acreage 10 **Open** April–October
Access Good **Site** Level
Sites available Total 65+.
Facilities
Nearby facilities
Tenby.
Near beaches, A.A. 2 pennants and listed site. Sky Television in club. Camping and Caravan Club Listed site.

TENBY

Manorbier Bay Caravanserai, A4139, Nr. Tenby, Dyfed, SA70 7SR.
Tel. 871235 Std. 01834
Nearest Town/Resort Tenby.
Directions We are directly on the A4139 Tenby to Pembroke coast road, approx ¼ mile east of Jameston Village.
Open 1st March–31st October
Access Good **Site** Level
Sites available Total 18.
Facilities
Nearby facilities
Manorbier.
Manorbier Sands accessible by public fooootpath. Ideal position for exploring South Pembrokeshire coastline.

TENBY

Rowston Holiday Park, New Hedges, Tenby, Dyfed, SA70 8TL.
Tel. 842178 Std. 01834
Nearest Town/Resort Tenby/Saundersfoot.
Directions 1½ miles north of Tenby, in village of New Hedges.
Acreage 8 **Open** March–December
Access Good **Site** Lev/Slope
Sites available Total 90.
Facilities
Nearby facilities
Tenby.
10 minutes walk through woods to secluded Waterwynch Cove. No dogs mid July/August.

TENBY

Tudor Glen Caravan Park, Jameston, Nr. Tenby, Dyfed, SA70 7SS.
Tel. 871417 Std. 01834
Nearest Town/Resort Tenby.
Directions From Tenby take the A4139 Coast Road west for 6 miles. Site is on the right before entering village of Jameston.
Acreage 6 **Open** March–October
Access Good **Site** Lev/Slope
Sites available Total 46.
Facilities
Nearby facilities
Manorbier.
Family run site, ideal touring base.

TENBY

Well Park Caravans, Tenby, Pembrokeshire, Dyfed.
Tel. 842179 Std. 01834
Nearest Town/Resort Tenby.
Directions On righthand side of main Tenby (A478) road 1¼ miles north of Tenby.
Acreage 4½ **Open** April–October
Access Good **Site** Lev/Slope
Sites available Total 100.
Facilities
Nearby facilities
Tenby.
Very central and convenient for the beautiful beaches and places of interest along the Pembrokeshire coast. Situated in pleasant surroundings. A family run site. Wales in Bloom Award Winning Park for Best Park in Dyfed.

TENBY

Wood Park Caravans & Country Club, New Hedges, Tenby, Dyfed. SA70 8TL. Tel. 843414 Std. 01834
Nearest Town/Resort Tenby.
Directions 1 mile north of Tenby off A478. West side of New Hedges bypass.
Acreage 2 **Open** Easter–September
Access Good **Site** Lev/Slope
Sites available Total 60.
Facilities S
Nearby facilities
Tenby.
No dogs end July/August, small dogs at other times. Ideally situated between Tenby and Saundersfoot. Waterwynch beach 1 mile, scenic views ideal touring, battery charging.

TENBY

Whitewell Camping Park, Lydstep Beach, Penally, Tenby, Dyfed SA70 7RY. Tel. 871569 Std. 01834
Nearest Town/Resort Tenby.
Acreage 13 **Open** April–September
Access Good **Site** Level
Sites available Total 120.
Facilities S
Nearby facilities
Tenby.
½ mile Lydstep Beach, green countryside on all sides.

TENBY

Windmills Camping Park, Narberth Road, Tenby, Dyfed, SA70 8TJ. Tel. 842200 Std. 01834
Nearest Town/Resort Tenby.
Acreage 4 **Open** Easter–September
Site Lev/Slope
Sites available Total 40.
Facilities I
Nearby facilities
Tenby.
Sea views, ¾ mile Tenby town centre.

GLAMORGAN

BARGOED

Parc Cwm Darran Caravan & Camp Site, Parc Cwm Darran, Nr. Deri, Bargoed, Mid Glamorgan, CF8 9AB. Tel. 875557 Std. 01443
Acreage 2 **Open** April–September
Access Good **Site** Lev/Slope
Sites available Total 30.
Facilities I
Nearby facilities
Bargoed.
Situated in 600 acre country park with woods, lake, visitor centre and cycle track.

BARRY

Fontygary Holiday Park, Rhoose, South Glamorgan, CF6 9ZT. Tel. 710386 Std. 01446
Nearest Town/Resort Barry.
Directions M4 to exit 33 onto A4232 and A4050. Drive through Rhoose Village and turn left opposite the Fontygarry Inn at west end of village.
Open March–October
Access Good **Site** Level
Sites available Total 25.
Facilities S I
Nearby facilities
Barry.
Ideal touring centre for many Vale of Glamorgan attractions and Wales capital city.

BARRY

Vale Touring Caravan Park, Port Road (West), Barry, South Glamorgan. Tel. 736604 Std. 01446
Nearest Town/Resort Barry Island.
Directions The park is located 2 miles west of Barry on the A4226. When you reach the roundabout with sculpture arrows turn left, park is on your right.
Acreage 2 **Open** April–October
Access Good **Site** Level
Sites available Total 40.
Facilities
Nearby facilities
Barry.
Ideal touring, beach 2 miles away.

COWBRIDGE

Llandow Touring Caravan Park, Llandow, Cowbridge, South Glamorgan, CF7 7PB. Tel. 794527 Std. 01446
Nearest Town/Resort Llantwit Major.
Directions From M4 junction 33. 3 miles from exit to the A48, Cowbridge. After the By-pass at Cowbridge take the first left to Llysworney and Llantwit Major (B4268). Do not go to Llandow Village. Keep on this road until you see the brown signs.
Acreage 5 **Open** 1st March–31st October
Access Good **Site** Level
Sites available Total 100.
Facilities S
Nearby facilities
Bridgend.
Level rural site, close to Heritage coast. Spotless modern amenities.

LLANMADOC

Llanmadoc Camping Site, Llanmadoc, Gower Coast, Swansea, West Glamorgan. Tel. 386202 Std. 01792
Nearest Town/Resort Swansea.
Directions M4 come off at junction 47 A483, signposted to Gower left at traffic lights Gorseinon, right at Gonerton.
Acreage 11 **Open** April–October
Access Good **Site** Lev/Slope
Sites available Total 250.
Facilities S I
Nearby facilities
Swansea.
Adjoining sandy beach and a National Trust and nature conservancy. Area of outstanding natural beauty.

LLANTWIT MAJOR

Acorn Camping and Caravanning, Rosedew Farm, Hamlane South, Llantwit Major, South Glamorgan, CF6 9RP. Tel. 794024 Std. 01446
Nearest Town/Resort Llantwit Major.
Directions From M4 junction 33 follow signs Cardiff Airport then B4265 for Llantwit Major. Approach site from the town centre via Beach Road or via Ham Lane East through Ham Manor Park.
Acreage 4 **Open** Easter–October
Access Good **Site** Level
Sites available Total 90.
Facilities S
Nearby facilities
Barry.
1 mile from beach, 1 mile from town, coastal walks, ideal base for touring. Holiday hire caravans available, one suitable for wheelchair.

MERTHYR TYDFIL

Grawen Caravan & Camping Park, Cwn Taff, Cefn Coed, Merthyr Tydfil, Mid Glamorgan. Tel. 723740 Std. 01685
Nearest Town/Resort Merthyr Tydfil.
Directions Easy access off A470 Brecon Beacons road. 1¼ miles from A465 known as the Heads of the Valleys. 1¼ miles from Cefn Coed, 4 miles from town of Merthyr Tydfil.
Acreage 4 **Open** April–October
Access Good **Site** Level
Sites available Total 50.
Facilities S I
Nearby facilities
Merthyr Tydfil.
Picturesque surroundings with mountains, forest and a reservoir. Walks from the park and fishing in the reservoir.

OXWICH

Oxwich Camping Park, Oxwich, Gower, Swansea, Glamorgan, SA3 1LS.
Tel. 390777 Std. 01792
Nearest Town/Resort Swansea.
Directions A4118 from Swansea, 10 miles turn left. 1¼ miles turn right at crossroads, ¼ mile on right hand side.
Acreage 10 **Open** April–September
Site Lev/Slope
Sites available Total 180.
Facilities
Nearby facilities
Swansea.
Near sandy beach. Water sports and nature reserve.

PENARTH

Lavernock Point Holiday Estate, Fort Road, Penarth, South Glamorgan, CF64 5XQ.
Tel. 707310 Std. 01222
Nearest Town/Resort Penarth.
Directions From Penarth follow coast road to the B4526. Travel 1 mile to a lane called Fort Road, turn left to find our estate.
Acreage 5¼ **Open** March–1 October
Site Lev/Slope
Sites available Total 120.
Facilities
Nearby facilities
Penarth.
Near beach, scenic views and country walks all nearby.

PORT EINON

Bank Farm Caravan Park, Bank Farm, Norton, Gower, West Glamorgan.
Tel. 390228 Std. 01792
Nearest Town/Resort Swansea.
Directions A4118 from Swansea, turn left in ½ mile from Port Einon, site is 200yds on your right.
Acreage 15 **Open** April–October
Access Good **Site** Sloping
Sites available Total 230.
Facilities
Nearby facilities
Swansea.
Overlooking beach, scenic views and a bar.

PORT EYNON

Newpark Holiday Park, Port Eynon, Gower, West Glamorgan, SA3 1NP.
Tel. 390292 Std. 01792
Nearest Town/Resort Swansea.
Directions From Swansea take the A4418 for 14 miles, down hill into Port Eynon, large splayed entrance into site on the left hand side.
Acreage 8 **Open** April–October
Access Good **Site** Level
Sites available Total 174.
Facilities
Nearby facilities
Swansea.
Scenic views, near beach. Britain's first area of outstanding natural beauty. B.H. and H.P.A and Welsh Tourist Board 4 Tick rating.

PORTHCAWL

Brodawel Camping Park, Brodawel House, Moor Lane, Nottage, Porthcawl, Mid Glamorgan.
Tel. Porthcawl 783231 Std. 01656
Nearest Town/Resort Porthcawl.
Directions 1 mile northwest Porthcawl, turn into Moor Lane off A4229 and along to site. M4 junction 37.
Acreage 4 **Open** April–October
Access Good **Site** Slight Slope
Sites available Total 80.
Facilities
Nearby facilities
Bridgend.
Convenient to all beaches, very central for touring area. Off Licence.

PORTHCAWL

Happy Valley Caravan & Camping Park, Wig Fach, Porthcawl, Mid Glamorgan, CF32 0NG.
Tel. 782144 Std. 01656.
Nearest Town/Resort Porthcawl.
Directions M4 junction 35, follow signs for Porthcawl. On the A4106, 1 mile on the left.
Acreage 10 **Open** April–September
Access Good **Site** Level
Sites available Total 100.
Facilities
Nearby facilities
Bridgend.
Good touring base. 2 miles to Porthcawl.

RHOSSILI

Pitton Cross Camping Site, Pitton Cross, Rhossili, Swansea, Glamorgan, SA3 1RH.
Tel. 390593 Std. 01792
Nearest Town/Resort Swansea.
Directions Leave Swansea via A4118, 16 miles to Scurlage. Turn right signposted Rhossili, 2 miles site on left.
Acreage 6 **Open** April–October
Access Good **Site** Level
Sites available Total 100.
Facilities
Nearby facilities
Swansea.
Scenic views, good walking, bird watching and beaches.

SWANSEA

Riverside Caravan Park, Ynysforgan Farm, Morriston, Swansea West Glamorgan.
Tel. 775587 Std. 01792
Nearest Town/Resort Swansea.
Directions Direct access to site from roundabout under motorway junction 45 on M4.
Acreage 7 **Open** All Year.
Access Good **Site** Level
Sites available Total 120.
Facilities
Nearby facilities
Swansea.
Alongside river, ideal touring, flat level grassy site. Indoor swimming pool and jaccuzi. Television room. Dogs are welcome but no dangerous breeds.

GWENT

ABERCARN

Cwmcarn Forest Drive Visitor Centre & Campsite, Cwmcarn, Newport, Gwent, NP1 7FA.
Tel. 272001 Std. 01495
Nearest Town/Resort Risca.
Directions M4 junction 28 for Risca, north on the A467 for 7 miles, Forest Drive is signposted. From A465 Heads of the Valleys road take the A467 south (Nantyglo). 3 miles beyond Crumlin is Forest Drive signpost. From A449 take Usk turn off (A472), drive to Pontypool onto Crumlin. Turn left onto the A467, 3 miles on is brown Forest Drive sign.
Acreage 3 **Open** All Year
Access Good **Site** Level
Sites available Total 36.
Facilities
Nearby facilities
Newport.
Scenic views, hill walking, central for many tourist attractions. Tranquil, wooded valley with trout fishing in a lake. Site is at the entrance to a famous Forest (scenic) Drive. Cafe/restaurant at weekends only.

ABERGAVENNY

Aberbaiden Caravan & Camping Park, Gilwern, Nr. Abergavenny, Gwent.
Tel. Gilwern 830157 Std. 01873
Nearest Town/Resort Abergavenny.
Directions A465 Head of the Valleys road, site adjacent to the Gilwern roundabout.
Acreage 9 **Open** April–October
Access Good. **Site** Lev/Slope.
Sites available Total 60.
Facilities
Nearby facilities
Abergavenny.
Situated in the National Park, very close to the Black Mountains and the Brecon Beacons.

ABERGAVENNY

Pyscodlyn Farm Caravan & Camping Site, Llanwenarth Citra, Abergavenny, Gwent, NP7 7ER.
Tel. 853271 Std. 01873.
Nearest Town/Resort Abergavenny.
Directions Situated on A40 to Brecon. 2 miles west of Abergavenny, approx 50 metres past telephone box on the left.
Acreage 4¼ **Open** 1st April–31st October
Access Good. **Site** Level.
Sites available Total 60.
Facilities
Nearby facilities
Abergavenny.
Ideal walking area, set in picturesque Usk Valley, in Black Mountain area.

ABERGAVENNY

The Offa's Tavern, Pandy, Abergavenny, Gwent, NP7 8DL.
Tel. 890254 Std. 01873
Nearest Town/Resort Abergavenny.
Directions 5 miles north of Abergavenny on the A465 to Hereford.
Acreage 1½ **Open** All Year
Access Good **Site** Level
Sites available Total 20.
Facilities
Nearby facilities
Abergavenny.
River, scenic views and Offa's Dyke Path.

MONMOUTH

Glen Trothy Caravan Park, Mitchel Troy, Monmouth, Gwent, NP5 4BD.
Tel. Monmouth 712295 Std. 01600.
Nearest Town/Resort Monmouth.
Directions From north M5, M50 then A40 taking the left turn after the traffic lights and before reaching road tunnel. From East Gloucester, A40 Ross on Wye, A40 Monmouth. From south and southeast M4 Severn Bridge, A466 Chepstow, Tintern and Monmouth turning left at traffic lights onto A40.
Acreage 6½ **Open** March–October
Access Good **Site** Level
Sites available Total 184.
Facilities
Nearby facilities
Aberganenny.
Alongside river, ideal touring. No arrivals between 1-2 pm.

MONMOUTH

Bridge Caravan Park & Camping Site, Dingestow, Monmouth, Gwent.
Tel. 740241 Std. 01600
Nearest Town/Resort Monmouth.
Directions A449 Trunk road, turn off at Raglan/Abergavenny junction, site signposted to Dingestow. 4mls from Monmouth.
Acreage 4½ **Open** Easter–October
Access Good **Site** Level
Sites available Total 64.
Facilities
Nearby facilities
Newport.
Riverside site, fishing, walking. W.T.B 5 Tick Rating. A.A 3 Pennants.

GWYNEDD

ABERDARON

Mur Melyn Camping Site, Mur Melyn, Aberdaron, Pwllheli, Gwynedd, LL53 8LW.
Nearest Town/Resort Pwllheli.
Directions Take A499 west from Pwllheli, then fork onto to B4133 at Llanbedrog about 3 miles before Aberdaron take Whistling Sand road. Turn left at Pen-y-Bont House to site ½ mile.
Acreage 2½ **Open** Whitsun–September
Access Good **Site** Level
Sites available Total 60.
Facilities
Nearby facilities
Pwllheli.
Near beach, scenic views, ideal touring, river nearby, ideal for Wales.

ABERDARON

Tir Glyn Caravan Park, Tirglyn, Aberdaron, Gwynedd.
Tel. 248 Std. 01758 760
Nearest Town/Resort Pwllheli.
Directions Pwllheli to Abersoch road, take the B4413 at Llanbedrog to Aberdaron. At Aberdaron Village turn right on the bridge and follow road to Uwchmynydd first left turn, site is on the left.
Acreage 3 **Open** May–October
Access Good **Site** Lev/Slope
Sites available Total 30.
Facilities
Nearby facilities
Pwllheli.
National Trust area with scenic views, near beach.

ABERSOCH

Bry Celyn Isaf, Cilan, Abersoch, Pwllheli, Gwynedd. LL53 7DD.
Tel. 713583 Std. 01758.
Nearest Town/Resort Abersoch.
Directions Come straight through Abersoch Village on the Cilan main road for about 2 miles until you reach Ty'r Lon B&B on right, turn right by B&B, site 200 yards from main road.
Acreage 2 **Open** Whitsun–September
Access Good **Site** Sloping
Sites available Total 50.
Facilities
Nearby facilities
Pwllheli.
Scenic views.

ABERSOCH

Deucoch Camping & Touring Site, Sarn Bach, Abersoch, Pwllheli, Gwynedd.
Tel. 713293 Std. 01758
Nearest Town/Resort Abersoch.
Directions Take Sarn Bach road out of Abersoch, continue on main road to Sarn Bach. Turn right in the square.
Acreage 12¼ **Open** March–October
Access Good **Site** Level
Sites available Total 65.
Facilities
Nearby facilities
Pwllheli.
Near the beach, ideal touring and scenic views.

ABERSOCH

Pant Gwyn Cottage, Sarn Bach, Abersoch, Gwynedd. LL53 7ET.
Tel. 2268 Std. 01758 71
Nearest Town/Resort Abersoch.
Directions 1½ miles from Abersoch centre.
Acreage 5 **Open** March–October
Access Good **Site** Lev/Slope
Sites available Total 62.
Facilities
Nearby facilities
Pwllheli.
Near beach, scenic views, ideal touring, safe for children family site. Tumble dryer and spinner available.

ABERSOCH

Sarn Farm Camping Site, Sarn Farm, Sarn Bach, Abersoch, Pwllheli, Gwynedd.
Tel. 712144
Nearest Town/Resort Abersoch.
Directions ¼ mile from Abersoch on the main road and signposted.
Acreage 3 **Open** Easter–October
Access Good **Site** Level
Sites available Total 50.
Facilities
Nearby facilities
Near the beach.

ABERSOCH

Sarnlys, Sarn Bach, Abersoch, Pwllheli, Gwynedd.
Tel. 712956 Std. 01758
Nearest Town/Resort Pwllheli.
Directions 1½ miles from Abersoch on A499.
Open Easter–October
Sites available
Facilities
Nearby facilities
Pwllheli.
Overlooking bay, six minutes walk to the beach.

ABERSOCH

Tan-y-Bryn Farm, Tan-y-Bryn, Sarn Bach, Abersoch, Gwynedd.
Tel. Abersoch 712093 Std. 01758
Nearest Town/Resort Abersoch.
Directions 1½ miles south of Abersoch on Sarn Bach road.
Acreage 2 **Open** Mid May–Mid September
Access Good **Site** Lev/Slope
Sites available
Facilities
Nearby facilities
Pwllheli.
Very popular seaside resort.

ABERSOCH

Haulfryn Camping Site, Abersoch, Pwllheli, Gwynedd.LL53 7AA.
Tel. Abersoch 2043 Std. 0175 871
Nearest Town/Resort Abersoch.
Directions 1 mile east of Abersoch on A499.
Acreage 9 **Open** Easter–September
Site Lev/Slope
Sites available Total 90.
Facilities
Nearby facilities
Pwllheli.

ABERSOCH

Tyn-y-Mur Camping Site, Abersoch, Gwynedd LL53 7UL.
Tel. Abersoch 2328 Std. 0175 871
Nearest Town/Resort Abersoch.
Directions A499 Pwllheli to Abersoch, on approaching Abersoch turn right at Land & Sea Services Garage, is then 1 mile on lefthand side.
Acreage 3 **Open** March–October
Access Good **Site** Level
Sites available Total 40.
Facilities
Nearby facilities
Pwllheli.
Superb, uninterrupted panoramic coastal views of Abersoch Bay and Hell's Mouth.

AMLWCH

Tyn Rhos, Penysarn, Amlwch, Gwynedd, LL69 9YR.
Tel. 830574 Std. 01407
Nearest Town/Resort Amlwch.
Directions A5025 turn off bypass to village of Penysarn. Take the first right after Y Bedol Public House and cross the cattle grid. 100yds up the drive.
Acreage 2 **Open** Easter–September
Access Good **Site** Level
Sites available Total 30.
Facilities
Nearby facilities
Bangor.
Near the village shops, post office and inn. Sports centre, beaches and swimming all 2 miles. Cafe/restaurant and licensed club within 200yds.

AMLWCH

Plas Eilian, Llaneilian, Amlwch, Anglesey.
Tel. Amlwch 830323 Std. 01407
Nearest Town/Resort Amlwch.
Directions Follow coastal road from Bangor for about 18 miles. Turn right by garage, continue straight until you reach the church.
Acreage 3 **Open** April–October
Access Good **Site** Level
Sites available Total 18.
Facilities
Nearby facilities
Bangor.

AMLWCH

Point Lynas Caravan Park, Llaneilian, Amlwch, Gwynedd, LL68 9LT.
Tel. 831130 Std. 01407
Nearest Town/Resort Amlwch.
Directions Turn off the A5025 at Twrcelyn Garage towards the sea. Follow signs for Llaneilian/Porth Eilian. Pass the phone box, entrance is 300yds on the left.
Acreage 1¼ **Open** Late March–October
Access Good **Site** Level
Sites available Total 15.
Facilities
Nearby facilities
Bangor.
200yds from Porth Eilian Cove. W.T.B. Graded 5 Tick.

ARTHOG

Garthyfog Camping Site, Garthyfog Farm, Arthog, Gwynedd LL39 1AX.
Tel. Fairbourne 250338 Std. 01341
Nearest Town/Resort Barmouth/Dolgellau.
Directions A493, 6 miles from Dolgellau, left by Village hall, look for signs on righthand side.
Acreage 2 **Open** All year
Site Lev/Slope
Sites available Total 20.
Facilities
Nearby facilities
Morfa Mawddach.
2 miles from Fairbourne, safe bathing sandy beach and shops. Beautiful scenery panoramic views. 300 yards from main road, sheltered from wind. Mains cold water. Plenty of room for children to play around the farm, rope-swing, little stream etc.

ARTHOG

Graig-Wen, Arthog, Gwynedd, LL39 1BQ.
Tel. 250482 Std. 01341
Nearest Town/Resort Fairbourne.
Directions Between Dolgellau and Fairbourne on the A493.
Acreage 42
Access Good **Site** Lev/Slope
Sites available
Facilities
Nearby facilities
Land reaching down to estuary with scenic views, woodlands and pastures. Ideal for touring and camping.

BALA

Berwyn Country Holiday Park, Llandderfel, Bala, Gwynedd. LL23 7RA.
Tel. 530212 Std. 01678
Nearest Town/Resort Bala.
Directions From A5 turn at Corwen onto the B4401 and continue 7¼ miles.
Acreage 40 **Open** March–7th Jan
Access Good **Site** Lev/Terraced
Sites available Total 20.
Facilities
Nearby facilities
Ruabon.
Snowdonia National Park, Bala Lake Water Sports.

BALA

Penybont Touring Park, Llangynog Road, Bala, Gwynedd. LL23 7PH.
Tel. 520549 Std. 01678
Nearest Town/Resort Bala.
Directions ½ mile from Bala on B4391 to Llangynog.
Acreage 6 **Open** April–October
Access Good **Site** Lev/Slope
Sites available Total 85.
Facilities
Nearby facilities

Ruabon.
300 yards from Bala lake, lakeside steam railway and sailing club. Ideal centre for windsurfing, sailing, canoeing, touring Snowdonia National Park and North Wales.

BALA

Penygarth Caravan and Camping Park, Rhos y Gwaliau, Bala, Gwynedd, LL23 7ES.
Tel. 520485 Std. 01678
Directions Take B4391 Bala to Llangynog road. 1½ miles from Bala fork right to Rhos-Y-Gwaliau. Site in 600yds.
Acreage 12 **Open** March–October
Access Good **Site** Level
Sites available Total 63.
Facilities
Nearby facilities
Ruabon.
Bala Lake, Sailing, Windsurfing, Snowdonia National Park, good touring centre. Barbecue and picnic area, 3 acre field for recreation or dog walks. AA 3 Pennants, B.H.P. 4 Ticks.

BALA

Tyisaf Camping Site, Tyisaf, Llangynog Road, Bala, Gwynedd.
Tel. 520574 Std. 01678
Nearest Town/Resort Bala.
Directions 2½ miles southeast of Bala, on B4391 road near telephone kiosk and post box.
Acreage 2 **Open** 1 April/Easter–October
Access Good **Site** Level
Sites available Total 30.
Facilities
Nearby facilities
Ruabon.
Ideal for touring, site alongside stream on a working farm.

BALA

Tyn Cornel Camping & Caravan Park, Frongoch, Bala, Gwynedd, LL23 7NU.
Tel. 520759 Std. 01678
Nearest Town/Resort Bala.
Directions Leave Bala on the A4212 Porthmadog road, turn left after 4 miles over river bridge.
Acreage 1¼ **Open** Mid March–Mid Oct
Access Good **Site** Level
Sites available Total 37.
Facilities
Nearby facilities
Llangollen.
Next to National White Water Centre on the River Tryweryn. Canoeing and white water rafting available.

BARMOUTH

Benar Beach Camping & Touring Park, Tal-y-bont, Barmouth, Gwynedd.
Tel. 247571 Std. 01341
Nearest Town/Resort Barmouth.
Directions Take A496 coast road from Barmouth towards Harlech, take left turn by Llanddwywe church after Talybont village. Site is on the left.
Acreage 10 **Open** March–October
Access Good **Site** Level
Sites available Total 225.
Facilities
Nearby facilities
Dyffryn Ardudwy.
100 yards from safe beach with miles of golden sandunes. Ideal family site. Electric, satellite and television hook-ups. A.A. and R.A.C. Appointed. Gas, Cafe/Restaurant and Licensed Club in ¼ mile.

BARMOUTH

Hendre Mynach Caravan Park, Barmouth, Gwynedd.
Tel. 280262 Std. 01341
Nearest Town/Resort Barmouth.
Directions ¼ mile north of Barmouth on the A496 Barmouth to Harlech road.
Acreage 10 **Open** March–October
Access Good **Site** Level
Sites available Total 245.
Facilities
Nearby facilities
Barmouth.
100yds from the beach, ½ mile from town centre. An excellent base for beach and mountain walks.

BEAUMARIS

Kingsbridge Caravan Park, Llanfaes, Beaumaris, Anglesey, Gwynedd, LL58 8LR.
Tel. 490636 Std. 01248
Nearest Town/Resort Beaumaris.
Directions 1¼ miles past Beaumaris Castle on the B5109. At crossroads turn left, 400yds to the site.
Acreage 9 **Open** March–October
Access Good **Site** Level
Sites available Total 48.
Facilities
Nearby facilities
Bangor.
Fishing, scenic views, historical sites. Ideal for touring and bird watching.

BENLLECH

Ad Astra Caravan Park, Brynteg, Nr. Benllech, Anglesey, Gwynedd.LL78 7JH.
Tel. Tynygongl 853283 Std. 01248
Nearest Town/Resort Benllech.
Directions Turn left up the hill from Benllech Village square on B5108. Drive 1½ miles to California Inn, turn left onto B5110. Park is 500 yards on right hand side.
Acreage 3 **Open** March–October
Access Good **Site** Level
Sites available

Facilities
Nearby facilities
Bangor.
Scenic views, ideal base for touring.

BENLLECH

Bodafon Caravan & Camping Park, Bodafon, Benllech, Anglesey, Gwynedd, LL74 8RU.
Tel. 852417 Std. 01248
Nearest Town/Resort Benllech Bay.
Directions A5025 through Benllech, $\frac{1}{4}$ mile on left.
Acreage 2 **Open** March–October
Access Good **Site** Lev/Slope
Sites available Total 50.
Facilities
Nearby facilities
Bangor.
Near to beach ($\frac{3}{4}$ mile), good views, quiet family site. Ideal touring.

BENLLECH

Bwich Caravan Park, Tynygongl, Benllech Bay, Anglesey.
Tel. Tynygongl 852914 Std. 01248
Nearest Town/Resort Benllech Bay.
Directions A5025. Menai Bridge to Benllech 8 miles, turn left B5110. $1\frac{1}{2}$ miles.
Acreage 4 **Open** March–October
Access Good **Site** Level
Sites available Total 12.
Facilities
Nearby facilities
Bangor.
Near beach, ideal touring, golf, riding (nearby).

BENLLECH

Garnedd Touring Caravan & Tent Park, Lon Bryn Mair, Brynteg, Anglesey, Gwynedd LL78 8QA.
Tel. 853240 Std. 01248
Nearest Town/Resort Benllech.
Directions From mainland Wales take A5 over Brittania Bridge. Keep on A5, then A5025 signed Amlwch/Benllech. Pass through Pentraeth then turn left at lay-by with AA phone and food stalls onto unclassified road signed Llanbedrgoch. In exactly 2 miles turn left at T junction onto B5108 signed Llangefni/Llanerchymedd. In 100 yards take first left onto Lon Bryn Mair, site $\frac{1}{4}$ mile on right at orange signs.
Acreage 5 **Open** Easter–September
Access Good **Site** Level
Sites available Total 35.
Facilities
Nearby facilities
Bangor.
$1\frac{1}{2}$ miles to beach. Very clean toilet facilities. Superb views. Farm, dairy, garden produce. No dogs, spin dryer and socket for ladies hair- dryers etc. Washroom for clothes and crockery.

BENLLECH

Nant Newydd Caravan Park, Brynteg, Nr. Benllech Bay, Gwynedd.
Tel. 852842/852266 Std. 01248
Nearest Town/Resort Benllech Bay.
Directions Leaving Britannia Bridge take the A5025 Amlwch and Benllech. Turn left at the square and take the B5108 towards Llangefni for approximately 2 miles. At crossroads turn left on the B5110. We are 1 mile on the right.
Acreage 7 **Open** March–October
Access Good **Site** Level
Sites available Total 65.
Facilities
Nearby facilities
Bangor.
Swimming, sailing, water ski-ing, fishing, boating, rambling, climbing, golf, pony trekking, sub-aqua diving. Dogs are permitted on leads.

BENLLECH

Plas Uchaf Caravan & Camping Park, Benllech Bay, Benllech, Gwynedd, LL74 8NU.
Tel. 763012 Std. 01407
Nearest Town/Resort Benllech.
Directions $\frac{1}{4}$ mile from Benllech, signposted just after fire sign on the B5108.
Acreage 8 **Open** March–October
Access Good **Site** Level
Sites available Total 80.
Facilities
Nearby facilities
Bangor.
Well sheltered, family park, under a mile from the beach. Tarmac roads, close mown grass, street lighting etc..

BETHESDA

Ogwen Bank Caravan Park, Bethesda, Gwynedd, LL57 3LQ.
Tel. 600486 Std. 01248
Nearest Town/Resort Bangor.
Directions Follow the A5 signposted for Betwys-y-Coed. Park is situated on the right just after the village of Bethesda.
Open March–October
Access Good **Site** Lev/Slope
Sites available

Facilities
Nearby facilities
Bangor.
Set in ancient woodlands, alongside a river and waterfalls. All individual pitches are level.

BETWS-Y-COED

Riverside Caravan & Camping Park, Old Church Road, Betws-y-Coed, Gwynedd, LL24 0BA.
Tel. 710310 Std. 01690
Nearest Town/Resort Betws-y-Coed.
Directions Enter Betws-y-Coed over Waterloo Bridge. Take first right after passing "Little Chef" Filling Station.
Acreage $3\frac{1}{2}$ **Open** 14 March–October
Access Good **Site** Level
Sites available Total 120.
Facilities
Nearby facilities
Betws-y-Coed.
Alongside river, adjacent to golf course. Ideally based as centre for touring Snowdonia.

BETWS-Y-COED

Rynys Farm Camping Site, Rynys Farm, Near Betws-Y-Coed, Llanrwst Gywnedd.
Tel. 710218 Std. 01690
Nearest Town/Resort Betws-y-Coed.
Directions 2 miles south of Betws-y-Coed Left by Conway Falls, 200yds from A5.
Acreage 3 **Open** Easter–October
Access Good **Site** Sloping
Sites available
Facilities
Betws-y-Coed.
Peaceful site, overlooking Snowdonia, central for touring.

BETWS-Y-COED

'Tanaeldroch' Farm, Pont-y-Pant, Dolwyddelan, Gwynedd.
Tel. Dolwyddelan 225 Std. 0169 06
Nearest Town/Resort Betws-y-Coed.
Directions Off A5 by Waterloo Bridge, Betws-y-Coed. Take A470. Site approx. $2\frac{1}{2}$ miles. ($\frac{1}{2}$ mile after rail bridge crosses road).
Acreage 6 **Open** All year
Site Lev/Slope
Sites available Total 120.
Facilities
Nearby facilities
Pont-y-Pant.
Alongside river, scenic views, ideal touring, walks. Toilets (not flush).

BRYNSIENCYN

Fron Caravan & Camping Site, Brynsiencyn, Anglesey, Gwynedd, LL61 6TX.
Tel. 430310 Std. 01248
Nearest Town/Resort Llanfairpwllgwyn.
Directions At start of Llanfairpwllgwyn turn left onto A4080 to Brysiencyn follow road through village site is on the right $\frac{1}{4}$ mile after village.
Acreage $5\frac{1}{4}$ **Open** Easter–September
Access Good **Site** Level
Sites available Total 70.
Facilities
Nearby facilities
Bangor.
Ideal for touring Angelsey and North Wales.

CAERNARFON

Bryn Gloch Caravan and Camping Park, Betws Garmon, Caernarfon, Gwynedd.
Tel. 650216 Std. 01286
Nearest Town/Resort Caernarfon.
Directions $4\frac{1}{2}$ miles south west of Caernarfon on A4085. Site on right opposite Betws Garmon church.
Acreage 12 **Open** Easter–October
Access Good **Site** Level
Sites available Total 100.
Facilities
Nearby facilities
Bangor.
Fishing, scenic views, ideal touring centre. Family owned and operated. WTB 5 Ticks Excellent. AA 4 Pennants. Award winning site.

CAERNARFON

Cadnant Valley Camping & Caravan Park, Llanberis Road, Caernarfon, Gwynedd.
Tel. 673196 Std. 01286
Nearest Town/Resort Caernarfon.
Directions $\frac{1}{4}$ mile from Caernarfon Castle on A4086 signposted for Llanberis. Entrance on left 150 yds after roundabout and just before the fire station. Drive slowly, easy to overshoot entrance.
Acreage $4\frac{1}{4}$ **Open** 14th Mar–31st October
Access Good **Site** Level
Sites available Total 60.
Facilities
Nearby facilities
Bangor.
Beautiful peaceful valley with attractive stream and trees. Everything clean and well maintained, terraced. Ideal touring centre. Swimming pool nearby.

CAERNARFON

Challoner Camping Site, Erw Hywel, Llanrug, Caernarfon, Gwynedd, LL55 2AJ.
Tel. 672985 Std. 01286
Nearest Town/Resort Caernarfon.
Directions A4086 from Caernarfon, 3 miles to Llanberis ½ mile west of Llanrug.
Acreage 2 **Open** March–October
Access Good **Site** Level
Sites available Total 35.
Facilities
Nearby facilities
Bangor.
Flat dry, touring, view of Angelesey. Quiet, flat site, very central for Snowdonia Mountains and the sea.

CAERNARFON

Glan Gwna Holiday Park, Caethro, Caernarfon, Gwynedd LL55 2SG.
Tel. 673456 Std. 01286
Nearest Town/Resort Caernarfon.
Directions 1¼ mile from Caernarfon on A4085.
Acreage 5 **Open** Easter–October
Access Good **Site** Lev/Slope
Sites available Total 100.
Facilities
Nearby facilities
Bangor.
Lakes, river, fishing.

CAERNARFON

Plas Gwyn Caravan Site, Plas Gwyn, Llanrug, Caernarfon, Gwynedd, LL55 2TD.
Tel. 672619 Std. 01286
Nearest Town/Resort Caernarfon.
Directions 3 miles from Caernarfon on the A4086, signposted on right.
Acreage 4 **Open** March–October
Access Good **Site** Level
Sites available Total 70.
Facilities
Nearby facilities
Bangor.
Snowdonia Mountains 3 miles, beach 2 miles, leisure complex ¾ mile Natural beauty within National Park Area. Art gallery on site. Tourist Board approved and graded caravan park 5 ticks. Dragon Award hire caravans. Bed and Breakfast available in the house. Telephone on site. FAX on the telephone line.

CAERNARFON

Riverside Camping, Caer Glyddyn, Pontrug, Caernarfon, Gwynedd LL55 2BB.
Tel. Caernarfon 672524 Std. 01286
Nearest Town/Resort Caernarfon.
Directions 2 miles out of Caernarfon on the righthand side of the A4086 (Llanberis road).
Acreage 4½ **Open** Easter–October
Access Good **Site** Level
Sites available Total 55.
Facilities
Nearby facilities
Bangor.
The campsite is bordered on two sides by a lovely river which is suitable for paddling and bathing. An ideal area for touring. Camp fires allowed. Dogs on leads at all times. Evening telephone number 01286 78781.

CAERNARFON

White Tower Caravan Park, Llandwrog, Caernarfon, Gwynedd. LL54 5UH.
Tel. 830649 Std. 01286
Nearest Town/Resort Caernarfon.
Directions From Caernarfon follow A487 Porthmaddog Road for approx ½ mile take the second turn on the right after Pioneer Supermarket signposted Saron 2 miles, we are 3 miles on right.
Acreage 3 **Open** March–October
Access Good **Site** Level
Sites available Total 52.
Facilities
Nearby facilities
Bangor.
2½ miles beach, 3¼ miles Caernarfon. Splendid views of Snowdon central for touring Llyn Peninsula, Anglesey and Snowdonia. W.T.B. 5 Ticks.

CAERNARFON

Tyn-yr-Onnen Mountain Farm Caravan & Camping Park, Waunfawr, Caernarfon, Gwynedd. LL55 4AX.
Tel. 650281 Std. 01286
Nearest Town/Resort Caernarfon.
Directions A4085 Caernarfon (A487) to Beddgelert, left at Waunfawr post office signposted from that point.
Acreage 4¼ **Open** S.B.Holiday–September
Access Good **Site** Lev/Slope
Sites available Total 70.
Facilities
Nearby facilities
Bangor.
A working farm at the foot of a mountain, secluded and peaceful, ideal touring and walking base. Please send SAE for a colour brochure. Park Quality Graded 4 Ticks and A.A. 2 Pennants.

CLYNNOG FAWR

Aberafon Camping Site, Aberafon, Gyrn Goch, Clynnog Fawr, Nr. Caernarfon, Gwynedd.
Tel. 660295 Std. 01286
Nearest Town/Resort Caernarfon.
Directions West of Caernarfon and east of Pwllheli on the A499.
Acreage 10 **Open** All Year
Access Poor **Site** Lev/Slope
Sites available Total 161.
Facilities
Nearby facilities
Pwllheli.
Own beach and scenic views.

CONWY

Conwy Touring Park, Conwy, Gwynedd.
Tel. 592856 Std. 01492
Nearest Town/Resort Conwy.
Acreage 70 **Open** Easter
Access Good **Site** Level
Sites available Total 300.
Facilities
Nearby facilities
Conwy.
Scenic views, ideal for touring Snowdonia. Evening entertainment during high season.

CRICCIETH

Cae-Canol Caravan & Camping, Criccieth, Gwynedd.
Tel. 522351 Std. 01766
Nearest Town/Resort Criccieth.
Directions Take the B4411 from Criccieth. 2 miles.
Acreage 3 **Open** April–October
Access Very Good **Site** Level
Sites available Total 25.
Facilities
Nearby facilities
Criccieth.
Ideal for touring. Private trout fishing available for caravanners and campers. Sheltered site.

CRICCIETH

Eisteddfa Farm Camp Site, Eisteddfa, Criccieth, Gwynedd.
Tel. 522104 Std. 01766
Nearest Town/Resort Criccieth.
Directions On A497, 3 miles Porthmadog. 1½ miles Criccieth.
Acreage 15 **Open** Easter–October
Access Good **Site** Lev/Slope
Sites available Total 150.
Facilities
Nearby facilities
Criccieth.
Ideally suited family site, centrally placed for climbing in Snowdonia. Wales Tourist Board – graded.

CONWY TOURING PARK

CONWY, GWYNEDD, LL32 8UX

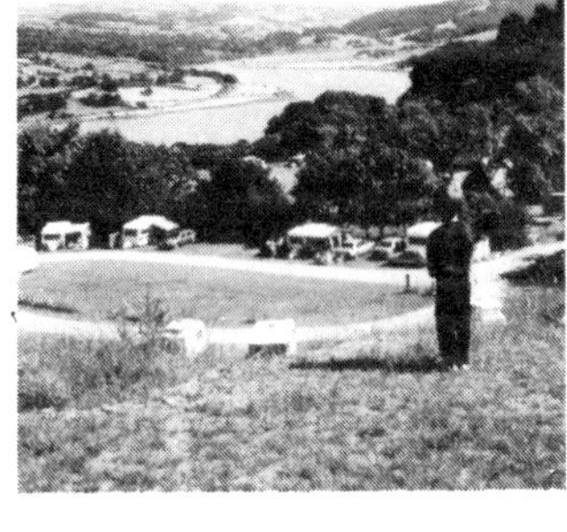

Set amidst spectacular scenery Conwy Touring Park is perfect for your touring or camping holiday, only 1 1/2 miles south of Conwy on the B5106 road. We are a spacious, impressively landscaped Park ideal for touring Snowdonia, Anglesey and the resorts of Llandudno and Betws-y-Coed.

Our facilities include FREE Hot showers - main luxury shower blocks heated during early and late season. **Clubhouse, Bar-food, Outdoor Adventure Playground with Indoor Playground plus Games Room, Launderette, Shop, Electric hook-ups.**

Evening Entertainment with Folk Groups, Morris Dancers, and more!

Tel: 01492 592856

Coastal Snowdonia

300 YARDS FROM LONG SANDY BEACH

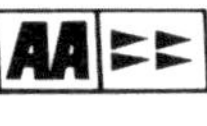

Enjoy the best of both worlds, between sea and mountains.

A 'Dragon Award' Park awarded by the Wales Tourist Board for high standards and facilities.

Luxury Holiday Homes for hire. All with Shower, Toilet, Fridge, Colour T.V. and Continental Quilts.

- ★ Beds cosily made up for arrival
- ★ Licensed Club House
- ★ Films twice daily for children
- ★ Entertainment
- ★ Heated Swimming Pool
- ★ Basket Meals
- ★ Take - Away Food
- ★ Disabled Toilet Facilities
- ★ Tourers & Campers on level grassland
- ★ Electrical Hook - ups available
- ★ Flush Toilets, Hot Showers
- ★ Washing up facilities
- ★ Children's Play Area
- ★ Supermarket
- ★ Launderette
- ★ Pets welcome under control

For colour brochure write or telephone:

Dinlle Caravan Park, Dinas Dinlle, Caernarfon. 01286 830324 Anytime.

Member of Thornley Leisure Group.

CRICCIETH

Gell Farm, Criccieth, Gwynedd, LL52 0PN.
Tel. 522781 Std. 01766
Nearest Town/Resort Criccieth.
Directions On the Criccieth/Caernarfon road (B4411), about 1 mile.
Acreage 5 **Open** March–October
Access Good **Site** Level
Sites available Total 40.
Facilities
Nearby facilities
Criccieth.

CRICCIETH

Llwynbugeilydd, Criccieth, Gwynedd, LL52 0PN.
Tel. 522235 Std. 01766
Nearest Town/Resort Criccieth.
Directions First site on the B4411, 1 mile north of Criccieth off the A497. From Caernarfon on the A487 turn right after Bryncir onto the B4411, the site is on the left in 3¼ miles.
Acreage 6 **Open** Easter–31st October
Access Good **Site** Level
Sites available Total 45.
Facilities
Nearby facilities
Criccieth.
Within easy walking distance to the beach and shop. Fine views of Cardigan Bay and Snowdonia.

CRICCIETH

Muriau Bach, Rhoslan, Criccieth, Gwynedd, LL52 0NP.
Tel. 530642 Std. 01766
Nearest Town/Resort Criccieth.
Directions Coming from Porthmadog on the A487, turn left onto the B4411. Fourth entrance on the left over a cattle grid, with a drive leading up to the side.
Acreage 1½ **Open** March–October
Access Good **Site** Level
Sites available Total 30.
Facilities
Nearby facilities
Criccieth.
Attractive site, central to all places of interest. Commanding the best views in the area, nice walks nearby.

CRICCIETH

Tyddyn Morthwyl, Criccieth, Gwynedd.
Tel. 522115 Std. 01766
Nearest Town/Resort Criccieth.
Directions 1½ miles north of Criccieth on B4411 main road to Caernarfon.
Acreage 6 **Open** March–October
Access Good **Site** Level
Sites available Total 40.
Facilities
Nearby facilities
Criccieth.
Central for mountains of Snowdonia and beaches of Lleyn Peninsula. Level and sheltered with mountain views.

DINAS DINLLE

Dinlle Caravan Park, Dinas Dinlle, Nr. Caernarfon, Gwynedd, LL54 5TW.
Tel. 830324 Std. 01286
Nearest Town/Resort Caernarfon.
Directions Take A487 south from Caernarfon then A499 for Pwllheli. 7 miles from Caernarfon turn right for Dinas Dinlle, 300yds along Beach Road turn right, park is 100yds on the left.
Acreage 10 **Open** March–October
Access Good **Site** Level
Sites available Total 240.
Facilities
Nearby facilities
Bangor.
Near beach.

DINAS DINLLE

Morfa Lodge Caravan Park, Dinas Dinlle, Near Caernarfon, Gwynedd. LL54 5TP.
Tel. 830205 Std. 01286
Nearest Town/Resort Caernarfon.
Directions Take the A487 south from Caernarfon which leads onto the A499. 7 miles from Caernarfon turn for Dinas Dinlle, turn right at the far end of Beach Road.
Acreage 15 **Open** March–October
Access Good **Site** Level
Sites available Total 220.
Facilities
Nearby facilities
Bangor.
¼ mile from Dinas Dinlle beach, central for touring Snowdonia, Anglesey and Lleyn Peninsula.

DOLGELLAU

Llwyn-Yr-Helm Farm, Brithdir, Dolgellau, Gwynedd.
Tel. 450254 Std. 01341
Nearest Town/Resort Dolgellau.
Directions Take loop road off A470 to A494 then ½ mile on minor road. At village telephone kiosk. 4 miles from Dolgellau.
Acreage 1½ **Open** Easter–November
Site Level
Sites available Total 20.
Facilities
Nearby facilities
Machynlleth.
Quiet small farm site in countryside, milk, eggs etc sold, ideal for children, friendly, good walking country. Dry ski slope in area.

DOLGELLAU

Tanyfron Camping and Caravan Park, Arran Road, Dolgellau, Gwynedd. LL40 2AA.
Tel. 422638 Std. 01341
Nearest Town/Resort Dolgellau.
Directions From Welshpool take A470, turn for Dolgellau by ARC Depot, off A470. ¼ mile on left – Dolgellau straight on ¼ mile from site.
Acreage 3¼ **Open** All Year
Access Good **Site** Level
Sites available Total 35.
Facilities
Nearby facilities
Barmouth.
10 miles beach, scenic views, walking, touring, fishing, walking distance of town. WTB Graded 5 Ticks. Snowdonia National Park Award 1993. Individual water/waste/TV hook-ups to touring pitches.

DYFFRYN ARDUDWY

Murmur-yr-Afon Touring Caravan & Camping Site, Dyffryn Ardudwy, Gwynedd, LL44 2BE.
Tel. 247353 Std. 01341
Nearest Town/Resort Barmouth.
Directions Take the A496 coast road from Barmouth towards Harlech. Site entrance is 100yds from the Esso Garage in Dyffryn Village on the right hand side.
Acreage 4 **Open** March–October
Access Good **Site** Level
Sites available
Facilities
Nearby facilities
Dyffryn.
1 mile from beach. Set in sheltered and natural surroundings, 100yds from village and shops, petrol stations and licensed premises.

FFESTINIOG

Llechrwd, Maentwrog, Blaenau Ffestiniog, Gwynedd.
Tel. Maentwrog 590240 Std. 01766
Directions On the A496. Blaenau Ffestiniog 3 miles, Porthmadog 8 miles.
Acreage 5 **Open** March–October
Access Good **Site** Lev/Slope
Sites available
Facilities
Nearby facilities
Blaenau Ffestiniog.
Riverside camp. Milk and eggs.

HARLECH

Woodlands Caravan Park, Harlech, Gwynedd, LL46 2UE.
Tel. 780419 Std. 01766
Nearest Town/Resort Harlech.
Directions Leave A496 at Harlech

railway crossing, site signposted at crossing at foot of castle.
Acreage 2 **Open** March–October
Access Good **Site** Level
Sites available Total 37.
Facilities
Nearby facilities
Harlech.
Near beach, shops and golfcourse. Harlech Castle adjacent. Swimming pool nearby, ideal touring.

HARLECH

Min-y-Don Caravan Park & Camping Sites, Min-y-Don, Beach Road, Harlech, Gwynedd, LL46 2UG.
Tel. 780286 Std. 01766
Nearest Town/Resort Harlech.
Directions Easily accessible off the A496 main road. Turn towards beach opposite Queens Hotel. Approx. 1 mile from Harlech. 5 minutes from the railway station and bus stop.
Acreage 2 **Open** Easter–October
Access Good **Site** Level
Sites available Total 100.
Facilities
Nearby facilities
Harlech.
Near the beach, Harlech Castle and swimming pool. Scenic views and ideal touring.

LLANBEDROG

Refail Caravan and Camping Park, Refail, Llanbedrog, Pwllheli. Gywnedd LL53 7NP.
Tel. 740511 Std. 01758
Nearest Town/Resort Pwllheli.
Directions Follow A499 from Pwllheli to Llanbedrog turn right onto B4413 at LLanbedrog, site situated 500 metres on the right hand side.
Acreage 1¾ **Open** Easter–October
Access Good **Site** Level
Sites available Total 33.
Facilities
Nearby facilities
Pwllheli.

Two mins from beach, scenic views, shops and 2 pubs. Welsh Tourist Board 5 Ticks. RAC approved, Caravan & Camping Club approved.

LLANBERIS

Snowdon View Caravan Park, Brynrefail, Nr. Llanberis, Caernarfon, Gwynedd.
Tel. Llanberis 870349 Std. 01286
Nearest Town/Resort LLanberis.
Directions 5 miles east of Caernarfon on the A4086 then turn north on the B4547 Bangor road for ¾ mile. We are situated on the right.
Acreage 12 **Open** March–January
Access Good **Site** Lev/Slope
Sites available Total 218.
Facilities
Nearby facilities
Bangor.
Scenic views, lake 300 yards away, ideal touring, walking, fishing, boating and climbing area.

LLANFWROG

Penrhyn Bay Caravan Park, Llanfwrog, Holyhead, Gwynedd. LL65 4YE.
Tel. 730496 Std. 01407
Nearest Town/Resort Holyhead/Valley.
Directions A5 to Valley, turn right at traffic lights through Llanfachraeth village then first left for Llanfwrog. At village turn left up hill by signpost Penrhyn keep on this road to end.
Acreage 15 **Open** Easter–October
Access Good **Site** Level
Sites available Total 60.
Facilities
Nearby facilities
Valley.
Quiet, family site in area of outstanding natural beauty. Long stretch of sandy beach and plenty of coastal walks. Indoor heated swimming pool. Clean, heated toilets and showers.

LLANGEFNI

Mornest Caravan Park, Pentre Bern, Gaerwen, Gwynedd, LL60 6HU.
Tel. 421725 Std. 01248
Nearest Town/Resort Llangefni.
Directions From Brittania Bridge 3 miles on A5 towards Holyhead 100yds. Leaving village of Gaerwen, entrance on the right hand side.
Open March–October
Access Good **Site** Level
Sites available Total 20.
Facilities
Nearby facilities
Bangor.
Ideal for touring Anglesey.

LLANGEFNI

Tregof Caravan, Cerrigceinwen, Boborgan, Anglesey, Gwynedd, LL62 5EH.
Tel. 720315 Std. 01407
Nearest Town/Resort Llangefni.
Directions 10 miles from Menai Bridge along A5 towards Holyhead signposted on lefthand side of road.
Acreage 10 **Open** April–October
Access Good **Site** Level
Sites available Total 48.
Facilities
Nearby facilities
Bodorgan.
Central Anglesey, easy reach most beaches by car. AA 3 pennant site.

LLANRWST

Bodnant Caravan Park, Nebo Road, Llanrwst, Gwynedd.
Tel. 640248/640683 Std. 01492
Nearest Town/Resort Llanrwst.
Directions Site faces A470. Entrance by 30 mile limit on Nebo Road. From Betws-y-Coed (A470). Sharp right at first crossroads to B5427, Nebo road.
Acreage 3 **Open** March–October
Access Good **Site** Level
Sites available Total 30.
Facilities
Nearby facilities
Llanrwst.
Lovely scenery, small, quiet, clean site. Ideal touring centre. 20 times Winner of Wales in Bloom.

LLANRWST

Glyn Farm Caravans, Trefriw, Nr. Llanrwst, Gwynedd, LL27 0RZ.
Tel. 640442 Std. 01492
Nearest Town/Resort Llanrwst.
Directions Follow the A470 to Llanrwst, over hump bridge onto the B5106 Betws-y-Coed to Conwy road. Trefriw is 1¼ miles from Gwydr Castle. Turn right opposite woollen mills, site 200yds.
Open March–October
Access Good **Site** Level
Sites available Total 28.
Facilities
Nearby facilities
Llanrwst.
Very centrally situated for Snowdonia and the sea. Beautiful country, lovely walks and ideal touring. Small family run site.

LLANRWST

Kerry's Orchard Camping Site, School Bank Road, Llanrwst, Gwynedd.
Tel. 640248/640683 Std. 01492
Nearest Town/Resort Llanrwst.
Directions From Betws-y-Coed A470, turn right at first crossroads by telephone box, entrance 300 yards on left.
Acreage 2 **Open** Easter–October
Access Good **Site** Level
Sites available Total 24.
Facilities
Nearby facilities
Llanrwst.
Ideal touring centre, quiet, well kept site. Pleasent views. Swimming pool nearby. 500yds from river Conway.

MARIANGLAS

Home Farm Caravan Park, Marianglas, Anglesey, Gwynedd LL73 8PH.
Tel. 410614 Std. 01248
Nearest Town/Resort Moelfre.
Directions Follow A5025 from bridge through Bennlech, keep left at roundabout, on left.
Acreage 20 **Open** April–October
Access Good **Site** Level
Sites available Total 61.
Facilities
Nearby facilities
Bangor.
Peaceful, scenic, near to several beaches, ideal for familes.

MOELFRE

Capel Elen Caravan Park, Lligwy, Dulas, Anglesey, Gwynedd, LL70 9PQ.
Tel. 410670 Std. 01248
Nearest Town/Resort Benllech.
Directions Take the A5025 after bridge onto Anglesey. 11 miles, through Benllech to village of Brynrefail, turn right at craft shop. Park is 300yds on the left.
Acreage 2 **Open** March–October
Access Good **Site** Sloping
Sites available Total 18.
Facilities
Nearby facilities
Bangor.
Quiet, family run site, ¾ mile from beach. Well kept, short grass, free showers and toilets.

NANT PERIS

Gwastadnant, Nant Peris, Llanberis Pass, Gwynedd, LL55 4UL.
Tel. 870356 Std. 01286
Nearest Town/Resort Llanberis/Betws-y-Coed.
Directions A4086 from Capel Curig to Llanberis.
Acreage ½ **Open** All year
Access Good **Site** Level
Sites available Total 20.
Facilities
Nearby facilities
Bangor.
Ideal for climbing, rambling and walks. Main attraction is Mount Snowdon and within easy reach of the seaside. £2.00 per person per night.

NEWBOROUGH

Awelfryn Caravan Park, Newborough, Anglesey, Gwynedd.
Tel. 230
Nearest Town/Resort Newborough.
Directions 10 miles from Menai Bridge on A4080 off A5.
Acreage 2¼ **Open** Easter–September
Access Good
Sites available Total 77.
Facilities
Nearby facilities
Bodorgan.
¾ mile from Newborough Warren (Nature Reserve), largest in West Europe. Also Llanddwyn Isle, a noted beauty spot.

PENMAENMAWR

Woodlands Camping Park, Pendffryn Hall, Penmaenmawr, Gwynedd. LL34 6UF.
Tel. 623219 Std. 01492
Nearest Town/Resort Penmaenmawr/Conwy.
Directions 200 yards off A55 between Bangor and Conwy, 3 miles from Conwy.
Acreage 9 **Open** March–October
Site Level
Sites available Total 100.
Facilities
Nearby facilities
Penmaenmawr.
Situated in Snowdonia National Park area. Ideal touring centre. Short walk to safe beach. S.A.E. for details. Families and couples only.

PENMAENMAWR

Trwyn Yr Wylfa Farm, Trwyn Yr Wylfa, Penmaenmawr, Gwynedd, LL34 6SF.
Tel. 622357 Std. 01492
Nearest Town/Resort Penmaenmawr.
Directions Leave A55 at roundabout for Penmaenmawr. Turn by Mountain View Hotel, farm is ¼ mile east.
Acreage 10 **Open** Spring Bank Holiday–End Aug
Site Sloping
Sites available Total 100.
Facilities
Nearby facilities
Penmaenmawr.
In Snowdonia National Park, secluded.

PENTRAETH

Rhos Caravan Park, Rhos Farm, Pentraeth, Gwynedd, LL75 8DZ.
Tel. 450214 Std. 01248
Nearest Town/Resort Red Wharf Bay.
Directions Through Pentraeth on A5025 main road. Site entrance on left 1 mile north of Pentraeth.
Acreage 6 **Open** March–October
Access Good **Site** Level

Sites available Total 40.
Facilities
Nearby facilities
Bangor.
Near beach and central location for Anglesey, good views of Snowdonia.

PONTLLYFNI
Llyn-y-Gele Farm & Caravan Park, Pontllyfni, Caernarfon, Gwynedd. LL54 5EL.
Tel. 660283 Std. 01286
Nearest Town/Resort Caernarfon.
Directions 7 miles south of Caernarfon on A499. First turning by garage and shop in the village of Pontllyfni. Site is signposted on main road.
Acreage 3½ **Open** Easter–October
Access Good **Site** Level.
Sites available Total 20.
Facilities
Nearby facilities
Bangor.
Near beach, in area of outstanding natural beauty ideal for touring Snowdonia.

PORTHMADOG
Black Rock Camping Park, Morfa Bychan, Porthmadog, Gwynedd.
Tel. 513919 Std. 01766
Nearest Town/Resort Porthmadog.
Directions After croosing Toll, turn left at Woolworths, and continue down the A492 to Black Rock Sands. Continue for 3 miles approx, and bear right.
Acreage 9 **Open** March–October
Access Good **Site** Level
Sites available Total 150.
Facilities
Nearby facilities
Porthmadog.
Adjacent to beach, ideal base for sightseeing, climbing, walking and water activities.

PORTHMADOG
Cardigan View Holiday Park, Morfa Bychan, Porthmadog, Gwynedd. LL49 9YA.
Tel. 512032 Std. 01766
Nearest Town/Resort Porthmadog.
Directions In Porthmadog turn off High Street by Woolworths, signposted to Black Rock Sands, follow road for 2 miles to Morfa Bychan, past the petrol station and small supermarket, turn left signposted Cardigan View. Park at the end of road on the right.
Acreage 2 **Open** Easter–October
Access Good **Site** Level
Sites available Total 32.
Facilities
Nearby facilities
Porthmadog.
Near beach, scenic views, ideal centre for touring. WTB 5 Ticks and a Dragon Award Park.

PORTHMADOG
Tyddyn Adi Camping Park, Morfa Bychan, Porthmadog, Gwynedd, LL49 9YW.
Tel. 512933 Std. 01766
Nearest Town/Resort Porthmadog.
Directions From Porthmadog take the Morfa Bychan road 2¼ miles. Follow to the end of village and there is a large red sign on the right.
Acreage 28 **Open** Easter–October
Access Good **Site** Level
Sites available Total 200.
Facilities
Nearby facilities
Porthmadog.
Close to Porthmadog attractions and ¼ mile from Black Rock Sands. Ideal for touring.

PORTHMADOG
Garreg Goch Caravan Park, Black Rock Sands, Morfa Bychan, Porthmadog, Gwynedd LL49 9YD.
Tel. 512210 Std. 01766
Nearest Town/Resort Porthmadog.
Directions Turn off A487 in Porthmadog, at Woolworths, follow signs for Morfa Bychan for 2 miles, turn left at sign for park.
Acreage 5 **Open** March–October
Access Good **Site** Level
Sites available Total 24.
Facilities
Nearby facilities
Porthmadog.
Near sandy beach, scenic views, ideal for touring places of interest.

PORTHMADOG
Gwyndy Caravan Park, Black Rock Sands, Morfa Bychan, Porthmadog, Gwynedd.
Tel. 512047 Std. 01766
Nearest Town/Resort Porthmadog.
Directions In Porthmadog turn at Woolworths to Black Rock Sands follow the road into the village of Morfa Bychan past the petrol station and little supermarket, turn first left and then second right into road leading into caravan park, exactly 2 miles from Porthmadog.
Acreage 4¼ **Open** March–October
Access Good **Site** Level
Sites available Total 15.
Facilities
Nearby facilities

Porthmadog.
Few minutes from beach, with backdrop of mountain views, ideal for touring Snowdonia area. Also 3 bedroom cottage for hire. British Graded 5 Tick Site.

PORTHMADOG

Ty Bricks Caravan Site, Traeth Mawr, Porthmadog, Gwynedd, LL49 9PP.
Tel. 512597 Std. 01766
Nearest Town/Resort Porthmadog.
Acreage 5 **Open** March–October
Access Good **Site** Level
Sites available Total 8.
Facilities
Nearby facilities
Porthmadog.
Small, quiet site, very scenic views.

PORTHMADOG

Tyddyn Llwyn Caravan Park and Campsite, Black Rock Road, Porthmadog, Gwynedd.
Tel. 512205 Std. 01766
Nearest Town/Resort Porthmadog.
Directions On high street turn bu the Post Office signposted golf course and Black Rock Sands. Park is on the right in under ¼ mile. Verge signs on left.
Acreage 52 **Open** March–October
Access Good **Site** Lev/Slope
Sites available Total 230.
Facilities S P
Nearby facilities
Porthmadog.
Only ¼ mile from Black Rock Sands. In a sheltered valley beneath Moel Y Gest mountain with beautiful wooded scenery.

PWLLHELI

Abererch Sands Holiday Centre, Pwllheli, Gwynedd, LL53 6PJ.
Tel. 612327 Std. 01758
Nearest Town/Resort Pwhelli.
Directions A497 Portmadog to Pwllheli road, 2 miles before Pwllheli.
Open March–October
Access Good **Site** Level
Sites available
Facilities S P
Nearby facilities
Abererch Halt.
Near beach, scenic views, safe swimming.

PWLLHELI

Crugan Holiday Park, Llanbedrog, Pwllheli, Gwynedd.
Tel. 2043 Std. 0175 871
Nearest Town/Resort Abersoch.
Directions On A499 Pwllheli – Abersoch, 2 miles from Abersoch.

Acreage 4 **Open** March–October
Access Good **Site** Level
Sites available Total 20.
Facilities P
Nearby facilities
Pwllheli.

PWLLHELI

Hendre Caravan Park, Efailnewydd, Pwllheli, Gwynedd.
Tel. 613416 Std. 01758
Nearest Town/Resort Pwllheli.
Directions Pwllheli A497, Efailnewydd left onto B4415, site 200yds.
Acreage 3 **Open** March–October
Access Good **Site** Level
Sites available Total 30.
Facilities P
Nearby facilities
Pwllheli.

RHOSNEIGR

Bodfan Farm, Rhosneigr, Anglesey, Gwynedd LL64 5XA.
Tel. 810563 Std. 01407
Nearest Town/Resort Rhosneigr.
Directions Turn left off A5 onto A4080. Site 4½ miles on.
Acreage 12 **Open** April–September
Access Good **Site** Lev/Slope
Sites available Total 80.
Facilities P
Nearby facilities
Rhosneigr.
Near beach, lake and river. Scenic views. Ideal touring.

RHOSNEIGR

Shoreside Caravan & Camp Park, Crigyll View, Station Road, Rhosneigr, Gwynedd, LL64 5QX.
Tel. 810279 Std. 01407
Nearest Town/Resort Rhosneigr.
Directions From A5 onto the A4080, site is opposite the golf club and next door to the riding centre.
Acreage 10 **Open** Easter–October
Access Good **Site** Lev/Slope
Sites available
Facilities S P
Nearby facilities
Rhosneigr.
2 minute walk to the beach, panoramic views of Snowdon. Riding centre, bowling green, tennis court, golf and wind-surfing on site. RAF Valley. Free hot water.

TALSARNAU

Barcdy Touring Caravan & Camping Park, Talsarnau, Gwynedd LL47 6YG.
Tel. 770736 Std. 01766
Nearest Town/Resort Harlech.
Directions From Bala A4212 to Trawsfynydd. A487 to Maentwrog. At Maentwrog left onto A496, signposted Harlech. Site 4 miles.
Acreage 12 **Open** April–October
Access Good **Site** Lev/Slope
Sites available Total 68.
Facilities S P
Nearby facilities
Talsarnau.
Walks from site to nearby mountains and lakes. Ideal touring Snowdonia.

TREARDDUR BAY

Gwyn Fair Caravan Site, Ravens Point Road, Trearddur Bay, Nr. Holyhead, Gwynedd.
Tel. 860289 Std. 01407
Nearest Town/Resort Trearddur Bay.
Directions Up A5 through Anglesey to Valley traffic lights. Turn left for 2 miles to Trearddur Bay, turn left up Ravens Point Road to the end.
Acreage 2 **Open** March–1 Nov
Access Good **Site** Level
Sites available
Facilities S
Nearby facilities
Holyhead.

TREARDDUR BAY

Valley of the Rocks Camping & Caravan Park, Porthdafarch Road, Nr. Trearddur Bay, Holyhead, Gwynedd.
Tel. 765787 Std. 01407
Nearest Town/Resort Holyhead.
Directions Up A5 through Anglesey, turn left at Valley traffic lights, 2 miles to Trearddur Bay. Turn left in Trearddur Bay after the shop to the South Stack. After 2 miles turn right at Cove for 800yds.
Acreage 12 **Open** March–1 Nov
Access Good **Site** Level
Sites available Total 24.
Facilities S P
Nearby facilities
Holyhead.
Near the sea and sandy Cove, beautiful countryside. Near a sports centre and swimming pool. Launderette service available, ask at shop.

TREFRIW

Plas Meirion Caravan Site, Gower Road, Trefriw, Gwynedd, LL27 0RZ.
Tel. Llanrwst 640247 Std. 01492
Nearest Town/Resort Llanrwst.
Directions Caravan park is off the B5106 look out for Woollen Mill in Trefriw Gower road is directly opposite. Halfway to Conway and Betws-Y-Coed.

Acreage 2 **Open** Easter–October.
Access Good **Site** Level
Sites available Total 25.
Facilities
Nearby facilities
Llanrwst.
Ideal touring Snowdonia National Park.

TYWYN

Caethle, Tywyn, Gwynedd, LL36 9HS.
Tel. 710587 Std. 01654
Nearest Town/Resort Aberdovey/Tywyn.
Directions A493 coastal road, between Tywyn and Aberdovey. 1¼ miles north of Tywyn, 2¼ miles south of Aberdovey.
Acreage 15 **Open** 28 March–October
Access Good **Site** Lev/Slope
Sites available Total 30.
Facilities
Nearby facilities
Tywyn.
Narrow Gauge Railway and a leisure centre. Near to beach with scenic views and ideal for touring.

TYWYN

Cwmrhwyddfor, Talyllyn, Tywyn, Gwynedd, LL36 9AJ.
Tel. 761286/761380 Std. 01654
Nearest Town/Resort Dolgellau.
Directions Situated on the A487 between Dolgellau and Machynlleth, at foot of Cader Idris mountain, right at the bottom of Talyllyn pass, a white house under the rocks.
Acreage 6 **Open** All year
Access Good **Site** Level
Sites available Total 40.
Facilities
Nearby facilities
Machynlleth.
Very central for Tywyn, Aberdovey, Barmouth. The site runs alongside a stream. Ideal for the mountains and sea. All kept very clean, excellent reputation. Public telephone and Cafe/Restaurant nearby.

TYWYN

Pall Mall Farm Caravan Park, Pall Mall Farm, Tywyn, Gwynedd.
Tel. 710384/710591 Std. 01654
Nearest Town/Resort Tywyn.
Directions ½ mile from town, first farm on left on the Tywyn/Barmouth Dolgellau main road A493.
Acreage 2 **Open** Easter–October
Access Good **Site** Level
Sites available Total 100.
Facilities
Nearby facilities
Tywyn.
Lovely sandy beach, safe bathing. Good centre for touring, walks, scenic views. Leisure centre and cinema in town. Free hot water, plug available for ironing, launderette close by, Calor Gas. Lots of other facilities in the town ½ mile. New development to a high standard.

TYWYN

Pant Y Neuadd, Aberdovey Road, Tywyn, Gwynedd.
Tel. 711393 Std. 01654
Nearest Town/Resort Tywyn/Aberdovey.
Directions A493, outskirts of Tywyn adjacent to hospital.
Acreage 1¼ **Open** Easter–30 October
Access Good **Site** Level
Sites available Total 32.
Facilities
Nearby facilities
Tywyn.

TYWYN

Waenfach Caravan Site, Waenfach, Llanegryn, Tywyn, Gwynedd, LL36 9SB.
Tel. Tywyn 710375 Std. 01654
Nearest Town/Resort Tywyn.
Directions 3 miles north of Tywyn on the A493.
Open Easter–October
Access Good
Sites available Total 20.
Facilities
Nearby facilities
Tywyn.
Small, working farm with beautiful views. 3 miles from the sea.

TYWYN

Woodlands Holiday Park, Bryncrug, Tywyn, Gwynedd, LL36 9UH.
Tel. 710471 Std. 0654
Nearest Town/Resort Tywyn.
Directions 3 miles inland from Tywyn off the B4405.
Open Easter–October
Access Good **Site** Level
Sites available Total 20.
Facilities
Nearby facilities
Tywyn.
Heated swimming pool.

VALLEY

Pen-Y-Bont Farm, Valley, Holyhead, Gwynedd.
Tel. 740481 Std. 01407
Nearest Town/Resort Holyhead.
Acreage 3¼ **Open** May–October
Access Good **Site** Level
Sites available
Facilities
Nearby facilities
Valley.

VALLEY

Sandy Beach Caravan Site, Llanfwrog, Nr. Holyhead Gwynedd, LL65 4YH.
Tel. 730302 Std. 01407
Nearest Town/Resort Holyhead.
Directions A5 to Valley, right at traffic lights onto A5025, 3 miles and take first left after passing through Llanfaechraeth for Llanfwrog, then follow Sandy Beach signs.
Acreage 10 **Open** March–October
Access Fair **Site** Level
Sites available Total 90.
Facilities
Nearby facilities
Valley.
Close to sandy beach.

POWYS

ABERHOSAN

Rhiwgam Farm, Rhiwgam, Aberhosan, Powys.
Tel. Machynlleth 703975 Std. 01654
Nearest Town/Resort Machynlleth.
Directions 4 miles from Machynlleth towards Dylife, turn right 2 miles up the valley.
Acreage 2 **Open** All year
Access Good **Site** Level
Sites available Total 20.
Facilities
Nearby facilities
Machynlleth.
Quiet site in the hills with scenic views.

BRECON

Brynich Caravan Park, Brecon, Powys.
Tel. 623325 (Also FAX) Std. 01874
Nearest Town/Resort Brecon.
Directions 1 mile east of Brecon on A470. 250 yards from A40/A470 roundabout.
Acreage 15 **Open** Easter–October
Access Good **Site** Level
Sites available Total 100.
Facilities
Nearby facilities
Abergavenny/Merthyr Tydfil.
Ideal centre for touring and discovering the many scenic views of central Wales. A.A. 3 Pennent, W.T.B. 5 Ticks, R.A.C. Appointed. Adventure playground, excellent facilities, including two shower blocks with free hot water and two disabled shower rooms. Baby room with bath.

BRECON

Llynfi Holiday Park, Llangorse Lake, Brecon, Powys.
Tel. Llangorse 283 Std. 0187484
Nearest Town/Resort Brecon.
Directions 4 miles south of Talgarth. B4560 6 miles east of Brecon A40.
Acreage 7 **Open** March–November
Access Good **Site** Level
Sites available Total 60.
Facilities
Nearby facilities
Abergavenny.
Flat, sheltered, grassy site in woodland. Close to Llangorse Lake in the Beacons National Park.

BRECON
Anchorage Caravan Park, Bronllys, Brecon, Powys.
Tel. Talgarth 711246 Std. 01874
Nearest Town/Resort Brecon.
Directions On A438, 8 miles northeast of Brecon on west side of village, behind Filling Station.
Acreage 8 **Open** All year
Access Good **Site** Lev/Slope
Sites available Total 110.
Facilities
Nearby facilities
Abergavenny.
Touring Brecon Beacons National Park, etc. AA 3 Pennants, WTB 5 Ticks.

BRECON
Bishops Meadow Caravan Park, Hay Road, Brecon, Powys, LD3 9SW.
Tel. 622051 Std. 01874
Nearest Town/Resort Brecon.
Directions 1 mile from Brecon on the B4602 to Hay-on-Wye.
Acreage 3¼ **Open** Easter–October
Access Good **Site** Level
Sites available Total 50.
Facilities
Nearby facilities
Scenic views and ideal touring.

BUILTH WELLS
Fforest Fields, Hundred House, Builth Wells, Powys.
Tel. 570220 Std. 01982
Nearest Town/Resort Builth Wells.
Directions 4 miles east of Builth Wells on A481 signposted Hundred House and New Radnor.
Acreage 7 **Open** Easter–October
Access Good **Site** Level
Sites available Total 40.
Facilities
Nearby facilities
Builth Road.
Lovely, quiet site, level mown pitches, wonderful views. Farm and woodland walks. A gem of a site ideal for exploring Mid Wales. Graded 4 Ticks.

BUILTH WELLS
Prince LLewelyn Inn, Cilmery, Builith Wells Powys LD2 3NU.
Tel. 552694 Std. 01982
Nearest Town/Resort Builth Wells.
Directions 2¼ miles west of Builth Wells on A483.
Acreage ¼ **Open** Easter–October
Site Lev/Sloping
Sites available Total 7.
Facilities
Nearby facilities
Cilmery.
Ideal touring, alongside pub/restaurant.

BUILTH WELLS
Irfon Caravan Park, Upper Chapel Road, Garth, Builth Wells, Powys LD4 4BH.
Tel. 620310 Std. 01591
Nearest Town/Resort Builth Wells.
Directions 500 yards along the B4519 out of Garth (Garth is 6 miles west of Builth Wells along the A483).
Acreage 6½ **Open** Easter–October
Access Good **Site** Lev/Slope
Sites available Total 36.
Facilities
Nearby facilities
Garth.
Quiet site alongside river. Scenic views, ideal touring in beauty of mountains and forest.

CARNO
Carno Caravan Park, Carno, Nr. Newtown, Powys, SY17 5JP.
Tel. 420259 Std. 01686
Nearest Town/Resort Newtown/Aberdovey.
Directions Newtown A489 to Caersws, A470 to Carno Village sign. 50yds turn left, over bridge right, continue uphill. Approx. ½ mile on the right.
Acreage 4 **Open** April–October
Access Good **Site** Level
Sites available Total 10.
Facilities
Nearby facilities
Caersws.
Alongside river with scenic views.

CHURCH STOKE
Daisy Bank Caravan Park, Snead, Church Stoke, Powys, SY15 6EB.
Tel. 620471 Std. 01588
Nearest Town/Resort Bishops Castle.
Directions Situated on the A489, 2 miles east of Church Stoke.
Acreage 3 **Open** All Year
Access Good **Site** Lev/Slope
Sites available Total 20.
Facilities
Nearby facilities
Scenic views, ideal touring and walking. Situated in the heart of the Camlad Valley. Dog walk.

CRICKHOWELL
Riverside Caravan and Camping Park, New Road, Crickhowell, Powys NP8 1AY.
Tel. 810397 Std. 01873
Nearest Town/Resort Crickhowell.
Directions Between A40 and A4077 at Crickhowell.
Acreage 3¼ **Open** March–October
Access Good **Site** Level
Sites available Total 65.
Facilities
Nearby facilities
Abergavenny.
Near river, mountain and canal walks, pony trekking, fishing. Town 5 mins walk, in National Park. New improved toilet, shower block with laundry (with drying facilities). Separate disabled shower, toilet and wash basin room. A.A. 3 Pennants, R.A.C. Appointed, WTB 4 Ticks. No hang gliders/paragliders.

CWMDU
Cwmdu Caravan and Camping Site, Cwmdu, Crickhowell, Powys.
Tel. Bwich 730441 Std. 01874
Nearest Town/Resort Crickhowell.
Directions Travelling north on the A40 turn right after 1 mile on to the A479, continue for a further 2 miles to the village of Cwmdu, then signposted right at Farmers Arms, further 400 metres to site.
Acreage 4 **Open** March–October
Access Good **Site** Lev/Slope
Sites available Total 50.
Facilities
Nearby facilities
Abergavenny.
Clean friendly site, ideal base for exploring the Brecon Beacons National Park.

DINAS MAWDDWY
Tynypwll Camping and Caravan Site, Dinas Mawddwy, Machynlleth, Powys.
Tel. 326 Std. 01650 531
Nearest Town/Resort Dolgellau/Machynlleth/Bala.
Directions Take A458 until you come to Mallwyd then take A470 for 1 mile, turn right by Red Lion in the village of Dinas Mwaddwy, site 400 yards away.
Open All year
Access Good **Site** Level
Sites available
Facilities
Nearby facilities
Only 15 miles from beach, alongside river, scenic views, ideal for touring north and mid Wales. Close to Machynlleth, Barmouth, Aberdovery, Dolgellau, Bala and Fairbourne. Very reasonable terms.

HAY-ON-WYE
Hollybush Caravan and Tenting Site, Hollybush Inn, Hay-on-Wye, Powys. HR3 5PG.
Tel. 847371 Std. 01497
Nearest Town/Resort Hay-on-Wye.

Directions 2 miles west of Hay-on-Wye on B4350 Brecon Road.
Acreage 3 **Open** Easter–October
Access Good **Site** Level
Sites available Total 22.
Facilities
Nearby facilities
Hereford.
Canoe launch.

LLANBISTER
Brynithon Caravan Site, Llananno, Llanbister, Nr. Llandrindod Wells, Powys, LD1 6TR.
Tel. 231 Std. 0159 783
Nearest Town/Resort Llanbister Village.
Directions 10 miles north of Llandrindod Wells, 15 miles south of Newtown. Signposted. On A483.
Acreage 2 **Open** March–October
Access Good **Site** Level
Sites available Total 30.
Facilities
Nearby facilities
Llandrindod Wells.

LLANDRINDOD WELLS
Disserth Caravan Park, Howey, Llandrindod Wells, Powys, LD1 6NL.
Tel. 860277 Std. 01597
Nearest Town/Resort Llandrindod Wells.
Open March–October
Access Good **Site** Level
Sites available Total 35.
Facilities
Nearby facilities
Llandrindod Wells.
Alongside river, Ideal touring, fishing. Two static caravans for hire.

LLANDRINDOD WELLS
Dalmore Caravan Park, Howey, Llandrindod Wells, Powys. LD1 5RG.
Tel. 822483 Std. 01597
Nearest Town/Resort Llandrindod Wells.
Directions 2 miles south of Llandrindod on main A483, towards Builth Wells.
Acreage 1 **Open** March–October
Access Good **Site** Lev/Gentle Slope
Sites available Total 6.
Facilities
Nearby facilities
Llandrindod.
Ideal base for hiking and touring Mid Wales, scenic views.

LLANDRINDOD WELLS
The Park Motel, Crossgates, Llandrindod Wells, Powys, LD1 6RF.
Tel. 851201 Std. 01597
Nearest Town/Resort Llandrindod Wells.
Directions 3 miles north of Llandrindod Wells. Follow the A483 to Crossgates, turn left at the roundabout onto A44 (Rhayader). Park is ¼ mile on the left.
Acreage 1 **Open** March–October
Access Good **Site** Level
Sites available Total 15.
Facilities
Nearby facilities
Penybont.
Set in 3 acres of beautiful Mid-Wales countryside yet conveniently situated on the A44. Ideal for touring.

LLANFYLLIN
Hernstent Caravan Park, Llangynog, Nr. Oswestry, Powys, SY10 0EP.
Tel. 860479 Std. 01691
Nearest Town/Resort Bala.
Directions Situated on the B4391. Follow signs for Bala from Oswestry. 18 miles from Oswestry, 12 miles from Bala.
Acreage 1 **Open** March–October
Access Good **Site** Sloping
Sites available Total 35.
Facilities
Nearby facilities
Gobowen.
Views of Berwyn Mountains. Alongside River Tanat, fishing and walking.

LLANGAMMARCH WELLS
Riverside Caravan Park, Llangammarch Wells, Powys, LD4 4BY.
Tel. 465/629 Std. 0159 12
Nearest Town/Resort Builth Wells.
Directions From Builth take A483 towards Garth, signposted in Garth Llangannarch 2 miles.
Acreage 3 **Open** April–October
Access Good **Site** Level
Sites available Total 25.
Facilities
Nearby facilities
Llangammarch Wells.
Alongside river, scenic views, ideal touring.

LLANGORSE
Lakeside Caravan Park, Llangorse, Nr. Brecon, Powys.
Tel. Llangorse 226 Std. 0187 484
Nearest Town/Resort Brecon.
Directions A40 Brecon/Abergavenny junction at B4560 at Bwlch to Llangorse village. Site adjacent to common leading to lake.
Acreage 14 **Open** April–October
Access Good **Site** Level
Sites available
Facilities
Nearby facilities
Abergavenny.
Best coarse fishing in Wales. We hire boats and give sailing and windsurfing instruction. A.A./R.A.C. appointed. Caravans available for hire.

LLANIDLOES
Dol-Llys Farm Caravan Site, Dol-Llys Farm, Llanidloes, Powys, SY18 6JA.
Tel. 412694 Std. 01686
Nearest Town/Resort Llanidloes.
Directions From Llanidloes take the B4569, past hospital, fork right onto the Oakley Park Road, Dol-Llys is the first farm on the right.
Acreage 3 **Open** March–October
Access Good **Site** Level
Sites available Total 20.
Facilities
Nearby facilities
Caersws.
Alongside the banks of the River Severn. Ideal for walkers, fishing and touring Mid Wales. Sports centre nearby.

LLANWDDYN
Fronheulog, Lake Vyrnwy, via Oswestry, Powys.
Tel. Llanwyddyn 662 Std. 0169 173
Nearest Town/Resort Lake Vyrnwy.
Directions 2 miles south of Lake Vyrnwy on B4393. 8 miles from Llanfyllin, Bala 18 miles.
Acreage 2 **Open** March–October
Access Good **Site** Level
Sites available Total 22.
Facilities
Nearby facilities
Pre-booking necessary. RSPB reserve nearby. Ideal centre for touring. Cold water tap.

MACHYNLLETH
Dovey Valley Caravan Park, Brynmelin, Llanwrin, Machynlleth, Powys, SY20 8QJ.
Tel. 511252 Std. 01650
Nearest Town/Resort Machynlleth/Aberdovey.
Directions Take A489 from Machynlleth. Take B4404 north and follow signs.
Acreage 4 **Open** April–October
Access Good **Site** Level
Sites available Total 30.
Facilities
Nearby facilities
Machynlleth.
Half hour drive to beaches. Ideal walking area.

MACHYNLLETH
Warren Parc, Penegoes, Machynlleth, Powys.
Tel. 702054 Std. 01654
Nearest Town/Resort Machynlleth.
Directions 2 miles east on A489, outside Penegoes village.
Acreage 2 **Open** March–October
Access Good **Site** Level
Sites available Total 10.
Facilities
Nearby facilities
Machynlleth.
Central for seaside resorts and touring in Dovey Valley and Snowdonia. BTA graded 5 ticks Excellent, Loo of the Year Award. Calor Award.

MIDDLETOWN
Bank Farm Caravan Park, Middletown, Welshpool, Powys, SY21 8EJ.
Tel. 570260/570526 Std. 01938
Nearest Town/Resort Welshpool.
Directions On A458 5½ miles east of Welshpool and 13¼ miles west of Shrewsbury.
Acreage 2 **Open** March–October
Access Good **Site** Lev/Slope
Sites available Total 20.
Facilities
Nearby facilities
Welshpool.
Scenic views, touring area.

NEWBRIDGE-ON-WYE
Pontarithon Caravan Site, Pont-ar-Ithon, Newbridge-on-Wye, Builth Wells, Powys, LD2 3SA.
Tel. 89203 Std. 01597
Directions Builth Wells 4 miles, Llandrindod Wells 5 miles and Rhayader 8 miles.
Open March–October
Access Good **Site** Level
Sites available
Facilities
Nearby facilities
River.

NEW RADNOR
Walton Caravan Site, Court Cottage, Walton, Presteigne, Powys.
Tel. 259 Std. 0154421
Nearest Town/Resort Kington.
Directions 4 miles from Kington on the A44.
Acreage 7 **Open** All Year
Access Good **Site** Level
Sites available Total 20.
Facilities
Nearby facilities
Knighton.
Scenic views and ideal touring.

NEWTOWN

Tynycwm Camping & Caravan Site, Tynycwm, Aberhafesp, Newtown, Powys, SY16 3JF.
Tel. 688651 Std. 01686
Nearest Town/Resort Newtown.
Directions 7 miles N.W. of Newtown via A489 to Caersws, then B4569 north signposted Aberhafesp, cross B4568 ignore sign for Aberhafesp and continue to next crossroads. Turn left signposted Bwlch y Garreg. Farm and site 1 mile on right.
Acreage 3 **Open** May–October
Access Good **Site** Level
Sites available Total 50.
Facilities
Nearby facilities
Caersws.
Scenic views, pony trekking close, farm site.

NEWTOWN

Smithy Caravan Park, Abermule, Newtown, Powys, SY15 6ND.
Tel. 711280 Std. 01584
Nearest Town/Resort Newtown.
Directions Leave A483 3 miles north Newtown and enter village of Abermule. Turn down lane opposite village shop and post office.
Acreage 4 **Open** All year
Access Good **Site** Level
Sites available Total 30.
Facilities S
Nearby facilities
Newtown.
Outstanding quality park maintained to highest standards. 2 miles of fishing on the park. Winter opening. Bowling nearby.

PRESTEIGNE

Rockbridge Park, Presteigne, Powys, LD6 2NT.
Tel. Whitton 300 Std. 0154 76
Nearest Town/Resort Presteigne.
Directions 1 mile west of Presteigne on the B4356.
Acreage 3 **Open** April–October
Access Good **Site** Level
Sites available Total 20.
Facilities
Nearby facilities
Knighton.
Alongside river, sceinc views, peaceful and un-commercialised.

RHAYADER

Gigrin Farm, South Road, Rhayader, Powys.
Tel. 810243 Std. 01597
Nearest Town/Resort Rhayader.
Directions $\frac{1}{4}$ mile south of Rhayader, just off the A470. Turn at Farm Trail sign.
Acreage 2 **Open** Easter–November
Access Good **Site** Level
Sites available Total 15.
Facilities
Nearby facilities
Llandrindod Wells.
Ideal touring area, beautiful views. Nature trail on a working farm. Fishing and RSPB reserve, near Elan Valley Dams.

TALGARTH

Riverside International Caravan Park, Bronllys, Talgarth, Nr Brecon, Powys, LD3 0HL.
Tel. 711320 Std. 01874
Nearest Town/Resort Brecon.
Directions Leave Brecon on A438 8 miles to Bronllys, turn right in the village for Talgarth, site $\frac{1}{4}$ mile on right – opposite Bronllys Castle.
Acreage $4\frac{1}{4}$ **Open** Easter–October
Access Good **Site** Lev/Slope
Sites available Total 85.
Facilities
Nearby facilities
Abergavenny.
Edge of Brecon Beacon National Park. Free freezer service and ice packs.

WELSHPOOL

Cefn Coch Caravan Park, c/o Cefn Coch Inn, Cefn Coch, Nr. Welshpool, Powys.
Tel. 810247 Std. 01938
Nearest Town/Resort Llanfair Caereinion.
Directions Enter Llanfair town centre, where you will pick up the signs for Cefn Coch (4 miles west of Llanfair).
Acreage 2 **Open** Easter–Mid October
Access Good **Site** Lev/SLope
Sites available Total 10.
Facilities
Nearby facilities
Welshpool.
Scenic views, pony riding, a beautiful and tranquil area.

WELSHPOOL

Derwen Mill Caravan & Chalet Park, Guilsfield, Nr. Welshpool, Powys, SY21 9PH.
Tel. 554365 Std. 01938
Nearest Town/Resort Welshpool.
Directions $2\frac{1}{4}$ miles north of Welshpool via A490 for 2 miles, then right fork on B4392.
Acreage 5 **Open** Easter–October
Access Good **Site** Level
Sites available Total 30.
Facilities
Nearby facilities
Welshpool.
Powys Castle, Llanfair Light Railway, canal boat trips.

WELSHPOOL

Maes-Yr-Afon Caravan Park, Berriew, Welshpool, Powys, SY21 8QB.
Tel. 640587 Std. 01686
Nearest Town/Resort Welshpool.
Directions A483 Welshpool to Newtown road, then 5 miles before Newtown take the B4390 to Berriew. Park is 2 miles towards Manafon on the left.
Acreage 2 **Open** March–October
Access Good **Site** Level
Sites available Total 20.
Facilities
Nearby facilities
Welshpool.

WELSHPOOL

Severn Caravan Park, Kilkewydd Farm, Forden, Welshpool, Powys SY21 8RT.
Tel. 580238 Std. 01938
Nearest Town/Resort Welshpool.
Directions $2\frac{1}{4}$ miles from Welshpool. Take the Newtown road out of Welshpool A438. First junction take the A490, over 2 bridges then left, first farm on the left.
Acreage 6 **Open** March–1 Nov
Access Good **Site** Level
Sites available Total 60.
Facilities M
Nearby facilities
Welshpool.
River, scenic views, ideal touring. Powys Castle, narrow gauge railway and canal.

SCOTLAND

BORDERS

COCKBURNSPATH

Chesterfield Caravan Park, The Neuk, Cockburnspath, Berwickshire, TD13 5YH.
Tel. 830459 Std. 01368
Nearest Town/Resort Eyemouth.
Directions From the A1 bypass, follow signs to Abbey St. Bathans. Caravan park is situated ¾ mile on the left from this junction.
Open April–Mid October
Access Good **Site** Level
Sites available
Facilities
Dunbar.
Quiet, tidy, clean, country site with scenic views. Within easy reach of the A1, Scottish Borders, Edinburgh, Berwick-on-Tweed. Nearest beach 3 miles.

COCKBURNSPATH

Pease Bay Developments Ltd, Pease Bay Caravan Park, Cockburnspath, Berwickshire, TD13 5YP.
Tel. 830206 Std. 01368
Nearest Town/Resort Dunbar.
Directions Signposted at Cockburnspath roundabout, 1¼ miles off the A1. 8 miles south of Dunbar, 22 miles north of Berwick-on-Tweed.
Acreage 1¼ **Open** April–October
Access Good **Site** Level
Sites available Total 16.
Facilities
Nearby facilities
Dunbar.
At the beach alongside a river, scenic views and country walks. Mobile butchers, disabled facilities in the clubhouse only. Parking by unit for tourers only. Surfing nearby.

HAWICK

Bonchester Bridge Caravan Park, Bonchester Bridge, Hawick, Borders.
Tel. 60676 Std. 01458
Nearest Town/Resort Hawick/Sedburgh.
Directions A68 Carter Bar then the A6088 to Bonchester. A7 Hawick.
Open Easter–1 October
Access Poor **Site** Sloping
Sites available Total 25.
Facilities
Nearby facilities
Edinburgh.
Scenic views, alongside a river.

HAWICK

Riverside Caravan Park, Hornshole, Hawick, Roxburghshire, TD9 8SY.
Tel. 73785 Std. 01450
Nearest Town/Resort Hawick.
Directions A689 Hawick/Kelso site 2 miles on left. A68 left 2 miles north of Jedburgh 8 miles on right.
Acreage 2 **Open** April–20th September
Access Good **Site** Level
Sites available Total 35.
Facilities
Nearby facilities

Berwick-on-Tweed.
Site on banks of River Teviot.

JEDBURGH

Jedwater Caravan Park, Jedburgh, Borders.
Tel. 840219 Std. 01835
Nearest Town/Resort Jedburgh.
Directions 3 miles south of Jedburgh on the A68.
Acreage 10 **Open** Easter–October
Access Good **Site** Level
Sites available Total 90.
Facilities
Nearby facilities
Scenic views on the river, Trout fishing, historic castles and abbeys. You can FAX us on 01835 840210.

KELSO

Springwood Caravan Park, Kelso, Borders, TD5 8LS.
Tel. 224596 Std. 01573
Nearest Town/Resort Kelso.
Directions 1 mile south west of Kelso on the A699 to St Boswells.
Acreage 2¼ **Open** 24 March 23 Oct
Access Good **Site** Level
Sites available
Facilities
Nearby facilities
Berwick.
Riverside walk, quiet area with lots of historic monuments and things to see.

PEEBLES

Crossburn Caravan Park, Edinburgh Road, Peebles, Borders.
Tel. 720501 Std. 01721
Nearest Town/Resort Peebles.
Directions ½ mile north of Peebles on A703.
Acreage 12 **Open** April–15th October
Access Good **Site** Lev/Slope
Sites available Total 35.
Facilities
Nearby facilities
Edinburgh.
Ideal touring centre in heart of Scottish borders, only individual motorcycles accepted not groups. A 5 tick British holiday park.

PEEBLES

Rosetta Caravan & Camping Park, Rosetta Road, Peebles, Borders, EH45 8PG.
Tel. 720770 Std. 01721
Nearest Town/Resort Peebles.
Directions 1 mile from Peebles, well signposted from all main roads.
Acreage 27 **Open** April–October
Access Good **Site** Level
Sites available Total 130.
Facilities
Nearby facilities
Edinburgh.
Scenic views, touring, fishing on the River Tweed, golf course adjacent.

CENTRAL

BLAIRLOGIE

Witches Craig Caravan & Camping Park, Blairlogie, Nr. Stirling, Central.
Tel. Stirling 474947 Std. 01786
Nearest Town/Resort Stirling.
Directions A91 Stirling to St. Andrews road.
Acreage 4 **Open** April–October
Access Good **Site** Level
Sites available Total 60.
Facilities
Nearby facilities
Stirling.
Scenic views. Hill walking.

CALLANDER

Mains Farm Camping Site, Main Farm, Thornhill, Stirling, Central.
Tel. Thornhill 850605 Std. 01786
Nearest Town/Resort Callander.
Directions In Thornhill village next to public park. 5½ miles south of Callander on B822.
Acreage 5 **Open** All year
Access Good **Site** Level
Sites available Total 50.
Facilities
Nearby facilities
Stirling.
Scenic views, ideal touring centre. Trossachs area.

KILLIN

Glen Dochart Caravan Park, Luib, By Crianlarich, Perthshire, FK20 8QT.
Tel. Killin 820637 Std. 01567
Nearest Town/Resort Killin.
Directions 6 miles west of Killin on A85.
Open Mid March–October
Access Good **Site** Level
Sites available Total 45.
Facilities
Nearby facilities
Crianlarich.
Peaceful park overlooking the River Dochart with beautiful scenic views. Ideal for walking.

KILLIN

Cruachan Caravan & Camping Park, Cruachan, Killin, Perthshire.
Tel. 820302 Std. 01567
Nearest Town/Resort Killin.
Directions 3 miles east of Killin on the A827.
Acreage 6 **Open** Mid March–October
Access Good **Site** Lev/Slope
Sites available Total 50.
Facilities
Nearby facilities
Crianlarich.
Forest walks, family farm and adjacent to a park. Horse riding next door. Ideal touring and hillwalking area.

KILLIN

High Creagan Caravan Park, Killin, Perthshire, FK21 8TX.
Tel. 449 Std. 0156 72
Nearest Town/Resort Killin.
Directions A827, 2¼ miles from Killin.
Acreage 4 **Open** March–October
Access Good **Site** Level

Sites available Total 30.
Facilities
Nearby facilities
Stirling.

STIRLING
Auchenbowie Caravan Site, By Stirling, Stirlingshire FK7 8HE.
Tel. 822141 Std. 01324
Nearest Town/Resort Stirling.
Directions ¼ mile south of junction 9 M80/M9 on A872 towards Denny turn right for ¼ mile.
Acreage 3¼ **Open** April–October
Access Good **Site** Lev/Slope
Sites available Total 60.
Facilities
Nearby facilities
Stirling.
Rural area ideal for touring.

STRATHYRE
Immervoulin Caravan & Camping Park, Strathyre, Central.
Tel. 384285 Std. 01877
Nearest Town/Resort Strathyre.
Directions On the A84, 8 miles north of Callander.
Acreage 5 **Open** Easter–October
Access Good **Site** Level
Sites available Total 60.
Facilities
Nearby facilities
Stirling.
Scenic park alongside a river. Centrally situated for touring Scotland. Popular with walkers.

DUMFRIES & GALLOWAY

ANNAN
Queensberry Bay Caravan Park, Powfoot, Annan, Dumfriesshire, DG12 5PU.
Tel. 700205 Std. 01461
Nearest Town/Resort Annan.
Acreage 5 **Open** Easter–October
Access Good **Site** Level
Sites available Total 50.
Facilities
Nearby facilities
Annan.
Near the beach, scenic views. Ideal for touring South West Scotland.

AUCHENMALG
Cock Inn Caravan Park, Auchenmalg, Nr. Glenluce, Newton Stewart, Wigtownshire.
Tel. Auchenmalg 227 Std. 0158 15
Nearest Town/Resort Stranraer.
Acreage 6½ **Open** March–October
Access Good **Site** Lev/Slope
Sites available Total 70.
Facilities
Nearby facilities
Stranraer.
Near beach. Thistle commadation 4 ticks.

BORGUE
Brighouse Bay Holiday Park, 5 Borgue Road, Borgue, Kirkcudbright, Dumfries & Galloway, DG6 4TS.
Tel. Borgue 267 Std. 0155 77.
Nearest Town/Resort Kirkcudbright.
Directions From Kirkcudbright take the A755 signposted Gatehouse of Fleet, west over river. On outskirts of town take B727 signposted Borgue. After 4 miles turn left at Brighouse Bay sign. Park is on the left, behind trees, in 2 miles.
Acreage 25 **Open** All Year
Access Good **Site** Lev/Slope
Sites available Total 180.
Facilities
Dumfries.
Beautifully situated on a quiet peninsula with its own sandy beach and working farm, this family park has exceptional on-site recreational facilities including an indoor complex, members lounge, spa facilities, water sports, bikes, golf, pony trekking centre and fishing. Graded "Excellent".

CAIRNRYAN
Cairnryan Caravan Park, Cairnryan, Wigtownshire, DG9 8QX.
Tel. 200231 Std. 01581
Nearest Town/Resort Stranraer.
Directions 4 miles north of Stranraer on the A77. Directly opposite P&O Ferry terminal for Larne.
Acreage ¾ **Open** April–October
Access Good **Site** Level
Sites available Total 25.
Facilities
Nearby facilities
Stranraer.
On Loch Ryan, sea angling, golf etc.

CASTLE DOUGLAS
Lochside Caravan & Camping Site, Lochside Park, Castle Douglas, Kirkcudbrightshire.
Tel. 502949 Std. 01556
Nearest Town/Resort Castle Douglas.
Directions Well signposted in town centre of Castle Douglas.
Acreage 6 **Open** Easter–October
Access Good **Site** Level
Sites available Total 161.
Facilities
Nearby facilities
Dumfries.
Beside Loch, ideal touring. Nearby squash courts, putting, swimming pool and bowling green.

CASTLE DOUGLAS
Loch Ken Holiday Park, Parton, Castle Douglas, Dumfries & Galloway.
Tel. Parton 282 Std. 016447
Nearest Town/Resort Castle Douglas.
Directions 7 miles from Castle Douglas on the A713.
Acreage 6 **Open** Late March–Early Nov
Access Good **Site** Level
Sites available Total 80.
Facilities
Nearby facilities
Dumfries.
Lochside suntrap park. Ideal touring centre. Fishing, sailing and water skiing on site or nearby.

CREETOWN
Castle Cary Holiday Park, Creetown, Newton Stewart, Wigtownshire, DG8 7DQ.
Tel. Creetown 820264 Std. 01671
Nearest Town/Resort Creetown.
Directions Entrance to park on right hand side approaching from the South, ¼ mile before Creetown Village on main A75 Euro-route.
Acreage 6 **Open** 1st March–31st October
Access Good **Site** Level
Sites available Total 80.
Facilities
Nearby facilities
Barrhill.
Superb parkland setting close to beaches, river and mountains. Ideal touring and camping park. New indoor heated swimming pool for 1994. Fully stocked coarse fishing loch. Mountain bike hire, crazy golf. You can FAX us on 01671 820670.

CROCKETFORD
Park of Brandedleys, Crocketford, Nr. Dumfries, Dumfries & Galloway, DG2 8RG.
Tel. Crocketford 0250 Std. 0155 669

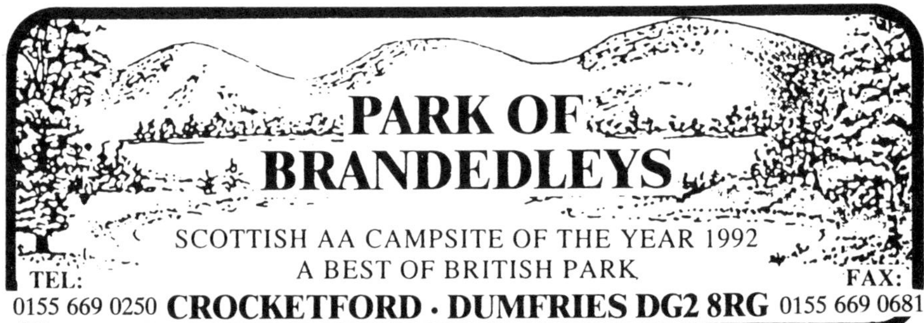

Nearest Town/Resort Dumfries.
Directions Turn left off A75 Dumfries/Castle Douglas road on edge of Crocketford village onto unclassified road. Site on right 150 yards.
Acreage 20 **Open** March–October
Access Good **Site** Lev/Slope
Sites available Total 80.
Facilities
Nearby facilities
Dumfries.
Ideal touring centre, set in beautiful countryside overlooking loch and hills. Indoor pool and sauna. AA Campsite of the Year Scotland 1992. You can FAX us on 0155 669 0681.

CROCKETFORD

Galloway Arms, Crocketford, Dumfries & Galloway.
Tel. 690248 Std. 01556
Nearest Town/Resort Dumfries.
Directions A75 to Stranraer.
Acreage ½ **Open** All Year
Access Good **Site** Level
Sites available Total 15.
Facilities
Nearby facilities
Dumfries.
Near beach, fishing, golfing. Scenic views, stalking.

DALBEATTIE

Sandyhills Bay Leisure Park, Sandyhills, Dalbeattie, Dumfries & Galloway.
Tel. Southwick 257 Std. 0138 778
Nearest Town/Resort Dalbeattie.
Directions On A710 coast road from Dumfries to Dalbeattie, next Sandyhills Village and Colvend Golf Course.
Acreage 6 **Open** 1st April–31st October
Access Good **Site** Level
Sites available Total 60.
Facilities
Nearby facilities
Dumfries.
A unique park only yards from Blue Flag sandy beach with golf, riding, fishing and eating out within ¼ mile. Magnificent coastal walks. Take-away food. Thistle Commended holiday caravans. Park graded 'Excellent'.

DALBEATTIE

Islecroft Caravan & Camping Site, Mill Street, Dalbeattie, Kirkcudbrightshire.
Tel. 610012 Std. 01556
Nearest Town/Resort Dalbeattie.
Directions Adjacent to Colliston Park, off Mill Street in the centre of Dalbeattie.
Acreage 3¼ **Open** Easter–September
Access Good **Site** Level
Sites available Total 74.
Facilities
Nearby facilities
Dumfries.
Ideal position for touring inland and coastal areas of the region.

DRUMMORE

Clashwhannon Caravan Site, Drummore, Stranraer, Dumfries and Galloway. DG9 9QE.
Tel. 840374/840632 Std. 01776
Nearest Town/Resort Stranraer.
Directions A75 from Dumfries (Carlisle) to Stranraer or A77 from Glasgow to Stranraer, then A716 to Drummore.
Acreage ¼ **Open** March–October
Access Good **Site** Lev/Slope
Sites available Total 6.
Facilities
Nearby facilities
Stranraer.
Near beach, scenic views. Good sea fishing, packages arranged. Wreck diving. Holiday caravans available (fully serviced). Gas locally. Licensed pub.

DUMFRIES

Mouswald Place Caravan Park, Mouswald Place, Dumfries, Dumfries & Galloway. DG1 4JS.
Tel. 83226 Std. 01387
Nearest Town/Resort Dumfries.
Directions The site lies just off the A75 approx 6 miles south of Dumfries and 11 miles north of Annan. It is signposted.
Acreage 4¼ **Open** March–October
Access Good **Site** Lev/Slope
Sites available Total 40.
Facilities
Nearby facilities
Dumfries.
Scenic views and ideal touring.

GATEHOUSE OF FLEET

Anwoth Caravan Park, Garden Street, Gatehouse of Fleet, Dumfries & Galloway, DG7 2JU.
Tel. 81433 Std. 01557
Nearest Town/Resort Gatehouse of Fleet.
Directions The site is situated at western end of Gatehouse of Fleet, just off A75. Follow international signposts.
Open Mid Apr–End September
Access Good **Site** Lev/Slope
Sites available Total 28.
Facilities
Nearby facilities
Dumfries.
Scenic views.

GATEHOUSE OF FLEET

Auchenlarie Holiday Farm, Gatehouse of Fleet, Dunfries and Galloway, DG7 2EX.
Tel. 251 Std. 0155 724
Nearest Town/Resort Gatehouse.
Directions 4 miles west of Gatehouse of Fleet on the A75.
Acreage 12 **Open** March–October
Access Good **Site** Level
Sites available Total 127.
Facilities
Nearby facilities
Dunfries.
Near beach, scenic views, main road access.

GATEHOUSE OF FLEET

Mossyard Caravan Park, Mossyard, Gatehouse of Fleet, Castle Douglas, Dumfries & Galloway, DG7 2ET.
Tel. 840226 Std. 01557
Nearest Town/Resort Gatehouse of Fleet.
Directions 4 miles west of Gatehouse of Fleet on the A75. Turn left at signpost to the caravan park.
Acreage 6¼ **Open** April–October
Access Good **Site** Lev/Slope
Sites available Total 55.
Facilities
Nearby facilities
Dumfries.
Sandy beaches within 200yds.

GLENLUCE

Glenluce Caravan Park, Glenluce Village, Dumfries & Galloway.
Nearest Town/Resort Stranraer.
Directions 10 miles east of Stranraer on A75 Dumfries/Stranraer road. Entrance at telephone kiosk in centre of village.
Acreage 2½ **Open** Mid March–Mid October
Access Good **Site** Lev/Slope
Sites available Total 40.
Facilities
Nearby facilities
Stranraer.
Secluded sun trap park in the private grounds of a former estate mansion house. Family operated, close to village. Near to the beach and golf, with bowling, pony trekking, fishing and superb walks all within 1 mile. Graded 5 Ticks Excellent.

GLENLUCE

Whitecairn Farm Caravan Park, Glenluce, Newton Stewart, Dumfries & Galloway.
Tel. Glenluce 300267 Std. 01581
Nearest Town/Resort Stranraer.

Directions 1½ miles north of Glenluce village.
Acreage 4 **Open** March–October
Access Good **Site** Level
Sites available Total 30.
Facilities
Nearby facilities
Stranraer.
Central location for touring Wigtownshire. Very peacful park, away from the main road. 2 miles from A75.

GRETNA

The Braids Caravan Park, Annan Road, Gretna, Dumfriesshire, DG16 5DQ.
Tel. 337409 Std. 01461
Directions From the M6 run straight onto the A74. Take the A75 signposted Dumfries/Stranraer. In 1 mile take the second left for Gretna (B721), park is 600yds on the left.
Acreage 5 **Open** All year
Access Good **Site** Lev/Slope
Sites available Total 84.
Facilities
Nearby facilities
Gretna.
Ideal touring centre, advice given. Fishing can be arranged. Good area for bird watching.

ISLE OF WHITHORN

Castlewigg Caravan Park, Whithorn, Newton Stewart, Wigtownshire, DG8 8DP.
Tel. 500616 Std. 01988
Nearest Town/Resort Newton Stewart.
Directions From roundabout at Newton Stewart turn onto the A714 to Wigtown. Just before Wigtown take the A746 to Whithorn. 3 miles after Sorbie site on the right.
Acreage 4¼ **Open** March–October
Access Good **Site** Level
Sites available Total 15.
Facilities
Nearby facilities
Stranraer.
Scenic views, central location. Award winning gardens, Graded 5 Ticks.

KIRKCOWAN

Three Lochs Holiday Park, Balminoch, Kirkcowan, Newton Stewart, Wigtownshire.
Tel. 830304 Std. 01671
Nearest Town/Resort Newton Stewart.
Acreage 15 **Open** Easter–October
Access Good **Site** Level
Sites available Total 80.
Facilities
Nearby facilities
Three Lochs for coarse or trout fishing, sailing, full size snooker.

KIRKCUDBRIGHT

Seaward Caravan Park, Dhoon Bay, Kirkcudbright, Dumfries & Galloway.
Tel. Kirkcudbright 331079 Std. 01557
Nearest Town/Resort Kirkcudbright.
Directions Take A755 signposted Gatehouse of Fleet, west from Kirkcudbright. On outskirts turn left onto the B727 signposted Borgue. Park is on the right in 2 miles.
Acreage 6¼ **Open** 1st March–31st October
Access Good **Site** Level
Sites available Total 50.
Facilities
Nearby facilities
Dumfries.
An exclusive park beautifully situated with exceptional views over Kirkcudbright Bay. Many on-site amenities plus all the activities at nearby Brighouse Bay. Sea adjacent for angling and sandy beach ½ mile away. Thistle Commended caravans for hire. Graded 'Excellent'.

KIRKCUDBRIGHT

Silvercraigs Caravan Site, Silvercraigs Road, Kirkcudbright, Dumfries & Galloway.
Tel. Kirkcudbright 330123 Std. 01557
Nearest Town/Resort Kirkcudbright.
Directions Turn left from St. Mary's Street to St. Mary's Place, follow Barrhill Road and Silvercraigs Road, site on left.
Acreage 5¼ **Open** Easter–October
Access Good **Site** Sloping
Sites available Total 50.
Facilities
Nearby facilities
Dumfries.
Ideal touring, near sea. Laundry facilities available. Wildlife Park nearby.

KIRKPATRICK FLEMING

Cove Estate Caravan and Camping Site, Cove Lodge, Kirkpatrick Fleming, By Lockerbie, Dumfries and Galloway.
Tel. 800285 Std. 01461
Nearest Town/Resort Gretna.
Directions Turn off A74 M74 at Kirkpatrick Fleming, then in Kirkpatrick follow all signs to Bruces Cave.
Acreage 80 **Open** All year
Access Good **Site** Level
Sites available Total 40.
Facilities
Nearby facilities
Annan.
In grounds of 80 acre estate, peacefull and quiet and secluded, famous ancient monument of King Robert the Bruce's cave in

grounds of site, free fishing on 3 mile stretch of river for Trout, Sea Trout, Salmon. New disabled toilet block and laundry room.

LOCKERBIE

Halleaths Caravan Park, Halleaths, Lochmaben, Lockerbie, Dumfries & Galloway.
Tel. 810630 Std. 01387
Nearest Town/Resort Lochmaben/Lockerbie.
Directions From Lockerbie on A74, take A709 to Lochmaben. ½ mile on right after crossing River Annan.
Acreage 8 **Open** March–November
Access Good **Site** Level
Sites available Total 70.
Facilities
Nearby facilities
Lockerbie.
Bowling, tennis, yachting, boating, golf and both coarse and game fishing, all within 1 mile of park.

LOCHNAW

Drumlochart Caravan Park, Lochnaw, Stranraer, Wigtownshire.
Tel. 870232 Std. 01776
Nearest Town/Resort Stranraer.
Directions Take Leswalt road from Stranraer. Turn left in Leswalt on B7043.
Acreage 22 **Open** March–October
Access Good **Site** Level
Sites available Total 24.
Facilities
Nearby facilities
Stranraer.
Own 10 acre trout loch. 4 pennant A.A. R.A.C. Appointed 5 Ticks.

MONREITH

Knock School Caravan Park, Monreith, Newton Stewart, Wigtownshire.
Tel. 700414/700409 Std. 01988
Nearest Town/Resort Port William.
Directions 3 miles south on A747 at crossroads to golf course.
Acreage 1 **Open** Easter–October
Access Good **Site** Lev/Slope
Sites available Total 15.
Facilities
Nearby facilities
Near sandy beaches and golf.

MONREITH

Monreith Sands Holiday Park, Newton Stewart, Wigtownshire DG8 9LJ.
Tel. 700218 Std. 01998
Nearest Town/Resort Port William.
Directions 2 miles south of Port William.
Acreage 2
Access Good **Site** Lev/Slope
Sites available Total 20.
Facilities
Nearby facilities
Stranraer.
Beach 200 yards, quiet site. Golf 1 mile.

NEWTON STEWART

Creebridge Caravan Park, Newton Stewart, Dumfries & Galloway.
Tel. 402324 Std. 01671
Nearest Town/Resort Newton Stewart.
Directions 300 metres from town centre, over Old Bridge.
Acreage 4 **Open** March–October
Access Good **Site** Level
Sites available Total 40.
Facilities
Nearby facilities
Barrhill.

NEWTON STEWART

Merrick Caravan Park, Glentrool, Nr. Newton Stewart, Wigtownshire.
Tel. 840280 Std. 01671
Nearest Town/Resort Glentrool.
Directions Take A714 from Newton Stewart to Girvan for 9 miles. Turn right towards Glentrool. site on left ½ mile from main road.
Acreage 3 **Open** March–October
Access Good **Site** Level
Sites available Total 14.
Facilities
Nearby facilities
Barhill.
On edge of forest, ideal touring.

PALNACKIE

Barlochan Caravan Park, Palnackie, Nr. Castle Douglas, Dumfries & Galloway.
Tel. Palnackie 256 Std. 0155 660
Nearest Town/Resort Dalbeattie.
Directions From Dalbeattie take A711 west. Left at T junction, park on right in 2 miles.
Acreage 8 **Open** April–October
Access Good **Site** Part/Slope
Sites available Total 30.
Facilities
Nearby facilities
Dumfries.
Overlooking river estuary. Own coarse fishing loch. Mini golf and dish wash-ups. Graded "Very Good". Thistle Award Holiday Caravans.

PORTPATRICK

Galloway Point Holiday Park, Portree Farm, Portpatrick, Stranraer, Wigtownshire DG9 9AA.
Tel. 810561 (Also FAX) Std. 01776
Nearest Town/Resort Portpatrick.
Directions A75 from Dumfries. A77 from Glasgow and Stranraer. ½ mile south of Portpatrick.
Acreage 17 **Open** Easter–Mid October
Access Good **Site** Lev/Slope
Sites available Total 100.
Facilities
Nearby facilities
Stranraer.
Overlooking Irish Sea. Only ten minutes walk to fishing village of Portpatrick. Botanical gardens nearby. British Holiday Parks Grading 4 Ticks, AA 3 Pennants and Environment Award, RAC Appointed, Thistle Award.

PORTPATRICK

Sunnymeade Caravan Park, Portpatrick, Nr. Stranraer, Wigtownshire, Dumfries and Galloway, DG9 8LN.
Tel. 810293 Std. 01776
Nearest Town/Resort Portpatrick.
Directions A77 to Portpatrick. First left on entering village, park is ¼ a mile on the left.
Open Easter–October
Access Good **Site** Lev/Slope
Sites available
Facilities
Nearby facilities
Stranraer.
Overlooking Irish Sea, near golf,beach, bowling, fishing etc. Hard standing.

ROCKCLIFFE

Castle Point Caravan Park, Barcloy Road, Rockcliffe by Dalbeattie, Dumfries and Galloway. DG5 4QL.
Tel. 630248 Std. 01556
Nearest Town/Resort Rockcliffe.
Directions In Dalbeattie take A710. 5 miles turn right to Rockcliffe. Sign for park in 1 mile near entrance to village.
Acreage 2 **Open** March–October
Access Good **Site** Level
Sites available Total 37.
Facilities
Nearby facilities
Dumfries.
Overlooking sea and Rockcliffe Bay, (shore 200yds), very quiet, and well kept. Lovely view.

SANDHEAD

Sands of Luce Caravan Park, Sandhead, Stranraer, Wigtownshire, DG9 9JR.
Tel. 830456 Std. 01776
Nearest Town/Resort Stranraer.
Directions From Stranraer follow the A77 to the A716. Site entrance is 1 mile south of Stoneykirk Village at the junction of the A716 and the B7084.
Acreage 5 **Open** Mid March–October
Access Good **Site** Lev/Slope
Sites available Total 36.
Facilities
Nearby facilities
Stranraer.
Site extends directly onto a wide sandy beach. Ideal for children and watersports.

STRANRAER

Aird Donald Caravan Park, Stranraer, Wigtownshire.
Tel. Stranraer 702025 Std. 01776
Nearest Town/Resort Stranraer.
Directions Off A75 entering Stranraer. Signposted.
Acreage 12 **Open** All year
Access Good **Site** Level
Sites available Total 100.
Facilities
Nearby facilities
Stranraer.
Ideal touring. Also tarmac hard standing for touring caravans in wet weather. Ideal site for ferry to Ireland. New toilet and shower block.

STRANRAER

Wig Bay Holiday Park, Loch Ryan, Stranraer, DG9 0PS.
Tel. 853233 Std. 01776
Nearest Town/Resort Stranraer.
Directions On entering Stranraer, follow the ferry signs. Take the Kirkcolm road A718, at roundabout take the road to the right along the coast road, about 4 miles from Stranraer.
Acreage 4 **Open** March–October
Access Good **Site** Level
Sites available Total 24.
Facilities
Nearby facilities
Stranraer.
Alongside beach, Loch Ryan. Scenic views across the Rhinns. Yachting, surfing, fishing, bird watching, golf and pony trekking.

THORNHILL

Penpont Caravan and Camping Park, Penpont, Thornhill, Dumfries and Galloway.
Tel. 330470 Std. 01848
Nearest Town/Resort Thornhill.
Directions 2 miles west of Thornhill on A702, on the left just before Penpont Village.

Acreage 1¾ **Open** April–October
Access Good **Site** Lev/Slope
Sites available Total 40.
Facilities
Nearby facilities
Dumfries.
Ideal touring centre in lovely countryside. Cycling, walking, fishing and bird watching.

FIFE

KINGHORN

Pettycur Bay Holiday Park, Burntisland Road, Kinghorn, Fife.
Tel. 890321 Std. 01592
Nearest Town/Resort Kinghorn.
Directions From Forth Bridge take the A921 cut off. Follow coast road to Burntisland. Park is ½ mile east.
Acreage 2 **Open** March–October
Access Good **Site** Level
Sites available Total 55.
Facilities
Nearby facilities
Kinghorn.
Overlooking 2 miles of golden sands. Panoramic seascape in a prime tourist area.

LEVEN

Letham Feus Caravan Park, Letham Feus, by Leven, Fife.
Tel. 350323 Std. 01333
Nearest Town/Resort Leven.
Directions On A916 Kennoway/Cupar road 1¼ miles east of Kennoway.
Acreage 1 **Open** April–September
Access Good **Site** Sloping
Sites available Total 11.
Facilities
Nearby facilities
Kirkcaldy.
Ideal touring.

ST ANDREWS

Cairnsmill Caravan Park, Largo Road, St. Andrews, Fife, KY16 8NN.
Nearest Town/Resort St Andrews.
Directions Follow A915 approx 1 mile.
Open April–October
Access Good **Site** Level
Sites available
Facilities
Nearby facilities
Leuchars.
Near beach, ideal touring.

ST ANDREWS

Clayton Caravan Park, Clayton, St. Andrews, Fife KY16 9YB.
Tel. 870242/870630 Std. 01334
Nearest Town/Resort St. Andrews.
Directions 4½ miles from St Andrew on A91, between Dairsie and Guardbridge.
Acreage 8 **Open** March–October
Access Good **Site** Lev/Slope
Sites available Total 30.
Facilities
Nearby facilities
Leuchars/Cupar.
Centrally situated for touring Scotland. Only 4 miles from beaches and golf courses. You can FAX us on 01334 870057.

ST ANDREWS

Craigtoun Meadows Holiday Park, No.5 Mount Melville, St. Andrews, Fife. KY16 8PQ.
Tel. 475959 Std. 01334
Nearest Town/Resort St. Andrews.
Directions 1¼ miles west of "West Port" of St. Andrews, bear left at Hepburn Gardens.
Open 1st March–31st October
Access Good **Site** Level
Sites available Total 98.
Facilities
Nearby facilities
Leuchars.
Close to beaches and many golfcourses.

ST. MONANS

St. Monans Caravan Park, St. Monans, Fife, KY10 2DN.
Tel. 730778 Std. 01333
Nearest Town/Resort St. Andrews.
Directions Park is on the A917 at east end of St. Monans.
Acreage 1 **Open** 21 March–October
Access Good **Site** Level
Sites available Total 18.
Facilities
Nearby facilities
Leuchars.
Small, quiet park, near the sea and small villages with harbours.

GRAMPIAN

ABOYNE

Aboyne Loch Caravan Park, Aboyne, Aberdeenshire, AB34 5BR.
Tel. 86244 Std. 013398
Nearest Town/Resort Aberdeen.
Directions ½ mile east of Aboyne village on the 1993 Aberdeen/Braemar trunk road.
Open April–October
Access Good **Site** Lev/Slope
Sites available Total 50.
Facilities
Nearby facilities
Aberdeen.
Situated on a wooded promentary of land, surrounded on three sides by a loch.

BANCHORY

Campfield Caravan Site, Banchory, Grampian.
Tel. 82250 Std. 013398
Nearest Town/Resort Banchory.
Directions On A980 road, 5 miles north of Banchory.
Acreage 2 **Open** April–September
Access Good **Site** Level
Sites available Total 14.
Facilities
Nearby facilities
Aberdeen.
Scenic views ideal for touring and exploring Deeside.

BANCHORY

Feughside Caravan Park, Strachan, Banchory, Kincardineshire.
Tel. 850669 Std. 01330
Nearest Town/Resort Banchory.
Directions Take B974 to Strachan, 3 miles. Continue straight on B976, 2 miles to Feughside Inn. Site is directly behind Inn, turn right directly after Inn.
Open April–Mid October
Access Good **Site** Level
Sites available Total 20.
Facilities
Nearby facilities
Stonehaven.
Scenic views. Near river. Ideal touring area. Good walks. Family site in country. Fishing nearby Trout Loch. Hotel 100 yards.

BANFF

Banff Links Caravan Park, The Links, Banff, Grampian.
Tel. 812228 Std. 01261
Nearest Town/Resort Banff.
Directions Follow the A98 from Banff to Elgin.
Acreage 3 **Open** April–September
Access Good **Site** Level
Sites available Total 115.
Facilities
Nearby facilities
Keith.
Scenic views over the sea and a large sandy beach.

BUCKIE

Findochty Caravan Site, Edindoune Shore, Findochty, Buckie, Grampian.
Tel. 835303 Std. 01542
Nearest Town/Resort Findochty.
Directions 2 miles east of Buckie on the A942.
Acreage 3 **Open** April–2 October
Access Good **Site** Level
Sites available Total 23.
Facilities
Nearby facilities
Elgin/Keith.
Attractive location adjacent to the harbour. Local attractions include watersports, golf, coastal walks, swimming and fishing. Disabled toilets on site.

BURGHEAD

Burghead Caravan Site, West Beach, Burghead, Moray, IV30 2UN.
Tel. 835799 Std. 01343
Nearest Town/Resort Burghead.
Directions Turn off the A96 2 miles west of Elgin onto the B9013, due north 5 miles.
Acreage 5¼ **Open** April–2 October
Access Good **Site** Sloping
Sites available Total 60.
Facilities
Nearby facilities
Elgin.
Within yards of a beautiful sandy beach. Local activities include watersports and bowling. Disabled toilets on site.

BURGHEAD

The Red Craig Hotel & Caravan & Camping Park, Burghead, Morayshire IV30 2XX.
Tel. Burghead 835663 Std. 01343
Nearest Town/Resort Elgin.
Directions Take signposted road to Burghead of A96 (main Elgin to Inverness road). Hotel and site situated approx. 300 yards east of B9013/B9040 junction, off B9040 Burghead/Lossiemouth road.
Acreage 2-3 **Open** April–October
Access Good **Site** Level
Sites available Total 38.
Facilities
Nearby facilities
Elgin.
Overlooking Moray Firth and near sandy beaches. British Caravan Park Graded 4 Ticks.

CULLEN
Logie Park Caravan Site, Logie Drive, Cullen, Grampian, AB56 2TW.
Tel. 840766 Std. 01542
Nearest Town/Resort Cullen.
Directions 5 miles east of Buckie on A942.
Acreage 4¾ **Open** April–2 October
Access Good **Site** Sloping
Sites available Total 65.
Facilities
Nearby facilities
Keith.
Attractive site with views across Cullen Bay and Moray Firth. Disabled toilets on site.

FOCHABERS
Burnside Caravan Site, Fochabers, Moray, Grampian.
Tel. 820362/820511 Std. 01343
Nearest Town/Resort Elgin.
Directions Situated in Fochabers on the A96 trunk road.
Open April–October
Access Good **Site** Level
Sites available Total 120.
Facilities
Nearby facilities
Elgin.
Ideal touring centre for north east Scotland.

FORRES
The Old Mill Holiday Park, Brodie, Forres, Morayshire, IV36 0TD.
Tel. 641244 Std. 01309
Nearest Town/Resort Forres/Nairn.
Directions On the A96 between Forres (3¼ miles) and Nairn (5 miles).
Acreage 2 **Open** April–October
Access Good **Site** Level
Sites available Total 49.
Facilities
Nearby facilities
Forres.
Alongside Burn countryside, Brodie Castle and Old Mill Inn. Quiet park with ideal touring.

HOPEMAN
Station Caravan Park, Hopeman, Nr. Elgin, Grampian.
Tel. 830880 Std. 01343
Nearest Town/Resort Elgin.
Acreage 3 **Open** April–October
Access Good **Site** Level
Sites available Total 37.
Facilities
Nearby facilities
Elgin.
On a beach on Moray Firth coast.

JOHNSHAVEN
Wairds Park Committee, Beach Road, Johnshaven, Montrose, Angus.
Tel. 362395 Std. 01561
Nearest Town/Resort Montrose.
Directions 10 miles north of Montrose ont he A92.
Acreage 6 **Open** April–15 October
Access Good **Site** Level
Sites available Total 60.
Facilities
Montrose.
On a beach, ideal for touring.

KEITH
Keith Caravan Site, Dunnyduff Road, Keith, Banffshire, AB55 3JG.
Tel. 882078 Std. 01542
Nearest Town/Resort Keith.
Directions 17 miles east of Elgin on the A96.
Acreage 1¾ **Open** April–2 October
Access Good **Site** Sloping
Sites available Total 24.
Facilities
Nearby facilities
Keith.
Small, attractive site situated on 'The Whisky Trail'. Swimming locally. Disabled toilets on site.

KINTORE
Hillhead Caravan Park, Kintore, Aberdeenshire. AB51 0YX.
Tel. 632809 Std. 01467
Nearest Town/Resort Kintore.
Directions In centre of Kintore turn off A96 onto road signposted Ratch Hill, in ¼ mile bear left onto road signposted Blairs/Hillhead Caravan Park. In ½ mile turn left into caravan park entrance. Or follow camping and caravan signs on B996 3 miles.
Acreage 1¼ **Open** Easter–October
Access Good **Site** Level
Sites available Total 29.
Facilities
Nearby facilities
Inverurie.
Ideally situated for joining Scotlands castle trail, near Whisky trail, Aberdeen and Royal Deeside. 4 Tick Grading. You can FAX us on 01467 633173.

LAURENCEKIRK
Brownmuir Caravan Park, Fordoun, By Laurencekirk, Grampian, AB30 1SJ.
Tel. 320552 Std. 01561
Nearest Town/Resort Stonehaven.
Directions From Laurencekirk, 4 miles north on the A90. At village of Fordoun turn right for 1 mile. Site is on the right. 10 miles south of Stonehaven, turn left at Fordoun, as above.
Acreage 3 **Open** April–October
Access Good **Site** Level
Sites available Total 30.
Facilities
Nearby facilities
Stonehaven.
At the foot of Grampian Hills. Ideal for Deeside, coast and wildlife. Fishing village.

LOSSIEMOUTH
Silver Sands Leisure Park, Covesea West Beach, Lossiemouth, Morayshire. IV31 6SP.
Tel. 813262 Std. 01343
Nearest Town/Resort Lossiemouth.
Directions Elgin/Lossiemouth A941, turn left 1 mile before Lossiemouth continue 1¼ miles, past R.A.F. camp, turn left, site beside lighthouse.
Acreage 14 **Open** April–October
Access Good **Site** Level
Sites available Total 140.
Facilities
Nearby facilities
Elgin.
Beautiful unspoilt golden beach next to park, no roads to cross. Ideal touring area for fishing villages, castles and distilleries.

LOSSIEMOUTH
East Beach Caravan Park, Seatown, Lossiemouth, Moray, IV31 6JJ.
Tel. 813980 Std. 01343
Nearest Town/Resort Lossiemouth.
Directions 6 miles north of Elgin on the A941.
Acreage 10 **Open** April–2 October
Access Good **Site** Sloping
Sites available Total 44.
Facilities
Nearby facilities
Elgin.
Overlooking the River Lossie, near an extensive white sandy beach. Good centre for a wide range of water based activities. Disabled toilets on site.

MACDUFF
Wester Bonnyton Farm Site, Gamrie, Banff, Grampian AB45 3EP.
Tel. Macduff 32470 Std. 01261
Nearest Town/Resort Macduff.
Directions 2 miles east of Macduff on B9031.
Acreage ¾ **Open** Easter–October
Access Good **Site** Level
Sites available Total 8.
Facilities
Nearby facilities
Keith.
Quiet site overlooking the Moray Firth. Ideal touring. Scenic views. Unspoiled countryside.

PETERHEAD
Aden Country Park Caravan Site, Aden Country Park, Mintlaw, Peterhead, Aberdeenshire.
Tel. 623460 Std. 01771
Nearest Town/Resort Peterhead.
Directions Take the A92 from Aberdeen or the A950 from Peterhead.
Acreage 4 **Open** April–September
Access Good **Site** Lev/Slope
Sites available Total 50.
Facilities
Nearby facilities
Aberdeen.
Aden Country Park and North East Scotland, Agricultural Heritage Centre.

PORTKNOCKIE

Portknockie Caravan Site, Seafield Terrace, Portknockie, Grampian.
Tel. 840766 Std. 01542
Nearest Town/Resort Buckie.
Directions 4 miles east of Buckie on the A942.
Acreage 2 **Open** June–August
Access Good **Site** Level
Sites available
Facilities
Nearby facilities
Keith.
Attractive village with attractions such as coastal walks and fishing.

PORTSOY

Sandend Caravan Park, Sandend, Portsoy, Banffshire.
Tel. 842660 Std. 01261
Nearest Town/Resort Portsoy.
Directions On the main A98, 8 miles west of Banff. Park is signposted ¼ mile off the A98, 3 miles from Portsoy.
Acreage 4¼ **Open** April–10 October
Access Good **Site** Level
Sites available Total 52.
Facilities
Nearby facilities
Keith.
On the edge of Sandend Beach (pure sand), winner of a 1994 Seaside Award. 5 Tick Graded.

ST. CYRUS

East Bowstrips Caravan Park, St. Cyrus, Nr. Montrose, Grampian DD10 0DE.
Tel. 850328 Std. 01674.
Nearest Town/Resort Montrose.
Directions Approx 6 miles north of Montrose. Follow A92, enter village of St. Cyrus, first left after Hotel, second right.
Acreage 4 **Open** April–October
Access Good **Site** Lev/Slope
Sites available Total 30.
Facilities
Nearby facilities
Montrose.
Quiet, family park by the coast. Ideal touring base. Very good facilities. Beautiful sandy beach and nature reserve approx. 1 mile. Special facilities for disabled visitors including adapted caravan for hire. A.A. Listed and Graded 4 Tick.

ST. CYRUS

Lauriston Caravan Park, St. Cyrus, By Montrose, Angus, Grampian.
Tel. 850316 Std. 01674
Nearest Town/Resort Montrose.
Directions Situated approx half way between Montrose and Inverbervie on the main A92. 1 mile north of St Cyrus Village, 7 miles north of Montrose.
Acreage 6¾ **Open** 1st April–18th Oct
Access Good **Site** Level
Sites available Total 60.
Facilities
Nearby facilities
Montrose.
Near beach, scenic views, ideal touring. Quiet country park on a bus route.

TURRIFF

McRobert Park, Parkview, Aberchirder, Huntly, Aberdeenshire, AB54 5RA.
Tel. 780260 Std. 01466
Nearest Town/Resort Aberchirder.
Acreage 1 **Open** June–September
Access Good **Site** Level
Sites available Total 15.
Facilities
Nearby facilities
Huntly.
Quiet site. Fishing can be arranged.

TURRIFF

Turriff Caravan Park, Station Road, Turriff, Grampian.
Tel. 562205 Std. 01888
Nearest Town/Resort Turriff.
Directions A947 from Aberdeen.
Acreage 2 **Open** April–2 October
Access Good **Site** Level
Sites available Total 50.
Facilities
Nearby facilities
Inverurie.
Sports centre, golf and swimming pool.

HIGHLAND

ACHARACLE

Resipole Farm Caravan & Camping Park, Loch Sunart, Acharacle, Argyll, PH36 4HX.
Tel. 617 Std. 01967 431
Nearest Town/Resort Fort William.
Directions Take A82 south from Fort William across Corran Ferry then A861 to Strontian and Salen. Site 7¼ miles west of Strontian on roadside.
Acreage 6 **Open** April–September
Access Good **Site** Level
Sites available Total 60.
Facilities
Nearby facilities
Fort William.
Scenic views, loch side, central for touring the area. Roomy site.

ARISAIG

Gorton Sands Caravan Site, Gorton Farm, Arisaig, Invernessshire.
Tel. 283 Std. 0168 75
Nearest Town/Resort Arisaig.
Directions A830 Fort William/Mallaig road, 2 miles west of Arisaig, turn left at sign 'Back of Keppoch', ¾ mile to road end.
Acreage 6 **Open** April–September
Access Good **Site** Level
Sites available Total 45.
Facilities
Nearby facilities
Arisaig.
On sandy beach, views of Isles of Skye, Eigg and Rhum. Boat trips to Isles, hill walking, ideal for bathing or boating.

ARISAIG

Camusdarach, Arisaig, Inverness-shire, PH39 4NT.
Tel. 221 Std. 016875
Nearest Town/Resort Arisaig/Mallaig.
Directions Take the Mallaig road from Fort William (A830) to Arisaig. After Arisaig, Camusdarach Campsite is signed on the left after high stone wall.
Acreage 3 **Open** March–October
Access Good **Site** Lev/Slope
Sites available Total 42.
Facilities
Nearby facilities
Arisaig.
Near a superb beach, views of the Inner Hebrides, Eigg, Rhum and Skye. Beautiful unspoilt surroundings.

ARISAIG

Portnardoran Caravan Site, Arisaig, Invernessshire, PH39 4NT.
Tel. Arisaig 267 Std. 0168 75
Nearest Town/Resort Mallaig.
Directions 2 miles north of Arisaig village, on Fort William – Arisaig road A830.
Acreage 2 **Open** Easter–October
Access Good **Site** Level
Sites available Total 40.
Facilities
Nearby facilities
Arisaig.
Beside silver sands, scenic views of inner Hebrides, safe for swimming.

AVIEMORE

Campground of Scotland, Coylumbridge, Nr. Aviemore, Invernesshire.
Tel. 120 Std. 0147 9810
Nearest Town/Resort Aviemore.
Directions From Aviemore take the ski road towards Glenmore. Park on right in 1¼ miles.
Acreage 4 **Open** All Year.
Access Good **Site** Level
Sites available Total 39.
Facilities
Nearby facilities
Aviemore.
Alongside river, in pinewood setting, close to Aviemore, ideal for ski-ing, boating, walking et cetera.

AVIEMORE

High Range Touring Caravan Park, Grampion Road, Aviemore, Inverness-shire, PH22 1PT.
Tel. 810636 Std. 01479
Nearest Town/Resort Aviemore.
Directions On the B9152 at the south end of Aviemore, directly opposite the B970 road.
Acreage 2 **Open** December–October
Access Good **Site** Level
Sites available Total 35.
Facilities
Nearby facilities
Aviemore.
Own birch woodland park at the foot of Craigellachie Nature Reserve. Scenic views of Spey valley. 500yds to Aviemore centre.

BALMACARA

Balmacara Woodland Campsite, Forest Enterprise, Balmacara, Kyle of Lochalsh, Ross-shire, IV40 8DN.
Tel. 321 Std. 0159986
Nearest Town/Resort Kyle of Lochalsh.
Directions 3 miles east on the A87.
Acreage 2¼ **Open** Easter–September
Access Good **Site** Level
Sites available Total 55.
Facilities
Nearby facilities
Kyle.
Scenic views, forest walks, orienteering, Pine Martens are resident on site, 5 minutes from sea.

BALMACARA

Reraig Caravan Site, Balmacara, Kyle of Lochalsh, Rosshire.
Tel. Balmacara 215 Std. 0159 986
Nearest Town/Resort Kyle of Lochalsh.
Directions On A87 1¾ miles west of junction with A890.
Acreage 2 **Open** May–September
Access Good **Site** Level

Sites available Total 45.
Facilities
Kyle of Lochalsh.
Hotel adjacent to site. Dishwashing sinks, hairdryers. Forest walks adjacent to site, no booking by telephone. Tent and awnings at discretion of warden.

BEAULY
Cruivend Caravan Park, Cruivend, Beauly, Highland IV4 7BE.
Tel. Beauly 782367 Std. 01463
Nearest Town/Resort Inverness.
Directions Northbound from Inverness to Beauly on A862 first left directly after crossing River Beauly. 1 mile south of Beauly.
Acreage 3 **Open** April–October
Access Good **Site** Level
Sites available Total 30.
Facilities
Nearby facilities
Inverness.
Peaceful riverside location ideal for touring the north and west Highlands. Award winning holiday caravans for hire.

BEAULY
Lovat Bridge Caravan Park, Lovat Bridge, Beauly, Inverness-shire, IV4 7AY.
Tel. 782374 Std. 01463
Nearest Town/Resort Beauly.
Directions 1 mile south of Beauly on the A862. 11 miles north of Inverness.
Acreage 12 **Open** 15th Mar–15th Oct
Access Good **Site** Level
Sites available Total 40.
Facilities
Nearby facilities
Muir of Ord.
Riverside site, ideal touring.

BETTYHILL
Craigdhu Caravan & Camping, Bettyhill, Nr. Thurso, Sutherland.
Tel. 521273 Std. 01641
Nearest Town/Resort Thurso.
Directions Main Thurso/Tongue road.
Acreage 4½ **Open** April–October
Access Good **Site** Lev/Slope
Sites available Total 90.
Facilities
Nearby facilities
Kinbrace.
Near beautiful beaches, river, fishing. Scenic views. Ideal touring. Rare plants.

BOAT OF GARTEN
Campgrounds of Scotland, Boat of Garten, Inverness-shire, PH24 3BN.
Tel. 831652 Std. 01479
Nearest Town/Resort Aviemore.
Directions 6 miles north of Aviemore in the village of Boat of Garten, off the A95.
Open All Year
Access Good **Site** Lev/Slope
Sites available Total 37.
Facilities
Nearby facilities
Aviemore.
Strathspey Steam Railway and RSPB Osprey Hide.

BROADFORD
Campbell's "Cullin View" Caravan & Camping Site, Breakish, Isle of Skye, Invernesshire.
Tel. Broadford 822248 Std. 01471
Nearest Town/Resort Broadford.
Directions 6 miles from Kyle/Kyleakin ferry at side of garage.

Acreage 4 **Open** All year
Access Good **Site** Lev/Slope
Sites available
Facilities
Nearby facilities
Kyle of Lochalsh.
Scenic views.

CANNICH
Bearnock Tearoom Caravan Site, Glenurquhart, Inverness, Highland.
Tel. 76353 Std. 014564
Nearest Town/Resort Inverness.
Directions West of Inverness on the A831, half way between Drumnadrochit and Cannich.
Acreage 2 **Open** March–October
Access Good **Site** Level
Sites available Total 20.
Facilities
Nearby facilities
Inverness.
Alongside river, scenic views. Ideal for walking, climbing and touring.

DORNIE
Ardelve, Dornie, Kyle, Highland.
Nearest Town/Resort Kyle of Lochalsh.
Directions Just off A87, Invergarry/Kyle road.
Acreage 2 **Open** May–September
Access Good **Site** Sloping
Sites available
Facilities
Kyle of Lochalsh.
Ideal for touring Skye. Near Eilan Donan Castle.

DORNOCH
Dornoch Caravan and Camping Park, The Links, Dornoch, Sutherland.
Tel. 810423 Std. 01862
Nearest Town/Resort Dornoch.
Directions From A9, 6 miles north of Tain, turn right into Dornoch. Turn right at the bottom of the square.
Acreage 25 **Open** April–22nd October
Access Good **Site** Level
Sites available Total 130.
Facilities
Nearby facilities
Tain.
Beach, championship golf course, cathedral town. Scenic views, ideal touring.

DORNOCH
Pitgrudy Caravan Park, Poles Road, Dornoch, Sutherland.
Tel. 810291 Std. 01862
Nearest Town/Resort Dornoch.
Directions From Dornoch take the B9168 north. Turn left at the War Memorial, park is approx. ¾ mile on the right.
Acreage 2 **Open** May–September
Access Good **Site** Sloping
Sites available Total 40.
Facilities
Nearby facilities
Ardgay.
Scenic views over Dornoch Firth. Near a beach and golf course. 5 Tick Park with first class facilities.

DORNOCH
Seaview Farm Caravan Park, Hilton, Dornoch, Sutherland, IV25 3PW.
Tel. Dornoch 810294 Std. 01862
Nearest Town/Resort Dornoch.
Directions From Dornoch square take Embo road. Site 1½ miles on right, entrance opposite telephone box.

Acreage 3½ **Open** May–September
Access Good **Site** Level
Sites available Total 25.
Facilities
Nearby facilities
Ardgay.
Near beach, scenic views, good centre for touring, small quiet site.

DRUMNADROCHIT
Borlum Farm Caravan and Camping Site, Drumnadrochit, Inverness, IV3 6XN.
Tel. 450220 Std. 01456
Nearest Town/Resort Drumnadrochit.
Directions Take A82 from Drumnadrochit towards Fort William site is on right.
Acreage 2 **Open** April–October
Access Good **Site** Lev/Slope
Sites available Total 25.
Facilities
Nearby facilities
Inverness.
Overlooking Loch Ness, Ideal touring centre. You can FAX us on 01456 450358.

DUNBEATH
Inver Caravan Site, Inver Guest House, Dunbeath, Caithness.
Tel. 252 Std. 015933
Nearest Town/Resort Wick.
Directions Roadside A9 south of Wick 21 miles.
Acreage 1 **Open** April–October
Access Good **Site** Level
Sites available Total 15.
Facilities
Nearby facilities
Helmsdale.
Ideal touring.

DURNESS
Sango Sands Caravan & Camping Site, Durness, Sutherland, Highland.
Tel. 511262 Std. 01971
Nearest Town/Resort Durness.
Directions In the centre of Durness Village, on the A838.
Acreage 10¼ **Open** April–15 October
Access Good **Site** Lev/Slope
Sites available Total 84.
Facilities
Nearby facilities
Lairg.
Overlooking the beach and Sango Bay. Ideal centre for touring North West Highlands. Lounge bar on site.

EDINBANE
Loch Greshornish, Borve, Arnisort, Edinbane, Isle of Skye.
Tel. 230 Std. 01470 582
Nearest Town/Resort Portree.
Directions 12 miles from Portree on the A850 Portree/Dunvegan road.
Acreage 5 **Open** April–October
Access Good **Site** Level
Sites available Total 130.
Facilities
Nearby facilities
Beside the sea, ideal centre for touring.

FORT AUGUSTUS
Fort Augustus Caravan & Camping Park, Market Hill, Fort Augustus, Inverness-shire.
Tel. 366360 Std. 01320
Nearest Town/Resort Fort Augustus.
Directions ¼ mile south of Fort Augustus on the A82.
Acreage 3¼ **Open** May–September
Access Good **Site** Level
Sites available Total 50.

Facilities

Nearby facilities

Spean Bridge.

Ideal touring alongside golf course, near Loch Ness, scenic views hill walking.

FORT WILLIAM

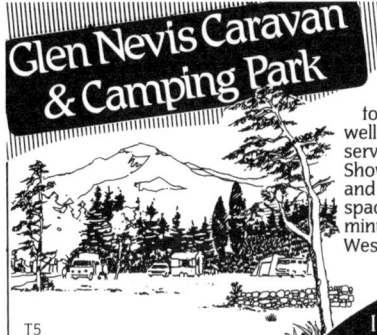

Glen Nevis Caravan & Camping Park, Glen Nevis, Fort William, Highland PH33 6SX.
Tel. 702191 Std. 01397
Nearest Town/Resort Fort William.
Directions On north side of Fort William (A82). East at Glen Nevis signpost. Site 2½ miles up Glen Nevis.
Acreage 19 **Open** April–October
Access Good **Site** Lev/Slope
Sites available Total 380.
Facilities
Nearby facilities
Fort William.
Close to Ben Nevis. Situated in Glen Nevis. Excellent centre for tours in all directions.

FORT WILLIAM

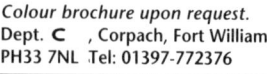

Linnhe Caravan Park, Corpach, Fort William, Invernesshire.
Tel. 772376 Std. 01397
Nearest Town/Resort Fort William.
Directions On A830, 1½ miles west of Corpach village.
Acreage 14 **Open** 15th Dec–31st Oct
Access Good **Site** Level
Sites available Total 85.
Facilities
Nearby facilities
Corpach.
The best in the west, Magnificent scenery from top quality park, private beach and boat slipway. Mains serviced pitches available. Hard standing toddlers play room.

GAIRLOCH

Sands Holiday Centre, Gairloch, Highland.
Tel. Gairloch 2152 Std. 01445
Nearest Town/Resort Gairloch.
Directions Turn west off the A832 onto the B8012. Site 3 miles on, beside sandy beach.
Acreage 55 **Open** April–September
Access Good **Site** Lev/Slope
Sites available Total 360.
Facilities
Nearby facilities
Achnasheen.
Site is near beach, scenic views, river, loch fishing and launching slip.

GLENCOE

Invercoe Caravans, Glencoe, Ballachulish, Highland PA39 4HP.
Tel. Ballachulish 210 Std. 0185 52
Nearest Town/Resort Fort William.
Directions On B863 (off A82) about ¼ mile from Glencoe crossroads.
Acreage 5 **Open** Easter–October
Access Good **Site** Level
Sites available Total 60.
Facilities
Nearby facilities
Fort William.
Ideal centre for touring West Highlands. Beautiful scenery. No advanced bookings. STB 5 ticks.

GLENCOE

Red Squirrel Site, MacColl Leacantuim Farm, Glencoe, Highland.
Tel. Ballachulish 256 Std. 0185 811
Nearest Town/Resort Fort William/Glencoe.
Directions Glencoe village up main street 1½ miles on passing place road.
Acreage 20 **Open** All year
Site Level
Sites available
Facilities
Nearby facilities
Fort William.
On River Coe by mountains, nature, birds and beasts. Fishing, sea pier 1½ miles. Small camp fires allowed. Very casual site, sheep graze. Historic and geological area. Scout group area, River swim pool.

GRANTOWN-ON-SPEY

Grantown-on-Spey Caravan Park, Seafield Avenue, Grantown-on-Spey, Highland.
Tel. 872474 Std. 01479
Nearest Town/Resort Grantown-on-Spey.
Directions From the town centre turn north at Bank of Scotland. Park is straight forward in ¼ mile.
Acreage 18 **Open** Easter–September
Access Good **Site** Level
Sites available Total 100.
Facilities
Nearby facilities
Aviemore.
Centrally located in beautiful surroundings.

INVERGARRY

Faichemard Farm Camp Site, A & D Grant, Faichemard Farm, Invergarry, Invernesshire PH35 4HG.
Tel. 314 Std. 01809 501
Nearest Town/Resort Fort William.
Directions Take A82 to Invergarry (25 miles) travel west on A87 for 1 mile, take side road on right at sign for Faichem, go past Ardgarry Farm and Faichem Park Camp Site to signpost A & D Grant.
Acreage 42 **Open** April–October
Access Good **Site** Lev/Slope

Sites available Total 40.
Facilities
Nearby facilities
Spean Bridge.
Hill walking, bird watching, space and quiet. Max price £5.00 nightly. Individual sites with picnic tables. Mountain bike hire.

INVERMORISTON

Loch Ness Caravan and Camping Park, Easter Port Clair, Invermorriston, Highland, IV3 6YE.
Tel. 351207 Std. 01320
Nearest Town/Resort Inverness-shire.
Directions Main A82 road between Inverness and Fort William. 35 miles either way.
Acreage 8 **Open** 15th March–15th October
Access Good **Site** Level
Sites available Total 85.
Facilities
Nearby facilities
Inverness.
Loch side site with scenic views. Ideal touring.

INVERNESS

Bunchrew Caravan Park, Bunchrew, Inverness, IV3 6TD.
Tel. 237802 Std. 01463
Nearest Town/Resort Inverness.
Directions Take A862 (Beauly) road from Inverness for 3 miles, park is on the right.
Acreage 20 **Open** March–End December
Access Good **Site** Level
Sites available Total 125.
Facilities
Nearby facilities
Inverness.
On the shores of Beauly Firth with scenic views and ideal for touring.

INVERNESS

Auchnahillin Caravan & Camping Centre, Auchnahillin House, Daviot East, Inverness, Highland, IV1 2XQ.
Tel. 772286 (Also FAX) Std. 01463
Nearest Town/Resort Inverness.
Directions Drive south on the A9 from Inverness for 5 miles, turn left onto the B9154. Park is 1 mile from this junction in Daviot East.
Acreage 6 **Open** Mid March–Mid Oct
Access Good **Site** Level
Sites available Total 100.
Facilities
Nearby facilities
Inverness.
Ideal touring area to discover grandeur of Highlands. Scenic views.

INVERNESS

Bught Caravan Park, Bught Park, Inverness, Highland.
Tel. 236920 Std. 0463
Nearest Town/Resort Inverness.
Directions A82 approx. 1 mile from the town centre, fully signposted.
Acreage 1 **Open** April–September
Access Good **Site** Level
Sites available
Facilities
Nearby facilities
Inverness.
Close to leisure facilities, adjacent to golf course and canal.

INVERNESS

Torvean Caravan Park, Glenurquhart Road, Inverness, Highland.
Tel. 220582 Std. 01463
Nearest Town/Resort Inverness.
Directions A82 signposted Fort William, turn right immediately after crossing Tomnahurich Canal bridge. Park is at the rear of caravan sales.
Open Easter–October
Access Good **Site** Level
Sites available Total 50.
Facilities
Nearby facilities
Inverness.
Secluded, 5 Tick park overlooking a golf course and a canal. Near Loch Ness. Ideal touring centre.

JOHN O'GROATS

John O'Groats Caravan and Camping Site, John O'Groats, Nr. Wick, Highland. KW1 4YS.
Tel. 329 Std. 0195 581
Nearest Town/Resort John O' Groats.
Directions End of A9 beside last house.
Acreage 4 **Open** April–October
Access Good **Site** Level
Sites available Total 75.
Facilities
Nearby facilities
Wick.
On sea shore with clear view of Orkney Islands. Day trips to Orkney by passenger ferry, jetty nearby. Hotel and snack bar within 150 yards. Cliff scenery and sea birds 1½ miles.

JOHN O'GROATS

Stroma View Huna, Wick, Highland.
Tel. John O'Groats 313 Std. 0195 581
Nearest Town/Resort John O'Groats.
Directions A9 to John O'Groats, 1½ miles west on A836 Thurso. Well signposted.
Acreage 1 **Open** April–October
Access Good **Site** Level
Sites available Total 30.
Facilities
Nearby facilities
Wick.
Near beach, sand. Views of Stroma, Orkney Isles. Dairy produce on site. Seal colony at Gills Bay, 1½ miles west of site. Ferry from Jog to Orkney daily. Free showers. Fast offshore sea cruises and fishing trips, weather permitting, on 105 "Tiger Lilly". 2-6 Berth caravans. All mod cons.

KINLOCHBERNIE

Oldshoremore Caravan & Camping Site, 152 Oldshoremore, Nr. Lairg, Sutherland.
Tel. 521281 Std. 01971.
Directions Take A838 Lairg to Rhiconich 49 miles. Join B801 to Kinlochbervie then take unclassified road to Oldshoremore, 6 miles.
Acreage 1 **Open** April–October
Access Good **Site** Sloping
Sites available
Facilities
Nearby facilities
Lairg.
Beach ten minutes walk, boating, beautiful scenery, walking, climbing.

LAIDE

Gruinard Bay Caravan & Camping Park, Laide, By Achnasheen, Ross-shire, IV22 2ND.
Tel. 731225 Std. 01445

Nearest Town/Resort Gairloch.
Directions 15 miles north of Gairloch on the A832.
Acreage 2¼ **Open** April–September
Access Good **Site** Level
Sites available Total 55.
Facilities
Nearby facilities
Achnasheen.
Beachside park, beautiful views. Ideal touring.

LAIRG

Dunroamin Caravan Park, Main Street, Lairg, Sutherland, IV27 4AR.
Tel. 402447 Std. 01549
Nearest Town/Resort Lairg.
Directions 300yds east of Loch Shin on the A839 on Main Street Lairg.
Acreage 4 **Open** April–October
Access Good **Site** Level
Sites available Total 60.
Facilities
Nearby facilities
Lairg.
Ideal centre for touring, fishing and sight seeing. Close to Loch Shin and all amenities.

LAIRG

Woodend Caravan and Camping Park, Woodend, Achnairn, Lairg, Highland.
Tel. 402248 Std. 01549
Nearest Town/Resort Lairg.
Directions A836 from Lairg onto A838 and follow site signs.
Acreage 4 **Open** April–September
Access Good **Site** Lev/Slope
Sites available Total 45.
Facilities
Nearby facilities
Lairg.
Overlooking Loch Shin, fishing, scenic views, ideal touring centre for north west. A.A. 3 Pennants, Scotish Tourist Board Graded 3 Tick.

MUIR OF ORD

Druimorrin Caravan Park, Orrin Bridge, Urray, Nr. Muir of Ord, Highland.
Tel. Urray 252 Std. 0199 73.
Nearest Town/Resort Muir of Ord.
Directions 2½ miles west of Muir of Ord on A832.
Acreage 5½ **Open** May–September
Access Good **Site** Level
Sites available Total 60.
Facilities
Nearby facilities
Muir of Ord.
Alongside river, ideal touring Highlands, set in very scenic countryside.

NAIRN

Delnies Woods Caravan Park, Delnies Woods, Nairn, Highland, IV12 5NT.
Tel. 455281 Std. 01667
Nearest Town/Resort Nairn.
Directions On the A96 Inverness to Aberdeen road. 13 miles east of Inverness.
Acreage 10 **Open** Easter–October
Access Good **Site** Level
Sites available Total 72.
Facilities
Nearby facilities
Nairn.
Touring centre for Highlands. Midway between Loch Ness (15 miles) and The Whiskey Trail (12 miles).

NAIRN

Spindrift Caravan & Camping Park, Little Kildrummie, Nairn, Highland, IV12 5QU.
Tel. 453992 Std. 01667
Nearest Town/Resort Nairn.
Directions From Nairn take the B9090 south for $1\frac{1}{4}$ miles. Turn right at the sharp left hand bend onto unclassified road and the entrance is 400yds on the left hand side.
Acreage 3 **Open** 1st April–31st October
Access Good **Site** Level
Sites available Total 40.
Facilities
Nearby facilities
Nairn.
A quiet grassy site, sheltered by trees, overlooking the River Nairn. Permits available from reception.

NEWTONMORE

Invernahavon Holiday Park, Glentruim, Newtonmore, Inverness-shire.
Tel. 673534/673219 Std. 01540
Nearest Town/Resort Newtonmore.
Directions From north on the A9, turn right about $1\frac{1}{4}$ miles past the B9150 junction into road Glentruim/Laggan.
Acreage 10 **Open** Mid March–Mid October
Access Good **Site** Level
Sites available Total 75.
Facilities
Nearby facilities
Newtonmore.
A beautiful site in the heart of the Highlands with breathtaking views of mountains and forest.

PORTREE

Torvaig Caravan and Camping Site, Torvaig, Staffin Road, Portree, Isle of Skye.
Tel. 2209 Std. 01478
Nearest Town/Resort Portree.
Directions 1 mile north of Portree on main Staffin road A855.
Acreage 3 **Open** April–November
Access Good **Site** Sloping
Sites available Total 120.
Facilities
Nearby facilities
Kyle of Lochash.
Scenic views and ideal base for touring Skye.

REAY

Dunvegan Euro Caravan & Camp Site, Dunvegan, Reay, Highland.
Tel. 405 Std. 01847 811
Nearest Town/Resort Thurso.
Directions 10 miles west of Thurso on the A836.
Acreage 1 **Open** Mid May–Mid October
Access Good **Site** Level
Sites available Total 15.
Facilities
Nearby facilities
Close to beach, harbour and cliffs. Scenic views and a golf course. Adjacent to a licensed club.

ROY BRIDGE

Inveroy Caravan & Camping Site, Inveroy, Roy Bridge, Inverness-shire, PH31 4AQ.
Tel. 712275 Std. 01397
Nearest Town/Resort Fort William.
Directions 10 miles north on the A82 from Fort William towards Spean Bridge. 2 miles east on the A86 to Newtonmore.
Acreage 2 **Open** April–September
Access Good **Site** Level
Sites available Total 20.
Facilities
Nearby facilities
Secluded, central Highlands, views of the Grampian Mountains. Ideal for touring West & North.

SCOURIE

Scourie Caravan & Camping Park, Harbour Road, Scourie, Sutherland IV27 4TG.
Tel. 2060/2217 Std. 01971
Nearest Town/Resort Scourie.
Directions On A894 Ullapool to Durness road, overlooking Scourie Bay.
Acreage 4 **Open** April–September
Access Good **Site** Level
Sites available Total 60.
Facilities
Nearby facilities
Lairg.
Ideal base for touring northwest Scotland. Bird watching, hill walking, loch and sea fishing. Restaurant closed on Sundays. No advance bookings except by phone day prior to or morning of arrival. Electrics, first come, first served.

SHIEL BRIDGE

Shielbridge Caravan Site, Shiel Bridge, By Kyle, Ross-shire.
Tel. Glenshiel 295 Std. 0159 981
Nearest Town/Resort Kyle.
Directions 15 miles east of Kyle on A87, site access adjacent Shiel Shop and Filling Station.
Acreage $2\frac{1}{4}$ **Open** Easter–September
Access Good **Site** Level
Sites available Total 65.
Facilities
Kyle.
Scenic area, ideal touring.

SPEAN BRIDGE

Gairlochy Holiday Park, Spean Bridge, Near Fort William, Invernesshire, PH34 4EQ.
Tel. 712711 Std. 01397
Nearest Town/Resort Fort William.
Directions Turn off A82 1 mile north of Spean Bridge at Commando Memorial onto the B8004 signposted Gairlochy. Site is 1 mile on the left and signposted.
Acreage 1 **Open** April–September
Access Good **Site** Level
Sites available Total 15.
Facilities
Nearby facilities
Spean Bridge.
Access to Loch Lochy for fishing and boating. Ideal touring centre and good for hill walking and canoeing.

SPEAN BRIDGE

Stronaba Caravan & Camping Site, Stronaba Farm, Spean Bridge, Highland, PH34 4DX.
Tel. 712259 Std. 01397
Nearest Town/Resort Fort William.
Directions On the main A82 Fort William to Inverness road. $2\frac{1}{4}$ miles north of Spean Bridge, on the left hand side just beyond A.A. phone box.
Acreage 4 **Open** Easter–October
Access Good **Site** Lev/Slope
Sites available Total 25.
Facilities
Nearby facilities
Spean Bridge.
Scenic views, ideal touring. Gas, telephone and cafe/restaurant all within $2\frac{1}{4}$ miles.

STAFFIN

Staffin Caravan & Camping Site, Staffin, Isle of Skye, Highland.
Tel. Staffin 213 Std. 01470 562
Nearest Town/Resort Portree.
Directions South side of Staffin village.
Acreage $1\frac{1}{2}$ **Open** April–September
Access Good **Site** Lev/Slope
Sites available Total 80.
Facilities
Nearby facilities
Kyle.
Sandy beaches 1 mile. Site overlooking Staffin Bay. Public telephone $\frac{1}{2}$ mile, local cafe/restaurant.

STRATHPEFFER

Riverside Caravan Site, Post Office, Contin, Strathpeffer, Rosshire IV1 9ES.
Tel. Strathpeffer 421351 Std. 01997
Nearest Town/Resort Contin.
Directions On A835 midway between Inverness and Ullapool.
Acreage 2 **Open** All year
Access Good **Site** Sloping
Sites available Total 30.
Facilities
Nearby facilities
Dingwall.
Alongside River Blackwater.

TAIN

Meikle Ferry Caravan Park, Meikle, Ferry by Tain, Highland.
Tel. Tain 892292 Std. 01862
Nearest Town/Resort Tain.
Directions 2 miles north of Tain, on A9.
Acreage $3\frac{1}{4}$ **Open** All year
Access Good **Site** Level
Sites available Total 30.
Facilities
Nearby facilities
Tain.
Near beach, good views. British Graded Holiday Parks 4 Ticks. Inn/restaurant adjacent.

THURSO

Thurso Caravan & Camping Park, c/o Director of Leisure & Recreation, Council Offices, Market Square, Wick, Highland, KW1 4AB.
Tel. Wick 3761 Std. 01955
Nearest Town/Resort Thurso.
Directions Adjacent to the A882 and within Thurso town boundary, heading west for Scrabster/Tongue/Durness.
Acreage $4\frac{1}{2}$ **Open** May–September
Access Good **Site** Lev/Slope
Sites available Total 92.
Facilities
Nearby facilities
Overlooking Pentland Firth to the Orkney Islands creating scenic views. Near the beach, ideal for sea and fresh water angling, canoeing, sub-aqua, sailing etc..

UIG

Uig Bay Camping & Caravan Site, 10 Idrigill, Uig, Isle of Skye, IV51 9XU.
Tel. 542360 Std. 01470
Nearest Town/Resort Portree.
Directions A850 from Kyleakin then join onto the A856 to Uig. We are 48 miles from Kyleakin and 17 miles from Portree (the Capital).
Acreage $2\frac{1}{4}$ **Open** April–End September
Access Good **Site** Level
Sites available Total 40.
Facilities

Nearby facilities

Kyle of Lochalsh.

Near sea shore and ferry for the Outer Hebrides. Excellent scenic views.

ULLAPOOL

Ardmair Point Caravan Site, Ullapool, Highland.
Tel. 612054 Std. 01854
Nearest Town/Resort Ullapool.
Directions 3½ miles north of Ullapool on A835.
Acreage 3½ **Open** May–September
Access Good **Site** Level
Sites available Total 45.
Facilities
Nearby facilities
Garve.
Boating centre, hire of boats. Beautiful location with panoramic views.

LOTHIAN

DUNBAR

Battleblent Hotel Caravan Park, Edinburgh Road, Dunbar, East Lothian. EH42 1TS.
Tel. 862234 (Also FAX) Std. 01368
Nearest Town/Resort Dunbar.
Directions Leave A1 at roundabout then 1 mile on A1087 to West Barns village and hotel. Caravan park right hand side (1 mile before Dunbar town centre).
Acreage 1 **Open** April–October
Access Good **Site** Level
Sites available Total 10.
Facilities
Nearby facilities
Dunbar.
Near beach, ideal touring stop.

HADDINGTON

The Monks' Muir, Haddington, East Lothian, EH41 3SB.
Tel. 860340 Std. 01620
Nearest Town/Resort Haddington/East Linton.
Directions Directly on the main A1 road, 3 miles east of Haddington, well signposted.
Acreage 7 **Open** All year
Access Good **Site** Level
Sites available Total 93.
Facilities
Nearby facilities
Dunbar/Drem.
Glorious views and no more than 15 minutes from 18 golf courses and beautiful beaches. 25 minutes from Edinburgh. Off License, some facilities for the disabled available.

MUSSELBURGH

Drum Mohr Caravan Park, Levenhall, Musselburgh, East Lothian.
Tel. 6656867 Std. 0131
Nearest Town/Resort Edinburgh.
Directions From Edinburgh take the A1, Berwick Upon Tweed turn off at slip road to Walleyford signposted caravan park and mining museum. From south on A1 turn off at A199 signposted Musselburgh and then as above.
Acreage 10 **Open** March–October
Access Good **Site** Lev/Slope
Sites available Total 120.
Facilities
Nearby facilities
Edinburgh.
Golf adjacent to site, near Edinburgh. STB Graded 5 Ticks.

STRATHCLYDE

ARDLUI

Ardlui Holiday Home Park, Ardlui Hotel, Loch Lomond, Strathclyde, G83 7EB.
Tel. 243 Std. 0130 14
Nearest Town/Resort Helensburgh.
Directions A82, Loch Lomond road. 25 miles from Helensburgh.
Acreage 1 **Open** April–November
Access Good **Site** Lev/Slope
Sites available Total 12.
Facilities
Nearby facilities
Ardlui.
On the shore of Loch Lomond.

ARROCHAR

Ardgartan Campsite, Forest Enterprise, Loch Long, Arrochar, Dunbartonshire G83 7AL.
Tel. 293/360 Std. 0130 12
Nearest Town/Resort Arrochar.
Directions From the A82 Glasgow to Crianlarich road, take the A83 at Tarbet signposted for Arrochar. The Ardgartan Campsite is situated 2 miles west of Arrochar on the A83 on the shores of Loch Long.
Acreage 16 **Open** 31 March–30 Oct
Access Good **Site** Level
Sites available Total 200.
Facilities
Nearby facilities
Tarbet.
Situated in the Argyll Forest Park on the shores of Loch Long. The site offers good sea fishing and facilities for launching small boats.

AYR

Sundrum Castle Holiday Park, Coylton, Ayr, KA6 6HX.
Tel. 570057 Std. 01292
Nearest Town/Resort Ayr.
Directions East on A70 from Ayr, before Coylton advance signs.
Acreage 3 **Open** Easter–October
Access Good **Site** Level
Sites available Total 52.
Facilities
Nearby facilities
Ayr.
'Talk of Ayr nightclub, excellent golfing area.

AYR

Middlemuir Park, Tarbolton, Nr. Ayr, KA5 5NR.
Tel. 541647 Std. 01292
Nearest Town/Resort Ayr.
Directions From Ayr take the B743 road for Mauchline, look for the international sign for Tarbolton and Park.
Acreage 4 **Open** March–October
Access Good **Site** Level
Sites available Total 30.
Facilities
Nearby facilities
Ayr.
Ayr beach, Racing, 18 golf courses within 18 miles, Culzean Castle, Robert Burns Heritage Trail and Cottage. Opening and closing dates may vary according to weather conditions.

AYR

Skeldon Caravan Park, Hollybush, By Ayr, Ayrshire. KA6 7EB.
Tel. 560502 Std. 01292
Nearest Town/Resort Ayr.
Directions From A77 (Ayr Bypass) turn onto A713 (direction of Castle Douglas) after 4 miles turn right after passing the Hollybush Inn and follow sign for caravan park (¼ mile).
Acreage 3 **Open** April–September
Access Good **Site** Level
Sites available Total 30.
Facilities
Nearby facilities
Ayr.
Sheltered southern aspect on Bank of River Doon.

BALLANTRAE

Laggan House Leisure Park, Ballantrae, Nr. Girvan, Ayrshire, KA26 0LL.
Tel. 1229 Std. 0146 583
Nearest Town/Resort Girvan.
Directions Going south on the A77, after leaving Ballantrae, cross over bridge and take the first left, follow signs.
Acreage 6 **Open** Early March–October
Access Good **Site** Level
Sites available Total 15.
Facilities
Nearby facilities
Girvan.
Walking, touring, bird watching, fishing and swimming. Indoor swimming pool, sauna and solarium.

BALLOCH

Tullichewan Caravan Park, Old Luss Road, Balloch, Loch Lomond, Strathclyde G83 8QP.
Tel. Alexandria 59475 Std. 01389
Nearest Town/Resort Balloch.
Directions Follow international direction signs from A82 4 miles north of Dumbarton.
Acreage 13 **Open** December–October
Access Good **Site** Level
Sites available Total 200.
Facilities
Nearby facilities
Balloch.
Loch Lomond, Glasgow, and West Highlands. You can FAX us on 01389 55563.

BIGGAR

Townfoot Garage, William Ramsay Engineers, Townfoot, Elsrickle, Biggar, Strathclyde.
Tel. 81200 Std. 01899
Nearest Town/Resort Biggar.
Directions On the A721 in the village of Elsrickle, at U.K. Petrol Station. Or from Biggar take the B7016 to Carnwath then fork right onto unclassified road. 1 mile from Biggar to Elsrickle, take right at junction with A721.
Acreage ½ **Open** April–October
Access Good **Site** Sloping
Sites available Total 10.
Facilities
Nearby facilities
Carstairs.

Quiet village. Ideal touring centre for Edinburgh, Borders, Glasgow etc. Telephone 200yds.

CARRADALE

Carradale Bay Caravan Park, Carradale, Kintyre, Argyll, PA28 6QG.
Tel. 431665 Std. 01583
Nearest Town/Resort Campbeltown.
Directions From Campbeltown B842, turn right onto the B879 (signposted Carradale). In ¼ mile at caravan park sign turn right onto a single track road. Site entrance within ½ mile.
Acreage 12 **Open** Easter–September
Access Good **Site** Level
Sites available Total 65.
Facilities
Nearby facilities
Situated on a safe, sloping, sandy beach with a river running alongside.

DUNOON

Stratheck Caravan Park, Loch Eck, By Dunoon, Argyll, PA23 8SG.
Tel. 472 Std. 01369 840
Nearest Town/Resort Dunoon.
Directions A815 to Glasgow from Dunoon, about 6 miles from Dunoon. ½ mile past entrance to Benmore Gardens.
Acreage 6 **Open** Easter–31st October
Access Good **Site** Level
Sites available Total 30.
Facilities
Nearby facilities
Gourock.
Alongside river, amidst magnificent Highlands mountains and Lochs.

GIRVAN

Bennane Hill Caravan Park, Lendalfoot, Girvan, Ayrshire.
Tel. 891233 Std. 01465
Nearest Town/Resort Girvan.
Directions 5 miles south of Girvan on the A77 Stranraer to Glasgow trunk road.
Acreage 2 **Open** March–October
Access Good **Site** Level
Sites available Total 25.
Facilities
Nearby facilities
Girvan.
Beach front, scenic views. Private slipway for the boating enthusiasts. Ideal touring.

GIRVAN

Carleton Caravan Park, Carleton Lodge, Lendalfoot, Girvan, Ayrshire, KA26 0JF.
Tel. Lendalfoot 215 Std. 01465 89
Nearest Town/Resort Girvan.
Directions Off A77 Girvan/Stranraer road at Lendalfoot village. 800 yards on unclassified road.
Acreage 9 **Open** March–October
Access Good **Site** Terraced
Sites available Total 10.
Facilities
Nearby facilities
Girvan.
Small quiet site , near sea, ideal touring area.

GIRVAN

Windsor Holiday Park, Barrhill, Nr. Girvan, Ayrshire, KA26 0PZ.
Tel. 821355 Std. 01465
Nearest Town/Resort Girvan.
Directions A714 Newton Stewart 17 miles, Girvan 11 miles.
Acreage 6 **Open** March–October
Access Good **Site** Level
Sites available Total 30.
Facilities M
Nearby facilities
Barrhill.
Ideal touring.

GLENBARR

Killegruer Caravan Site, Woodend, Glenbarr, Tarbert, Argyll.
Tel. 241 Std. 015832
Nearest Town/Resort Campbeltown.
Directions 12 miles north of Campbeltown on the A83.
Acreage 1¼ **Open** April–September
Access Good **Site** Level
Sites available Total 25.
Facilities
Oban.
Overlooks a sandy beach with views of the Inner Hebrides and the Mull of Kintyre.

GLENDARUEL

Glendaruel Caravan Park, Glendaruel, Argyll, PA22 3AB.
Tel. 820267 Std. 01369
Nearest Town/Resort Tighnabruaich.
Directions 13 miles south Strachur on A886 or by ferry to Dunoon and then on B836. B836 not recommended for touring caravans – 1 in 5 gradient.
Acreage 6 **Open** April–October
Access Good **Site** Level
Sites available Total 25.
Facilities S

Nearby facilities
Gourock.
Peaceful secluded country park. Kyles of Bute 5 miles. Bicycles for hire. Ideal centre touring and walking. Dogs by arrangement only. Within 22 acre park. Sea trout and Salmon fishing. Thistle Award, Graded 5 Ticks.

INVERBEG

Inverbeg Holiday Park, Luss, Dunbartonshire, G83 8PD.
Tel. 860267 Std. 01436
Nearest Town/Resort Luss.
Directions n A82 3 miles north of Luss.
Acreage 5 **Open** April–October
Access Good **Site** Level
Sites available Total 30.
Facilities
Nearby facilities
Balloch.
On Loch Lomond, with large beach, good boat launching and excellent fishing. Thistle Award caravans for hire. Adventure playground, cycle hire.

IRVINE

Cunningham Head Estate Caravan Park, Cunningham Head, Nr. Kilmarnock, Ayrshire.
Tel. 850238 Std. 01294
Nearest Town/Resort Irvine.
Directions From Irvine take A736 Glasgow road at Stanecastle roundabout turn east onto B769 Stewarton road. Park is 2 miles on left.
Acreage 20 **Open** April–September
Access Good **Site** Level
Sites available Total 90.
Facilities
Nearby facilities
On grounds of mansion house (now gone). Ideal for touring Burns country and Clyde coast resorts. Near Magnum Leisure Centre.

LANARK

Clyde Valley Caravan Park, Kirkfieldbank, Nr. Lanark, Strathclyde.
Tel. 663951 Std. 01555
Nearest Town/Resort Lanark.
Directions M74 to A73, ¼ mile north of Lanark.
Acreage 5 **Open** April–October
Access Good **Site** Level
Sites available Total 50.
Facilities
Nearby facilities
Lanark.
Golf, fishing, horse riding and historic New Lanark.

LANARK

Newhouse Caravan & Camping Park, Ravenstruther, Lanark. ML11 8NP.
Tel. Carstairs 870228 Std. 01555
Nearest Town/Resort Lanark.
Directions On A70 Edinburgh road from Lanark, 3 miles east on left.
Acreage 4 **Open** March–October
Access Good **Site** Level
Sites available Total 45.
Facilities
Nearby facilities
Ideal touring, near Clyde Valley, 40 minutes from Edinburgh and Glasgow. Near New Lanark Conservation Village.

MAYBOLE

Culzean Bay Holiday Park, Knoweside, By Maybole, Ayrshire, KA19 8JS.
Tel. 500444 Std. 01292
Nearest Town/Resort Ayr.
Directions 7 miles south of Ayr on the A719 coast road.
Acreage 1 **Open** March–October
Access Good **Site** Level
Sites available Total 12.
Facilities
Nearby facilities
Maybole.
Sandy beach and scenic views.

MAYBOLE

Sandy Beach Caravan Park, 25 Ardlochan Road, Maidens, Ayrshire, KA26 9NS.
Tel. 31456 Std. 01655
Nearest Town/Resort Girvan.
Open March–October
Access Good **Site** Level
Sites available Total 7.
Facilities
Nearby facilities
Girvan.
Directly across the road from beach, scenic sea views. 2 miles to Culzean Castle. Ideal for touring Burns Country. Motorcycles are only accepted if pulling a small van.

OBAN

Oban Caravan and Camping Park, Gallanachmore Farm, Oban, Argyll.
Tel. 62425 Std. 01631
Nearest Town/Resort Oban.
Directions From Oban town centre (roundabout) follow sign for Gallanach. Pass ferry terminal road. Site is 2 miles along coast road on left.
Acreage 15 **Open** Easter–Mid October
Access Good **Site** Lev/Slope
Sites available Total 200.
Facilities
Nearby facilities
Oban.
Beside the sea, scenic views, ideal location for touring the west coast.

OBAN

Ganavan Sands Caravan Park, Ganavan Sands, Oban, Strathclyde.
Tel. 62179 Std. 01631
Nearest Town/Resort Oban.
Directions From Oban town centre follow Esplanade coast road keeping the sea immediately adjacent on the left for 2 miles.
Acreage 2 **Open** Easter–October
Access Good **Site** Lev/Slope
Sites available Total 80.
Facilities
Nearby facilities
Oban.
Beside beach, launching slip and dive shop.

ROSNEATH

Rosneath Castle Caravan Park, Rosneath, Nr. Helensburgh, Dunbartonshire, G84 0QS.
Tel. 831208 Std. 01436
Nearest Town/Resort Helensburgh.
Directions 1 mile south of Rosneath on the B833.
Acreage 4 **Open** March–30th October
Access Good **Site** Level
Sites available Total 50.
Facilities
Nearby facilities
Helensburgh.
55 acres of parkland at the entrance to Gare Loch opposite Helensburgh. Superb sea fishing, childrens mini club, sailing school, cycle hire and luxurious bistro bar and restaurant. New toilet/shower block for tourers (July 1994). Static caravans also to rent.

SKELMORLIE

Skelmorlie Mains Caravan & Camping Site, Skelmorlie Mains, Skelmorlie, Ayrshire.
Tel. 520794 Std. 01475
Nearest Town/Resort Largs.
Directions ½ mile from A78 south of Skelmorlie.
Acreage 4 **Open** April–October
Access Good **Site** Sloping
Sites available Total 100.
Facilities
Nearby facilities
Wemyss Bay.
Scenic view of Cumbrae, Arran, Bute Islands and Firth of Clyde.

SOUTHEND

Machribeg Caravan Site, Southend, By Campbeltown, Argyll, PA28 6RW.
Tel. 830249 Std. 01586
Nearest Town/Resort Campbeltown.
Directions Take the B843 from Campbeltown for 10 miles. Site is situated 250yds through Southend Village on the left by the beach.
Acreage 4 **Open** Easter–September
Access Good **Site** Sloping
Sites available Total 80.
Facilities
Nearby facilities
Near the beach with good views, very quiet location. 18 hole golf course.

TARBERT

Escart Bay Caravan Park, Tarbert, Argyll, PA29 6YF.
Tel. 820873 Std. 01880
Nearest Town/Resort Tarbert.
Directions 2 miles south of Tarbert on the A83 Campbeltown road.
Acreage ¼ **Open** April–October
Access Good **Site** Lev/Slope
Sites available Total 20.
Facilities
Nearby facilities
Glasgow.
Quiet site with beautiful views over West Loch, adjacent to a beach. Ferry terminals in the vicinity.

TARBERT

Loch Lomond Holiday Park, Inveruglas, Near Tarbert, Dunbartonshire.
Tel. 224 Std. 0130 14
Nearest Town/Resort Tarbert.
Directions 3 miles north of Tarbert on the A82.
Acreage 1 **Open** March–October
Access Good **Site** Level
Sites available Total 26.
Facilities
Nearby facilities
Tarbert.
Own beach in a superb location. Ideal for hill walking and touring.

TAYINLOAN

Point Sands Holiday Park, TayinLoan, Argyll, PA29 6XG.
Tel. 263 Std. 015834
Nearest Town/Resort Tarbert.
Directions A83 17 miles south of Tarbert.
Acreage 14 **Open** April–October
Access Good **Site** Level
Sites available Total 65.
Facilities
Nearby facilities
Oban.
On superb sandy beach opposite Isle of Gigha. Ideal for visits to Hebredian Islands + Arran, magnificent views of Jura.

TAYNUILT

Crunachy Caravan & Camping Park, Bridge of Awe, Taynuilt, Argyll. Strathclyde.
Tel. Taynuilt 612 Std. 0186 62.
Nearest Town/Resort Oban.
Directions Alongside main A85 Tyndrum to Oban 14 miles east of Oban outside the village of Taynuilt.
Acreage 9 **Open** March–November
Access Good **Site** Level
Sites available Total 80.
Facilities
Nearby facilities
Taynuilt.
Alongside the River Awe at the foot of Ben Cruachan.

TAYSIDE

ABERFELDY

Glengoulamdie Deer Park, Glengoulamdie, Foss, By Pitlochry, Perthshire, PH5 6NL.
Tel. 830261 Std. 01887
Nearest Town/Resort Aberfeldy.
Directions B846 road from Aberfeldy to Kinloch Rannoch for 8 miles, on left hand side.
Acreage 3 **Open** April–1 Nov
Access Good **Site** Level
Sites available Total 10.
Facilities
Nearby facilities
Pitlochry.
Adjoining wildlife park and stocked Rainbow Trout fishing.

ABERFELDY

Kenmore Caravan & Camping Park, Aberfeldy, Perthshire EH15 2HN.
Tel. Kenmore 830226 Std. 01887
Nearest Town/Resort Aberfeldy.
Directions 6 miles west on A827 from Aberfeldy to Killin.
Acreage 14 **Open** April–October
Access Good **Site** Level
Sites available Total 160.
Facilities
Nearby facilities
Pitlochry.
By river near loch. Touring centre. All outdoor pursuits and water sports. 4 pennant site. Excellent Par 70 golf course on site.

ARBROATH

Red Lion Caravan Park, Dundee Road, Arbroath, Tayside.
Tel. 872038 Std. 01241
Nearest Town/Resort Arbroath.
Directions When entering Arbroath on the A92, park is on the left.
Acreage 18 **Open** April–October
Access Good **Site** Level
Sites available Total 300.
Facilities
Nearby facilities
Arbroath.
Adjacent to the promenade and beach.

BLAIRGOWRIE

Beech Hedge Caravan Park, Cargill, Perth, Tayside.
Tel. Meikleour 249 Std. 0125 0883
Nearest Town/Resort Blairgowrie.
Directions 8 miles north of Perth on A93 Breamar road.
Acreage 2 **Open** March–October
Access Good **Site** Level
Sites available Total 20.
Facilities
Nearby facilities
Perth.
Scenic views, ideal touring centre.

BLAIRGOWRIE

Blairgowrie Caravan Park, Rattray, Blairgowrie, Perthshire, PH10 7AL.
Tel. 872941 Std. 01250
Nearest Town/Resort Blairgowrie.
Directions 1 mile north of Blairgowrie town centre off the A93. Turn right past Keathbank Mill and the petrol station. Park is on the left in 250yds following international signs.
Acreage ¾ **Open** March–October
Access Good **Site** Level
Sites available Total 30.
Facilities
Nearby facilities
Perth.
Ideal centre for touring Perthshire, Angus, Glens and royal Deeside. Local swimming pool.

BRECHIN

Glenesk Caravan Park, Edzell, Brechin, Angus, DD9 7YP.
Tel. 648565 Std. 01356
Nearest Town/Resort Edzell.
Directions From the A94 take the B966 to Edzell. 2 miles north of Edzell turn off at sign Glenesk and Tarside. Site is 1 mile on the right.
Acreage 8 **Open** April–October
Access Good **Site** Level
Sites available Total 45.
Facilities
Nearby facilities
Montrose.
A quiet, woodland site featuring a small lake. Ideal for walkers and wildlife enthusiasts as well as many local visitor attractions.

BRECHIN

Eastmill Road Caravan Site, Eastmill Road, Brechin, Tayside.
Tel. 622810/622487 Std. 01356
Nearest Town/Resort Brechin.
Directions A90 Perth to Aberdeen road, follow signs for Brechin and Montrose. Approx. 10 miles north of Forfar.
Acreage 3¼ **Open** April–October
Access Good **Site** Level
Sites available Total 50.
Facilities
Nearby facilities
Montrose.
Alongside the River South Esk, with easy access to Angus Glens. Sandy beaches approx. 15 minutes by car.

BRIDGE OF CALLY

Corriefodly Holiday Park, Bridge of Cally, Perthshire, PH10 7JG.
Tel. 886236 Std. 01250
Nearest Town/Resort Blairgowrie.
Directions From Blairgowrie take A93 north for 6 miles. Turn onto A924 Pitlochry road, site approx 200yds from junction of A93 and A924.
Acreage 5 **Open** December–October
Access Good **Site** Sloping
Sites available Total 110.
Facilities
Nearby facilities
Perth.
Ideal touring base, riverside setting, scenic views. Private bowling on site.

COMRIE

West Lodge Caravan Park, Lawers, Comrie, Perthshire. PH6 2LS.
Tel. 670354 Std. 01764
Nearest Town/Resort Comrie.
Directions On A85, 5 miles from Crieff. 1 mile from Comrie.
Acreage 3 **Open** Easter–October
Access Good **Site** Level
Sites available Total 20.
Facilities
Nearby facilities
Perth.
Sheltered friendly site, ideal for touring, set in beautiful country area.

COMRIE

Twenty Shilling Wood Caravan Park, St. Fillans Road, Comrie, Perthshire PH6 2JY.
Tel. 670411 Std. 01764
Nearest Town/Resort Crieff.
Directions ¼ mile west of Comrie on A85.
Acreage 10¼ **Open** Late March–20 Oct
Access Good **Site** Level
Sites available Total 30.
Facilities
Nearby facilities
Perth.
Peaceful sheltered park in woodlands visted by deer and many woodland birds. Family run, spotless. All season.

CRIEFF

East Buchanty, Glenalmond, Perth, Tayside.
Tel. 880293 Std. 01738
Nearest Town/Resort Crieff.
Directions 7 miles north east of Crieff, A85 Gilmerton, then B8063 at Buchanty.
Acreage 12 **Open** All Year.
Site Level
Sites available
Facilities
Perth.
Scenic views, ideal touring. No Dogs.

CRIEFF

Crieff Holiday Village, Turret Bank, Crieff, Perthshire PH7 4JN.
Tel. Crieff 653513 Std. 01764
Nearest Town/Resort Crieff.
Directions Follow A85 Crieff/Comrie road, turn left ¼ mile from Crieff at first crossroads. Site 300 yards on left, well signposted.
Acreage 2 **Open** All year
Access Good **Site** Level
Sites available Total 45.
Facilities
Nearby facilities
Gleneagles.
Beautifully situated, bounded by River Turret. Adjacent to public parks. Ideal touring centre.

DUNKELD

Kilvrecht, Forest Enterprise, Inver Park, Dunkeld, Tayside.
Tel. 727284 Std. 01796
Nearest Town/Resort Kinloch Rannoch.
Acreage 17 **Open** 21 March–21 October
Access Good **Site** Level
Sites available Total 90.
Facilities
Nearby facilities
Pitlochry.
Surrounded by a large forest area for numerous forest walks. Plus boating and fishing on the nearby Loch Rannoch.

DUNKELD

Erigmore House Holiday Park, Birnam, Dunkeld, Perthshire. PH8 9XX.
Tel. 727236/727677 Std. 01350
Nearest Town/Resort Dunkeld.
Directions From Perth 12 miles north on the A9 take the right turning to Birnam, park entrance on right 400 yards from A9.
Acreage 4 **Open** Easter–October
Access Good **Site** Level
Sites available Total 34.
Facilities
Nearby facilities
Dunkeld.
Spectacular scenery, indoor pool, weekend entertainment, bar and restaurant.

FORFAR

The Glens Caravan & Camping Park, Memus, By Forfar, Angus, DD8 3TY.
Tel. 860258 Std. 01307
Directions Take the B9128 from Forfar bypass A90. Follow signs for Memus. Please take care crossing by-pass. From south site is 4 miles from the bypass.
Acreage 1 **Open** 15 March–October
Access Good **Site** Level
Sites available Total 24.
Facilities
Nearby facilities
Dundee.
Fishing, golf, walking and cycling.

KINROSS

Gairney Bridge Caravan Site, Gairney Bridge Farm Ltd, By Kinross, Kinrosshire KY13 7JZ.
Nearest Town/Resort Kinross.
Directions Leave M90 at junction 5 (Glenrothes) on B996 to monument.
Acreage 1 **Open** June–September
Access Good **Site** Level
Sites available Total 25.
Facilities
Cowdenbeath.
Hills, scenic views, ideal touring.

KIRRIEMUIR

Drumshademuir Caravan Park, Roundyhill, By Glamis, Forfar, Tayside, DD8 1QT.
Tel. 573284 Std. 01575
Nearest Town/Resort Kirriemuir.
Directions Turn off the A90 or the A94 onto the A928. Park is situated 3 miles north of Glamis Castle, 2 miles south of Kirriemuir.
Acreage 2 **Open** Mid March–October
Access Good **Site** Level
Sites available Total 80.
Facilities
Nearby facilities
Dundee.
Scenic views and Angus Glens for all outdoor activities. Glamis Castle 3 miles and gliding ¼ mile.

PERTH

Cleeve Caravan Site, Glasgow Road, Perth, Tayside.
Tel. 39521 Std. 01738
Nearest Town/Resort Perth.
Directions 350 metres east of A9 (Perth By-pass intersection).
Acreage 5¼ **Open** April–October
Access Good **Site** Sloping
Sites available Total 120.
Facilities
Nearby facilities
Perth.
Secluded woodland setting; 5 minutes from the thriving and beautiful City of Perth. Ideal for sport and touring. Sports retail and Senior Citizen discounts. Bookings accepted.

PITLOCHRY

Blair Castle Caravan Park, Blair Atholl, Pitlochry, Perthshire PH18 5SR.
Tel. 481263 Std. 01796.
Nearest Town/Resort Pitlochry.
Directions Follow A9 north past Pitlochry, after 6 miles turn off following signs to Blair Atholl. After 1¼ miles turn right into caravan park.
Acreage 35 **Open** April–Late Oct
Access Good **Site** Level
Sites available Total 250.
Facilities
Nearby facilities

Blair Atholl.
Blair Castle. Queens view and the road to the Isles.

PITLOCHRY

Milton of Fonab Caravan Site, Bridge Road, Pitlochry, Tayside.
Tel. 472882 Std. 01796
Directions $\frac{1}{4}$ mile south of Pitlochry, opposite Bells Distillery.
Acreage 15 **Open** March–October
Access Good **Site** Level
Sites available Total 250.
Facilities S
Nearby facilities
Pitlochry.
On the banks of the River Tummel, spectacular scenery, hill walking.

WESTERN ISLES

HARRIS

Laig House Caravan Site, 10 Drinnis Hadder, Harris, Western Isles.
Tel. 511207 Std. 01859
Nearest Town/Resort Tarbert.
Directions $4\frac{1}{2}$ miles south of Tarbert on east coast.
Acreage $2\frac{1}{2}$ **Open** April–October
Access Good **Site** Level
Sites available Total 20.
Facilities M I
Nearby facilities
Kyle of Lochalsh.
Ideal touring, free fishing on coast. Hill walking and excellent beaches.

HARRIS

Minch View Caravan Site, 10 Drinishader, Isle of Harris, Western Isles, PA85 3DX.
Tel. 511207 Std. 01859
Nearest Town/Resort Tarbert.
Directions South east of Tarbert along the A859 (5 miles). Turn off the A859 at Drinishader road end. $2\frac{1}{4}$ miles south of Tarbert. From car ferry turn left at all junctions.
Acreage 3 **Open** April–October
Access Good **Site** Level
Sites available Total 26.
Facilities M
Nearby facilities
Kyle of Lochalsh.
Ideal touring, alongside the sea and a fresh water loch. Scenic views.

Dealers and Retailers Section

A Nationwide Directory of Caravan and Camping Centres, Accessory Shops and Equipment Suppliers.

Sponsored By

AVON

BATH Oswald Bailey Ltd 8 The Mall, Southgate, Bath, BA1 1TB. (01225) 463202. Cut price tents. Rucksacks, Sleeping bags, Hike boots, Waterproof clothing. Everything for the great outdoors.

BRISTOL Avon County Caravans 97 Bridgewater Road (A38), Bedminster Down, Bristol, Avon, BS13 8AE. (01934) 642030. Main dealer in the Bristol and Bath areas for ABI Caravans. Fully stocked accessory shop, workshop, all makes of awnings sold and a good selection of used caravans. Part of the Davan Group.

BRISTOL Camping and Outdoor Centre 9/10 Transom House, Victoria Street, Bristol, BS1 6AH. (0117) 926 4892. Leading outdoor specialists with 80 years camping experience. Large ranges of tents, sleeping bags, stoves, lanterns, camping accessories, rucksacks, walking boots and outdoor clothing.

BRISTOL Oswald Bailey Ltd 61 Horsefair, Bristol, BS1 3JP. (0117) 929 3523. Cut price tents. Rucksacks, sleeping bags, hike boots and waterproof clothing. Everything for the great outdoors.

CHIPPING SODBURY Chipping Sodbury Caravans Badminton Road, Chipping Sodbury, Avon, BS17 6LH. (01454) 318374.

KEYNSHAM G.B. Camping Jarretts Garden Centre, Bath Road, Willsbridge, Near Bitton, Bristol, BS15 6EE. (0117) 932 9660. Tents, frame, ridge, dome and tunnel. Trailers and all accessories. Camping Gaz and Calor Gas refills.

KINGSWOOD Kingswood Caravan & Camping Centre 137-145 High Street, Kingswood, Bristol, BS15 4AQ. (0117) 967 4706/960 0205.

WESTON SUPER MARE Davan Caravans Ltd St Georges, Weston Super Mare, Avon, BS22 0XF. (01934) 510606.

BEDFORDSHIRE

WOBURN Tony Wild Camping Woburn Park, Bedfordshire, MK43 0TP. (01525) 290477. Tents, trailer tents and folding campers - new and used. Lightweight tents, baggage, trailers, caravan awnings and Gas. Large accessory shop.

BERKSHIRE

ALDERMASTON Colins Caravans of Berkshire Ltd Bath Road (A4), Aldermaston, Reading, Berks, RG7 5JD. (01734) 712424. Touring caravan retailers. Caravan and camping accessory shop, awnings. Service and repair workshops. Caravan hire. 5 Star RAC/NCC Approved.

READING Berkshire Caravans 16a Church Lane, Three Mile Cross, Reading, Berkshire, RG7 1HB. (01734) 882590. We specialise in accessories and spares for most makes of touring caravans. Calor Gas and Camping Gaz. New and used caravan sales and awnings.

READING Berkshire Caravans 247 Wokingham Road, Earley, Reading, Berks, RG6 2DU. (01734) 265233. New and used caravan sales. Calor Gas, Camping Gaz, awnings and accessories.

BUCKINGHAMSHIRE

MILTON KEYNES Keyne Camping & Leisure 15 Stacey Bushes Business Centre, Milton Keynes, Bucks, MK12 6HS. (01908) 227090. Tents by Kyham, Freeman, Outbound, Freetime, Lichfield and Relum. Camping trailers, sleeping bags, rucksacks, outdoor clothing, walking boots, shoes and rainwear. A comprehensive range of camping accessories.

CAMBRIDGESHIRE

GREAT SHELFORD Hills Stores 134 Cambridge Road, Great Shelford, Cambs, CB2 5OU. (01223) 842943.

PETERBOROUGH Camping and Outdoor Centre 97 Bridge Street, Peterborough, Cambs, PE1 1HG. (01733) 61000. Leading outdoor specialists with 80 years camping experience. Large ranges of tents, sleeping bags, stoves, lanterns, camping accessories, rucksacks, walking boots and outdoor clothing.

PETERBOROUGH Pioneer Caravans Thorney Road, Eye, Peterborough, Cambs. (01733) 222244. Sale of new and used tourers and holiday statics. Large accessory shop. Calor Gas. Heated showroom. Open seven days a week.

PETERBOROUGH Welland Holiday Hire & Sales Centre Ltd Postland Road, Crowland, Peterborough, Cambs, PE6 0JB. (01733) 210560.

ST IVES St Ives Caravans Old Ramsey Road, St Ives, Cambs, PE17 4LL. (01480) 300621.

ST NEOTS St Neots Calor Gas (1991) Ltd Alington Industrial Estate, Eynesbury, St Neots, Cambs, PE19 2RD. (01480) 213007.

CHESHIRE

CHEADLE HULME North Western Caravans Earl Road, Cheadle Hulme, Cheshire, SK8 6QE. (0161) 437 4255.

CHESTER Barretts of Feckenham 33 Pepper Row, Chester, Cheshire, CH1 1EA. (01244) 317076.

CHESTER Caseys Camping (Chester) Grosvenor Garden Centre, Wrexham Road, Belgrave, Chester, Cheshire, CH4 9AB. (01244) 682002.

ELLESMERE PORT The Camping Shop 76-80 Station Road, Ellesmere Port, South Wirral, Cheshire, L65 4BQ. (0151) 355 4887. Tents, camping equipment, rucksacks, walking boots. Gas Heater sale and repair. Second hand goods bought and sold.

KNUTSFORD Spinney Motorcaravans Chelford Road, Ollerton, Knutsford, Cheshire, WA16 8SB. (01565) 634011.

NORTHWICH Harringtons Caravans Ltd Chester Road, Delamere Forest, Nr. Northwich, Cheshire, CW8 2HE. (01606) 882032.

WARRINGTON Cheshire Outdoor Leisure 30-42 Knutsford Road, Warrington, Cheshire, WA4 1AG. (01925) 30554.

WIDNES Hugh Lewis & Son Ltd 29-31 Moor Lane, Widnes, Cheshire, WA8 0NW. (0151) 424 7316.

WIDNES Widnes Caravans Croft Street, Widnes, Cheshire, WA8 0NQ. (0151) 424 3378. Caravan repairs, spares and accessories.

CLEVELAND

HARTLEPOOL A19 Camping & Leisure 13 Park View Industrial Estate, Brenda Road, Hartlepool, Cleveland, TS25 1PE. (01429) 869811.

THORNABY ON TEES Hadrian Caravans Ltd Hadrian House, Thornaby Place, Thornaby, Cleveland. (01642) 679527.

CORNWALL

REDRUTH Caraleisure Cornwall Scorrier, Redruth, Cornwall, TR16 5EG. (01209) 820451. FAX (01209) 820116.

CUMBRIA

CUMWHINTON Reston Motorhome Hire Oakwood, The Stripes, Cumwhinton, Cumbria, CA4 0AP. (01228) 561143. Motorcaravan self drive hire. Caravan and motorcaravan site.

HARKER Carlisle Caravan Centre Ltd Harker, Nr. Carlisle, Cumbria, CA6 4DS. (01228) 74570.

PENRITH Westmorland Motorway Services Ltd Orton, Penrith, Cumbria, CA10 3SB. (015396) 24511.

ULVERSTON Bardsea Leisure Park Priory Road, Ulverston, Cumbria, LA12 9QE. (01229) 584712. Large selection of camping and caravan accessories including a vast display of awnings. Calor Gas and Camping Gaz stockists. New Abi Tourers in stock. Witter Towbars fitted. Open 363 days a year.

DERBYSHIRE

ALFRETON Yeomans Army Stores 5/7 Rodgers Lane, Alfreton, Derbys. (01773) 831486. Tents, air beds, sleeping bags, water carriers and crockery, camp furniture, groundsheets. Lights and stoves, rucksacks and all tent accessories. Footwear and clothing.

ASHBOURNE Rileys Outdoor Centre 10 Shawcroft Centre, Ashbourne, Derbys, DE6 1GF. (01335) 346364.

ASHBOURNE Yeomans Army Stores 3 Victoria Square, Ashbourne, Derbys. (01335) 42468. Tents, air beds, sleeping bags, water carriers and crockery, camp furniture, groundsheets. Lights and stoves, rucksacks and all tent accessories. Footwear and clothing.

BELPER Yeomans Army Stores 47 King Street, Belper, Derbys. (01773) 829259. Tents, air beds, sleeping bags, water carriers and crockery, camp furniture and groundsheets. Lights, stoves, rucksacks and all tent accessories. Footwear and clothing.

BUXTON Yeomans Army Stores Scarsdale Place, Buxton, Derbys. (01298) 70087. Tents, air beds, sleeping bags, water carriers and crockery, camp furniture, groundsheets. Lights and stoves, rucksacks and all tent accessories. Footwear and clothing.

CHESTERFIELD Yeomans Army Stores Beetwell Street, Chesterfield, Derbys. (01246) 559072. Tents, air beds, sleeping bags, water carriers and crockery, camp furniture, groundsheets. Lights and stoves, rucksacks and all tent accessories. Footwear and clothing.

DERBY J.R. Leisure (Don Amott Caravans) Hilton, Derbys. (01283) 733525.

DERBY Yeomans Army Stores 20 Osmaston Road, The Spot, Derby. (01332) 384684. Tents, air beds, sleeping bags, water carriers and crockery, camp furniture, groundsheets. Lights and stoves, rucksacks and all tent accessories. Footwear and clothing.

GLOSSOP Glossop Caravans Brookfield, Glossop, Derbys, SK13 9JE. (01457) 865215/868011.

HEANOR Yeomans Army Stores 5 Market Street, Heanor, Derbys. (01773) 533804. Tents, air beds, sleeping bags, water carriers and crockery, camp furniture, groundsheets. Lights and stoves, rucksacks and all tent accessories. Footwear and clothing.

ILKESTON Yeomans Army Stores 51 Bath Street, Ilkeston, Derbys. (0115) 932 4853. Tents, air beds, sleeping bags, water carriers and crockery, camp furniture, groundsheets. Lights and stoves, rucksacks and all tent accessories. Footwear and clothing.

LONG EATON Yeomans Army Stores Market Place, Long Eaton, Derbys. (0115) 946 3458. Tents, air beds, sleeping bags, water carriers and crockery, camp furniture, groundsheets. Lights and stoves, rucksacks and all tent accessories. Footwear and clothing.

MATLOCK Yeomans Army Stores 5 Crown Square, Matlock, Derbys. (01629) 56727. Tents, air beds, sleeping bags, water carriers and crockery, camp furniture and groundsheets. Lights, stoves, rucksacks and all tent accessories. Footwear and clothing.

SPONDON Goodalls Caravans Nottingham Road, Spondon, Derbys, DE2 7NJ. (01332) 663191. Abbey, Swift, Bailey and Bessacarr new sales and a huge selection of used caravans. Five Star service centre. Indoor awnings display and leisure shop.

STAVELEY Yeomans Army Stores 16 Market Place, Staveley, Derbys. (01246) 472339. Tents, air beds, sleeping bags, water carriers and crockery, camp furniture, groundsheets. Lights and stoves, rucksacks and all tent accessories. Footwear and clothing.

DEVON

ASHBURTON Ashburn Caravan Sales Ltd Chuley Road, Ashburton, Devon, TQ13 7DQ. (01364) 652377.

EXETER Martins Caravans Pinhoe (on B3181), Exeter, Devon, EX1 3TH. (01392) 466211. FAX (01392) 464544. Lunar and Sprite dealers. Quality used caravans and a super accessories shop. Four Star workshop, service and insurance repairs. Well worth a visit.

NEWTON ABBOT Compass Caravans (Devon) Higher Brocks Plantation, Teigngrace, Newton Abbot, Devon. (01626) 832792. Avondale main dealers, accessory shop. Full workshop and mobile breakdowns.

PLYMOUTH Camping and Outdoor Centre 4/6 Royal Parade, Plymouth, Devon, PL1 1HB. (01752) 662614. Leading outdoor specialists with 80 years camping experience. Large ranges of tents, sleeping bags, stoves, lanterns, camping accessories, rucksacks, walking boots and outdoor clothing.

WINKLEIGH West Britain Caravan Centre Oaktree Corner, Winkleigh, Devon, EX19 8EJ. (01837) 83101. Touring caravan sales, spares and accessories. Touring caravan storage. Closed on Mondays.

DORSET

BLANDFORD County Caravans Lady Baileys, Winterbourne White Church, Blandford, Dorset, DT11 0HS. (01258) 880786.

BOURNEMOUTH Camping and Outdoor Centre 7 Gervis Place, Bournemouth, Dorset, BH1 2AL. (01202) 558797. Leading outdoor specialists with 80 years camping experience. Large ranges of tents, sleeping bags, stoves, lanterns, camping accessories, rucksacks, walking boots and outdoor clothing.

BOURNEMOUTH Dolphin Leisure 1621 Wimborne Road, Kinson, Bournemouth, Dorset. (01202) 572413.

BOURNEMOUTH Oswald Bailey Ltd 106 Commercial Road, Bournemouth, Dorset, BH2 5LR. (01202) 552742. Cut price tents. Rucksacks, sleeping bags, hike boots and waterproof clothing. Everything for the great outdoors.

BOURNEMOUTH Oswald Bailey Ltd 403 Wimborne Road, Winton, Bournemouth, Dorset, BH9 2AJ. (01202) 528001. Cut price tents. Rucksacks, sleeping bags, hike boots and waterproof clothing. Everything for the great outdoors.

CHARMOUTH Dorset Leisure Centre Newlands Bridge, Charmouth, Dorset, DT6 6QZ. (01297) 560473.

CHRISTCHURCH Oswald Bailey Ltd 2 Saxon Square, Christchurch, Dorset, BH23 1QA. (01202) 483043. Cut price tents. Rucksacks, sleeping bags, hike boots and waterproof clothing. Everything for the great outdoors.

POOLE Oswald Bailey Ltd 317 Ashley Road, Parkstone, Poole, Dorset, BH14 9DZ. (01202) 740724. Cut price tents. Rucksacks, sleeping bags, hike boots and waterproof clothing. Everything for the great outdoors.

POOLE Oswald Bailey Ltd 31 Kingland Crescent, Poole, Dorset, BH15 1TA. (01202) 675495. Cut price tents. Rucksacks, sleeping bags, hike boots and waterproof clothing. Everything for the great outdoors.

WIMBORNE The Forest Camping Centre John Brown Garden Centre, Ringwood Road, Three Legged Cross, Near Wimborne, Dorset. (01202) 826822.

WIMBORNE Oswald Bailey Ltd 5 Crown Mead Centre, Wimborne, Dorset, BH21 1ED. (01202) 880366. Cut price tents. Rucksacks, sleeping bags, hike boots and waterproof clothing. Everything for the great outdoors.

WIMBORNE Wimborne Caravans Ltd Lake Gates, Dorchester Road, Wimborne, Dorset, BH21 3HA. (01202) 888601. Sales, repairs and accessories.

ESSEX

CANVEY ISLAND Camping and General Charfleets, Canvey Island, Essex, SS8 0PL. (01268) 692141. Frame, Ridge and Dome tents, Caravan Awnings, Porches and Motor Annexes on permanent show in our indoor showroom. Thousands of camping and caravan accessories. Walking and Hiking Boots, Waterproof Clothing all at discount prices. Repairs undertaken in our own factory. Unigas, Shell and Camping Gaz stockists. Open all year - Tuesday to Saturday 9am-6pm, Sunday 10am-3pm (March to September).

COLCHESTER Anglia Caravans Ltd 475 Ipswich Road, Colchester, Essex, CO4 4HQ. (01206) 841111.

COLCHESTER Camping and Outdoor Centre 16 Short Wyre Street, Colchester, Essex, CO1 1LN. (01206) 577040. Leading outdoor specialists with 80 years camping experience. Large ranges of tents, sleeping bags, stoves lanterns, camping accessories, rucksacks, walking boots and outdoor clothing.

COLCHESTER Leisure & Camping (Colchester) Ltd 61 North Station Road, Colchester, Essex, CO1 1RQ. (01206) 766056.

HORNCHURCH Hornchurch Motor Caravan Centre 5-7 Broadway Parade, Elm Park Avenue, Hornchurch, Essex, RM12 4RS. (01708) 444791. New and used motorcaravan sales, repairs and servicing. Accident repairs. Hire Fleet operators.

MARKS TEY Camperite Flyover Nurseries, Marks Tey, Colchester, Essex, CO6 1LJ. (01206) 210551.

ROMFORD P J Camping Ltd The Open Site, Collier Row Road, Collier Row, Romford, Essex, RM5 2BJ. (01708) 722937. Ridge, Dome, Frame and Trailer tents by Marechal, Relum, Lichfield, Vango, Sunncamp, Jamet, Combi-Camp, Comanche, and Raclet. PLUS Folding Campers and a fully stocked accessory shop. Open April to September, Monday, Thursday and Friday 10am to 8pm. Saturday 10am to 6pm and Sunday 12 noon to 6pm. Tent repairs on site.

SHOEBURYNESS A & B Leisure (Arlen & Brand Southend Ltd) 101 Ness Road, Shoeburyness, Essex, SS3 9DA. (01702) 292348. Camping equipment and caravan accessories. Backpacking equipment, outdoor and leisure clothing. Hiking and walking boots etc. Calor and Camping Gas Exchange Service.

SOUTHEND-ON-SEA Camping and General 126 Arterial Road, Southend-On-Sea, Essex. (01702) 525536. Ridge and Dome tents on permanent show. Walking and Hiking Boots, Waterproof Clothing, camping and caravanning accessories all at discount prices. Unigas, Shell Gas and Camping Gaz stockists. Open Monday to Saturday 9am-5.30pm, closed all day Wednesday.

SOUTHEND-ON-SEA TAH Leisure Sales (TAH Services Ltd), TAH House, Aviation Way, Southend-on-Sea, Essex, SS2 6UN. (01702) 547225.

UPMINSTER Cranham Caravans Old Gailey Park, Southend Arterial Road, Upminster, Essex, RM14 1TS. (01277) 215159.

WEELEY Homestead Caravan & Accessory Centre Thorpe Road (B1033), Weeley, Essex, CO16 9JN. (01255) 830229. Abbey and Swift caravans, quality used tourers, workshops and a massive accessory showroom. Awnings, tents and trailers. "The Cabin" Snack Bar.

GLOUCESTERSHIRE

GLOUCESTER Oswald Bailey Ltd 24 Oxebode, Gloucester, GL1 1SA. (01452) 305555. Cut price tents. Rucksacks, sleeping bags, hike boots and waterproof clothing. Everything for the great outdoors.

LYDNEY Forest of Dean Caravans Parkend, Lydney, Gloucestershire, GL15 4JN. (01594) 562206. Retail sales of new and used touring caravans. Awnings, caravan and camping accessories. Servicing and repairs.

WHITMINSTER Attwooll's Camping and Leisure Bristol Road, Whitminster, Gloucester, GL2 7LX. (01452) 740278.

GREATER MANCHESTER

MANCHESTER Camperlands Ltd Mill Lane, Northenden, Manchester, M22 4HI. (0161) 998 8523.

MANCHESTER Camping and Outdoor Centre 7 Oldham Street, Manchester, M6 1LG. (0161) 835 1016. Leading outdoor specialists with 80 years camping experience. Large ranges of tents, sleeping bags, stoves, lanterns, camping accessories, rucksacks, walking boots and outdoor clothin

MANCHESTER Castlecroft Camping & Caravans Eton Hill Road, Radcliffe, Manchester. (0161) 724 9922.

MANCHESTER City Autogas Manchester Ltd The Camping Centre, Norton Street, Miles Platting, Manchester, M10 8HB. (0161) 205 9127.

HAMPSHIRE

EASTLEIGH Oswald Bailey Ltd 15-17 Market Street, Eastleigh, Hants, SO5 5RJ. (01703) 613238. Cut price tents. Rucksacks, sleeping bags, hike boots and waterproof clothing, Everything for the great outdoors.

FAREHAM Castle Camping (Fareham) 137 Gosport Road, Fareham, Hants, PO16 0PZ. (01329) 280697.

LYNDHURST Leisure Fayre 60 High Street, Lyndhurst, Hampshire, SO43 7BJ. (01703) 283445. Full range for hikers and campers. Tent pegs, waterproofs, hike boots, air beds, cold boxes, stoves and lights.

LYNDHURST Leisure Fayre 36 High Street, Lyndhurst, Hampshire, SO43 7BJ. (01703) 282401. For all caravan accessories and Aerotex Awning Carpet. BBQ's and kites.

NEW MILTON Dolphin Leisure 63 Old Milton Road, New Milton, Hants. (01425) 621191.

PORTSMOUTH Hants and Dorset Caravan Centre Ltd London Road, Purbrook, Portsmouth, Hants, PO7 5AE. (01705) 374921. New Swift, Abbey and Bailey. Used tourers. Accessories, awnings and workshop services. Insurance repairs.

SOUTHAMPTON Green Pennant Caravans West End Road, Hursledon, Southampton, Hants, SO3 8BP. (01703) 405122.

SOUTHAMPTON Leisure Trail (Solent) Ltd Haskins Garden Centre, Mansbridge Road, Gatershill, West End, Southampton, SO3 3HW. (01703) 463903.

SOUTHAMPTON Oswald Bailey Ltd 60/62 Shirley High Street, Shirley, Southampton, Hants, SO1 3NF. (01703) 772460. Cut price tents Rucksacks, sleeping bags, hike boots and waterproof clothing. Everything for the great outdoors.

SOUTHAMPTON Oswald Bailey Ltd 109 Above Bar Street, Southampton, Hants, SO1 0SH. (01203) 333687. Cut price tents. Rucksacks, sleeping bags, hike boots and waterproof clothing. Everything for the great outdoors.

WATERLOOVILLE Waterlooville Camping 157a London Road, Waterlooville, Hants, PO7 7RJ. (01705) 252610.

HEREFORD & WORCESTERSHIRE

BROMSGROVE Oswald Bailey Ltd 67 High Street, Bromsgrove, Hereford & Worcester, B61 8AQ. (01527) 871562. Cut price tents. Rucksacks, sleeping bags, hike boots and waterproof clothing. Everything for the great outdoors.

HEREFORD Hereford Caravan Centre Holmer Road, Hereford, HR4 9RX. (01432) 269476.

REDDITCH Barretts of Feckenham 5 Astwood Road, Feckenham, Redditch, Worcestershire, B96 6HQ. (01527) 892935.

STOURPORT-ON-SEVERN Chichester Caravans Vale Road, Stourport-on-Severn, Worcester, DY13 8YJ. (01299) 825221.

HERTFORDSHIRE

BISHOPS STORTFORD Essex Motorcaravan Centre Dunmow Road, Takeley, Near Bishops Stortford, Herts. (01279) 870755. Calor and Gaz sales, large accessory shop.

HATFIELD G.T. Herts & North London Caravan Co. Ltd Great North Road, Hatfield, Herts, AL9 5SD. (01707) 262875. New Bailey and Avondale caravans together with quality used stock. Caravan servicing, repair and accessories.

HITCHIN Hitchin Caravan Centre Ltd Harkness Rose Gardens, Cambridge Road, Hitchin, Herts, SG4 0JT. (01462) 452856.

POTTERS BAR G.T. Towing Ltd 6 Hatfield Road, Potters Bar, Herts, EN6 1HP. (01707) 658312/3. Witter towing brackets fitted or DIY, all types of trailers and trailer parts. Roof racks and boxes, cycle carriers.

ST ALBANS J.R. Leisure Notcutts Garden Centre, Hatfield Road, Smallford, St Albans, Herts. (01727) 850901.

HUMBERSIDE

DRIFFIELD Robert Traves Holiday Homes Swifts Corner, Barmston, Driffield, North Humberside, YO25 8PR. (01262) 674144/468371.

SCUNTHORPE Armstrong Caravan Sales North Street, Winterton, Scunthorpe, South Humberside, DN15 9QS. (01724) 733114.

KENT

CHATHAM Kent Camping, Outdoor Enthusiasts One-Stop-Store 39/41 High Street, Chatham, Kent, ME4 4EN. (01634) Medway 845152/402255. Vast range of camping and caravanning equipment. Frame tents, caravan awnings. Specialist lightweight camping and clothing department. Open 7 days a week in the season.

GILLINGHAM Camping International Watling Street, Gillingham, Kent, ME7 2YX. (01634) 577326. 40,000 square feet of indoor showroom.

MAIDSTONE Camping and Outdoor Centre 2-4 Granada House, Gabriels Hill, Maidstone, Kent, ME15 6JG. (01622) 763008. Leading outdoor specialists with 80 years camping experience. Large range of tents, sleeping bags, stoves, lanterns, camping accessories, rucksacks, walking boots and outdoor clothing.

MAIDSTONE Lee Davey Caravans Ltd East Street, Harrietsham, Near Maidstone, Kent, ME17 1HN. (01622) 859301.

ORPINGTON Orpington Caravan Centre Green Street Green, Orpington, Kent, BR6 7LR. (01689) 855661. New and used caravans, large accessories shop and workshop (service and repairs).

WEST MALLING Songhurst Caravans 242 London Road (A20), West Malling, Kent, ME19 5AU. (01732) 845399.

LANCASHIRE

BLACKBURN Harringtons Caravans & Leisure Ltd Whitebirk Drive, Blackburn, Lancs, BB1 3HS. (01254) 54222.

BLACKBURN Outdoor Action 26 King Street, Blackburn, Lancs. (01254) 671945. Frame, ridge and dome tents, camping equipment and a vast range of waterproof clothing.

CARNFORTH Callender Caravans Scotland Road, Carnforth, Lancs, LA5 9RF. (01524) 732224.

CHORLEY Barrons Great Outdoors Chapel Lane, Coppull, Chorley, Lancs, PR7 4NB. (01257) 793377.

CHORLEY Tourers U.K. Chapel Way, Coppull, Chorley, Lancs, PR7 4NO. (01257) 793123.

CLAYTON-LE-WOODS Ken Dyson Caravans Park View Garden Centre, 600 Preston Road, Clayton-Le-Woods, Near Chorley, Lancs, PR6 7EH. (01772) 34000. FAX (01772) 620487.

MOSSLEY Shipley Caravans Roaches Loch, Manchester Road, Mossley, Lancashire, OL5 9BU. (01457) 835553. New and used tourers and leisure homes, large indoor showrooms, awning display, accessories, coffee shop and 5 Star workshops.

ORMSKIRK Ormskirk Camping Warbreck Garden Centre, Lyelake Lane, Lathom, Near Ormskirk, Lancs, L40 6JW. (01695) 21388. New and used trailer tents sold. Recent trailer tents bought or sold on commission. Accessories. Usually 20 to 30 second hand trailer tents on display and 20 to 30 frame and ridge tents. Part exchanges welcome.

PRESTON Campbells Caravans Watkin Lane, Lostock Hall, Preston, Lancs, PR5 5RD. (01772) 627627.

PRESTON Camping and Outdoor Centre 23 Miller Arcade, Preston, Lancs, PR1 2QA. (01772) 250242. Leading outdoor specialists with 80 years camping experience. Large ranges of tents, sleeping bags, stoves, lanterns, camping accessories, rucksacks, walking boots and outdoor clothing.

PRESTON W & A Hartley Ltd Blackpool Road (A583), Kirkham, Nr. Preston, Lancs. (01772) 685592/683868. Adria, Bessacarr, Compass, Castleton, 100 used stock. Largest walk round accessory shop, customer permanent parking. All year or Winter workshop.

PRESTON Todds Leisure Coote Lane, Lostock Hall, Preston, Lancs, PR5 5HS. (01772) 35360.

ROCHDALE Progress Caravans 1050 Manchester Road, Castletown, Rochdale, Lancs, OL11 2XJ. (01706) 44095.

WIGAN Bradburn Camping Abbey Lakes Hall, Orrell Road, Orrell, Near Wigan, Lancs. (01695) 622250.

LEICESTERSHIRE

HINCKLEY Dodwell's Leisure A5 Watling Street, Hinckley, Leicester, LE10 3ED. (01455) 632625.

LEICESTER J.R. Leisure World Oswin Road, Brailsford Industrial Estate, Off Hinckley Road, Leicester, LE3 1HR. (0116) 255 1595.

LEICESTER J.R. Leisure Byron Street, Off Lee Circle, Leicester. (0116) 253 6044.

MARKET HARBOROUGH Fairfield Caravans Rockingham Road, Market Harborough, Leics, LE16 7QE. (01858) 432602. Fleetwood range of new caravans, used tourers, accessory shop, workshop facilities and Calor Gas stockist.

MEASHAM Barretts of Feckenham Burton Road, Measham, Leicestershire, DE12 7QX. (01530) 270555.

SHEPSHED Priory Caravans Ashby Road Central, Shepshed, Leics, LE12 9BE. (01509) 508951.

LINCOLNSHIRE

BOSTON Sutterton Caravan Centre Post Office Lane, Sutterton, Boston, Lincs, PE20 2EB. (01205) 460485.

GAINSBOROUGH Kirton Caravans Ltd Station Road, Kirton Lindsey, Nr. Gainsborough, Lincs, DN21 4JR. (01652) 648569.

GRANTHAM Yeomans Army Stores 76 Westgate, Grantham, Lincs. (01476) 592431. Tents, air beds, Sleeping Bags, Water Carriers and Crockery, Camp Furniture, Groundsheets. Lights and Stoves, Rucksacks and all tent accessories. Footwear and clothing.

LINCOLN Brayford Leisure Caravan Centre, Tritton Road, Lincoln, Lincs, LN6 7QY. (01522) 686996.

LINCOLN Yeomans Army Stores 352 High Street, Lincoln, Lincs. (01522) 545630. Tents, air beds, sleeping bags, water carriers and crockery, camp furniture, groundsheets, lights, stoves, rucksacks and all tent accessories. Footwear and clothing.

TORKSEY Torksey Caravans Lincoln Road, Torksey, Lincs, LN1 2EL. (01427) 718226.

LONDON

CENTRAL LONDON Camping and Outdoor Centre 27 Buckingham Palace Road, London, SW1W 0PP. (0171) 834 6007. Leading outdoor specialists with 80 years camping experience. Large ranges of tents, sleeping bags, stoves, lanterns, camping accessories, rucksacks, walking boots and outdoor clothing.

CENTRAL LONDON Camping and Outdoor Centre 41 Ludgate Hill, London, EC4M 7JN. (0171) 329 8757. Leading outdoor specialists with 80 years experience. Large ranges of tents, sleeping bags, stoves, lanterns, camping accessories, rucksacks, walking boots and outdoor clothing.

CROUCH END Crouch End Camping 59 Park Road, London, N8 8SY. (0181) 348 5455.

CRYSTAL PALACE Crystal Palace Camping 15-17 Central Hill, Crystal Palace, London, SE19 1BG. (0181) 766 6060. Camping equipment, tents, clothing and caravan accessories.

ENFIELD Enfield Leisure Centre Caravan Accessories, Jute Lane, Enfield, Middlesex, EN3 7PJ. (0181) 804 5486.

HARROW Camping and Outdoor Centre 104 Hindes Road, Harrow, Middlesex, HA1 1RP. (0181) 427 3809. Leading outdoor specialists with 80 years experience. Large ranges of tents, sleeping bags, stoves, lanterns, camping accessories, rucksacks, walking boots and outdoor clothing.

HILLINGDON Bartletts (Hillingdon) Ltd 1-2 Rosslyn Parade, Uxbridge Road, Hillingdon, Middlesex, UB10 0NP. (0181) 573 2076.

WEST DRAYTON West Drayton United British Caravans Colnbrook-by-Pass (A4), Nr. West Drayton, Middlesex, UB7 0HE. (01753) 682606. Touring caravan retailers, Elddis, Bailey and Sprite. Service and repair workshops. 5 Star RAC/NCC Approved. Large caravan and camping accessory shop, awnings, Calor Gas and Gaz.

MERSEYSIDE

BURTON Campers World Waterworld, Chester High Road, Burton, South Wirral, L64 8TF. (0151) 353 0550.

WIRRAL Wirral Caravans Ltd 389 Hoylake Road, Moreton, Wirral, Merseyside, L46 0RW. (0151) 605 0770. Main agents for A.B.I. Touring Caravans.

NORFOLK

DEREHAM Greentree Caravans Norwich Road, Dereham, Norfolk, NR20 3PX. (01362) 696434.

DISS Waveney Leisure Station Road, Diss, Norfolk. (01379) 644070.

GREAT YARMOUTH Great Yarmouth Caravan Centre North Quay, Great Yarmouth, Norfolk, NR30 1JT. (01493) 844143/853982.

GREAT YARMOUTH Simpsons Motorcaravan Centre Suffolk Road, Great Yarmouth, Norfolk, NR31 0LN. (01493) 601778/601696.

GREAT YARMOUTH Stuart Day Caravan Services Ferry House Workshops, South Denes Road, Great Yarmouth, Norfolk, NR30 3PN. (01493) 854038.

KINGS LYNN H.J. Malletts Caravan Centre Ltd Hardwick Road, Kings Lynn, Norfolk, PE30 4HT. (01535) 773876.

NORWICH Leisure & Camping Ltd 4 Upper Goat Lane, Norwich, Norfolk, NR2 1EW. (01603) 610987.

NORWICH Norwich Camping Company Ltd 17 South Hill Road, Thorpe St Andrew, Norwich, Norfolk, NR7 0PQ. (01603) 34394/36120.

SWAFFHAM Peter Wells Caravans Station Street, Swaffham, Norfolk, PE37 7NP. (01760) 722277. All types of used caravans bought and sold. Accessory shop, servicing and repairs, Calor Gas and Camping Gaz.

NORTHAMPTONSHIRE

BILLING AQUADROME Camping Accessories Shop Billing Aquadrome, Northampton, NN3 4DA. (01604) 410197.

KETTERING J.R.Leisure Victoria Street, Kettering, Northants. (01536) 81071.

NORTHAMPTON Civilised Camping Wye Vale Garden Centre, Newport Pagnell Road, Northampton, NN4 0HP. (01604) 765061.

RUSHDEN White Arches Caravans Ltd Wellingborough Road, Rushden, Northants, NN10 9AY. (01933) 50042.

WATFORD GAP Broad Lane Caravans (Daventry) (Go Camping), Toll House, A5 Watling Street, Watford Gap, Northants. (01327) 703371. U.K's Number One Adria dealer, Abbey and Bailey. Awnings by Trio and NR. Large accessory supermarket, used caravans.

WELLINGBOROUGH Bestbuys Camping Centre Irthlingborough Road, The Embankment, Wellingborough, Northants. (01933) 272699.

WELLINGBOROUGH Tower Caravans Irthlingborough Road, Finedon, Wellingborough, Northants, NN9 5EJ. (01933) 680555.

WELLINGBOROUGH Tradewinds 8 Park Road, Wellingborough, Northants, NN8 4PG. (01933) 276632.

NOTTINGHAMSHIRE

ARNOLD Yeomans Army Stores 108 Front Street, Arnold, Notts. (0115) 967 4787. Tents, air beds, sleeping bags, water carriers and crockery, camp furniture, groundsheets. Lights and stoves, rucksacks and all tent accessories. Footwear and clothing.

BEESTON Yeomans Army Stores 118 High Road, Beeston, Notts. (0115) 925 5177. Tents, air beds, sleeping bags, water carriers and crockery, camp furniture, groundsheets. Lights, stoves, rucksacks and all tent accessories. Footwear and clothing.

BULWELL Yeomans Army Stores 16 Commercial Road, Bulwell, Nottingham. (0115) 975 6210. Tents, air beds, sleeping bags, water carriers and crockery, camp furniture and groundsheets. Lights, stoves, rucksacks and all tent accessories. Footwear and clothing.

EASTWOOD Yeaomans Army Stores 24 Nottingham Road, Eastwood, Notts. (01773) 760360. Tents, air beds, sleeping bags, water carriers and crockery, camp furniture, groundsheets. Lights, stoves, rucksacks and all tent accessories. Footwear and clothing.

HUCKNALL Yeomans Army Stores 11 High Street, Hucknell, Notts. (0115) 963 0347. Tents, air beds, sleeping bags, water carriers and crockery, camp furniture, groundsheets. Lights, stoves, rucksacks and all tent accessories. Footwear and clothing.

KIRBY-IN-ASHFIELD Yeomans Army Stores The Precinct, Kirby-In-Ashfield, Notts. (01623) 756516. Tents, air beds, sleeping bags, water carriers and crockery, camp furniture, groundsheets. Lights, stoves, rucksacks and all tent accessories. Footwear and clothing.

MANSFIELD Mansfield Outdoor Leisure Centre 21 Chesterfield Road, South Mansfield, Notts, NG19 7AB. (01623) 25236. Calor Gas dealers, camping and caravan equipment, tents, trailer tents and campers. Dealers for Conway, Pennine and Dandy.

MANSFIELD Yeomans Army Stores 14 White Heart Street, Mansfield, Notts. (01623) 23095. Tents, air beds, sleeping bags, water carriers and crockery, camp furniture, groundsheets. Lights, stoves, rucksacks and all tent accessories. Footwear and clothing.

NEWARK Brownhills Ltd A46 Farndon Road, Newark, Notts, NG24 4SG. (01636) 704201.

NEWARK Yeomans Army Stores 48a Cartergate, Newark, Notts. (01636) 640596. Tents, air beds, sleeping bags, water carriers and crockery, camp furniture, groundsheets. Lights, stoves, rucksacks and all tent accessories. Footwear and clothing.

NOTTINGHAM Camping and Outdoor Centre 3/7 St James's Street, Nottingham, NG1 1BA. (0115) 948 4571. Leading outdoor specialists with 80 years experience. Large ranges of tents, sleeping bags, stoves, lanterns, camping accessories, rucksacks, walking boots and outdoor clothing.

NOTTINGHAM J.R. Leisure Floralnads Garden Centre, Catfoot Lane, Off Plaines Road, Lambley, Nottingham. (0115) 920 4152.

NOTTINGHAM Kimberley Caravan Centre EastwoodRoad, Kimberley, Nottingham, NG16 2HX. (0115) 938 2401.

NOTTINGHAM Lowdham Caravans Lowdham, Nottingham, Notts, NG14 7EN. (0115) 966 3838.

NOTTINGHAM Nottingham Camping Centre 43/45 Alfreton Road, Canning Circus, Nottingham. (0115) 942 4920. Tents, airbeds, sleeping bags, water carriers and crockery, camp furniture and groundsheets. Lights, stoves, rucksacks and all tent accessories. Footwear and clothing.

NOTTINGHAM Yeomans Army Stores Mansfield Road, Nottingham. (0115) 941 3617. Tents, air beds, sleeping bags, water carriers and crockery, camp furniture, groundsheets. Lights, stoves, rucksacks and all tent accessories. Footwear and clothing.

RETFORD Yeomans Army Stores 1 Churchgate, Retford, Notts. (01777) 710539. Tents, air beds, sleeping bags, water carriers and crockery, camp furniture, groundsheets. Lights, stoves, rucksacks and all tent accessories. Footwear and clothing.

SELSTON Selston Caravans Mansfield Road, Selston, Notts, NG16 6BD. (01773) 810536. FAX (01773) 810535.

SUTTON-IN-ASHFIELD Sutton Supply Stores The Camping Centre, 9 Market Street, Huthwaite, Sutton-in-Ashfield, Notts, NG17 2HE. (01623) 511181.

SUTTON-IN-ASHFIELD Yeomans Army Stores Portland Square, Sutton-In-Ashfield, Notts. (01623) 511339. Tents, air beds, sleeping bags, water carriers and crockery, camp furniture, groundsheets. Lights, stoves, rucksacks and all tent accessories. Footwear and clothing.

WORKSOP Yeomans Army Stores 96 Bridge Street, Worksop, Notts. (01909) 500798. Tents, air beds, sleeping bags, water carriers and crockery, camp furniture, groundsheets. Lights, stoves, rucksacks and all tent accessories. Footwear and clothing.

OXFORDSHIRE

OXFORD Camping and Outdoor Centre 16 Turl Street, Oxford, OX1 3DH. (01865) 247110. Leading outdoor specialists with 80 years camping experience. Large ranges of tents, sleeping bags, stoves, lanterns, camping accessories, rucksacks, walking boots and outdoor clothing.

OXFORD Touchwood Sports Ltd 426 Abingdon Road, Oxford, OX1 4XN. (01865) 246551.

WITNEY C.T.C. Leisure 89-91 Corn Street, Witney, Oxford, OX8 7DH. (01993) 771080. Camping and caravan specialists. Accessories and service.

SHROPSHIRE

SHREWSBURY Brackley Motorhomes Ltd T/A Minster Motorhomes, Station Road, Minsterley, Shrewsbury, Shropshire. (01743) 790000. New and used motorcaravan sales, service, M.O.T's and repairs.

SHREWSBURY Camping & Outdoor Centre 50 Castle Foregate, Shrewsbury, Shropshire, FY1 2DJ. (01743) 355168.

SHREWSBURY Jabez Barker Caravans Montford Bridge, Shrewsbury, Shropshire, SY4 1EF. (01743) 850423. New and used caravan sales, awnings and accessories. Open 7 days a week.

WEM Lower Lacon Caravan Park Wem, Shropshire, SY4 5RP. (01939) 232376. Second hand caravans sold on commission. Holiday homes new and second hand.

SOMERSET

BURNHAM-ON-SEA Edwards & Rees Home Farm Caravan Park, Edithmead, Burnham-on-Sea, Somerset, TA9 4HD. (01278) 780196/794989.

BURNHAM-ON-SEA Northam Farm Touring Centre Brean, Burnham-on-Sea, Somerset, TA8 2SE. (01278) 751244.

CASTLE CARY Castle Cary Caravans Main A371, Castle Cary, Somerset, BA7 7PF. (01963) 351014.

STREET Elmside Caravans Farm Road, Street, Somerset, BA16 0BJ. (01458) 43151.

YEOVIL Southfork Caravan & Leisure Centre Ltd Parrett Works, Martock, Somerset, TA12 6AE. (01935) 825661. FAX (01935) 825122. Caravan sales, servicing and repairs. Sale of caravan accessories, spares and parts. Tow bars supplied and fitted. Sale of Calor Gas and Camping Gaz. Carver agents. Caravan valet service.

STAFFORDSHIRE

GAILEY Gailey Park Caravan Ltd Gailey Caravan Centre, Saxon Cross House, Gailey, Nr. Stafford, Staffs, ST19 5PP. (01902) 790246.

NEWCASTLE UNDER LYME North Staffordshire Caravans Stonewall Place, Silverdale, Newcastle under Lyme, Staffs, ST5 6NR. (01782) 622581.

STOKE-ON-TRENT Hi-Peak Leisure Ltd Stafford House, Clough Street, Hanley, Stoke-on-Trent, Staffs, ST1 4AS. (01782) 268102

SUFFOLK

GLEMSFORD Fuller Leisure Lower Road (A1092), Glemsford, Near Sudbury, Suffolk, CO10 7QU. (01787) 280263.

IPSWICH Camping and Outdoor Centre 7/9 Tacket Street, Ipswich, Suffolk, IP4 1AU. (01473) 254704. Leading outdoor specialists with 80 years camping experience. Large ranges of tents, sleeping bags, stoves, lanterns, camping accessories, rucksacks, walking boots and outdoor clothing.

IPSWICH Falcon Caravans 273 Main Road, Kesgrave, Ipswich, Suffolk, IP5 7PL. (01473) 611112.

IPSWICH Barry Sharman Caravans Ltd The Caravan Centre, Colchester Road, Ipswich, Suffolk, IP4 4RX. (01473) 713284/728238 or FAX (01473) 273166. 4 Star rated workshop and insurance repairers. On site maintenance. Fully stocked shop, Electrolux, Porta Pottis Fiammi. Witter Tow Bars. Used Caravans. New caravans to order. Spacemaker awnings. Calor Gas, Shell Gas and Camping Gaz.

NEW HAW Falcon Leisure Centre 303 Woodham Lane, New Haw, Surrey, KT15 3NY. (01932) 353040.

SAXMUNDHAM Brian Fuller Caravans (Farnham) Ltd Farnham, Saxmundham, Suffolk, IP17 1LE. (01728) 602858.

STOWMARKET Stowmarket Caravan Leisure Centre Bury Road, Stowmarket, Suffolk, IP14 1JF. (01449) 677445.

SURREY

CAMBERLEY Sandhurst Caravans 414 York Town Road, College Town, Camberley, Surrey, GU15 4PR. (01276) 32121.

CROYDON Camping and Outdoor Centre 37-39 St Georges Walk, Croydon, Surrey, CR0 1YL. (0181) 688 1730. Leading outdoor specialists with 80 years camping experience. Large ranges of tents, sleeping bags, stoves, lanterns, camping accessories, rucksacks, walking boots and outdoor clothing.

NEW MALDEN TAM Leisure Ltd 180-186 Kingston Road, New Malden, Surrey. (0181) 949 5435.

SUSSEX

BRIGHTON Camping and Outdoor Centre 24 St James's Street, Brighton, East Sussex, BN2 1RF. (01273) 684281. Leading outdoor specialists with 80 years camping experience. Large ranges of tents, sleeping bags, stoves, lanterns, camping accessories, rucksacks, walking boots and outdoor clothing.

BRIGHTON John's Camping New England Street, Brighton, Sussex, BN1 4GQ. (01273) 685226.

CHICHESTER Chichester Caravans Main Road (A259), Nutbourne, Nr. Chichester, West Sussex, PO18 8RL. (01243) 377441. The South's Number One caravan retailer. Sales centres at Nutbourne Chichester, Colden Common Winchester and Uckfield. Large accessory shop, new and used awnings. We specialise in new Lunar and Compass tourers. Large range of used caravans.

EASTBOURNE Coastal Caravans & Camping 24 Lottsbridge Drove, Eastbourne, East Sussex, BN23 6NS. (01323) 639449.
Conway Trailer Tents, Relum Tents. Camping and caravan accessories. Tent and awning repairs, tent hire, caravan repairs and service.

HALLAND D.D. Motorhomes Ltd Eastbourne Road, Halland, East Sussex, BN8 6PS. (01825) 840723.

LITTLEHAMPTON The Base Camp 67 High Street, Littlehampton, West Sussex, BN17 5EJ. (01903) 723853. All your camping and walking requirements, small range of caravan accessories. Tilley, Vapalux and Bialaddin Lantern specialists.

UCKFIELD Chichester Caravans London Road, Uckfield, East Sussex, TN22 2EA. (01825) 764151.

WORTHING Camping and Outdoor Centre 20-22 Brighton Road, Worthing, West Sussex, BN11 3ED. (01903) 232028. Leading outdoor specialists with 80 years camping experience. Large ranges of tents, sleeping bags, stoves, lanterns, camping accessories, rucksacks, walking boots and outdoor clothing.

TYNE & WEAR

SUNDERLAND Reynolds Outdoor Centre 6 Derwent Street, Sunderland, Tyne & Wear, SR1 3NT. (0191) 565 7945.

WASHINGTON Roper Caravans Glover East Industrial Estate, Washington District 10, Tyne & Wear, NE37 2PA. (0191) 419 1631.

WIDEOPEN Newcastle United British Caravans Sandy Lane, Wideopen, Tyne & Wear, NE3 5HA. (0191) 236 3156. Touring caravan retailers, Swift, Bailey and Elddis. Service and repair workshops. 5 Star RAC/NCC Approval. Large caravan and camping accessory supermarket, awnings, tents, Calor Gas and Gaz.

WARWICKSHIRE

ALCESTER Broad Lane Caravans (Alcester) Birmingham Road, Alcester, Warwickshire. (01789) 763432. New caravans by Elddis and Swift. Used caravans, awning showroom and accessory megastore.

EXHALL Pedleys Caravans 289 Goodyears End Lane, Exhall, Nr. Coventry, Warwicks. (01203) 644883. Superb selection of new and used caravans in stock. Large well stocked accessory shop. Calor Gas stockists.

KENILWORTH Broad Lane Caravans (Kenilworth) Old Warwick Road, Leek Wootton, Kenilworth, Warwickshire, CV35 7RD. New caravans by Abbey, Adria, Bailey and Swift. Accessory shop, awning showroom and used caravans.

WEST MIDLANDS

BIRMINGHAM Camping and Outdoor Centre 62 New Street, Birmingham, B2 4DU. (0121) 643 0885. Leading outdoor specialists with 80 years camping experience. Large ranges of tents, sleeping bags, stoves, lanterns, camping accessories, rucksacks, walking boots and outdoor clothing.

BIRMINGHAM Harlew Caravans 41 Alumrock Road, Saltley, Birmingham, B8 1LR. (0121) 327 5369. Caravan and camping accessories, Calor Gas and Calor Gas appliances, Primus Camping Gaz, Cadac Leisure, Bulldog Leisure Craft, Gimeg UK Ltd, Joy & King, Burdens etc.

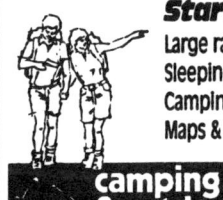

BIRMINGHAM Oswald Bailey Ltd 18 Alcester Road South, Kings Heath, Birmingham, B14 7PU. (0121) 444 4572. Cut price tents. Rucksacks, sleeping bags, hike boots and waterproof clothing. Everything for the great outdoors.

BIRMINGHAM Oswald Bailey Ltd 111 Bull Ring Centre, Birmingham, B5 4QW. (0121) 643 2474. Cut price tents. Rucksacks, sleeping bags, hike boots and waterproof clothing. Everything for the great outdoors.

COVENTRY Jacksons of Old Arley Arley Industrial Estate, Spring Hill, Old Arley, Coventry, CV7 8FL. (01676) 540878.

COVENTRY Raymond James Caravans 245 Torrington Avenue, Tile Hill, Coventry, CV4 9AP. (01203) 471567.

CRADLEY HEATH Black Country Caravans Grangers Lane, Cradley Heath, West Midlands, B64 6AL. (01384) 61995.

SOLIHULL Barretts of Feckenham 17 Station Road, Solihull, West Midlands, B91 3TG. (0121) 704 9292.

SOLIHULL Oswald Bailey Ltd 48 Station Road, Solihull, West Midlands, B91 3RX. (0121) 705 3226. Cut price tents. Rucksacks, sleeping bags, hike boots and waterproof clothing. Everything for the great outdoors.

SUTTON COLDFIELD Barretts of Feckenham 63 Boldmere Road, Sutton Coldfield, West Midlands, B73 5XA. (0121) 355 6751.

SUTTON COLDFIELD Canwell Caravans Ltd A38 London Road, Canwell, Sutton Coldfield, West Midlands, B75 5ST. (0121) 308 0583.

SUTTON COLDFIELD Midwest Camping Ltd Wyndley Nurseries, Lichfield Road, Sutton Coldfield, West Midlands, B75 4AH. (0121) 308 7279. The premier outdoor displays in the Midlands. Open March to October, 7 days a week. Major stockists of Conway, Cabanon and other big brand names. Comprehensive range of accessories. Expert advice, repairs and part exchange. (See also Wolverhampton - Open all year).

WALSALL D.J. Motorcaravans 119-121 Darlaston Road, Walsall, West Midlands, WS2 9RD. (01922) 611248.

WOLVERHAMPTON Barretts of Feckenham 58-60 Victoria Street, Wolverhampton, West Midlands, WV1 3NX. (01902) 21240.

WOLVERHAMPTON Midwest Camping Ltd Codsall Garden Centre, Wergs Hall Road, Codsall, Near Wolverhampton, WV8 2DB. (01902) 845404. The premier outdoor displays in the Midlands. Large accessory/tent showroom. Open 7 days a week, all year round. Major stockists of Conway, Cabanon and other big name brands. Expert advice, repairs and part exchange.

WILTSHIRE

CORSHAM Pickwick Caravans Bradford Road, Corsham, Wiltshire, SN13 0QT. (01249) 713572.

SALISBURY Oswald Bailey Ltd Old George Mall, Salisbury, Wilts, SP1 2AG. (01722) 328689. Cut price tents. Rucksacks, sleeping bags, hike boots and waterproof clothing. Everything for the great outdoors.

SALISBURY PLAIN Tilshead Caravans & Motorcaravans Tilshead Garage, Tilshead (A360), Salisbury Plain, Wilts, SP3 4SB. (01722) 324421.

SWINDON Folding Caravan Centre (Swindon) Ltd 24 Turnpike Road (A419), Blunsdon, Swindon, Wiltshire, SN2 4EA. (01793) 726717. Main agents for Fleurette, Rapido, Esterel, Conway and Dandy. Large selection of new and previously owned models plus parts and a large accessory shop. Mail Order facilities.

SWINDON Swindon Caravan Centre Greatfield, Wootton Bassett, Swindon, Wiltshire. (01793) 772096. Dealer for Bessacarr, Abbey and Elddis caravans. Full workshop and accessory facilities.

TROWBRIDGE BCH Camping & Leisure 8-12 Islington, Trowbridge, Wilts, BA14 8QE. (01225) 764977.

NORTH YORKSHIRE

CATTERICK BRIDGE Roper Caravans Gatherley Road, Catterick Bridge, North Yorks, DL10 7SL. (01748) 818666.

FILEY Bridlington Caravan & Accessory Centre Bridlington Road, Reighton, Near Filey, North Yorks, YO14 8XX. (01723) 891715.

RICHMOND Catterick Caravan & Camping Centre Catterick Bridge, Richmond, North Yorks, DL10 7JB. (01748) 818391.

RIPLEY Yeomans Army Stores Oxford Street, Ripley, North Yorkshire. (01773) 748044. Tents, air beds, sleeping bags, water carriers and crockery, camp furniture and groundsheets. Lights, stoves, rucksacks and all tent accessories. Footwear and clothing.

SCARBOROUGH Leisureways 38 Victoria Road, Scarborough, North Yorkshire. (01723) 368777. Camping, walking, climbing and caravan equipment.

YORK Camping and Outdoor Centre 3 Queens House, Micklegate, York, North Yorkshire, YO1 1DG. (01904) 653567. Leading outdoor specialists with 80 years camping experience. Large ranges of tents, sleeping bags, stoves, lanterns, camping accessories, rucksacks, walking boots and outdoor clothing.

YORK H.C. Fawcett Caravan Centre 201 Acomb Road, York, North Yorkshire, YO2 4HD. (01904) 798321.

SOUTH YORKSHIRE

BARNSLEY Knollbeck Caravan Service Centre Pontefract Road, Brampton, Wombwell, Barnsley, South Yorkshire, S73 0YG. (01226) 753956. Manufacturers of Scorpion Motorhomes. New and second hand caravans. Towbar fitting, mains fitting, service's to caravans. Full quality repairs, both private and insurance claims. Complete accessories shop. Carver agent. Member of Guild of Master Craftsmen.

DONCASTER Don Valley Sports Littleworth Lane, Old Rossington, Doncaster, South Yorkshire DN11 0HJ. (01302) 868408.

DONCASTER Yorkshire Caravans of Bawtry Ltd Doncaster Road, Bawtry, Doncaster, South Yorkshire, DN10 6DG. (01302) 710366. Full range of Abi new tourers, used tourers. NR, Bradcott, Trio and Isabella awnings. 5 Star service centre. Large leisure shop.

ROTHERHAM Glentworth Caravans Lidget Lane, Thurnscoe, Rotherham, South Yorkshire, S63 0DA. (01709) 893332.

ROTHERHAM Rotherham Caravans Bawtry Road, Brinsworth, Rotherham, South Yorks, S60 5DN. (01709) 370877.

SHEFFIELD C.C.C. Camping & Caravan Centre Hill Street, Bramall Lane, Sheffield, S2 4SZ. (0114) 272 9733.

SHEFFIELD Caravan Supplies 531-535 Attercliffe Road, Sheffield, South Yorks, S9 3RA. (0114) 244 2447.

SHEFFIELD Sheffield Caravans Chesterfield Road, Swallownest, Sheffield, South Yorks, S31 0TL. (0114) 269 4027.

SHEFFIELD Yeomans Army Stores 698 Chesterfield Road, Woodseats, Sheffield, South Yorkshire. (0114) 258 9103. Tents, air beds, sleeping bags, water carriers and crockery, camp furniture and groundsheets. Lights, stoves, rucksacks and all tent accessories. Footwear and clothing.

SHEFFIELD Yeomans Army Stores 502 London Road, Sheffield, South Yorkshire. (0114) 255 1408. Tents, air beds, sleeping bags, water carriers and crockery, camp furniture and groundsheets. Lights, stoves, rucksacks and all tent accessories. Footwear and clothing.

WEST YORKSHIRE

BRADFORD Albion Caravans Leeds Road, Idle, Bradford, West Yorks, BD10 9SX. (01274) 611867.

CASTLEFORD Pleasuretime Caravans Ltd Cambridge Street, Castleford, West Yorkshire, WF10 5BL. (01977) 557798. Dealer in new Lunar touring caravans and any make of used touring caravan. Self Tow hire fleet. Caravan four star service centre. Calor Gas centre.

GARFORTH Barretts of Feckenham Selby Road, Garforth, Near Leeds, West Yorkshire, LS25 2AQ. (0113) 286 7976.

HUDDERSFIELD Goodalls Caravans Crossland Hill, Huddersfield, West Yorks, HD4 5NU. (01484) 642613.

KEIGHLEY Silsden Caravans & Leisure Keighley Road, Silsden, Keighley, West Yorkshire, BD20 0EA. (01535) 652577.

LEEDS Camping and Outdoor Centre 62 The Headrow, Leeds, Yorkshire, LS1 8ET. (0113) 245 7273. Leading outdoor specialists with 80 years camping experience. Large ranges of tents, sleeping bags, stoves, lanterns, camping accessories, rucksacks, walking boots and outdoor clothing.

MIRFIELD Tourer World Huddersfield Road, Mirfield, West Yorks, WF14 9DA. (01924) 498313.

OTLEY Caseys Camping c/o Stephen Smith Garden World, Pool Road, Otley, West Yorks, LS21 1DY. (01943 465462/462195.

WAKEFIELD Mitchells Practical Campers Exhibition Centre, Hostingley Lane, Middlestown, Nr. Wakefield, West Yorks, WF4 4PZ. (01924) 272877.

WAKEFIELD Victoria Motors 129 New Road, Middlestown, Wakefield, West Yorks, WF4 4PA. (01924) 272087. Motorcaravan hire (2 to 5 Berth), sale of new and used motorcaravans. Speciality "Sportsman Conversion" based on Bedford Rascal Van.

WETHERBY A1 Caravans Unit 435, Thorp Arch Trading Estate, Wetherby, West Yorkshire, LS23 7BJ. (01937) 842845. Caravan service and repair specialists. Spares, accessories, Calor Gas and Camping Gaz.

WALES

CLWYD

PRESTATYN Tan-Y-Don Caravans 269 Victoria Road, Prestatyn, Clwyd, LL19 7UT. (01745) 853646/853749.

QUEENSFERRY Flintshire Caravan Sales 76 Station Road, Queensferry, Deeside, Clwyd, CH5 2TE. (01244) 830438.

TOWYN The Handyman & Caravan Stores 10 Penisaf Avenue, Towyn, Abergele, Clwyd, LL22 9LL. (01745) 331902.

WREXHAM Campwise c/o Waterways Garden Centre, Wrexham Road, Lavister, Near Wrexham, Clwyd, LL12 0DF. (01244) 571282. Trigano and Comanche trailer tents. Ridge, frame and dome tents by Trigano and Relum. Large range of camping accessories. Some caravan spares also available. Open 7 days a week, March till end of September. Gaz and Calor stocked.

DYFED

LLANELLI C.S.E. Caravans The Caravan Centre, Carmarthen Road, Crosshands, Llanelli, Dyfed. (01269) 832381.

LLANELLI Continental Caravans Ltd Crosshands Business Park, Crosshands, Llanelli, Dyfed, SA14 6RE. (01269) 831151.

GLAMORGAN

BARRY Barry Caravans & Motorcaravans Cardiff Road, Barry, South Glamorgan, CF6 6QW. (01446) 720011.

BRIDGEND Pyle Caravan & Camping Centre Unit 1 Plot 56, Village Farm Industrial Estate, Pyle, Mid Glamorgan, CF33 6NU. (01656) 743267. Quality used touring caravans, camping equipment, accessories, Calor Gas and a tow bar fitting service.

CARDIFF Camping and Outdoor Centre 10 Duke Street, Cardiff, Glamorgan, CF1 2AY. (01222) 390887. Leading ourdoor specialists with 80 years camping experience. Large ranges of tents, sleeping bags, stoves, lanterns, camping accessoies, rucksacks, walking boots and outdoor clothing.

GOWER Bank Farm Caravan Park Bank Farm, Horton, Gower, West Glamorgan, SA3 1LL. (01792) 390228. Caravan and camping park. New and used tourers and statics sold. Statics for hire.

PONTYPRIDD Pontypridd Caravan Sales Cardiff Road, Treforest, Pontypridd, Glamorgan, CF37 5RF. (01443) 402629.

SWANSEA Blazers Caravan & Camping Co Ltd Baldwins Crescent, Fabion Way, Swansea, Glamorgan, SA1 8QJ. (01792) 643326. Touring caravans, caravan accessories and awnings. Avondale, Bailey, Bessacarr and Perle caravans. Servicing and repairs. Towbars.

SWANSEA Mike Davies Leisure Ltd 665 Gower Road, Upper Killay, Swansea, West Glamorgan. (01792) 203177/208954. Caravan awnings and accessories. Trailer tents. Frame tents. Lightweight tents. Backpacking tents and equipment. Camping accessories. Barbecue gas and charcoal. Marine accessories. Outdoor clothing. Ski wear and waterproofs. Calor Gas and Camping Gaz. Canvas repair service.

SWANSEA Sunnyhaven Caravans Gorseinon Road, Penllergaer, Swansea, Glamorgan. (01792) 892884. Caravans sales. Towbar fitting. Accessories, Gas and awnings. 5 Star workshop.

GWENT

NEWBRIDGE Newbridge Caravan Centre Ltd New Bryngwyn Road, Newbridge, Gwent, NP1 4NF. (01495) 249242.

NEWPORT Gwent Camping and Awnings Pavilion Showroom, 136-140 Stow Hill, Newport, Gwent, NP9 4GA. (01633) 211403.

NEWPORT Leeway Leisure Leeway Industrial Estate, Newport, Gwent. (01633) 276611. Caravans and motor caravans, parts and all associated equipment.

GWYNEDD

PORTHMADOC Gwynedd Caravans and Accessories Madoc Street, Porthmadoc, Gwynedd, LL49 9YA. (01766) 513589. The caravan, camping and Calor centre. Extensive range of equipment and spares.

SCOTLAND

BORDERS

PEEBLES Crossburn Caravans Crossburn Caravan Park, Edinburgh Road, Peebles, Borders, EH45 8ED. (01721) 720501. New and used caravan sales and service. Agents for Coachman and Fleetwood, towbar fitting. Calor and Camping Gaz dealer.

DUMFRIES & GALLOWAY

DUMFRIES Dumfries Caravan Centre Brasswell, Annan Road, Dumfries, Dumfries & Galloway, DG1 3JZ. (01387) 52917/53399.

FIFE

KIRKCALDY Kirkcaldy Caravan Centre Randolph Industrial Estate, Kirkcaldy, Fife, KY1 2YX. (01592) 651969.

GRAMPIAN

BANCHORY Dee Valley Caravans Drumoak, By Banchory, Grampian, AB31 3AU. (01330) 811351.

FRASERBURGH Greenbank Motorhomes & Caravans Hillhead, Fraserburgh, Grampian, AB43 4BL. (01346) 514747.

HIGHLAND

INVERNESS Caravan Sales Glenurquhart Road, Inverness, Highland, IV3 6JL. (01463) 233051.

LOTHIAN

DALKEITH Scotts Caravans Mayfield Industrial Estate, Dalkeith, Mid-Lothian, EH22 4AD. (0131) 663 1471.

EDINBURGH Camping and Outdoor Centre 77 Southbridge, Edinburgh, EH1 1HN. (0131) 225 3339. Leading outdoor specialists with 80 years camping experience. Large ranges of tents, sleeping bags, stoves, lanterns, camping accessories, rucksacks, walking boots and outdoor clothing.

EDINBURGH Camping Ecosse Ltd Ingliston Road, Ingliston, Edinburgh, EH28 8NB. (0131) 333 2574. Folding campers, trailer tents, frame tents, ridge tents and camping and caravanning accessories.

LIVINGSTON Knowepark Caravans Ltd Hardie Road, Deans Industrial Estate, Livingston, West Lothian, Scotland, EH54 8BA. (01506) 411827.

STRATHCLYDE

HURLFORD Hurlford Caravans 71-75 Mauchline Road, Hurlford, Strathclyde, KA1 5DE. (01563) 23559.

MOTHERWELL Strathclyde Caravans Ltd 341 Windmillhill Street, Motherwell, Strathclyde, ML1 2UB. (01698) 269418.

STRATHAVEN Strathaven Caravan Centre Darvel Road, Strathaven, Strathclyde, ML10 6QD. (01357) 22444.

TAYSIDE

DUNDEE Grants (Craigmills) Caravans Strathmortine, Dundee, Tayside, DD3 0PH. (01382) 817979.

ERROL Perthshire Caravans Dundee Road, Errol, Perth, Tayside. (01821) 670212.

CADE'S FIFTY PENCE

50p

CAMPING, TOURING & MOTORCARAVAN SITE GUIDE 1995

PRESENT THIS VOUCHER TO THE SITE OPERATOR WHEN PAYING TO RECEIVE A FIFTY PENCE DISCOUNT PER VOUCHER PER NIGHT. SEE CONDITIONS OVERLEAF. VALID UNTIL 31-12-95

CADE'S FIFTY PENCE

50p

CAMPING, TOURING & MOTORCARAVAN SITE GUIDE 1995

PRESENT THIS VOUCHER TO THE SITE OPERATOR WHEN PAYING TO RECEIVE A FIFTY PENCE DISCOUNT PER VOUCHER PER NIGHT. SEE CONDITIONS OVERLEAF. VALID UNTIL 31-12-95

CADE'S FIFTY PENCE

50p

CAMPING, TOURING & MOTORCARAVAN SITE GUIDE 1995

PRESENT THIS VOUCHER TO THE SITE OPERATOR WHEN PAYING TO RECEIVE A FIFTY PENCE DISCOUNT PER VOUCHER PER NIGHT. SEE CONDITIONS OVERLEAF. VALID UNTIL 31-12-95

CADE'S FIFTY PENCE

50p

CAMPING, TOURING & MOTORCARAVAN SITE GUIDE 1995

PRESENT THIS VOUCHER TO THE SITE OPERATOR WHEN PAYING TO RECEIVE A FIFTY PENCE DISCOUNT PER VOUCHER PER NIGHT. SEE CONDITIONS OVERLEAF. VALID UNTIL 31-12-95

CADE'S FIFTY PENCE

50p

CAMPING, TOURING & MOTORCARAVAN SITE GUIDE 1995

PRESENT THIS VOUCHER TO THE SITE OPERATOR WHEN PAYING TO RECEIVE A FIFTY PENCE DISCOUNT PER VOUCHER PER NIGHT. SEE CONDITIONS OVERLEAF. VALID UNTIL 31-12-95

CADE'S FIFTY PENCE

50p

CAMPING, TOURING & MOTORCARAVAN SITE GUIDE 1995

PRESENT THIS VOUCHER TO THE SITE OPERATOR WHEN PAYING TO RECEIVE A FIFTY PENCE DISCOUNT PER VOUCHER PER NIGHT. SEE CONDITIONS OVERLEAF. VALID UNTIL 31-12-95

CADE'S FIFTY PENCE

50p

CAMPING, TOURING & MOTORCARAVAN SITE GUIDE 1995

PRESENT THIS VOUCHER TO THE SITE OPERATOR WHEN PAYING TO RECEIVE A FIFTY PENCE DISCOUNT PER VOUCHER PER NIGHT. SEE CONDITIONS OVERLEAF. VALID UNTIL 31-12-95

CADE'S FIFTY PENCE

50p

CAMPING, TOURING & MOTORCARAVAN SITE GUIDE 1995

PRESENT THIS VOUCHER TO THE SITE OPERATOR WHEN PAYING TO RECEIVE A FIFTY PENCE DISCOUNT PER VOUCHER PER NIGHT. SEE CONDITIONS OVERLEAF. VALID UNTIL 31-12-95

CADE'S FIFTY PENCE

50p

CAMPING, TOURING & MOTORCARAVAN SITE GUIDE 1995

PRESENT THIS VOUCHER TO THE SITE OPERATOR WHEN PAYING TO RECEIVE A FIFTY PENCE DISCOUNT PER VOUCHER PER NIGHT. SEE CONDITIONS OVERLEAF. VALID UNTIL 31-12-95

CADE'S FIFTY PENCE

50p

CAMPING, TOURING & MOTORCARAVAN SITE GUIDE 1995

PRESENT THIS VOUCHER TO THE SITE OPERATOR WHEN PAYING TO RECEIVE A FIFTY PENCE DISCOUNT PER VOUCHER PER NIGHT. SEE CONDITIONS OVERLEAF. VALID UNTIL 31-12-95

CONDITIONS OF USE

Vouchers will only be redeemed by those sites featuring a £ symbol in their county entry. Presentation of this voucher to the Site Operator at the time of paying your balance will entitle you to a fifty pence discount per voucher, per night (only one voucher per night). Vouchers may be used in multiples i.e. five vouchers presented for a five night stay will entitle you to a discount of £2.50.

A CADE'S CAMPING, TOURING & MOTORCARAVAN SITE GUIDE 1995 EDITION must be presented at the time of payment. Vouchers are valid for accommodation only. Vouchers may not be exchanged for cash. Valid until 31-12-95.

CONDITIONS OF USE

Vouchers will only be redeemed by those sites featuring a £ symbol in their county entry. Presentation of this voucher to the Site Operator at the time of paying your balance will entitle you to a fifty pence discount per voucher, per night (only one voucher per night). Vouchers may be used in multiples i.e. five vouchers presented for a five night stay will entitle you to a discount of £2.50.

A CADE'S CAMPING, TOURING & MOTORCARAVAN SITE GUIDE 1995 EDITION must be presented at the time of payment. Vouchers are valid for accommodation only. Vouchers may not be exchanged for cash. Valid until 31-12-95.

CONDITIONS OF USE

Vouchers will only be redeemed by those sites featuring a £ symbol in their county entry. Presentation of this voucher to the Site Operator at the time of paying your balance will entitle you to a fifty pence discount per voucher, per night (only one voucher per night). Vouchers may be used in multiples i.e. five vouchers presented for a five night stay will entitle you to a discount of £2.50.

A CADE'S CAMPING, TOURING & MOTORCARAVAN SITE GUIDE 1995 EDITION must be presented at the time of payment. Vouchers are valid for accommodation only. Vouchers may not be exchanged for cash. Valid until 31-12-95.

CONDITIONS OF USE

Vouchers will only be redeemed by those sites featuring a £ symbol in their county entry. Presentation of this voucher to the Site Operator at the time of paying your balance will entitle you to a fifty pence discount per voucher, per night (only one voucher per night). Vouchers may be used in multiples i.e. five vouchers presented for a five night stay will entitle you to a discount of £2.50.

A CADE'S CAMPING, TOURING & MOTORCARAVAN SITE GUIDE 1995 EDITION must be presented at the time of payment. Vouchers are valid for accommodation only. Vouchers may not be exchanged for cash. Valid until 31-12-95.

CONDITIONS OF USE

Vouchers will only be redeemed by those sites featuring a £ symbol in their county entry. Presentation of this voucher to the Site Operator at the time of paying your balance will entitle you to a fifty pence discount per voucher, per night (only one voucher per night). Vouchers may be used in multiples i.e. five vouchers presented for a five night stay will entitle you to a discount of £2.50.

A CADE'S CAMPING, TOURING & MOTORCARAVAN SITE GUIDE 1995 EDITION must be presented at the time of payment. Vouchers are valid for accommodation only. Vouchers may not be exchanged for cash. Valid until 31-12-95.

CONDITIONS OF USE

Vouchers will only be redeemed by those sites featuring a £ symbol in their county entry. Presentation of this voucher to the Site Operator at the time of paying your balance will entitle you to a fifty pence discount per voucher, per night (only one voucher per night). Vouchers may be used in multiples i.e. five vouchers presented for a five night stay will entitle you to a discount of £2.50.

A CADE'S CAMPING, TOURING & MOTORCARAVAN SITE GUIDE 1995 EDITION must be presented at the time of payment. Vouchers are valid for accommodation only. Vouchers may not be exchanged for cash. Valid until 31-12-95.

CONDITIONS OF USE

Vouchers will only be redeemed by those sites featuring a £ symbol in their county entry. Presentation of this voucher to the Site Operator at the time of paying your balance will entitle you to a fifty pence discount per voucher, per night (only one voucher per night). Vouchers may be used in multiples i.e. five vouchers presented for a five night stay will entitle you to a discount of £2.50.

A CADE'S CAMPING, TOURING & MOTORCARAVAN SITE GUIDE 1995 EDITION must be presented at the time of payment. Vouchers are valid for accommodation only. Vouchers may not be exchanged for cash. Valid until 31-12-95.

CONDITIONS OF USE

Vouchers will only be redeemed by those sites featuring a £ symbol in their county entry. Presentation of this voucher to the Site Operator at the time of paying your balance will entitle you to a fifty pence discount per voucher, per night (only one voucher per night). Vouchers may be used in multiples i.e. five vouchers presented for a five night stay will entitle you to a discount of £2.50.

A CADE'S CAMPING, TOURING & MOTORCARAVAN SITE GUIDE 1995 EDITION must be presented at the time of payment. Vouchers are valid for accommodation only. Vouchers may not be exchanged for cash. Valid until 31-12-95.

CONDITIONS OF USE

Vouchers will only be redeemed by those sites featuring a £ symbol in their county entry. Presentation of this voucher to the Site Operator at the time of paying your balance will entitle you to a fifty pence discount per voucher, per night (only one voucher per night). Vouchers may be used in multiples i.e. five vouchers presented for a five night stay will entitle you to a discount of £2.50.

A CADE'S CAMPING, TOURING & MOTORCARAVAN SITE GUIDE 1995 EDITION must be presented at the time of payment. Vouchers are valid for accommodation only. Vouchers may not be exchanged for cash. Valid until 31-12-95.

CONDITIONS OF USE

Vouchers will only be redeemed by those sites featuring a £ symbol in their county entry. Presentation of this voucher to the Site Operator at the time of paying your balance will entitle you to a fifty pence discount per voucher, per night (only one voucher per night). Vouchers may be used in multiples i.e. five vouchers presented for a five night stay will entitle you to a discount of £2.50.

A CADE'S CAMPING, TOURING & MOTORCARAVAN SITE GUIDE 1995 EDITION must be presented at the time of payment. Vouchers are valid for accommodation only. Vouchers may not be exchanged for cash. Valid until 31-12-95.

CADE'S FIFTY PENCE

50p

CAMPING, TOURING & MOTORCARAVAN SITE GUIDE 1995

PRESENT THIS VOUCHER TO THE SITE OPERATOR WHEN PAYING TO RECEIVE A FIFTY PENCE DISCOUNT PER VOUCHER PER NIGHT. SEE CONDITIONS OVERLEAF. VALID UNTIL 31-12-95

CADE'S FIFTY PENCE

50p

CAMPING, TOURING & MOTORCARAVAN SITE GUIDE 1995

PRESENT THIS VOUCHER TO THE SITE OPERATOR WHEN PAYING TO RECEIVE A FIFTY PENCE DISCOUNT PER VOUCHER PER NIGHT. SEE CONDITIONS OVERLEAF. VALID UNTIL 31-12-95

CADE'S FIFTY PENCE

50p

CAMPING, TOURING & MOTORCARAVAN SITE GUIDE 1995

PRESENT THIS VOUCHER TO THE SITE OPERATOR WHEN PAYING TO RECEIVE A FIFTY PENCE DISCOUNT PER VOUCHER PER NIGHT. SEE CONDITIONS OVERLEAF. VALID UNTIL 31-12-95

CADE'S FIFTY PENCE

50p

CAMPING, TOURING & MOTORCARAVAN SITE GUIDE 1995

PRESENT THIS VOUCHER TO THE SITE OPERATOR WHEN PAYING TO RECEIVE A FIFTY PENCE DISCOUNT PER VOUCHER PER NIGHT. SEE CONDITIONS OVERLEAF. VALID UNTIL 31-12-95

CADE'S FIFTY PENCE

50p

CAMPING, TOURING & MOTORCARAVAN SITE GUIDE 1995

PRESENT THIS VOUCHER TO THE SITE OPERATOR WHEN PAYING TO RECEIVE A FIFTY PENCE DISCOUNT PER VOUCHER PER NIGHT. SEE CONDITIONS OVERLEAF. VALID UNTIL 31-12-95

CADE'S FIFTY PENCE

50p

CAMPING, TOURING & MOTORCARAVAN SITE GUIDE 1995

PRESENT THIS VOUCHER TO THE SITE OPERATOR WHEN PAYING TO RECEIVE A FIFTY PENCE DISCOUNT PER VOUCHER PER NIGHT. SEE CONDITIONS OVERLEAF. VALID UNTIL 31-12-95

CADE'S FIFTY PENCE

50p

CAMPING, TOURING & MOTORCARAVAN SITE GUIDE 1995

PRESENT THIS VOUCHER TO THE SITE OPERATOR WHEN PAYING TO RECEIVE A FIFTY PENCE DISCOUNT PER VOUCHER PER NIGHT. SEE CONDITIONS OVERLEAF. VALID UNTIL 31-12-95

CADE'S FIFTY PENCE

50p

CAMPING, TOURING & MOTORCARAVAN SITE GUIDE 1995

PRESENT THIS VOUCHER TO THE SITE OPERATOR WHEN PAYING TO RECEIVE A FIFTY PENCE DISCOUNT PER VOUCHER PER NIGHT. SEE CONDITIONS OVERLEAF. VALID UNTIL 31-12-95

CADE'S FIFTY PENCE

50p

CAMPING, TOURING & MOTORCARAVAN SITE GUIDE 1995

PRESENT THIS VOUCHER TO THE SITE OPERATOR WHEN PAYING TO RECEIVE A FIFTY PENCE DISCOUNT PER VOUCHER PER NIGHT. SEE CONDITIONS OVERLEAF. VALID UNTIL 31-12-95

CADE'S FIFTY PENCE

50p

CAMPING, TOURING & MOTORCARAVAN SITE GUIDE 1995

PRESENT THIS VOUCHER TO THE SITE OPERATOR WHEN PAYING TO RECEIVE A FIFTY PENCE DISCOUNT PER VOUCHER PER NIGHT. SEE CONDITIONS OVERLEAF. VALID UNTIL 31-12-95

CONDITIONS OF USE

Vouchers will only be redeemed by those sites featuring a £ symbol in their county entry. Presentation of this voucher to the Site Operator at the time of paying your balance will entitle you to a fifty pence discount per voucher, per night (only one voucher per night). Vouchers may be used in multiples i.e. five vouchers presented for a five night stay will entitle you to a discount of £2.50.

A CADE'S CAMPING, TOURING & MOTORCARAVAN SITE GUIDE 1995 EDITION must be presented at the time of payment. Vouchers are valid for accommodation only. Vouchers may not be exchanged for cash. Valid until 31-12-95.

CONDITIONS OF USE

Vouchers will only be redeemed by those sites featuring a £ symbol in their county entry. Presentation of this voucher to the Site Operator at the time of paying your balance will entitle you to a fifty pence discount per voucher, per night (only one voucher per night). Vouchers may be used in multiples i.e. five vouchers presented for a five night stay will entitle you to a discount of £2.50.

A CADE'S CAMPING, TOURING & MOTORCARAVAN SITE GUIDE 1995 EDITION must be presented at the time of payment. Vouchers are valid for accommodation only. Vouchers may not be exchanged for cash. Valid until 31-12-95.

CONDITIONS OF USE

Vouchers will only be redeemed by those sites featuring a £ symbol in their county entry. Presentation of this voucher to the Site Operator at the time of paying your balance will entitle you to a fifty pence discount per voucher, per night (only one voucher per night). Vouchers may be used in multiples i.e. five vouchers presented for a five night stay will entitle you to a discount of £2.50.

A CADE'S CAMPING, TOURING & MOTORCARAVAN SITE GUIDE 1995 EDITION must be presented at the time of payment. Vouchers are valid for accommodation only. Vouchers may not be exchanged for cash. Valid until 31-12-95.

CONDITIONS OF USE

Vouchers will only be redeemed by those sites featuring a £ symbol in their county entry. Presentation of this voucher to the Site Operator at the time of paying your balance will entitle you to a fifty pence discount per voucher, per night (only one voucher per night). Vouchers may be used in multiples i.e. five vouchers presented for a five night stay will entitle you to a discount of £2.50.

A CADE'S CAMPING, TOURING & MOTORCARAVAN SITE GUIDE 1995 EDITION must be presented at the time of payment. Vouchers are valid for accommodation only. Vouchers may not be exchanged for cash. Valid until 31-12-95.

CONDITIONS OF USE

Vouchers will only be redeemed by those sites featuring a £ symbol in their county entry. Presentation of this voucher to the Site Operator at the time of paying your balance will entitle you to a fifty pence discount per voucher, per night (only one voucher per night). Vouchers may be used in multiples i.e. five vouchers presented for a five night stay will entitle you to a discount of £2.50.

A CADE'S CAMPING, TOURING & MOTORCARAVAN SITE GUIDE 1995 EDITION must be presented at the time of payment. Vouchers are valid for accommodation only. Vouchers may not be exchanged for cash. Valid until 31-12-95.

CONDITIONS OF USE

Vouchers will only be redeemed by those sites featuring a £ symbol in their county entry. Presentation of this voucher to the Site Operator at the time of paying your balance will entitle you to a fifty pence discount per voucher, per night (only one voucher per night). Vouchers may be used in multiples i.e. five vouchers presented for a five night stay will entitle you to a discount of £2.50.

A CADE'S CAMPING, TOURING & MOTORCARAVAN SITE GUIDE 1995 EDITION must be presented at the time of payment. Vouchers are valid for accommodation only. Vouchers may not be exchanged for cash. Valid until 31-12-95.

CONDITIONS OF USE

Vouchers will only be redeemed by those sites featuring a £ symbol in their county entry. Presentation of this voucher to the Site Operator at the time of paying your balance will entitle you to a fifty pence discount per voucher, per night (only one voucher per night). Vouchers may be used in multiples i.e. five vouchers presented for a five night stay will entitle you to a discount of £2.50.

A CADE'S CAMPING, TOURING & MOTORCARAVAN SITE GUIDE 1995 EDITION must be presented at the time of payment. Vouchers are valid for accommodation only. Vouchers may not be exchanged for cash. Valid until 31-12-95.

CONDITIONS OF USE

Vouchers will only be redeemed by those sites featuring a £ symbol in their county entry. Presentation of this voucher to the Site Operator at the time of paying your balance will entitle you to a fifty pence discount per voucher, per night (only one voucher per night). Vouchers may be used in multiples i.e. five vouchers presented for a five night stay will entitle you to a discount of £2.50.

A CADE'S CAMPING, TOURING & MOTORCARAVAN SITE GUIDE 1995 EDITION must be presented at the time of payment. Vouchers are valid for accommodation only. Vouchers may not be exchanged for cash. Valid until 31-12-95.

CONDITIONS OF USE

Vouchers will only be redeemed by those sites featuring a £ symbol in their county entry. Presentation of this voucher to the Site Operator at the time of paying your balance will entitle you to a fifty pence discount per voucher, per night (only one voucher per night). Vouchers may be used in multiples i.e. five vouchers presented for a five night stay will entitle you to a discount of £2.50.

A CADE'S CAMPING, TOURING & MOTORCARAVAN SITE GUIDE 1995 EDITION must be presented at the time of payment. Vouchers are valid for accommodation only. Vouchers may not be exchanged for cash. Valid until 31-12-95.

CONDITIONS OF USE

Vouchers will only be redeemed by those sites featuring a £ symbol in their county entry. Presentation of this voucher to the Site Operator at the time of paying your balance will entitle you to a fifty pence discount per voucher, per night (only one voucher per night). Vouchers may be used in multiples i.e. five vouchers presented for a five night stay will entitle you to a discount of £2.50.

A CADE'S CAMPING, TOURING & MOTORCARAVAN SITE GUIDE 1995 EDITION must be presented at the time of payment. Vouchers are valid for accommodation only. Vouchers may not be exchanged for cash. Valid until 31-12-95.

MAP SECTION

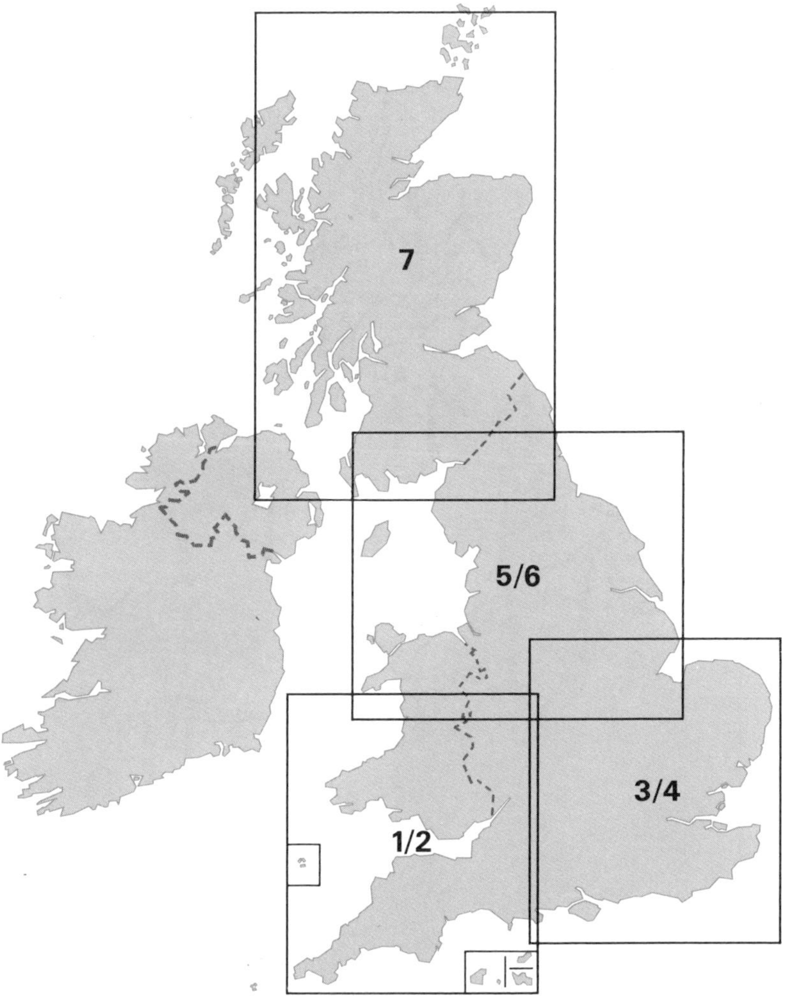

7

5/6

3/4

1/2

Maps designed and produced by GEOprojects (UK) Ltd., Reading, Berkshire. RG1 4QS.

1

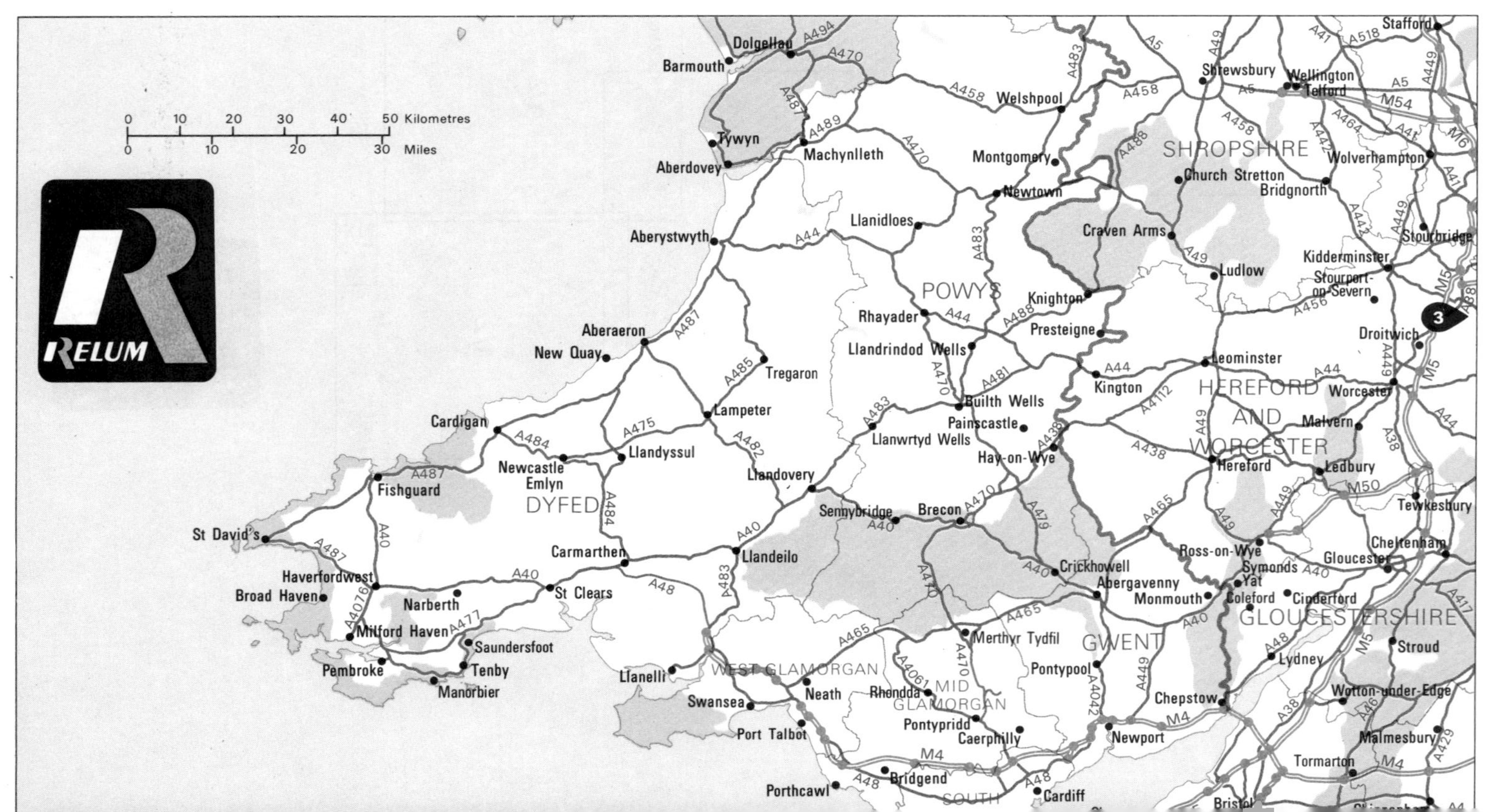
RELUM
0 10 20 30 40 50 Kilometres
0 10 20 30 Miles
DYFED
POWYS
WEST GLAMORGAN
MID GLAMORGAN
SOUTH
GWENT
HEREFORD AND WORCESTER
SHROPSHIRE
GLOUCESTERSHIRE
Dolgellau
Barmouth
Tywyn
Aberdovey
Machynlleth
Aberystwyth
Aberaeron
New Quay
Cardigan
Fishguard
St David's
Haverfordwest
Broad Haven
Milford Haven
Pembroke
Narberth
Saundersfoot
Tenby
Manorbier
St Clears
Carmarthen
Newcastle Emlyn
Llandyssul
Lampeter
Tregaron
Llandovery
Llandeilo
Llanelli
Swansea
Port Talbot
Neath
Porthcawl
Bridgend
Rhondda
Pontypridd
Caerphilly
Cardiff
Merthyr Tydfil
Pontypool
Newport
Chepstow
Sennybridge
Brecon
Crickhowell
Abergavenny
Monmouth
Llanidloes
Rhayader
Llandrindod Wells
Llanwrtyd Wells
Builth Wells
Painscastle
Hay-on-Wye
Kington
Presteigne
Knighton
Newtown
Montgomery
Welshpool
Craven Arms
Ludlow
Church Stretton
Shrewsbury
Wellington
Telford
Bridgnorth
Wolverhampton
Stafford
Stourbridge
Kidderminster
Stourport-on-Severn
Droitwich
Worcester
Leominster
Hereford
Malvern
Ledbury
Tewkesbury
Ross-on-Wye
Symonds Yat
Coleford
Cinderford
Gloucester
Cheltenham
Lydney
Stroud
Wotton-under-Edge
Malmesbury
Tormarton
Bristol
3
A494
A470
A487
A489
A458
A483
A5
A49
A41
A518
A464
A442
M54
M6
A488
A44
A456
A449
M5
A38
A4112
A438
A465
A40
A479
A481
A482
A485
A475
A484
A4076
A477
A48
A4061
A4042
M4
M50
A417
A46
A429
A4

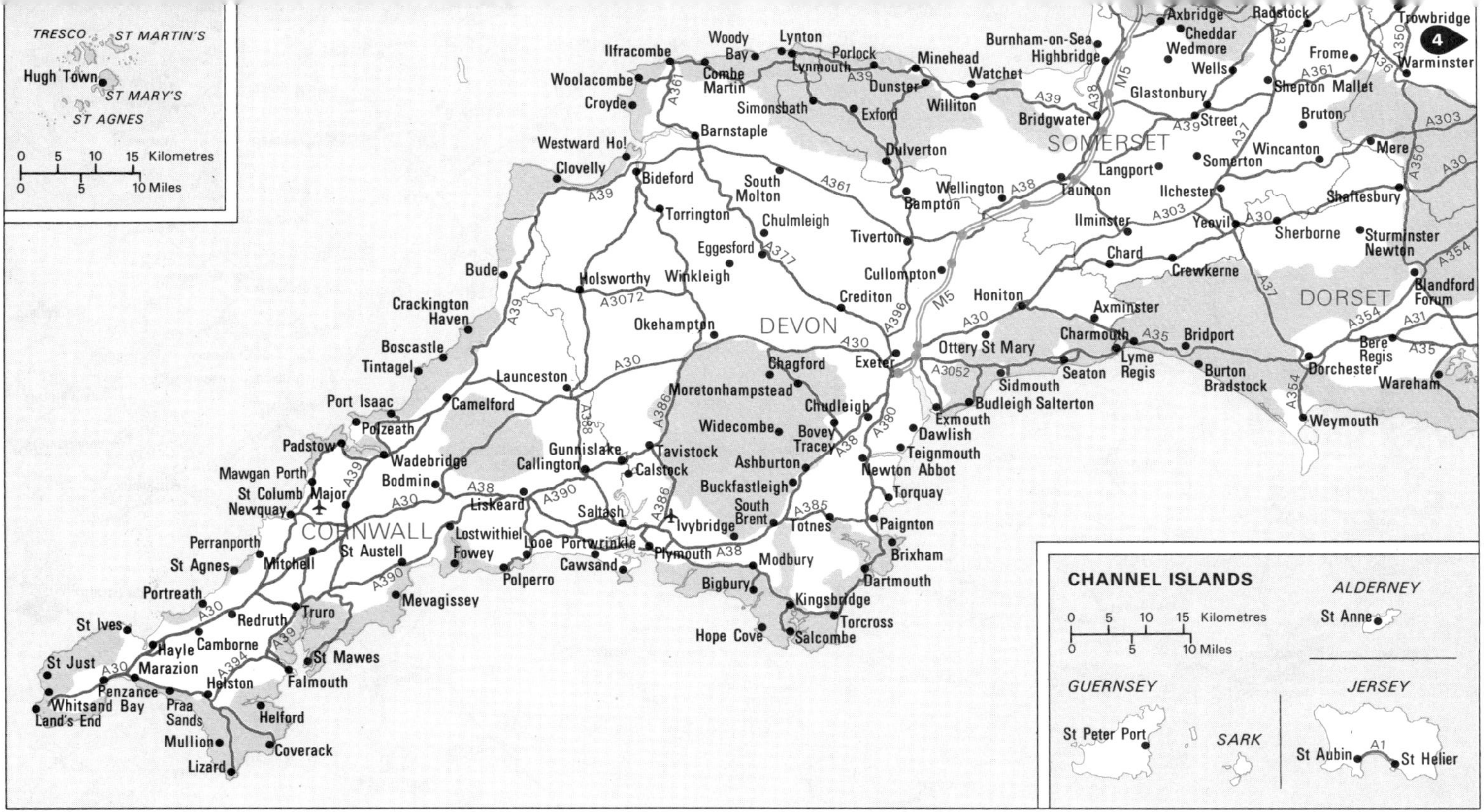

TRESCO
ST MARTIN'S
Hugh Town
ST MARY'S
ST AGNES
0 5 10 15 Kilometres
0 5 10 Miles

CORNWALL
DEVON
SOMERSET
DORSET

Ilfracombe
Woody Bay
Lynton
Lynmouth
Porlock
Minehead
Burnham-on-Sea
Highbridge
Axbridge
Cheddar
Wedmore
Radstock
Trowbridge
Frome
Warminster
Woolacombe
Combe Martin
Dunster
Watchet
Wells
Shepton Mallet
Croyde
Simonsbath
Exford
Williton
Glastonbury
Bridgwater
Street
Bruton
Barnstaple
Westward Ho!
Clovelly
Dulverton
Wincanton
Somerton
Mere
Langport
Bideford
South Molton
Wellington
Taunton
Ilchester
Bampton
Shaftesbury
Torrington
Chulmleigh
Ilminster
Yeovil
Sherborne
Tiverton
Sturminster Newton
Eggesford
Chard
Crewkerne
Bude
Holsworthy
Winkleigh
Cullompton
Crediton
Honiton
Blandford Forum
Axminster
Crackington Haven
Okehampton
Ottery St Mary
Charmouth
Bridport
Bere Regis
Boscastle
Exeter
Lyme Regis
Tintagel
Launceston
Chagford
Seaton
Burton Bradstock
Dorchester
Wareham
Sidmouth
Moretonhampstead
Port Isaac
Camelford
Chudleigh
Budleigh Salterton
Polzeath
Exmouth
Weymouth
Widecombe
Bovey Tracey
Dawlish
Padstow
Gunnislake
Tavistock
Teignmouth
Wadebridge
Callington
Calstock
Ashburton
Newton Abbot
Mawgan Porth
Bodmin
Buckfastleigh
St Columb Major
Torquay
Newquay
Liskeard
Saltash
South Brent
Ivybridge
Totnes
Paignton
Lostwithiel
Fowey
Looe
Portwrinkle
Perranporth
St Austell
Plymouth
Brixham
St Agnes
Mitchell
Cawsand
Modbury
Polperro
Dartmouth
Portreath
Bigbury
Mevagissey
Kingsbridge
Truro
Redruth
St Ives
Torcross
Hope Cove
Salcombe
Hayle
Camborne
St Mawes
St Just
Marazion
Helston
Falmouth
Penzance
Whitsand Bay
Land's End
Praa Sands
Helford
Mullion
Coverack
Lizard

A30 A39 A361 A38 M5 A37 A350 A36 A303 A3072 A377 A396 A354 A31 A35 A3052 A380 A386 A388 A390 A385 A394

4

CHANNEL ISLANDS
0 5 10 15 Kilometres
0 5 10 Miles
ALDERNEY
St Anne
GUERNSEY
St Peter Port
SARK
JERSEY
St Aubin
A1
St Helier

2

Bakewell
Mansfield
Leek
Matlock
Alfreton
NOTTINGHAMSHIRE
Newark
Skegness
DERBYSHIRE
LINCOLNSHIRE
Ashbourne
Boston
Sleaford
Nottingham
Hunstanton
Wells-next-the-Sea
Blakeney
Sheringham
Cromer
STAFFS
Uttoxeter
Derby
Grantham
Holt
Overstrand
Mundesley-on-Sea
East Midlands
North Walsham
Stafford
Burton-upon-Trent
Fakenham
Stalham
Melton Mowbray
Loughborough
Spalding
King's Lynn
NORFOLK
Hemsby
Wroxham
Horning
East Dereham
Lichfield
LEICESTERSHIRE
Stamford
Wisbech
Downham Market
Norwich
Acle
Caister
Oakham
Swaffham
Great Yarmouth
Tamworth
Leicester
Uppingham
Peterborough
Watton
Wolverhampton
Sutton Coldfield
WEST MIDLANDS
Lowestoft
Nuneaton
Market Harborough
Corby
Bungay
Beccles
Birmingham
National Exhibition Centre
Thetford
Diss
Harleston
Kessingland
Solihull
Coventry
Ely
Rugby
Kettering
CAMBRIDGESHIRE
Halesworth
Southwold
Bromsgrove
Huntingdon
Warwick
Leamington Spa
NORTHAMPTONSHIRE
Bury St Edmunds
Framlingham
Saxmundham
WARWICKSHIRE
Daventry
Northampton
Newmarket
Stowmarket
SUFFOLK
Cambridge
Aldeburgh
Stratford-upon-Avon
Towcester
Bedford
Lavenham
Woodbridge
Evesham
Haverhill
Shipston on Stour
Banbury
Brackley
BEDFORDSHIRE
Sudbury
Hadleigh
Ipswich
Broadway
Milton Keynes
Buckingham
Baldock
Felixstowe
Moreton-in-Marsh
Dedham
Harwich
Chipping Norton
Hitchin
Stow-on-the-Wold
Stevenage
Braintree
Colchester
Cheltenham
Kingham
Luton
Stansted
Walton-on-Naze
Bicester
BUCKS
Dunstable
Bishop's Stortford
Bourton-on-the-Water
GLOS
HERTFORDSHIRE
ESSEX
Burford

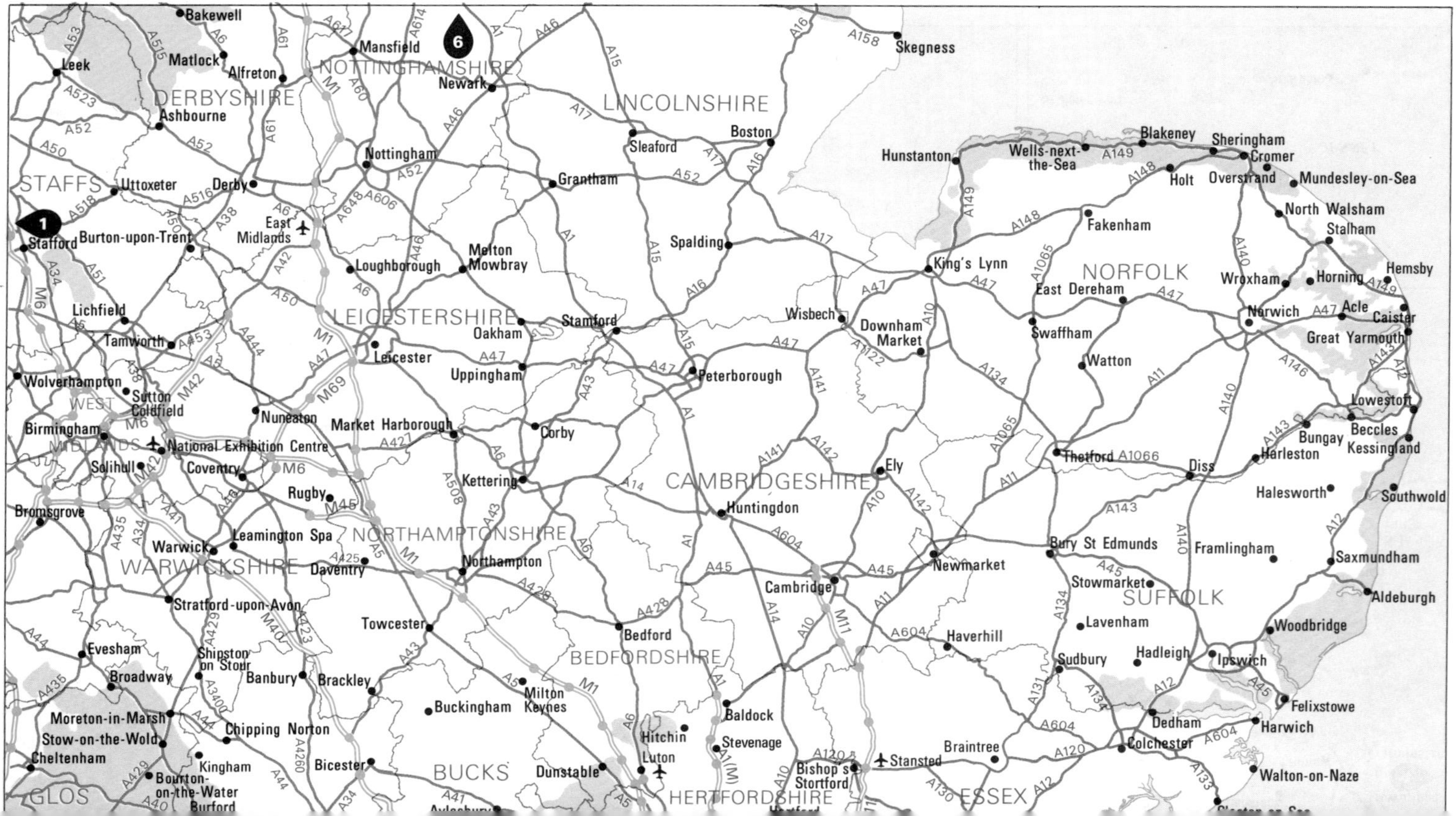

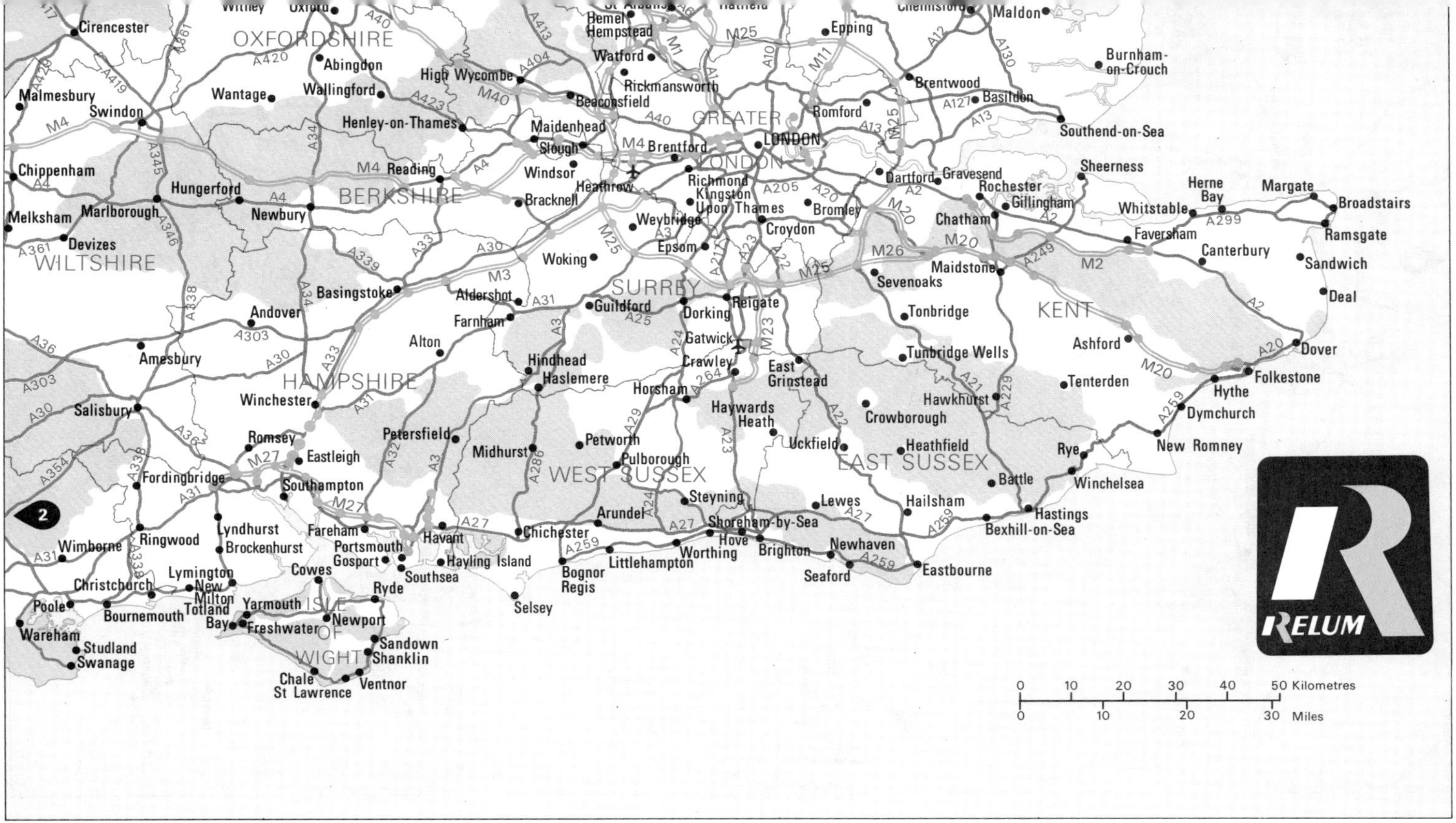

OXFORDSHIRE
BERKSHIRE
WILTSHIRE
HAMPSHIRE
SURREY
GREATER LONDON
WEST SUSSEX
EAST SUSSEX
KENT
ISLE OF WIGHT

Cirencester, Malmesbury, Swindon, Chippenham, Melksham, Marlborough, Devizes, Hungerford, Newbury, Wantage, Abingdon, Wallingford, Henley-on-Thames, Reading, High Wycombe, Beaconsfield, Maidenhead, Slough, Windsor, Bracknell, Heathrow, Hemel Hempstead, Watford, Rickmansworth, Brentford, Richmond, Kingston upon Thames, Weybridge, Epsom, Croydon, Bromley, LONDON, Romford, Epping, Brentwood, Basildon, Maldon, Burnham-on-Crouch, Southend-on-Sea, Dartford, Gravesend, Rochester, Gillingham, Chatham, Sheerness, Whitstable, Herne Bay, Margate, Broadstairs, Ramsgate, Faversham, Canterbury, Sandwich, Deal, Dover, Folkestone, Hythe, Dymchurch, New Romney, Ashford, Tenterden, Maidstone, Sevenoaks, Tonbridge, Tunbridge Wells, Hawkhurst, Crowborough, Heathfield, Uckfield, East Grinstead, Haywards Heath, Crawley, Gatwick, Reigate, Dorking, Guildford, Woking, Aldershot, Farnham, Alton, Basingstoke, Andover, Amesbury, Salisbury, Winchester, Romsey, Eastleigh, Southampton, Fordingbridge, Ringwood, Wimborne, Christchurch, Bournemouth, Poole, Wareham, Studland, Swanage, Lymington, New Milton, Lyndhurst, Brockenhurst, Fareham, Gosport, Portsmouth, Southsea, Havant, Hayling Island, Petersfield, Midhurst, Hindhead, Haslemere, Petworth, Pulborough, Horsham, Chichester, Selsey, Bognor Regis, Arundel, Littlehampton, Worthing, Steyning, Shoreham-by-Sea, Hove, Brighton, Lewes, Newhaven, Seaford, Eastbourne, Hailsham, Battle, Bexhill-on-Sea, Hastings, Rye, Winchelsea, Cowes, Ryde, Yarmouth, Totland Bay, Freshwater, Newport, Sandown, Shanklin, Chale, St Lawrence, Ventnor

M4, M3, M25, M27, M40, M1, M11, M20, M23, M26, M2, A4, A30, A31, A33, A34, A36, A303, A338, A339, A345, A346, A361, A354, A419, A420, A423, A404, A413, A10, A12, A13, A127, A130, A205, A20, A2, A21, A22, A23, A24, A25, A217, A229, A249, A259, A264, A27, A29, A286, A299, A3, A32, A40

RELUM

0 10 20 30 40 50 Kilometres
0 10 20 30 Miles

DUMFRIES AND GALLOWAY
Girvan
New Galloway
Dumfries
Lockerbie
Langholm
Newton Stewart
Castle Douglas
Dalbeattie
Gatehouse of Fleet
Annan
Gretna
Longtown
Brampton
Carlisle
Wigtown
Kirkcudbright
Silloth
Port William
Wigton
Maryport
Cockermouth
Bassenthwaite
Workington
Penrith
Keswick
Thornthwaite
Whitehaven
Ennerdale Bridge
Ullswater
CUMBRIA
Shap
Appleby
Kirkby Stephen
Gosforth
Little Langdale
Ambleside
Troutbeck
Hawkshead
Coniston
Windermere
Seascale
Ravenglass
Kendal
Sedbergh
Broughton-in-Furness
Newby Bridge
Millom
Ulverston
Grange-over-Sands
Barrow-in-Furness
Carnforth
Morecambe
Lancaster
ISLE OF MAN
Ramsey
Peel
Douglas
Port Erin
Castletown
Port St Mary
Fleetwood
Clitheroe
LANCASHIRE
Blackpool
Lytham St Annes
Preston
Blackburn
Southport
Chorley
Formby
Ormskirk
Wigan
GREATER MANCHESTER
MERSEYSIDE
Liverpool
Hoylake
Birkenhead
Warrington
Widnes
ANGLESEY
Amlwch
Holyhead
Llanerchymedd
Llandudno
Colwyn Bay
Prestatyn
Rhyl
Menai Bridge
Beaumaris
Llangefni
Conwy
Abergele
Ellesmere Port
Northwich
Knutsford
Bangor
Chester
CHESHIRE
Caernarvon
Denbigh
Mold
Llanrwst
Llanberis
Ruthin
Betws-y-Coed
CLWYD
Nantwich
Wrexham
GWYNEDD
Corwen
Newcastle-under-Lyme
Nefyn
Portmadoc
Ffestiniog
Llangollen
Whitchurch
Criccieth
Penrhyndeudraeth
Bala
Ellesmere
Pwllheli
Llanbedrog
Harlech
Oswestry
Wem
Market Drayton
Abersoch
Aberdaron
SHROPSHIRE
Dolgellau
Barmouth
Welshpool
Shrewsbury
Wellington
Telford
POWYS
Tywyn
Machynlleth
A77
A713
A76
A701
A74
A7
A75
A69
A689
A596
A595
M6
A6
A686
A66
A5086
A591
A592
A685
A684
A590
A65
A683
A585
M55
A59
A666
A570
A565
M61
M58
M62
M53
M56
A5
A55
A470
A494
A54
A49
A41
A51
A483
A487
A525
A495
A53
A458
A493

0 10 20 30 40 50 Kilometres
0 10 20 30 Miles
RELUM
NORTHUMBERLAND
DURHAM
CLEVELAND
NORTH YORKSHIRE
WEST YORKSHIRE
SOUTH YORKSHIRE
HUMBERSIDE
DERBYSHIRE
NOTTINGHAMSHIRE
LINCOLNSHIRE
LEICESTERSHIRE
STAFFORDSHIRE
Morpeth
Ashington
Whitley Bay
Tynemouth
South Shields
Corbridge
Hexham
Newcastle-upon-Tyne
Sunderland
Washington
Consett
Durham
Peterlee
Hartlepool
Bishop Auckland
Middleton-in-Teesdale
Middlesbrough
Stockton-on-Tees
Redcar
Saltburn-by-the-Sea
Barnard Castle
Darlington
Guisborough
Whitby
Stokesley
Richmond
Northallerton
Leyburn
Middleham
Thirsk
Helmsley
Pickering
Scarborough
Cayton Bay
Filey
Ripon
Castle Howard
Malton
Flamborough
Grassington
Huby
Sledmere
Bridlington
Knaresborough
Driffield
Skipton
Harrogate
Stamford Bridge
Wetherby
York
Hornsea
Keighley
Ilkley
Bingley
Beverley
Bradford
Leeds
Selby
Heptonstall
Halifax
Hull
Withernsea
Wakefield
Goole
Huddersfield
Scunthorpe
Grimsby
Holmfirth
Barnsley
Cleethorpes
Oldham
Doncaster
Glossop
Rotherham
Gainsborough
Market Rasen
Louth
Sheffield
Castleton
Worksop
Mablethorpe
Buxton
Alford
Chesterfield
Lincoln
Bakewell
Horncastle
Matlock
Mansfield
Woodhall Spa
Skegness
Leek
Alfreton
Newark
Ashbourne
Sleaford
Boston
Nottingham
Uttoxeter
Derby
Grantham
East Midlands
Stafford
Burton-upon-Trent
Loughborough
Melton Mowbray
Spalding
Lichfield
Stamford
Wisbech
Tamworth
Oakham
Leicester
Uppingham
Peterborough
3

6

7

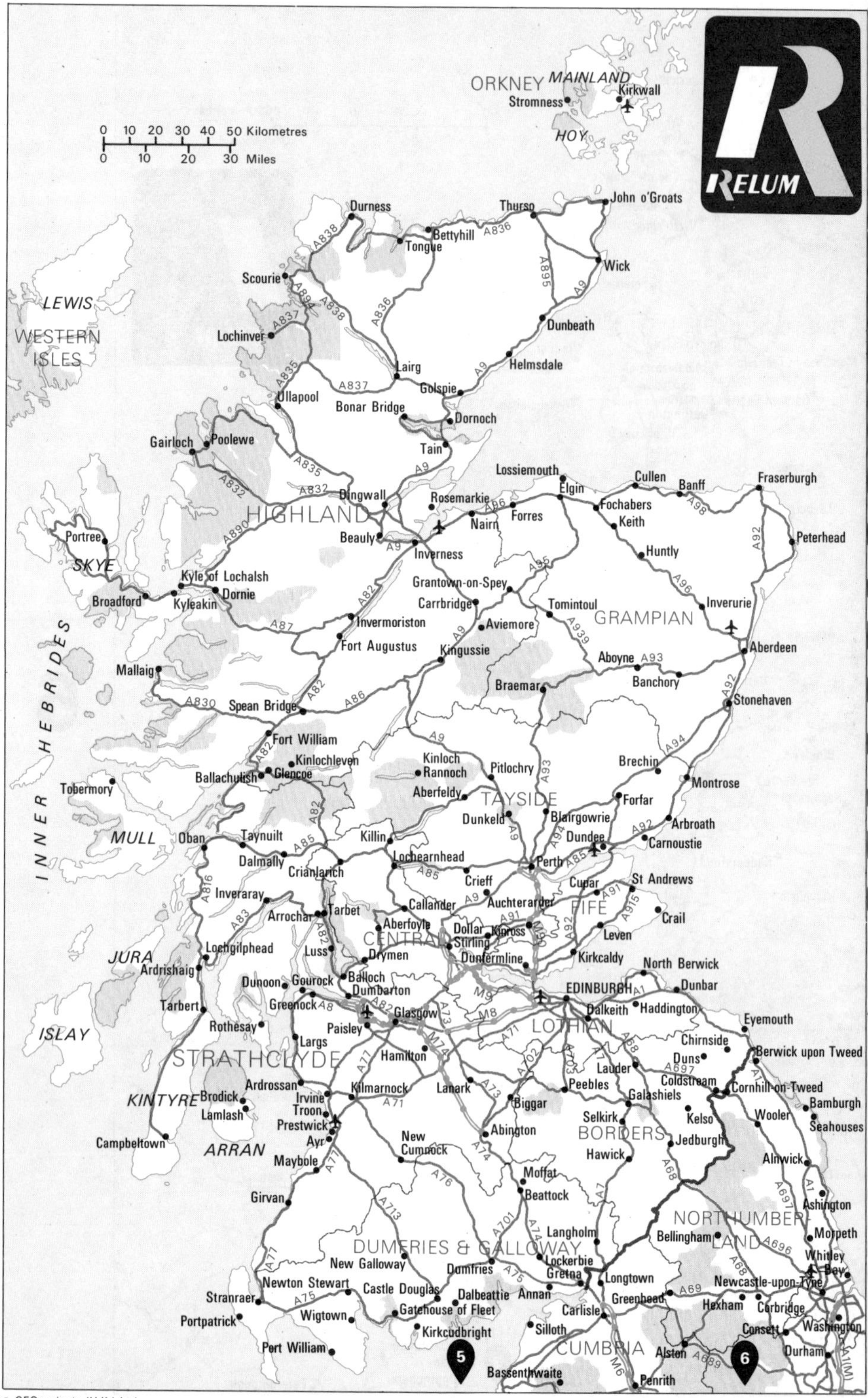
0 10 20 30 40 50 Kilometres
0 10 20 30 Miles
RELUM
ORKNEY
MAINLAND
Kirkwall
Stromness
HOY
John o'Groats
Thurso
Durness
Bettyhill
Tongue
Wick
Scourie
LEWIS
WESTERN ISLES
Lochinver
Dunbeath
Helmsdale
Lairg
Golspie
Ullapool
Bonar Bridge
Dornoch
Gairloch
Poolewe
Tain
Lossiemouth
Cullen
Banff
Fraserburgh
Dingwall
Rosemarkie
Elgin
Fochabers
Keith
HIGHLAND
Nairn
Forres
Peterhead
Portree
Beauly
Inverness
Huntly
SKYE
Kyle of Lochalsh
Grantown-on-Spey
Broadford
Kyleakin
Dornie
Carrbridge
Tomintoul
GRAMPIAN
Inverurie
Invermoriston
Aviemore
INNER HEBRIDES
Fort Augustus
Kingussie
Aberdeen
Aboyne
Mallaig
Banchory
Braemar
Spean Bridge
Stonehaven
Fort William
Kinlochleven
Kinloch Rannoch
Pitlochry
Brechin
Ballachulish
Glencoe
Tobermory
Montrose
Aberfeldy
TAYSIDE
Forfar
Dunkeld
Blairgowrie
Arbroath
MULL
Oban
Taynuilt
Killin
Dundee
Carnoustie
Dalmally
Lochearnhead
Crianlarich
Perth
Inveraray
Crieff
Cupar
St Andrews
Arrochar
Tarbet
Callander
Auchterarder
FIFE
Crail
Aberfoyle
Dollar
Kinross
Luss
CENTRAL
Stirling
Leven
JURA
Lochgilphead
Drymen
Dunfermline
Kirkcaldy
Ardrishaig
North Berwick
Dunoon
Gourock
Balloch
Dumbarton
EDINBURGH
Dunbar
Tarbert
Greenock
Glasgow
Dalkeith
Haddington
Paisley
Eyemouth
Rothesay
LOTHIAN
Largs
ISLAY
Chirnside
Hamilton
Duns
Berwick upon Tweed
STRATHCLYDE
Lauder
Coldstream
Cornhill-on-Tweed
Ardrossan
Kilmarnock
Lanark
Peebles
Galashiels
Bamburgh
KINTYRE
Brodick
Irvine
Biggar
Kelso
Wooler
Lamlash
Troon
Selkirk
Seahouses
Prestwick
Abington
BORDERS
Campbeltown
Ayr
New Cumnock
Jedburgh
ARRAN
Hawick
Maybole
Alnwick
Moffat
Beattock
Girvan
Ashington
NORTHUMBERLAND
Langholm
Morpeth
Bellingham
DUMFRIES & GALLOWAY
New Galloway
Lockerbie
Whitley Bay
Newton Stewart
Dumfries
Gretna
Longtown
Newcastle-upon-Tyne
Castle Douglas
Dalbeattie
Annan
Stranraer
Greenhead
Hexham
Corbridge
Carlisle
Wigtown
Gatehouse of Fleet
Portpatrick
Silloth
Consett
Washington
Kirkcudbright
CUMBRIA
Alston
Durham
Port William
5
6
Bassenthwaite
Penrith
A838
A836
A895
A9
A894
A837
A836
A835
A832
A890
A82
A87
A830
A86
A96
A98
A92
A95
A939
A93
A94
A85
A816
A83
A82
A91
A915
A90
M9
M8
M74
A73
A71
A77
A76
A74
A702
A703
A7
A68
A697
A1
A701
A713
A75
A69
A689
A696
M6
A1(M)

© GEOprojects (U.K.) Ltd
Crown Copyright Reserved